PENGUIN B

DUNKIR

'For readable wartime history, you can't just leave it to Holmes and Beevor' *Observer*

'Sebag-Montefiore has added significantly to our knowledge . . . a marvellous tribute to these men who helped create a legend' John Crossland, *Sunday Times*

'The author has brought together scores of personal accounts to impressive, moving effect' Max Hastings, *Sunday Telegraph*

'Sebag-Montefiore is at his best with "set pieces" such as the massacres at Wormhout, Vinkt and Le Paradis, his description of the capture of Eben Emael or the Mechelen Incident. He writes crisply and the series of small-scale actions are related with considerable verve. A fine book . . . immaculately researched, well written, and has much in the way of pathos and human interest' *BBC History*

'Sebag-Montefiore brings a wealth of fresh revelation and detail to this most familiar tale. By the time he is done, the evacuation of Dunkirk seems more miraculous still' Tim Gardam, *The Times*

'The use of anecdote to tell the story and the author's gift for characterization help move the plot along quickly; this is an eminently readable book' Simon Heffer, *Literary Review*

'Absorbing . . . helps put the record straight' *Scotsman*

'Is there anything left to say about the big subjects of World War 2? Yes, provided you give enough time and effort as proved by . . . Hugh Sebag-Montefiore' *Liverpool Daily Post*

'This weighty tome is masterly and scholarly, yet its fast, clear pace makes this definitive work highly readable' *Leicester Mercury*

'It amounts not just to a prodigiously thorough tribute to the "forgotten heroes", but to a landmark work which will take its place among the best examples of serious yet compellingly written military history' *Soldier*

'Many historians have written about Dunkirk, and others (including myself) about the earlier war in France, in 1940. But nobody has done such a masterly job of telling the whole story as Hugh Sebag-Montefiore. He brought much new material to light, not least the unsung heroism of the French forces that guarded the approaches to Dunkirk so desperately in May 1940, without which the BEF would never have been able to escape' Sir Alistair Horne

'A first-rate panoramic history, and highly affecting worm's-eye account, of Britain's absolutely all-time favourite disaster . . . The particular brilliance of this book lies in the manner in which Sebag-Montefiore interleaves the military with the political' Christopher Hitchens, *New York Times*

'In his compelling new study . . . Sebag-Montefiore focuses unerringly on the front line, presenting violence on the field of battle as vivid, harrowing, horrific, ubiquitous' *Washington Post*

'Well-judged and fascinating . . . the definitive account of Dunkirk. While explaining overall strategy, Sebag-Montefiore has expertly interwoven individual tales of heroism and occasional cowardice' *New York Sun*

ABOUT THE AUTHOR

Hugh Sebag-Montefiore was a barrister before becoming a journalist and then an author. He has written for the *Sunday Times*, the *Sunday Telegraph*, the *Observer*, the *Independent on Sunday* and the *Mail on Sunday*. His bestselling book *Enigma: The Battle for the Code* describes how the Polish, French and British cryptographers cracked the German Enigma code. In his quest to find the truth about Dunkirk he has travelled extensively within Europe. In the process he has discovered interesting facts about his own family: two relations were evacuated from the Dunkirk beaches. He lives in North London with his wife and three children.

Dunkirk

Fight to the Last Man

Revised Edition

HUGH SEBAG–MONTEFIORE

PENGUIN BOOKS

For Aviva Burnstock, my wife,
and for Saul, Esther and Abraham, my children

PENGUIN BOOKS

UK | USA | Canada | Ireland | Australia
India | New Zealand | South Africa

Penguin Books is part of the Penguin Random House group of companies
whose addresses can be found at global.penguinrandomhouse.com.

Penguin
Random House
UK

First published by Viking 2006
Published in Penguin Books 2007
Reissued in this edition 2015
001

Copyright © Hugh Sebag-Montefiore, 2006, 2015

The moral right of the author has been asserted

Printed in Great Britain by Clays Ltd, St Ives plc

A CIP catalogue record for this book is available from the British Library

ISBN: 978-0-241-97226-7

www.greenpenguin.co.uk

MIX
Paper from
responsible sources
FSC® C018179

Penguin Random House is committed to a
sustainable future for our business, our readers
and our planet. This book is made from Forest
Stewardship Council® certified paper.

Contents

All sections in this Contents section which are marked with an ⋆ are not included in this 75th Anniversary Edition of this book. They are to be found in the original edition of this book, which can either be purchased while stocks last or which can be found in libraries, or they can be found on Hugh Sebag-Montefiore's website: http://www.hughsebagmontefiore.com.

List of Illustrations

All photographs other than those from archives open to the public and agencies were printed from originals by Steve Aldridge at Sky Imaging (UK) Limited, London. The picture source is given in brackets. An asterisk (*) indicates that the inset shows just a portion of the original photograph.

Section 1

1 Colonel Hans Oster (supplied by his daughter Barbara)
2 Major Gijsbertus Sas (de Spiegel/Spaarnestad Fotoarchief, Haarlem, Holland)
3 Oster's and Sas' children (Oster's daughter Barbara)
4 Erich Hoenmanns (his family)
5 Hoenmanns' crashed plane (Jeroen Huygelier, archivist at Centre de Documentation Historique, Brussels)
6 Colonel Georges Goethals and Vicomte Davignon (*Le Soir*, Brussels)
7 Hore-Belisha on the Gort Line (Imperial War Museum [IWM])*
8 Churchill with French and British generals (Établissement de communication et de production audiovisuelle de la défense [ECPAD/France])
9 French generals (ECPAD/France)
10 Belgians surrender at Veldwezelt bridge (Martina Caspers, archivist at Bundesarchiv-Bildarchiv, Koblenz [Bundesarchiv-Bildarchiv])
11 Aerial view of Albert Canal bridge (Flight Lieutenant Mary Hudson at the Ministry of Defence Air Historical Branch [Air Historical Branch])
12 German armour crosses Veldwezelt bridge (Bundesarchiv-Bildarchiv)
13 A Fairey Battle bomber in France (Air Historical Branch)
14 Dick Marland's burning plane (Air Historical Branch and Michael Pitt)
15 Dick Marland (his daughter Margaret)
16 Tom Gray (IWM)*
17 Generals Corap and Brooke, November 1939 parade (ECPAD/France)
18 Weir at Houx, Belgium (Peter Taghon [Taghon])
19 French B1 bis tank (IWM)*
20 Bridge over Meuse near Dinant (Bundesarchiv-Bildarchiv)
21 General Heinz Guderian (Bundesarchiv-Bildarchiv)
22 Captain R. J. Hastings (Kate Thaxton at the Royal Norfolk Regimental Museum, Norfolk Museums and Archaeology Service, Norwich [Royal Norfolk Regimental Museum])
23 British light tanks advance through Belgium (IWM)*
24 French Somua S-35 tank (IWM)*

Section 2

Section 3

List of Maps

Introducing This Special 75th Anniversary Edition

It is not generally appreciated that the May–June 1940 evacuation of the British Expeditionary Force from Dunkirk would almost certainly have been thwarted if British soldiers had not defended the series of fortified strongpoints and perimeters which obstructed the German advance towards the coast with such courage and tenacity. That being the case, I felt it would be fitting in this special edition of this book, whose main focus has always been the rearguard actions around Dunkirk, to mark Dunkirk's 75th Anniversary by revealing for public scrutiny some of the most exceptional accounts of the heroic last stands which made the evacuation possible.

Although short extracts from these documents were quoted in this book's first edition, I did not there have the space to include all the passages I would have liked. The reason why room is available in this special edition is that Eleo Gordon, my editor at Penguin, and I have decided to move this book's voluminous chapter end notes, as well as other information not usually consulted by the general reader, onto my website on the Internet (see p. xxvi).

One of the criteria for the three accounts in this category which I have chosen to highlight is that they should all describe what any military historian will agree is a rare commodity: descriptions of the action in the front line. That in itself makes the account by Captain Nick Hallett of the 2nd Battalion, the Royal Norfolk Regiment, valuable (see Personal Account 1 on pp. 646–50). However, there is an additional factor which increases its value. He has told his story without in any way seeking to embroider or dramatize the actions in which he and his men participated. His tale is told so matter of factly one has the feeling that, if he were alive today, he would probably have categorized what he and his men did as merely the normal execution of their duty. Yet his story, which describes how he fought on until he was literally the last man on his sector of the battlefield, includes instances of true heroism, while at the same time providing a fascinating snapshot of what so many men had to endure in the front line.

2nd Lieutenant Roy Creswell's account (Personal Account 2 on pp. 652–6) has been included for a slightly different reason. Like so many schoolboys in the 1960s, I was entranced by the bravery exhibited by the redcoats at Rorke's Drift, a last stand immortalized in the film *Zulu*. When I read about what happened in the blockhouse outside Cassel, it reminded me of that earlier fight which so exemplified the British soldiers' willingness to fight with their backs to the wall even when facing up to a much stronger enemy. Although the defence of the block-house was a much smaller-scale version of what occurred at Rorke's Drift, it shared many of its characteristics and showed at least one facet of what we now refer to as 'the Dunkirk spirit' in operation.

The last-ditch stands at the strongpoints, two of which are described in the Hallett and Creswell accounts, could not have effectively shielded the evacuation on their own. Similar fortitude had to be shown by sol-diers ringing the perimeter boundary that encircled Dunkirk itself if the evacuation was not to be interrupted. That is why I felt readers might like to read more of Captain Francis Waldron's account (Personal Account 3 on pp. 657–66) than was included in this book's first edition. As readers of the first edition will remember, it describes the torment which he, along with other members of the 4th Battalion, the Royal Berkshire Regiment, bore as they struggled to overcome their exhaus-tion and fear while at the same time ensuring that no Germans crossed over into their part of the front line on the Furnes–Nieuport Canal. It is the focus on the devastating effects of human frailty when the guns are firing which makes Captain Waldron's narrative so unusual. In such an account, those rash desperados who, like Waldron himself, wanted to lead bayonet charges to throw back the enemy, or who like 2nd Lieutenant Partridge, proposed waking up the Germans by lobbing grenades over onto the other side of the canal, are branded reckless. Instead the emphasis is on profiling the troops who ran away from their post when they were mortared, the officer who was so shell-shocked he was said to be 'useless', and Waldron himself who darted around the coun-tryside looking for Germans, not because he was brave, but because he feared he would go mad if he remained a minute longer at his battalion's HQ where a shell had just landed. Because of the dearth of detailed descriptions of what British soldiers were thinking as they held the line, I cannot say definitively that Waldron's feelings were typical. However, I suspect that many of the soldiers manning the edge of the perimeter around Dunkirk had to overcome similar demons. If I am correct, then Waldron's unique history is essential reading for those who wish to appreciate what they achieved.

Many of the British soldiers who fought on until the bitter end were either captured, wounded or killed. But there were some who battled on, walking at night and hiding by day until they eventually made it to the coast just in time to be evacuated along with everyone else. If one is attempting to describe all the consequences of the rearguard actions, it would be wrong to omit stories of such escapes. That is why I have decided in this special edition to highlight the account by 2nd Lieutenant Julian Fane of the 2nd Battalion, the Gloucestershire Regiment (Personal Account 4 on pp. 667–71). The long list of obstacles that he had to overcome to make it back to Dunkirk after participating in the rearguard action at Cassel emphasizes just how much luck and valour were needed if a man was to successfully break through the German lines. After reading his chronicle, it is easy to see why in the course of my research I never found a similar report to rival it.

Not surprisingly, many of those who were wounded during those desperate rearguard actions ended up in one of Dunkirk's casualty clearing stations. The doctors and medical orderlies caring for them had to risk losing their own liberty or even their lives. As a tribute to all such men, who decided that doing their duty was paramount, I have highlighted in this special edition a moving account by one of them: the surgeon Major Philip Newman (Personal Account 5 on pp. 672–81) who cared for the amputees and the maimed at the 12th Casualty Clearing Station in Rosendaël, a Dunkirk suburb. Newman was one of the medics who stayed behind to look after the wounded at Dunkirk until the Germans took over the evacuated town. In some ways one can say that his self-sacrifice at Dunkirk was even more admirable than the soldiers'. Unlike the soldiers who fought in the rearguard actions, he probably never anticipated that his military service would bring him into contact with Germans, yet when it came to the crunch he was steadfast. That did not mean he did not experience moments of weakness. The depiction of his abject misery as he watched his fellow countrymen abandoning him at the end of the evacuation is all the more poignant because in some respects he was not a natural do-gooder. He was mortified when his name was seventeenth out of the hat during the medics' ballot held to decide which of the CCS medical team should look after the wounded until the Germans took over. The emotional impact of his testimony makes an enduring point, which perhaps is the most important theme running through all the new material in this special edition: courage is not just the preserve of the recklessly daring. True bravery requires a painful struggle to quell one's baser instincts in order to do an act which could have disastrous consequences.

As well as including text which celebrates such bravery, I would like this special edition, being published as it is during the centenary of the First World War, to highlight the most important repercussions of the lessons learned between 1914 and 1918 which affected the outcome in 1940.

Of those fighting in 1940, the German commanders appear to have learned more than anyone from their successes and failures during the First World War. For example, their experience on the defensive during the 1916 Battle of the Somme had taught them that if sufficient shells or bombs were rained down on soldiers in trenches, then a quick follow-up infantry attack would be able to capture even the best dug-in positions. Because they had acted on this lesson learned, and had manufactured thousands of planes whose bombs could reach the French side of the River Meuse, they were able to terrorize the French troops dug in alongside the river in May 1940, thereby rendering vulnerable positions which would otherwise have been impregnable.

The Germans also showed the world how to make the most of their tanks. Having learned from the British failure to exploit their tanks decisively on the Somme – one lesson derived from the fighting in 1916 being that tanks were a relatively ineffective weapon against a well-armed position if used in small numbers against it – they revolutionized tank warfare by attacking with a large number in one location. The fact that the adoption of this tactic played a significant role in the 1940 German Panzer divisions' success is all the more apparent when one contrasts it with the failure of the French tanks, which far from being concentrated in one area, were spread thinly over the battlefield.

Unlike the French, the British had not invested in enough tanks before the fighting started, but because they had learned something from their tank experiences in the First World War, albeit not as much as the Germans, and because that persuaded their commanders to deploy enough of them together during the critical fighting around Arras on 21 May 1940, they were able to alarm the German high command to such an extent that it postponed the Panzers' advance on 22 May and then again between 24 and 26 May 1940. This turned out to be crucial. If the advance had not been halted in this way, it is highly unlikely that the evacuation from Dunkirk would have succeeded, notwithstanding the heroism of the British soldiers at the strongpoints and around the Dunkirk perimeter, and the resulting loss of the British Expeditionary Force might well have changed the whole course of the War. Partly for that reason, and partly because many people still wonder whether the sole reason for Hitler's famous halt order on 24 May 1940 was to enable the British Army to escape so that he could negotiate peace with a country which was not on its knees, I thought readers might be interested in seeing the raw evidence behind my conclusions: I concluded that the German general Gerd von Rundstedt, Army Group A's commander, appears to have made the decision to halt the tanks on military grounds, and that Hitler merely confirmed what von Rundstedt had already decided. The relevant extract from the document I relied on, a translation of von Rundstedt's Army Group A war diary, is laid out in the Postscript on pp. 681–85.

There are many other documents and accounts featured in this book which I could have selected instead of those I have mentioned. Perhaps they will appear in a subsequent new edition to commemorate the next important Dunkirk anniversary, possibly alongside other documents which readers bring to my attention after inheriting them from their forebears. By the time of the next big Dunkirk anniversary there will probably be no living witnesses of the campaign, just as today there are no living witnesses of the First World War. However, for the moment, I will conclude by explaining where the block of personal accounts and postscript that I have mentioned above is to be found. So that readers who have previously read the book can go straight to the new material, my publisher and I have decided to leave the original text more or less unaltered, except where mistakes have been identified, and to put all new material between the Maps and the Bibliography and Sources near the end of this book. That is where readers should look for the newly added text.

Introduction

Many books have already been written about the evacuation of the British Army from Dunkirk, and they all have one characteristic in common: they all stress that it was thanks to the Royal Navy and the little ships that the British Expeditionary Force (the BEF) was saved. But there is another aspect of the story that has not been properly understood. Without in any way belittling the contribution of Vice-Admiral Ramsay and the Royal Navy, not to mention those who took their launches and motor cruisers to Dunkirk, it is now clear that the evacuation would never have succeeded had it not been for those who remained behind to fight on while the rest of the Army retreated.

The crucial part of the battle took place outside Dunkirk. On 24 May 1940 the German panzer divisions that had bludgeoned their way through France had halted at the line of canals twenty to thirty miles to the south of Dunkirk. However, on 27 May they advanced again, intending to encircle and capture half a million Allied soldiers, many of them British. They would almost certainly have succeeded, had it not been for the BEF battalions who were ordered to stand in their path. Their job was to shield the safety zone or corridor behind them down which the rest of the Army was retreating to Dunkirk, and they were not to give way until they had fired their last bullet. They were to fight to the last man. Hardly any of these brave men made it back to the beaches or the Dunkirk 'mole'. Most remained in the front line until it was too late to flee, and were either killed or captured at their posts. They are the forgotten heroes of Dunkirk, and it is their valiant exploits that form the core of this book.

But why was the evacuation necessary in the first place? There were many reasons. The majority were the consequence of mistakes made by French generals and politicians. These fundamental errors are described in the first ten chapters of this book. One of the most important was the failure by French generals to adapt their war plans to take account of the fallout from the so-called 'Mechelen incident': on 10 January 1940 the Belgians captured the German plan to invade their country after a plane carrying it crash-landed near Mechelen in Belgium. Although the Belgians told the French and British what was in the plan – the main focus of the attack was to be in north-east Belgium – the French, who were in charge of the Allies' military strategy, failed to appreciate that the Germans would seek to do something different once the plan had been seen by the enemy. As a result the French carried on concentrating their best forces – including the BEF – so that they were ready to repulse an attack on north-east Belgium, while the Germans were deciding to concentrate their main thrusts further to the south in southern Belgium and around French Sedan.

The Mechelen incident has been written about before. It is covered by most books dealing with the May–June 1940 campaign. But the discovery of the top-secret Reichskriegsgericht (German War Tribunal) file on the affair, which had been gathering dust in the Czechoslovakian Army files in Prague for more than fifty years, together with matching files in the Belgian military archive in Brussels, has enabled me to fill in many of the gaps: previous writers have not been able to determine whether the incident was part of a hoax – as was feared by the British – set up by the Germans to persuade the Belgians to call in the Allies to protect them, thereby giving Hitler a pretext to invade neutral Belgium. Nor could previous writers be sure whether Major Erich Hoenmanns, the pilot of the plane, was a traitor, as was feared by the Germans, who was defecting to the Allies from Nazi Germany. Those who have described the incident before have also had to do so without knowing about Hoenmanns' private life, which appears to have had a bearing on the crash, and they have not been able to write up what happened to him after he was repatriated and arrested by the Germans. The Reichskriegsgericht and Belgian files, along with the report written by Hoenmanns while he was a prisoner-of-war and given to me by his family, tell the whole story, and it is published for the first time in this book.

Another equally important factor that contributed to the French and Belgian defeats, and to Dunkirk, was the failure to react judiciously to the warnings from Berlin issued by the German 'traitor' Colonel Hans Oster about when the attack against France and Belgium would commence. The warnings were passed to the Allies via Major Gijsbertus Sas, the Dutch Military Attaché in Berlin. Once again, this is not a new topic. The warnings have been described in Jean Vanwelkenhuyzen's book *Les avertissements qui venaient de Berlin: 9 octobre 1939–10 mai 1940*. But there are gaps, and some were filled in by Oster's daughter Barbara when I interviewed her. For example, she told me how Oster befriended the Sas family, how Oster's nervous disposition affected him as the Nazis established an iron grip on Germany, and she also confirmed the disastrous effects of her father's love affair with a brother officer's wife: not only did it nearly lead to the break-up of his marriage, but it also led to his having to leave the Army, and to his embarking on a new career in the Abwehr (military intelligence). As is explained in Chapter 4 of this book, Oster's job was one of the main reasons why his intelligence was mistrusted.

The stands made by BEF troops as they withdrew to Dunkirk to avoid being encircled and the deliberations by British politicians and generals have also been referred to in previous books. Major L. F. Ellis's official history *The War In France and Flanders 1939–1940*, and Gregory Blaxland's *Destination Dunkirk: The story of Gort's army*, are the classic accounts. They endeavour to cover all the principal actions that were fought by British troops during the campaign and most of the relevant discussions by the politicians and generals directing them. Covering the whole military campaign in this way was some achievement, given the number of skirmishes and engagements. However, it was achieved at a price. The only way these authors managed to fit so many actions into one book was by relying for the most part on war diaries and regimental histories with the object of presenting not much more than the stark facts.

Not wishing to replicate what Blaxland and Ellis have done so professionally, I have adopted a different strategy: I have confined myself to describing the most important and most heroic actions, and have dealt with them in detail where interesting and vivid reports exist. I have not mentioned actions at all where such reports could not be found unless it was necessary to do so in order to explain manoeuvres by the entire British force. My object has been to give the reader a feel for what it was like to be in the British front line as the great events were unfolding even if this has meant that regretfully I have had to exclude some actions for want of space and others for want of dramatic accounts. Perhaps those readers whose relations took part in battles that have been omitted will send me their accounts, thereby enabling me to cover them in subsequent editions of this book.

Notwithstanding all the praise lavished on those whose Dunkirk spirit made the evacuation a success, it should not be forgotten that the campaign represented a disaster for the British Army. It would almost certainly have ended with the capture of most of the BEF had not Hitler and his generals reined in their panzer divisions at least three times between 20 and 30 May 1940. Some of the lessons that can be learned from what went wrong from the British point of view are as relevant today as they were then. First and foremost, the campaign showed that politicians must never, even in peacetime, deprive their armed forces of the equipment they need. Complacently assuming that the equipment can be manufactured once war is declared is demonstrably unwise. By the time the BEF's Commander-in-Chief Lord Gort realized that his well-protected infantry tanks were able to force back the Germans, it was too late to ask for more. He had to make do with just seventy-four, two thirds of which were knocked out during their first engagement near Arras on 21 May.[1] From that moment, the BEF were effectively pinned down and deprived of the opportunity to mount a viable counter-attack.

Another lesson that can be learned relates to what should be done when, as so often is the case, Britain is the junior partner in a military alliance. Britain's politicians and generals should never agree to put her troops under an ally's command without first auditing and analysing the way in which the ally proposes to deploy its troops as well as Britain's, without insisting on ongoing audits of the ally's plans, and regular reports from British battalions and liaison officers in the front line on the way the ally's troops are shaping up. If this had been done in France between September 1939 and 10 May 1940, Lord Gort and the British Prime Minister (who was Neville Chamberlain until Churchill took over on 10 May) would have seen that France was not leaving herself enough reserves to repulse the German units that eventually broke through the French principal line of resistance, and could have done something about it: in his memoirs Churchill bemoaned the fact that the British Government and the War Office had not taken this lesson on board before the battle started.[2]

Also, British officers in France had seen clear signs indicating that many French soldiers were undisciplined, poorly trained, and that morale in the French Army was very low. If these findings had been properly circulated, it is just possible that after the German breakthrough on the

Meuse, British politicians and generals would not have entertained the unrealistic hope that the French would recover, and an earlier decision might have been made to evacuate the British troops from France.

All of this raises the question: was Gort cowed by Churchill's demand that he should counter-attack into waiting too long before letting it be known that the evacuation from Dunkirk was the only answer? Gort has rightly been praised for making the decision on 25 May 1940 to call off the planned counter-attack; this freed up British units that were then used to protect the corridor to Dunkirk (see Chapter 19). However, the evidence presented in this book suggests he should have stood up to Churchill and General Ironside, the Chief of the Imperial General Staff, four days earlier, once he had realized that the counter-attack was unlikely to succeed. As is demonstrated in Chapter 36, Churchill was perfectly willing to back down from his insistence that British troops should remain in France when in relation to the 2nd BEF General Alan Brooke stood up to him resolutely, refusing to be browbeaten by the arguments put forward by his prime minister.

Perhaps Gort would have done the same if, on 21 May, he had had the opportunity to talk to General Weygand, the French Commander-in-Chief, about his plans. However, he missed the 21 May meeting with Weygand, not through any fault of the French but because, as often happened during the campaign, Gort failed to organize communications so that he was always in contact with his GHQ and his liaison officers at French headquarters. His liaison officer at the French Army Group 1 headquarters attempted to tip him off about the meeting but was told that Gort was out.

Gort's failure to call off the counter-attack until the last possible moment did not make the French any more accommodating about the BEF's departure. I was astonished to discover from the French veterans I interviewed that many French soldiers are still very bitter about what they refer to as the British desertion at Dunkirk. A symbol of the anti-British sentiments that were inflamed during 'Operation Dynamo' (the code name for the evacuation from Dunkirk) is the extraordinary document in the French military archives purporting to be a transcript of the heated discussions on 31 May 1940 between the British General Alexander and the French admiral and commanders at Dunkirk.[3] At first sight the document makes it look as if Alexander was welching on a promise given by Gort to hold the Dunkirk perimeter.

It is only when British records are consulted that a more balanced version of the events is revealed. War Cabinet minutes show that, far from merely asking the British troops to hold on while the French were evacuated, the British were being asked to sacrifice their troops so that Dunkirk could be held indefinitely. This was clearly an unreasonable demand, given the small number of equipped and trained units available in Britain to repulse the expected invasion: another document in the British archives shows that on that day there were just three divisions in Britain with more than twenty-five per cent of their guns in their hands.[4]

One reason why Dunkirk has such resonance for British people today is that, in spite of all the mistakes made by the politicians and generals, it showed the nation at its best, with so many people from all walks of life coming together to demonstrate that famous all-conquering spirit. Nearly every British family either has or had a relative or acquaintance who was there. My family is no exception. I have often heard about my cousin Denzil Sebag-Montefiore's precious ivory hairbrushes engraved with his initials, which were thrown into the sea at Dunkirk along with other heavy items in his backpack so that he would be more buoyant in the water. My search for veterans quickly led me to men who had known him and who had stories to tell about what he did in France during the 1940 campaign. Fortunately he was a benevolent platoon commander, and earned undying devotion from his men by sharing with them the contents of the Fortnum and Mason food hamper his parents sent to him in France at Christmas 1939. His men paid him back in kind at Dunkirk when he was spotted having difficulty climbing into the rowing-boat that had come in to pick them up from the sea. Rather than deserting him in his hour of need, a group of men rushed to heave him up over the side and into the boat.[5] He duly made it back to England, and eventually resumed his career as a stockbroker in Sebags, the family firm.

Basil Jaffé, another cousin, on my mother's side, also spent hours queuing in the water off the Dunkirk beaches. He only survived by ditching all his equipment, and by reading a miniature edition of Shakespeare's plays, which helped to pass the time until he was picked up.

Of course even for my family much more was at stake at Dunkirk than the lives of these two cousins. If Britain had lost her army, Hitler might have been tempted to invade, whether or not he had first established air superiority over the English Channel. That would probably have spelt disaster for all British people given the small number of fully equipped troops in the country. It would have resulted in even more catastrophic consequences for all Anglo-Jewish families, such as mine, who would almost certainly have been rounded up and exterminated once Hitler took control of Britain. Dunkirk and the men who fought to make it happen saved us from this fate, and for that my family, and I, will be eternally grateful.

Note to Readers

In order to make room for the extended quotations from soldiers' accounts and the Postscript which have been included in this Dunkirk 75th Anniversary special edition, the chapter Notes, together with the Appendices, Dramatis Personae and Abbreviations, all of which appeared in the first version of this book, have been omitted from this edition. Those wishing to read them can either purchase a copy of the original text, or they can consult a copy in a library. Alternatively they will be posted on my website on the Internet: http://www.hughsebagmontefiore.com. The pages on the Internet will have the same page numbers on them as they had in the first edition of this book.

The references to names, places and military units which appear in the newly added Personal Accounts and Postscript are not reflected in the index.

Readers who want to follow a particular chapter's action on the maps which are at the end of this book should refer to the map(s) specified at the beginning of each chapter, and to the maps specified at various points in the body of that chapter's main text. Alternatively readers who want to know the whereabouts of a particular town or village can look at its entry in the index in order to find the chapter end note which specifies where the town or village is located.

Because many of the accounts and other documents in this book were not written for publication, words and punctuation necessary to make them comprehensible and easy to read have often been omitted by their authors. Alternatively the grammar is faulty. I have taken the liberty of correcting punctuation where this has occurred, but when I have added a word to help the sense, I have placed it in square brackets, and when I have omitted or moved a word, I have marked the omission or changes by inserting three dots.

PART 1: THE GERMAN ATTACK

1: Moment of Truth

La Ferté, Paris and London, 14–16 May 1940
(See Maps 1 and 5)

At 3 a.m. on 14 May 1940, events at Château des Bondons, headquarters of the French Commander-in-Chief of the North-East Front, were unfolding, which, if observed by a British general, would have made his blood run cold. Just four days after the German attack on France, Belgium and Holland had commenced, the French commander, General Alphonse Georges, who was supposed to be leading French, Belgian and British troops into battle, had broken down and was crying. Most of his staff had been stunned into silence by the bad news they had received.

A French captain who entered the house, situated in La Ferté-sous-Jouarre, twenty-five miles east of Paris, recorded what he witnessed as the section of the French general staff responsible for the entire front in North-East France and Belgium threatened to implode:

All the lights are out, except in this room [which had been converted into a map room, and] which is only half lit. Commandant Navereau is talking to someone on the telephone, and repeats in a quiet voice the intelligence he is receiving. The others in the room are silent. General Roton, the chief of [Georges'] staff, is slumped in an armchair. It is like attending a family wake. Georges jumps up, and steps forward to greet [Major-General Aimé] Doumenc. He [Georges] is very pale. 'Our front has caved in at Sedan!' [Georges says]. 'There have been disasters . . .' He falls into an armchair, and is choked by a sob. It was the first time I saw a man crying during the battle. It would not be the last . . . Georges, still pale, explains: two mediocre divisions have run away after the terrible bombing raids. Xth Corps has signalled that its front line has been pierced, and German tanks arrived at Bulson just before midnight. All the other witnesses remain silent, overwhelmed by what has happened.[1]

At last someone spoke: 'Come on, General,' said Doumenc. 'There are routs in every war. Let's look at the map. We're going to see what can be done!' Doumenc then walked over to the map, and proceeded to plan counter-measures. The three French armoured divisions were still intact. The one in Charleroi, Belgium, could attack from north to south; another south of Sedan from south to north, and the third, on its way northward, from west to east.[2] The German bridgehead could thus be attacked from three sides, and thrown back eastwards over the River Meuse, which, until the Germans attacked, had been the French front line. Unless there was an unexpected hitch, the status quo that had existed before the German attack would be quickly re-established.

Doumenc's pep talk evidently resulted in a mood swing at Georges' headquarters: later that morning, the information Georges sent to his superior, General Maurice Gamelin, the overall Commander-in-Chief of all Allied troops, played down the crisis to such an extent that it was as if the breakdown of confidence at Les Bondons had never happened.

The general's report included the following misleading information: '2nd Army – The breach at Sedan has been blocked on the stop line . . . Counter-attack with formidable means started this morning at 4.30 a.m.'[3]

It was only after lunch on 14 May that the French Government caught its first whiff of the crisis that was rapidly turning into a disaster. Paul Baudouin, the French Cabinet Secretary, described how he discovered what was happening:

I went to a lunch in honour of the Prime Minister and the Foreign Minister of Luxembourg, and of the Belgian Foreign and Finance Ministers, and I was just coming out when Colonel de Villelume [the French Prime Minister's military adviser] said that he wanted to speak to me urgently. At that moment I was walking on the big lawn at the Quai d'Orsay in glorious sunshine, but a chill came over me . . . The news was very bad: [General Charles] Huntziger's [2nd] army had been violently attacked, and some fortifications in the Sedan district had been lost . . . The Prime Minister [the Président du Conseil, Paul Reynaud] came in and asked Colonel de Villelume if the order to fall back had been given to our armies which were advancing in Belgium. The Colonel . . . replied in the negative. We felt that the situation had suddenly become tragic.[4]

Later that afternoon, Reynaud rang a message through to Winston Churchill, who, four days earlier, in the wake of the abortive attempt to seize Norway before the Germans, had replaced Neville Chamberlain as the British Prime Minister. Reynaud, who, had it not been for the 10 May German attack, would himself have stepped down as premier because of a split in the French Cabinet over how to react to the Norway fiasco, asked Churchill for ten squadrons of fighter planes in addition to the ten Hurricane squadrons already operating in France 'to allow our counter-attack to succeed', and while he awaited Churchill's response, there was still hope.[5] Reynaud's pleading was to be successful. Although Sir Hugh Dowding, Fighter Command's Air Officer Commanding-in-Chief, reported to the Chiefs of Staff that sending the extra squadrons to France would leave him with just twenty-nine, too few to protect Britain securely, after much debate it was eventually agreed that France should have her planes. (See note 6 for details of the agreement.)[6]

Reynaud was only given this good news on 16 May. By then there had been other developments. During the evening of 14 May, General Georges had told Air Marshal Arthur Barratt, commander of the British Air Forces in France, that the British air raids that day had enabled General Huntziger to 'contain' the German bridgehead so effectively that he felt the centre of the attack would switch to Dinant the next day.[7] The full implications of the disaster were only finally appreciated by Reynaud on the morning of 15 May, by which time the capitulation of Holland had been announced, thereby freeing up yet another panzer division to be used against French, Belgian and British forces.[8] That was when he famously woke Churchill with his 7.30 a.m. telephone call, and proceeded to tell him, as it turned out correctly: 'We are beaten. We have lost the battle.'[9]

On the same day, there were also signs that staff at the headquarters of General Gaston Billotte, commander of Army Group 1, believed that the battle might be lost. This was not to be taken lightly since Billotte's Army Group 1 was the entity through which General Georges exercised control over all the Allied units facing the principal German thrusts: the French 1st, 7th and 9th Armies, and until 13 May the 2nd Army, as well as the Belgian Army and the British Expeditionary Force in France (the BEF). (See Map 1 on pp. 508–9 for the positions held by these armies prior to the German attack.)[10] Major Osmund Archdale, Britain's liaison officer between Lord Gort, the BEF's Commander-in-Chief, and Billotte, wrote in his diary for 15 May: 'Today for the first time I saw the Headquarters 1st [Army] Group start to crack.' He went on to paint an alarming picture: 'My doubts about General Billotte started to take definite shape,' he wrote. He described Billotte's chief of staff as 'inarticulate', and spotted other officers with tears rolling down their cheeks. Most worrying of all, Archdale began to suspect that the French had no 'strategic reserves'. The only straw that could be clutched at was the claim that they were about to counter-attack.[11] Unfortunately the French counter-attacks did not succeed, and on 16 May Billotte was forced to order British and French forces, which had just advanced into Belgium, to retreat as quickly as possible, in order to avoid being surrounded by German panzers that had broken through the French line to the south.[12]

The parlous state in which the French Army found itself and the unrealistic expectations of politicians who were supposed to be running it were highlighted at 8.40 p.m. on the night of 15–16 May during a meeting between Édouard Daladier, the French Defence Minister, and William Bullitt, America's Ambassador in Paris. Their meeting was interrupted by a desperate telephone call from General Gamelin, who had rung to report the depth of the German advance. 'Daladier was totally incredulous and stupefied,' Bullitt informed President Franklin D. Roosevelt. 'As the information came over the wire from Gamelin, he [Daladier] kept exclaiming: "It cannot be true." "Impossible." '[13] But not only was it possible. It was the truth, and whatever Churchill or his generals said in an attempt to restore French morale, it was clear to the French Government and its generals that they were about to be the victims of a humiliating defeat.

The next day Major-General Hastings Ismay, who flew with Churchill to Paris, was 'flabbergasted' when told by officers collecting them from the Le Bourget airfield that the Germans were expected in the French capital in a few days at most.[14] And that was an optimistic forecast compared with the rumours sweeping through the corridors of the French Assembly that morning, where at least one politician was overheard telling a friend: 'I advise you to leave Paris before two o'clock.'[15] 'It was obvious that the situation was incomparably worse than we had imagined,' Churchill wrote in his memoirs. Churchill's party was driven to the Quai d'Orsay (the Foreign Ministry) where the meeting with Reynaud, Daladier and Gamelin was due to take place. According to Churchill: 'Everybody was standing. At no time did we sit down around a table. Utter dejection was written on every face. In front of Gamelin on a student's easel was a map about two yards square with a black line purporting to show the Allied front. In this line there was drawn a small but sinister bulge at Sedan.'[16]

Baudouin wrote acidly of Gamelin's contribution to the proceedings: 'He explained, but he made no suggestions. He had no views on the future . . . While this was going on M. Daladier [who, just before the battle started, had refused to allow Reynaud to dismiss Gamelin] remained apart, red in the face, drawn. He sat in a corner like a schoolboy in disgrace.'[17]

Churchill, in one of the most celebrated passages written on the campaign, has described what happened next:

I then asked: 'Where is the strategic reserve?' and, breaking into French, which I used indifferently . . . 'Où est la masse de manoeuvre?'

General Gamelin turned to me and, with a shake of the head and a shrug, said: 'Aucune.'

There was another long pause. Outside in the garden of the Quai d'Orsay clouds of smoke arose from large bonfires, and I saw from the window venerable officials pushing wheel-barrows of archives on to them. Already . . . the evacuation of Paris was being prepared.[18]

It took those present some time to digest the terrible significance of the simple words 'strategic reserve' and '*aucune*'. Churchill's reaction is to be found in his memoirs:

I was dumbfounded. What were we to think of the great French Army and its highest chief? It had never occurred to me that any commanders . . . would have left themselves unprovided with a mass of manoeuvre . . . This was one of the greatest surprises I have had in my life.[19]

So how had the French Army, supposedly one of the strongest military forces in 1940, with as many divisions and tanks as the Germans under its command, fallen so quickly? (See note 20 for comparative numbers of divisions and tanks.)[20] And why was its fall such a surprise to the British, whose Expeditionary Force had for months been standing shoulder to shoulder with its French ally along the Franco-Belgian border?

2: The BEF Arrives in France

The French ports, Lille and the Franco-Belgian border,
October 1939–April 1940
(See Map 2. Also Map 1)

Advance elements of the BEF had started out on their journey to France on 4 September 1939, just one day after war was declared. The first convoy of troopships carrying BEF soldiers steamed out of the ports at Southampton and Bristol five days later. By 27 September, more than 152,000 British soldiers had arrived in France, most of them landing at ports south of the River Somme including Cherbourg, St Nazaire, Nantes, Le Havre and Dieppe.[1] These men, and those who followed, were to become the victims of the French defeat at Sedan and north of Dinant. Yet they could not all be said to be innocent. Long before the battles started, they had seen abundant evidence suggesting that the French Army had little in common with the force that had held up the Germans in the First World War, and if politicians had served in the ranks with their troops, the British Government would have been in the know as well.

However, doubts about their French allies were far from British soldiers' minds when, on 3 October, the first two BEF divisions moved into the front line on the Franco-Belgian border. The British sector was east of Lille, and was to run from Maulde in the south to Halluin in the north, before curling round to Armentières.[2] The next two divisions arrived in the British sector on 12 October. Each division, which in theory was supposed to contain around 13,600 men, included three infantry brigades, each brigade holding around 2500 men, as well as support troops such as artillery and signal units. For example, 1 Division included 1, 2 and 3 Brigades, and 2 Division had 4, 5 and 6 Brigades under its command. There were three infantry battalions in each brigade, each battalion containing around 750 to 800 men.[3] French troops held the Franco-Belgian border on either side of the British, the idea being that a continuous line of Allied soldiers would be deployed along France's north-east frontier from the southern end of the Maginot Line near Basle, Switzerland, to the sea east of Dunkirk. (The line is shown in

Maps 1 and 2 on pp. 508–9 and 511.) The units guarding it – which constituted Army Groups 1, 2 and 3 – were under the Commander-in-Chief of the North-East Front: General Georges.

It should be pointed out that French and British generals and politicians would have preferred it if their defence line had run through Belgium. However, the Belgians would not allow this. Although Belgium was to become Britain's and France's ally as soon as Germany attacked in the west, the Belgian Government had decided their country should remain neutral until then. As a result the British and French Governments had to leave their forces on the French side of the Franco-Belgian border until Belgium was invaded. Nevertheless their troops made the best of a bad job, digging trenches and building blockhouses. If the Germans attacked France after passing through Belgium or Luxembourg, the French Army and the BEF would be dug in and waiting for them. At any rate, that was the theory. General Gamelin was not planning to use the trenches at all if he could avoid it. As soon as the Germans attacked, he wanted the BEF and the French Army to march into Belgium and Holland to take on the Germans well away from French territory.

The first four British divisions to arrive in France were made up of regular soldiers, and were supposed to represent the cream of the British Army. But although they included battalions from famous regiments such as the Grenadier and Coldstream Guards, their effectiveness was hampered because they were extraordinarily badly equipped and trained. The difficulties experienced by one of 5 Brigade's anti-tank platoons, a unit manned by men from the 1st Battalion, the Queen's Own Cameron Highlanders, mirrored similar problems in other units. There were anti-tank platoons in each brigade, and they had a crucial role to play. Most infantry soldiers were armed with mere rifles and Bren guns, which, though adequate for fighting against German infantry, could not penetrate the panzers' armour. Some soldiers had hand-held anti-tank rifles, but they proved ineffective when they came up against real tanks rather than the imaginary 'cardboard' versions referred to by British propaganda. (Some British propaganda published before the German attack suggested that Germany was passing off cardboard mocked-up tanks as the real thing to make her panzer divisions appear more powerful than they really were.) Thus, once the panzers had evaded the heavy British artillery, and other guns controlled by divisional commanders, the 25mm guns-on-wheels deployed by the brigades' anti-tank platoons represented the British Army's best chance of stopping them.

Given their importance, one might have expected that the anti-tank platoons at least would have been properly provided for. They were not. Their makeshift transport was indicative of the British Army's failure across the board to make adequate preparations for war. It consisted of a motley selection of trucks and vans from post offices, butchers, bakers and other British shops and companies, whose only military addition was a lick of khaki paint. Worse still, the anti-tank platoons arrived in France before they had had the opportunity to fire their newly issued 25mm Hotchkiss guns. The men had to work out how to fire them from the accompanying manuals after they had arrived in France.[4]

Similar stories abound in relation to the other infantry battalions. The BEF's tank units were even less well endowed. The all-important 1st Armoured Division, Britain's only answer to Germany's panzer divisions, had so few of the new cruiser tanks it had been promised that Lord Gort initially refused to accept the division in France, saying it should wait until at least 50 per cent of its existing Mark VI light tanks – light referring to the thickness and weight of their armour rather than their colour – were replaced with heavier cruisers armed with two-pounder (40mm) guns.[5] The two-pounder guns were essential because they were the only weapons mounted on British tanks that could penetrate the panzers' armour. Light tanks had to make do with two machine-guns. But if anyone expected cruiser tanks to save the BEF when they finally reached France during the battle, they were living in a fool's paradise. The cruisers were far from invincible. Their 1.2-inch-thick armour provided better protection than that on light tanks, but it could not repel well-aimed anti-tank gun shells.[6]

As for the fifty thickly armoured Mark I infantry tanks that accompanied the BEF to France, their armour was thick enough to ward off German anti-tank shells, but they only carried machine-guns, which made them as useless as the BEF's ninety-six Mark VI light tanks when it came to penetrating the panzers.[7] As if that was not bad enough, when the light tanks arrived in France, many were not ready to fight; for example, of the twenty-eight supporting 1 Division, only twelve had shoulder pieces for their guns.[8]

The reason why the first sections of the BEF to arrive in France were in this shocking state is clear: the British Government had waited for a long time before increasing the size of its army. It had only finally agreed to do so in February 1939.[9] Nevertheless by the time the Germans attacked, there were ten more or less complete British infantry divisions in France, in addition to three incomplete divisions whose soldiers' principal task was to act as labourers.[10] By then at least some of the former units were properly trained and better equipped. Strengthening the armour supporting the BEF was harder. Although fifty extra infantry tanks arrived in May 1940, only twenty-three were armed with a two-pounder gun.[11] Given that the war was likely to be won by the side that made the best use of its armour in tank-versus-tank combat, it is small wonder that British soldiers, backed up by just twenty-three tanks properly equipped for the task, hoped the French would make up for the BEF's deficiency.

Had the BEF been attacked in 1939, such deficiencies might have proved disastrous. Fortunately, there was an eight-month period of 'peace', known as 'the phoney war', during which many British soldiers were more interested in making the most of the 'facilities' offered by the French, and improving their living conditions, than in what might be done to compensate for the lack of effective equipment and training. The living conditions were in some cases even more primitive than the equipment. The memoirs of Private Gregor MacDonald of the 4th Battalion, the Queen's Own Cameron Highlanders, give us a good idea of what some infantrymen had to put up with when they arrived in France.[12] MacDonald was from the island of Harris in the Scottish Highlands and was used to inclement weather, but his first day in France, after arriving at Dieppe on 10 January 1940, taxed even his powers of endurance.

First, he and his comrades had to make a ten-mile route march through the snow, carrying all their equipment. During the march they were comforted by the idea that they could at least rest their weary backs and feet in the farm where they were to be billeted. 'Imagine our feelings,' wrote MacDonald, 'when we arrived at a group of broken-down sheds, all of which housed lean, hungry cattle, and it was clear that no attempt had been made to clean the sheds out.' By the time they had persuaded the farmer to produce a cart of damp smelly hay, a poor substitute for the mattresses they normally slept on, it was dark. That being the case, there was nothing each man could do but eat his share of the rations cooked on a pressure burner, and lie down on one of the shed floors. MacDonald has described how he was allotted a single blanket for the night, and how he tried to ignore his freezing cold feet, which were wet and dirty after tramping through the mud churned up by the cattle. He finally went to sleep on the hay just feet away from the cows in their stalls. He and the other men in his company endured these uncomfortable conditions for three weeks, before moving to a slightly more civilized half-built house near Lille.

MacDonald and his comrades were not the only soldiers who suffered in this way. But their experiences were by no means universal. Other men had a more cushy landing. When the 1st East Riding Yeomanry, a unit equipped with light tanks and Bren-gun carriers, landed at Le Havre in February 1940, they were told they could do as they pleased during their first evening in France.[13] After eating a snack in the field kitchen set up in a dockside warehouse, the younger soldiers debated what they should do next. It did not take them long to decide. They had all heard about France's licensed brothels, which did not exist in England. While some balked at the idea of paying for sex, others reasoned that since they might not survive the conflict, it was now or never. Much of the action in Le Havre's red-light district took place in rue des Galions, where some brothels displayed their girls in the window. Lance-Corporal Richard Harvey, an advertising executive from Hull before he joined the East Riding Yeomanry, has written about the welcome the young Englishmen received when they entered one such establishment. They found themselves in a bright, airy room with a highly polished wooden floor, and with chairs and tables around the walls. It was as if they had walked into a dance hall. They were greeted by the plump, beaming Madame. On the other side of the room pretty young girls were chatting to a dozen young sailors. One of Harvey's companions went scarlet when a dainty dark-haired girl in a bright red dress walked up to him and asked him something in French.

'Christ, Corporal! What did she say?' he asked Harvey.

'She's only asking us what we'd like to drink, Jack,' Harvey replied. Then all of the other girls abandoned the sailors, sashayed over to Harvey and his friends and sat on their laps.

'Upstairs, Tommy. You come upstairs *avec moi* for a good time,' Harvey's young lady suggested.

He declined, but five of his companions disappeared with their girls, reappearing shortly afterwards. By that time the remaining girls had abandoned those soldiers who were less game so that they could renew their assault on the sailors. 'This was our first taste of the French way of life,' wrote Harvey.

Rue des Galions quickly became a favourite haunt for troops arriving in France, and when they went there, it was not just for sex. Captain Forde Cayley, a medical officer, started his first night out in France by having a meal with his senior officer in rue des Galions' Lion d'Or restaurant.[14] Afterwards they went next door into the La Lune brothel where they succumbed to temptation. In their case their temptresses were 'Fifi' and 'Mimi', who had perched on their knees as soon as they arrived. Cayley was surprised to discover that his girl was pregnant; his memoirs record that she was married by the time his medical unit left Le Havre. Later that same evening he and his friend went into another brothel opposite the first where they came across a sporty variation on the same theme. One girl was dressed for tennis, another was wearing a swimsuit, two were in evening dresses, and the other girls wore very short skirts, which they lifted to reveal that they were wearing no knickers. Cayley did not mention whether he and his friend went upstairs for a second time that night.

Similar facilities were laid on at the other ports where British soldiers were landing. In September 1939 when gunner William Harding arrived at Cherbourg, an experienced married reservist warned him off the brothels, saying, 'What you've never had you'll never miss.'[15] But on his third night in France, he ended up at a brothel too. It was called L'Avion, and for those who could not read French its name and location were advertised by a neon light shaped to look like an aeroplane. Outside, a queue of around two hundred soldiers stretched along the street. As Harding gazed down the alley running alongside the house, he thought for a moment that it had begun to rain, until he realized that dozens of soldiers were urinating out of the windows. When he finally went in, he was overwhelmed by the sight of girls with long black hair wearing nothing but G-strings and high-heeled shoes. 'I couldn't resist once inside,' he confessed in his memoir. It only cost him ten francs, twice the price of the beer he had bought while he was waiting. The beer was not the only distraction laid on. Fearing perhaps that the soldiers might lose interest before it was their turn, a girl emerged from one of the upstairs rooms every now and then, and wiped her vagina with a rag before throwing it to the men below. According to

Harding, the soldiers scrambled to pick up the rag covered with her odour and their compatriots' semen 'like a rugby scrum fighting for a ball'.

The visits to brothels did not stop when the men moved up into the line on the Franco-Belgian border. On their nights off, the men would hop into a truck known as 'the passion wagon', which took them to the fleshpots of Lille and Tourcoing.[16] Lille was particularly well set-up for sex-starved soldiers: the red-light district was concentrated in rue ABC. It was a narrow cobbled street, full of brothels with 'stable doors', of which the top half could be opened while the bottom remained shut.[17] Its mysterious charm was accentuated by the semi-blackout then in force. No street-lights were illuminated. The only light came from the houses on either side of the road. Soldiers of all ranks used the brothels in rue ABC, but because officers did not like their men to see them with their trousers down, a separation of ranks was maintained. Some brothels bore a sign saying, 'Officers only'. Others were set aside for 'Warrant Officers and Sergeants', while the remainder accepted all comers. 2nd Lieutenant Toby Taylor, an officer serving with the 1st Battalion, the East Surrey Regiment, has described what he observed in one of the smarter officer-only establishments: girls in evening dress stood to attention like men on parade, so that the officers could walk down the line to choose the one who took their fancy.[18] Taylor must have found it hard to forget this seductive scene when he next lined up the men in his platoon to inspect them.

Visits to Lille did not take place every night. Taylor and his fellow officers, Captain 'Buck' Buchanan and 2nd Lieutenants 'Foxy' Brooke-Fox and 'Peck' Andrews, usually preferred to have dinner near their billets in Roubaix. Then they only had to jump into a taxi, and mouth, 'Girls,' to the driver, who would whisk them off to one of the many *estaminets* − bars − that provided women as well as drink. You could usually tell if a bar doubled as a brothel because such establishments more often than not displayed a sign in the window on which the words '*tous conforts*' were written. On one occasion, Foxy returned to his billet only to discover that his watch, a valuable heirloom given to him by his grandfather, was missing. Next morning he and Taylor hailed another taxi, somehow found the right *estaminet*, and eventually discovered the watch under the bed where he had been entertained. After that, both Taylor and Foxy agreed it would be safer to visit one establishment regularly, rather than ending up at a different brothel each time. They settled on one to which they were introduced by a girl they had met in a bar. It was called Le Soleil and, apart from a few officers, it was normally half empty. Here they established something approaching real friendships with the girls, which did not always lead to better sex. Taylor found his ardour dampened somewhat when, on asking one girl why she had letters tattooed on to her inner thigh, she told him they were her boyfriend's initials, and that she 'belonged' to him.

In the end, the young officers who had first visited Le Soleil because they were hungry for sex became as interested in the alcohol on offer as the girls; Taylor had discovered quite quickly that they were not particularly exciting once he had got to know them properly. He and his brother officers liked to challenge each other to have a drink from each bottle behind the bar, which guaranteed that they staggered out roaring drunk. If this had occurred in any other house, he and his friends would have had to make it back to their billets under their own steam, but Le Soleil's Madame, a pretty woman called Denise, took it upon herself to mother these young men, who must have appeared so innocent beside her sexually experienced girls. Whenever she felt they had drunk too much, she would insist on driving them home.

The British soldiers' partiality for French prostitutes led to some comic scenes. 2nd Lieutenant Jimmy Langley, whose Coldstream Guards' platoon was to play an important role on the perimeter at Dunkirk, has described how while stationed at Pont-à-Marcq, six miles to the south of Lille, he was walking back to his billet after paying his men their wages when his commanding officer, Lieutenant-Colonel Lionel Bootle-Wilbraham, drew up beside him in his car, and addressed him thus:

'I did not know, Jimmy, that No. 3 Company were having a cross-country run this afternoon.'

Nor did I, and my face must have showed it. [Wilbraham continued:] 'I have just come back from Brigade Headquarters and have passed most of the company running in the general direction of Templeuve [a village some three miles away]. No. 15 Platoon was well in the lead. You might find out and let me know what it is all about.'

I was fully aware of the attractions that were to be found in Templeuve, and suddenly understood why my platoon were so grateful when I paid them first. Colonel Bootle laughed when I told him [before concluding], 'A pity

Templeuve is not farther away, but I must say No. 15 Platoon appeared remarkably fit. They were setting an absolutely cracking pace.'[19]

Thus the lure of sex at least improved the fitness of some BEF soldiers. It must also have relieved the monotony of digging trenches along the frontier, which was all they had to keep them occupied during working hours. But not all of the side effects were as beneficial: some men used girls outside the licensed brothels, and many caught venereal disease. On 15 November 1939 one of the BEF's youngest generals, the fifty-one-year-old Major-General Bernard Montgomery, tried to deal with the problem affecting his 3rd Division by circulating a memorandum on sexual behaviour. It started with the words: 'Subject: Prevention of Venereal Disease', and continued:

I am not happy about the situation regarding venereal disease in the Division. Since the 18 October, the number of cases admitted to Field Ambulances in the Divisional area totals 44 . . . My view is that if a man wants to have a woman, let him do so by all means: but he must use his common sense, and take the necessary precautions against infection – otherwise he becomes a casualty by his own neglect, and this is helping the enemy. Our job is to help him by providing the necessary means.[20]

Montgomery wanted the men to be given the chance to buy 'French letters' in their army unit's shop, and he said that a room for cleaning up afterwards should be made available within each company, rather than in each battalion: 'The man who has a woman in a beetroot field near his coy. billet will not walk a mile to the battalion E.T. room,' he explained, adding that the men should be given French lessons so that they knew how to ask for a French letter, a '*capote anglaise*', in a chemist. He went on:

There are in Lille a number of brothels, which are properly inspected, and where the risk of infection is practically nil. These are known to the military police, and any soldier who is in need of horizontal refreshment would be well advised to ask a policeman for a suitable address.

His words seem sensible and uncontroversial today, but in the relatively repressed 1930s, they were so provocative that BEF Commander-in-Chief Lord Gort told 2 Corps' Lieutenant-General Alan Brooke that Montgomery must publicly withdraw them.[21] In fairness to Gort, the wives and girlfriends left behind in England would not have been happy to learn what Montgomery had said, and was thus tacitly encouraging, while their men were under his command in France. General Brooke was not being unreasonable when, on 23 November 1939, he told Montgomery that his language was 'obscene', and must on no account be repeated. However, he refused to diminish the general's authority by making him withdraw the circular.[22]

Whether it was the women in the beetroot fields or in the brothels who were responsible for the VD outbreak, extreme measures were taken thereafter to encourage the British soldiers to be more careful. 2nd Lieutenant Taylor remembers going with Dr Bird, the 1st East Surrey's medical officer, to buy condoms from the local pharmacy. He was amused, if somewhat embarrassed, by the raised eyebrows of the girl behind the counter when Dr Bird asked her to wrap up twelve dozen. Then, as Dr Bird marched out of the shop carrying a large box, Taylor thought he heard the girl mutter admiringly, '*Quel homme!*'[23]

As Montgomery had suggested, condoms alone were insufficient, given that many soldiers lacked the presence of mind to use them. Some medical officers maintained the 'prophylactic rooms' mentioned by 3 Division's commander where men were encouraged to clean themselves after visiting brothels. It was found that men who applied an ointment referred to as 'dreadnought' within an hour of visiting a prostitute were almost immune to VD.[24] Other doctors terrified the men in their units into taking care of themselves. One doctor showed the men in his battalion horrific pictures of infected genitals, which put many off their food as well as sex.[25] A verbal description of possible treatments for venereal disease dissuaded some from indulging. One man remembers being told that if a soldier had syphilis, a probe covered with Calomel ointment would be inserted into his penis, a painful procedure in itself, but one that would have been made worse thanks to the stinging induced by chemicals within the ointment.[26] The same man was also told of an equally unpleasant treatment to combat gonorrhoea: it involved pumping two pints of Condy's fluid, a disinfectant, into the penis. This would have forced the unfortunate sufferer to empty his bladder, by which time it was hoped that the disease would have been eradicated.[27] Army records do not reveal whether it was the fear of these procedures, or the actual treatments utilized that were most effective. But some men fell through the net.[28] William Harding heard an unsympathetic medical officer telling a friend, 'It serves you right. You put it in a dirty place, and now you're going to suffer for it. It'll teach you not to do it again.'[29]

Harding must have taken the warnings to heart: he stopped visiting brothels, and spent his free time with the daughter of the thirty-eight-year-old woman who did his ironing. However, when his unit had to move to another town, he failed to say goodbye, and the mother made a scene as they departed. Harding then had to suffer the taunts of his mates, who accused him of sleeping with both women.

Ensuring that the men were not sexually frustrated while helping them to avoid venereal disease was an important step forward. But these were not the only difficulties encountered during the early days in France. Persuading the average beer-swilling soldier that he could not carry on drinking the same quantities if he switched to French brandy was equally important. The Glaswegians in the Queen's Own Cameron Highlanders were a particular menace when drunk. The military police found that the only way to control them, short of building a military prison, was to handcuff their hands together, then tie them up to stakes that had been driven into the ground. They were then left overnight until they sobered up. The number of men subdued in this manner only fell to more manageable proportions when British beer was shipped in and made available.[30]

The time it took to provide acceptable food and cigarettes also caused problems. 8 Brigade's war diary entry for 8 October 1939 reported:

There has been a bad shortage of cigarettes. The troops have not taken to the French brand, and this has been a real hardship. To-day the first cigarette ration was issued.

The fresh meat ration since our arrival has consisted of horse. This was quite eatable and would have escaped identification but for the fact that the head was left on in one case![31]

Sexual adventures occupied the soldiers' free evenings well enough, but there was plenty of time during the day, while they were digging trenches and building pillboxes, to think about what would happen when the Germans attacked. Many went to France believing that the

French Army would look after them, whatever the limitations of the BEF. British officers trained at Sandhurst accepted what they had been taught: that the French had far and away the best army in the world.[32] But after they had seen French troops in France, some officers were not so sure. 2nd Lieutenant Donald Callander, in charge of the three-gun anti-tank platoon manned by the 1st Battalion, the Cameron Highlanders, noticed their lack of discipline. French soldiers were allowed to smoke on duty, they were carelessly dressed, and their sentries wore shoes, sometimes even bedroom slippers, rather than army boots. If they were seen on a route march, the men lagged behind if they felt like it. Because Callander and his battalion, sandwiched as they were on the Franco-Belgian border between two British battalions, rarely saw the French, he decided that perhaps he had been unlucky to come across an unrepresentative group of bad apples. But he became worried when he and his platoon were summoned to watch a demonstration by the French that was supposed to show them how to operate their 25mm Hotchkiss anti-tank guns. Because the guns were French, much was expected, but although six men operated the gun, two more than the four the British used, the exercise took a farcical turn when the gun became stuck in an unworkable position, and the French soldiers were reduced to shouting at each other rather than firing at their imaginary enemy.

The French method of holding the positions in the Saar area of Lorraine, in front of the Maginot Line forts, was even more farcical. BEF troops observed what was happening after a November 1939 arrangement required each British brigade to go into the line under French command for a short period to gain some front-line experience. The French operated under a rule that could be summarized as 'live and let live'. John MacKenzie, a sergeant in the 2nd Battalion, the Seaforth Highlanders, which relieved a French unit in April 1940, was amazed to learn that small parties of less than six men were never fired at by either side, and that nothing was done to obstruct the movement of ration trucks provided that neither side attempted to bring in more than two each day.[33] Artillery was only ordered to shell the enemy if larger groups appeared, or more than two ration trucks were spotted.

During the Seaforth Highlanders' first night in the position, MacKenzie alarmed his French hosts, who were supposed to show him the ropes, by fixing his bayonet. They insisted he should unfix it immediately, and in case he was tempted to fix it again during the night, they hid his rifle. He was told on no account to interfere with German patrols that might be wandering around in the dark in no man's land, unless the attackers cut the barbed wire enclosing the front-line position. His French hosts recommended that he should remove a vital part from each of his platoon's Bren guns so that they could not be fired. On no account was he to let loose a mortar: the French had fired one of theirs in January 1940, and this had led to fierce German shelling, and the death of fifteen Frenchmen.

MacKenzie's experience was merely an extension of the extraordinary welcome given to Major Murray Grant from the same battalion. Grant had travelled to the front line in advance of his brigade so that their takeover from the French could be discussed at leisure. When he and the men accompanying him arrived, the French attempted to break the ice by laying on a rowdy and boozy lunch, which ended in back-slapping, toasts, and the French lobbing grenades over a fence.[34] 'The remainder of the recce was just a hilarious party,' Major Grant recalled. 'Had it occurred a few days later [that is after the start of the German attack], we'd have all been shot!!'

Worse was to come. It quickly became clear to Grant that the French had not been patrolling in front of their positions. His account reveals that when he asked whether there would be any objection to British officers going out on patrol during the next few nights, the commandant 'nearly fainted. [He] shouted at me that there must be no movement at night, and no contact with the enemy until they, the French, got out of the Ligne de Contact.' Grant responded that he and his officers had only come down to the front line in advance of their units to learn from the French, but, as he noted in his diary, it was to no avail. He also recorded that the French were amused by the British attempt to clean the billets where his men were to sleep when off duty. 'They had lived in utter filth,' he concluded.

In the notes General Alan Brooke completed after the campaign he wrote that he, too, was uneasy about the state of the French Army. This feeling came to a head on 5 November 1939 during a parade to mark the anniversary of the arrival of German armistice envoys in Allied lines in 1918.[35] The parade was presided over by General André-Georges Corap, commander of the French 9th Army. If Brooke had known then that Corap and his 9th Army would face, in the front line, one of the main German thrusts to the north of Sedan on the River Meuse and that, consequently, the fate of all the Allied armies, including the BEF, would rest on the general's shoulders, he would have been even more disturbed by what he saw. 'Seldom have I seen anything more slovenly and badly turned out,' Brooke wrote. 'Men unshaven, horses ungroomed, clothes and saddlery that did not fit, vehicles dirty, and complete lack of pride in themselves or their units. What shook me most however was the look in the men's faces, [their] disgruntled and insubordinate looks, and, although ordered to give "Eyes left", hardly a man bothered to do so.' Afterwards, Corap showed Brooke some of the defences dug by his soldiers. Brooke saw a poorly constructed anti-tank ditch and asked Corap how he would support it with covering fire, only to be told, 'We'll deal with that later. Let's go and have some lunch.'

Brooke's disquiet might have turned to panic had he listened to a private conversation between General Billotte and one of the French tank generals:[36] Billotte admitted that French optimism on the outcome of the war was unjustified – the state of the army was much worse than was generally known. He emphasized that 'our soldiers and equipment are inferior to Germany's,' referred to the 'crushing superiority' of the Luftwaffe, and predicted that a German attack 'will lead to a disaster on a scale which is unthinkable, because in spite of our limited number of soldiers relative to our long front, we do not have sufficient reserves to stabilize the front if there is a breakthrough'.

British concerns about the French Army increased when it was discovered that the two senior French generals did not get on. On 10 February 1940, General Sir Edmund Ironside, who as Chief of the Imperial General Staff was the most senior general in the Army, in charge of all British forces at home and abroad, wrote to tell Lord Gort, his subordinate in France, that the relationship between Generals Gamelin and Georges was 'very strained'.[37] According to Ironside, the problem was that although Georges was directly in charge of the British sector of the front, Gamelin had failed to consult him before agreeing that two British territorial divisions earmarked for France could be retained in England, pending a decision on whether they should be sent instead to Scandinavia. At the time the French and British Governments were contemplating sending a second expeditionary force, firstly to relieve the Finnish Army that was attempting to repulse the Russian invasion of Finland, and secondly to secure Swedish iron ore supplies before they could be seized by the Germans. Gamelin had also agreed, without reference to Georges, that one of the five regular divisions with the BEF – 5 Division having joined 2 Corps at the end of 1939 – would also be sent to Scandinavia, if required. Either Gamelin had 'omitted to do so', wrote Ironside, or 'he regards himself as the direct superior of the BEF.'[38] This raised an important question: which of the two generals was supposed to be giving Lord Gort his orders?

Two days later Gort replied to Ironside: 'We should be a little wary of raising this question formally at this juncture . . . Like you I am most anxious that any show down between Gamelin and Georges should not be on the subject of the BEF. It would be a disaster for our present good relations with the French High Command were we to find ourselves the shuttlecock in this game.'[39]

Regardless of Gort's plea, Ironside talked to Gamelin about who should give orders to the BEF, and the escalating confusion was only resolved when Gamelin agreed to leave it to Georges until the British Army in France was large enough to be regarded as an independent force.[40]

On 22 February 1940, Gort's Chief of Staff, Lieutenant-General Henry Pownall, in his diary, analysed why the two French generals had disagreed: 'It is based almost certainly on [the] jealousies of Gamelin who "thinks he is overshadowed" and so "his riposte is to try and take everything away from Georges".'[41] However, neither Pownall, Gort nor Ironside had put his finger on a much more fundamental disagreement between the two men. Although Georges was too decorous to mention in the presence of the British that he did not agree with Gamelin's defence plan, he was secretly antagonistic to the idea that valuable French troops would be marched into the area around Breda in Holland if the Germans attacked: for a start it was too risky. The fact that the Dutch did not intend to defend the south of Holland where the French were to operate made it all the more so. Another reason for opposing it was that it occupied French units that could otherwise have been used to increase Georges' reserves.[42] Nevertheless Pownall was aware that the upset caused by Gamelin's failure to talk to Georges about the BEF might well only represent the thin end of the wedge. 'I fear that there are other frictions of which we have heard nothing . . .' Pownall wrote in his diary on 3 March 1940.[43]

There were other factors that should have disqualified both Gamelin and Georges from their posts at the top of the French Army. Georges, aged sixty-four, was a First World War veteran. He had been badly wounded by splinters from the bomb that had been used during the 1934 assassination of King Alexander of Yugoslavia and the French Foreign Minister, and had never fully recovered. He had been told he must not fly, and he always wore a woollen glove to cover the damage to one of his hands. But nothing could repair the psychological damage and, as we have seen, this irrevocably affected his ability to keep cool in a crisis. Nevertheless, he could not have been a more unsuitable candidate for the top job than Gamelin. By 1940, the French Commander-in-Chief was sixty-seven years old. That would not have mattered had he been endowed with the right attitude and vigour. Unfortunately he had none of the attributes of a great soldier. He was small, quiet, and had little charisma. Reynaud, who tried to sack him on several occasions, famously said of him, 'He might be all right as a prefect or a bishop, but he is not a leader of men.'⁴⁴ Even Daladier, Gamelin's protector, issued a damning indictment of his inability to give clear concise opinions and orders: 'When you speak, one has something; as for Gamelin, it is like sand running through one's fingers.'⁴⁵

There were also tensions within the British Army. In November 1939, the row that became known as the Pillbox Affair blew up after the Secretary of State for War, Leslie Hore-Belisha, had visited the BEF in France.⁴⁶ When he was back in England, he asked a member of Gort's staff to pass on his concern at the time it took to build concrete pillboxes in the British line when, Hore-Belisha claimed, the French were only taking three days to build each of the pillboxes in their sector. Gort was furious, not only because he knew that Hore-Belisha's criticism was unjustified, but also because it had been relayed to him via a subordinate. It transpired later that Hore-Belisha had misunderstood a comment made to him by Gamelin, who had in fact said that the pillboxes could be built three days after the site had been prepared and the materials were available; the French spent three weeks building each pillbox. Hore-Belisha compounded his error by comparing the pillboxes to the left of the British line favourably with those he had seen in the British area, not realizing that his troops had also constructed those he had praised. His criticism was soon known and resented throughout the higher echelons of the BEF, as generals, ministers and even the King came to view the controversial defences.

Had the Secretary of State for War made a heartfelt public apology

the Pillbox Affair would probably have been buried once and for all.
Normal relations could have been quickly re-established between him
and the generals if he had only reassured them that he would not criticize
them again without first talking to them face to face so that he could
check his facts. That done, even his harshest critics would have been
forced to admit that the subject matter of the row did not warrant
any more time being expended on it. The small number of pillboxes
completed was hardly the most pressing problem for the BEF. After all,
the number of pillboxes built was unlikely to affect the outcome of any
conflict, given that Gamelin's plan was to send Allied troops, including
the BEF, into Belgium as soon as the Germans invaded. The Pillbox
Affair was certainly less important than the positive measures that Hore-
Belisha had introduced to help the Army: they included making the
Army an attractive career for young men, pushing through conscription
and a doubling of the Territorial Army, and persuading the Cabinet in
February to March 1939 that a force should be equipped and trained so
that it was ready to go to France.[47]

It was perhaps the fact that he had done so much for the Army that
convinced Hore-Belisha an apology was unnecessary. He appears not to
have understood how important it was that he and Britain's leading
soldiers supported each other both in private and in public, and his
failure to do so on this issue only reinforced the generals' view that he
was not their friend. His behaviour in relation to the pillboxes was just
the latest in a line of mistakes, as far as they were concerned. In their
eyes, he had already blotted his copybook by relying on the views of
Captain Basil Liddell Hart, military correspondent of *The Times*, a man
who no doubt had interesting ideas, but who was, as far as the generals
were concerned, an outsider and, worse still, a journalist. They had also
come to believe that Hore-Belisha was more interested in boosting his
own popularity as a politician rather than doing what was best for the
Army. Eventually the Prime Minister, Neville Chamberlain, decided
that Hore-Belisha would have to be moved from the War Office if
Gort was to feel confident that his own position was secure. Hore-
Belisha might have become Minister of Information in the 4 January
1940 ministerial reshuffle, had not the Foreign Secretary, Lord Halifax,
pointed out that the appointment of a Jew would play into Joseph
Goebbels' hands. The Foreign Secretary apparently feared that Hore-
Belisha's semitic roots would have presented the German propaganda

supremo, who specialized in mocking the Jews, with an additional opportunity to ridicule anything that came out of the British Information Ministry. Instead he was offered the Board of Trade, a post he rejected because it did not give him a seat in the Cabinet. So at a time when the British generals should have been concentrating on how to improve the Army, rather than on how to destroy the man who had done so much to build it up, Hore-Belisha was sent into the political wilderness.[48]

The British newspapers were full of speculation about the personality clashes between Hore-Belisha and the generals, and about what had led to his resignation. The French Ambassador in Britain, who knew about the row, presented a measured analysis to his government.

Even in a country where anti-Semitism is almost unknown, M. Hore-Belisha should have been more prudent given his origins. For example he upset some people by praising the French army, and declaring that British officers would never be as good as ours. M. Churchill often says the same thing, but what is permissible for a descendant of Marlborough, is not permissible for M. Hore-Belisha. On the eve of one of his trips to Paris, Lord Derby himself said to me: 'I hope you and your people do not take M. Hore-Belisha to be a true Englishman.'

The Ambassador concluded:

We should regret the departure of M. Hore-Belisha who perhaps because he 'is not a real Englishman' understood us better than many of his compatriots, and often supported our ideas.[49]

Unfortunately Hore-Belisha's departure did not mean that Gort was never undermined again. General Ironside was equally culpable: just as Gamelin had not consulted with Georges about the holding of the two British divisions in England, pending a decision being made about their use in Scandinavia, so Ironside had not consulted with Gort. Ironside's inconsiderate act, combined with his having talked to Gamelin about the leadership of the BEF even though Gort had asked him not to, provoked Pownall into penning a series of angry notes in his diary, including comments such as: Ironside's 'clumsiness has to be seen to be believed', and 'he has no more circumspection than a bull in a china shop'.[50] This last description was especially appropriate, given that

Ironside, who was fifty-nine years old when the events complained about took place, was a huge man of six feet four. Inevitably he was nicknamed 'Tiny'. At the time, neither Gort nor Pownall could have foretold how Ironside's willingness to take decisions without first speaking to Gort would later increase the danger facing the BEF at Dunkirk. But Pownall quite correctly suspected that no good would come of it.[51]

Equally worrying was the low regard in which Gort was held by some of his most senior commanders. This was not because he had anything in common with the uninspiring Gamelin: rather, he was the ultimate dashing hero: a viscount and Grenadier Guardsman who had been awarded several decorations for valour, including the Victoria Cross at the end of the First World War. It was probably his record and his youthful vigour rather than his abilities as a commander that had persuaded Hore-Belisha to make him Chief of the Imperial General Staff in 1937, at the age of fifty-one, and subsequently Commander-in-Chief of the BEF. He was still only fifty-three years old when his first troops landed in France. Unfortunately he failed to adapt his methods to fit in with the demands of his new job. The attention to detail that had stood him in good stead as a more junior officer was inappropriate in such a senior post where he was required to focus on a bigger picture. General Alan Brooke, who was three years older than Gort, was appalled by his commander-in-chief's habit of concentrating on relatively unimportant issues, while leaving vital matters of principle to his subordinates. During a trip to the positions held by British brigades in the Saar area of Lorraine in front of the Maginot Line, Brooke thought that Gort should have been considering how to change the system of defence, which included isolated weak outposts manned by the British several miles in front of the Maginot forts. But Gort – whose eyes, according to Brooke, were still twinkling with the excitement of discussing patrols, the importance of reading tracks in the snow, the noises made by birds when alarmed, and how each platoon's logbook should be maintained – brushed aside Brooke's suggestion, saying, 'Oh, I have not had time to think of that, but look, what we must go into is the proper distribution of sandbags.'[52]

Brooke began seriously to question whether Gort was the right man to lead the BEF when he heard that Gort had ignored a comment made by Lieutenant-General Sir John Dill, commander of the BEF's 1 Corps, about the original plan to advance to the River Escaut in Belgium when the Germans attacked. Dill had pointed out that asking Brooke's 2 Corps, which then included just 3 and 4 Divisions, to hold a seventeen-mile front 'made serious resistance impossible'. Notwithstanding Gort's point that the BEF's resistance on the Escaut would be stiffened by the arrival of the French before the Germans reached it, Brooke agreed with Dill, and he was not meaning to be complimentary when he wrote that Gort's plan was 'fantastic'. He went on in his Notes to give the following damning verdict: it 'could only have resulted in a disaster'.[53] It was this kind of disagreement that made Brooke wish that Dill was the BEF's Commander-in-Chief. According to Brooke, Gort was no more than a 'glorified boy scout'.[54]

3: The Mechelen Affair

Vucht and Mechelen-sur-Meuse, Belgium, January 1940
(See Map 3. Also Map 1)

It was not just the quarrelsome French generals and their failure to discipline their soldiers that helped the Germans to make their break-through on the River Meuse. Equally important was the French high command's failure to adapt their war plans to cope with fallout from one of the best-known incidents of the phoney war: the Mechelen affair. At midday on 10 January 1940, everything was still quiet on the western front that separated Belgium from neutral Holland and Nazi Germany. But as Belgian border guards at Vucht, near Mechelen-sur-Meuse (Maas-mechelen), huddled over the stove in their guardhouse, away from the snow and the freezing conditions outside, a drama was taking place in the air above their heads that was to have the gravest consequences not only for Belgium, but also for England, France and for Germany.

It began with a mistake made by German aviator Major Erich Hoen-manns, the fifty-two-year-old airbase commander at Loddenheide air-port, near Münster. He had been flying a Messerschmitt BF.108 Taifun, a plane used for reconnaissance, from Loddenheide to Cologne when he lost his way in fog. While searching for the River Rhine, which, he hoped, would enable him to regain his bearings, he flew too far west and ended up circling Vucht near the River Meuse in Belgium.[1] It was then that he appears inadvertently to have cut off the fuel supply to the plane's engine by moving a lever inside the cockpit.[2] The engine spluttered, then stopped, and Hoenmanns quickly decided that he must attempt to land in a nearby field. The subsequent descent terminated with what was more of a crash than a landing: as he came down, the plane narrowly missed an electricity cable, and its wings hit two trees as it sped between them. But although the plane was a write-off, Hoenmanns survived more or less unscathed.

Had Hoenmanns been alone in the plane, there would have been no traumatic consequences. He would have been interned for landing without permission in a neutral country, and that would have been the end of the affair. But he was not alone. As has been confirmed by documents recently discovered in Reichskriegsgericht (German War Tribunal) files in the former Czechoslovakia, he had a passenger. It was the fifty-year-old Major Helmuth Reinberger, whose position on the staff of Fliegerführer 220 made him responsible for masterminding the supplying of Fliegerdivision 7, the élite unit that was to land paratroopers behind Belgian lines on the first day of the imminent attack. Reinberger was going to Cologne to make sure everything was ready.[3]

Reinberger had planned originally to take the train to Cologne, and had even purchased a ticket, but the night before he was due to travel, he had bumped into Hoenmanns at the Loddenheide barracks, and had been unable to resist Hoenmanns' offer of a lift. Hoenmanns was pleased to have a passenger, being unaware that Reinberger would have with him Germany's plan for its attack on Belgium.[4] This document was at the heart of Germany's war strategy. On the very day when the two majors landed at Vucht, Hitler decided that his attack, based on that same plan, should take place seven days later.[5]

The newly discovered Reichskriegsgericht files highlight difficulties Hoenmanns was experiencing that may well have contributed to the errors he made in the cockpit. Some appear to have been the indirect result of his physical separation from his wife. She had remained in Cologne when, at the end of September 1939, he had taken the job in Loddenheide. Her absence had given him the opportunity to acquire a mistress. Nevertheless he kept the marriage going by frequently flying himself down to visit his wife. The flying he did on these trips was not just to preserve marital harmony. He wanted to escape from his desk job by becoming a full-time Luftwaffe pilot. Although he had a licence to fly civil aircraft, his military pilot's licence had lapsed, and he needed to fly a certain number of hours to regain it. The flying hours clocked up during the flights to and from Cologne were helping him reach this target. His bosses at Loddenheide usually allowed him to borrow a plane for these trips, but the Reichskriegsgericht documents suggest that they only sanctioned the flights because they believed the flying enabled him to do his job more efficiently. As he flew over other airports he could see how their runways had been camouflaged, and his bosses hoped this would give him some new ideas on how camouflage should be arranged at Loddenheide.[6]

However, on the morning of 10 January, this synergy, which had in the past kept everyone happy, began to fall apart, and Hoenmanns found himself pulled in two directions. On the one hand, he knew that Reinberger had an important meeting to attend in Cologne, and was relying on him to fly him there on time. He had told Reinberger that he hoped to take off at 10 a.m. His wife was also expecting him in Cologne. On the other hand, one of Hoenmanns' bosses wanted him to show some troops round the airport at Loddenheide; thanks to Hoenmanns, the airport had been camouflaged so creatively that from the sky it looked like a working farm, and he was supposed to tell his visitors how he had achieved this effect. Hoenmanns' attempt to resolve the conflict by instructing a subordinate to show the troops round ended with his being reprimanded by his superior officer. That precluded Hoenmanns from asking for permission to fly to Cologne, and also delayed his and Reinberger's take-off. No doubt feeling guilty on both counts, Hoenmanns nevertheless went ahead, and borrowed a plane for the flight without asking his boss.

Witnesses interviewed subsequently by German investigators inquiring into whether Hoenmanns and Reinberger should be prosecuted, for what at one time was thought to be treason, stated that he was in a great hurry when he and his passenger climbed into the Taifun at about midday. They claimed he had failed to follow his normal practice of requesting a weather check, and had jumped down from the plane to fetch a map he had forgotten.[7] By all accounts he was somewhat flustered, and it is possible that this might have distracted him from his map reading and navigation when he finally took off, leading him to fly off-course. All went well during the flight until he reached Cologne's industrial area. It was only then that things began to go badly wrong. It was so foggy that he could not see the Essen to Cologne main road, which normally helped him navigate. Consequently he turned west, hoping to skirt round the fog before turning south again towards Cologne. As he flew, he peered out of the cockpit trying to spot the Rhine, a landmark that in normal conditions would have prompted him to turn south. However, as he might have anticipated had he not been so preoccupied, the river was frozen and covered with snow, and therefore hard to differentiate from the surrounding countryside. That explains how he came to fly over it, ending up in Belgian air space.[8] His upset mental state might also have played its part once he realized he was lost: perhaps he would not have flown so far west if he had been more alert, and if that had been the case maybe he would not have inadvertently moved the lever shutting off the petrol supply – if that was what happened – thereby stalling the plane's engine.

Hoenmanns only discovered that Reinberger was carrying secret documents when, after they had landed, they asked a farmer where they were. When they learned they were in Belgium, Reinberger went as white as a sheet, and rushed back to the plane after exclaiming that he had secret documents with him which he had to destroy immediately. He intended to do this using matches borrowed from the farmer, a pipe-smoker. Hoenmanns moved away from the plane acting as a decoy.

But while Reinberger was struggling to burn the documents behind a hedge, Belgian soldiers arrived, and seeing smoke coming from where Reinberger was hiding, they rushed over to capture him before all the papers could be destroyed. Hoenmanns was also captured. The drama reached its climax in the Belgian soldiers' watchhouse near the bridge at Mechelen-sur-Meuse where the two men were taken. There, on catching sight of the remains of the documents, which the Belgian soldiers had unwisely left lying on a table, Reinberger and Hoenmanns used a combination of whispers and signals to hatch a plan that they hoped would give Reinberger a second chance to burn them. Hoenmanns would go to the other side of the room where he would ask to be escorted to the washroom. While the guards were attending to him, Reinberger was to seize the documents and stuff them into the lit stove. Unfortunately their plan did not cater for the fact that the lid on the stove was very hot. After Hoenmanns had carried out his part of the plan, Reinberger picked up the lid and put the documents into the stove. But the lid burnt his hands, and he dropped it, thereby alerting the guards to what he was doing. The officer in charge rushed up to Reinberger, pushed him out of the way, then plunged his hands into the stove and scooped out the smouldering, but still undestroyed, documents. They were then locked away in another room – as they should have been in the first place.[9]

Whatever one might feel about a man who supports a plan to attack a neutral country, it is hard not to feel sorry for Reinberger. According to Hoenmanns' account, his companion began to sob, and banged his head against a nearby cupboard, evidently believing that enough of the documents remained to reveal to Belgium that she was about to be attacked, and fearing that there would be unpleasant repercussions. There would be an international outcry. The Allies might invade Belgium –

even Germany. Hermann Göring and Hitler would be told of how Reinberger had endangered his country's security by taking secret documents on an aeroplane. Heaven help him if Hitler's henchmen ever got hold of him!

Realizing the hopelessness of his position, Reinberger asked the Belgian officer for his gun, saying, 'I'm finished. I want to put an end to this affair right now.' The officer naturally refused to comply with Reinberger's demand, even after Hoenmanns intervened, saying: 'You can't blame him. He's a regular officer. He's finished now.' Undaunted, Reinberger attempted to take the gun by force, but when he was roughly pushed back into his chair, he collapsed, and once more began to sob. 'Not realizing how important the documents were, I thought he was overdoing it a bit, and was not behaving like a man,' Hoenmanns commented later, then described how, with a relatively clear conscience, he ate the meal he was given while Reinberger wept beside him.

Interestingly, both the Germans and the Belgians thought that Reinberger and Hoenmanns were trying to deceive them over the documents. The Germans feared that the two men were traitors, and were intentionally handing the highly secret documents to the enemy. An investigator was dispatched to interrogate Hoenmanns' wife, Annie, and to search their Cologne apartment. Annie Hoenmanns told the investigator that if her husband had been about to betray Germany, she would have known about it. However, when she added that she and her husband kept no secrets from each other and were not having any marital problems, it was clear that she was an unreliable witness.[10]

The Belgians' anxiety revolved around their fear that the Germans were using bogus papers to provoke them into calling in the British and French, thereby giving the Germans a pretext to invade Belgium. However, after they had reviewed all the evidence, and being particularly influenced by the fact that the German aviators had only narrowly escaped from the landing with their lives, the Belgians concluded that it was unlikely that the crash had been premeditated. That conclusion tempted them to stage a hoax of their own. They decided to trick Reinberger into believing that the most important sections of the plans had been destroyed, then give him the opportunity to pass this on to the German authorities.

In the first part of the deception, the Belgian investigators asked Reinberger what was in the plans, and informed him that he would be treated as a spy if he did not tell them. 'From the way this question was asked, I realized he [the interrogator] could not have understood anything from the fragments of the documents he had seen,' Reinberger testified later.[11] The second part of the plan involved permitting the German Air and Army Attachés, Lieutenant-General Ralph Wenninger and Colonel Rabe von Pappenheim, to see the majors while their conversation was secretly recorded. It was 12 January before the recording equipment was in place at the Brussels police station where the interview was to take place. Only then could the meeting be sanctioned. The report describing what was overheard during the meeting is still in the Belgian archives. It contains the following disclaimer from the man responsible for doing the recording: 'I cannot claim to have heard everything because the five people often formed two groups of conversation that I could not follow simultaneously. But I have certainly recorded most of what was said.'[12]

The meeting began with innocuous questions that had no bearing on international relations with Germany. For example, Reinberger was asked whether he needed a toothbrush. The important questions were asked only after the Belgian major, who was supervising the interview, left the room. As soon as the Germans were alone, Wenninger told Reinberger: 'The day before yesterday I went to the General Headquarters who sent me here to speak to you. According to the press you managed to burn the papers. Is that correct?'

Reinberger replied, 'Yes, Herr General.'

At that point, the Belgian major returned, only to leave again when asked whether Hoenmanns and Reinberger might be isolated from other prisoners. While he was absent, Reinberger told the attachés the full story: how Hoenmanns lost his way in the fog, how they had mistaken the Meuse for the Rhine, how they had had to make an emergency landing, how they had borrowed matches from the Belgian farmer on the pretext they needed to smoke a cigarette, how they had burned the documents, and how a soldier had taken a few charred pieces from the fire. When Reinberger had finished, Hoenmanns mentioned the two matters that were worrying him. He wanted to know what Göring had said about the accident, and asked whether he could give Wenninger a letter for his mistress in Münster to avoid a marital drama. Later, Hoenmanns wrote asking the German authorities to remove any objects belonging to his mistress from the room near Loddenheide where he had been living so that his wife would not find out about his affair when his personal effects were delivered to the family home in Cologne.[13]

Hoenmanns' complicated domestic arrangements were evidently the last subject that concerned the attachés and the German generals waiting to hear what Wenninger and von Pappenheim had discovered. The generals that constituted the German high command were horrified by what had happened to their attack plan. On the day of the attachés' first meeting with Reinberger and Hoenmanns, General Alfred Jodl, the Wehrmacht's (Armed Forces) Chief of Operations, gave Hitler his grim assessment of what the Belgians might have learned from it. A note in Jodl's diary for 12 January summed up what Jodl had said: 'If the enemy is in possession of all the files, situation catastrophic!'[14]

In view of the hostile reaction to the two majors, and the feeling that if Hoenmanns was not a traitor, he was certainly a reckless adventurer who, by his disobedience, had endangered the lives of thousands of German soldiers about to go into battle, it is not surprising that, whether by mistake or by design, his instructions about his personal effects were forgotten, and his wife was handed a pile of his mistress's letters along with the rest of his possessions.

The Belgian Government's act of deception was more successful, at least in the short term. After the meeting at the police station, His Excellency Vicco von Bülow-Schwante, Germany's Ambassador in Belgium, telegraphed to his superiors: 'Major Reinberger has confirmed that he burned the documents except for some pieces which are the size of the palm of his hand. Reinberger confirms that most of the documents which could not be destroyed appear to be unimportant.'[15] This convinced General Jodl. His diary for 13 January included the entry: 'Report on conversation of Luftwaffe Attaché with the two airmen who made the forced landing. Result: dispatch case burned for certain.'

There was another reason why the Belgians eventually concluded that the plan was genuine: on 13 January, a message from Colonel Georges Goethals, Belgium's Military Attaché in Berlin, but based on information provided by an informant who was in touch with the Dutch Military Attaché, included the following words: 'Were there tactical documents or references to them on Malines [*sic*] plane? A sincere informer, whose intelligence may be suspect, claims that this plane was carrying plans from Berlin to Cologne in relation to the attack on the West. Because these plans have fallen into Belgian hands, the attack will happen tomorrow before counter-measures can be taken.'[16]

General Raoul Van Overstraeten, the King of Belgium's military adviser, was astonished that the informant appeared to know about the capture of the plan. It had not been mentioned in any press reports describing the crash. It was possible that the informant's tip-off was part of the same German hoax, but also that it was genuine.[17] Acting on the assumption that it should be taken seriously, Van Overstraeten altered the warning that the Belgian Chief of the General Staff Lieutenant-General Édouard Van den Bergen had drafted that was about to be sent to all Belgian Army commanders on 13 January so that instead of stating that an attack on the next morning was 'probable', it stated that the attack was 'quasi-certain'.[18]

Van Overstraeten's change, made without reference to Van den Bergen, left the Belgian Chief of the General Staff with a difficult dilemma. That night, a popular current-affairs programme was about to be broadcast on Belgian radio, and Van den Bergen realized that if he moved quickly, he could ask for an announcement to be made that all 80,000 Belgian soldiers on leave should return immediately to their units. This would enable many to be in the front line before dawn, when any attack by the Germans was likely to come. Without discussing the broadcast with Van Overstraeten or the Belgian King, and without knowing about the decision that had been taken earlier that day to leave the Germans in the dark as to whether or not Belgium had their attack plans, Van den Bergen ordered the announcement to be made.[19] Two hours later he made another dramatic gesture, once again without obtaining the agreement of Van Overstraeten or the King.[20] Realizing that the freezing weather conditions would make it difficult to move aside quickly all the barriers that had been erected on the country's south-western border with France, he ordered them to be removed immediately. The idea was that at least some would be out of the way before the Germans attacked, thereby enabling British and French troops to march into Belgium as soon as they were summoned.[21]

If the Germans had attacked on the morning of 14 January, Van den Bergen would probably have been congratulated for his quick thinking. But because they did not attack then, or three days later – Hitler had called off the attack scheduled for 17 January because of the weather – Van den Bergen was in disgrace for acting in this way without the King's permission. King Leopold was the Belgian Commander-in-Chief.[22] Van

Overstraeten rebuked Van den Bergen so harshly for what he had done that the Belgian Chief of Staff's reputation never recovered, and at the end of January he was forced to resign.

One of Van Overstraeten's complaints was that Van den Bergen had given the Germans grounds for believing that the Belgians had their plans. The Belgian Government's desire to keep the possession of the plans a secret was, however, to be further undermined by a second attempt to protect the country. This time King Leopold was to blame. During the morning of 14 January, he had sent a message to Winston Churchill, then First Lord of the Admiralty, via Admiral Sir Roger Keyes asking for certain guarantees. Keyes, referred to by the Belgians as 'Mr X', had established himself as the secret link man between the British Government and the King.[23] The guarantees included an undertaking that the Allies would not open negotiations for a settlement of any conflict without Belgium's agreement.[24] Keyes added a rider that he believed Leopold might be able to persuade his government to call in the Allies immediately if the guarantees were forthcoming. This was of interest to the Allies because both Britain and France had been trying to persuade Belgium to allow them to move in since war had been declared.

There is no transcript of Keyes's conversation with Churchill, but if Keyes really did state accurately what he meant to say, his message, like Chinese whispers, was altered the further down the line it went.[25] By the time it reached the French later that afternoon, there was no reference to the fact that Keyes was only giving his opinion about the calling in of the Allies. The French record of what was on offer stated that 'the King would ask his government to invite the Allied armies to occupy defensive positions inside Belgium immediately', if the Belgians received satisfaction in relation to their requested guarantees.[26] Édouard Daladier, the French Président du Conseil in January 1940, quickly told the British Government that, as far as France was concerned, the guarantees could be given.

The upshot was that the French believed the Belgians would receive a satisfactory response from the British Government in relation to the guarantees, and would then immediately invite the Allied armies to march in. With that in mind, General Gamelin issued the order during the night of 14–15 January that the Allied troops under his control should move up to the Franco-Belgian border so that they would be ready to enter at a moment's notice. During the night, the Belgians were told of this manoeuvre. It was only at 8 a.m. on 15 January that Gamelin saw the British response to the request for guarantees: they were offering a watered-down version that was most unlikely to be acceptable to Belgium.[27] Three hours later Daladier, prompted by a desperate Gamelin, told Pol Le Tellier, Belgium's Ambassador in Paris, that unless the French had an invitation to enter Belgium by 8 p.m. that night, they would not only withdraw all British and French troops from the border but would refuse to carry out similar manoeuvres during future alerts until after the Germans had invaded.[28]

The rising tension between France and Belgium is underlined by France's decision to install a tap on the telephone line that connected the Belgian Embassy in Paris with Belgium, an extreme step given that the two countries were allies in everything but name. A transcript reveals what was said when the Belgian Foreign Minister, Paul-Henri Spaak, spoke to Le Tellier at 5.20 p.m. on 15 January – just two hours and forty minutes before the French deadline expired. The French telephone tapper, who identified as Spaak the speaker named 'X' in the transcript, noted that 'Minister X appears to be in a very bad temper'. The conversation ran as follows:

X [Spaak]: 'I will keep you informed.'
Le T: 'But the big chief is waiting for my reply.'
X [Spaak]: 'Are they able to concentrate their troops in one night?'
Le T: 'Yes, but if the enemy sees or hears about the concentration!'
X [Spaak]: 'Believe me, I will do my best.'
Le T: 'I don't want to be rude, but will I have some news from you to-night?'
X [Spaak]: 'I cannot take this kind of decision in one and a half hours. If they cannot, or will not, wait for our reply, they must act as they see fit. In any case, I'm going to deal with the problem. I'm doing nothing else at the moment, but I don't know if I'll have a reply before 8 p.m.'[29]

At 8.05 p.m. the telephone tapper heard Spaak giving Le Tellier the Belgian Government's response:

S [Spaak]: 'It's very simple. We cannot reply in the affirmative. A long note will be sent tomorrow. It's absolutely impossible.'

Le T: 'Will they have to take steps as a result of this reply? They are in the open and concentrated.'

S [*Spaak*]: 'There's nothing stopping them.'

Le T: 'But they are concentrated.'

S [*Spaak*]: 'What do you want me to do? I know the situation, but they are speaking of different dates. It could be tomorrow, or the 17th or the 20th. This problem you are talking about is a technical matter. If they cannot remain where they are, it's just too bad. Let them decide what to do. Don't repeat that. Tell them simply that I cannot reply in the affirmative. I am adding, for your ears only, from all points of view, it's impossible.'

Le T: 'Must they remove their troops from the frontier?'

S [*Spaak*]: 'If they have to remove them all, then they must go ahead and do that. I've no problem about that. They have not understood all the political consequences it would cause. What they've asked is extraordinary.'

Le T: 'Understood. I'll pass on what you said just now, and nothing else, and I'll call you back with their reaction.'[30]

Apart from some bitter recriminations, there was nothing more that Daladier and Gamelin could do to coax the Belgians into letting the Allied armies into Belgium. They were forced to order the British and French troops back to their original positions.

In the short term, no harm appeared to have been done. But in the long term, the manoeuvre was disastrous. The Belgians felt obliged to tell the Germans they had the attack plan. When Joachim von Ribbentrop, Germany's Foreign Minister, retorted that it was out of date, he was being more truthful than he intended, as is demonstrated by what follows. The entry in General Jodl's diary for 13 February 1940 reveals the fundamental change to the plan that had been made after Reinberger's and Hoenmanns' accident. Instead of being committed to the attack detailed in the captured documents, whose principal thrust was on Belgium's north-eastern frontier, Jodl recorded that Hitler wanted the German panzer divisions concentrated further south: 'We should let them attack in the direction of Sedan,' Hitler told Jodl. 'The enemy is not expecting us to attack there. The documents held by the Luftwaffe officers who crash landed have convinced the enemy that we only intend to take over the Dutch and Belgian channel coasts.' Within days of this discussion, Hitler had talked to General Erich von Manstein, the former Chief of Staff of the German Army Group A, who for some time had been championing this new plan, and the Führer had given it the green light. The plan that had caused so much mayhem when it was captured by the Belgians in January 1940 was to be quietly shelved.[31]

The adoption of the revised Plan Yellow (Fall Gelb) by the Germans, while the Allies were still expecting Hitler to go ahead with the captured version, meant that the Germans could set a trap. An attack would still be made on Belgium's north-eastern frontier, but as one writer has vividly described it, it would merely be 'the matador's cloak', tempting the Allied armies to move as many troops as possible into Belgium, thereby carrying out in full the plan that had been aborted on 14–15 January.[32] Once the Allied 'bull' was safely in Belgium, the main German thrust – backed by most of the panzer divisions – would pass through the Ardennes, cross the Meuse between Sedan and the area north of Dinant, then cut across France to the coast, thereby isolating and surrounding the armies in Belgium, separating them from their supplies and forcing them to surrender.

Clever as this ruse was, it would only work if Gamelin stuck to his original strategy. That was asking a lot, given that until 14 January 1940 his intuition had been impeccable. Had he not guessed correctly the content of the German generals' original Plan Yellow?[33] But after the capture of the German plan, everything had changed. It did not take a genius to conclude that the Germans might devise a new plan now that the Allies had seen the original version. But for some inexplicable reason, Gamelin failed to adapt his strategy to take into account the new circumstances, and in their turn Gort and the British Government failed to point this out. Perhaps notwithstanding the Belgian verdict on the captured documents, British generals and politicians, like the British Ambassador in Brussels, still believed they were a German 'plant'.[34] Or perhaps they were so embarrassed by the small contribution Britain was making to the coming ground war that they did not feel entitled to question French strategy. Whatever the reason, by blindly obeying French orders, they were not appreciating that their plan, which required them to charge into Belgium as soon as the Germans invaded, represented a disaster waiting to happen.

4: The Final Warning

The Hague and Berlin, October 1939 to 9 May 1940
(See Map 1)

The Dutch Military Attaché in Berlin, whose warning had led to the 14–15 January 1940 crisis, was the forty-seven-year-old Major Gijsbertus Sas. The tip-off to his counterpart at Belgium's Berlin Embassy was just one of a series of similar warnings he had been sending to the Dutch and Belgian Governments since October 1939.[1] However, like so many tip-offs emanating from concerned insiders, Sas' warnings seemed suspect to say the least. He had told the Dutch Armed Forces Commander-in-Chief, General Izaak Reynders, that he was receiving his intelligence from a man in the German Abwehr (military intelligence). But he had refused to disclose his source's name.[2] It was the fact that the man worked in the Abwehr that bothered Reynders. As he stated quite reasonably, it was the Abwehr's job to deceive the enemy, so how could they be sure that Sas' source was not attempting to deceive them?[3]

The Dutch Commander-in-Chief's suspicions were strengthened by Sas' hysterical reaction to questioning. Reynders' initial doubts were also reinforced by what happened in November 1939. On 7–8 November 1939, Sas had warned both the Dutch and Belgian Governments that his informant had told him the German attack was scheduled for 12 November.[4] On the eighth he had travelled to The Hague to back up the verbal warning he had sent to the Dutch on the previous day via his wife who was still living in Holland.[5] The trip was a terrible mistake. On 7 November, the day on which the whistle-blower had revealed the date to Sas, Hitler and his generals postponed the attack from the twelfth to after the fourteenth, and Sas had departed for The Hague by the time the whistle-blower discovered the change.[6] Unaware that the intelligence had been superseded, and also that a British diplomat had already warned the Dutch Government of the 12 November date, Sas was upset when the ministers convened in The Hague to hear his report were unmoved by the information that he considered vitally important.[7] Infuriated by the scepticism that greeted his 'revelation', he threw restraint to the wind and swore that he was sure the attack would take place on 12 November. One minister responded: 'How can you be sure of something that has not yet happened?'[8] On hearing this, Sas lost his temper and, gesticulating wildly, walked out of the room.

Two days later Sas was even more disturbed because no preparations were in hand to repulse the predicted attack. Tortured by the realization that he had been entrusted with intelligence that might save his country from ruin, and by the feeling that he had not exhausted all possibilities, he took it upon himself to visit some of the great and the good in Holland in an attempt to persuade them to reinforce his warning. After receiving short shrift from the first man he saw, the former head of the Dutch Navy, Sas talked to Dr Hendrik Colijn, the former Minister-President (Prime Minister).[9] But when Colijn rang up Sas' boss, Reynders, they both agreed that Sas was too excitable to be a credible witness. The next man on Sas' list was Major-General van Oorschot, head of Dutch intelligence. However, rather than being grateful for the information, Oorschot stated bluntly that he did not believe Sas' informant. At this point Sas totally lost control of himself, and told the intelligence chief exactly what he thought of him. His tirade only terminated when he marched out of Oorschot's office, slamming the door behind him.[10] On the way out, he revealed unwisely that he was going right to the top: he was going to talk to the Dutch Queen. That enabled the intelligence chief to warn Reynders, who in his turn spoke smartly to the palace gate-keepers so that when Sas arrived, he was told by the Queen's adjutant that Reynders had forbidden him to see her. Nevertheless Sas left a message for her with her staff, and eventually the action he had suggested was taken: the floodgates were opened so that many routes into Holland from Germany were flooded, and leave for 40,000 Dutch soldiers was cancelled.[11] By 12 November, largely thanks to Sas and his whistle-blower, Holland was as ready as she could be, given her limited armed forces, to receive the enemy.

But as the whistle-blower would have told Sas, had he remained in Germany, the attack had been postponed, and Sas was left with mixed feelings when, on 12 November and the following days, it did not materialize. Sas was glad, of course, that Holland was still intact, but horrified that he had committed himself so strongly, only to be let down by the intelligence. He was even more unhappy when he discovered how he was being mocked by his Dutch colleagues, one of whom asked him, 'So, SOS, how is your mental state today?'[12] The Dutch were not alone in questioning his informant's reliability: according to the Belgian Military Attaché in The Hague, Sas had 'blind faith' in his source, and even after the November intelligence was shown to be flawed, he was still vouching for the trustworthiness of his friend.[13] The British Military Attaché in Brussels also believed that Sas' source could not be trusted, and Sas even suspected that the British intelligence service were tailing him in Holland, presumably because it was feared that he might have become a double agent.[14]

But Sas must have felt that Reynders was the main stumbling block. Shortly before Christmas 1939, their relationship collapsed in the wake of another warning given by the informant to Sas on 7 December. It specified that the attack would take place on the seventeenth, but was then contradicted two days before the due date by another message claiming that this latest attack was also being postponed.[15] Reynders summoned Sas to his office. During what must have been a stormy meeting, Sas insisted that Reynders should tell him what he thought of the intelligence. Eventually the long-suffering Reynders exploded: 'Goddammit, that bullshit about you and your connection! I don't believe a bloody word of it! You give me all of this data, but what the hell am I supposed to do with it?'[16] Sas was told that he was to be replaced as Military Attaché in Berlin.

Unfortunately for Sas there was no easy way, short of adopting a more restrained approach, to have made the intelligence more convincing. Revealing the source's identity had been ruled out because it was too dangerous – and, anyway, it probably would not have helped. The whistle-blower was Colonel Hans Oster, a high-flying soldier, whose promising military career had been cut short by a scandal. During the early 1930s, he had been obliged to leave the German Army after it was discovered he had betrayed his wife and a brother officer by having an affair with that officer's wife.[17] If that did not of itself mark him out as untrustworthy, there was something else about his family life that might have led intelligence analysts to a similar conclusion. Oster had two sons in the German Army. Was it likely, in these circumstances, that he would pass military secrets to the enemy?

On the other hand certain factors made him less likely than most Germans to stand by while Hitler ruined his country and attacked its neighbours. Intelligence chiefs in Belgium and Holland might have surmised that his father, a clergyman, would not have approved of Hitler, and that Hans Oster would be of the same opinion. They might also have been interested to learn that Oster's family had strong links with French Alsace-Lorraine, and that during his youth Oster had at one stage adopted the name 'Jean'. Furthermore his parents-in-law had lived in England for many years.[18]

Oster, himself a keen horseman, had made friends with Sas and his family when he had been asked to escort them to equestrian events at the 1936 Berlin Olympics. Sas was attending the Games to provide official support for the Dutch team. At first the fifty-two-year-old Oster was the height of discretion, not revealing any of his true feelings about Hitler and the Nazis. His daughter Barbara, then a fifteen-year-old schoolgirl, remembers the lecture he gave her before they met the Sas family: 'I don't know this man,' he told her, 'so I don't want you to say anything about politics. If I hear you say one word which criticizes the Nazis, I will send you straight home.' Oster was a strict father who meant what he said, and Barbara made sure she complied with his instructions.[19]

At home Oster was more relaxed when it came to airing his political opinions. According to his daughter, he was always talking about 'those bloody Nazis', and when he heard clicking while talking on the telephone, he would tell the person he was talking to, 'The pigs are listening in again.' However, he was careful to counterbalance what he must have hoped would pass for irreverent humour by always ending his telephone conversations with 'Heil Hitler!' His strategy in helping Jewish friends and acquaintances also combined daring with prudence. On Kristall-nacht, 9–10 November 1938, for example, when Nazis attacked Jews in the streets as well as their synagogues, he made no attempt to stop the violence, but he quickly invited his Jewish neighbours to take refuge in his flat in Berlin's Bayerische Strasse.[20]

His daughter never forgot what happened on 1 April 1938 shortly after the legal proceedings exonerating General Werner von Fritsch, the former Commander-in-Chief of the German Army who had been forced to resign to defend himself against the trumped-up charge that he was a practising homosexual. The von Fritsch witchhunt was one of the events that transformed Oster's attitude towards the Nazis. Until then, he had been a passive opponent. Thereafter he became an active member of the German resistance movement. He could not stand by and watch Hitler and his cronies attack the Army, one of the last pillars of civilized society that had the power to halt the Nazis' excesses. Not realizing how strongly her father felt about the von Fritsch affair, Barbara Oster decided to use it as part of an April Fool joke. Early that morning while her father was still in bed, she tinkered with the receiver on one of the telephones in the Bayerische Strasse apartment so that another phone near her parents' bedroom tinkled as if someone was ringing. Before her father had a chance to get up, Barbara stopped tinkering, and then, after a brief pause, ran to tell her father that they had been telephoned by one of von Fritsch's friends. Fearing that the 'telephone call' meant more bad news, the colour drained from her father's face, and he leaped out of bed, demanding to know what had happened. His shocked reaction was just what Barbara had wanted, and she roared with laughter, shouting, 'April, April!', the German equivalent of 'April Fool'. But Hans Oster did not laugh. He was furious, and slapped her so hard that she had to wear a scarf to hide the bruise at school. Later that evening, he explained why he had lashed out: he had feared that von Fritsch might commit suicide, and had been so preoccupied, he had forgotten himself briefly when his daughter had involved the former Commander-in-Chief in her joke. He was normally a kind, considerate father, although somewhat reserved with his children.[21]

Sas had been absent from Germany during the von Fritsch affair, but on his return in 1939, he said to Oster, 'I wish you'd told me how bad things are.'

Oster replied, 'I couldn't talk about it until you said something. It would have been dangerous.' That was a crucial moment. Only then had Oster felt it safe to reveal to Sas his true feelings.[22] A real deep friendship developed, and in October 1939 it encouraged Oster to turn to Sas when he wanted to warn the Allies about the planned German attack.

Notwithstanding Sas' failure to get along with Reynders, and Reynders' decision to replace him, Sas was ordered to remain at his post in Berlin until a replacement was found. However, before a satisfactory candidate turned up, Reynders himself was driven to resign from his post following a series of disagreements with Adriaan Dijxhoorn, the Dutch Defence Minister, and Sas was reprieved, following the appointment of General Henri Winkelman as the new Commander-in-Chief.[23]

As a result, Sas was still in place when, on Tuesday, 2 April 1940, Hitler decided to invade Norway and Denmark seven days later.[24] This gave Sas, who had received yet another warning from Oster, the opportunity to redeem himself in the eyes of the Dutch Government. After the war, Sas described the method he used: on 3 April he telephoned Captain Hendrik Kruls of the Dutch Intelligence section in The Hague. While they were talking, Sas told Kruls he was coming to the Netherlands on 9 May, and would like to meet for dinner. It would have been hard for anyone intercepting this mundane telephone conversation to read anything significant into it. On the surface, it was just two colleagues arranging a dinner date. However, the carefully chosen words were full of hidden meaning. The reference to a planned visit to Holland told Kruls that Holland was to be 'visited', or attacked, by Germany. The reference to 9 May meant that Sas' informant was predicting that the attack would take place on Tuesday 9 April, a month earlier than the date specified by Sas.[25]

Sas had decided to use this primitive code because the only man who knew the more sophisticated diplomatic code, which was supposed to be used by staff at the Dutch Legation in Berlin when communicating with Holland, was the Legation's Minister, Henri Haersma de With, and he was out. It was only later, after his return, that Sas' full message was transmitted using the diplomatic code. It indicated that the invasion of Denmark and Norway was likely to take place in the first half of the following week, and it was possible, but by no means certain, that the attack on the West might occur at the same time.[26]

It was this forecast, borne out as it was on 9 April 1940 when Germany invaded Denmark and Norway, that gave Sas' reputation a vital boost. Although, in spite of the warning, a British expeditionary force was only landed in Norway four days later, to be followed by a French force, and although the Allies were not able to dislodge the Germans from Norway during the weeks of fighting that ensued, the new Dutch Commander-in-Chief, General Winkelman, congratulated Sas on what was an astounding intelligence coup. But Winkelman's praise was qualified: next time Sas was to use the diplomatic code with the aid of the Legation and the minister. According to the general, the primitive code Sas had used was not specific enough and, as a result, unnecessary counter-measures had been taken by the Government in The Hague.[27]

This coup meant that, in spite of all the reverses, Sas and his whistle-blower were regarded as well worth listening to when, in May 1940, Hitler finally decided to invade France, Belgium and Holland. Heinz Renk, a young staff officer serving in Germany's 2nd Panzer Division, remembered the historic moment on 9 May 1940 when the final German order to attack was passed to the troops who were to execute it. At around 1.30 p.m., he was having lunch at the Diehls Hotel in Koblenz, General Heinz Guderian's XIX Corps' headquarters, when Guderian's Chief of Staff, Colonel Walter Nehring, was summoned to leave the dining room to take a telephone call. When he came back, there was an expectant hush as all those present waited to hear what he had to say. He announced that the password '*Eisfrei*' had been given, which meant that the attack was to take place at dawn the next day. 'We must now all do our duty,' he concluded. Within minutes the dining room was empty, as the German officers rushed off to prepare for the long-awaited attack.[28]

It was 8.30 p.m. Belgian time (an hour behind German time), before the first attempt was made to warn Belgium. That was when the intelligence office in Brussels received a coded message from Colonel Georges Goethals, the Belgian Military Attaché in Berlin. It started with a tell-tale reference to 'the usual source', but the rest was indecipherable. Goethals was asked to repeat the message, which he did: only then could the warning predicting the attack in the early morning of 10 May be deciphered.[29] It conveyed what Oster had mentioned to Sas when they had met earlier that evening. In the course of that meeting, Oster pointed out that the attack had been postponed on three earlier occasions, and told Sas not to raise the alarm until 9.30 p.m. German time, the last moment at which German generals could call off the night-time manoeuvres leading up to the attack.[30] This prompted Goethals to add a rider to his warning, stating that a counter-order might still be given.[31]

Sas has described what happened next. He and Oster had dinner at a Berlin restaurant so that Sas could be in contact with his friend when the crucial deadline passed. During the meal, Oster told him that an inquiry was being set up to discover who had leaked the date of the attack on Denmark. According to Oster, Goethals was the prime suspect: the Germans conducting the inquiry feared he had been tipped off by the Vatican. Fortunately for Sas and Oster, their names had not yet been mentioned. 'So,' Oster said to Sas, 'we've played our cards right. No one knows who was behind it.' Nevertheless Oster's next move was heroic to the point of being reckless. They went together to the German Armed Forces' Headquarters and Oster coolly walked in. Twenty minutes later, he reappeared, and said, 'My dear friend. It really is going ahead. No counter-order has been given. The pig has gone to the West.' Sas' account does not record the emotion the two friends must have experienced as they bade each other farewell, only Oster's hope that they would meet again after the war.

Goethals, whom Sas had tipped off about the meeting with his informant, was already waiting at the Dutch Legation when Sas returned at around 10 p.m. (German time). After hearing Sas' news, he rushed off to tell the Belgian Government. Sas spent twenty nail-biting minutes trying to get through to the Defence Ministry in The Hague. He was finally connected to Lieutenant Post Uiterweer, the Defence Minister's aide. Sas described their conversation when he gave evidence to the post-war Dutch inquiry which, among other matters, analysed the exploitation of his intelligence:

'I said: "Post, you know who you are speaking to, don't you. This is Sas in Berlin. I only need to give you one message. Tomorrow morning, early at the break of day. Good luck. Do you want me to repeat it, or do you understand what I am telling you?" Post repeated what I had said, and added: "So letter 210 has been received." I said: "Yes, letter 210 has been received." That was the code. 200 meant that the invasion was to happen. The last two digits gave the date in May when the invasion would take place.'[32]

About an hour later Major Jacobus van der Plaasche, head of the foreign section of Dutch Intelligence, telephoned Sas. Again Sas' testimony to the Dutch inquiry is the best source for what was said:

'I've heard the bad news about your wife's operation,' he [van der Plaasche] said, before adding mistrustfully: 'It's terrible news. Have you seen all the doctors yet?' I was very angry, and replied: 'Yes, but I don't understand why you are bothering me. You know about the operation. There's nothing more that can be done. I've seen all the doctors. It will take place tomorrow morning at the break of day.' Having said that, I angrily hung up.

The final warning had been given.

5: The Matador's Cloak

Albert Canal Bridges, and Fort Eben-Emael, Belgium, 10–11 May 1940
(See Map 3. Also Map 1)

The countdown to the German attack on Belgium – the matador's cloak that was to tempt British and French forces away from the main thrust in the south – started during the evening of 9 May. At 8.30 p.m., the élite paratroopers and engineers, who had been isolated for some time in hangars at two of Cologne's airports, were ordered to put on their combat jackets and trousers, and write final letters to their families.[1] At 9 p.m., the Junker 52 planes, which were to tow the DFS 230 gliders carrying the paratroopers and engineers on the first stage of their journey towards their as yet undisclosed targets, arrived at the airports, and the gliders were pulled on to the runway. At 11 p.m. the paratroopers and engineers were finally given their targets, which had not been disclosed previously to avoid leaks. They were also told when their mission was to start. The forty-two gliders and the planes towing them were to commence take-offs at 3.25 a.m. on 10 May so that they would reach their targets as dawn was breaking. Then the 450 men, whose task was to capture the three bridges over the Albert Canal near Veldwezelt, Vroenhoven and Canne, to the west and south-west of Maastricht, and the nearby fort a mile from Eben-Emael, would be on their own.[2]

This time Sas' warning had been spot-on. The question now was whether the forewarned Belgians would be able to use what they had been told to help them repel the invaders. Unfortunately for the Allies the contrast between Sas' frantic message – telephoned to Brussels by Georges Goethals at 10.30 p.m. on 9 May – and the sluggish Belgian response could not have been more extreme.[3] This was partly because the Belgian soldiers had lived through so many alerts that they had become blasé, but also because General Oscar Michiels, the new Chief of the General Staff, had encouraged his troops to be off their guard by announcing on 9 May that leave was to be increased from two to five days per month. Although this was decided before Goethals' 9 May warning, it was an ill-advised action. Two days earlier, Goethals had warned the Belgians that the 'usual source' was saying that the attack, planned for 8 May, was to be postponed for one or two days.⁴ Other evidence was also suggesting that the Germans might be on the move at last.

This other evidence was admittedly not as clear-cut as that contained in Goethals' warnings, but it was consistent with them. On 5 May, a notice had been published in German newspapers stating that during the feast of Pentecost (Pentecost being on 12 May that year), all railway journeys should be avoided.⁵ On the same day, Sas was told by the Greek Naval Attaché in Berlin that a woman had revealed to him that her boyfriend in the German Grüne Polizei had been told to report to Utrecht in Holland on 12 May.⁶ Even more alarming was the news that on 7 May the German Foreign Ministry had asked the Dutch Legation in Berlin to provide an immediate visa for Major Werner Kiewitz so that he could attend to urgent business in The Hague. It was thought he wanted to deliver an ultimatum to the Dutch Queen. Dutch diplomats' suspicions were heightened by the warning Sas sent during the night of 6–7 May that the Germans planned to attack during the morning of 8 May.⁷

None of this intelligence was passed on to Belgian soldiers in the front line. The only event that concerned them on 9 May was the re-establishment of the five days' leave per month, signalling that an imminent attack was unlikely. Their guard was duly lowered – and nowhere was this more graphically illustrated than in the area around the bridges over the Albert Canal, which, unbeknown to the Belgians, were to be the principal targets for the German attack. During the afternoon of 9 May, a Belgian major inspected the defences near the concrete bridge at Vroenhoven. He was astonished to discover that while there were some soldiers dotted around, the majority were attending a concert in honour of Queen Elisabeth, King Leopold's mother. Later that evening, he reported what he had seen to his superior officers, only to be told that they were not in the least concerned. They pointed out that the re-establishment of the five days' leave meant there was no immediate danger.⁸

The same complacency prevailed at the fort near Eben-Emael. Its commander, Major Jean Jottrand, had been woken at around 12.40 a.m. on 10 May by the sound of his doorbell being rung.⁹ He slept outside the fort precincts. The major was still wearing his pyjamas when he received the note from the soldier who had been ringing. It contained the unambiguous words 'Real alert.' Nevertheless, half an hour after he had received what appeared to be a clear warning, he was still discussing the note with his officers at the fort. Some believed that the alert was not genuine, and that it might have something to do with the 7th Belgian Division's training manoeuvres, which everyone had been talking about for several days. Others thought it might be genuine, but it would probably turn out to be another false alarm. Even Jottrand, whose job it was to discipline his men into smartly taking up their positions just in case, failed to summon up the necessary enthusiasm. Instead, he further dampened down any sense of urgency he might otherwise have been able to foster by remarking that it seemed strange that an alert should come so soon after the five days' leave order, which he had only just heard about that night.

A gunner at the fort was supposed to fire twenty cannon shots whenever there was a genuine alert to warn soldiers and civilians in the vicinity, but in the early hours of 10 May, Jottrand's officers were so sceptical that they told the gunner to wait until they had confirmation from their commander. Notwithstanding Jottrand's own doubts, he eventually decided that the gun should be fired, but it was 2.20 a.m. before he gave this order, and the firing was delayed for an hour because the gun in question was out of order, and had to be repaired. The delay had a knock-on effect. Officers who would have ordered their men to race to their combat positions in the fort had they believed the alert was genuine instead told some of the gun crews to help first with the transportation of food and other supplies into the fort's kitchen. As a result six out of the seven gun positions that could be fired at troops attempting to land on the fort's roof either lacked the full complement of men to operate them, or were unmanned altogether.[10] Furthermore, the reaction time for at least one of the manned guns was drastically lengthened by the ruling that none of the ammunition stored in boxes in the deep well beneath the gun room was to be brought up into the casemate until a specific order to that effect had been received.[11]

The Belgian high command had made other crucial mistakes. The lack of discipline at the fort was the indirect result of the generals' decision to man the Eben-Emael garrison with second-rate and inexperienced officers and soldiers, who in many cases had been rejected by other army units. Other mistakes by Belgian generals compromised the defences near the Albert Canal bridges. One of the most glaring omissions concerned the protection offered to Commandant Giddeloo, who was in charge of the men guarding the bridges.[12] Giddeloo had on more than one occasion requested that a bombproof bunker should be built at his headquarters, in the army barracks at Lanaeken, a mile and a half to the north-east of the bridge near Veldwezelt. But his suggestion was never taken seriously, even though it should have been obvious to the generals that the headquarters would be one of the Luftwaffe's first targets when they attacked the bridges.[13]

Difficulties that arose from the generals' instructions concerning the bridges' defences were equally debilitating. One general asked Sergeant Crauwels, who, during a German attack, would have to decide whether or not to blow up the bridge at Vroenhoven, what he would do if he was told that two Germans had been spotted near the bridge. When the sergeant replied that he would check first whether the Germans really were there, then get ready to open fire, the general replied, 'No, that is not correct. You should blow up the bridge.' Another general gave the sergeant contradictory orders, saying that such a small German presence did not justify such an extreme move.[14]

Thus were the Belgian defences fatally weakened, but their weakness was exacerbated by the failure to arm the bridges' guards with equipment they obviously needed. Troops on one side of the road leading up to the northern bridge near Veldwezelt were given grenades, but the elements needed to prime them were supplied to their comrades on the other side of the road. At least that was better than the state of affairs at the southern bridge near Vroenhoven, where some of the front-line units had no grenades at all. None of the troops guarding the bridges had easy access to the machine-gun ammunition that was essential if they were to pin down a group of well-armed invaders.[15]

The complacency of soldiers in the front line might have been eradicated had their generals been convinced by the intelligence they were receiving. Unfortunately that was far from the case. After the January 1940 alert, General Van den Bergen had lost his job, and General Van Overstraeten's judgement had been called into question. So, when an officer in the Belgian intelligence service passed the latter general a report stating that German soldiers near the Dutch border were on the move, he should not have been surprised by Van Overstraeten's reaction: the King's military adviser asked whether they were heading east or west, and on hearing that there was no evidence they were marching into Holland, he remarked dismissively that they must in that case be less ready to attack than before.[16]

But Van Overstraeten's initial scepticism on 9 May was gradually overcome. He, like the intelligence section, was entitled to see information collected by so-called reconnaissance officers (ROs) attached to Belgium's 3rd Regiment of Chasseurs Ardennais, who had been patrolling for months along the Belgian–German frontier. These ROs, who were more intelligence gatherers than fighting soldiers, had struck up working relationships with the German border guards in the hope that their German counterparts would give them clues about when and where an attack would be launched. On 9 May, the ROs' patient watching at last began to pay off when they picked up signs that something was amiss. At first the signs were ambiguous. One unit reported that German guards were not allowing them to approach a couple of bridges in the border area that had never been out of bounds before.[17] At 5 p.m., another unit reported German couriers on motorcycles moving around on the German side of the border in combat uniform. This was significant: in the past couriers had invariably been seen in civilian apparel.[18]

As afternoon and evening turned into night a pattern emerged. What had been identified at first as the clanking of individual tanks being driven from north to south had become a 'dull continuous rumble which never stopped'.[19] All along the Belgian–German border, shouts, orders and songs could be heard, as well as the sounds of vehicles on the move. Lanterns, lamps and headlights were visible where none had been seen before. The message carried by the sinister noises and illumination was reinforced by news from Brussels: thick smoke was pouring out of the chimney at the German Embassy, leading some Belgian intelligence officers to conclude that the Ambassador was burning confidential documents so that he could leave in a hurry. All of this intelligence, which was consistent with Sas' warning, persuaded the officer on duty in Belgium's intelligence section that his country was about to be invaded. His verdict was immediately passed on to General Van Overstraeten.[20]

Notwithstanding the compelling evidence, the warnings Van Overstraeten passed to Belgian commanders of units in the front line were much more restrained than the one he had circulated during the January 1940 alert. At 11.10 p.m. on 9 May, he told one commander that the tip-off about an attack at dawn the next day 'might be true'. However, the warnings other commanders received between 11.30 p.m. and midnight could more accurately be described as pre-alerts, suggesting that a full alert might come later that night. It was 1.30 a.m. on 10 May before a general alert was given to the entire Belgian Army.[21] Even then, the fallout from the January 1940 alert, and from General Van den Bergen's dismissal for having acted too quickly on that occasion, restricted and slowed the General Staff's reaction. When General Michiels was urged to broadcast a radio message recalling all those on leave, he retorted, 'Do you know what you are asking? Do you want me to have the same problems as General Van den Bergen?'[22] As a result, the order to end all soldiers' leave was only cleared for broadcast between 3 and 3.20 a.m., minutes before the German parachutists took off in their gliders from Cologne.[23]

The first gliders reached the Albert Canal bridges near Vroenhoven and Veldwezelt, and Fort Eben-Emael shortly after 4 a.m.[24] Although Major Jottrand was criticized subsequently for not drilling his men so that they were ready to repel a surprise attack, he cannot be faulted for the steps he took once the gliders appeared. No one can blame either him or his men for thinking initially that the gliders were a flock of birds: they certainly looked like crows when seen circling in the distance. However, when the 'crows' descended he realized quickly that they were in fact German planes, and immediately rushed to his command post inside the fort after an urgent telephone message told him that one was about to land on the roof.[25] Once there, he promptly ordered that the nearby bridge at Canne should be blown up, thereby ensuring that a substantial part of it was lying in the canal by the time the German paratroopers reached it. There was nothing he could do to prevent eight more gliders following the first on to the fort's roof.[26]

If only the guards at the other Albert Canal bridges had acted as decisively. When the first glider landed near the southern bridge at Vroenhoven, a policeman, evidently believing that one of the circling planes had been shot down, approached it without taking any precautions to arrest its pilot. He was greeted by a burst of machine-gun fire, as the paratroopers inside the glider leaped out.[27] In spite of being hit in the leg, he hobbled back to the shelter at the western end of the bridge, where he joined a group of fifteen to twenty Belgian soldiers who had also taken refuge there.[28]

It was then that Sergeant Crauwels, the Belgian soldier who, prior to the attack, had been confused by the generals' instructions, made a fatal error. Instead of concealing himself in the shelter's vestibule, where the fuse for exploding the bridge was situated, he left the outer (front) door open as he lit the fuse. This permitted the Germans climbing out of their glider to see what he was up to. As Crauwels hurried through the shelter's inner door, which he locked after him, and as he ran down the stairs to join his comrades in the basement, hoping no doubt that this would protect him from the impending explosion, a German paratrooper dived towards the open door upstairs and extinguished the fuse before it detonated the explosives under the bridge.[29]

Meanwhile Crauwels had reached the shelter's basement where, instead of being congratulated on having lit the fuse, he was criticized for what he had done: 'Sergeant, you should not be blowing up the bridge for the sake of three Germans. We will all be locked up for life,' one soldier said.[30] Crauwels' first reaction was to reply, 'It's too late. I've lit the fuse.'[31] But then, as if suddenly remembering the instruction given to him by the general about not blowing up the bridge for just a few Germans, he panicked and, after pushing aside another soldier who tried to stop him, raced upstairs.[32] He was followed by two others, including the man who had criticized him. However, before any of them could reach the vestibule, they were stopped in their tracks by a powerful explosion that blew a hole in the inner door, killing the three men on the spot. The other Belgians who tried to escape through the door were shot by Germans standing outside. The only survivors were those who, though incapacitated at first by their wounds, or by the smoke and flames that engulfed the interior of the shelter, managed to crawl out later, burned and coughing, without attracting further German bullets.[33]

There was still a chance that the German attack could be contained. As the first gliders appeared, one of the soldiers in the shelter had telephoned the unit's headquarters at Lanaeken and reported that three German planes had landed nearby.[34] However, the line was cut before any orders could be given. Lieutenant Boyen, the officer at Lanaeken who received the disturbing news from Vroenhoven, was told by Commandant Giddeloo to notify their commanders at Tongres, ten miles to the south-west. Boyen then attempted to warn the men occupying a similar shelter at the western end of the bridge near Veldwezelt, but that line was dead too so he rang another shelter under the bridge. The man who answered the phone gasped that he and his comrades were suffocating – they were trapped inside the shelter. Desperate for orders, Boyen ran to where Commandant Giddeloo had last been seen, and arrived in time to see German planes dropping bombs on to the barracks. Commandant Giddeloo was among those killed.[35]

We know the fate of soldiers who took refuge in the shelter at the western end of the Veldwezelt bridge thanks to the testimony of Willem Vranken, the only survivor.[36] The soldiers in the shelter fired at the German paratroopers as they emerged from their gliders, but their resistance was interrupted by a bombing raid that extinguished the lights. The Belgians ran down to the basement. Vranken never found out whether the corporal in charge of the shelter managed to light the fuse in the vestibule upstairs. The next thing he remembered was hearing German voices telling them to come out. The corporal in charge of the bridge defences called back that they would only surrender if the Germans promised not to shoot. It was not the response the Germans had wanted to hear, and they fired flame-throwers through holes in the shelter wall that had originally been constructed to enable those inside to throw grenades at their attackers. In his account Vranken described how he and two of his comrades raced up the stairs to escape the 'unbearable heat', but they were thrown against the wall by an explosion that killed one of them outright. Vranken was lucky to survive: he stumbled outside and was hit by a hail of German bullets. The other men inside who were not killed by the explosion must have been cooked alive as the interior of the shelter went up in flames.

The Belgian soldiers in the area around the bridge fared no better. One survivor has described how he was nearly decapitated as a glider landed near the trench where he was waiting. Shortly afterwards, he saw Germans further along the trench but he was unable to shoot them because they were concealed by the smoke from their smoke bombs. The smoke does not appear to have inhibited the German attackers, and the Belgian fell to the ground after being shot in the stomach. He was one of the lucky ones: out of forty-four men in his unit, twenty-four were killed.[37]

It was not just the smoke that impeded the Belgian defenders. Time and again Belgian soldiers with Germans in their sights squeezed their triggers only to find that their guns would not fire. The fact that the

Belgians' inability to defend themselves properly resulted from negligence – the unreliability of the Belgian guns having been brought to their commander's attention a long time before the attack – made the injuries suffered even harder to bear. One Belgian soldier has vividly described the terrible moment when one of his comrades called to him that his legs had been blown off by a German grenade. The soldier would have tied a tourniquet round his friend's bloody stumps, had he not been forced to take evasive action to save his own life as two more German grenades were lobbed in their direction.[38] As has already been mentioned, the Belgians had no primed grenades, which would have enabled them to give the Germans a taste of their own medicine.

The German ability to mop up the Belgian infantry around the bridges at Vroenhoven and Veldwezelt was doubtless helped by the defenders' inadequate preparations. The troops at Vroenhoven had only reached their defensive positions an hour before the attack. At both bridges, the soldiers had left most of their ammunition in their lorries, which could not be reached before they were overrun.[39] That did not stop the Belgians making several attempts to counter-attack. But each time Belgian infantry congregated for an attack, they were dispersed by the Luftwaffe's bombs, which could be called in at a moment's notice.[40] During the late morning and early afternoon, the paratroopers' firepower was boosted by the first German reinforcements, and that night, German troops in the bridgehead over the Albert Canal were so sure they could hold on to the captured bridges that the surviving paratroopers were told their mission was accomplished, and by 8.45 p.m. they had been sent back towards Maastricht.[41] The relative losses of the two sides highlighted the difference between them: the attackers' war diary notes that 69 of the 250 paratroopers who attacked the Vroenhoven and Veldwezelt bridges were killed or wounded, whereas an estimated 750 Belgians had suffered the same fate. Another 500 Belgian soldiers were taken prisoner.[42]

Meanwhile, a more prolonged, but equally one-sided, battle was taking place two miles south-east of Vroenhoven at Fort Eben-Emael. Each group of paratroopers that emerged from the nine gliders that landed on the fort's roof was supposed to capture, or put out of action, the guns to be found in one or two of the fort's gigantic casemates. They had to succeed: the most powerful guns, if left in Belgian hands, could pulverize any soldiers or tanks passing over the captured bridges.

The fort was not a conventional building: its internal corridors and cellars had been hollowed out of the limestone hill that overlooked the Albert Canal, and the gun casemates and cupolas, which were accessible from the corridors via internal staircases, were dotted around the large field that constituted the fort's 'roof'. This roof measured 900 yards from north to south, and 800 yards from east to west – large enough to contain many football pitches. The fort's interior was equally vast: it took almost twenty minutes to walk from the main entrance on its western side to the most distant gun position on the roof.

A description of the attack carried out by those German paratroopers who had been ordered to knock out casemate Maastricht (Ma) 1, a large structure containing three 75mm guns that could be fired at targets more than six miles away, gives an idea of what was going on all over the fort's roof as the commando-style raid commenced.[43] As soon as their plane landed, the men leaped out and followed their commander Sergeant Arendt towards the casemate thirty yards away.[44] It was near the south-western edge of the roof. Their task might have been considerably more difficult if the casemate had been surrounded with coils of barbed wire, and if even some of the guns in Ma 1 or other casemates had been fired at the attackers. Incredibly, not one of the six positions with guns capable of firing at targets on the roof engaged either Arendt's group or any of the other paratroopers. This was not because the guns could not be aimed at attackers on the fort's roof. Five of the positions were not manned or armed in time to repulse the attack, while the sixth had only received a general command to open fire, and proceeded to shoot at other targets.[45] Nevertheless, Arendt and his men must have feared that the Belgian guns would open up on them at any minute as they rushed towards Ma 1. They were carrying two 'hollow' charges weighing 25 pounds and 110 pounds, charges that had been specially designed to blast a hole in the fort's concrete carapace. They decided to use the smaller charge on the ball joint that supported one of the guns in the casemate. The blast blew all of the German attackers to the ground and made a one-foot-square hole in the casemate, from which billowed clouds of black smoke. When Arendt and his men picked themselves up and approached the casemate, the only sounds emanating from the interior were the groans of wounded Belgian soldiers.

No detailed description of the casemate's interior after the explosion has been located, but the scene inside must have been horrific. Four of the seven men who made up the gun crews had been severely wounded, and a fifth had been crushed against a wall by the gun barrel, which the blast had catapulted into the interior. As one of the survivors helped two wounded men down the stairs leading to the well beneath the gun position, Arendt and his men made the Belgian soldiers' progress even more terrifying by firing their machine-guns through the hole in the casemate that their explosion had created. Then, without waiting to see if the Belgians would retaliate, he and two others clambered inside. They must have been impressed by the devastation they had caused, but their immediate concern was the sound of voices coming from the bottom of the ammunition lift shaft. They were silenced after a grenade was thrown down the shaft. Then, taking a Belgian prisoner with him as a human shield, Arendt courageously climbed down the 118 steps to the well at the bottom of the shaft, only to be halted by locked steel doors, which isolated the captured casemate from the rest of the fort. Having been foiled, if only temporarily, by this strong barrier, he climbed back up to the casemate with his prisoner.

Any Belgian who climbed up to the gun room, occupied by the Germans, had to take his life in his hands. The only way up was via the staircase. Nevertheless, Commandant Van der Auwera, an officer in the fort, and the fort's chaplain, who was determined to bring succour to any wounded Belgians in the casemate, insisted they should go up.[46] After passing through a steel door at the bottom, which gave them access to the staircase, they in their turn heard voices coming from the top of the stairs. On hearing them, Van der Auwera bravely, if somewhat recklessly, called out, 'Who's there?' only to be almost overcome by the boom made by the exploding grenade the Germans tossed down. The two men, who were deafened by the blast but relieved to be alive, stumbled back down the stairs and stepped through the steel barrier at the bottom. The steel door was then slammed shut and locked behind them, isolating the Germans again.

Ma 1 was just one of several gun casemates captured by the Germans almost simultaneously as the first wave of gliders landed on the fort's roof. But after these initial successes, a kind of stalemate ensued. The Belgians were too timid to send strong patrols out on to the fort's roof to try to overwhelm their attackers. At the same time, the Germans feared they would suffer large losses if they attempted to storm the rabbit warren of corridors that made up the unconquered interior. Thus, although the Germans could walk with impunity almost anywhere on the roof, they could not yet say the whole fort was in their hands. Also, even after many of the gun casemates had been captured, others were still in Belgian hands, including two that faced the Albert Canal, thereby protecting the fort against attacks from the east.[47] Frustrated by their failure to capture these remaining gun positions using the methods adopted hitherto, the Germans on the roof decided to terrorize the fort's garrison into surrendering. Anything to avoid a hand-to-hand battle and the taking of the fort by force, which would doubtless have led to large casualties on both sides.

Sergeant Arendt and his team began by throwing hand grenades down Ma 1's lift shaft. Then they went down the stairs so that they could place and explode heavier charges in the well beneath the guns. This carried on throughout the night of 10–11 May, and reached its climax the following morning. It was the devastating explosion of a 110-pound charge on the stairwell of Ma 1 at around 8.30 a.m. on 11 May that was to damage Belgian morale within the fort irreparably. The main psychological damage was not caused by the injuries to the men manning the barricade at the bottom of the Ma 1 stairwell, although that was bad enough: the explosion blew away the steel doors separating the stairwell from the rest of the fort, and the sandbags that had been placed to strengthen the barricade. Four of the soldiers who were standing behind it were killed by the blast, and most of the Belgians in the corridors behind the barricade were either knocked unconscious or at least swept off their feet. One got up to find that Major Van der Auwera, who until then had been a tower of strength, was having a breakdown and was shouting orders to imaginary soldiers.[48]

But it was the knowledge that the defences had been breached, and that the Germans could now try to force their way into the fort, that was so upsetting. This fear was exacerbated as the soldiers felt themselves grow drowsy and began to suffer from headaches, symptoms that were probably caused by the splitting open of the barrels of lime chloride stored inside the fort as a cleaning agent. Equally demoralizing was a rumour passed on by the fort's chief surgeon, who had heard a sinister knocking coming from under the fort's sick bay. According to the rumour, Germans were tunnelling under the fort so that they could blow up the whole structure, and all the men inside.[49]

During the early morning of 11 May, the Germans also managed to neutralize one of the guns that had been covering the area to the north-east. This was an important development because it enabled German troops, who until then had been unable to approach from the east, to cross the Albert Canal and more or less to surround the fort. It was only then that Jottrand, after realizing that prolonged resistance could only lead to pointless bloodshed, convened the fort's defence council to decide what they should do. At around 10.15 a.m., they agreed to ask the Germans for terms under which they could surrender.[50]

Even that was carried out clumsily. The officer sent out to parley with the Germans was supposed to buy time. Jottrand was still able to speak with his superiors on the telephone, and had been instructed to explode the remaining weapons in the fort so that they could not be turned against the Belgians. He also wanted to redeem himself by leading his garrison out of the fort, and back to Belgian lines.[51] But before his negotiator, who had walked out of the fort's front door, had even spoken to the German commander outside, he turned around and saw, to his horror, that the garrison was following him out of the fort with their hands up. The soldiers had decided to surrender the fort without waiting for their officers' orders.

For the Belgians, it was a humiliating end to the siege. For the Germans it was an important victory, since for them more than the taking of a fort was at stake. If the matador's cloak was to flap convincingly, and if it was to tempt the French and the British to send their troops into Belgium, something spectacular had had to be achieved quickly. And there was nothing more so than the piercing of the Belgian front-line defences on the second day of the attack by just 450 men.

The surrender represented the insertion of the final piece in the German northern-attack jigsaw. Although the Dutch had blown up the bridges at Maastricht before the Germans could capture them, new bridges spanning the River Meuse had been built, enabling the German panzers within the northern army group (Group B) to drive westward towards the Albert Canal. The surrender of the fort meant that the captured Albert Canal bridges were also safe to cross. There was now nothing to stop the panzers and the supporting infantry thrusting into the heart of Belgium . . . or was there?

6: Charging Bull

River Dyle, Gembloux, Belgium, 10–15 May 1940
(See Map 3. Also Maps 1, 2 and 4)

During the early hours of 10 May the BEF's Captain David Strangeways, whose battalion was stationed in the village of Bachy, near Lille in northern France, had his first inkling that he and his men were about to go into battle.[1] The news reached him in almost farcical circumstances. He had begun to rebuke the battalion's orderly room clerk, who had woken him by rushing into his bedroom, shouting, 'David, sir, David!' before he realized that the poor man had not committed the unforgivable crime of addressing an officer by his first name but was instead referring to 'Operation David', the code word given to the British Army's move up to the River Dyle in Belgium. He got up smartly, and began to prepare for war.[2]

Similar hurried preparations were being made by everyone along the British sector of the Franco-Belgian border, as soldiers in BEF divisions, acting in response to Belgium's call for assistance, gathered up their possessions and equipment. It was a large-scale manoeuvre. The ten infantry divisions in France, making up the BEF's main fighting force, were manned by some 237,000 men. They were backed by around 150,000 other troops, who had been transported to France to carry out line-of-communication, medical or other supporting duties.[3] Most of the men in the main fighting force were to follow the armoured cars driven by the 12th Royal Lancers and the light tanks and carriers manned by divisional cavalry regiments into Belgium with the object of occupying the British front line on the Dyle, which was to run from north of Louvain to Wavre in the south.[4] Only three divisions were to hold the front line itself. Five of the others were to halt at various points west of the Dyle so that there would be troops in position all the way back to the River Escaut. The French were to make equivalent manoeuvres so that they could move forward to hold a line to the south of the BEF, while Belgian forces were to hold the line to the BEF's north.

The Royal Lancers, the BEF's spearhead, were only permitted to

cross the Belgian frontier at 1 p.m., so while they were kicking their
heels on the French side of the border, the boisterous cavalry officers
celebrated their call to arms by knocking back a bottle of champagne
for lunch. Suitably fortified, they motored over the border, inspired, no
doubt, by one of their men blasting out the 'Charge!' signal on his
trumpet, as each troop of three armoured cars sped past.[5] Thus did the
horns of the proverbial bull charge into Belgium, mesmerized by a
flourish of the matador's cloak.

Two accounts of the move, written by middle-ranking officers from
the 2nd Battalion, the Royal Norfolk Regiment, are particularly poignant because most of the men mentioned in them were never to see
their homes and families again. Little did the writers realize, as they
accepted the accolades of the Belgian people, that their battalion, and a
large part of their division (2 Division), would be rewarded for the
heroism of its soldiers over the next three weeks with virtual annihilation.
The accounts also contain the first hints that the British Army was
marching into a trap.

In the account by Captain Nick Hallett, the battalion's transport
officer, he describes how, before driving into Belgium, he stopped at
Raymond's, a shop in a village near Orchies, to buy some shaving soap.[6]
'This was a good thing,' he wrote, 'as it was the last time I was to see
an occupied shop for some time.' He went on to describe how, as the
battalion moved out of Orchies, 'the expected bombers arrived'. Their
bombs hit the station. 'My first experience of this sort of thing, and
decidedly unpleasant, as about 200 yards is much too close for comfort,'
commented Hallett. He and his men crossed the frontier at 1.20 a.m.
on 11 May. 'I felt very excited,' he wrote, 'as this was what we had been
waiting for since the beginning of the war. Action was imminent . . .
We all expected to be bombed on the way . . . Actually we saw no
enemy aircraft all day.'

Captain R. J. Hastings, the second-in-command of the Royal
Norfolks' D Company, was similarly amazed by the surprisingly small
number of German aircraft in the skies. Neither officer realized that
Hitler and his generals were doing everything in their power to persuade
the British and French to advance quickly into Belgium. Like Hallett,
Hastings mentioned the comforts he would miss over the coming days:
'It certainly did not occur to me as I got up and dressed that I had worn
pyjamas for the last time for five months, that the shirt I then put on

would have to do duty night and day for that period, and that I should not be properly undressed again for nearly four weeks.'[7] He also mentioned the 'atmosphere of subdued excitement' running through the battalion, excitement fuelled by the 'wild enthusiasm' of the Belgian people at the sight of British soldiers coming to their aid: 'In towns and villages, they lined our route, and little children ran along with the trucks, throwing flowers to the troops . . . people in motor cars drove up and down the convoy distributing cigarettes and chocolate, and whenever we stopped, the women came out of houses with hot coffee . . . No expressions of a nation's goodwill could have been more enthusiastic or complete.'

But Hastings was soon to discover that war also brought with it fear and its unfortunate consequences. His account reveals that a short distance to the west of the Dyle, at a point which he initially presumed was where men from another battalion had to disembark from their trucks, 'a rather bad thing occurred'. The troop trucks had stopped in a line at the side of the road when a single German plane appeared above them. It dropped several bombs, which landed about 150 yards away. According to Hastings:

The orders regarding bombing on the line of march had been very definite. They were that in the event of an air attack, there was to be no debussing [disembarking from trucks], and trucks were to continue to move. But on looking down the road now, I was horrified to see that a large number of men were getting out of the trucks, and scattering to both sides of the road. I yelled at them to get back, but our convoy occupied a long stretch of road, and many were out of earshot. It was obvious that there would be considerable delay before I got moving unless men were to be left behind. Another salvo of bombs from more aircraft hovering above settled the matter. I ordered everyone into cover at the side of the road . . . Part of the trouble was caused by two boys who lost their heads, and the others followed like sheep. I found these two cowering under some bushes without their rifles. They looked abject, and ashamed of themselves. My civilian self might have said 'Poor devils', but that was not what I said to them . . . For most of these men, it was a baptism of fire, and I never saw at any time such incidents again.

It was only when Hastings spoke to another officer that he realized they had in fact reached his own battalion's 'debussing point' after all.

The Royal Norfolks' initial task at the Dyle was to act as part of the BEF's advance guard at the southern end of the British sector. This involved Hastings's battalion holding a front that would subsequently be taken over by a whole brigade. His men were placed in trenches at the foot of the steep, wooded slopes that ran down to the river, while he and another officer placed themselves near the top of a hill overlooking their troops' positions. When they first arrived, Hastings believed that the Belgian Army was holding up the Germans along the Albert Canal. He was also comforted by the thought that light tanks and carriers within the divisional cavalry units had fanned out east of the river so that they could further obstruct any Germans who broke through the Belgian lines. Consequently the prospect of being involved in a battle during the night of 11–12 May, their first in the front line, seemed to be remote. That did not make the transition from peace to war any easier, as the following extract from his account demonstrates:

We . . . stood down at 22[00] hrs. [Major] Richardson [D Company's commander] and I spent that night in the open . . . I used my new lilo and . . . sleeping bag . . . We only removed our boots . . . and ties. We were awakened early by the sound of heavy, continuous gunfire. We concluded, quite rightly, that the Belgian line had broken. I got up. It was one of the finest and most glorious mornings I can ever remember. The sun was blazing through the remnants of a light morning mist, and the hills opposite looked superb. Birds warbled in the trees as if nothing was amiss. It was Whitsunday. Everything looked most peaceful, and except for the rumble of artillery in the distance, it was difficult to believe we were at war. How I hated the rumble of artillery! All of the civilian in my nature was stirred deeply. I saw a long silver hair glistening in the sun on my sleeping bag, and remembered how my wife had laughingly insisted on trying herself in it when it arrived new from the shop. I twisted the hair round a small photograph of its owner I had in my wallet, and had a struggle with myself to get back to the idea of being a soldier.

This he had to do swiftly, since his battalion was to be relieved during the day, and had to move to their new position near Wavre, which was expected to be their first combat area.

Later that morning, on the way to this new position on the right of the British line, Hastings saw the first ominous sign of German superiority:

I saw thousands of Belgian troops . . . All the soldiers looked unkempt, and were unshaven, and the eyes of many were shining and staring as if they had been through a frightening experience . . . One of the Belgians, an officer, told Jallop that his company commander had been killed. The second-in-command had then turned and run, and he and the rest of the company had followed.

As Hastings and his men settled into their positions, he observed that Lieutenant-Colonel Gerald de Wilton, the battalion's commanding officer, looked unwell. De Wilton told Hastings that he was very tired, and could not carry on much longer. 'If only they'd give me a house, I could manage it,' he said. Eventually he was evacuated, having suffered a mental breakdown, and thirty-seven-year-old Major Lisle Ryder, who was to play such an important role in the heroic fighting that was to come, was promoted to be second-in-command under Major Nicolas Charlton, the new commanding officer.[8] The attitude of Major Richardson, Hastings's immediate superior, was another cause for concern:

Richardson was a man who, one imagined, had always liked to do himself well. He was slightly fat, a bachelor, quick thinking and very intolerant of views that were opposed to his own . . . This morning he was in a very bad temper . . . Lack of sleep, the rather harassing time we had had, together with the sudden disturbance from his normal habit, were making him very difficult to deal with. Only that morning, I had seen one bad result of a too hasty temper. The driver of the ration lorry was manoeuvring in a very narrow archway, and one of his front wings looked like grazing the wall. Richardson rounded on him most viciously, and as a result the driver lost his head, and drove backwards demolishing all but one of the platoon water cans. This was to cause a lot of inconvenience later, as they could not be replaced.

Thus Hastings, like so many of the British officers who had moved up into what was soon to become a battle zone, chafed at the difficulties he encountered, difficulties that would soon pale into insignificance beside the terrible cataclysm that was to engulf them all.

During the first hours after the German attack began, British soldiers' difficulties were nothing compared with the suffering endured by the ill-equipped men in the Royal Air Force. Two independent RAF units were operating in France. One, the Royal Air Force component of the

British Expeditionary Force, was expected to work with the BEF. The other, known as the Advanced Air Striking Force (AASF), had also to protect the French. (See note 9 for details of the two units.)[9] It was hoped that its Fairey Battle and Blenheim bombers would disrupt any German advance. However, long before the Germans attacked, Air Vice-Marshal Pip Playfair, the AASF's commander, must have realized that even this might not be feasible: since the first month of the war, it had been apparent that the Fairey Battles were vulnerable when attacked by the Luftwaffe's Messerschmitt (Me) fighters. On 30 September 1939, a force of six Fairey Battles had set out to conduct reconnaissance over German lines. Four were shot down by Me.109 fighters, and the fifth was so badly damaged that it caught fire after landing back at its base. The sixth returned to base with engine trouble. After that, the eight Fairey Battle squadrons in the AASF were never again asked to fly over Germany during the phoney war.[10]

However, when the Germans attacked, the Fairey Battles' and Blenheims' limitations had to be forgotten if the RAF was to attempt to hold them up. At the time no suitable alternative bombers were available.[11] At midday on 10 May Air Marshal Arthur Barratt, commander of the British Air Forces in France, had tired of waiting for the French to order an attack and took it upon himself to throw the first of the AASF's 135 serviceable Fairey Battles and Blenheims into the fray.[12] It was soon obvious that the AASF would suffer heavy casualties. The first bombing raid on the German columns advancing along the Luxembourg–Dippach road set the pace for British losses that day. Of eight aircraft that took off, one had returned to base with malfunctioning wheels and three were shot down.[13] The decision to fly low to avoid the Me.109s had made the British planes vulnerable to another form of attack: German anti-aircraft flak. In the course of making thirty-two sorties on 10 May, thirteen aircraft failed to return, and virtually all of those that did were damaged.[14]

These were just the figures. Behind the impersonal statistics there are stories of such horror experienced by young airmen that it is sometimes hard to comprehend how pilots and their crews summoned up the courage to carry on flying. There was no braver group of men than the crews who flew the aircraft in 12 Squadron, the 'Dirty Dozen', in the playful language of the air force. At dawn on 10 May its Fairey Battle aircraft on the Amifontaine airfield, near Rheims, narrowly escaped being shot up by marauding German planes, possibly because the German pilots incorrectly assumed that the British planes were dummies.[15] Any Luftwaffe bombing in the area was confined to the nearby French airfield. However, by the end of the day, the crews of at least two 12 Squadron Fairey Battles, which took off in order to attack German columns on the Luxembourg–Junglinster road, must have been wishing that the Germans had put their planes out of action while they were still sitting unmanned on the Amifontaine airfield, given what happened to them during their foray.

Flight Lieutenant Bill Simpson was the commander of the attack, and the pilot of one of the two planes.[16] They took off at around 4.25 p.m., and after crossing the frontier separating Luxembourg from Belgium, descended to an altitude that meant they were just skimming the tree tops. Simpson spotted the German column he was to bomb, standing in a clearing within a large wood. Before he attacked it, he saw the other plane with him disappear behind some trees with a trail of white smoke billowing from its engine. Undaunted, he made his approach, and dropped his four 250-pound bombs on to the leading vehicles from a height of just thirty feet. Then, zigzagging sharply to avoid the heavy flak coming from the undergrowth around the column, he sped away. As he did so, he heard and felt what he later described as a 'heavy thud'. To his dismay, he saw that flames were leaping out of the left side of his engine. Although he was able to escape from the German gunfire, he knew that the engine would cut out at any moment. As he was too low to parachute, a forced landing was the only option. The plane was back over Belgium by the time he spotted a suitable clearing and made a 'belly landing' on a sandy track running across it.

But his problems were only just beginning. In the air, the flames had been blown clear of the cockpit. After he had landed and brought the plane to a halt, there was nothing to stop the fire reaching the petrol vapour that had escaped from the fuel tanks and, as he reported, 'there was a tremendous "woof"' as the vapour ignited.

My hands were searching frantically for the release clip holding my straps together. Great sheets of searing flames rushed between my legs and up to thirty feet above me. In that first rush of heat, my hands were burned and they seized up . . . I was trapped . . . The awful realization that I was about to be burned to death took possession of my mind . . . I could feel my flesh burning . . . My whole mind was full of a bloodcurdling scream; but no sound came.

Simpson was only saved thanks to the efforts of his crew, who rushed to his rescue. 'I heard Odell's gasp of horror,' Simpson wrote, referring to his observer's reaction when he saw Simpson's injuries. 'There was a peculiar drawn feeling about my face; the left side of my nose and my left eye felt completely distorted – as indeed they were . . . What horrified me most of all was the sight of my hands . . . I stared at them with an unbelieving terror . . . The skin hung from them like long icicles . . .'

Although Simpson survived, and his face and hands were reconstructed by plastic surgeons, the commander of the AASF should have taken on board another hard lesson. Ordering Fairey Battle pilots to attack a German column during daylight was almost like sending them on a suicide mission.

Meanwhile, it had become clear that Royal Norfolk officers Hastings and Hallett were not the only soldiers surprised by the Luftwaffe's restrained response to the British and French march into Belgium. Concern that the Germans were tacitly encouraging the Allies' move was passed to the French high command at their headquarters in Vincennes, near Paris. On 12 May Lieutenant-Colonel Paul de Villelume, Paul Reynaud's military adviser, told General Gamelin that he thought Germany was setting 'a trap' for the French, and begged his commander-in-chief to consider halting the advance while there was still time. De Villelume's diary note for that day recorded that Gamelin could not think of one sensible reason for suggesting that de Villelume's analysis was incorrect. Instead Gamelin concluded lamely: 'When we took the decision to go into Belgium, we decided to accept all of the risks. Now it's too late merely to support the Belgians on the Escaut.'[17]

The French archives do not record Reynaud's reaction to Gamelin's complacent reasoning, but he must have been indignant. When Reynaud had attempted to resign as premier on the eve of the German attack (see Chapter 1), the issue that had divided the Cabinet had been Gamelin's competence. Reynaud had wanted to sack him after seeing the French Army's slow response to the German invasion of Norway, and had decided to tender his resignation when Daladier opposed the change. Reynaud's majority was so small he could not carry on as premier without Daladier's support. Now Reynaud's worst fears about Gamelin's indecisiveness and lack of vigour were being borne out at a time of national crisis.

By 12 May it was also too late to hold back the divisions within General Henri Giraud's 7th Army, which, notwithstanding General Georges' and Giraud's opposition, had been sent into Holland to provide the link between the Belgian and Dutch armies.[18] On 11 May, the forward elements of the 7th Army, which included the 160 tanks in the 1ière Division Légère Mécanique, had not only reached the Breda–St-Lenaarts line, that Gamelin had decreed they should hold, but had already been attacked by German armour.[19] This contact took place much more quickly than had been expected, thanks to a successful German trick: the Dutch guards at the bridge spanning the River Maas at Gennep had been overcome after three fifth-columnists dressed in Dutch policemen's uniforms marched up to the bridge with a group of 'captured' German 'PoWs', fully equipped with machine-pistols and grenades under their greatcoats.[20]

Although the subsequent retreat by the French troops to Antwerp on 12–13 May effectively sealed Holland's fate, since the 9th Panzer Division was then free to besiege Fortress Holland, where the Germans already had a bridgehead thanks to the capture by paratroopers of the large bridge at Moerdijk, Gamelin must have been relieved to see his 7th Army escape.[21] At least the nightmare scenario feared by Giraud, with divisions of French troops being surrounded and captured by the Germans, had been averted. It was only after the withdrawal, when Georges was crying out for reserves and, in particular, armour to stage a counter-attack against the main German thrust to the south, that the scale of the disaster represented by the Breda manoeuvre could be appreciated.

The same comment would be made in relation to the use of French tanks in Belgium. This step, like the Breda manoeuvre, was criticized by the general who was to carry out the operation. The original instructions given to General René Prioux specified that until 15 May, he and the crews manning the 415 tanks in his Cavalry Corps should attempt to hold the Germans to the east of the so-called Gembloux gap, the line running between Wavre and Gembloux, and from Gembloux to Namur, where there was no natural anti-tank barrier.[22] This would give French infantry in General Georges Blanchard's 1st Army, who, like the BEF, were to advance into Belgium, time to dig themselves in along this line. But on 11 May Prioux was upset by the discovery that the Belgians, without informing the French, had moved the anti-tank defences, consisting of 'de Cointet' metal barriers, which he had been given to understand would be in place to the east of Gembloux, some five miles to the east, and the barriers had not yet been made into an uninterrupted line. This, combined with the fact that the Belgian line had been penetrated on the Albert Canal, and that his tanks were to have minimal air support, persuaded him that he could no longer guarantee that his Cavalry Corps could hold the Germans until the specified date.[23] General Billotte listened to Prioux's concerns, then told him his men had to hold back the Germans until 14 May – a day less than had been specified in the original order. But, like Gamelin, he refused to rescind the order requiring French troops to march into Belgium.

By 12 May, Prioux's tanks, the majority being embodied in the 2ième and 3ième Divisions Légères Mécaniques (2 and 3 DLMs), were in action against the tanks and anti-tank guns in General Erich Hoepner's XVI Corps – 3rd and 4th Panzer Divisions – on the line running from Tirlemont via Hannut to Huy.[24] It is difficult to follow the thrusts and localized counter-attacks that take place in any battle involving two groups of tanks, but a sample of the kind of combat the French crews experienced has been described by an eighteen-year-old tank driver, who was caught up in some of the most fiercely fought encounters involving 3 DLM at the north of the French line.[25] Jean-Marie de Beaucorps had joined the division's 2ième Régiment de Cuirassiers and had been trained to drive one of its heaviest tanks, a Somua-35. Unlike the even more heavily armoured Char B1 bis tanks with their 2.4-inch-thick armour and their two cannons, which were used by the Divisions Cuirassées (armoured divisions), the DLMs relied for their firepower on the lighter Somua tanks. Somuas had armour 1.6 inches thick, a machine-gun, and one 47mm cannon, making them better protected and armed than the Panzer 3 models, but less well protected and armed than the Panzer 4s.[26] In common with the French armoured divisions, the DLMs also used Hotchkiss tanks, which were protected by armour 1.6 inches thick, but whose 37mm guns lacked the punch of the armament on Somuas.[27] The divisions also had even thinner-skinned armoured cars, more suitable for reconnaissance than for the tank-versus-tank combat that was the *raison d'être* of the armoured divisions.[28] So, from the Germans' viewpoint, de Beaucorps was in one of the division's most threatening vehicles.

However, even the Somua's armour provided insufficient protection against well-aimed bombs dropped by a Stuka. This is confirmed by what de Beaucorps observed during the first Stuka attack on his tank regiment, which occurred on 12 May, shortly after he and his crew had survived their first tank battle to the west of Thisnes, the latter location being around two miles west of Hannut:

The planes approach us in a close formation. We immediately accelerate and disperse. I close my shutter. The planes have arrived. They are going to bomb us. But no, they topple over as if they have been hit and dive down towards the ground. A mournful sound, a long scream combined with the growling sound of their motors. I feel they are going to dive on to my head. And then there are explosions that make one believe that the whole world is being thrown into the air. Our tank is thrown on to its side . . . I think we are going to topple over. I panic and turn off the motor. We fall down on to our tracks again. There is silence. Then some way away from me, powerful explosions are to be heard: the ammunition lorry which has just supplied us is lying on its side and the ammunition is exploding. Twenty metres away from us, one of our tanks has turned over and has come to rest on its turret. The Lieutenant shouts, 'Get going, goddammit, full speed ahead!'

After the first air raid, and two more, which followed in quick succession, de Beaucorps and the other tanks in his squadron took cover in a wood. He was upset to discover that only nine out of the sixteen that had started out that morning were still in working order. His own tank would have been knocked out too if the armour had been any thinner: the white paint inside had been burned brown in several places by the heat generated by shells as they hit the exterior. De Beaucorps counted twenty such marks after his first tank battle, but felt quite secure because his tank's armour had not given way. However, while he was inspecting his tank's tracks for damage, he saw something that horrified him:

In the chains there is a sticky bloody mass of skin and tissue. When I was crossing the road, I must have crushed some men who were taking cover in the ditch. I vomit. Suddenly Gérard [his friend] is beside me. I see him close his eyes, but he controls himself. I cannot do the same. I tremble and sob. Gérard does not hesitate. He slaps me hard. I find it hard to breathe, and lie down. I remember managing to sit up. Then nothing . . . Gérard later tells me he laid me down like a baby, rolled up in a blanket. In the middle of the night, I wake up crying. Then I sleep again. The next morning the weather is beautiful and everything is bright. Gérard smiled at me, and said: 'Now, you are a man.'

But it was only the next day, after his regiment had retreated from the original front line, that he and his comrades received their true blooding when they were attacked by more than two hundred tanks, backed up by artillery, near Merdorp.[29] De Beaucorps later described what he witnessed:

Smoke, dust. I cannot see much. I try to drive in a straight line, and then there is a terrible crash. Our tank is lifted off the ground, and then falls back down again on its tracks. My legs are slammed into the inner tank shell and I fear that they might be broken. Behind me the light has gone out. The turret has been torn off. It was probably hit by a large shell. In front of me the curtain of dust and smoke is still thick. I don't know where I am, nor where I can find friend or foe. I turn around. Our gunner has been flattened at the back of the tank. He must have been crushed when the turret fell off. The lieutenant has completely disappeared. He has flown away along with the turret . . . Then all of a sudden a German tank appears close to mine, about twenty metres away. The presence of my tank, immobile, half destroyed, does not deter him. A second tank joins him . . . They are smaller than my tank. Their guns are relatively small calibre. They must be light tanks, Mark 1s or Mark 2s. I start my motor . . . I engage the clutch. My tank must have jumped forward because without the turret I can go much faster. They have no time to move, and I crash into them. All I can hear is the sound of the tracks grinding into the metal. They cannot escape. As if in a dream, I light my burning grenade, and place it on my seat. In five seconds it will emit flames and intense heat and burn my tank. After it has been turned into a burning torch, it will in its turn burn the two enemy tanks. I scurry to the rear of my tank. One jump, and I am outside.

In this way, de Beaucorps lived to tell his tale, but by the time he returned to the French line, it was known that only twenty-four out of eighty-two tanks in his regiment were still available for combat. During the battles, which continued until the French tanks retired behind their infantry line – running from Wavre to Namur – during the afternoon and evening of 14 May, 105 French tanks were put out of action.[30] The German losses were even higher. By 16 May at least 135 German tanks within the 4th Panzer Division were unusable, more than double the number out of service in the 3rd Panzer Division. The two panzer divisions had started the battles with more than 620 tanks, although some 498 were Panzer 1s and 2s whose armour (0.5 and 1.2 inches thick respectively) and armament (two machine-guns, and a machine-gun and 20mm cannon respectively) were far inferior to that on the French Hotchkiss 39s and Somuas.[31] But because the French Cavalry Corps retreated, the Germans, who were left holding the battlefield, were able to recover many of their tanks so that they could be repaired.

Nevertheless at 3.30 p.m. on 15 May, having heard that the French had employed strong artillery to hold their line, XVI Corps' General Hoepner sent out a terse signal: 'Suspend the offensive . . .'[32] He wanted the attack to be recommenced the following morning backed up with infantry.[33] But his resolve to carry on advancing was shaken by an alarming report from the 4th Panzer Division mentioning its heavy losses.[34] Its commander's judgement that it was not worth attacking again the next day since the strong French artillery was given extra emphasis, thanks to the account delivered by the officer in charge of the 5th Panzer Brigade, who had just come in from the front line. This officer, who had been wounded in the face, related how he had been forced to lie in a shell hole for three hours and had only survived by pretending to be dead. He had never seen such concentrated artillery fire, even in the last war, and in his opinion to attack the next day would be 'suicidal'.[35] Even though the 3rd Panzer Division, notwithstanding the previous halt order, had not only broken through the French infantry's front line at Ernage and Perbais but had reached the back-up line at Cortil-Noirmont, Hoepner finally ordered that there should be no further advance by the panzers the next day. This order reached the 3rd Panzer Division at 10 p.m. on 15 May.[36] It marked the end of the tank battle: on 18 May Hoepner was ordered to take his panzers to support the southern attack. The French 1st Army had been saved from a mauling. But the terrible news from the south prompted Allied generals to wonder, For how long?[37]

7: Into Battle

Veldwezelt Bridge, and the River Dyle, 12–15 May 1940
(See Map 3. Also Map 1)

While the French Cavalry Corps was commencing its battle against German tanks near Hannut, Britain's Advanced Air Striking Force made a valiant attempt to cut the 3rd and 4th Panzer Divisions' lines of communication by bombing the captured Albert Canal bridges. During the early hours of 12 May, the commanding officer of the AASF's 12 Squadron, which was still based at Amifontaine, north-west of Rheims, was told he must attack the Vroenhoven and Veldwezelt bridges at 9.15 a.m.[1]

Shortly afterwards, all the pilots, observer navigators and wireless-operator air-gunners in the squadron were summoned to attend a meeting in the operations room, a Nissen hut near the Amifontaine airfield. The officer who gave the briefing explained the dangerous nature of the mission: only the day before, the Belgian air force had lost six out of the nine planes that had attacked the two bridges and a third at Briegden.[2] He then asked all men who would volunteer for the mission to raise their hands. Every man in the squadron put up his hand so that the crews whose turn it was according to the normal rota were selected.[3]

As the five Fairey Battles took off – a sixth plane had to drop out due to malfunctioning equipment – those fortunate enough to have remained on the airfield waved at their comrades, and interspersed their thumbs-up signals with the V-for-victory. At least some on the planes were less sanguine about their prospects, as can be seen from an account written by one of the wireless-operator air-gunners who survived to tell his tale: Gordon Patterson, whose plane was one of two that were to attack the southern bridge at Vroenhoven, made sure his gun was loaded before take-off. Then he strapped on his parachute chest pack, and cut through the strings that normally had to be broken when the ripcord was pulled after jumping out of the plane.[4] It is possible that this precaution, which ensured the parachute was 'cocked', saved his life. His plane was shot up by German fighters on the way to the Albert Canal, and he was knocked unconscious while baling out. Nevertheless his parachute opened, and his only injury on landing was a broken foot. The other members of his crew also survived, as did those in the second plane, which was shot down.

No one lived to describe the most celebrated part of the raid on the northern bridge at Veldwezelt. The story goes that twenty-one-year-old flight leader Don 'Judy' Garland dived down to bomb the bridge, and either dropped his bombs on to it before he crashed, or crashed his plane into it. He and his crew were all killed. However, testimony provided by Neville Harper, the twenty-seven-year-old navigator of one of the other two planes under Garland's command, at least gives an insight into the terrifying conditions they had to endure when they made the low-level attack. Garland had decided to go in low to avoid the Luftwaffe – he disagreed with the tactics advocated by Flying Officer Thomas, the leader of the planes that attacked the bridge near Vroenhoven, who decided it would be safer to divebomb the bridge from a higher altitude.

The first sign that they were approaching the bridges came when Harper's plane began to lurch. At first he put this down to atmospheric turbulence, but soon realized the true cause: the plane was being hit by German flak. Then he saw that the fuel pipes under the pilot's seat were on fire having been severed by a bullet. Before he could shout a warning, he was punched in the face by a ball of fire, as the airstream coming through the open canopy blew the flames towards him. He later likened it to being attacked by a blowtorch. Harper quickly gave up all hope of living, and prayed, 'Please hurry up', hoping that if God existed He would end his life before his suffering became unbearable. But before his prayer was answered, the pilot slammed shut his canopy, and the flames returned to the fuel pipes. Harper had almost been cooked, but was thankful to be alive. The plane landed in a nearby field, and it was as he climbed out that he noticed the skin that had once covered his hands was dangling down from his cuticles like rubber gloves, a common phenomenon among badly burned air crews.[5]

Nevertheless, he took cover in a ditch with the rest of the crew. From there, they watched the third plane in their flight zooming overhead with smoke pouring out of its tail. Shortly afterwards, it shot up vertically into the sky, as if the pilot was making one final attempt to regain control, before plunging down to hit the ground with a sickening crash two hundred yards away. When the Germans arrived to pick up Harper and his crew, one said, 'You British are mad. We capture the bridge early Friday morning. You give us all Friday and Saturday to get our flak guns up in circles all around the bridge, and then on Sunday, when all is ready, you come along with three aircraft and try and blow it up.'[6] Their captors were more reticent when it came to answering the question posed by Pilot Officer Ian McIntosh, Harper's pilot, about whether either of the bridges was damaged. But McIntosh noted with satisfaction that their German driver made a detour to another crossing-point when they had to traverse the Albert Canal, leading him to assume that the loss of life and injuries suffered during the raid had not been in vain.[7]

He was right. The bridge was damaged. If Garland did not in fact crash into it, either he or Sergeant Marland – who was flying the plane that had crashed as Harper watched – had dropped a bomb that had damaged the bridge's western lateral truss.[8] McIntosh's plane had been shot down before it reached the bridge. In the short term, this may have stopped the Germans crossing the bridge as effectively as if it had been destroyed.

Although it is possible that Sergeant Marland's bombing had damaged the truss, the British authorities appear to have decided that Garland, who had led the attack, provided better copy: he, rather than Marland, was awarded the Victoria Cross. This highest award for bravery also went to Tom 'Dolly' Gray, Garland's observer – whose good looks had already featured in a publicity shot for the Ministry of Information.[9] Gray's involvement in an unpleasant incident a few days before was hushed up. He had been arrested for firing his revolver at a British lorry which had somehow offended him, and would probably have been court-martialled had he not been killed.[10] Curiously Lawrence Reynolds, the wireless-operator air-gunner, was passed over.

Whatever the gloss put on the raid, it represented another defeat for the RAF, which should not have been sacrificing its valuable pilots by sending them in vulnerable bombers over well-defended German positions. The losses over France and Belgium that day spiralled to twenty-nine Blenheim and Fairey Battle bombers, and ten Hurricane fighters, leaving the AASF with just 72 out of the 135 operational bombers it had possessed on 10 May.[11] It was these sobering statistics that prompted Sir Cyril Newall, Chief of the Air Staff, to send the following note to Air Marshal Barratt that evening: 'I am concerned at the heavy losses incurred by the medium bombers. I must impress on you that we cannot continue at this rate of intensity. If we expend all our effort in the early stage of the battle, we shall not be able to operate effectively when the really critical phase comes.'[12]

The next day, Barratt used his bombers on one small-scale mission in Holland, permitting the Germans to approach the BEF defences in the north without opposition from the air.[13]

★　★　★

Long before German soldiers made contact with the dug-in British troops, the security of British positions in their front line along the River Dyle came under threat, not as a result of enemy action, but thanks to a misunderstanding on the part of the Belgians. Although the French high command had ordered British generals to place their men around Louvain at the north of the British sector, the Belgian generals believed that they should be holding this area. When General Montgomery's 3 Division arrived to take over its positions at the northern end of the British line, the general commanding Belgium's 10th Division refused to move. On 12 May General Alan Brooke, who, as commander of the British 2 Corps, was Montgomery's superior officer, tried to sort out the mix-up at a meeting with the King of Belgium. Their discussion, in English, was interrupted by a Belgian officer who, prior to his intervention, had been standing unobserved in the same room. Without introducing himself, this gentleman told the King in French that the Belgian 10th Division could not be moved. Brooke in his turn interrupted 'the officer', and told him in French that the King was not being presented with all the facts. As Brooke recorded in his diary:

He ['the officer'] then turned to me and said: 'Oh! Do you speak French?' I assured him I did and that I happened to have been born in France. By that time he had interposed himself between me and the King. I therefore walked round him and resumed my conversation with the King in English. This individual then came round again, and placed himself between me and the King, and the King then withdrew to the window. I could not very well force my presence a third time on the King, and I therefore discussed the matter with this individual, who I assumed [incorrectly] must be the Chief of Staff. [Unbeknown to Brooke, this officer was General Van Overstraeten.] I found that arguing with him was [a] sheer waste of time. He was not familiar with the dispositions of the BEF and seemed to care little about them. Most of his suggestions were fantastic. I finally withdrew.[14]

The Belgians only moved after General Georges ordered them to do so, Georges having been tipped-off about the confusion by a liaison officer sent by Brooke.

The line that was eventually given to the BEF to hold ran, as originally expected, for twenty-two miles along the western banks of the River Dyle from the area just north of Louvain to Wavre further to the south-west. (The British line is shown on Map 3 on pp. 512–13.) After the Belgians had left Louvain, the BEF's 3 Division was alone responsible for the north of the British line. 1 Division was on its right. The southernmost British troops were in 2 Division, including the 2nd Royal Norfolks, as mentioned in Chapter 6, and on 2 Division's right were the French. Their principal line of resistance ran from Wavre to Namur, then followed the line of the River Meuse, passing through Sedan. The Belgians held the line to the north of the BEF, and the British front line was temporarily screened by the light tanks and carriers that had crossed to the eastern side of the river.[15] This screen of light armour, like the heavier armour used by the French in front of Gembloux, mentioned in Chapter 6, was merely intended to delay the Germans until the line of principal resistance, which in the BEF's case was the Dyle, was securely held.

The British light tanks and carriers may have been unsuitable for offensive operations, but they were eminently suited to the kind of reconnaissance missions given to them east of the Dyle. Thanks to their presence, the BEF infantry advanced to the river without interference from German ground forces. By the evening of 14 May, the infantry being in place, all British light armour that had not been damaged or captured was back west of the river.

The following day the Germans mounted their first strong attacks on the BEF's front line. Compared with those against the French between Yvoir and Sedan (described in Chapter 8), they were mere pinpricks. Nevertheless they still packed enough of a punch to threaten penetration, particularly at the northern end of the line. These thrusts were, however, quickly reversed, thanks to 3 Division's smartly delivered counter-attacks.[16]

Holding on to the southern end of the line turned out to be much harder. Included within 2 Division's sector was the hilly, wooded area surrounding the Belgian village of Gastuche. It was in the countryside between Gastuche and the ominously named La Tombe that one of the most celebrated actions of the campaign was carried out by Dick Annand, a twenty-five-year-old 2nd Lieutenant serving in the 2nd Battalion, the Durham Light Infantry (DLI).[17] His bravery under fire was to win him the Victoria Cross.

Annand was in charge of one of the DLI platoons that arrived at the Dyle during the night of 11–12 May and dug themselves in along the river's west bank.[18] As well as making sure that Germans did not swim or row across, he and his men had to ensure that no enemy troops used the bridge almost opposite his platoon's position. That was more easily said than done because Belgian refugees, alarmed by the piercing of the Belgian line on the Albert Canal, were streaming across, making it hard for British soldiers to determine whether or not Germans were with them. Annand's job was further complicated by an instruction he had received telling him that anyone carrying a red blanket might be a fifth-columnist. So many Belgians were carrying red blankets that Annand decided to let them all pass, fearing that his men would be swamped with prisoners if he ordered his men to arrest them. On 14 May the British soldiers were relieved when, after being told that the division's cavalry had crossed to the British side of the Dyle, they were permitted to blow up the bridge. It subsided into the river following a loud explosion.

The first groups of German troops to the east of the river were spotted at 4 p.m. that afternoon.[19] The British soldiers were ordered to hold their fire: a few hours earlier, a man in another platoon had fired at and killed a soldier he spotted in a tree to the east of the river, only to be told it was a British artillery observer. This time the men in the trees were German snipers, and when they fired at the British, the British fired back.[20]

British soldiers who kept their heads down in their trenches soon discovered they were relatively safe. But one young soldier was so disturbed by the gunfire that he climbed out of his trench, and attempted to run away. He was immediately cut down by an enemy machine-gunner. Luke Bowden, a twenty-two-year-old former miner, was unsympathetic: 'It's his own fault,' he said to the man beside him in his trench. The young man's body was left where it had fallen until dark, a potent reminder to anyone else tempted to flee that he was safer in the trenches with his comrades.

The River Dyle around Gastuche represented an effective tank obstacle, but because it was only around fifteen feet wide, and because the DLI was defending a 2000-yard front – double the distance recommended 'as a rough guide' by military manuals for a battalion – it was obvious that a determined attempt to cross it would not be easily resisted.[21] The first crossing in the DLI's sector took place at around 6 a.m. on 15 May to the right of Annand's platoon, the Germans making use of a lock that could not be destroyed without lowering the level of the river. They rushed across it and annihilated the DLI platoon holding the position, every man being killed or wounded except 2nd Lieutenant John Hyde-Thompson, its commander.[22] He escaped after shooting the German who had called on him to surrender, and dispersed the remaining German soldiers in the vicinity by lobbing a hand grenade into their midst. Later he linked up with another platoon, and it was under his command that the German advance was checked.[23]

Annand and his men were likewise forced to move back from their riverside positions. This gave German soldiers the chance to build a new crossing-point, incorporating rubble from the old bridge. Annand's Victoria Cross citation, which mentions his 'most conspicuous gallantry', includes a description of the British response:

About 11 a.m. the enemy again launched a violent attack and pushed forward a bridging party into the sunken bottom of the river. Second Lieutenant Annand attacked this party, but when ammunition ran out, he went forward himself over open ground with total disregard for enemy mortar and machine-gun fire. Reaching the top of the bridge, he drove out the party below inflicting over 20 casualties with hand grenades. Having been wounded he rejoined his platoon, had his wound dressed and then carried on in command. During the evening another attack was launched and again Second Lieutenant Annand went forward with hand grenades and inflicted heavy casualties on the enemy. When the order to withdraw was received, he withdrew his platoon, but learning on the way back that his batman was wounded and had been left behind, he returned at once to the former position and brought him back in a wheelbarrow before losing consciousness as a result of his wounds.[24]

In fact the citation was inaccurate, and probably so were many of the tales told by the men who fought alongside Annand, who helped to transform a brave action into another VC legend. The citation under-played Annand's heroism on the battlefield, while spicing up the story about his batman's rescue. He later told his fiancée he had in fact rushed down to the bridge three times to 'bomb' German bridging parties. He carried the grenades that had been primed by his men, including Luke Bowden, in sandbags, and was so confused by the bullets fired at him that on one occasion, while running back, he had a vision that led him to believe he was already dead, and therefore safe at last. He only came to himself after his heroic exploit was over.

There was also a sadder truth behind the wounded-batman story. The citation correctly stated that Annand brought Joseph Hunter, his batman, back from the front line in a wheelbarrow, but unfortunately Annand was so weakened by loss of blood from his own shoulder wound that he was unable to lift Hunter, or the wheelbarrow, over a fallen tree they came across in woodland to the west of the front line. Consequently, Annand had to leave Hunter in a ditch beside the path while he went off to search for help. He had hoped to obtain assistance at his company's headquarters to the rear, but on reaching it, he discovered it had been abandoned. When he finally found members of his battalion further back, his mind was so befuddled due to his injury that he could not explain to the stretcher-bearers exactly where he had left Hunter. After doing his best, he fainted, and was himself carried away from the scene before he could provide a better description. As a result Hunter was abandoned in no man's land, and only received medical attention for his wounded leg after the Germans overran the position, the DLI having retreated from it pursuant to orders issued at 1.30 a.m. on 16 May. (The reason for the retreat, and the fact that neither it, nor the subsequent retreat by the other BEF forces on the Dyle, was caused by German attacks on British positions, is explained in note 25.)[25] Hunter never recovered and died while being treated in a Dutch hospital.[26]

8: Over the River Meuse

Dinant, Yvoir, Houx and Sedan, 12–13 May 1940
(See Maps 4, 5 and 6. Also Map 1)

If there was one decisive factor behind the débâcles in the Sedan and Dinant sectors of the River Meuse, it was the French high command's insistence that the Ardennes was impracticable for, if not impenetrable by, German tanks.[1] Out of this single misconception sprang many of the problems that were to cost France and the BEF so dear: the French failure to allocate enough well-trained troops to protect these sectors, the failure to arm those positioned there with enough guns and mines, or to shelter them with enough pillboxes and bunkers, and the failure to send to the east of the Meuse strong cavalry units to delay the advancing panzers long enough to allow the troops on the south and west banks of the river sufficient time to dig themselves in. Given that General Gamelin did not believe a strong thrust would be made through the Ardennes, it did not seem worth expending too much effort on the defences in the Sedan and Dinant sectors.

Another damaging consequence of Gamelin's 'impracticable Ardennes' theory was the failure to ensure that the full complement of defenders and guns allocated to these sectors was in position behind the river line before the Germans arrived. This was particularly important in relation to the stretch of the Meuse inside Belgium. Just as the BEF had to transport its troops from the Franco-Belgian border to its principal line of resistance along the River Dyle, so the French had to do the same in order to guard the Belgian portion of the Meuse between Namur and Givet. Unfortunately the French generals responsible for transport did not provide sufficient vehicles. As a result many of the soldiers who should, like British soldiers on the Dyle, have been guarding their front line by 12 May were on that day still marching towards their riverside positions.

The French attitude to speedy deployment of forces was diametrically opposite to that advocated by the panzer generals, Heinz Guderian and Erwin Rommel, whose XIX Corps and 7th Panzer Division were to make the initial breakthroughs. They believed they had to race the

French to the river. Guderian insisted his men must be there within five days of the start of the campaign, if all was to go according to plan.[2] Incredible as it must have seemed to some of their colleagues, both generals were counting on either taking French positions on the west side of the Meuse by rushing past the unsuspecting guards of an undestroyed bridge, or on arriving at the river so quickly that, while their attack would not surprise those French soldiers already dug in, their thrust would be made before all the front-line troops had arrived, and before reserves were in place to counter-attack.

The first attempts to cross the southern section of the Belgian River Meuse fell into the former category. One attempt was made after 4 p.m. on 12 May in the Dinant sector of the river.[3] Earlier that day, while the panzer divisions were still advancing through the Ardennes, other bridges over the Meuse had been blown up.[4] But from the heights overlooking the river, officers in Rommel's 7th Panzer Division saw that the Dinant bridge was still standing. Four German tanks, commanded by Captain Steffen of the 7th Panzer Division, were ordered to dash down to capture this bridge before it could be destroyed. Steffen's driver, Michael Berthold, has described what he witnessed during the attack:

Steffen and I were like members of the same family. We had worked together in tanks since 1936. We'd been to Austria and Poland together, and now we were in Belgium. I called Steffen 'the Chief', and everyone referred to me as 'Steffen's Bride'. We were that close.

During the attack I'd to drive his four-man Czechoslovakian tank down the cobbled streets of Dinant to the bridge. But as we drove through the main shopping street in Dinant, we were shot at from a butcher's shop on our left by an anti-tank gun. The shell made a hole in the tank, and it hit Steffen in his throat, severing his jugular vein. I only discovered that later, after I had driven the tank to safety. At the time I only knew he had been wounded because I felt him fall on to the back of my neck. Our gunner was also wounded. His head was split open. I could not hear what was going on behind me since it was so noisy. I just carried on driving towards the bridge, not realizing that some of the tanks behind me had also been shot up. I got to within ten yards of the bridge before it exploded. I then had to turn around quickly, and I drove back out of the firing line. It was only then that Steffen was carried out of the tank. His body was placed on the ground and a cover was put over him. I became very emotional when I saw how it had ended, and I began to cry.[5]

All was not lost, however. That same afternoon aerial reconnaissance had revealed that another Meuse bridge was still standing near Yvoir, which is five miles north of Dinant. News of this discovery was relayed back to Colonel Paul Werner, commander of the 5th Panzer Division's 31st Panzer Regiment, who quickly decided that seven armoured vehicles should be used in an attempt to capture it.[6]

The rushed attack came at a particularly bad time for the Belgian soldiers who were still holding the bridge: they had just been told by Colonel Tachet des Combes, commander of the French 5 Division's 129th Regiment, that they were about to be relieved by his men, and this, combined with the proprietorial way that he and another French officer had strolled across the bridge, to check where enemy sharp-shooters might hide, appears to have distracted them.[7] Had they been alert and well disciplined, they would have stood-to as soon as they noticed that the torrent of refugees on the east bank of the river who, minutes before, had been streaming down the road that led over the bridge, had dried up. This should have told them that the enemy might be approaching. However, at least one Belgian soldier assumed that the refugees were taking cover from a German aircraft whose guns had been heard firing in the vicinity.

When the German vehicles appeared from behind a screen of trees on the eastern side of the river, most of the Belgian soldiers were resting behind the concrete shelter opposite the bridge on the west bank of the river rather than inside it. The alarm had barely been shouted before the Germans opened fire, killing the two French officers who had reached the other side of the bridge. Most of the Belgian soldiers ran inside their shelter in the expectation that their commander, Lieutenant René De Wispelaere, would quickly blow up the bridge. This he tried to do, but when he pressed the plunger, nothing happened.

It was then that one of De Wispelaere's men, Corporal Desmet, showed that if the Belgians were not always disciplined some were certainly very brave. Although the only available Belgian anti-tank gun, a powerful 4.7cm cannon on wheels, was placed in an exposed position, directly in front of the bridge, he ran forward from the shelter to man it. As he did so, the driver of the armoured car at the front of the German column overshot the turning on to the bridge, and had to back up before driving on to it. The few seconds it took him to perform this manoeuvre gave Desmet just enough time to reach the gun and load it.

The German gunner in the leading armoured car fired first, but the shell flew harmlessly over Desmet's head, and hit the shelter behind him. Desmet waited until the armoured car reached the middle of the bridge before he fired. The shell slammed into the car's bonnet, killing the driver and causing the vehicle to slew across the bridge with thick black smoke belching out of its engine.

For the moment at least the bridge was blocked, but the Belgians had not yet won the battle. Another German soldier, carrying cutting equipment, climbed down from one of the following vehicles and began to search for the wires linked to the explosives packed under the bridge. However, before he succeeded, Desmet shot him. In the meantime, Lieutenant De Wispelaere raced to a shelter near the one where his men were hiding to light the fuse linked to the explosives. No one knows whether he was successful, or whether flames ignited by a German shell lit the fuse or explosives for him. Whatever happened, the Germans in their tanks were startled by a gigantic flame that leaped towards the heavens accompanied by a deafening bang. Everyone in the area took cover, as metal debris and paving-stones rained down on them. When the clouds of dust had settled, the German soldiers peering out of their vehicles on the east bank saw that the bridge had caved in, and the two armoured cars, which just minutes before had posed such a threat to the defenders of the bridge, had disappeared into the river. There were no survivors.

The Belgian gunners were equally upset: when the bridge exploded, a heavy object thudded on to the road beside them, and as the smoke cleared, they found themselves looking at the maimed corpse of Lieutenant De Wispelaere whose face had been blackened, and whose limbs had been blown off by the explosion.

There would have been still more bloodshed if the Belgian gun had not jammed as Desmet tried to fire it once more at a panzer that had been about to follow the armoured cars on to the bridge. Unaware that their lives were to be spared, the terrified German crew remained huddled inside the tank for the rest of the day, expecting to be shot up at any moment. It was only after darkness fell that, having failed to complete their mission successfully, they climbed out of the tank and sneaked away into the night.[8]

These abortive attempts to storm bridges with armoured vehicles were not the only attempts to cross on to the western side of the Meuse that afternoon. Shortly after 2.35 p.m. when the railway bridge between Yvoir and Houx was blown up, an attempt was made to scramble across the rubble.[9] Most of the German soldiers were shot by the Belgian defenders before they reached the west bank. However, one German wearing just a shirt and underpants made it to the Belgians' side of the river. After clambering up on to the western river bank, he raised his hands and shouted that the Belgians should not fire at poor French prisoners. This appears to have been a trick designed to confuse the defenders. They were not fooled, and he was shot as well. He may well have been the first German to cross the Meuse during the campaign.[10]

When the initial attempts to establish a bridgehead failed, the 5th Panzer Division's Colonel Werner sent motorcyclists along the bank to see whether they could find suitable points for a more organized crossing.[11] One of the patrols, while passing through the village of Houx, about two miles south-east of Yvoir, noticed that the island in the middle of the Meuse was still connected to both sides of the river by a weir and a lock. The French could not destroy them without lowering the water level, thereby making the Meuse fordable.[12] That would not have mattered if they had positioned soldiers on the west bank who could have repulsed any Germans attempting to walk across. But they had not taken this elementary measure, an omission which was the indirect result of the slow movement of French troops from the Franco-Belgian border to the Meuse. Only five of the nine battalions in the French 18 Division, which had been ordered to hold the Anhée to Insemont portion of the principal line of resistance within the Dinant sector, were in position by the evening of 12 May.[13]

To compensate for this sluggish reaction, a sixth battalion from the neighbouring division to the north was ordered to bolster the north of 18 Division's sector, and it was this unit, the 2nd Battalion of the French 5 Division's 39th Regiment, which was given the riverbank west of the lock at Houx to hold. While this extra battalion was marching towards Houx, the German patrol that had discovered the undefended lock waited patiently until it was dark. Then, shortly before 11 p.m., the men in the patrol stepped quietly across the weir to the island, and then via the lock to the west bank.[14] They were part of the first German group to make the crossing, and ironically, after all the blood spilled during the three failed attempts earlier that day, not one shot was fired at them.

It is not clear who was responsible on the French side for allowing this to happen. If Commandant Cadennes, of the 39th Regiment's 2nd Battalion, was ever given specific instructions to post sentries on the bank beside the lock, then he was at fault since none were posted. Instead the battalion covered the line of the river from a hill some way back from the river. Whoever was at fault must have felt very guilty, since of the many mistakes the French made in the course of the campaign, this one had by far the most memorable consequences.

However, the Germans must take some credit for the confusion within the French ranks. A report by a Lieutenant Gamber of 5 Division's 129th Regiment has described how the division's engineering colonel pointed out to him the danger posed by the undestroyed lock and weir. Gamber went to pass on this information to his colonel, who was none other than the same Tachet des Combes referred to above in connection with the action at Yvoir. Gamber waited for the colonel at his headquarters from 4.30 p.m. until 6 p.m. on 12 May, little realizing that the reason he never showed up was that he had been killed in the course of the Yvoir attack. If the Yvoir attack had never taken place, and if Tachet des Combes had been given the information mentioned by Gamber, it is quite likely that he would have inspected the lock and weir, noticed they were not properly covered, and would have pointed this out to an officer in 18 Division, the unit responsible for it. The lock and weir would then surely have been guarded correctly. This reasoning leads to the conclusion that the panzer attack on the Yvoir bridge may not have been as unsuccessful as it might have appeared to be at first sight. Had it not taken place, the crossing at Houx might have been impossible.[15]

At first, the crossing at Houx was on a small scale. But even after the French fired at the crossing-point, the Germans persisted in using it – at a price. A German who ran the gauntlet of the guns and who reached the west bank of the river at 8 a.m. on 13 May has reported seeing several dead soldiers in the water beside the lock. He carried on regardless despite heartrending cries for help from wounded men who had also fallen into the water.[16] However, his testimony suggests that the Germans might have found it difficult to establish a strong presence on the west bank had they not been helped by the French: if the French commanders had acted decisively once they had seen what was happening, there is little doubt that the incursion could have been repelled. But the hours it took for the message to creep up the chain of command made this increasingly unlikely.

At 5 a.m. Commandant Boulanger of the 66th Regiment, the 18 Division unit holding the sector to the south of the lock, was told that Germans had crossed the river.[17] But the news only appears to have reached General Camille Duffet, his divisional commander, between 6 and 7 a.m., and the content of a note confirming what had happened was only relayed through to General Julien Martin, who as commander of the French XI Corps was Duffet's superior officer, between 8 and 9 a.m.[18] There was then another long delay because the telephone line connecting Martin with his superior, General Corap, commander of the 9th Army, was out of order. Corap only heard the news after 11 a.m., and it was 12.05 p.m. before it reached General Georges' staff. (The positions held by the 9th Army units are specified in Map 5 on pp. 516–17, and note 19.)[19] As a result of this shocking delay, General Gamelin and his officers in the command centre at Vincennes not only slept soundly during the night of 12 May, but carried out their duties the next morning oblivious to the disaster developing in the 9th Army's sector after being reassured by the following summary of events issued by General Georges: 'Defence now seems well assured on the whole front of the river.'[20]

He could not have been more wrong. Not only was the west bank of the River Meuse inadequately protected by Corap's 9th Army at Houx, but the French 2nd Army's defences in the Sedan sector of the river further to the south, where the main German thrust was scheduled to take place the next day, were also far from ready. Around Sedan, the flaws in the defences were manifold. It was not just the alarming shortage of anti-tank, anti-aircraft and machine-guns, or the failure to make available enough mines to create no-go areas that made the French line so vulnerable. Nor was it the lack of pillboxes, and bunkers, or that many that had been built were either not completed or lacked armoured shields to protect the gun embrasures. (See details in note 21.)[21] Nor was it just that German reconnaissance had identified a gap in the line of pillboxes and bunkers that overlooked the river in the Sedan sector. The one-mile gap was opposite Gaulier, north-west of Sedan.[22] Nor was it even the mistaken belief that the second-rate 'B' divisions in the Sedan sector, and the fortress regiment, whose best men had been cherry-picked by other units, to be replaced by elderly untrained substitutes, could hold the French line along the Meuse notwithstanding complete German air supremacy.[23] It is likely that none of these flaws would have been decisive had the French high command and subordinate generals used the soldiers and equipment at their disposal to create the necessary reserves, and then ensured that these reserves counter-attacked promptly following the inevitable breakthrough.

The first error concerning reserves, which was to help the Germans establish a foothold south of the Meuse in the first place, was committed by General Huntziger, the 2nd Army's commander. Although it had been generally agreed that an extra division should be inserted into the Sedan section of the front line when the Germans attacked, Huntziger had positioned his reserve division, the 71st, which was to have bolstered up the overstretched Sedan sector defences, thirty-five miles to the rear, without making available sufficient lorries to bring it to the front as soon as the German Army invaded.[24] He compounded this error by failing to insist that this extra division should march to the front as fast as possible. It was the same error that had led to the disaster at Houx in the north. The tanks in Guderian's 1st Panzer Division had already broken through the French cavalry screen in the 'impracticable' Ardennes before Huntziger, during the night of 11–12 May, ordered that 71 Division's progress to the front should be hastened.[25] (See note 26 for a description of the German advance through the Ardennes.)[26]

Unfortunately for the French, the order reached General Charles Grandsard of X Corps, the unit under Huntziger's command which was responsible for the Sedan sector, too late for 71 Division to be hurried into position during that night. Consequently, a single division, the 55th, backed up by fortress units, was left to hold the critical portion of the twelve-mile front until the night of 12–13 May, when 71 Division took over one section of the sector.[27] This was early enough for 71 Division to be in position prior to the Germans' 13 May attack, but too late for the two freed-up 55 Division battalions to move and dig in at their new area – in La Boulette, some two miles south-west of Sedan – in time to oppose the German thrust. (The positions held by the 2nd Army's units at the time of the German attack are specified on Map 5, pp. 516–17, and in note 28.)[28] The freed-up 55 Division battalions could have made it to La Boulette during the night of 13–14 May, but by then the battle to cross the Meuse had already been lost and won.[29]

The ordeal for the uninitiated, elderly, reservist troops in the Sedan sector began early on 13 May. Between 7 and 8 a.m. the first of many air raids was carried out by the pick of the 1500 planes available to the Luftwaffe.[30] It was these attacks, more than any other factor, that tore the heart out of the front-line French troops cowering in their blockhouses. There is no better account of how it felt to be on the receiving end of this carpet-bombing than the one contained in the following report from Lieutenant Michard, an intelligence officer in the 147th Fortress Infantry Regiment, whose headquarters on 13 May were on the La Marfée heights above Sedan:

The whistling sounds and the explosions are approaching. They are over us! Each man tenses his back, jaws set. The earth trembles and seems to break up. These first five minutes are terrible, but others are to follow. Then it is the turn of Étadon [another area near Sedan].[31] We look around nearly ecstatic: they have gone!

I get out of my trench to inspect the damage; but I jump straight back in it again. A second wave is coming. It is just the beginning of a methodical bombardment which we are to experience for six hours . . . The noise of the explosions now takes over . . . You feel they are aiming their bombs at you. You wait, your muscles tensed up. The explosion is a liberation. But then there is another bang, then two more, ten more . . . the individual blasts merging together to form one continuous wall of thunder . . .

We are still, silent, our backs are bent, turned in on ourselves, our mouths open so that our ear drums do not burst. Our shelter shakes . . . The bombs are of all sizes . . . The big ones do not whistle. As they fall, they sound like an approaching train. On two occasions I have aural hallucinations. I am in a station; a train is coming. The noise of an explosion shakes me out of my dream, and brutally brings me back to real life.

The Stukas join the heavy bombers.[32] The siren of the dive-bombers bores into one's ears and puts one's nerves on edge. They make you want to scream . . . My cipher expert looks haggard; his wide open eyes are staring . . . Half leaning on his elbows his whole body shakes after each explosion, and he repeats over and again in a quiet trembling voice: 'This one's going to land on us. This is it. It's going to hit us.'[33]

A German diarist, who was watching what he referred to as this 'incredible spectacle', described what it looked like from the east side of the Meuse:

The Stukas dive down vertically out of a cloudless sky . . . They dive down with a deafening whistle like birds of prey, and then climb up, before disappearing from the scene to make space for their circling sisters. More and more appear. The house basements shake, windows burst. There is explosion after explosion. Bunker after bunker, position after position begins to feel the destructive consequences of the bombing. Fountains of earth are spat up into the air, crater after crater appears. How do the French feel now? Can they still be confident in their 'impregnable' line?[34]

His question was answered by the ferocious artillery and machine-gun fire that was put down on to the river when at 3 p.m. German troops attempted their first crossings.[35] Although the bombing had certainly demoralized the French troops in the front line, it had not destroyed their defences. The Germans were still left with the difficult task of crossing a waterway, some sixty metres wide, when faced by lines of French soldiers and their artillery, the seven Sedan bridges having been blown up the previous day.[36]

Ironically, it was troops attached to the 10th Panzer Division, the unit that had suffered most at the hands of the French gunners − 81 out of 96 rubber boats being shot up near Bazeilles before they even reached the east bank of the river − that were to provide the most devastating response.[37] Although the damage inflicted demonstrated that the French gunners could disperse the men making the kind of massed attack that was being prepared by the 10th Panzer Division's Schützenregiment (Rifle Regiment) 69 when the boats were hit, they were to prove less adroit when coping with small-scale commando-style raids. This was possibly because smaller raiding parties were concealed from the watching defenders by thick smoke and dust thrown up by the bombardment, which effectively blinded the French in certain areas.[38] A series of such raiding parties, two being from groups under the command of the 10th Panzer Division, held the key that would unlock the French defences.

One such raid has been immortalized by the same German diarist who had been so struck by the Stuka attacks. His report describes the crossing south of Sedan's Pont de la Gare made by troops from the 10th Panzer Division's Schützenregiment 86 acting under the command of Lieutenant Heinrich Hanbauer.[39] The account does not mention the exact number of men involved, but it was evidently only a section of the company, and it epitomizes the way these courageous groups of professional soldiers terrorized the much larger number of Frenchmen on the opposite side of the river. Even before the attack was launched, Hanbauer impressed the diarist with his fighting spirit: he complained to his superior when he heard that he and his men had been relegated to the second wave. Minutes before the action was due to start, Hanbauer was given the go-ahead to lead an attack after all. Shortly after 3 p.m. the group ran down to the east bank of the river, carrying their rubber boats on their shoulders. The diarist, who appears to have been in one of the first boats, described what happened next:

We push off from the bank, and row as fast as possible. When the first boat reaches the middle of the river, the enemy opens fire. Another four boats are pushed off from the bank, but are carried off by the current . . . One man falls into the water, and only saves himself by swimming back to the river bank. Several engineers quickly jump into a third boat, and come across without any losses. But the last two boats are shot to pieces by fierce machine-gun fire coming from a bunker. The crew fall into the water, but they all survive except for two men who are swept away by the current. Three boats succeed in crossing the river without any losses.

According to the writer of the report, the men from the three boats led by Hanbauer had to cut their way through barbed wire before they could get at the bunkers near their crossing-point. 'In spite of the fact that the French soldiers put their hands up to surrender, hand grenades are thrown, and the Frenchmen killed,' he concluded, before describing the resistance encountered at another bunker.

Some rifle shots are fired at us . . . The marksman is quickly spotted concealed in a tree, and one of the NCOs knocks him down from his lofty seat with a well-aimed shot. Meanwhile our lieutenant, covered by our fire, works his way towards the bunker. The soldiers in the garrison are firing with all their weapons. Because it is a hot day, the French have left the back door of the bunker open. Our heavy weapons [from across the river] also shoot at the bunker . . . but they stop firing . . . And then, with a giant leap, the lieutenant rushes across the road, raises his machine pistol, and shouts out the first French words he has uttered during the campaign: 'À bas les armes!' [Drop your weapons.]

As if bitten by a tarantula spider, the French soldiers in the bunker turn around, and stare in astonishment at the lieutenant who stares back with flashing eyes. They raise their hands above their heads . . . One after the other, they walk out of the bunker past the lieutenant. Seizing this opportunity to get at the enemy, one of the Frenchmen crouches down, and then jumps on to the lieutenant from behind, gripping him by the throat, and pulling him to the ground. He tries to grab the machine pistol, but the lieutenant fights back. One moment the lieutenant is on the ground. Then it is the turn of the Frenchman. The other French soldiers join in. But several shots ring out, and the Frenchmen fall down dead. It is also the end for the Frenchman who started the fight. The gunfire causes him to hesitate for a moment, and this gives the lieutenant the chance to grab the machine pistol. He pulls the trigger several times, and the last Frenchman bites the dust.

Lieutenant Hanbauer carried on living dangerously. When he approached another bunker, his pistol jammed as he pulled the trigger, and he was only saved by the action of one of his men who instantly gauged the situation, and threw a grenade at the French soldiers just in time. Eventually the three Frenchmen in the bunker were also captured, but they too were shot later when they tried to escape. More and more Frenchmen came out of their foxholes to give themselves up as this small group of Germans advanced, and in the end Height 246 overlooking the river from the L'Étadon district was seized by just seven men.[40]

Lieutenant Hanbauer's attack was matched by an even more decisive hit-and-run raid led by Sturmpionier Feldwebel Walter Rubarth, leader of a group of sappers attached to the 10th Panzer Division.[41] He and his small group of just eleven men crossed the Meuse near to where Hanbauer's group were to make their crossing.[42] A German gunner provided cover after Rubarth had asked him to fire at the bunker near the crossing-point. Rubarth's account is short on detail concerning the resistance he encountered, but it does explain briefly how his group dealt with one of the bunkers they captured: 'We seize the next bunker from the rear. I use an explosive charge. The blast tears off the back of the bunker. We grab our opportunity and attack the occupants with hand grenades. After a short fight, a white flag appears, and over the bunker we hang our flag with a swastika on it. From the other bank of the river we hear our comrades cheering.'[43] Rubarth's account went on to describe how, encouraged by these cheers, he and his comrades waded through marshy ground with water 'up to our hips' to take two more riverside bunkers.

Not content with having broken through the front line of bunkers overlooking the Meuse, Rubarth and his men, reinforced by four more soldiers, began to work their way through the second line of bunkers, which ran at right angles to the line of the river. (The bunkers he captured are specified in Map 6 on p. 518.) By the time he and his men had taken their seventh, he and Lieutenant Hanbauer had punched a hole in the French defences. This enabled the larger 10th Panzer Division infantry units to cross, and turned what had at one point looked like defeat into victory. By 5.45 a.m. on 14 May, the 10th Panzer Division had even built a bridge over the river south of the destroyed Pont de la Gare.[44]

The 10th Panzer Division was not the only unit that struggled to overcome the French resistance. Its attacks between Sedan and Remilly-Aillicourt (some four miles south-east of Sedan) were hampered by the lack of cover on the river's east banks, and also by the fact that most of XIX Corps' artillery was supporting the 1st Panzer Division.[45] The 2nd Panzer Division on the northernmost wing was equally disadvantaged, and for similar reasons also failed to cross the river at first.[46]

Accounts by French defenders in the area around Donchery have described how the 2nd Panzer Division's tanks on the north side of the river shot up the artillery casemate at Bellevue, the largest gun shelter in the sector on the French side, at 2.45 p.m. This temporarily put the casemate's guns out of action, but even before they started firing again seventy-five minutes later, the attackers remained pinned down on the north side of the river because they had failed to put enough blockhouses out of action to make it safe to cross.[47] That was only achieved thanks to the efforts of another small group of storm engineers who, along with the 1st Panzer Division's Schützenregiment 1, had crossed the river in the so-called Gaulier gap. (The details of this attack, and the thrust by a second unit under the 1st Panzer Division's command are described in note 48.)[48] The steps taken by the storm engineers cleared the way for the main German thrust towards the south, but also enabled troops within the 2nd Panzer Division to start crossing: at 7 p.m. the first troops in a rubber boat made it across the river in the Donchery sector, and by 9.20 p.m. French resistance had been quelled sufficiently for a regular ferrying service to be in operation.[49] Thus did the French defences collapse like a house of cards, completely justifying Guderian's decision to allocate the easiest approach to the Meuse, and most of his corps' artillery, to the 1st Panzer Division. The rationale was that if one division crossed the river, its troops could clear the way for the other two.[50]

Lieutenant Drapier, commander of the 147th Fortress Infantry Regiment company in position between the Bellevue artillery casemate and Blockhouse 102 (marked on Map 6 on p. 518), found himself in the path of the main thrust during the late afternoon and early evening of 13 May.[51] The following extracts from his testimony highlight the difficulties faced by French officers, given the badly trained and demoralized men at their disposal as the Germans first bombed them and then advanced with ground forces:

The bombers arrived around midday. I was eating a sardine on some bread. Several bombs fell near me. My bread was covered with dust from the roof of my command post . . . But no one was hurt.

[Later that afternoon] I watch Germans getting out of their lorries on the other side of the Meuse on the Montimont road.[52] I telephone for an hour in a vain attempt to get the artillery to fire at them. Only one shell comes over. Our guns, which are attacked without respite by German planes, remain silent.

I then see the German tanks assembling in and around Donchery. Our 75mm gun in the casemate quickly fires fifty shells. The tanks respond from the village, firing short of the casemate at first. But one big tank hits the target with its fourth shot killing the sous-lieutenant in the casemate. The gun nevertheless starts firing at the Germans again. However, this time at least ten tanks take it on. It is the end.

Tanks firing from the north bank attempt to neutralize my area. Shelter C . . . just to the south of the [Bellevue] crossroads is all but decapitated.[53] My observatory is also fired at. I can only look out through a hole. The bullets crack around me, and the shells keep on coming. I wonder whether the shelter will stand up to all of this . . .

Fortunately it does, which is more than can be said for the French soldiers. They turn out to be the weak element in the defences.

All of a sudden, while looking at Blockhouse 102 I see a group of Germans going inside. I can't understand what's happening at first. None of my sections open fire on them from the crossroads.

Blockhouse 103, to the north of the crossroads, is taken without anyone resisting. [Another officer reported that this blockhouse was captured after its defenders were swamped by French soldiers who had thrown down their weapons. This is said to have denied the garrison the chance to defend themselves when Germans approached.][54] . . . Seeing the enemy behind me, I run to my command post to assemble my men . . . At that moment some other ranks arrive. I find myself surrounded by a crowd of soldiers who will not let me out of their sight . . . It is with great difficulty that I get them into good firing positions . . .

The men in my command post have had hardly any training, many of them having arrived just one month ago from the 55th Division . . . I notice that when faced with danger, they want to remain near me. When I move away, they rush after me . . . Some of them run away into the wood . . . Germans emerge from Blockhouse 102 and start walking towards me, carrying a flag marked with a swastika, driving prisoners in front of them. My men panic. They do not want to shoot their own comrades. Some of them say: 'Let's surrender.' However, I manage to fire my gun, and the enemy returns to the shelter . . .

I place some of the men so that they are facing the Meuse, and I take up a position 50 metres behind them on the edge of the wood . . . But the men whom I have placed facing the river are panic-stricken by my absence, and this enables a group of Germans to advance . . . The men rush back to me. Some of them fall over in the process. Others stop once they are out in the open, and throw their hands up in the air.[55]

Eventually Drapier realized they could not hold out any longer, and he finally took flight, as so many of his men had done before him, abandoning his post to the Germans.

The taking of all these bunkers and blockhouses enabled the 1st Panzer Division's Schützenregiment 1 to make a deep thrust three miles to the south-west of its Gaulier crossing-point that same night. At 10.40 p.m., Lieutenant-Colonel Hermann Balck, its commander, had his telegraphist send the following message to the headquarters of the 1st Panzer Division: 'Schützenregiment 1 has at 22.40 taken high hill just to the north of Cheveuges [Height 301, marked on Map 6 on p. 518].[56] Last enemy blockhouse in our hands. Complete breakthrough.'[57]

The unexpected speed and depth of the German attack as well as the lack of control and discipline in the French combat zone are highlighted by the following incident that occurred later that night. Lieutenant Wolff-Rüdiger Guercke, of Schützenregiment 1, whose company had also seized a French bunker beside the Meuse, was resting with his comrades in a house near the captured heights when they heard steps outside. The men leaped up, grabbing their guns. But when the door was flung open and the light switched on, it was not vengeful Frenchmen with machine-guns as they had feared. Instead they were confronted by a beautiful Frenchwoman, dressed immaculately in a fur coat, stockings and high heels, and smelling of the most intoxicating perfume, who said she had come from Paris to visit her lover, a captain in the artillery. After bringing her into the house to be interrogated, the Germans struck up quite a jolly rapport with her, and Guercke's report on this incident concluded: 'She began to laugh at her predicament, and so did we. She had ended up with twenty-five soldiers instead of the one she had been expecting, and she certainly had more balls than her Frenchman who had fled.'[58]

9: Flight

Bulson, 13–14 May 1940
(See Map 5. Also Maps 4 and 6)

The French gunner who fled before his girlfriend arrived from Paris was not the only soldier who deserted his position in the Sedan sector during the evening of 13 May. He might even have been a participant in what a post-mortem report referred to as the 'unexpected and unpleasant incident' that occurred at 6 p.m.[1]

The incident was observed by staff officers standing outside the French 55 Division's headquarters, situated near the Bulson to Chémery road, at Fond Dagot (see the number 6 linked with caption 6 on Map 5, pp. 516–17).[2] They were astonished to see a column of fleeing soldiers, who, all of a sudden, poured out of Bulson and headed south, away from the Germans. According to the writer of the report:

They speed past, with clusters of men hanging on to the vehicles like grapes. They are panic-stricken, and shout that the enemy and their tanks have just arrived at Bulson. Some of these fugitives are completely out of control, and fire their guns in all directions. Shots whistle through the branches [of the trees] at the very moment when General [Pierre] Lafontaine [commander of 55 Division] comes out of his headquarters on hearing the commotion ... Most of the fugitives have no weapons, and many of them are clutching suitcases.[3]

Some of the fugitives were approached and interviewed. Most were gunners who had been in position between Bulson and Haraucourt.[4] They all claimed that German armoured vehicles or tanks had been just 250 metres away when they had left Bulson, and would have captured them had they not fled.[5] The long procession of fleeing men was only stopped after vans and lorries had been driven into the road to create a barrier. This was reinforced by Lafontaine's infantry commander, Colonel Fernand Chaligne, who stood in front of the roadblock brandishing his pistol.[6] While the men were rounded up into groups to defend the area around the divisional headquarters, in case the Germans really were in Bulson, the artillery officers who had also retreated merely watched without offering any assistance. They included Lieutenant-Colonel Dourzal, who was supposed to be in charge of the heavy artillery around Bulson: he walked up and down with his hands behind his back.[7]

Fortunately, all the men obeyed the commands of their general and his colonel, and at around 7 p.m., when no Germans, let alone any German tanks, had appeared over the horizon, and after a report had arrived from the infantry commander in charge of the area to the north of Bulson that confirmed all was relatively quiet on the road leading from Chaumont to Bulson, these gunners, who just an hour before had run for their lives, made their way somewhat shamefacedly back to their positions.[8]

Lafontaine and Chaligne must have hoped they had nipped the panic in the bud. But men all over the countryside at the back of 55 Division were fleeing from these same phantom tanks, tanks that so many reported but which no one had actually seen. Shortly before the incident south of Bulson, a French infantry captain witnessed a similar scene at Maisoncelle. He reported seeing:

A wave of lorries, cars, cyclists, motorbicyclists, horse riders, artillery vehicles, as well as troops on foot without any weapons, pass at top speed down the main road, coming from Raucourt and Bulson, and moving towards Artaise and Chémery.[9] I alert my men on sentry duty. The crowd is so thick at the crossroads by the western exit from the village that I order all my sections to leave, so they can be protected from this defeatist atmosphere . . . This panic has been caused by a lieutenant engineer, or someone who claimed to be a lieutenant engineer, mounted on a side car, who shouted out again and again in the middle of the crowd which surrounded him: 'Save your lives. They are coming! They are chasing us from Bulson.'[10]

An almost identical scenario was observed at Vendresse, three and a half miles west of Chémery, where an officer reported having seen an artillery captain mounted on the running-board of a lorry, shouting to anyone he passed, 'Run! The Boches are coming!'[11] Echoes of this incident reached General Huntziger's ears at the 2nd Army's head-quarters in Senuc at around 9 p.m. that night.[12] According to a witness who was present when the report was made, Huntziger treated the men who made the claims as if they were liars, and pointed out that they appeared to have mistaken the French 7th Tank Battalion, which was moving up to assist 55 Division, for the enemy.[13]

The anarchic scenes were not confined to villages and towns immediately behind 55 Division's front line. Colonel Sarin, a military policeman attached to 55 Division, was amazed to discover how far south the panicking soldiers had fled. He has described how, on the way from Grandpré to Buzancy on 13–14 May, he tried to shunt a lorry off the road and was nearly lynched:

When I intervened, one of these men, a colossus – who had seen my adjutant's, my driver's and my uniform – advanced towards me, waving his gun high over his head so that he could hit me with its butt. 'You bastard!' he said to me. I took out my pistol. But one of his men, whom I heard referred to as 'My adjutant', placed himself between us, and said: 'Leave him. We're all going to end up being put in prison.' Meanwhile, a large crowd which had gathered around us . . . let me know what they intended to do. 'Kill him!' some of them shouted, pointing at me. Any resistance would have been hopeless, and would only have resulted in a one-sided massacre.

A bloody end to the incident was only avoided because Sarin and his men, realizing that discretion was the better part of valour, ran away from those threatening them, and made good their escape.[14]

The next day Sarin witnessed more anarchy: at Vouziers, he saw soldiers going on the rampage.[15] They began by stealing food, sometimes from homes still inhabited by their owners. But then events spiralled out of control, with the men indulging in an orgy of destruction. They smashed absent householders' furniture, crockery and works of art, and tore up their precious photographs before defecating and urinating on the beds, where they had fallen asleep after finding nothing else to destroy.

Notwithstanding all this mayhem and hysteria, it is now generally agreed that there were no German tanks on the French side of the Meuse during the early evening of 13–14 May when the trouble behind the front line started. That is not to say that no German armour was seen. It is just possible that the vehicles which had caused such terror were German armoured cars: after the campaign, a repatriated French prisoner reported that at one point during the evening some of these vehicles were spotted crossing the river on rafts.[16] It seems unlikely this was before the 6 p.m. panic at Fond Dagot. When the captured commander of Blockhouse 103 was taken across the river on a pontoon pulled by a boat at 7 p.m., there was not a tank or armoured car to be seen.[17] The first reliable sighting of a tank on the French side of the river appears to have been that made by a Lieutenant David of the 147th Fortress Infantry Regiment who saw twenty panzers between Glaire and Bellevue before he was taken over the river on a bridge at 8.30 p.m.[18] Even then they do not appear to have advanced to the south. At about 10 p.m. the chief of staff of one of 55 Division's infantry regiments assured General Lafontaine that he had not seen any of 'these phantom tanks' by the time he left Chaumont between 8 and 8.30 p.m.[19]

So who was responsible for the rout, given this verdict? It seems that the panic may have had its genesis in a report made by an artillery commander at 5.30 p.m. on 13 May. According to this report, German armoured vehicles were patrolling several hundred metres away from his headquarters south of Chaumont.[20] This intelligence was quickly demonstrated to be wrong after it had been checked with the officer commanding the Frénois district, whose headquarters were in Chaumont.[21] But the French gunners in the area appear not to have believed the denial, and continued to experience a malaise concerning their security.

An hour later a similar message reached Lieutenant-Colonel Dourzal, the sector's heavy-artillery commander, at his headquarters in Bulson.[22] He was told that guns – possibly attached to tanks – had been heard firing 400 to 500 metres from the artillery batteries deployed at Chaumont.[23] Dourzal's reaction to this disturbing message was to be critical. If he had done his duty, and had coolly checked whether German tanks really were in the vicinity, the chain of events that led to disaster might have been broken there and then. Instead, he inflamed the situation by telephoning Colonel Poncelet, his superior officer based at Flaba, to tell him a battle was being fought 500 metres from his headquarters.[24] He then sought permission to retreat. On being asked whether he could confirm that the firing was German, he confirmed it was. Shortly afterwards, another officer in Dourzal's headquarters rang Colonel Poncelet to say that they were about to be surrounded.[25] This latter report appears to have been provoked by a report from a French motorcyclist who at 6.55 p.m. told someone in Dourzal's headquarters that there were tanks in the woods near Bulson, and they should get out while they could.[26] On hearing all this from officers he trusted, Colonel Poncelet readily agreed that Dourzal and his artillery should retreat.

Poncelet, who was X Corps' heavy artillery commander, subsequently moved out of his own headquarters without warning Dourzal and, on his way south, he repeated what Dourzal had told him to the officer in charge of the artillery with the neighbouring 3 North African Division, adding that by the time he left Flaba, the tanks had arrived there too.[27] Poncelet's move extended the depth of the rout. Later that night when Dourzal arrived at the Flaba headquarters, he found them empty, and continued south – that is, away from the position where, given that there were in fact no German tanks near Bulson, he should have been holding the line. He only halted at around 5 a.m. the next morning when he bumped into Colonel Poncelet. Poncelet had been told by the head of X Corps' artillery based at La Berlière to return to his position at Flaba, given that the intelligence he had received was wrong.[28] But by then the rout was in full flow, and it was too late to stop it.

Since German stormtroopers and sappers were already taking control of the French side of the River Meuse before the French artillery began to flee, it seems unlikely that the Bulson incident affected the outcome of the German attempt to establish a bridgehead across the river. However, there is little doubt that the clogging up of the roads behind the front line, and the slowing down of the movements of the 2nd Army's reserves – exacerbated by their commanders' fear that they might be ambushed if German tanks really were approaching – played a crucial role in hampering the French attempts to counter-attack.

These difficulties were aggravated a hundred times by the style of French leadership. The soldier who should have had most influence on the way in which the first counter-attack was mounted was X Corps' commander General Grandsard, who had direct control over the divisions in the Sedan sector. He was a general of the old school, who had not understood that French strategy must change in line with Guderian's new mobile tactics. It was this failure to move with the times that persuaded him on 13 May to conclude that it would take the Germans several days to mount a serious attack on the Meuse.[29] He later claimed that his analysis would have been different had he realized the Germans would have air superiority during the attack.[30] The Luftwaffe's support enabled Guderian's panzer divisions to proceed without the artillery that they would otherwise have needed to pound the French into submission.

Although General Huntziger was partly to blame for not sending the French 71 Division up to the Sedan front in time, Grandsard's complacent acquiescence with the 2nd Army commander's slow reaction to the German attack made him equally responsible. Also, no one but Grandsard could be blamed for his decision to base his headquarters at La Berlière, some twelve miles to the south of the front line at Sedan. This, combined with the fact that he allowed his subordinates to believe they must report back to him before taking any important decisions, was to put French troops at a serious disadvantage in comparison with those fighting under his opposite number in the German hierarchy.

General Guderian, the German XIX Corps commander with responsibility for the attack at Sedan, took enormous risks during the battle to be with, or near, his soldiers at the front. He was nearly killed or captured at least twice as the Germans approached the Meuse. A French shell had narrowly missed him at Bouillon, north of the river, and while he was flying near the front line, the pilot had lost his way and had flown over the French positions in a slow, unarmed Fieseler-Storch plane, a situation that might well have enabled French gunners to shoot down and capture not only the new German attack plan, but their general as well.[31]

But keeping up with the troops brought with it important advantages. Apart from anything else, the presence of the general near the front line boosted his men's morale and was reassuring. Schützenregiment 1's Lieutenant Colonel Balck seems to have been very glad to see him when he insisted on crossing the Meuse on one of the first boats. Balck greeted him with the words, 'Joyriding in canoes on the Meuse is forbidden', referring to an earlier pep talk delivered by Guderian stating that crossing the Meuse would be no picnic.[32] There was another valid reason for Guderian's stance. It meant that whenever there was a hitch, his subordinates could seek his advice straight away.

The need to refer back to Guderian was, however, limited by the entrepreneurial culture he fostered: German officers were expected to make up their own minds on how to achieve the objectives Guderian set, and how to act in a crisis. An example of this occurred during the evening of 15 May. The men in Schützenregiment 1 were wilting, following some of the hardest fighting of the campaign at La Horgne,

two miles north-east of Bouvellemont, when, notwithstanding opposition from his officers, Balck ordered them to take Bouvellemont
itself. Bouvellemont is fourteen miles south-west of Sedan. Balck later
described his response to his officers' opposition in the following terms:
'It was one of those situations where whatever orders were given, the
men would not obey them. So I said, "If you don't want to advance, I
will take the village by myself," and I set off towards Bouvellemont . . .
I had walked . . . 100 metres. Then everyone got moving. Men and
officers who, seconds before, could not carry on, caught up.' Balck's
persistence was rewarded with the capturing of the village without a
bullet being fired.[33] Guderian was too modest to claim that his guiding principles inspired Balck, but whether or not they did, it is likely
that some of the entrepreneurial spirit advocated by Guderian filtered
down to at least some of the small groups of men who made the initial
breakthrough.

Knowing how important it was to act quickly, given the rapid
response rate of the Germans, it is almost painful to read about the slow
build-up of the French counter-attack. Crucially, Grandsard had failed
to impress upon the commanders of his reserves that they must be ready
to move at a moment's notice. As a result, although he gave his first
order between 2.45 and 3.15 p.m. on 13 May – that is, before he even
knew that any Germans had crossed the Meuse – telling the 213th
Infantry Regiment to advance to a position around Bulson, there were
extraordinary delays before it was put into effect.[34] It took over an hour
for the written order to travel from Grandsard's headquarters at La
Berlière to the 213th Regiment's headquarters at Chémery, another hour
for Lieutenant-Colonel Pierre Labarthe, the regiment's commander, to
call in his three battalion commanders from the surrounding countryside
where their men were deployed, and another ninety minutes before
these same commanders could get their men on the move after returning
to their battalions.[35] Consequently it was around 7 p.m. before the
regiment was even ready for action.

If only Grandsard had been present once these French troops began
their march northwards, he could have insisted that they continued to
advance despite the news passed to Labarthe by a staff officer from 55
Division that German vehicles armed with machine-guns were advancing from Chaumont to Bulson. He might also have told Labarthe that
the long line of French vehicles heading south out of Chémery during

the night of 13–14 May were relying on incorrect rumours. As it was, in Grandsard's absence, Labarthe was persuaded that the march should be suspended until he had a clearer picture.[36]

Similar reasons held up the advance of the three other units within Grandsard's reserves: the 205th Infantry Regiment, and the 4th and 7th Tank Battalions, whose commanders had also been ordered to go with their men up to the Bulson line. (The delays are explained in note 37.)[37] Grandsard only heard about the delays at his headquarters between 9 and 10 p.m. on 13 May, when a X Corps staff officer made it back from Chémery after an excruciating journey through crowds of fleeing French soldiers.[38] The delays might not have been fatal, had Grandsard been able to telephone 55 Division's commander, Lafontaine. Unfortunately when Lafontaine asked permission to move his headquarters back from Bulson to Chémery, so that, as ordered by Grandsard, he could command the counter-attack, Grandsard had not mentioned that Lafontaine should maintain the telephone connection between La Berlière and the old headquarters until another had been established with the new headquarters. Lafontaine failed to take this basic precaution on his own initiative. Because of the omission the telephone equipment at the Fond Dagot headquarters was dismantled and, at this critical time, Grandsard's only contact with Lafontaine was by messenger, a slow method of communication, given the congested roads.

Even at this late stage, the French could have advanced in time and secured the Bulson heights if Lafontaine had been decisive. Admittedly, he had a difficult decision to make. The commander of the 7th Tank Battalion, who had arrived in Chémery at around 10.30 p.m. on 13 May, had told him that his tanks would probably not arrive before 6 a.m. the next morning. His excuse was that the roads were still full of retreating soldiers and vehicles. Also, Lafontaine had no idea where 205th Infantry Regiment and the 4th Tank Battalion had harboured for the night. This led him to wonder whether he had enough troops and equipment to hold back the Germans at Bulson.[39] Although at around 10 p.m. he was assured by an officer who had been at Chaumont that not one German tank had been sighted there prior to the officer's departure shortly after 8 p.m., Lafontaine's position was made still more difficult by another depressing report.[40] At 1 a.m. on 14 May, Colonel Chaligne warned him that the troops north of Bulson were not strong enough to hold back the Germans without the support of the 213th Regiment.[41] This must have led him to fear that if he ordered his infantry to advance during the night, they really might meet German tanks.

Nevertheless, a more pugnacious character might have seized the opportunity to advance to the Bulson line in the knowledge that his troops might at least stall the Germans until reinforcements arrived – and perhaps Lafontaine would have acted in this way, had he been told that the 3ième Division Cuirassée (the 3rd Armoured Division) had been ordered to come to the rescue. Grandsard, who was given this welcome news during the early hours of 14 May, does not appear to have passed it on to Lafontaine.[42] But Lafontaine was not feeling bullish on the night of 13–14 May. Whereas a German in Guderian's corps, faced with similar choices, might have realized that his commander would expect him to give the offensive option a chance, Lafontaine appears to have been guided by the French practice, which required an officer to check with his superior before attempting anything risky. So it was that Lafontaine, rather than charging forward towards the Germans while he still could, left Chémery at around 2 a.m., and drove southward, away from the enemy, in an attempt to reach General Grandsard at La Berlière.

Perhaps if the roads had been clear, his action would not have seemed so ill advised. But the roads were far from being clear. After being held up by numerous traffic jams, his progress was finally halted altogether near Stonne by mines that had been placed across the road and by French soldiers who, not realizing that he was on their side, fired at his car. By 3 a.m. he was back at Chémery and, once there, he merely carried on waiting.[43]

In the meantime, General Grandsard, who had been left wondering whether the Germans were about to emerge from Bulson, finally spoke to one of his commanders on the telephone. Colonel Chaligne, whose telephone at Fond Dagot had been connected, rang at 2.15 a.m. on 14 May to tell Grandsard that his men were still holding the line to the north of Bulson.[44] This enabled Grandsard to order that the counter-attack should go ahead at dawn, and that Chaligne should take charge of it if Lafontaine failed to return in time.

During the telephone conversation, the first intimation that 55 Division was to counter-attack, Grandsard told Chaligne that his written orders were already on their way to the division's headquarters at Chémery. That prompted Chaligne to drive there with his verbal version. Both arrived at around 4 a.m., and it was only then, more than twelve hours after Grandsard had first ordered his reserves to advance, that Lafontaine finally sat down to work out the details of the counter-attack.[45] It was 5.30 a.m. before the final written order was handed to Lieutenant-Colonel Labarthe.[46] He was, if anything, even less keen on the attack than General Lafontaine. On being handed the order, Labarthe commented that he and his men were being sent on a 'suicide mission'.[47] However, at 6.30 a.m. his troops began at last to move towards Bulson and Connage, to be followed a quarter of an hour later by the tanks that were to support each of the 213th Regiment's three battalions.[48]

The rapid German response to the threat posed by the counter-attack only serves to underline the slowness of the French. At 6.50 a.m. on 14 May, intelligence from a reconnaissance plane told Lieutenant-General Friedrich Kirchner, commander of the 1st Panzer Division, that the French counter-attack, consisting of tanks and infantry, was forming up.[49] Shortly after 7 a.m., the first German tanks set out to meet the French armour. In other words, the Germans began their own counter-attack within ten minutes of identifying their target, whereas it had taken the French more than twelve hours to launch their troops into the attack. At the time Kirchner was inside the bridgehead on the French side of the Meuse, and therefore could send his tanks to attack the French as they rolled off the bridge spanning the river at Gaulier. He was supported by Guderian, who, on visiting the bridge, had ruled that tanks should be sent across before any other vehicles.[50]

The first group of German tanks consisted of one company commanded by a Lieutenant Heinrich Krajewski. His report, describing as it does how close the French came to winning the race to capture the heights south-west of Bulson, highlights the importance of moving quickly:

Carefully we drive through Bulson, which is not occupied by the enemy, and drive slowly up the heights, one hundred metres south-west of the village. As soon as the first vehicles reach the top, we come under heavy fire. Two of our tanks are hit by an anti-tank gun and burn ... One of the fires is extinguished ... I stand twenty metres behind the burning tank with shells flying all around me, and try in vain to see where the enemy is hiding ... Wild thoughts cross my mind. Two of my tanks have already been destroyed ... Should I go back to the division to report the attack? But if we go, we would be leaving the infantry behind to face the tank attack alone. So I decide to carry on.

Krajewski's account records the evasive action he took as the French carried on firing:

I run towards my company with my arms spread wide. My men understand what I want them to do, and fan out on the right side of the road. The French tanks have to climb up a steep hill, and already the first of these tanks appears on the edge of the hill. The fight against them starts 300 to 400 metres away. I run back to my tank, climb into it and give orders to shoot. But my tank is hit. Its gun is out of action. We are being overcome. I jump down, and run to the next tank. It has already been hit, and is also out of action. One of the other vehicles is also out of the fight. The nearest tank to me is 400 metres away. I cannot reach it, so I hide in the grass and watch the battle which now involves just three of our tanks . . .

These tanks shoot one tank after another, but these last parts of my company are not strong enough to cope with the enemy which is growing stronger all the time. My tanks must be short of ammunition already. Suddenly I realize that two of our remaining tanks are out of action after being hit. There is only one left . . . It must run out of ammunition any minute. Then all of a sudden everything changes. I suddenly see numerous shells exploding near the enemy . . . I look around, and behind a trench I see the cannon and turret of a German tank. I sigh with relief. The reinforcements have arrived just in time.[51]

What Krajewski had seen was the arrival of the next batch of tanks that had driven to the rescue immediately after crossing the Gaulier bridge over the Meuse. Minutes later, the French tanks were retreating, and the French infantry, who must have had such high hopes of victory after the Germans' initial losses, had to watch the sad spectacle of their countrymen in flight once again, this time pursued by real tanks spitting fire.

Thus did the German panzers deal with the eastern arm of the French counter-attack. Meanwhile the 1st Panzer Division's General Kirchner had ensured that the western arm was obstructed by a thin line of anti-tank guns. Reports written after the action by Lieutenant Beck-Broichsitter, commander of an anti-tank platoon attached to the

Grossdeutschland regiment, suggest that if his six-gun platoon had not been intercepted by Kirchner at one of the crossroads on the French side of the Meuse as it travelled south, and diverted to the south-west, the French tanks they encountered to the east of Connage would have been minutes away from the German bridge over the Meuse with no opposition in their path apart from infantry.

Lieutenant Beck-Broichsitter has described how his men spotted the French tanks as they emerged from a wood 800 metres away to their right.

They push through the willow trees as if they are big game coming out of the forest. Everyone has to be very disciplined, and we have to hold our fire, or we will reveal where we are hiding. Somehow everyone stays calm, and this gives us a sort of inner superiority. One of our comrades even takes out his camera and takes a picture before putting it away again. We count at least eight tanks. We can now hear their engines and the clanking of their chain tracks. They are moving directly towards us. They are 350 metres away. One of the platoon leaders happens to look at me. I nod. Fire! A flame shoots up out of one of the tanks. Another tank turns in circles. The next tank stops but carries on firing. From another tank smoke comes up. The next tank is evacuated by its crew.

In spite of their losses, the French tanks carried on attacking, but each time they advanced, they were knocked out by the German gunners. Beck-Broichsitter's account criticizes the French tactics, which saw them sending in the tanks one at a time, or in small groups: 'Simultaneous attacks would have been very difficult for us. But attacking in waves in this manner means they lose their courage after seeing their burning comrades.'[52]

According to Beck-Broichsitter, 'The gunners usually hit with their first shots. Then they aim at different spots on the tank until they find a weak area which can be penetrated by our shells.' His admission that the anti-tank guns could not always penetrate the 1.6-inch thick armour of the FCM tanks employed by the 7th Tank Battalion suggests that the German guns might have been even less successful against the French Char B1 bis tanks of the 3rd French Armoured Division, whose armour was almost an inch thicker (see note 53 for tank details).[53] The latter would have been counter-attacking during the night of 13–14 May if the French generals had not dithered. Eventually the French attack was beaten off, thanks to anti-tank-gun reinforcements and assistance from more German tanks, which had at last crossed the Meuse, and come up to support the gunners.[54]

Back at Chémery, Lieutenant-Colonel Labarthe, commander of the 213th Infantry Regiment, was wounded by one of the German tanks he had hoped his comrades would shoot up during the counter-attack. He managed to limp away, hidden in the smoke from some burning petrol cans, which had been hit by a shell that had narrowly missed him.[55] His escape was only temporary, however. At 4 p.m., he was captured in the house in Chémery where he had taken refuge.

General Grandsard's fate, and that of the commanders of the heavy artillery and two of the divisions under his control, was just as ignominious. General Lafontaine, having seen his 55 Division melt away under the onslaught, evaded the Germans, only to be relieved of his command two days later. General Joseph Baudet, commander of 71 Division who, during the Bulson incident, had taken even the French practice of keeping well clear of the front line to extreme lengths by abandoning his headquarters and fleeing many miles to the south, also lost his job, after his division, deprived of its leader, failed to fight to the finish.[56]

As for Colonel Poncelet, he was inconsolable. Having realized that the steps he and his officers had taken fell well short of the standard expected of a French officer, he made his report, then committed suicide on 24 May.[57] These events resulted in Grandsard being left in command of a mere shell, consisting of just one division. It was taken out of his hands and passed to General Jean Flavigny, the man who, because he had also been handed the 3rd Armoured Division, represented the last French hope of stopping the panzers before they left their bridgehead at Sedan, and driving them back over the Meuse.[58]

10: Battle of the Bulge

Mont Dieu, Sedan, Flavion, 14–15 May 1940
(See Map 5. Also Map 1)

On that dreadful night of 13–14 May, when General Doumenc found General Georges weeping at Château des Bondons, the first step Doumenc took to resolve the crisis was to order the three French armoured divisions to come to the rescue. Had these units been able to counter-attack swiftly, there was every chance that the German tide could have been turned. If, for example, General Flavigny had been able to order the French 3rd Armoured Division to mount its counter-attack alongside Lieutenant-Colonel Labarthe during the early hours of 14 May, it is just possible that the bulge in the French line at Sedan would have been substantially diminished, if not wiped out entirely, by the end of that day.

On paper at least the 3rd Armoured Division was formidable. Its 160 tanks included seventy of the huge B1 bis models, whose armour was thicker than the thickest armour on the heaviest German tank. (The most vulnerable areas on a Char B1 bis were protected by armour that was 2.4 inches thick while the armour on a Panzer 4 was nowhere in excess of two inches thick.)[1] B1 bis tanks also carried not just one, but two powerful cannons: a 47mm gun in the turret, and a 75mm monster in the hull, in addition to its two machine-guns. That made the Char B1 bis the pride of the French Army.

But at 4 a.m. on 14 May, when Flavigny met General Antoine Brocard, the Armoured Division's commander, to plan the counter-attack, he was shocked to discover that the tanks were not only not ready to start advancing immediately, but they would not be ready for another twelve hours. They could not even be expected in their first assembly area at Le Chesne, fifteen miles south-west of Sedan, until 6 a.m. It would then take around six hours to fill them with petrol, another two to move the five miles to their positions to the north of the Mont Dieu forest, and two more hours to refuel them again.[2] In short, they would not move forward from the designated counter-attack start line until 4 p.m.[3] It is no wonder that General Georges, who had already committed the 1st and 2nd French Armoured Divisions and General Prioux's Cavalry Corps to the northern arm of the German attack, in the mistaken belief that the main thrust was in the north, burst into tears of despair after hearing about the Sedan breakthrough in the south (see Chapter 1). So, how had this unexpected delay come about?

If the French high command had been doing their job, they would at the very least have concentrated their 3rd Armoured Division as soon as the German attack commenced, and might even have moved it to within striking distance of one section of the front line so that it could be ready to advance at a moment's notice. This was particularly important, given General Georges' concern about the sparse reserves. However, as late as 12 May, the division was still in the Rheims area, its tanks dispersed over fifteen miles of countryside. When the order was given to move to Le Chesne during the late afternoon of 12 May, General Brocard worked out that the tanks could not be assembled there until two days later.[4]

Gamelin's and Georges' failure to marshal their forces represented a dereliction of duty and led to a stand-off between Flavigny and Brocard when they met at 4 a.m. on 14 May at the 2nd Army's headquarters in the village of Senuc.[5] Flavigny refused to accept that the tanks could not be made ready more rapidly, while Brocard believed that Flavigny's expectations were unrealistic. Their simmering disagreement was brought to a head by Flavigny's demand that the tanks should be ready by 11 a.m. After Brocard had explained why that was impossible, Flavigny reluctantly agreed to delay the advance until after midday but told Brocard to stop making excuses and to comply with his instructions.[6]

To understand what happened next, it is important to take into account Flavigny's personality and his frame of mind during the afternoon of 14 May, as he attempted to carry out his mission. At about 10 p.m. the previous night General Huntziger had ordered him to hold the 2nd Army's back-up line, north of the forest of Mont Dieu, between Stonne and the Canal des Ardennes, then to advance towards Sedan to recapture the lost ground.[7] The 5ième Division Légère de Cavalerie, also under Flavigny's command, was to advance with the counter-attack on the west side of the Canal des Ardennes, at the same time holding the bridges over the canal so that the Germans could not break out to the west. The infantry element of the counter-attack was to be provided by the 3ième Division Motorisée, whose troops on 13 May were in and around Briquenay, Thénorgues, Savigny-sur-Aisne and Monthois, the latter, the furthest south, being nineteen miles south-west of Mont Dieu.[8] Even as he was being given these orders, Flavigny had felt uncomfortable. From the moment on 12 May when he had first heard that the French cavalry had retired across the Meuse, he had sensed that something was wrong. 'The resistance offered appeared rather short,' he noted later in his report.[9] The report also records his anxiety concerning the troops placed at his disposal: 'Was it possible to pull off the second part of my mission [the counter-attack] with such weak forces and with infantry which had to move more than 40 kilometres? I realized that war was not always straightforward, and I would have some ups and downs, but I never dreamed that with just a few officers, without services or communications, I would be asked to lead an army corps into battle with the assistance which was less than is normally allocated to the commander of a battalion.'[10]

During the early hours of 14 May, he caught up with the 3ième Division Motorisée, which was moving to the front to assist with the counter-attack, and was so struck by the order and discipline of the troops that, as he wrote later, 'My hopes were raised.' But they were soon dashed by the long lines of French soldiers fleeing in the opposite direction, and by the demoralizing and demoralized reports from 3 Division's officers, who told him that German tanks were already on the way from Chémery to Tannay, and were unstoppable because French anti-tank guns could not penetrate their armour.[11] Flavigny was himself forced to take cover on several occasions from German air attacks targeting the area south of Chémery as well as the front line.[12]

By the time he arrived at Les Alleux, where he discovered that the 3rd Armoured Division's tanks had still not arrived at the counter-attack's start line, he was already in a very negative, even defeatist, frame of mind. He tore a strip off Brocard for the delay, and demanded to know why the tanks were so late. His frustration was not assuaged by more of General Brocard's excuses. According to Brocard, the division could not be expected to operate like an experienced well-trained unit: its men had not completed their training programme; the division had rudimentary radio communications; some of the tank gunners had had little practice in firing the guns; and there were no personnel attached who could repair the tanks quickly when they broke down.

All of these factors contributed to what Flavigny did next. Even though the French high command was relying on him to send in the tanks immediately, and in spite of the fact that the armoured division might never have a better chance to thwart the German attack, he decided that it would be unsafe to proceed into battle during the late afternoon and early evening. His conviction that this was so can only have been strengthened by the knowledge that if he ordered the tanks to advance, they would come up against the same panzers that had repulsed, and eventually decimated, the 7th Tank Battalion that morning. When Brocard protested that the time of day should not make a difference because the evenings remained light until late, Flavigny ignored him. The attack was called off. Flavigny then exacerbated what has generally been seen as his mistake by ordering the tanks to take up defensive positions across the front in the area to be covered by his corps. They were to act as 'corks', bottling up German attempts to advance down all the main roads over a twelve-mile area.[13] This was how he interpreted Huntziger's order that he must block the German advance, and counter-attack. The only problem was that his blocking made it impossible to mount a quick counter-attack the next morning.

By the early hours of 15 May when Huntziger, urged on by a frustrated General Georges, told Flavigny to get on with the counter-attack, some of the tanks had been sucked into local battles at the positions allocated to them the night before. Thus, at 9 a.m. when Flavigny summoned Brocard to his Senuc headquarters to tell him the attack must get under way at 1 p.m., he was told that fewer Char B1 bis tanks were available for action than there had been the night before – twenty-seven compared with sixty-two – and that it would be impossible to assemble even this number by his deadline.[14] Some of the twenty-seven needed petrol, a repetition of the problem that had infuriated Flavigny the day before. The only difference this time was that the delay had resulted from his own orders. Others had been caught up in the fighting at Stonne, and it would take time to extricate them from the battle.

Flavigny was forced to agree that the attack could not take place until 3 p.m. His report describes what happened as the second deadline approached:

You can imagine my astonishment when at 14.30 the general commanding the 3ième Division Motorisée [General Paul Bertin-Boussu] and the commander of the Armoured Division's tank brigade walked into my office. 'The attack cannot start at 1500 hours,' the former said to me, 'because the tanks have not been able to take on supplies. There are only eight [Char B1 bis] tanks available.' I replied sharply: 'You have an order. Carry it out. You have twenty Hotchkiss tanks [lighter H39 tanks whose 37mm guns were no match for those on the Char B1 bis].[15] Attack with them.'[16]

But by this time, Flavigny's authority appears to have evaporated. Notwithstanding his orders, the counter-attack was adjourned once more, and was finally called off at 5.15 p.m.

Worse still, the commander of one of the heavy tank companies had moved his tanks forward before he heard that the order had been rescinded. By that time two more tanks had been put out of action by German anti-tank guns, and all the other tanks in the company had been damaged. The company commander was missing.[17] It was a sorry end to what had seemed the best chance to cut off the German panzers as they advanced out of the bridgehead towards the west.

The 3rd Armoured Division was not the only force called upon to attack the Germans in their Sedan bridgehead. On the night of 13–14 May, General François d'Astier de la Vigerie, Commander-in-Chief of Forces Aériennes de la Zone d'Opérations Nord (ZOAN), met up with Air Marshal Arthur Barratt in Chauny, and asked him if his planes could bomb the bridges over the Meuse in the area around Sedan.[18] At first Barratt, no doubt remembering how he had been reined in twenty-four hours earlier by Air Marshal Sir Cyril Newall after the attacks on 12 May, demurred. But, as d'Astier de la Vigerie recalled after the war, when he quoted the words of General Billotte, 'Victory or defeat is passing over those bridges', Barratt's hard-boiled exterior softened. 'I will send six Battles at dawn,' he told d'Astier de la Vigerie. 'Let me have the targets.' But when d'Astier de la Vigerie asked Barratt to let him see the British pilots' reports on their return, Barratt replied pessimistically, 'There won't be any reports since none of them will return.'[19]

The number of planes Barratt was prepared to risk over Sedan was dramatically increased during the afternoon of 14 May, after all of those used during the first early-morning flight returned safely.[20] No fewer than seventy-one bombers were sent to attack the German bridges and columns. No one who witnessed the performance of the AASF could have called into question the British pilots' bravery, as time and again their diving attacks were met with a hail of anti-aircraft fire, and plane after plane was shot down. However, their success rate was less clear-cut. Although General Georges congratulated the British aviators on slowing the German advance, there was no confirmation that they had destroyed any German bridges over the Meuse.[21]

An interesting insight into what it was like to be in a British air crew over the Meuse on that day has been provided by Len Clarke, a twenty-one-year-old wireless-operator air-gunner in 12 Squadron, whose plane was among the first wave sent in during the afternoon. At 3 p.m. Clarke, along with all surviving members of 12 Squadron, was called into the operations hut near the Amifontaine airfield and told the situation was 'critical'. His flight's mission was to bomb one of the bridges erected by the Germans over the Meuse near Donchery. After the meeting large brown envelopes were handed round into which the crews were to put their personal belongings. They would be handed to their next of kin if they did not return. Clarke held on to his watch, cigarettes and lighter. He also retained a crucifix he had been given on the outbreak of war by a friend, who had told him to keep it with him at all times. It was a kind of lucky charm.

The squadron's five planes took off at about 3.30 p.m., and minutes later the three Fairey Battles within Flight A reached the Meuse.[22] As Clarke's plane, flown by Sergeant Reg Winkler, and two other Fairey Battles approached their target, Clarke was puzzled to observe the German fighters pursuing them turning away. He soon realized why as the plane was buffeted by flak. 'For the first time I was really frightened,' Clarke wrote. The flak made an eerie sound as it hit the plane. It was the rattling sound of stones being dropped into a tin can, and there were a lot of stones being dropped. It was not just the noise that was unnerving. While looking around for German fighters, Clarke saw the Fairey Battle on their right drop its bombs, then dive, trailing smoke. 'Well, we can't hang around for him,' said Winkler, and added, 'Hang on, chaps, here we go.' Clarke hung on as Winkler, who had almost overshot the target, put the plane into a dive so deep that Clarke was moved to inquire if he was OK. He was relieved when Winkler replied that he was.

Clarke felt the plane shudder as its four bombs were released. Then it swept upwards. Clarke looked down at the bridge and noted that two houses at its eastern end were on fire. Smoke was wafting over the bridge. 'I think you hit it,' he told Winkler.

'Good,' Winkler replied.

But they were soon being buffeted by flak again, to such an extent that Winkler gave up his attempt to take evasive action. Then Clarke saw debris falling off the plane leading their flight. Seconds later it plunged to the ground. His concern for the crew was abruptly diverted by a loud bang he heard inside their own plane, followed by the sight of flames sweeping into the cockpit from the engine. Clarke watched as Winkler, who had received a flesh wound in his neck, smartly slid back the hood, and attempted to stay clear of the flames by standing up in the cockpit like a jockey riding in a steeplechase. That prompted Clarke to ask if he could control the plane. Winkler's response was terse. 'Bale out!' he shouted. 'And make it snappy!'

Clarke was the first of the three men to jump, and his account describes what happened next:

I experienced that unique sensation of falling into a bottomless pit before being jerked into silent downward flight. Looking across, I could see the smoke trail left by our aircraft, and two parachutes close to the ground in the distance. Shortly afterwards, I almost dropped into the canal leading from the River Meuse, all my weight going on my right-leg, as I hit the canal towpath, my left leg sinking deeply into soft ground . . .

A German motorcycle combination was fast approaching, and feeling rather ludicrous, I put up my hands as directed by the two Germans holding Tommy guns . . . I was the first British airman the Germans had encountered . . . Naturally they regarded me with some curiosity . . . I had a cut on the back of my head which they bandaged, and I was plied with cigarettes, fruit and some coffee. The English speakers introduced me to that familiar phrase of later days, 'For you the war is over.'

During this time a Hurricane flew over, and the Germans let rip with their rifles. The pilot, recklessly I thought, did a few aerobatics at low level, for which the Germans cheered, then flew off. Soon after a Fairey Battle . . . came streaking past at ground level on full boost, smoke pouring from its exhausts. The aircraft showed signs of damage, and the rear position was unmanned. The tanks and other guns opened up, and surrounded the aircraft with shell bursts, but it disappeared over a ridge. A few seconds later a column of smoke shot up into the air, and the sound of an explosion followed. The Germans shrugged and exclaimed: 'Es ist Krieg.' [That's war.][23]

The planes Clarke had seen shot down were just a few of the British and French aircraft lost that day. Forty out of the seventy-one British bombers failed to return to their bases, which persuaded Barratt that the Fairey Battle bombers should never again be used for daylight raids, except in the most exceptional circumstances.[24]

That decision, combined as it was with Flavigny's failure to send the 3rd Armoured Division into battle, marked the end of the battle for Sedan. During the afternoon of 14 May, Guderian famously asked a 1st Panzer Division staff officer whether he thought the division should head off towards the west or remain on the eastern banks of the Canal des Ardennes, facing south. The staff officer replied, 'Boot them. Don't just spatter them,' meaning that the former option was preferable.[25] Guderian evidently agreed, and the 1st and 2nd Panzer Divisions' commanders were both ordered to turn west to break through the remaining layers of French defences. Although fierce fighting continued at Stonne for several days (described in note 26), the French had been comprehensively defeated.[26]

But what had happened to the second tumour that had been swelling at Houx ever since the night of 12–13 May? As at Sedan, efforts to cut it off were made by local corps commanders – in this case, 2 Corps' General Jean Bouffet and XI Corps' General Martin, whose 5 Division (2 Corps) and 18 Division (XI Corps) were respectively responsible for the fronts to the north and south of the railway bridge near Houx.[27] However, once again, French officers demonstrated they were unequal to the task of mounting a quick counter-attack. The result was that XI Corps' only threat to the German bridgehead on 13 May came from a company of relatively light tanks, which, after several delays, finally attacked that evening. The infantry commander who had been ordered to support them was unable to marshal his forces in time to participate at the start and the tanks' effort was inconclusive. Lacking the thick protective armour of the heavier tanks in the armoured divisions, and the number of vehicles that might have been on hand had the French high command not been deceived by the matador's cloak, the available armour captured its first objective, a wood near Grange, but never received the reinforcements that were needed if its second objective, the previous front line along the Meuse, was to be recaptured. (Details of XI Corps' and 2 Corps' unsuccessful counter-attacks are in note 28.)[28]

The second counter-attack, planned by 2 Corps, was also delayed by the French inability to call up infantry quickly. This attack, when it finally went ahead at dawn on 14 May, also succeeded in taking its initial target, the village of Haut-le-Wastia, a mile and a half to the north-west of XI Corps' counter-attack's first objective. But by then, the Germans were already pushing XI Corps' troops further back from the river. In order to fall into line with the retreating troops to the south, 2 Corps' victorious tanks were ordered to withdraw from the village they had captured before they could drive on to the Meuse.

As if that was not bad enough, a third swelling was growing at Bouvignes, three miles to the south of Haut-le-Wastia. A German crossing was made there at dawn on 13 May, thanks in part to the bravery of infantry in Schützenregiment 7 from Rommel's 7th Panzer Division, but as at Houx, it was also due to the French failure to bring troops swiftly to the river line from the Franco–Belgian border. Because of this, there were not enough French soldiers in place to secure the western banks of the river, and even if there had been, those available had not been furnished with enough heavy weapons to ensure a sufficiently stout resistance. For example, only twenty-one of the fifty anti-tank guns that 18 Division's troops were supposed to possess ever made it to the front line.

Nevertheless, as the war diary for the 2nd Battalion, Schützenregiment 7 records, the French gunfire at Bouvignes was so intense that ten and a half hours passed after the initial crossing before other companies within the battalion were able to follow. For several hours after the first crossing, which was made by a twenty-man force, French gunfire sank any boats that the Germans attempted to row across the Meuse. Eighty-seven Germans lost their lives or were wounded during the fighting. Notwithstanding this, the Germans carried on probing as they destroyed more and more French guns until they eventually succeeded in clearing the way for other companies within the battalion to cross.

The almost reckless bravery exhibited by the Germans can be contrasted with the safety-first and ill-thought-out tactics of the French defenders. The 2nd Battalion, Schützenregiment 7 war diary describes how French armour cornered the attackers at 9 p.m. when they were still vulnerable with their backs to the river. Although the Germans retreated to sloping ground where it was difficult for the tanks to operate, there was nothing to stop the French calling up infantry reinforcements and heavier weapons to annihilate the invaders while still in a contained area. Instead, the war diary reports that the French tanks just turned round and left the battlefield, thereby permitting the Germans to consolidate their bridgehead.[29] The next day, the resulting bridgehead was extended to include Onhaye, and with tanks as well as German infantry across the river, the French XI Corps' infantry disintegrated.[30] By the end of 14 May, some of the panzers that had been ferried across the river into the bridgehead had reached Anthée, five miles to the west, cutting off XI Corps' troops to the north from those to the south, and preparing the way for Rommel's great thrust, which, on the night of 16–17 May, was to take the 7th Panzer Division to the French frontier (see Chapter 11).

The rout of XI Corps was to have disastrous consequences for General Emmanuel Libaud's XLI Corps, which was still holding the line of the Meuse between the XI Corps' Dinant sector and X Corps' Sedan sector.[31] At midnight during the night of 14–15 May, Corap telephoned Libaud to instruct him to abandon his front line along the western banks of the Meuse, so that the troops in XLI Corps could stand shoulder to shoulder with XI Corps' new position further to the west. The 9th Army's new line stretched from Marcinelle (south of Charleroi) to Signy-l'Abbaye in the south. (It is shown in Map 5 on pp. 516–17.)[32] This order appears to have caused the disintegration of the units in XLI Corps, many of which were fortress troops armed with guns that could not easily be transported to a new position.

Corap's order also appears to have opened the floodgates in so far as General Georg-Hans Reinhardt's XLI Panzer Corps was concerned. Until the night of 14–15 May, XLI Corps' 6th Panzer Division had been bottled up within the area enclosed by the loop of the Meuse south of Monthermé.[33] The French troops had maintained their line across the neck of the loop, thereby frustrating Reinhardt's attempts to exploit the crossing of the Meuse that his men had achieved on 13 May.[34] At 5 a.m. on 15 May, German flame-throwers finally broke through the French cordon, which, because of the retreat order, was no longer being supplied with ammunition or reinforcements, and the way was opened for the third principal panzer thrust to the west.[35] By the end of the day the 6th Panzer Division had reached Montcornet, a staggering thirty-five miles to the south-west, leaving in its wake a trail of destruction every bit as devastating as Rommel's more celebrated thrust on the night of 16–17 May. The 6th Panzer Division's breakthrough heralded the

1. *Above* Colonel Hans Oster, the German spy who tipped off the Allies about Hitler's plans to invade France, Belgium and Holland

2. *Above* Major Gijsbertus Sas, the Dutch Military Attaché in Germany (with his back to the car), saluting as he prepares to lay a wreath at the Berlin war memorial. He was disbelieved when he passed Oster's warnings to the Dutch Government

3. *Right* Sas' son Bert (*left*) with Oster's son Harald during the 1936 Berlin Olympics where the families met for the first time. After the meeting Bert Sas acted as a go-between for his father and Oster

4. and 5. *Above* Major Erich Hoenmanns, the wannabe Luftwaffe pilot, at a pre-war air show. He crash landed his plane (*right*) near Mechelen in Belgium on 10 January 1940 thereby permitting Belgian soldiers to seize the top-secret German attack plans which his passenger was carrying

6. *Left* The statement by Colonel Georges Goethals, the Belgian Military Attaché in Berlin (on the right, next to his ambassador, Vicomte Jacques Davignon) that a 'sincere informer' (Oster) was claiming that the German attack plans were on board the crashed plane helped convince the Belgians that the informer was genuine, and that the attack forecast by the informer was imminent

7. *Left* Complaints by Secretary of State for War Leslie Hore-Belisha (*third from right*), seen here during his November 1939 visit to the 'Gort Line'), about the BEF's defences upset General Pownall (*far left*) and Lord Gort (centre with stick) and eventually led to Belisha's dismissal. General Montgomery is on the extreme right

8. and 9. *Middle* A photograph commemorating the award in January 1940 of the Légion d'Honneur to British generals 'Tiny' Ironside (*far left*) and Lord Gort (*far right*) in the presence of Winston Churchill (*centre*). Their comments about the French generals Alphonse Georges (on Churchill's right) and Maurice Gamelin (on Churchill's left), and about Generals Georges Blanchard and Gaston Billotte (seen respectively on Gamelin's right and left in *photo 9 right*) were somewhat less flattering after the Germans had broken through the French defences on 13–14 May, thereby endangering the BEF

10. *Left* Surrendering Belgian soldiers emerge from the bunker under the Albert Canal bridge near Veldwezelt after the surprise raid by German paratroopers on 10 May

11. *Right* One of the destroyed Albert Canal bridges (near Locht, three miles north-west of Veldwezelt) and the pontoon on the right of the bridge erected by the Germans. They are believed to have been photographed from a British plane on 15–16 May. The photograph shows how small the bridges looked when viewed from a plane

12. *Below* German armour is driven over the captured Veldwezelt bridge

13. *Above* A Fairey Battle bomber (*right*) similar to those used in 12 Squadron's 12 May raid on the Albert Canal bridges

14. and 15. *Left* The burning wreckage of one of the Battle bombers that was shot down during the raid. Fred Marland, its twenty-eight-year-old pilot (*below*), was still inside when it crashed

16. *Left* Tom 'Dolly' Gray VC, the photogenic observer in the Battle bomber piloted by Don Garland VC. He might have been court-martialled for an earlier shooting incident had he not died during the raid

17. *Top left* Generals Alan Brooke (*left*) and André Corap, commander of France's 9th Army (*foreground*), salute during the November 1939 parade to commemorate the end of the First World War. It was during this parade that Brooke noticed the lack of discipline in the French Army

18. *Top right* The weir connecting the island in the middle of the Meuse (*foreground*) with the western side of the river. Because it was not properly guarded by the 9th Army, Germans were able to walk across it during the night of 12–13 May

19. *Above* An abandoned Char B1 bis, one of the huge French tanks that terrified the Germans until they discovered its Achilles heel

20. *Left* Germans crossing one of the bridges their engineers had laid across the Meuse near Dinant after the initial 13 May breakthrough

21. *Top left* General Heinz Guderian whose XIX Panzer Corps spearheaded the assault on French positions west of the Meuse near Sedan on 13 May

22. and 23. *Top centre* The Royal Norfolks' Captain Hastings whose diary describes the 'wild enthusiasm' of the Belgian people at the sight of the British Army coming to their aid: *see top right* where Belgians are seen waving at British soldiers in their Mark VI light tank

24. *Above left* An abandoned Somua S-35 French tank similar to those that took on the German panzers in the 'Gembloux gap' on 12–14 May

25. *Above right* 2nd Lieutenant Dick Annand, seen with his fiancée Shirley, on the day he was presented with his Victoria Cross for 'conspicuous gallantry' west of the River Dyle in Belgium on 15 May

26. and 27. *Above* Two Victoria Crosses were awarded for courageous acts on the River Escaut on 21 May. *Left* The Royal Norfolks' Sergeant-Major George Gristock who won a posthumous VC for knocking out a machine-gun post north of Calonne although he had been wounded in both legs. *Right* The Grenadier Guards' Lance-Corporal Harry Nicholls (seen here on the right in his prison camp) who won his for an equivalent act south of Pecq

28. *Above* Germans cross the Escaut on 23 May after the British withdrawal

beginning of the end for the French 9th Army, which broke up as different units and parts of units retreated to different defence lines. During 15 May, General Corap was relieved of his command and replaced by General Giraud.[36]

But where was the armoured division that could be used against Rommel? General Georges' diary shows that on 13 May he had been inclined to send the 1ière Division Cuirassée de Réserve (1st French Armoured Division), which had been harbouring near Charleroi, some thirty miles south-east of Brussels, in case it was needed against the northern arm of the German attack, to Corap's 9th Army. The 13 May entry in Georges' diary suggests he would have thus strengthened Corap's hand if the local counter-attacks ordered by the French XI and 2 Corps had been mounted, and shown to be inadequate, more quickly.[37] The next morning Billotte protested that he needed it as his reserve when Georges asked for it to be sent to relieve Corap.[38] Half an hour later Billotte relented, and it was agreed that the armoured division should be released to move against Rommel immediately.[39]

If Georges had been directly in touch with the 1st Armoured Division's General Marie Bruneau, the tanks could have been given their 'marching' orders at 11 a.m. on 14 May. Unfortunately the French command structure did not cater for such a rapid response. It was 1 p.m. before the order was passed to Bruneau via General Blanchard's 1st Army.[40] The armoured division's progress was further delayed by the crowds of refugees on the roads, and the first heavy Char B1 bis tanks arrived in the area around Flavion at around 8 p.m.[41] Bruneau's initial plan, squared with XI Corps' General Martin, was to make a thrust towards the Bois de Weillen, one mile to the north of the Dinant to Anthée road, during the evening of 14 May.[42] The idea was to take the pressure off Martin's front line, and to destroy some German tanks in the process.

Martin hoped that at least some of his infantry would hold long enough to be in place to exploit the thrust, but he was to be disappointed. The report by 18 Division's General Camille Duffet records how, after learning that his men were not standing up to the Germans, Martin exploded: 'All I ask is that they don't b— off [as soon as the Germans appear].'[43] However, before the evening was over, he realized his troops were on the run to such an extent that his first priority had to be the shoring up of his defences. He therefore issued the order that required

Bruneau to cancel the counter-attack so that the 1st Armoured Division could be used to bolster what was to become XI Corps' portion of the 9th Army's new Marcinelle to Signy-l'Abbaye defence line. Martin's portion ran from Jamagne, a mile and a half north-west of Philippeville, down to Forge du Prince, eighteen miles south-west of Givet.[44] It was another example of a French general attempting to use the one weapon that might have stopped the German panzers for an inappropriate task. Ironically the effect of Martin's gaffe was nullified by the communication problems that were making it so hard to reorganize the retreating French forces. Bruneau did not receive the order until after his armour had made contact with the Germans.

However, Bruneau's plan to counter-attack was hampered by the basic problem built into all the French armoured divisions: the heavy tanks needed refuelling even after relatively short moves, yet the French had not devised a speedy method of achieving this. The Germans overcame their refuelling difficulties by transporting petrol to the front in cans. Once the cans were in the vicinity of the panzer divisions, all the tanks nearby could be refuelled simultaneously on any terrain. The French, on the other hand, had the petrol brought to the front in lorries, which, not being tracked, could not be used over rough ground. Even when the French armour was refuelled on a road, the vehicles' petrol tanks had to be filled up consecutively rather than simultaneously, which took much longer than the German method. If the tanks harboured on bumpy terrain, the refuelling time was even more protracted. The problem was exacerbated by the fact that the Char B1 bis tanks used up their petrol more quickly than the German panzers.[45]

General Bruneau had to cope with an additional complication during the night of 14–15 May. In the rush to deploy, contact was not maintained with the petrol tanker lorries, which went missing during the move. Because of this, the plan to send the tanks on to counter-attack near Dinant that day had to be abandoned, and the tanks, which were short of fuel, remained in and around Flavion, their commanders no doubt hoping that the tankers would find them and give them the petrol they needed before the Germans appeared.

The French fuel tankers were finally tracked down at Oret, some five miles north-west of Flavion, at 7 a.m. the next morning, but this was too late for them to be able to replenish the petrol supplies of many of the tanks.[46] Shortly after 8 a.m., the French B1 bis tanks to the west of the Ermeton-sur-Biert to Flavion road were discovered by reconnaissance units from Rommel's 7th Panzer Division, which, by the end of 14 May, had taken control of the area from Dinant to Anthée.[47] However, the expected full-on clash between French and German tanks did not take place immediately because Rommel had ordered his tank commanders to avoid being sucked into a time-consuming battle; their first priority was to carry on towards Philippeville. After the first bruising encounter, the French tank crews watched Rommel's panzers speeding off to the west before they were assaulted by a second wave of tanks from the 5th Panzer Division.

The incomplete records of units involved in the ensuing battle and the limited number of witness statements left behind by participants only permit a snapshot of the fighting near Flavion to be presented. One such account by Sergeant Nökel, a twenty-two-year-old tank commander from the 5th Panzer Division, describes events indicative of what was going on all over the battlefield. His Panzer 3 was ferried across the Meuse at Houx notwithstanding the earlier difficulties in sending tanks across the river: a Panzer 4 tank toppled off its ferry into the river with one member of the tank crew inside. He survived by jumping into the water before the tank sank, but after that incident many of the 5th Panzer Division's heavy- and medium-weight tanks had to cross at the bridge built in the 7th Panzer Division's sector near Dinant.[48]

The Panzer 3 was a medium tank, having thinner armour (1.2 inches thick) and a less powerful gun (37mm) than those on the heavy Char B1 bis tanks it came up against near Flavion.[49] That explains Nökel's misgivings, revealed in the following extract from his account, when he saw a group of Char B1 bis tanks lumbering towards him for the first time; there were twenty-five of them and they seemed even more menacing once it was realized that German shells were bouncing off their armour as if they were harmless peas.

The tanks' silhouettes was getting larger, and I was scared. Never before had I seen such huge tanks . . . My company commander gave clear instructions over the radio describing which targets to aim at, and the enemy tanks were just 200 metres away before he gave the order to fire. As if they had been hit by lightning, three of the enemy tanks halted, their hatches opened and their crews jumped out. But some of the other tanks continued towards us, while some turned . . . presenting their broadsides to us. On the . . . side of the tank there was an oil radiator behind some armour. At this spot, even our [smaller Panzer 2] tanks' 20mm guns could penetrate the armour, and the French tanks went up in flames immediately if they were hit there. It was then that our good training made such a difference. The information about the vulnerability of the enemy tanks was quickly circulated to all our tanks. Then we shot bullet after bullet at the French tanks, so that within the fifteen minutes it took us to repulse the attack, nineteen enemy tanks were either burning or immobile.

But the French tanks were not beaten yet. As Nökel's account reveals, some outflanked the Germans and shot up four panzers from the rear, including the tank commanded by Nökel's best friend.

His tank received a direct hit and then it brewed up. There was nothing I could do to save him . . . I was glad when our company commander ordered us to move. I could not see anything to the front as the wind was blowing black smoke towards us . . . All I knew is that I wanted to escape from this inferno. Then my driver suddenly shouted: 'Everyone get out! French tank ahead!' I turned, and saw there was an enemy tank just five metres away from us. You can never know in advance how quickly you can move until you have been in danger. The crew leapt out of our tank, and took cover behind it. But nothing stirred in the enemy tank. The engine was off, the hatches closed.

It was only then that Nökel, suspecting he might be safe after all, moved his tank out of the line of fire of the French gun. Then they moved in for the kill. His gunner fired at the tank at point-blank range, presumably aiming at the weak point in its armour, and the French colossus blew up as its ammunition caught fire. 'The enemy's crew appeared to have abandoned their tank,' wrote Nökel, omitting to mention the significant point that the French tank, like so many others on the battlefield, was stranded, having run out of petrol.

Nökel's account also records the moment when, shortly afterwards, he and his tank crew were themselves on the receiving end of shells fired by a French tank's guns:

I saw the muzzle flash of the third shot. I told my driver to reverse immediately. All I could hear was the grinding of the gears. That was quickly followed by a blue, yellow and red flame which flashed up before me. I felt the tank being thrown back, and I smelt the sulphurous odour which I have never forgotten

. . . After my tank was hit my eardrums were hurting, and I couldn't hear anything.

According to Nökel, that did not stop him and three of his five-man crew scrambling out of the tank yet again. Only the driver was missing: 'I approached the front of my tank, and saw that the upper part of the front hull was buckled inwards behind the driver, where there was a hole in the armour. The driver's body was hanging half out of the hatch.'[50]

Fortunately the driver was still alive, and after he had been pulled out and placed on the back of the tank, Nökel climbed in, doing his best not to be distracted by the blood on the driver's seat, and drove the tank back to the German lines, where it was repaired. Others remained to carry on the fight, however. Eventually, after General Bruneau finally received the order telling him that his division was supposed to be retreating to a new line rather than standing and fighting, the order to withdraw trickled down to the front line, and those French crews still manning tanks complied, leaving the Germans in control of yet another battlefield.[51]

There were precious few French tanks left. Only thirty-six of the 160-odd tanks deployed by the 1st Armoured Division at the beginning of the battle drove away. The battalions of Char B1 bis tanks had been decimated: only eleven limped off the battlefield.[52] Many of the abandoned tanks had merely run out of fuel, like the one encountered by Nökel. Consequently the full strength of the division was never properly tested. Even more importantly, another opportunity to make a decisive counter-attack had been lost.

At least the 1st Armoured Division had gone down fighting. Like the 3rd Armoured Division, the 2ième Division Cuirassée de Réserve (2nd Armoured Division) did not even have that consolation.[53] Having been bamboozled by the matador's cloak, General Georges had initially ordered the 2nd Armoured Division to join the 1st Armoured Division near Charleroi, which would have been a good launching pad for a timely intervention in the northern tank battle. But there were not enough railway wagons to take the whole division, so while the tanks were transported by rail, the artillery and supply vehicles took to the roads. Thus the division was split up, and on 14 May, at the most critical stage in the battle, its commander General Albert Bruché was forced to admit to General Blanchard that he had no idea where his tanks were.

Nevertheless General Bruché was told that when the tanks reappeared, he should use them to support General Corap's 9th Army. However, when his liaison officer reported to Corap's headquarters, the officer discovered that the 2nd Armoured Division had been reassigned to another commander.[54] In the meantime General Georges had redirected the road column to Signy-l'Abbaye at the southern end of Corap's new defence line. The tanks were to proceed by rail to Hirson and then go to Signy-l'Abbaye by road.[55] The division's units were just executing this manoeuvre when they were hit by the tanks of Reinhardt's XLI Panzer Corps which were heading towards the west. After one of the 2nd Armoured Division's artillery batteries had been decimated by the panzers during the late afternoon on 15 May, the artillery retreated to the south, while the French tanks, which retreated as soon as they unexpectedly made contact with the Germans, were scattered around the French countryside to the north without any means of support. Thus yet another of Georges' aces from his fast-dwindling pack was squandered before it could be played, and there were not many left.

11: Lambs to the Slaughter

Clairfayts to Le Cateau, Neuville-Vitasse, Doullens and Amiens,
15–20 May 1940
(See Maps 7 and 8. Also Maps 1 and 5)

Ironically, on the very day when Reynaud was despairingly telling Churchill that France was defeated, the Germans were themselves beginning to worry about France beating them. On 15 May, General Gerd von Rundstedt, who as commander of Army Group A was in charge of the southern arm of the German attack, began to ask whether he should halt his armour on the Oise.[1] In his war diary for that day, he stated: 'The enemy should not be allowed to achieve any kind of success. That would have an effect which would be more detrimental to the conduct of our attack than would be the case if our tanks were to be slowed down.'[2]

On 16 May von Rundstedt finally ordered his 4th Army (responsible for XV Corps' 5th and 7th Panzer Divisions) and the 12th Army (responsible for XLI Corps' 6th and 8th Panzer Divisions, and XIX Corps' 1st, 2nd and 10th Panzer Divisions) to stop all of their tanks, except those representing the vanguard, only giving them back their freedom of movement four days later.[3] This important development particularly frustrated Guderian, who on 14 May had decided to advance to the west from his Sedan bridgehead without waiting for the infantry. (See details in note 4.)[4] However, it was to be just the first of a series of such halt orders culminating in the most celebrated halt order of all, given ten days later as the panzers approached Dunkirk.

On 17 May Hitler backed the order, overruling General Franz Halder, the Army's Chief of Staff, who disapproved. This fundamental disagreement, which threatened to compromise the whole attack, was summed up as follows, with uncharacteristic understatement, in Halder's diary for that day: 'Apparently little mutual understanding. The Führer insists that main threat is from the south. (I see no threat at all at present!)'[5] On 17 May he concluded: 'Rather unpleasant day. The Führer is terribly nervous. Because he is frightened by his own success, he is afraid to take any chance, and so would rather pull the reins in on us. He puts forward the excuse that it is all because of his concern for the left flank.'

Hitler might have been even more concerned had he known about the counter-attack carried out by Colonel Charles de Gaulle's 4ième Division Cuirassée de Réserve (4th Armoured Division) on 17 May. De Gaulle's eighty-five tanks, representing half of the 4th Armoured Division which would subsequently be assembled, had driven some fifteen miles from the area east of Laon to Montcornet to mount the counter-attack.[6] The thrust, which might have succeeded had it been backed by infantry, artillery and air support, showed that when they were attacking the French were hard to stop. Two waves of tanks made it into Montcornet, destroying anti-tank guns and German supply lorries that they encountered on the way, only to be forced to retreat when they ran out of fuel. (Details of the 4th Armoured Division's attack, and its subsequent attempt to capture the bridges over the Serre at Crécy and Mortiers two days later, are in note 7.)[7]

Hitler's behaviour on 17 May was nothing compared to his violent reaction the next day, after he had heard about Halder's suggestion that they should consider going south as well as west to defeat both the remainder of the French army south of the Somme and the troops to the north. 'The Führer unaccountably keeps worrying about the south flank,' wrote Halder on 18 May. 'He rages and screams that we are doing our best to ruin the whole campaign, and we will end up by being defeated.'

Guderian was not the only general who refused to accept von Rundstedt's 16 May halt order with good grace. Rommel appears to have worked out a way to sidestep the ruling: he exploited the time it took for orders to filter down from the Army Group to him at the front. At 1.45 p.m. on 16 May General Hans-Günther von Kluge, commander of the 4th Army, told the XV Panzer Corps' commander, General Hermann Hoth, that the 7th Panzer Division should pierce the French fortifications at the Franco-Belgian border.[8] This order was passed verbally to Rommel so that he could prepare his move, but by the time the written order with certain restrictions added arrived at his division's headquarters, he had already set off on what became one of the most exhilarating thrusts of the whole campaign.[9]

His tanks started from the hills west of Cerfontaine, and reached the Franco-Belgian frontier near Clairfayts at around 6 p.m. that day.[10]

Instead of waiting until morning, he ordered his engineers to cut through the barbed wire that fenced off the French positions, then blow up their blockhouses and anti-tank obstacles placed across the road.[11] His tanks were then to drive through the small gap thereby created firing on both sides to keep the French soldiers' heads down.

As Rommel and his tanks passed through the line of fortifications and out the other side, he was obviously savouring the moment, a sentiment reflected in the following extract from his memoirs:

We were through the Maginot Line! It was hardly conceivable. Twenty-two years before we had stood for four and a half long years before this self-same enemy and won victory after victory, and yet finally lost the war. And now we had broken through the renowned Maginot Line, and were driving deep into enemy territory. It was not just a beautiful dream. It was reality.[12]

Rommel's account, which stresses that the French did not resist as hard as he had expected, leaves out the French side of the story. French archives make it clear that Rommel was in fact very lucky. Yet another French error made it possible for his tanks and engineers to approach the anti-tank obstacles. The French commander in charge of the artillery that might have decimated the enemy had failed to stock up his positions with shells. Consequently, German tanks and engineers were not exposed to the barrage that would have rained down on them if the gunners had had sufficient ammunition.[13]

Rommel did not stop after breaking through the frontier defences. He urged his tank commanders to drive on to Landrecies and Le Cateau via Avesnes, which they duly did, spreading panic on both sides of the road as the following report by a German soldier demonstrates: 'Hundreds of soldiers and French civilians are woken by the armoured regiment driving at full speed on the roads; lying in the holes and ditches to the right and left of the tanks, their faces are deformed with fear. The firing by the armoured regiment reaches out on both sides of the road and sows panic into the night.'[14]

A German soldier who passed down the road, after the initial attack, described the havoc that had resulted:

I have never seen anything like it on Rommel's route. His tanks had come across a French division. And it had simply carried on without pausing. Over the ten following kilometres there were hundreds of lorries and tanks; some of them had been driven into the ditches, others were burned out, many of them were full of corpses or wounded men. Frenchmen emerged from the fields and forests, their hands in the air, a terrible fear etched on their faces. Ahead I could hear the abrupt barking of the tanks' cannons, tanks that Rommel personally was leading. He stood up in his command vehicle with two staff officers, his cap hanging from around his neck as he urged on the attack.[15]

At Avesnes, Rommel's tanks met up with the sixteen Char B1 bis tanks from the French 1st Armoured Division that had not been put out of action during the battle at Flavion. This relatively small force had guns that might have stopped Rommel's surge. But the threat was snuffed out after some of his tanks ambushed them from the rear. In the end only three of the sixteen French tanks escaped.[16]

Most of the Frenchmen the panzers encountered were almost anxious to surrender, terrified of what the tanks might do to them. But of one French lieutenant-colonel, captured in his car near Landrecies, Rommel wrote, 'His eyes glowed with hate and impotent fury. Colonel Rothenburg [commander of Panzer Regiment 25] . . . signed to him to get in his tank. But he curtly refused to come with us, so, after summoning him three times to get in, there was nothing for it but to shoot him.'[17]

It is interesting to note that Rommel's radio link with the 7th Panzer Division's headquarters was cut at moments when it would have been most inconvenient for him to listen to his superiors. At 9.30 p.m. on 16 May a written order from XV Corps' General Hoth had arrived at the 7th Panzer Division's headquarters, still many miles to the east of Rommel's vanguard, forbidding Rommel to attack Avesnes until seven the next morning.[18] By the time the order arrived, Rommel was conveniently out of touch with his headquarters, and appears to have remained off air until 2.40 the next morning, by which time he had already made it to Avesnes, nineteen miles to the west of where he had started the previous day.[19] At 4.20 a.m. another urgent request from XV Corps that reached the 7th Panzer Division's headquarters stated: 'Don't go beyond Avesnes.'[20] But by this time Rommel was off air again.[21]

Rommel only appears to have realized that his dazzling advance had left him in mortal danger after he reached Le Cateau, which he did at 5.15 a.m. on 17 May, an hour and three quarters before he was supposed to start advancing towards the areas he had already captured:[22] he discovered then that the main part of his division had failed to follow him, leaving him and his advanced tanks isolated. Another commander might have told a junior officer to go back and tell the men lagging behind to catch up, but Rommel insisted that he should retrace his steps. He set off in an armoured car with only one Panzer 3 as an escort.[23] When the tank broke down, Rommel carried on alone. During the journey he came across a column of some forty French lorries emerging from a side road near Marbaix, six miles east of Landrecies. Undaunted, he flagged it down. Then, with his aide mounted in the first French lorry, and his armoured car at the front, he led the column, armed as it was with anti-aircraft guns, into Avesnes. There, he handed over his captives to a unit that had remained in the town following its capture. His division's headquarters staff appeared at 4 p.m. that afternoon, and they were then able to complete the occupation of the places he had captured so audaciously.[24]

The fact that no French reserves were in place to stop the panzers that had pierced the French front line was apparently not mentioned to staff officers at the Arras branch of the British General Headquarters (Rear GHQ) until after they had worked out for themselves what had happened.[25] Incredibly, although Churchill had been told the bad news on 16 May during his meeting with General Gamelin and Paul Reynaud, no one had passed it on to the staff officers masterminding the movement of BEF troops. The GHQ staff officers at Arras only began to understand the scale of the problem on 17 May when General Georges asked whether the British 23 Division, a so-called 'digging division' sent out to France to provide manual labour rather than to fight, could hold a stretch of the Canal du Nord south of Arleux.[26] This request, which would have been unnecessary if France had had enough fighting troops of her own, shocked Lieutenant-Colonel Robert Bridgeman, the officer in charge at Rear GHQ, to such an extent that he immediately asked a colleague to carry out what he referred to as an 'intelligence appreciation' on the French Army. It says a lot about the quality of communications between the Allies that he had to ask for intelligence on the French, but it turned out to be necessary, as is confirmed by his account of the campaign. Twenty minutes later the full 'horror of the situation' was known: 'There had been a major breakthrough, and there were no French troops to stop it,' he wrote.[27]

The French difficulties were compounded by what had happened in

Dunkirk

the north around Gembloux. Although the halting of the German thrust appeared at first sight to represent a victory for the French, in strategic terms it was a defeat. The Germans had tempted the French into playing one of their aces in an area far removed from the main attack, and had then weakened them by knocking out so many tanks. When on 19 May General Dill, the Vice Chief of the Imperial General Staff since April, was told by the French that they were hoping to use the remnants of the Cavalry Corps in the south, Gamelin and Georges made it quite clear that they were not expecting very much from the counter-attack.[28]

The breakthrough in the south brought with it serious consequences for the BEF. 'At about 10 a.m. [on 16 May] I received . . . orders for a withdrawal [from the Dyle] to the Escaut,' Lord Gort recorded in his Despatches.[29] There were equally important measures in store for the RAF. The AASF units, which were ordered to move their bases away from around the River Aisne on 15 May, ended up in the area around Troyes (south-east of Paris). By 17 May, the aircraft and ground crews in the BEF's RAF Component were also on the move, westward. Two days later it was agreed that the Component units should leave France altogether, and operate from the south of England. The speed of their subsequent evacuation led to aircraft losses that, given the shortage, were verging on the disastrous. Of 261 fighters that had operated with the Component, seventy-five had been destroyed or written off in the course of combat. That was bad enough. However, to add insult to injury, an additional 120 damaged but repairable Hurricanes were left behind in France when the Component was evacuated. Only sixty-six made it back to England, a pitifully small remnant.[30] The 195 fighters lost in and over France and Belgium may not have seemed a large number to the French, but for Britain's Fighter Command, which by 20 May only had some 480 Hurricanes and Spitfires available, it was a major blow.[31]

At least the ground and aircraft crews and pilots in the RAF were fortunate enough to be spirited away from the line of the German advance. There was no such preferential treatment made available to some of the BEF's digging divisions. Because Lord Gort and his Chief of Staff General Pownall were in their advanced headquarters in Renaix, seven miles south of Oudenarde in Belgium, it was left to Bridgeman to try to fill the gap with some of these units. He asked Major-General Roderick Petre, commander of 12 Division – one of three digging divisions that were eventually called into action – to command an *ad hoc* force that could stand in the Germans' path to stop them attacking British lines of communication. As well as having 23 Division placed under his command, General Petre, who was to be based in Arras, was to have the assistance of a battalion of Welsh Guards. He was also to command 36 Brigade from his own 12 Division, part of which was to be positioned south of 23 Division on the Canal du Nord.

Given the panic that had occurred at Rear GHQ when the true state of affairs was discovered, the written order that confirmed General Petre's appointment contained some excessively optimistic, and misleading, statements: 'Indications point to a hardening by the French on both flanks of the gap created by the German armoured divisions. It is believed that only small German detachments have penetrated very deeply.'[32] Whether or not General Petre believed it, the same message was passed to his brigadiers.

Their subordinates were equally ill-informed. An account by Major Arthur 'Tim' West, an officer within the 5th Battalion, the Buffs, a unit of 12 Division's 36 Brigade, has highlighted the lack of hard information, which was also causing problems lower down the hierarchy.[33] 'It was surprising how little we knew of the progress of the war,' Major West wrote.

All the time we had been in France, out of a British zone, we had not found it easy to procure newspapers, and when we did . . . they did not really tell one anything.[34] We were now under the fond impression that we were going into the British army area, and that therefore all would be all right . . . But we were very much mistaken. It was just after midday [on 18 May] when we entered Doullens.[35] There we received our first disillusion. Doullens was deserted, dead. Every house and shop was shuttered and closed. Only two or three civilians were to be seen, and they were making their preparations for departure. A car was being loaded, a hand cart or perambulator filled with the few possessions it was possible to bear away. The foreboding of ill was reinforced in this sinister place.

West's search for a suitable venue for the officers' mess took him into a convent within the town. 'It was evident that the good sisters and their pupils had left hastily, and but a short time before,' he reported. 'Life there had stopped and suddenly: clothes were still in cupboards; a handkerchief dropped and left in a desk, and the subject of the day's lessons still on the blackboard. In the kitchen the stove was still alight, and the remains of coffee and breakfast were on the table.'

He went on to describe how, over the next twenty-four hours, the Buffs set up a series of roadblocks on the principal roads leading into the town.

All these preparations might have seemed overdone to cope with a handful of tanks which, as the reports would have it, had broken through. But we didn't quite believe that story, though we had nothing to tell us a contrary tale, except for the unceasing, especially towards nightfall, streams of French soldiers, now for the most part on foot, which flowed through the town. It did not seem credible that what must have been the greater part of an army corps at least could retreat without valid reason; and retreat in no sort of order, singly, in twos and threes, unarmed and unkempt, shambling despondently along the street . . . Some rode bicycles gathered on the way, or drove a farm wagon. Others rode horses . . . These scenes were hardly calculated to fill us with any sort of exhilaration.

During the lull before the storm, West moved the mess from the convent to a hotel, where some of the men prepared themselves for the worst. 'At 1800 hours [on 19 May] there was a communion service behind the front café,' West wrote. 'The tables were moved to one side. Here, surrounded by such incongruities as advertisements for . . . calvados, marble-topped tables and trays and aspidistras, the two or three able to get away from duties . . . received what might well be, for all we knew, a last sacrament.'

West was right to be concerned for their safety. Early in the morning on 20 May, troops from 36 Brigade, including the 5th Buffs, moved into their positions in front of the road running north-east from Doullens to Arras. The line that was formed was a ridiculously weak island of resistance given the force that was approaching. According to West, the Buffs were particularly vulnerable. Even if they had possessed all the equipment and guns that a fighting battalion was supposed to carry, the width of the six-mile front they were expected to hold would have precluded them from preventing a breakthrough. They were certainly not properly armed. They had no artillery, and none of the anti-tank guns on wheels that a unit needed if it was to have a chance of repulsing a group of tanks. Their weapons could hardly have been more rudimentary: each man had a rifle of some sort, but ordinary rifles were not much use against tanks, and according to Major West, there were only fourteen anti-tank rifles within the entire battalion. On their right, they were supported by another 36 Brigade unit, the 6th Battalion, the Queen's Own Royal West Kent Regiment, but their left flank was dangling in the air, an open invitation for any attacker to move round them in order to attack from the rear.[36]

It was hoped that the 1st Battalion, the Tyneside Scottish Regiment, from 70 Brigade, part of 23 Division, whose call-up by General Georges had first alerted the British staff officers to the danger, would arrive in time to reinforce the thin line that had been manned. But before it arrived, it was sucked into its own vortex. Its commanding officer, Lieutenant-Colonel Hugh Swinburne, has described how he and his men were initially ordered to guard a section of the Canal du Nord, as requested by General Georges. However, when they arrived there on 18 May they discovered that the term 'canal' was misleading: there was no water in it, and the deep ditch that was supposed to hold up the German armour would not have challenged a car in some places, let alone a tank. Fortunately, although Swinburne saw and was fired at by a few armoured vehicles on the east bank, which he took to be German, no full-scale attack was launched. So his men's ability to hold the line was not put to the test. These tank sightings, however, unnerved him. He became even more jumpy when, on 19 May, he discovered that an engineer who had been ordered to blow up a bridge spanning the 'canal' had failed to do so. His campaign account explains what followed:

[When] I . . . asked him why on earth he had not blown it up (to fall into the canal 60 feet below) as ordered, he replied: 'I cannot stop refugees crossing from the other side. [Could you] . . . send two men over to hold them?' I said: 'What, and lose them. Not damn likely! Blow it', whereupon he burst into tears (he was very young and junior), much to my horror, and I had to push down the plunger myself, much as I too hated to do it with people still on the bridge. But orders are orders, and sentiment comes nowhere in war.[37]

Swinburne's account reveals that he became even more uneasy when, having been told to retreat from the canal, he had a most unsatisfactory discussion with the brigade staff handing out the orders.

We were told that the situation was very much easier, and that there were only a few enemy armoured cars in the vicinity, and that they had probably run out of petrol and ammunition. No one would listen to either myself, or the colonel of the battalion which had been next to me on the canal, when we said we had seen tanks on several occasions, and had been fired on by them. We were told they must obviously be French tanks which had 'made a mistake'!

Swinburne's response to this might have been even more forceful, had he known about the action involving British forces that had taken place during the night of 18–19 May. The 7th Battalion, the Queen's Own Royal West Kent Regiment, which had been guarding the bridge connecting the road running from Péronne to Cléry, had repulsed a raid by some German armoured vehicles, and in the process put one of them out of action.[38]

Swinburne had demonstrated a ruthless streak when he blew up the Canal du Nord bridge, but his anxiety about the impending danger appears to have made him even more militant, if the following extract from an account by Company Sergeant-Major C. Baggs is anything to go by: 'They bring in a spy to Headquarters, and take him to the commanding officer Colonel Swinburne, who with our French liaison officer interrogates him. Result: Sergeant Dick Chamber has orders to shoot him. It was done OK.'[39]

The punishment Swinburne handed out to a member of his own battalion, who was helplessly drunk on duty, might have been regarded as only marginally less severe, if one remembers that some soldiers believed that the Germans were not taking any prisoners. 'I said take all his papers [and possessions] from him, except his identity disc [hung round his neck], but including his arms and ammunition,' wrote Swinburne, 'chuck him into the Gendarmerie cell, and lock him in.'[40]

Swinburne's malaise increased when he saw fires blazing on the horizon and the flash of ammunition dumps blowing up, which told him that the Germans must be approaching. He spent part of the night of 19–20 May with his men at Neuville-Vitasse.[41] This was to be a staging-post on the way to the line held by Major West and his 5th Buffs. The final goal was Saulty, just to the north-west of this line.[42] The next morning, Swinburne was told that refugees had seen tanks to the north, between Neuville-Vitasse and Arras. He took these reports with a pinch of salt until, while standing in the local cemetery, he saw what appeared to be tanks in the distance.

If Swinburne's brigadier had only taken into account these tank sightings, he might have insisted that the battalion's trucks take his men to the west first rather than the stores.[43] Also if the move had started immediately they arrived in Neuville-Vitasse, the trucks might perhaps have carried the men out of the danger zone before it was too late. Instead, the stores were given priority, and consequently the first lorry full of men did not set off until after 7 a.m. on 20 May. Swinburne went ahead in his car hoping to report to the brigadier.

Neither Swinburne nor his troops were destined to reach their goal. As he approached Ficheux, his windscreen was shattered by a burst of machine-gun fire, which set his car's engine on fire.[44] He had been driven into an ambush. He managed to escape by crawling through the corn beside the road, but was captured later. His men were less fortunate. Although they fought hard against the German infantry, they had no way of beating off the tanks. Reports suggest that only around eighty of 450 Tyneside Scottish soldiers escaped. The remainder were either killed or taken prisoner, many of the prisoners having first been wounded.[45]

It has certainly been hard to find clear and vivid reports describing the battle in which so many lives were lost. In the circumstances, we have to be content with reading the following raw account by Company Sergeant-Major Baggs, which records the torment endured by so many Tyneside Scottish soldiers:

I could see the boys fighting like hell with tanks all around them simply going over the men. What a terrible sight. I was quite happy controlling my men. A German MG [machine-gun] opened out on my left flank . . . Did he do his stuff. He simply raked us with MG fire, and to complete his work, two tanks came up behind us and positioned themselves about twenty yards away. They opened out with their shells, and simply blasted us out of the embankment. We were at last surrounded, and within a minute or two, I had 14 killed and 6 wounded. To hear those lads moaning made one feel rather sick. I myself didn't feel too grand, having been hit myself in the foot. When hit, I rolled down the bank, and just missed being blown to hell by a tank shell. It burst just where I had been lying. Thank God for that. What was left of us were signalled by the German tank commander to group together in the field.

Sergeant Rutherford carried me over his back, and after cutting off my boot, laid me down among the rest of the boys. We were told to sit together, and really, we expected to be wiped out.[46]

Afterwards, Baggs and his comrades were driven away on a tank. Only then did he take in the scale of the carnage:

It was a sad sight seeing our dead comrades lying all over the field on each side of the road. What a sacrifice! . . . We passed a barn. It was an inferno . . . blazing like hell, and some of our boys are inside burned to death. We saw at least two bodies half in and half out of the barn door burned black. God, what a sight!

So it was that 36 Brigade had to hold its line without Tyneside Scottish support. In fact, von Kleist's panzer group, including Guderian's XIX Corps, moved so quickly on 20 May that even if the Tyneside Scottish had not been attacked between Neuville-Vitasse and Ficheux, it would have been too late to help 36 Brigade's 7th Battalion, the Queen's Own Royal West Kent Regiment, which was overrun by the Germans at Albert, some fifteen miles south-east of Doullens. Like Swinburne, the battalion's commanding officer, Lieutenant-Colonel Basil Clay, had been given information suggesting that most of the panzers were miles away. Consequently the orders he passed on to his companies at 3.15 that morning were nothing if not optimistic. The orders started with the misleading words 'Situation on our front materially improved . . .', before going on to announce that the battalion was to deploy east of Albert armed with anti-tank rifles with a view to halting the German AFVs (armoured fighting vehicles).[47]

It was not long, however, before the colonel saw evidence that his men might be attacked sooner rather than later. While he was visiting the platoon holding the road leading from Albert to Cléry-sur-Somme, a German motorcyclist appeared, and then made off after being fired at by one of Clay's men. Clay was also machine-gunned by an enemy plane, as were some of the other units moving into position on the other roads near the town. 'I don't like the look of this,' Clay told Captain Newbery, the officer accompanying him. Shortly afterwards Newbery spotted a second German motorcyclist on another road, who was also put to flight by a fierce volley of rifle fire.

Notwithstanding all these warning signs, Newbery appears to have been surprised when shortly after 7 a.m. reports that panzers had been sighted came in to his headquarters situated to the west of the front-line units. A runner from one platoon rushed in to report that thirty tanks had been seen. Before Newbery could send a reply, a message from another platoon told him that they had counted twenty tanks. He hurried back to the square in Albert to inform the colonel, but their conversation was interrupted by the arrival of a German plane that swooped down to fire at them. As they took cover, a tank entered the square, to be greeted by gunfire from all directions. 'Get your company back as quickly as you can,' Clay instructed him.

Thanks to Clay's rapid response, Newbery escaped with around seventy men, and eventually made it back to England, via Boulogne. The rest of the battalion were hemmed in before they could break away. Like the Tyneside Scottish, they fought bravely but, like their comrades, they lacked the hardware that might have enabled them to make a proper stab at resistance against so many tanks. Within hours, the resistance at Albert had been quelled, and most British soldiers there had been either killed, wounded or captured. The prisoners-of-war included Colonel Clay who, along with his men, had been badly let down by the British Army's failure to provide adequate equipment and intelligence from aerial reconnaissance.[48]

Two British officers from Albert made it back to warn the brigadier and the remaining 36 Brigade battalions that the Germans were approaching.[49] These battalions were therefore ready and waiting when, between 12.30 p.m. and 2 p.m. on the same day, the tanks of the 2nd and 6th Panzer Divisions arrived, commencing their attack to the north of Doullens in the area held by the 6th Royal West Kents and 5th Buffs, before Doullens was itself invested. (Details are in note 50.)[50]

Although a stronghold at Doullens held out until 8.30 p.m., 36 Brigade's Brigadier George Roupell, who had counted on his headquarters, in a château at Lucheux, being tucked away behind the cover provided by his battalions' companies, swiftly discovered that he was in the front line.[51] From there he could not see the battle raging in front of him, but a desperate phone call from Lieutenant-Colonel Nash, commanding officer of the 6th Royal West Kents, who were holding the right side of the line, prepared him for the worst, as he recalled in his memoirs: 'Colonel Nash rang me to say that a German tank had just stopped outside his HQ. "We are just getting our Boys rifle into action," he said. "Wait a moment, and you will hear it go off." I did hear a bang, and that was the last noise I heard on that telephone. It was disconnected from then on.'[52]

Yet when another officer ran in breathlessly to report that he had been forced back by the tanks, and had seen the rest of the battalion routed, Roupell, who knew a thing or two about bravery, having won the Victoria Cross during the First World War, uttered the immortal line, 'Never mind the Germans. I'm just going to finish my cup of tea.'[53]

Even Brigadier Roupell's feathers were ruffled, however, when a report came in at around 6.30 p.m. that three German armoured vehicles were approaching his headquarters.[54] He and his staff watched as a Buffs soldier manning the barricade at the château gates was told by an officer to hold his fire until the leading car was just a hundred yards away. Then the soldier opened fire, hitting each car and bringing the column to a grinding, and bloody, halt.[55] The surviving Germans in the leading vehicle did not wait to check whether the British soldier had more ammunition. They quickly clambered out of it, leaving behind one of their comrades whose blood-spattered corpse lay half in and half out of the vehicle. It was perhaps this gruesome sight that deterred the crew in a heavier tank, which appeared on the scene shortly afterwards, from launching an attack. Whatever the true reason, the heavy tank kept its distance, thereby giving the brigadier, and the others who had congregated at the château, time to beat a hasty retreat out of the back door.

Few of the men who had served under Roupell's command shared his good fortune. Only seventy-five of the 6th Royal West Kents returned to England; the remaining 503 were posted as missing.[56] The 5th Buffs were hardly better off, with just eighty out of 605 men eventually going home.[57]

If anything, the difficulties experienced by the soldiers in another 12 Division unit, the 7th Battalion, the Royal Sussex Regiment, near Amiens, were even more extreme. Their troubles started even before they reached the battlefield where they were to make their first and last stand. On 18 May, the train carrying them from Rouen to Amiens was moving slowly through the station at St Roch, to the west of Amiens, when it was bombed, causing at least sixty casualties. Horrific injuries were inflicted. One officer lost an arm when the front carriage in which he was travelling and the train's engine were thrown on their sides by a direct hit from one of the bombs. But that was nothing compared to what Jim Brook, a Royal Engineer, observed when he tried to escape the bombs by crawling under some nearby carriages. One of his comrades was already lying there motionless, the top of his head sliced off. 'I could not stop myself looking at him,' Brook recalled. 'His brain had been exposed, and it was already covered by a thick layer of dust.'[58] Another soldier reported seeing a man who had been in the engine walk past him with half of his face missing.[59]

The survivors were hurried away from the train, and collected in a wood in case the bombers returned. Later that night they were disturbed by what sounded like a howling wolf. This terrified some of the men, who were still trying to recover from the shock caused by the bombing. However, when the first man approached the area of the wood whence the sound was emanating, he found one of his comrades. He was lying prostrate on the ground with his face buried in the earth, and he was alternately howling, and shouting, 'Oh my God! We're surrounded! The Germans are going to get me!' The soldiers told their medical officer that he had gone mad, but in fact it was just mild shell-shock. The medical officer led him away, further reducing the battalion's already depleted manpower.[60]

The battalion was eventually put into a position near the Amiens–Poix road on 20 May, the day on which the Tyneside Scottish and the 36 Brigade soldiers were overrun. At least the commanders of these latter battalions were given some advance warning that the Germans were approaching. It seems that Lieutenant-Colonel Gethen, the Royal Sussex's commanding officer, had had no idea that the panzers were so close. He had relied initially for his intelligence on what he had been told by a French commandant in Amiens, who assured him that the gap opened by the fighting at Sedan had been closed, and the isolated units that had broken through had been cleaned up. According to this Frenchman, there were 'no Germans between us and Sedan'.[61] This intelligence appears to have led to the series of extraordinary conversations recorded in a report filed at the National Archives in London with the battalion's war diary. When he was told that the Germans were approaching, Gethen is said to have retorted, 'Don't talk rot!', and when another man claimed the Germans were just five miles away, he replied that the enemy was forty miles away. Another man who voiced an equally pessimistic opinion was threatened with a court-martial. Even after a reconnaissance party returned from Amiens and reported that the Germans had arrived, Gethen said that it was all 'lies', and he did not want to hear any more about it. He was equally dismissive concerning artillery firing in Amiens. According to Gethen, the French were having a firing practice.

Whether or not Gethen really did react in this way, there certainly were tanks in the area, belonging to Guderian's 1st Panzer Division. That division had left the 2nd Panzer Division at Albert to mop up the final resistance there, and it had then moved on to capture Amiens, which was to be an important launching pad for the subsequent German attack south of the Somme. When a Royal Sussex officer heard a report confirming that the tanks were in Amiens after all, he remarked sardonically with reference to the French commandant's intelligence that there were no Germans west of Sedan: 'Fast moving from Sedan to Amiens overnight.'[62] The German tanks finally appeared over the brow of the hill in front of Gethen and his men during the early afternoon of 20 May, and when at around 4 p.m. the panzers attacked, there was little the poorly armed 'digging' battalion could do to stop them. Doug Swift, a private in A Company who observed the slaughter of many comrades, later wrote:

A lorry load of the lads – D Company I think – were crossing the front diagonally along an old cart track, and were hit by a heavy mortar. The whole lot went up killing them all . . . At one point I caught sight of one of our companies advancing on my right, possibly to try and relieve the pressure on our A Company. They advanced with bayonets fixed, bloody heroes the lot of them, against tanks. Bayonets! I don't know what happened to them, must have been mown down.[63]

After the panzers had overrun A Company, Swift, who had been captured, was horrified to see the battlefield littered with his comrades' corpses. His account records what he witnessed:

Some had been run over by tank tracks . . . A sergeant, chest up from the ground, stared with sightless eyes, a look of pained surprise on his face and a bullet through his heart. Men I knew had bloody holes where their eyes had been, bullets in their guts, heads [and] hearts. They [were] lying spreadeagled in their bloodstained uniforms, the stillness of death upon them.

Meanwhile Guderian's 2nd Panzer Division had moved on from Albert to Abbeville, before finally making it to the sea, overrunning another 'digging' brigade, the 35th, in the process. It was a historic moment. The Allied armies in the north, including the BEF in Belgium, were now cut off from the troops south of the Somme and their lines of communication. Four days earlier, before Rommel's and Guderian's tanks had started their spurt westwards, General Pownall had observed in his diary: 'I hope to God the French have some means of stopping them, and closing the gap, or we are bust.'[64] Now on hearing that the Germans were at the coast, he gave the British Army one final chance: 'We attack tomorrow [the British Royal Tank Regiment was to counter-attack on 21 May near Arras – see Chapter 12], and if it comes off, it might well be the turning point. If it doesn't, we may be foutu [stuffed].'[65]

12: The Arras Counter-Attack

Lens and Arras, 20–21 May 1940
(See Map 8. Also Maps 1, 2 and 7)

The planning of the two-pronged attack that was supposed to send British tanks to the south of Arras and French armour to Cambrai commenced inauspiciously on 20 May.[1] The principal problem from the British point of view was the French generals' disintegrating morale. Even before the full implications of the growing catastrophe were taken on board by the French, Major Archdale, the British liaison officer between GHQ and Army Group 1, was describing General Billotte in the most unflattering terms. The Army Group 1 commander was written off as a large man with a 'rather shuffling walk', who failed to create 'an atmosphere of command and confidence' at his headquarters in Folembray.[2]

Difficulties between Billotte and Lord Gort over the precise times of the British and French retreat from the Dyle to the River Escaut only served to back up Archdale's original analysis. (See note 3.)[3] But notwithstanding Billotte's procrastination, the retreat was accomplished with remarkably few infantry casualties between 16 and 19 May, thanks in part to staunch rearguard actions by the BEF's light cavalry. (See note 4.)[4] Archdale reported that while all this was going on he could not complain about Billotte's manners – Billotte was as suave and courteous as ever. But Archdale feared that the 'pleasant façade' concealed 'hesitation and perhaps despair, and not the calm confidence that I had hoped'. On 18 May, he visited the British GHQ at Wahagnies (seven miles south of Lille) and told General Pownall of his concerns, mentioning the 'supine futility' Billotte exhibited, and the 'malignant inaction' at the general's headquarters. According to Archdale, Colonel Humbert, Billotte's right-hand man, 'had almost completely broken down and was no longer capable of acting as a chief of staff'. The imperturbability of Colonel de Hesdin who had stepped into the breach 'carried no conviction and was unaccompanied by practical action'. At first Pownall brushed aside Archdale's comments, stating that the French would recover, and suggesting that Archdale was exaggerating the problem because he was tired.

But Pownall must have understood what Archdale had meant after Gort met Billotte at GHQ's command post at Wahagnies that night.[5] Archdale, who was there too, described how Gort jauntily asked Billotte in his best schoolboy French, 'Eh bien, mon général, qu'est-ce que vous avez à me dire?' (Well, General, what do you want to tell me?). According to Archdale, Billotte replied that he had 'no reserves, no plan, and little hope!' If further evidence was needed to show how low Billotte's morale had sunk, it was provided during the drive from Gort's headquarters at Wahagnies to Billotte's own – which had been moved from Folembray to Douai – when Billotte admitted to Archdale: 'Je suis crevé de fatigue . . . et contre ces panzers je ne peux rien faire.' (I am exhausted and I can't do anything about these tanks.) The latter phrase was to be repeated again and again by Billotte over the next days, until it became a kind of mantra. It was almost as if Billotte believed that if he repeated it often enough, the problem would miraculously disappear.

The Billotte meeting appears to have persuaded Gort and Pownall that the battle for France might already be lost. The tidings he brought were so pessimistic that a staff meeting was held at GHQ after he left to decide how the BEF might retreat to Dunkirk, the first minuted discussion on this subject.[6] On 19 May, Pownall twice rang Major-General Dewing, Director of Military Operations and Plans at the War Office, to warn him what was being considered: the BEF might be forced to 'withdraw' to Dunkirk 'whence it might be possible to get some shipping to get some troops home'. During their first conversation in the morning, Pownall spoke 'in camouflaged language', presumably fearing that the line might be tapped. But prior to the conversation during the afternoon, he summoned Lieutenant-Generals Alan Brooke and Michael Barker so that these officers, respectively in command of 2 and 1 Corps, might witness what was said. The message this time was clearer: if the French failed to close the gap in the south, the withdrawal 'might become inevitable'.[7]

After Gort's 18–19 May meeting with Billotte, the French general's despair cannot have come as any surprise to the other BEF generals. However, by the time Generals Tiny Ironside and Pownall met their French counterparts at General Blanchard's 1st Army's headquarters in

Lens on 20 May, Billotte's morale had reached a new low.[8] Ironside had travelled to France to find out whether the BEF should abandon the Escaut and the Belgians to fight its way down to the Somme where it could link up with the remaining British and French forces. While he had been talking to Churchill in London, he had accepted that this might be a good idea but when he consulted with Gort in France he realized that it was impossible.[9] The meeting in Lens was supposed to work out whether a co-ordinated counter-attack might take place instead.

The British generals found Billotte 'in a proper dither' as he shouted and trembled over his inability to stop the panzers. It was obvious to everyone at the meeting that his hysteria was preventing him doing his job properly.[10] Clearly, unless he was brought to his senses, there would be no counter-attack. His spineless performance so infuriated Ironside that the huge British general seized him by one of the buttons on his tunic and gave him a good shaking.[11] It was only after strong arguments for an immediate counter-attack had been presented by the British generals, and backed up by equally strong words from the seventy-three-year-old General Maxime Weygand, who had taken over that day from Gamelin as the Commander-in-Chief of the Allied forces, that Billotte and Blanchard finally agreed that the French would counter-attack towards Cambrai on 21 May. The French generals were told that the BEF would stage its own counter-attack on the same day, targeting the area to the south of Arras.[12]

A fascinating glimpse into the workings of the British Commander-in-Chief's mind at this stage has been provided in a report by Captain Melchior de Vogüé, Army Group 1's liaison officer at GHQ. De Vogüé has described how, during the afternoon of 20 May, he was summoned to meet Lord Gort and other members of his staff at Gort's headquarters. Gort, who had just learned that the Germans had taken Cambrai without any serious opposition, opened the meeting by asking de Vogüé if the French Army was refusing to fight. He told de Vogüé that when he asked British soldiers to attack, they immediately obeyed his orders. Would the French Army do the same? If not, the Germans would get to Abbeville and Calais, and Gort would have no choice but to retreat to Dunkirk so that he could transport the BEF back to England. On being told that the order to attack Cambrai had not yet been given, Gort asked de Vogüé, 'What is the French Army waiting for?' He added that it was nothing like the French Army he had known in 1918, whose commanders would have taken it upon themselves to eject the weak advance German guard that had just taken Cambrai.[13]

This meeting, and other contacts between French and British generals on 20 May, appears to have represented a watershed in Anglo-French relations. For the first time during the campaign, the British high command's customary reserve was ripped away, revealing to the French the BEF generals' true feelings. The French attitude to the British changed too. When Captain Miles Reid, British liaison officer between GHQ and the French First Army, told Colonel Vignolles, the 1st Army's Deputy Chief of Staff, that the French in the north had to join up with the troops south of the Somme so that the BEF did not become a 'beleaguered garrison', Vignolles inquired 'acidly' whether this meant that the BEF would be evacuated. Reid replied that it had not come to that yet.[14]

The British generals' worst suspicions about the French unwillingness to counter-attack appeared to be confirmed when, later that afternoon, Gort was handed a copy of Blanchard's written order. Rather than stipulating that the attack should be made the next day, as Billotte and Blanchard had agreed that morning, it stated that it should take place 'on or after 21 May'. A complaint was sent to the 1st Army via its liaison officer, and a corrected order was eventually delivered to General René Altmayer, commander of the French V Corps, who was in charge of the attack. But it only reached him at 2.30 a.m. on 21 May, just hours before the attack was supposed to commence.[15] Further disheartening signals revealing the French generals' inability to act decisively were received by the British liaison officers. Archdale was told by a French liaison officer in Lens that the French generals were not even trusted by their own men. 'There is no one in command here,' the liaison officer told Archdale, and added that Lord Gort should take over.

However, this comment was counterbalanced by Archdale's discovery that even though the 2ième and 3ième Divisions Légères Mécaniques (2nd and 3rd Light Cavalry Divisions) could only muster around thirty-five Somua tanks following their bruising battles in the north, the crews were raring to have another go at the Germans. But no sooner were Archdale's hopes raised, than they were dashed by General Billotte, now in his new headquarters in Béthune. Rather than spending his time making sure that the all-important counter-attack went ahead, he was wasting it on long discussions about whether an ammunition dump should be left for the Germans or blown up. 'I left the room in the bitter knowledge that the fates of the Armies of the North East . . . were indeed in the hands of one who had lost all power to command,' wrote Archdale.[16]

Meanwhile the first signs that the French would not be able to attack after all were being picked up by Captain Reid at General Blanchard's 1st Army headquarters. Reid had watched Blanchard brief General Altmayer and seen how Blanchard appeared to accept Altmayer's view that V Corps' troops might be too tired to fight on 21 May.[17] This worried Reid – but he would have been even more concerned if he had witnessed what was seen by his opposite number in the French liaison section later that night.

General Altmayer, who seemed to be exhausted and demoralized, was sitting on his bed and was crying silently. He said we must realize the truth: his troops were worn out. He was ready to take the responsibility for refusing to obey orders, and he was quite prepared to take control of a battalion, and to die fighting. But he was not prepared to sacrifice his corps, which had already lost half of its men.[18]

At 11.30 p.m. Archdale finally learned that Altmayer was not going to attack the next day. He spent the next two hours trying in vain to telephone Gort, then gave up, consoling himself with the thought that his Commander-in-Chief must have discovered the French change of plan from another source.[19] In fact General Pownall heard the news from Captain de Vogüe – but not until the morning of 21 May.[20]

The British attack, commanded by 5 Division's Major-General Harold Franklyn, nevertheless went ahead at 2 p.m. on 21 May. It consisted of two discrete arms, which were both to skirt round to the west and south of Arras before going east towards the River Sensée. (Extra details concerning Franklyn's orders are in note 21.)[21] The commander of each arm had an infantry battalion and a battalion of Matilda infantry tanks under his control. (Troop details are in note 22.)[22] The force was, however, more impressive on paper than in practice. Although all seventy-four tanks made available were as heavily armoured as the best French ones, most were the inferior Mark 1 model, whose maximum speed was just eight m.p.h., and whose armament was a mere machine-gun.[23] The newer Matilda Mark 2s with Franklyn's

'Frankforce' were much more formidable. They were protected by even thicker armour (3.1 inches thick), and could be driven at almost twice the speed of their older sisters. Most important of all, they were armed with two-pounder (40mm) cannons, which meant that their shells would be sure to penetrate the most heavily armoured German tanks.[24] But there were only sixteen of them – and the failure to lay on artillery and air support further weakened the British force's potential.[25]

The thrust made by the right wing of the attack, consisting of tanks from the 7th Battalion, the Royal Tank Regiment (7 RTR), backed up by the 8th Battalion, the Durham Light Infantry (8 DLI), appears to have caused the Germans most concern, although the attack's left wing captured more prisoners and destroyed more vehicles. The crisis for the Germans in the path of the right wing of the British attack occurred in the area around Wailly.[26] If the tanks in Rommel's 7th Panzer Division had been available to help protect the village, the Germans might have coped more easily. But by the time the 7 RTR's tanks reached Wailly, Rommel's armour had already headed off to the area north-west of Arras, leaving German infantry and artillery to fend for themselves.[27]

The British tanks approaching Wailly terrorized the German infantry, as Rommel's account of the action reveals:

The enemy tank fire had created chaos and confusion among our troops in the village, and they were jamming up the roads and yards with their vehicles, instead of going into action with every available weapon to fight off the oncoming enemy. We tried to create order. After notifying the divisional staff of the critical situation in and around Wailly, we drove off to a hill 1000 yards west of the village, where we found a light AA [anti-aircraft] troop and several anti-tank guns located in hollows and a small wood, most of them totally under cover. About 1200 yards west of our position, the leading enemy tanks, among them one heavy, had already crossed the Arras–Beaumetz railway, and shot up one of our Panzer IIIs.[28] At the same time several enemy tanks were advancing down the road from Bac du Nord, and across the railway line towards Wailly.[29] It was an extremely tight spot, for there were also several enemy tanks very close to Wailly on its northern side. The crew of a howitzer battery, some distance away, now left their guns, swept along by the retreating infantry. With [Lieutenant] Most's help, I brought every available gun into action at top speed against the tanks. Every gun, both anti-tank and anti-aircraft, was ordered to open rapid fire immediately, and I personally gave each gun its target. With the enemy tanks so perilously close, only rapid fire from every gun could save the situation. We ran from gun to gun. The objections of gun commanders that the range was still too great to engage the tanks effectively, were overruled. All I cared about was to halt the enemy tanks by heavy gunfire. Soon we succeeded in putting the leading enemy tanks out of action.[30]

Had it not been for Rommel's personal intervention, it is possible that the German panic might have turned into a rout, replicating what happened to the French at Sedan. However, Rommel's insistence on leading from the front could also have had disastrous consequences. After the battle he described how his aide, Lieutenant Most, was shot and killed yards away from where he was standing: 'Suddenly Most sank to the ground behind a 20mm anti-aircraft gun close beside me. He was mortally wounded, and blood gushed from his mouth. I had had no idea that there was any firing in our vicinity at that moment, apart from that 20mm gun . . . Poor Most was beyond help, and died before he could be carried into cover beside the gun position.'[31]

Rommel's telegraphist has described an even more dangerous encounter.[32] At one point during the fighting, he and Rommel were cornered by a British tank in a shell hole without any means of defending themselves. But rather than advancing to shoot Rommel or take him prisoner, the British tank crew jumped out and gave themselves up. By some lucky chance, the driver had been killed, and the tank immobilized. So, Rommel remained at liberty, and was able to complete the marshalling of the German troops who somehow halted the British armour.

Rommel was fortunate enough to be confronted in the main by Matilda 1 tanks. An even more audacious raid was made by 7 RTR's Matilda 2s commanded by Major John King, which appear to have bypassed Wailly and carried on towards Mercatel.[33] King started the day with seven Mark 2 tanks under his command.[34] But oil leaks, and engine and track troubles – caused, no doubt, by the long retreat from Brussels – put three out of action even before the first shell was fired. Two of the remaining four were disabled, at least one thanks to enemy action, during the counter-attack. Thus when it came to the crucial stage of the battle, only two were available, the first commanded by King, and the second, appropriately named Good Luck, driven by King's Sergeant Doyle.

The astonishingly successful odyssey through German-held territory that these two tanks made, for much of the time without support, highlighted the appalling planning that had seen Britain go to war with so few of these very effective vehicles in its arsenal. Fired up by the Germans having killed at least one of their comrades, the two tank commanders and their crews rushed through the countryside, shooting any Germans who were unfortunate enough to find themselves in their path. To many of these Germans who fired their 37 mm anti-tank guns at the tanks, only to see the bullets bounce off like peas hitting a brick wall, these tanks, which they had never encountered before, must have seemed indestructible. Finding testimony from the tanks' victims has turned out to be impossible, but King's and Doyle's own reports, handed in after they had returned to England from prisoner-of-war camps, provide an eloquent account of what they achieved.

King's first kills occurred shortly after he passed through the counter-attack's start line:

The Matilda 1s had deployed, and I followed up in the rear centre of two parties. Suddenly we came under [the] fire of 3 or 4 AT [anti-tank] guns about 300 yds to our front. They did not penetrate, so we went straight at them, and put them out of action. My tank ran over one, and I saw another suffer the same fate . . . Small parties of enemy machine-gunners and infantry now kept getting up in front of us, and retreating rapidly, giving us good MG targets for about 10 minutes. There must have been about 150 altogether.

He encountered more threatening opposition when he and his crew came across four enemy tanks about 300 yards away with a roadblock behind them.

They were about the same size as my Matilda 2, and carried a gun and two MGs, and were stationed two on each side of the road with a gap in the middle. They were firing at the Matilda 1s and when they saw me, the two rear tanks swung their guns round in my direction. We opened fire together, and I advanced up the road, Sgt Doyle following, but unfortunately with his fire masked by my tank. Their shells did not penetrate, [but] . . . my 2-pdrs went right through them. By the time I reached them, two were in flames, and some men from one of the others were running over the fields. I passed between them, and went hard at the weakest part of the roadblock, which was composed of a traction engine and some farm wagons. We crashed through the farm carts . . .

King's progress might have been even faster, had he and his crew not been tormented by the fumes and smoke sucked into the fighting chamber of their tank due to a design flaw. King's account explains why this occurred:

Some burning substance got through the louvres of my large forward tool-box, which is inaccessible from inside the tank . . . through which fresh air is drawn into the inside of the tank, and set fire to the oily waste, overcoats, etc. So we sucked in fumes and smoke, instead of fresh air from then onwards . . . My loader couldn't stand the fumes inside, and had to put on his gas mask . . . [My driver] found the red-hot tool-box by his right side so unpleasant that he . . . opened his front visor, and put on his steel visor and crouched [down] low . . . I opened the top to get some air and free some of the fumes and smoke from inside, [but] . . . immediately the lid was hit, and some burning stuff fell into the tank, and on to my head, [causing] slight burns, and a splinter of metal [lodged itself] in the back of [my] neck. We put the fire out with Pyrene.

King's account goes on to describe how, after shutting the turret lid for a while, he was forced to reopen it in spite of the danger 'as the fumes and smoke were getting us down'. He closed it again when he discovered that the Germans were shooting at it and the 'occasional round' was falling inside the tank.

He must have been relieved to find that he was still being backed up by Sergeant Doyle. Doyle's own account describes how King

called me up and when I got to him, he was on fire. His words were 'Doyle, let's finish the job.' So in again we went, knowing we were outnumbered, and never had a chance of coming out of it . . . Then the fun started. I know at least five German tanks he put out [of action] and a number of trucks etc. You see we met a convoy, and did we have some fun! We paid the jerry back for the loss of the rest of the Company, and [at] about 8 o'clock, I saw him get hit in the front locker, but still he kept going. I myself was then on fire, but [he] must have been on fire for an hour or so. [He] would not leave his tank because we were surrounded by German tanks etc, so we just kept on, letting them have it.[35]

It was the Matilda 2's engine rather than anything done by the Germans that eventually turned out to be King's undoing. Shortly after they crashed through the German roadblock, it, as he put it, 'conked out'. King has described what happened next.

We were then hit by something heavier, and the power traverse of the turret put out of action. At the same time, the force of the impact crashed my gunner [Corporal Holland] against the turret side, his left arm breaking the hand traverse mechanism off the turret, and breaking his forearm in doing so. The turret was thus jammed with the guns pointing to the rear, having swung round to finish off the four tanks . . . [However, Holland] said he could carry on, and the driver was able to restart the engine.

At this point a less gallant tank commander might have called it a day, and would have discreetly motored back to Vimy Ridge using Doyle's tank to cover his retreat. But King by this time appears to have turned his back on prudence. Perhaps he was still upset at the way his other tanks had been dealt with by the Germans, or perhaps he was just exhilarated by the heat of battle. Whatever the explanation, he rejected the chance to turn back and, like a man possessed, insisted on pushing on for one last action. This is also covered in his account:

I was following a track across country when, on topping a rise, we came upon a German 88mm AA gun – 30 yds off the track. He immediately started to depress on to me, and I speeded up into a sunken part of the track whose banks gave us complete protection. There were no signs of Sgt Doyle, so I decided to run out the other end of the sunken road, and hope that our direction would bring the gun in our jammed turret to bear on the AA gun. He knocked the top off the bank while we were stationary, but did not hit us. As we came out at the other end, we were lucky enough to get a burst of MG fire on to the gun, and he only fired one round which missed us. Then Sgt Doyle appeared, and opened up with his 2-pdr and put him out of action. We stopped for a breather, and opened up the top which was almost immediately struck by MG fire, and this time the burning stuff that fell in seemed to ignite the fumes, and the whole thing flared up, and then settled down to steady burning. We scrambled out, and dragged the driver from the front seat.

At this point King was down, but he did not yet regard his section as out, and after allowing Doyle to drive him and his crew to the next village, Doyle was ordered to carry on 'his good work'. In the end even Doyle's tank was hit, presumably by something stronger than an anti-tank shell, and he was wounded in the hand. His report mentions as an afterthought that he 'lost' two fingers from his right hand at this stage. Unfortunately neither Doyle, King nor any member of their crews made it back to the Vimy area whence they had started: they were all picked up by the Germans, joining the growing band of British soldiers who were greeted with the demoralizing phrase 'For you the war is over', and taken into captivity.

7 RTR was eventually ordered to retreat. By then at least ten of its twenty-three Matilda Mark 1 tanks and all of the Mark 2s were out of action, and Lieutenant-Colonel Hector Heyland, the battalion's commanding officer, was among those killed; he was shot when he climbed out of his tank to pass an order to another tank commander, a loss that was all the more tragic because it would not have happened if the radio equipment had been adjusted properly before the tanks went into battle.[36]

The 4th Battalion, the Royal Tank Regiment (4 RTR), was to suffer even higher losses. However, before disaster struck, its thrust on the left wing of the counter-attack left the Germans in disarray. Shortly after crossing the Doullens–Arras line, Captain David Hunt, commander of a section of three infantry tanks, came across a column of some fifteen German half-track vehicles (wheels in front and tracks at the back) towing anti-tank guns, and enjoyed watching his corporal's infantry tank drive down the side of the column firing at each in turn. 'Most of the vehicles were put out of action, and lots were burning,' Hunt reported.[37] Twenty-three-year-old Lieutenant Peter Vaux, another 4 RTR officer, reported a further twenty-five German vehicles on fire after 4 RTR's tanks had attacked.

Nevertheless, even during the early stages, there had been scary moments. During one encounter with a German column, an enemy soldier jumped on to Vaux's tank. 'I was looking out of the periscope and saw him looking in – I suppose he saw me looking out!' Vaux wrote later. 'Then a neighbouring tank very kindly turned his machine-gun on me, and that removed my passenger.'[38] The progress made by 4 RTR was helped by the fact that the shells fired by the German 37mm anti-tank guns on wheels could not penetrate the Matildas' armour. Had this been appreciated before the attack started, it would have spared the crews a lot of anxiety that day. 'It's quite an experience seeing guns getting trained on your tank, and wondering if the shell is going to come through,' wrote a soldier who was in one of 4 RTR's tanks during the battle.[39]

However, the tide turned when the 4 RTR tanks moved towards the south-east after reaching Beaurains.[40] Everything had been fine when Vaux peeled off from the rest of the battalion; Lieutenant-Colonel Fitzmaurice, on spotting a heavy German tank, had sent Vaux back to Beaurains to ask the commander of a French tank whether he would come to their aid. But, as Vaux later recalled, the French commander refused to help and Vaux was on his way back to report this to Fitzmaurice when he began to suspect that all was not as it should be:

As I went down the hill, I saw that some of the tanks were moving, but by the time I was 50 yards away, I sensed that something was not quite right. As I approached, I saw that some of the tanks had their tracks knocked off, some of the turrets were crooked, some had smoke pouring out of them, and some had chaps hanging out of the turrets. There were around 15 to 20 tanks, and all of them were 'dead'. I saw my colonel's light tank with a flag on it; the front of the tank was smashed in, and the engine was pushed right back. No one in the tank could have survived.[41]

Vaux ordered his driver to drive to the front of the burned-out tanks where he found Captain Robert Cracroft, the battalion's adjutant, trying to crush some German anti-tank-gun trails with his tank's tracks. While Vaux was standing on the seat inside his own light tank's turret to tell his gunner where the German anti-tank gun crews were hiding, he narrowly missed being added to the casualty list: a brave, or foolhardy, German, who had been manning one of the anti-tank guns until its crew were scattered by the British, reappeared and prepared to shoot him. Vaux's life was only saved thanks to Cracroft, who drew his revolver and shot the German just in time.

The remaining 4 RTR tanks were ordered to assemble on the cross-roads near Achicourt.[42] Only then did the full horror of what had happened sink in. They had started out with forty-two tanks; the battalion had been decimated.[43] But there was still a chance that some of the Matilda 2s, which had been acting independently, would show up, and as dusk turned into night, Vaux and Cracroft sighed with relief, when they heard the unmistakable sound of tanks rumbling and clanking towards them from the east. As the first two large tanks roared up to the crossroads, Captain Cracroft walked up to the leading vehicle and waved his maps in front of the driver's visor. The tank stopped, and it was only when the hatch on top of the turret was opened, and a man in a German uniform popped up, that Cracroft realized the tanks were German. Within seconds, the German tanks were firing at the British, who fired back, both sides somehow missing Cracroft, who ran like a hare to his own tank on the 'British' side of the crossroads. Had it been daylight, 4 RTR might have suffered further losses, but fortunately the battle was only illuminated by moonlight, and a blazing truck, which had been hit by one of the first shells fired. Eventually the Germans withdrew, and the British also beat a hasty retreat.[44] By the time 4 RTR formed up again in Vimy, it only had twelve of the thirty-five Mark 1s that had started out that morning.[45]

Meanwhile, the two Durham Light Infantry (DLI) battalions that were following in the wake of the British tanks had also been suffering. At first, 8 DLI's officers, whose battalion was backing up the western arm of the RTR's thrust, had seen their men's spirits raised by the sight of so many burned-out guns surrounded by German corpses, and because a large number of Germans surrendered without offering any determined resistance.[46] On 21 May they took about four hundred prisoners. 6 DLI, supporting the eastern arm of the thrust, fared even better. Whereas 8 DLI were stopped by German tanks and infantry at Warlus, to the west of Arras, 6 DLI made it round to Agny and Beaurains, to the south of Arras, before being stopped by German gunfire.[47] If the promised artillery and air support had arrived, they might even have broken through the lines of German guns. But the artillery never reached the moving front, and when planes arrived they were German Stukas, whose bombing raids terrified the untested troops in both battalions. (See note 48 for details.)[48]

During the early evening, after the order had been given that the DLI should retreat to Vimy Ridge, some of the 8 DLI troops had the indignity of realizing that, far from being triumphant victors, they themselves were now on the run. They were grateful to be rescued by some tanks from the French 3ième Division Légère Mécanique. It had itself suffered and inflicted heavy losses while repulsing an attack from Rommel's 7th Panzer Division tanks which had hastily returned from the north-west.[49] The French tanks escorted all surviving DLI men whom they found at Warlus, including wounded soldiers who could be moved, through the German roadblocks to Vimy Ridge. The fact that soldiers from the 6 DLI, who had been supporting the left wing of the attack, were extricated from the areas around Achicourt and Beaurains was largely down to a heroic action fought by Y Company, the 4th Royal Northumberland Fusiliers, many of whom sacrificed their lives and liberty to allow their comrades to escape; only a handful of those who fought in this courageous rearguard action returned to the British line from which they had started.[50]

It had been a fiercely contested battle, but in spite of the heroism displayed by the British tank commanders and their men, none of their objectives had been achieved. British soldiers still controlled Arras. However, far from cutting off the German panzers from their supplies and infantry, the counter-attackers had not even managed to hold any of the ground to the south of Arras that they had 'invaded'. Nor had they put enough Germans out of action to impair their fighting capability. Rommel's 7th Panzer Division sustained 378 casualties on 21 May, including those captured.[51] That probably did not include all the foot-soldiers from other units who were killed, wounded or taken prisoner. Whatever the precise figure, the Germans had enough resources to replace those they had lost. The British, on the other hand, were less well endowed: they had no reserves when it came to tanks. Of the seventy-four British infantry tanks that had started out that morning, only thirty-one were available for action the next day.[52] It was an attack that could not be repeated. In other words, all realistic hopes of an independent British force counter-attacking again with their own tanks from the north, and thereby interrupting German progress, had evaporated into thin air. In strategic terms at least, the British appeared, at first sight, to have suffered a devastating defeat.

13: We Stand and Fight

The River Escaut, 21 May 1940
(See Map 9. Also Map 1)

By 20 May, an enormous gulf separated what British generals knew about the mortal peril that endangered the BEF from the south and what the foot-soldiers knew as they fought in the north. On 20 May Lord Gort was so worried that he warned General Billotte that the BEF could not be maintained in its current position if the planned counter-attack against the southern arm of the German offensive failed. Yet on that day, British soldiers who had retreated from the River Dyle and who had been ordered to hold back the northern arm of the German attack along the River Escaut were doing just that, oblivious to the scale of the danger approaching from their rear.[1] Their suspicion that the BEF was in trouble was allayed by a series of deceptive messages coming from their own Commander-in-Chief. The most misleading of all, circulated to battalion commanders on 21 May, stated: 'News from the south reassuring. We stand and fight. Tell your men.'[2]

Gort's troops had been ordered to hold a thirty-two-mile front along the west and south banks of the 'canalized' River Escaut. As on the Dyle, British troops were sandwiched between Belgian forces to the north, and French to the south. However, whereas just three divisions had held the BEF's twenty-two-mile front on the Dyle, seven were guarding the British sector of the Escaut, which ran from north of Oudenarde to Maulde.[3] (See Map 9 on p. 521.) One soldier on that long stretch of riverbank, whose attitude might have been different had he known the full story, was Captain Peter Barclay of the 2nd Battalion, the Royal Norfolk Regiment. On 21 May, his company was holding one of the positions north of Chercq allotted to 2 Division, having reached the Escaut the previous evening.[4] For some time after his unit had dug in there was no combat and, after the war, he described how he had passed the time while waiting for the Germans to arrive:

My batman reported that he'd seen some black rabbits in the park of a château . . . [where] my positions were. Not only that, but he'd found some ferrets and retrievers shut up in the stables. So we thought we'd get in a bit of sport before the fun began. I had a shotgun with me, and we popped these ferrets down a big warren. We were having a rare bit of sport as these rabbits bolted out of [their] burrows when, after about an hour and a half, the shelling started along the river line.[5]

At 7.30 a.m. that same morning, German artillery began to soften up the troops holding another sector of the Escaut, which it intended to overrun: the area to the east of Bailleul held by the 3rd Battalion, the Grenadier Guards.[6] The moment when German artillery started firing at that battalion's 4 Company, its left-hand unit along the Escaut, was recorded by Private Arthur Rice:

We were in trees by the canal. We were all eating breakfast, when suddenly there were explosions all around us. I remember seeing the Company Runner, Guardsman Brind, showered with earth and thought 'Well that's just ruined his breakfast!' I took cover with Guardsman Chapman on 4 Company's extreme left flank. [Then] we were hit by a bomb, and all that was left of Chapman was his pack. I remember thinking: 'Funny, he was wearing that a second ago.'[7]

Les Drinkwater, a stretcher-bearer based in 4 Company's head-quarters, situated in a barn further to the rear of the company's front-line position, has also described the attack:

Suddenly, all hell was let loose. The enemy [had] opened up with artillery, trench mortar and machine-gun fire. The left flank had taken a . . . battering, and Major West [4 Company's commander] became very worried about their position. He ordered Sgt Bullock and myself to proceed at once to that extreme left flank.

When we arrived, we realized the enemy was determined to wipe out this flank. We were lying down behind a bush, bullets were cracking over our bodies, trench mortar bombs and shrapnel shells were exploding. The din was terrible. To our amazement, through all this noise, we could hear the familiar sound of a Bren gun, firing as if it was defying the whole German Army. The Bren was positioned on the other side of the bush, on the canal bank. I admired the guts of the two men operating the gun, but realized they were the reason for the very high concentration of enemy fire.

Suddenly a terrific explosion rent the air. The Bren gun had received a direct hit. It blasted Guardsman Arthur Rice clean through the bush. He looked in a dreadful mess. His knee was smashed, his leg and arm riddled with shrapnel. He also had a head wound. The sergeant and I set to with shell dressings in an effort to stop the bleeding. In the meantime, the other guardsman on the Bren gun lay somewhere on the canal bank. Terrible screams of agony and fear came from him. He had received a nasty head wound, and blood had seeped into his eyes, temporarily blinding him. Sgt Bullock . . . applied a shell dressing . . . After the Bren had been knocked out, all firing by the enemy at this flank had ceased. He [Bullock] soon found [out] the reason for this, for on the opposite bank of the canal, the Germans were launching inflatable rafts. He made a quick decision, and came through the bush leading the soldier with the head wound by the hand. He looked at the severity of Arthur Rice's wounds, and decided that if we took Rice with us, our progress would be so slow that the four of us would either be killed or captured. 'Leave him, pull back!' he said. I [nevertheless] continued to give Rice what attention I could. On looking up, I could see the sergeant leading the blinded soldier by the hand. They were running like blazes. He turned once, and waved me on. They then disappeared over a rise in the ground.[8]

Les Drinkwater's account can be contrasted with the post-action report written by Hauptmann Lothar Ambrosius, an officer in the German 31 Division's 12th Regiment's 2nd Battalion, which was spear-heading the attack. According to Ambrosius:

The carrying of rafts to the river, and the attack itself is very difficult. Crossing the river is worse still. The closer we get to the river, the heavier the artillery fire, and at times, the firing develops into a continuous barrage. English troops fire at us with their machine-guns and rifles from every direction. They shoot from very impressive, well-built and well-concealed positions on the other side of the river. In spite of our many losses . . . and in spite of having to cross at this very unsuitable and very steep river embankment, all the small rafts cross at the ordered positions, and then break the resistance on the other side of the river . . .

The most difficult task is still to be carried out. On the other side of the Schelde [the Flemish name for the Escaut], the terrain is like a swamp. Every-body who has to wade through it has water up to his stomach, and the enemy firing is so strong that, in spite of the high level of effort, and in spite of covering fire from our side of the river, only a few men reach the wood on the other side, about 200 metres from the Schelde. [The wood, on a small hill known as Poplar Ridge, was to be at the epicentre of the fighting that was to come.] Our casualties include 40 killed and 100 wounded.[9]

Les Drinkwater, who had remained with Rice even though it meant he would probably end up being captured, has described how he watched the Germans advancing after they had crossed the river. He then realized that he and Rice might be able to escape after all:

It was obvious to me that it would be foolhardy for the enemy to follow us along the canal back into their own fire. This proved to be correct, as on crossing the canal, they proceeded out from the canal bank, and were now veering slightly to their left.

Again Rice said: 'Leave me, I've had it.' Yet he never complained about his wounds. As we progressed, blood was running down my hand . . . [I thought] 'Hell! I've been hit,' but I wasn't at this stage. The blood came from Rice's arm . . . As we moved along, a couple of guardsmen pulled out of a trench. Then two more. I thought 'Good – here's some assistance,' but these fellows were in no state to help anyone. Then I spotted Major West, running along the canal bank towards us, exposing himself to enemy fire. When I looked again, he had disappeared.[10]

Drinkwater appears to have witnessed the tragic death of Major Reggie Alston-Roberts-West, 4 Company's commander, who had come forward with Lieutenant George Percy, the Duke of Northumberland, to see what could be done to halt the German advance. During their recce, the two officers had visited the Grenadier Guards' 2 Company's positions, on 4 Company's right, along the riverbank. There, they found Lieutenant the Master of Forbes lying helplessly on the ground in a pool of his own blood. He had been hit in the leg. According to Nigel Forbes:

Reggie [Alston-Roberts-West] told me that he wanted to try and make contact with Battalion HQ, so as to organize a counter-attack aimed at pushing the Germans back over the canal. He then asked whether I would like to be left where I was and taken prisoner, or . . . to risk being pulled back towards the Regimental Aid Post. Without any hesitation, I opted for the latter. Next moment Reggie and George, crouching down to avoid being an obvious target, were pulling me along the ground by my shoulder straps, rather like a dead stag is pulled off the hill by its antlers. We had not gone far when I passed out.[11]

Lieutenant Forbes was evacuated successfully, but as Les Drinkwater's account demonstrates, he found that extricating himself and Private Rice was more complicated.

We eventually got to Company HQ at the barn. I found a stretcher for Arthur Rice, and a nice pile of straw for myself where I [lay down] . . . completely exhausted . . . Hearing a voice calling my name, I moved across to the stretcher. Arthur gripped my hand, and said 'Thanks pal!' . . . I returned to my pile of straw with the knowledge we were surrounded. The shelling of my company's position had ceased, [but] bullets could be heard ricocheting off the roof and walls of the barn. The enemy were closing in. Drastic action had to be taken to enable us to escape.

Two company trucks, loaded with equipment, stood in the centre of the barn. It was decided to offload the trucks. Two senior NCOs set up a Bren gun outside the large double doors. Once they started firing, we had to start the vehicle motors. The noise of the Bren would deaden the sound of the motors starting. The stretcher with Arthur lay diagonally across the vehicle. Except for the driver's position, there was no cover at all, apart from the side and tail boards. I crouched alongside the stretcher, my rifle at the ready. We were very fortunate. The large double doors faced the [river] bank. The enemy were closing in from the rear. A decision had been made for the first truck out to turn left, the other to the right in case the leading truck was put out of action. On clearing the barn, we ran straight into the enemy. The essence of surprise was with us. At this stage, the enemy dared not fire in case they hit each other. Once we were through, however, a hail of bullets hit the truck, wounding our driver. But we continued, and were soon over a ridge of high ground and out of sight of the enemy.[12]

Drinkwater and Rice, who both made it back to England, were luckier than many of the other men in 4 Company, who were told to fix their bayonets so they could counter-attack. Most of them were mowed down by German gunfire either before or after they rushed into a cornfield behind their company's former riverside positions which the Germans had occupied.[13]

The following extract from Hauptmann Ambrosius' account confirms that his men were indeed behind what had once been the British front line:

The remaining men in the attacking companies have moved through the wood [the Poplar Ridge wood mentioned above] to maintain the bridgehead and have dug themselves in . . . There are about 70 men in this position. They've been fired at from 9.30 [a.m.] until 5.30 p.m., and have had to defend themselves again and again against the enemy's attacks.[14]

By 11.30 a.m. on 21 May they had already beaten off two British counter-attacks. Then came the third. It was made by the Grenadier Guards' 3 Company, which had been held back in the area around the battalion's headquarters to deal with a German breakthrough. The infantry were backed up by a group of carriers, also manned by Grenadier Guards. Lieutenant 'Tommy' Reynell-Pack, in command of these carriers, was particularly courageous. He and his men managed to silence one German machine-gun position, which was holding up the left arm of the counter-attack. Then he decided they should try to overpower another, on the ridge. Instead of acting within the limitations of his vehicle, he ordered his driver to charge the gun, an action which might well have been successful had he and his men been inside a well-armoured tank, but which was tantamount to committing suicide given that they were in a thin-skinned carrier with no secure chamber for its driver and passenger. Witnesses have reported that the vehicle was hit when it was just fifty yards away from Poplar Ridge. Reynell-Pack was killed, as was the Duke of Northumberland, who, while leading one of the platoons attacking on the right, bravely, but rashly, failed to take cover, preferring to stand up in the face of the German fire, so that he could wave his men forward with his ash stick.[15]

The attack by the carriers evidently made an impression on the Germans on the ridge. Hauptmann Ambrosius' account specifically mentions that

Three [British] armoured vehicles suddenly emerged in front of their own positions in a wheat field. They were followed by an English [infantry] company. The three vehicles were destroyed, and their passengers killed. Two other vehicles were forced to retreat, as they could not go over the trenches, and the English [infantry] company had to retreat with them . . . Our men stood their ground as the vehicles moved towards them, shooting and throwing hand grenades . . . until there was hardly any ammunition left . . . After the attack, only about 40–50 men were left in our battalion [on the ridge].

Ambrosius' account also refers to 'a most unfortunate event' that resulted from the counter-attack: 'The attack by these English vehicles led to a panic 300 metres behind us on the Schelde, and parts of the 5th and 6th Companies rushed back across the river.'[16]

Hauptmann Ambrosius and his men appear to have been particularly struck by the English carriers. But it was the heroism of another Grenadier Guardsman, Lance-Corporal Harry Nicholls, which bolstered the flagging spirits of the counter-attacking foot-soldiers and made a crucial contribution to the British efforts in the front line, a fact which was later recognized when he was given the highest award for valour in the face of the enemy: the Victoria Cross. After the covering artillery stopped firing, the British attack faltered. This allowed the Germans on Poplar Ridge to raise their heads out of the pits they had dug. They then picked off the British infantry one by one. What Nicholls did to save his pinned-down comrades from annihilation has been described in his Victoria Cross citation:

At the very start of the advance, he was wounded in the arm by shrapnel, but continued to lead his section forward. As the company came over a small ridge, the enemy opened heavy machine-gun fire at close range. Lance-Corporal Nicholls, realizing the danger to his company, immediately seized a Bren gun, and dashed forward towards the machine-guns firing from the hip. He succeeded in silencing first one machine-gun, and then two other machine-guns, in spite of being severely wounded. Lance-Corporal Nicholls then went on up to a higher piece of ground, and engaged the German infantry massed behind, causing many casualties, and continuing to fire until he had no more ammunition left. He was wounded at least four times, but absolutely refused to give in. There is no doubt that his gallant action was instrumental in enabling his company to reach its objective, and in causing the enemy to fall back across the River Scheldt. Lance-Corporal Nicholls has since been reported to have been killed in action.[17]

Guardsman Percy Nash provided a more personal account of what happened:

Harry just turned to me and said: 'Come on Nash, follow me!' So I did. He had the Bren, firing from the hip, and I had my rifle. I fed Harry ammunition, and we attacked by means of short rushes forward. Harry was hit several times, and hurt bad, but he wouldn't stop. He just kept on shouting: 'Come on Nash, they can't get me!' Once the enemy guns in the poplars were out of action, we fired on Germans who were crossing the River Escaut. Harry said: 'Wait till they're half way across, then we'll sink 'em. I reckon we sank two boats, each containing about ten men, before Harry turned the Bren on the other Germans located both sides of the Canal. By then we were drawing a lot of small arms fire ourselves.[18]

Nicholls's extraordinarily brave foray only ended when, weakened by his wounds, he collapsed in the cornfield.

Guardsman Lewcock later recalled how he and his comrades benefited from Nicholls's attack: 'I met up with Harry Nicholls and Percy Nash in the corn. I could see that Harry was badly wounded, but appeared just about conscious. At that moment, a Lysander flew over, and the enemy turned their attention to it. This enabled the few of us left to drop behind a low bank at the back of the field. The CSM was almost in tears as he counted us: 39 alive out of over 100 men.'[19]

By the time the Guards retreated, German casualties had risen to 199, including sixty-six killed.[20] Hauptmann Ambrosius concluded:

The Regiment believes that the large numbers of casualties caused by the heavy attacks mean that the bridgehead cannot be held. This is backed up by the fact that no other battalion is able to establish itself across the Schelde. As a result the divisions and corps involved decide to sort themselves out on the eastern side of the Schelde, and to relaunch their attacks after softening up the enemy with artillery . . .

The 2nd Battalion of the 12th Infantry Regiment receives the order to return to their initial positions, but the battalion commander only agrees after receiving the order for a second time, and after Lieutenant Kuthe tells him that the Luftwaffe had seen two enemy columns marching towards the Schelde from the south-west . . . The battalion commander then gives the order to retreat to save the lives of his remaining men.[21]

By then the British casualties were on a par with those suffered by the Germans. Ambrosius' report describes how, two days later, after the BEF's withdrawal from the Escaut, one of his officers 'buries 60 of the English soldiers who died in front of our bridgehead. Amongst them there is a Lieutenant, and a Major West, the leader of the English counter-attack, and . . . the Duke of Northumberland.[22] It is very seldom that the English leave behind their dead, and never so many in one place.'

When Ambrosius and his men retreated, they took with them sixty British soldiers captured during the fighting. 'These prisoners are Grenadier Guards,' Ambrosius reported, adding that the prisoners were 'the best British professional soldiers. They are all 1.80 metres tall, and the youngest have served six, and the oldest 18 years.'[23] They had 'fought to the last man', he said. The sixty prisoners mentioned by Ambrosius were probably included among the 188 Grenadier Guardsmen who, according to the regimental history, had been killed or wounded during the battle.[24] The sixty must also have included Harry Nicholls, who had in fact survived, and recovered.

Later that night, Grenadier Guards patrols were sent down to the Escaut to find out why the area was so quiet. Sneaking through the positions where so many comrades had been killed was an eerie experience, which tested the courage of at least one guardsman. Lance-Sergeant Constantine, who had been involved in the first abortive counter-attack, described what he saw:

I led the Section through the ditch from where we had started the attack on the cornfield. Trying our hardest to make as little noise as possible, we made our way to the end nearest the river. We then slowly climbed out, and moved right towards the cottage that was behind the trench that we had vacated that morning. Everything was silent except the noise of artillery. When we reached the cottage, I signalled that half of the men were to go round to the right, the other half with me to the left. We moved around the building without a sound. When I drew level with the door, I heard a slight creak, and fired a shot at where the noise had come from. I must have re-loaded . . . and got the door open, but there was nobody there. I felt that I had over-reacted, as the shot had made a terrific noise due to the overall surrounding silence. We managed to continue without further mishap, however, and re-occupied the trench.[25]

The battle east of Bailleul was won.

But it was not the only fiercely fought battle on the Escaut on 21 May. Further south, German commanders must have been equally dismayed by the spirited defence put up by the 2nd Royal Norfolks south of Tournai, and particularly by Captain Barclay's A Company on the British battalion's right flank north of Chercq.[26] Barclay has described how, after his early-morning hunt for rabbits was thwarted by German artillery, he proceeded to use hunting tactics against the first Germans who tried to cross the river opposite his company's positions:

After a few more hours, the Germans appeared on the far bank. They were totally oblivious of our presence in the immediate vicinity. I told my soldiers on no account to fire until they heard my hunting horn. A German officer appeared, and got his map out, and appeared to be holding an 'O' Group [order group] with his senior warrant officers. Then they withdrew into the wood, and we heard a lot of chopping going on, and saw the tops of trees flattening out. What they were doing was cutting down young trees to make a number of long hurdles, and they proceeded to lay these across the rubble and remains of concrete blocks in the canal. We kept quiet, and they still had no idea we were there. I reckoned we'd wait until there were as many as we could contend with on our side of the canal before opening fire . . . When we'd enough, about 25, I blew my hunting horn. [On hearing this our] soldiers opened fire with consummate accuracy, and disposed of all the enemy personnel on our side of the canal, and also the ones on the bank at the far side. [This] brought the hostile proceedings to an abrupt halt . . .

Then of course we came in for an inordinate amount of shelling and mortar fire. After the initial burst of fire and their enormous casualties, they knew pretty well where we were. Their mortar fire was very accurate. Not so long after, I was wounded in the guts, back and arm. I had a field dressing put on each of my wounds. We'd had several casualties, and all the stretchers were out. My batman, with great presence of mind, ripped a door off its hinges and, in spite of my orders to the contrary, tied me to this door. He wouldn't take any orders from me from then on, except to go where I told him to go. There I was, tied to this door, and I said, 'Right, well, now you've got to take me round on this door, you've not only my weight to contend with but the door as well!' Of course that took four people and they took me round to deal with a very threatening situation.[27]

In spite of Barclay's bravery, the Germans crossed the river and established themselves on A Company's right flank. Barclay's response was to bring up his small reserve to deal with the breakthrough:

I put my Sergeant-Major [George] Gristock in charge of this small force, which was about ten men including a wireless operator, a company clerk and various other personnel from Company Headquarters. They were not only to hold my right flank, but [they were to] deal with a German post that had established itself not very far off on my right ... Fire came from another German post on our side of the canal. Gristock spotted where this was, and he left two men to give him covering fire. He went forward with a Tommy gun and grenades to dispose of this party, which was in position behind a pile of stones on the bank of the canal itself. When he was about 20–30 yards from this position, which hadn't seen him, he was spotted by another machine-gun post on the enemy side of the canal. They opened fire on him, and raked him through, [and] smashed both his knees. In spite of this, he dragged himself till he was within grenade-lobbing range, then lay on his side and lobbed the grenade over the top of this pile of stones, belted the three Germans, turned over, opened fire with his Tommy gun and dealt with the lot of them. So in fact with that heroic display of his, and the good work done by the rest of that tiny party, the two enemy groups that crossed the canal were disposed of.[28]

Barclay's romanticized version of Gristock's action – an action that earned Gristock the second Victoria Cross won on the Escaut that day – suggests that Barclay might not have witnessed it himself. But a report by Ernie Leggett, a twenty-year-old private in Barclay's company, reveals that he at least saw some of what had gone on from his position on the second floor of a nearby cement factory:

Just over a hundred yards away, I saw a solitary figure crawling towards a machine-gun post set up on the other side of the river. I saw the figure stop and raise his rifle. I heard shots ring out, and almost immediately afterwards, saw the machine-gun post blow up. As this was happening, I saw another machine-gun post being set up on the soldier's right-hand side, this, without doubt, out of his view. It opened fire and the soldier lay still. I then had to turn away.[29]

The Victoria Cross citation gives a complete account of what took place:

Realizing that an enemy machine-gun had moved forward to a position from which it was inflicting heavy casualties on his Company, Company Sergeant-Major Gristock went on, with one man acting as connecting file, to try to put it out of action. Whilst advancing, he came under heavy machine-gun fire from the opposite bank, and was severely wounded in both legs, his right knee being badly smashed. He nevertheless gained his fire position, some 20 yards from the enemy machine-gun post, undetected, and by a well-aimed rapid fire killed the machine-gun crew of four, and put their gun out of action. He then dragged himself back to the right flank position, from which he refused to be evacuated until contact with the battalion on the right had been established, and the line once more made good.[30]

Eventually Gristock was evacuated with Captain Barclay, but Leggett remained in the front line for long enough to witness some of the Germans' massed attacks: 'We saw the Germans coming at us through the wood . . . They also had light tanks,' Leggett reported.

We let them have all we'd got, firing the Bren, rifles and everything. I was on the Bren gun firing from the cover of these old benches, tables and God knows what on this veranda. We killed a lot of Germans. They came almost up as far as the river. We really gave them hell, and they retreated. They attacked us again, and the tanks were coming over their own dead men. To us that was repulsive, and we couldn't understand why they did that. We put them back again; we just fired at them. They weren't the heavy tanks, [and] there was no bridge near me so they couldn't get across the river. We managed to keep them on their side. They attacked us three times, and three times we sent them back. We were being shelled by their artillery, but the mortars were the things which were causing the most damage. It was terrible, just terrible. You can more or less hear the thing sort of pump off, and the next thing you know there's an explosion. Out of my section in the end there was myself, two other privates and a lance corporal.[31]

The Germans' failure to cross the river in strength persuaded their commanders to alter their tactics. Rather than rushing the British defences, they fought a battle of attrition, in the hope that they could mortar and shell the BEF's soldiers into submission. During this part of the action, Leggett was himself hit, and the following extract from his account is a rare example of a man describing how he was wounded.

The Lance Corporal said to me 'Ernie, nip across [to] see if the bastards are penetrating on our left flank.' I left my rifle, and I walked across the floor of this second storey building. The next thing I knew, I'd hit the ceiling. Then I heard a loud bang. I . . . came down and hit the floor. I realized I'd been hit. It was one of those blasted mortars. We'd got no roof. It had come down . . . My left leg was absolutely numb. I was bleeding all over the place. My back was numb from the waist downwards. I couldn't move my legs, and all I saw was the blood coming round on the floor.[32]

He had been shot through the left buttock and also had a hole in his groin where the piece of shrapnel must have exited after it had passed through his body. 'My pals . . . got their and my field dressings,' wrote Leggett.

We only had one each. It was no good just tying them round. It was insufficient. So they bunged one into the wound at the back, pushed it up, put another one into the wound at the front, and they tied the other two on the outside. They then got a piece of rope, and tied a tourniquet. I was bleeding a lot. Fortunately I was numb. I had no pain. That's the amazing thing about it. I just thought of my home and family, and what they were going to do when they heard the news.

After Leggett had been bandaged up, he was carried down to the ground floor of the cement factory. There, he was abandoned by his comrades, who had to return to their positions, and left to make his own way back to Company Headquarters.

I crawled and crawled. They'd taken my trousers off. All I'd got was a rough old pair of pants and battledress top. [In the] meantime they were bombing from above. I was being covered with earth, everything and God knows what . . . As I was crawling along, I was conscious that my finger nails had been worn down so that they were bleeding. My hands were bleeding pulling myself along. [I was determined] to get away, like a wounded animal. It took me ages. It was about . . . 120 yards away from our headquarters. I was almost at my last gasp [when] there was one hell of a big explosion . . . I was covered with earth, and I said: 'Please God, help me . . .' I don't know how long I was out, but I then remember my hands and arms being tugged, and I heard someone say: 'Bloody hell, it's Ernie!' I looked up into the faces of two bandsmen. They take the job of stretcher-bearers . . . They pulled me out, and I heard [one of] them . . . [saying]: 'Bloody hell, he's had it!'

But Leggett survived, and joined the growing number of men who were evacuated to England. There, he ended up in the same hospital as Sergeant-Major Gristock. Unfortunately Gristock, who had both his legs amputated, died before hearing that he had been awarded the Victoria Cross.[33]

There were many courageous acts on the River Escaut on 21 May for which no medals were awarded. Hundreds of British soldiers lost their lives in trying to hold back the Germans. One of the bravest unrewarded actions, and one that had the most upsetting outcome, featured Lieutenant-Colonel Reginald Baker, whose unit, the 8th Royal Warwickshire Regiment (part of 48 Division's 143 Brigade), had been holding the Calonne–Antoing sector, a few miles to the south of the Royal Norfolks' positions, since dawn on 19 May.[34] It is sad to relate that Baker's battalion, mostly novice territorials, should not even have been in the front line on 21 May. They were to have been relieved the night before, having withstood the German artillery barrage for much of 20 May. But as the new day dawned without the expected reserve battalion materializing, Baker and his men had to resign themselves to dodging German bullets and shells for what was to become another thirty-six gruelling hours. (See note 35 for the reason for the delayed relief.)[35]

Not many of these hours had elapsed before Baker learned that the Germans had crossed the Escaut on his right.[36] He reacted in an unconventional way. It is debatable whether a counter-attack was ever feasible, given the number of men at Baker's disposal. Even had it been, most commanding officers would have directed their subordinates to carry it out. Baker decided against this and, after making up a scratch force using battalion headquarters personnel, he announced that he would personally lead it into battle, a reckless and dangerous strategy since it ran the risk of leaving the battalion with no commanding officer. The account by Captain Neil Holdich, a brother officer, has revealed what may have been the true reason for Baker's action, though he did not witness the events:

It appears that Col. Baker was not aware of the full state of disintegration of his forward companies until well on the 21st. He then seems to have gone over to see Col. [Douglas] Money commanding the 1st Royal Scots [who had just relieved Holdich's battalion, the 1st/7th Royal Warwicks, on 8 Royal Warwicks' left]. Exactly what for, I have never been able to discover, but they had a disagreement, at the end of which Col. Money is alleged to have said: 'If my positions had gone like yours, I would have counter-attacked them out long before now,' or words to that effect. This remark was fatal . . . By that time the Germans had already been several hours on the [west] bank, and had consolidated their positions. It was hours too late for an immediate counter-attack. What followed next is little short of fantastic. Col. Baker formed up any available person of his Bn [Battalion] HQ in one enormous widespread 'arrowhead', himself at the point. He seems to have literally got hold of anyone; his intelligence officer . . . his Mess corporal, in all some 40–50 bodies. At a given signal they moved forward, Col. Baker checking dressing and spacing. Thus they moved over the several thousand yards behind Calonne. [They were moving eastwards towards the Escaut from the Battalion Headquarters at Warnaffles Farm, to the west of Calonne.] The ground [there] dips steeply to the river bank. The Germans waited till they had come a certain way down the slope, then opened a withering fire at close range.

After a fierce fire fight, during which many German as well as British soldiers were hit, the British advance was halted, and Baker's force was more or less annihilated. 'Col. Baker [also] fell, shot through the head . . . The Light Brigade at Balaclava . . . may have had some chance of success,' Holdich wrote, adding, 'Baker's [men] had none.'[37]

The following testimony provided by another witness reveals that more lives might have been lost had it not been for the bravery of Major George Byam-Shaw serving with the Royal Scots on the Royal Warwicks' left:

We were in a position on a ridge overlooking the town [Calonne] and the river . . . The situation had become rather desperate, for the forward companies were just managing to hold on . . . Dawn had hardly broken when groups of wounded men were seen to be staggering back evidently trying to reach our regimental aid post . . . In fact they were making straight for enemy MG positions farther down the canal, which took a sharp turn towards our line at this point. Major Byam-Shaw . . . saw the danger they were in. He immediately climbed out of our trench and started to run out to them . . . Everyone in my platoon held his breath . . . The whole of our front was being swept with MG fire and heavily shelled . . . None of us ever thought he could make it . . . The distance must have been at least a quarter-mile. Yet on he went, gaining on them every second, until . . . he caught [up with them], and turned them back to our lines and safety. Even then he had to run the gauntlet in getting back. I remember him climbing up the ridge, rather out of breath but quite calm, as if it were all in an ordinary day's work. Some of the troops were so overcome that they jumped out of their trenches, and slapped him on the back as they congratulated him. At this point our spirits were a bit low . . . but this deed . . . raised them to the highest pitch, and made us feel ready for anything.[38]

Even Major Byam-Shaw's tragic death minutes later – he was hit by a shell while enjoying a cigarette after his long run – failed to demoralize the men, who proceeded to hold the line in the Royal Scots' sector in spite of several German attempts to break through.

Later that night, all Germans on the British side of the river in the Calonne sector were ordered to return to the east bank, which leads one to question whether Baker's costly counter-attack had really been necessary.[39] Unfortunately the losses during that action represented a small proportion of those killed, wounded and missing. By the time the 8th Royal Warwicks withdrew from the Escaut during the night 22–3 May, they could only muster 366 men.[40] The Royal Scots had also suffered, losing nearly two hundred of their soldiers.[41] One consolation was that the Germans had been equally hard hit: for example, the 3rd Battalion of 18 Division's 54th Infantry Regiment that had been attacking Calonne reported 156 men killed, wounded and missing.[42] These, and other heavy losses at different points along the front line, are likely to have been one of the prime factors that persuaded the Germans they could not break through the British troops unless they were first softened up by the artillery.

Whether or not Baker's action had any effect on the Germans, there was no doubting that he had exhibited a dogged determination to do his duty – a determination that was also in evidence in countless other actions along the BEF's front. (See note 43.)[43] It is this steadfastness, this willingness to stand and fight, that differentiates the BEF's performance from the defeatist behaviour of the French at Sedan. It enabled the British Army to hold the line on and behind the Escaut until orders were given to retreat to the Franco-Belgian frontier, the so-called Gort Line, during the night of 22–3 May.

Ypres and Arras, 21–4 May 1940
(See Map 8. Also Maps 1, 2, 7 and 10)

Even while British tanks were making their counter-attack to the south of Arras, a last-ditch attempt was being made by Allied generals to stitch together a more powerful multinational thrust towards the south. But the 21 May meeting convened by General Weygand, which eventually took place at Ypres town hall, turned out to be a disaster from start to finish. A long catalogue of problems was encountered, starting with the most fundamental problem of all: Lord Gort, whose troops were to play a crucial role in the counter-attack, could not be contacted during the early hours of 21 May, and tracking him down was all the harder because his Advanced Headquarters were being moved from Wahagnies (seven miles south of Lille) to Prémesques (five miles west of Lille).

A further complication was caused by Gort's decision to attend a conference with his corps commanders at Wambrechies (five miles north-west of Lille), and his failure to ensure that his liaison officer at Army Group 1 knew at all times where he was.[1] Gort's absence left Weygand with the choice of either aborting the meeting or carrying on regardless. He chose the latter option.

Because Billotte was also late, Weygand, unbriefed as he was, started the meeting with the King of Belgium and General Van Overstraeten without the necessary support. As if that was not enough to highlight the lack of co-ordination between the Allies, it soon became apparent that Weygand and the King of Belgium disagreed over how troops should be made available for the counter-attack.[2] Weygand, quite reasonably, suggested that the best military solution required the Belgians to retreat to the River Yser, so that the Allies would be left holding a shorter line than on the Escaut; this would have enabled Weygand to take some British troops out of the line for the counter-attack without significantly weakening Allied defences. The King and Van Overstraeten replied that they did not like that solution, and told Weygand that their troops were too tired for such a move. They also feared that their men would become demoralized if they were forced to abandon so much

Belgian territory.³ However, the true reason for the King's opposition
is likely to have been more complicated: he was concerned that his
troops were being used to support a counter-attack whose principal
object was to help the British escape from the encirclement. After the
meeting he told Van Overstraeten that he believed the Belgians would
be abandoned as soon as they had served the British and French purpose.⁴

The King had solid grounds for suspecting that the British might not
have Belgium's best interests at heart. On the previous day, he had been
told of the plan calling for British forces to abandon the Escaut so that
they could counter-attack towards the south.⁵ (See Chapter 12.) This
plan, which would have left the Belgians in the lurch, prompted Ironside
to confide to his diary: 'What is to happen to the Belgians I really don't
know. They have the longest wheel to make, and are very unwilling
to evacuate Belgium completely. I daresay that they will never get out
at all.'⁶

Nevertheless, Weygand might have at least attempted to silence the
King's opposition by informing him that the battle was already lost if he
did not back down. Had Weygand only dared to reject all other plans
after explaining that they would fatally weaken the front line, a different
outcome might have been achieved. This approach would have isolated the King since, as Weygand well knew, the Belgian Government
supported the French Commander-in-Chief's strategy rather than the
King's.⁷ However, Weygand, fearing perhaps with good reason that
his bluff might be called, and not wanting to be sucked into a long-
winded stand-off when he knew he was expected in Paris, backed down.
Instead he put forward a compromise that took the King's position into
account: the Belgian Army, which was then west of the Oudenarde–
Ghent stretch of the Escaut, and west of the canal between Ghent and
Terneuzen, would not be asked to retreat as far as the Yser.⁸ It would
withdraw to the River Lys, where it would take over part of the British
line. The French Army would take over from the British a portion of
the Allied line to the south, which was to run along the Franco-Belgian
border. Thus, British troops could be released notwithstanding Belgian
intransigence.

The King at once accepted this solution, and a deal was struck, which,
in the short term, held together the Franco-Belgian alliance. But the
plan, which would stretch the Belgian Army's limited resources to
breaking point, was to benefit no one in the long term, and Weygand's

decision to fit in with it was to be an important factor in the Belgian inability to hold the northern sector of the Allied line. Ironically, in attempting to save the Allied armies, Weygand had sown the seeds of an even greater catastrophe than had happened eight days earlier at Sedan: the capitulation of the Belgian Army, which, following this agreement, would only be a matter of time.

Weygand left the meeting before Gort had been contacted. Although the BEF's Commander-in-Chief immediately agreed to come to Ypres when he heard his presence was required, he and General Pownall, who accompanied him, never had the opportunity to talk to Weygand about the dangers inherent in the French general's compromise solution. Their failure to voice their opposition to it may also have been influenced by a misunderstanding that, according to Pownall's diary, occurred during their meeting at Ypres later that day with Billotte and the Belgian King. Pownall has recorded how, at the end of this meeting, Billotte asked the King, who until that point had stated that he would not retreat from the Lys, whether he would withdraw to the Yser once the Lys could no longer be held. The King replied 'apparently regretfully' that he would, and it was this reply that appears to have convinced the British generals that the King had, albeit unwillingly, agreed to retreat to the Yser after all.[9]

Whatever the King had said, this British interpretation certainly did not accord with what Van Overstraeten and the King believed they had agreed. They had intended to reserve their position about whether they ever would agree to withdraw from the Lys, the pre-condition that needed to be fulfilled before their agreement to go to the Yser was triggered. The next morning, long after the Allies' generals had gone their separate ways, the King told Van Overstraeten that he could not countenance such a retreat.[10]

Even before this misunderstanding occurred Gort had grounds for refusing to support what Weygand and the King had agreed. As Gort and Pownall explained at the Ypres meeting, the British divisions that were to be taken out of the line were not among the BEF's best, and would be even less effective given the shortage of ammunition that had resulted from the BEF's cut lines of communication.[11] In view of this, it was unlikely that a counter-attack using these divisions would succeed.

Perhaps if the more ruthless General Alan Brooke had been in Gort's shoes, he would have insisted that the Germans could not be beaten by the force at Weygand's disposal and, that being the case, he would have told Churchill that it was better to evacuate the BEF immediately, rather than waiting until a worse crisis occurred. Brooke was to adopt this approach successfully when, after the Dunkirk evacuation, he was the Commander-in-Chief of the 2nd BEF. (See Chapter 36.) Perhaps Gort might have reached the same conclusion if Churchill had not, two days earlier, pugnaciously, but on this occasion impractically, urged the Commander-in-Chief via Ironside to link up with other troops south of the Somme, rather than proposing an evacuation.[12] Ironside, by supinely agreeing with Churchill's suggestion without first taking soundings from the BEF's GHQ, had only made it harder for Gort to say what should be done. Had Ironside contacted Gort's staff, he would have discovered that during the night of 18–19 May they were already thinking seriously about how to extricate the BEF. An evacuation was still being considered three nights later: after returning from Ypres to the Advanced GHQ, Pownall had instructed Lieutenant-Colonel Bridgeman to draw up an evacuation plan.[13]

But Brooke was not the Commander-in-Chief during the night of 21–2 May, and Gort, who had missed seeing Weygand because of his failure to organize his headquarters so that he was always in touch with Army Group 1 and the French Commander-in-Chief, did not yet have the conclusive evidence he felt he needed to stand up to the Prime Minister. Encouraged by the French General Robert Fagalde, who said, in his best English, 'You must do it, sir,' and against his own better judgement, Gort finally agreed to the plan proposed by Weygand, confining himself to telling the King of Belgium on his way out of the meeting, 'It's a bad job.'[14] Bridgeman's evacuation plan, which advocated lifting the BEF off the beaches between Dunkirk and Nieuport, with extensions of the evacuation area to Ostend and Calais, was made redundant by this decision – for the moment at least. It was duly put on ice on 23 May.[15]

In the course of the meeting at Ypres, it was also agreed that the BEF could retreat from the Escaut to the Franco-Belgian frontier line, which they had held before the Germans' 10 May attack; the British corps commanders had insisted this was necessary if the Germans were not to break through the existing line.[16] The withdrawal, which was to start on the night of the 22–3 May, would be followed the next night by the relief of three British divisions, two by the French and one by the

Belgians, which meant that the counter-attack could not take place before 26 May.[17] The withdrawal represented another setback for the Belgians: while the British were to occupy prepared positions, the Belgians were retreating to the River Lys, where little had been readied for what was to come. This relative inequality in the state of the positions prompted Gort, on leaving the conference, to ask Admiral Keyes whether the Belgians thought the British were 'awful dirty dogs'.[18] Keyes replied diplomatically, but incorrectly, that the King wanted to do whatever he could to help the British escape the disaster they faced if they became encircled.

The downbeat end to the conference was not the last blow to hit the Allies that night. The next morning one of Billotte's aides staggered into Major Archdale's office, his head swathed in bandages, to report that he and Billotte had been involved in a car crash.[19] Billotte never recovered consciousness and died in hospital, leaving Army Group 1 with no one who had heard Weygand's plan at first hand.

The high-level discussions at Ypres certainly did not help the British garrison in Arras, which now had to remain in place for several days in case it was needed as a launch pad for Weygand's counter-attack. Neither did the French counter-attack towards Cambrai on 22 May provide any more comfort. Like the Arras attack by the British tanks, it was repulsed, after a promising start. That left the Arras garrison exposed. Between 17 and 22 May Gort had placed a line of BEF troops along the canals stretching from Millonfosse (west of St Amand) in the east to Gravelines in the west.[20] They were to cover the southern and south-westerly flanks of the BEF forces on the Escaut. But the line, including La Bassée, Béthune, Aire and St Omer, did not protect Arras, which stuck out from the newly established cordon like a vulnerable sore thumb.

This was one of several reasons why defending Arras was never going to be easy. As Eric Cole, a member of the British garrison from 17 May, remembered, his battalion, the 1st Welsh Guards, had to hold the town despite obstacles placed in their path by the many retreating civilians.

There were literally thousands of people, a never ending stream of refugees, some pulling hand carts, others with prams, [and] horse[s] and cart[s]. Young people, old people; it was a shambles; all rushing to get as far away from the enemy as possible. One poor old man threw himself in front of our truck. He wanted us to run [him over]. With difficulty, we got him to one side . . . [We wondered] how . . . an army [could] manage to put up a line of defence with such a crowd everywhere.[21]

As the British Army's defences were put in place, the situation became increasingly dangerous for soldiers and civilians alike. Lance-Sergeant George Griffin, from the Welsh Guards' carrier platoon, which was to play such a significant role in the subsequent escape from the town, has described how the danger was increased by the laying of anti-tank mines across main roads leading into Arras: 'A dear old French lady came waddling to the outer fringe of the mines wanting to come through. I shouted at her to stop. Then holding her hands, [I] brought her through the minefield in a nerve racking "pas de deux". She was quite oblivious of the risk.'[22]

Roadblocks were also built up across minor roads leading into the town. 2nd Lieutenant Tony Younger, a Royal Engineer, was instructed to place his unit's anti-tank mines across three such roads to the east of Arras, where it was initially assumed the Germans would attack first. After the mines had been put into position he went to sleep in a nearby house, only to be woken up at around 1 a.m. by a loud explosion that shattered his bedroom windows: 'What had happened was that a huge French lorry, wanting to go eastwards, had refused to obey our sentry's order to stop, and had driven over a mine,' wrote Younger:

The French driver was miraculously alive, although suffering from severe shock, but our sentry, who had jumped out of his slit-trench in a last attempt to stop the lorry, was desperately wounded . . . I told one of our drivers to take the wounded man to the Welsh Guards' medical post at once, and two of his friends volunteered to go with him. He never complained as we laid him in the back of the truck, although we could see from his face the pain he was in. His friends returned a couple of hours later with the news, which I had been expecting, that he had died before reaching the doctor. We were all deeply affected.[23]

To prevent another such accident, Younger requisitioned some cars from a nearby garage, after giving the owners notes to say they would be compensated by His Majesty's Government, and had them placed across the road on the Arras side of the mines.

Younger was to see many more injuries before he left Arras. The

most extreme carnage was caused by bombs dropped near the railway
station on 19 May. Two trains carrying civilian evacuees were hit.[24] An
extract from Younger's account reveals what he witnessed as he
attempted to drive past the railway station after the bombing, only to
find his path blocked by a building that had collapsed on to the road:
'Our sappers worked fast to open up a way through, and as I climbed
back into my truck, I saw a man carrying a young girl along the pavement
next to us. She was six or seven years old, and I remember that she was
wearing a white skirt. The expression of utter horror on [the father's]
face has stayed with me to this day, and it was only when I looked down
and saw that the girl had no head that I realized why.'

Shortly after the British soldier had been blown up by the mine,
Younger saw German tanks for the first time. But they were put off by
the obstacles placed in their path, and retreated without attempting to
pierce the British line. They were not the only armoured vehicles that
reached the outskirts of Arras. There were frequent probing attacks,
which were invariably called off once the Germans discovered that the
roadblocks were staunchly defended. One such hit-and-run raid was
made on 20 May at the crossroads that had to be passed by anyone
driving south-east from Arras to Cambrai or south to Bapaume, where
a barricade had been built round an upturned bus.[25] The first 'invader'
was a cow, which, it was thought, the attackers released to draw British
fire. A Welsh Guard shot it before it could set off one of the anti-tank
mines in front of the barricade.[26] Next, an open-topped car driven by
Germans appeared. Most of the occupants, who ran for their lives when
the British soldiers opened fire, were hunted down and dispatched in
the back-streets where they had taken refuge.

By this stage, the Welsh Guards had abandoned their barricade near
the crossroads, and they fired at the six tanks following the car, and at
infantry sheltering behind them, from loopholes made in the walls of
surrounding houses. One of the best positions was on the third floor of
a house above a café. Although the tanks never made a determined
attempt to break through the barricade, their shells paved the way for
such an attack. The British soldiers above the café were almost suffocated
by the acrid black smoke caused by fires ignited on the floors below,
and after the flames had made the staircase impassable, they only escaped
by jumping down from a first-floor window at the back of the house
on to a shed, whence they climbed down to the garden.[27] The defenders

overlooking the crossroads realized that they were outgunned. Bullets fired by the platoon's most powerful weapon, an anti-tank rifle, made no impression on the tanks' armour. Fortunately for the defenders, the tanks did not follow up their initial attack, and eventually withdrew. But there were fears on the British side that they would soon return, and Private Williams, one of the defenders above the café, noted ominously that there were 'large gaps' in the barricade.[28]

On 20 May reinforcements arrived in the form of a battalion of Royal Northumberland Fusiliers and another of Green Howards.[29] The Green Howards had barely moved into their and the Welsh Guards' head-quarters at the Palais St Vaast in the centre of town when their attempt to unpack was disturbed by two deafening bangs. Almost simultaneously those inside the Palais saw a large flash, and a sheet of flame leaped into the sky as four of the battalion's trucks exploded. Eleven British soldiers were killed or injured, according to an account by the 5th Green Howards' Captain Denis Whitehead, who had been inside the Palais and was shielded from the blast. While he was sympathetic to those who had been hurt, he took a rather hard line when dealing with his 'terrified' batman, who had lost a finger in the explosion, telling him that 'it was bound to hurt, but there were lots worse off'.[30] Some of the men had been killed, and the injuries suffered by many of the survivors can only be described as horrific: the blasts had stripped off their clothing, and flayed them alive.

By this time Arras was a completely different town from that seen by the Welsh Guards on their arrival. The crowds of refugees had either left or retreated to cellars. There, they lived a subterranean existence, hidden from the troops guarding the town. Whitehead remembers being surprised by this when he arrived on the night of 20–21 May: 'I tramped up the empty ghostly streets [with their] modern shops on both sides [displaying] . . . gents' natty suitings, shoes . . . boots [and] groceries . . .' he wrote.

We passed a dead dog, [which had] four legs sticking straight up, and then a tailor's dummy in a shop doorway which made me jump! Broken glass . . . helped to make our tramping almost ear-splitting, and all the time, one felt one ought to be quiet. We passed a house surrounded by a high brick wall, and up went a green star shell. I asked what it was, and the I.O. [Intelligence Officer] said: 'Oh, 5th Column . . .' It was the first time that I had considered that civilians might still be about . . . They were though . . . They used to snipe our sentries at Bn HQ from across the street. We had 'sniper hunts' each evening. It was not until the third day that I found a cellar full of women and kids in some other large building not 100 yards away from Bn HQ. What they lived on God knows. Few came above ground while we were there.

Each night while the Green Howards were in Arras, there were discussions at the evening conference convened by the garrison commander, General Petre, about whether orders would be received to evacuate the town. But each night arrangements made in the expectation that there would be an evacuation were called off. Meanwhile, the British soldiers in the garrison huddled in the cellars of the Palais or residential houses during the bombing, and waited for peace to return to the town again. Even this was no insurance that they would not be hurt. On 20 May, thirteen Welsh Guards were crushed and killed when their air-raid shelter caved in after it was hit by three bombs.[31] On the same day another twenty men were killed or wounded, including fifteen Welsh Guards, when the building they were in was struck.[32] The repeated air raids and the officers' realization that they were unlikely to escape made some maudlin and depressed.[33] Although British troops had been lined up to the north-west and the east of the town, the Germans were gradually either capturing or killing them, or forcing them to pull back. By the evening of 23 May, it became obvious that if the garrison was not pulled out soon, all escape routes would be closed and Arras surrounded. (Details are in note 34.)[34]

That night, according to Captain Whitehead's account, the evacuation conference was interrupted by one of General Petre's staff officers, who put his head round the door, and said, 'Excuse me, sir. Message from the Commander-in-Chief. Arras will be held to the last.'[35] That message had a strange effect on all who heard it. If not a death sentence, it was confirmation that everyone present would probably be captured if they survived. Yet men who, minutes before, had been downcast and dejected, all of a sudden perked up and began to behave like heroes, saying, 'Well, at least we know where we are now,' and 'There'll always be an England.' The message that reached the Welsh Guards around the perimeter was even more dramatic: they were to 'fight to the last man and last round'.[36]

After the message had been circulated, Lieutenant Christopher

Furness, a Welsh Guards' officer, whose actions that night were to be even more heroic than his brother officers' stirring words, got ready for the battle that lay ahead. Twenty-eight-year-old 'Dickie' Furness was one of the most popular men in the regiment, and one of the richest. The eldest son of a viscount, he was the heir to a vast fortune that, in 1940, was valued at £1 million.[37] He was also very well connected: during the late 1920s his stepmother, Thelma Furness, had been the lover of the then Prince of Wales (who later became Edward VIII, and after his abdication the Duke of Windsor). Even after the love affair ended, Thelma had remained on friendly terms with the Prince and Dickie had benefited from the connection. When he joined the Welsh Guards in 1932, it was probably no coincidence that the Prince of Wales was the regiment's colonel. In 1936 Dickie Furness was among the select few called upon to guard George V's coffin in Westminster Hall, and received a note of thanks from the new monarch. Dickie Furness himself had broken plenty of girls' hearts, but in 1940 he was engaged to be married to Princess Natasha Bagration, a cousin of Marina, Duchess of Kent. The fact that he had lots of female admirers was not surprising. He was very dashing and liked to drive around in fast cars, but he was known especially for his sporting prowess: he shot five bull buffalo within as many minutes when he had visited Kenya as a nineteen-year-old. In Ireland, he had been joint master of the Limerick Hunt and was said to be a fearless rider.[38]

It was clear to anyone who saw him getting on to the train that was to take him on the first stage of his journey to France in 1940 that he did not intend to stop being sporty just because he was joining the BEF. He had two sleek greyhounds with him, and when asked whether he was allowed to keep them, he pointed proudly to the labels attached to their collars, which were engraved with the words, 'By order of Lord Gort'.[39] He had not always been so punctilious about asking his superior officers' permission before committing rash acts. In 1935 he had been asked to leave the Welsh Guards after he was caught *in flagrante* with another officer's wife.[40] But if he did not always give his brother officers the respect that was their due, he certainly had the common touch with his men, and that may explain why, after war was declared, the Welsh Guards welcomed him back. When the man who took care of the dogs for him in France was caught poaching, Furness ticked him off and ordered him to keep the dogs on a lead in future but, in the same breath, he told him where he could find more rabbits.[41]

During the evening of 23 May, Furness's response to the news brought to his battalion's headquarters that a German machine-gunner, who had escaped from a downed plane, had been firing at British patrols, was typically robust: he tossed a coin with another officer for the privilege of going out with the carriers to bring the man in. He won the toss and insisted on sitting in the front of his carrier with the Bren gun so that he would be in the thick of any action. As they approached the area to the north of Arras where the machine-gunner was supposed to be concealed, Furness fired his gun to see whether the German would reveal his position. Seconds later, the carrier was struck by a shell, whereupon Furness, who had been hit by splinters in one of his legs and in one buttock, stood up and shouted, 'Who in the hell did that?' The 'culprit', a British anti-tank gunner, who had been narrowly missed by Furness's original burst, then appeared, and Furness and his crew had to return empty-handed to Arras, their carrier having been put out of action.[42]

There they learned that the garrison had finally received the order to abandon the town. General Franklyn had telephoned Gort's head-quarters at around 10 p.m., and told one of Gort's staff that if the garrison troops did not evacuate Arras that night, they would all be taken prisoner, only to be informed that the evacuation order had already been given: two officers who were supposed to hand it to General Franklyn were on their way to Vimy, where Franklyn's headquarters were situated, via Douai, and had evidently been delayed.[43]

At 2 a.m. on 24 May, the Welsh Guards, including Furness, followed the other troops out of the town, but on approaching the road to the north-east of Arras, which led to Douai, they found that the bridge over the railway had been destroyed. Although soldiers on foot could climb over the rubble and continue down the road, the motor transport, consisting of around forty trucks, was diverted to another road that branched off to the south. Unfortunately for the drivers, German gunners already had this southern road in their sights, and the column was halted by their fire.

According to the account by the Welsh Guards' quartermaster, Lieu-tenant Buckland, Furness then approached him in his carrier, and asked:

'What have you got, and where are you making for?' I answered that I had the whole Bn transport and MT [Motor Transport] personnel, and was making for Douai, those being my orders. He said: 'You cannot go down this road, or you'll be shot up, as Jerry is there; you'll have to turn round and proceed N [North].' I then explained it would be impossible in the short time [available] to turn the transport around in such a narrow road, particularly the three tonners, and that, as the mist was lifting, I would be seen by the enemy. I had only Bren guns to protect the column. It had been impressed on me that the Germans should not be aware of the fact that Arras was being evacuated. He said: 'Don't worry about Jerry. I'll go and shoot him up and keep him busy while you turn and get out' . . . I was amazed at Lieut. Furness' calmness and composure, for only a few hours previously, I had dressed his wounds, and on my suggesting he should see the Medical Officer, [he] smiled and said he couldn't be bothered. He was too busy fighting the Germans.

After this discussion, Furness disappeared in the direction of the firing. 'This was the last I saw of Lieut. Furness,' Buckland reported.[44]

The most detailed account of the ensuing action, which resulted in Furness being awarded the Victoria Cross and in Buckland and his forty lorries being saved, was by Lance-Sergeant George Griffin, commander of one of the four carriers that followed Furness's into battle. The account confirms that all of the carriers reached the main Arras–Douai road without being troubled by any Germans. Further along this road, they saw four light tanks, and Furness asked their commander what they were going to do. The tank commander replied that he was going to attack the machine-guns, whereupon Furness said, 'Then I shall come too.' However, before he could move, his carrier stalled, being out of petrol, and he ordered the commander of another carrier to step down so that he could take his place. This carrier, with Furness inside, was then driven off, with two other carriers following about fifty yards behind. The fourth had to drop out, its gun having jammed.

Griffin's account continues:

On mounting the ridge [to the north of the Arras–Douai road], we could see there was a German strong-post on the crest. Mr Furness bore to the right, so as to take the position in the flank. As we approached the top, Griffiths, my driver, said, 'I'm wounded.' I looked at him, and he seemed so casual that I asked him if he would carry on, and he said 'Yes', but from then on he could only use his left arm. I had followed Mr Furness, and on bearing round to the left of the post, I saw one of the tanks with Mr Furness' carrier close behind it. Neither [was] firing. Griffiths could hardly control the machine by this time, and it continued in a circle down the ridge, and back again. I kept firing whenever we were facing the right way. We came round to the post a second time, and this time managed to stop close to Mr Furness' carrier. Griffiths was again hit, this time in the thigh. I saw Mr Furness stand up in his carrier, grappling with a German over the side. Mr Furness shot him with his revolver, and he fell to the ground. Fire was very hot by this time, pinging on the plates. It was suicide to stand up.[45]

We then moved off again on another circle. This time, as we came in, Griffiths was so weak that he crashed into the back of Mr Furness' carrier, and stalled his engine. I said 'Start up again Griffiths.' The starter is on the right, so he had to do this with his wounded arm. He managed it though, but the engine refused to start . . . While this was going on, four Germans came out from the post, and started walking up to us. Perhaps they thought we were finished. Anyway I had a lovely clear shot, and finished them . . . [off] with a full magazine. All of a sudden, the engine started, and Griffiths managed to back away. There was no sign of life either in the tank, or in Mr Furness' carrier, bar the . . . [German] squirming on the ground that he had shot. I depressed the muzzle of the Bren to finish off the German . . . [But] I could not get to him, and on reflection, I am glad I didn't.

Somehow they made it back to the Arras–Douai road, with Griffin in the driver's seat. But that was not the end of their ordeal, according to Griffin: 'When I looked over the back of the carrier, it was all on fire: the other side [from where] Roberts [was sitting]. He was holding Williams in his arms. I shouted to him: "Put out the fire Roberts!" He said: "I'm wounded, I can't." I grabbed hold of his Pyrene, and squirted it on the fire, but [it] did not make any difference.'

Meanwhile Corporal Jones, who had stepped down from his carrier to allow Furness to take over, had been peering through the mist to see what was happening to his comrades. His account, which also survives, describes what he saw: 'All of a sudden we noticed a carrier coming up the hill with red flames streaming out behind it. We could see it was Sjt. Griffin, because he was driving standing up. He seemed to be trying to help Griffiths at the same time. He drove up so fast, I thought he was going to run us down. I ran up to him. He was shouting at us to hurry up, [while] helping Griffiths out at the same time.'[46]

As Griffin's report reveals, Griffiths had been incredibly brave: 'His most serious wound was to the upper arm. The flesh [had been] shot away revealing the white bone,' Griffin reported. Roberts was also wounded: a bullet had passed through both of his ankles. There was nothing they could do for Williams. When they opened up his jacket, they found a big hole in his chest. This extremely courageous man, who had insisted on accompanying the men in Griffin's carrier in spite of being told to get out, was dead. Jones's account also mentions some of the other casualties:

A tank came up the road out of the battle, tearing along as fast as it could go. When it got near, we could see . . . the chap on top had his head and shoulders out of the turret, [and he was] supporting himself with his elbows on the edge of it . . . He shouted to me as he went past: 'Give us a hand' . . . [Then] I could see him sinking back, and his head falling on one side . . . Lewis [a gunner for one of the carriers] . . . lifted the chap into a sitting position on the top of the turret, and I climbed up to help him down. We saw that his leg was blown half away, with his foot dangling loose. He was holding it up with his finger hooked in his gaiter. He had bags of guts. The driver climbed out on his own. He had been wounded in the shoulder. He had left his engine running, so I said to him, 'I think I had better switch it off.' He said, 'Don't go too near. The ammo is still going off.'

He told Jones that it was the exploding ammunition which had done for his comrade's leg. They laid the injured man on the side of the road just across from where Williams was lying. Those who could then jumped on to the one carrier that could still be driven, and drove off to report what they had seen and done.

But that was not quite the end of this extraordinary saga. The gunner in the third carrier to have reached the German machine-gun post – who, confusingly, was also called Griffiths – has described how he arrived back at the Arras–Douai road shortly after the other carrier departed:

We saw the Sjt Major [the officer with the injured leg] lying in the ditch with two men giving him rum out of a bottle. We put the Sjt Major on the tool box, and I [lay] beside him, and the two others got into the gunner's seat. We started off with the tank back the way we had first come. We were crossing a field, when . . . [the Germans] started firing at us out of a wood to our rear with an AT [anti-tank] gun. I was struck in the behind with a splinter, and the next shot went through the back of the carrier. The engine gradually stopped. I saw the tank stop too, and the officer and another man got out, and ran round the back to have a look at it. Then they ran across the field, and so did the other four out of the carrier, leaving me alone with the Sjt Major. I lifted him down on to the grass, and put a blanket underneath him. He was moaning, [but] I could not do anything for him. So I took my rifle and left him there, and went off after the others.[47]

Of the ten men whose carriers took on the Germans during that action, four were killed, including all of the men in Furness's vehicle, and five wounded or taken prisoner. Only Lance-Sergeant Griffin was unscathed. Because the witnesses could not be contacted when the Welsh Guards returned to England, no awards were given for some time. It was only in 1946 that Furness's bravery during the evacuation from Arras was recognized. Thanks to the carriers' attack, which he had led, the battalion's transport escaped before it could be shot up by German guns. As a belated tribute to his courageous act, Furness was rewarded with a posthumous VC.[48] Curiously, none of the other men involved received an award, although some appear to have been equally brave.

PART 2: THE EVACUATION

15: Boulogne and the Useless Mouths

Arras and Boulogne, 17–23 May 1940
(See Map 11, and inset on Map 12. Also Maps 1 and 2)

Boulogne was first sucked into the growing débâcle because it was thought to be a safe haven. That is why BEF Adjutant-General Sir Douglas Brownrigg decided to send Rear GHQ from Arras to Boulogne on 17 May, as soon as he learned the true nature of the German breakthrough.[1] However, nowhere on France's north-west coast was safe, and this decision, made without consultation with the French, not only jeopardized the safety of the BEF's pen-pushers, but undermined the already deteriorating Anglo-French relationship.

Captain de Voguë has written about the 'very cordial' relations that existed between the two nations until the Germans broke through the French 9th Army.[2] From then on, French liaison officers had to put up with 'a coldness bordering on insolence' from their British counterparts, and their presence in Gort's command post at Wahagnies was 'barely tolerated'. According to de Voguë, British officers at GHQ 'became obsessed by the fear that they might be cut off from their bases on the French coast', and this prompted them to 'turn in on themselves'.

A report by Paul Le Tallec, a liaison officer with Rear GHQ in Arras, demonstrates how the worsening Anglo-French relationship impinged on him.[3] Before the German breakthrough, the British could not have been more welcoming. He and his boss, Commandant Comte Henri Marty, were invited to set up their office in a small house in Arras that had been allocated to the British. Since it was just fifty metres away from the main GHQ offices at Palais St Vaast, they had no difficulty in fulfilling their duties. They were even allowed to have their meals in the British canteen. But everything changed after the German panzer divisions crossed the Meuse. During the night of 14–15 May, the Luftwaffe bombed the Hôtel de l'Univers in Arras, where many British staff had been billeted, killing around fifty of them. The next day, Le Tallec visited GHQ's offices to ask whether he and the French liaison staff could take refuge in the Palais St Vaast cellars, but his request was turned down on the grounds of 'security' and 'secrecy'. 'It was the first sign I saw of the infighting which was to come,' he reported.

It was the move from Arras to Boulogne that irreparably damaged the liaison network. No one on the British side deigned to tell the French liaison officers that GHQ was about to leave Arras, although it would have been easier to disclose the news than to hide it given that Le Tallec and his staff were still eating in the British canteen. Le Tallec only found out about the move from a French secretary. He might have overlooked that slight, had it not been followed with another. GHQ's staff refused to tell Marty their destination, once again fobbing off the French liaison officers with the excuse that it was a 'military secret'. A complaint to General Voruz, head of the French Liaison Service, revealed that even he was powerless to help: he was experiencing similar problems. When Voruz had first inquired why GHQ was moving, Brownrigg had told him that only the small section under the Duke of Gloucester was going. It was only later that Voruz learned the whole administrative section was leaving.[4] Voruz's own report confirms that he had received 'numerous' complaints from his agents. They all alleged that the British were 'very disagreeable', and held the French responsible for their forced retreat. Even Voruz's staff were 'given the cold shoulder'.[5] Le Tallec only discovered 'by chance' that the planned destination for Rear GHQ was 'Boulogne-sur-mer'.

Rear GHQ left Arras during 17–18 May.[6] Due to the difficulties in tracing their whereabouts, Le Tallec and his staff only caught up with them two days later. The French liaison team set themselves up in an empty room in the Hôtel Impérial, which the British were also using as their offices. Only then did Le Tallec learn that Rear GHQ had not merely moved in order to carry on operating at a safer location: the entire section was to be evacuated to England. The decision had been taken by Gort and communicated to Brownrigg on 19 May, the day after Gort's revealing, and depressing, night-time meeting with General Billotte. Brownrigg was ordered to evacuate all 'useless mouths' from Boulogne, and that unflattering description also referred to Rear GHQ.[7] The only softening in the British stance towards the French liaison group was represented by an offer to allow Marty to accompany the GHQ staff on the boat; they could not find room for Le Tallec and the rest of his team. The inadequate peace-offering was rejected.

On the night of 19–20 May, as if to demonstrate that Boulogne was not safe, the Luftwaffe bombed Hôtel Impérial, causing part of the building to collapse, and killing around fifteen people. That was enough to convince the French liaison team that they, too, should arrange to leave. They drove to Abbeville the next day, crossing the Somme just before the Germans captured the town.

During the evacuation of the GHQ staff, the French were still hoping to defend Boulogne, but their good intentions evaporated during the night of 20–21 May. The naval officer in charge of the garrison was Commandant Dutfoy de Mont de Benque. At around 2 a.m. on 21 May, he ordered the 1100 French sailors in Boulogne to retire to the citadel in the old sector of the town, the so-called Haute Ville, situated east of the River Liane, which bisects the new town's centre. There, protected by the thick walls that had been built to withstand a medieval siege, they would have the best chance of holding out until reinforcements were sent to relieve them.[8] However, during the night, Dutfoy had what a subsequent French inquiry referred to as an 'incredible change of mind'. In the early morning he decided that all the sailors under his control should be evacuated from Boulogne, and the large-calibre naval guns that were supposed to protect the town from a seaborne invasion destroyed.[9]

The catalyst for this abrupt decision appears to have been a conversation he had with General Jean Pelissier de Féligonde, whose unit had been attacked by German panzers at Hesdin, just thirty miles south-east of Boulogne. According to a report made during Dutfoy's post-war appeal against his 26 May 1940 condemnation by a court-martial:

The general was very depressed . . . [and] what he had to say was alarming . . . He had witnessed the destruction of our tanks and his own artillery, and he was lucky to escape from the enemy which had gone on to Abbeville . . . [His experiences made it clear] it was not just light tanks and motorcyclists who might arrive during the next night . . . but motorized divisions with tanks [and] artillery, supported by a powerful air force.[10]

The court-martial report reveals that Dutfoy's evacuation order was backed by a series of hysterical commands from his subordinates. The statement, 'If you wait ten seconds, it will be too late to depart,' was repeated again and again in an attempt to persuade Boulogne's garrison that they should hurry down to the port where ships were waiting for them.[11] Commands such as this transformed the French sailors' dutiful resolve to stand and fight into what one witness referred to as 'indescribable chaos'. The situation was exacerbated by the absence of officers who might have been able to restore order. It was not just the 'drunken sailors', often seen with young women in tow, who were responsible: the report also mentions 'lorries full of men driving in every direction, [and] vehicles and material of every kind piled up wherever the eye could see at the Gare Maritime [the naval station adjacent to the Quai Chanzy, both of which are shown in Map 11 on p. 525]'.[12]

During the early morning Dutfoy departed, heading for Dunkirk; once he was gone, the situation in Boulogne's harbour took a turn for the worse after some sailors and civilians broke into the naval storeroom.[13] They must have found enough alcohol for a good party, for a group of sailors were discovered dead drunk, having consumed what they had stolen. As boats full of refugees steamed out of the harbour, those remaining began to panic. Some kind of order was only re-established when the commander of the sea front appeared, waving his pistol in the air to show he meant business.[14] But at 10 a.m., even he left Boulogne.

The spiking of the town's naval guns was only interrupted when two French sailors questioned the order that had reached them. They managed to send a message to Admiral Leclerc, Dutfoy's immediate superior, in Dunkirk. Leclerc told them he knew nothing of any evacuation, and confirmed that the guns should be preserved to help the remaining sailors defend the town.[15] Alarmed, no doubt, by what he had been told, Leclerc visited the naval gunners still in Boulogne during the morning of 22 May. According to Leclerc, the only opposition coming their way consisted of some isolated armoured vehicles cut off from their supplies. He ordered the gunners to 'fight to the last man', and die, rather than yield the town to the Germans: they would eventually be relieved by British and French soldiers.[16] The instructions from Admiral Jean Abrial, who was based in Dunkirk but was ultimately responsible for all of the Channel ports, were even more graphic: 'You are to die at your posts one by one rather than give in.'[17]

If the German high command had known about the chaos in Boulogne, they might have sanctioned an immediate advance on 21 May when there would have been little opposition. Fortunately for the Allies, they missed this golden opportunity. By the time the order was given to advance on 22 May, it was too late for them to take the town without a fight. The French were already marshalling their troops. Even more significantly, at 6.30 a.m. on 22 May, the first ship carrying British reinforcements to Boulogne – from the 2nd Battalion, the Irish Guards – docked in the harbour.[18]

The number of British soldiers sent from Dover on 22 May with instructions to hold the town during the evacuation was only just superior to the number of French sailors deemed inadequate by Dutfoy. Some 1400–1500 men from two battalions of Irish and Welsh Guards landed in Boulogne that morning. They and the anti-tank gunners accompanying them constituted the core of 20 Brigade. The scene which greeted the Irish Guards, the first troops to land, has been described in their regimental history: 'The quay was a scene of squalid confusion. It looked as if thousands of suitcases had been emptied on the ground by maniac customs officers, and trampling over this sodden mass of clothes, bedding and filthy refuse was a horde of panic-stricken refugees and stray soldiers waiting to rush the ships.'[19]

According to 20 Brigade's war diary, the 'shambles of MT [Motor Transport], discarded equipment, refugees, and troops trying to leave the Harbour' was made even less appealing by the weather: 'It was deluging with rain.'[20] The only blessing was that 'everywhere was quiet on shore and there was no firing. Buildings along the shore had obviously been bombed, and the late General Headquarters, a large white hotel, had been shattered.'[21] One Irish Guard who was on the first ship also noted the civilians' desperation: 'Men, women and children all seemed to be trying to get aboard ships standing by the quayside. I saw one poor lady hanging on to a naval officer with her arms around his neck apparently pleading to let her on to his ship. Such was the confusion that we were ordered to force a way through them, and both naval ratings and guardsmen were obliged to fix bayonets in order that we could move on.'[22] When the Welsh Guards arrived at 10 a.m., the commanding officer, Lieutenant-Colonel Sir Alexander Stanier, noticed the distress written all over the face of the groom escorting Lord Gort's and the Duke of Gloucester's 'chargers'. 'Later I was told that they were shot on the quayside,' he reported.[23]

20 Brigade's Brigadier Billy Fox-Pitt reported to General Brownrigg's Wimereux HQ at around 7 a.m.[24] Brownrigg was of the opinion that

Boulogne would be most easily defended from well outside the town, but lack of personnel prevented Fox-Pitt from complying with this suggestion. He eventually decided to hold the shortest possible perimeter, which without placing his front-line troops inside the town enabled them to block the major roads outside the town centre.[25] Even so, it was impossible with the men at his disposal to form a continuous line of soldiers. His only option was to set up islands of resistance dug in on the hills outside the town. He placed the Irish Guards to the west of the Liane, and the Welsh Guards to the east of the river. 20 Brigade ended up attempting to hold a 10,000-yard perimeter, an area that could easily have absorbed the nine battalions in a division as well as divisional artillery.[26] Unfortunately, Fox-Pitt's men were not to be protected by sufficient artillery. (The Guards' initial positions were as shown in Map 11 on p. 525.) They were sent to Boulogne with the brigade's anti-tank guns, but the only extra fire-power allocated to the force was eight two-pounder guns, which were also dumped on the quay during 22 May.[27]

However, Brownrigg had some reassuring news. He told Fox-Pitt the Germans were expected to approach from the south where his front line was screened by three battalions from the French 21st Division. These French troops were thought to be deployed along the line Neufchâtel–Samer–Wirwignes.[28] He also mentioned that two additional British battalions, one infantry, the other equipped with tanks, were to be landed in Calais during the night of 22–3 May, and Fox-Pitt could count on them to beef up the Boulogne defences the following morning.[29] There was little psychological comfort to be gained from the French troops already in Boulogne. A French officer told Fox-Pitt that the soldiers in the citadel were short of rifles and ammunition, 'and . . . were for the most part untrained'.[30]

In fact, Brownrigg's intelligence was deeply flawed. The trains carrying the three battalions of French soldiers, from 21 Division's 48th Regiment, had been delayed. As a result, when a refugee drove into Nesles-Neufchâtel at 11.30 a.m. on 22 May to announce that he had seen a German tank column crossing the river at Étaples, the only soldiers separating the panzers from Boulogne were the 48th Regiment's headquarters staff and the gunners manning four 75mm and four 25mm guns.[31] Much has been written about the defeatist, even cowardly, attitude of French soldiers during the 1940 campaign. However, the commanders of this minuscule force, fleshed out as it was with drivers, telephonists and secretaries, who never expected to find themselves in the front line, were to be the exception to the rule. Given the unit's weakness, these officers might have been excused if they had admitted that they could not hope to stop a German panzer division, and had retreated to the north. Instead, to their credit, they dutifully set up their guns on the Nesles–Neufchâtel crossroads, and waited for the panzers to arrive.

Guderian had allocated the task of capturing Boulogne to the 2nd Panzer Division. Its commander, Lieutenant-General Rudolf Veiel, decided to besiege the town with two principal thrusts. The south was to be attacked by a group led by Oberst von Prittwitz und Gaffron, while Oberst von Vaerst was to lead a flanking movement that would ensure Boulogne was attacked simultaneously from the east and north. It was von Prittwitz's group that had to pass through the French screen of guns at Nesles–Neufchâtel.

The opposition they encountered as they drove up to the crossroads in the centre of that town during the early afternoon of 22 May has been described by Oberleutnant Rudolf Behr, a tank commander, whose platoon led the German column:

They are shooting [at us] from the left, and dust rises on the right. I also see that a gun is firing ahead [of us]. Where should I fire first? . . . While I look for the French positions, I notice a small cloud of dust and smoke coming out of the tank in front of me. It has been hit. The driver quickly tries to escape. He falls down on to the crossroads, and lies still. Two other men get out of the tank, and take cover behind my tank. The tank driver, who seems to have been wounded, crawls to a house where he can take cover. Shortly afterwards, my tank is hit, and sparks shoot around the combat compartment as if there is a firework inside it. Our driver slumps forward in his seat with his head hanging down. Although I am still half blinded, I peer through the dim light, and see that he has blood running down his face. We have no choice but to get out. The gunner positions the turret so that we can do this without being seen by the enemy. I call out to the driver, but he does not move; he is probably dead.[32]

It quickly became clear that the Germans could not pass the crossroads without knocking out the anti-tank guns. This they eventually achieved after outflanking the defenders, and only then was the German column able to move on, leaving behind the two German tanks smouldering at the crossroads. Behr described what happened next:

As soon as the first panzers drive past the crossroads, we return to our vehicle. There is nothing that can be done in my tank. My driver is sitting in his seat just as we left him . . . In the first tank, Jochum 2, the gunner is lying . . . dead. The wireless operator has had his foot blown off, and is heavily wounded in the leg. The tank is on fire. The ammunition and fuel tank might blow up at any minute. A junior officer achieves the impossible. He puts on his gas mask, and climbs into the combat compartment so that he can pull out the wounded wireless operator . . . The tank itself cannot be saved. Our attempt to extinguish the fire fails. As the tank 'brews up', there are loud bangs caused by the ammunition exploding. The dead gunner is still inside. We can do nothing to help him. The tank has literally become his iron grave.

That was not the only resistance obstructing the 2nd Panzer Division's progress. Another French anti-tank gun knocked out two more tanks on the road leading from Montreuil to Samer, the valiant gunner remaining at his post until a third tank crushed him and the gun.[33] But in spite of these brave acts, and more losses, which occurred when the right-hand column of the 2nd Panzer Division was bombed by the RAF on the same road further south, the Germans were delayed for less than two hours.[34] Shortly after 5 p.m. that afternoon the last tank within Behr's platoon was driven up to the British front line at Manihen (three miles to the south of the Gare Maritime), a Boulogne suburb. Arthur Evans, an Irish Guard in the line, later described what he saw and heard:

The distinct rumble of tanks could be heard approaching our position, and sure enough, one appeared unconcernedly round the bend and then stopped. I could clearly see the tank commander's head above the open turret with field glasses to his eyes. We opened fire, and the tank rocked as we scored two direct hits. The crew baled out, and abandoned it. Soon a second [tank] appeared, and that too was disposed of.[35]

Behr's account reveals what it was like to be on the receiving end of the Irish Guards' shelling:

When the tank goes round the bend, there is a flash, and the tank is hit. The tank commander, who has seen the well-concealed anti-tank gun, wants to see it shot, and stops the tank. But the tank keeps on rolling forward without anyone at the wheel. The driver down below is dead. He was shot in the head by the first shell. His foot however is still on the accelerator. The tank knocks down a wall at the side of the road. But it eventually stops. Other shells hit the tank, partly tearing it apart. Get out! . . . The men scramble out. Only the radio man cannot make it. He was nearly out when he was hit in the head by a machine-gun. He also is dead.[36]

But by adopting the same tactics that had been employed so successfully against the French, the Germans were able to outflank the gun position and to overcome it. As Sergeant Evans recorded in his account, he and his men were lucky to escape: 'There was a deafening explosion, the blast from which knocked me to the ground. My first thought was that one of our guns had blown up. But then I noticed the potato mashers – German hand grenades – sailing through the air towards our position. We were in imminent danger of being surrounded. So I gave the order to disable the guns and withdraw.'[37]

Evans's retreat saved him, but according to the Irish Guards' war diary, at 10 p.m. that night the Germans put in 'a more vicious attack', and this time the forward platoon was 'outflanked, and but few escaped'.[38] The German attack resumed at 7.30 a.m. on 23 May, and after another platoon was overrun, the Irish Guards retreated some five hours later into Boulogne's town centre itself.[39]

The Irish Guards' regimental history includes a description of an incident that occurred while they were taking refuge in and around the town centre:

The officers and sergeants, sheltering in the doorways, heard the rattle of tank tracks on the cobbles, and then saw five German medium tanks coming slowly down the street. In front of them walked a man dressed in civilian clothes, waving his hands, and shouting that the tanks were French. The man and the three leading tanks went on down the hill; the two rear ones remained in the street. One halted outside a house in which a section [of Irish Guards] was sheltering. The other was immediately in front of Battalion HQ. The sergeant [in the former house] was wondering what to do, when a civilian walked in the back door. The stranger quickly unbuttoned his mackintosh to show a

French uniform, pointed to the front door and said: 'Français.' The sergeant opened the door cautiously to have a look at the tank which was noisily turning round. The 'French officer' fled out of the back door, and taking time from him, the section flung themselves on their faces just as the tank's shots rocketed down the passage.[40]

Fortunately for the holed-up Irish Guards, the tank's shells failed to connect with them, and there was no German infantry on the street to press home the attack. Within half an hour, all five tanks had withdrawn, and the Guards were free to retreat once more to a new line around the harbour.

Meanwhile, the Welsh Guards had marched off to guard the area to the north and east of the town. They suffered their first casualty long before they met any Germans. The injury, which was self-inflicted, was described in the following terms by 2nd Lieutenant Peter Hanbury in his report: 'On the shore Davies blew his thumb off, and I was very nearly sick. He suffered frightfully . . . Sgt Gould was sick. Know[ing] that other people felt worse than me *made me feel much better.*'[41]

The next day, as the Welsh Guards were also pushed back by probing tank attacks, Lieutenant Hanbury was confronted with more serious injuries:

I talked to a sergeant . . . who was walking back with one arm off and a bloody tourniquet around [the stump]. He said this was a change from Public Duties in London. I was sitting beside him during an air raid when he died. [It was the] first time I had heard the rattle in someone's throat as they died. We went into a building during [an] air raid, and I found a French nurse in the cellar with 3 badly wounded British soldiers. One asked me to promise I would get him on a boat. He had been shot through his insides, and the nurse said he would not live more than a few hours. But [he] was in no pain as she had filled him with morphia. He asked me to get the photograph of his girlfriend out of his pocket, which I did, and propped [it] up [with] his arm on his chest so he could die looking at it. I promised I would get him on a boat. Another soldier had had his jaw shot away and his tongue cut off. He kept swallowing the stump and choking. The nurse thrust her fingers down his throat and pulled the stump back. She suggested I did this. I don't know whether I could have, but, thank God [before I was put to the test], we received new orders.[42]

The most welcome order of all required the Welsh Guards to retreat to the quay around the harbour.

General Pierre Lanquetot, 21 Division's commander, who had taken control of the French troops in the citadel, heard the British troops singing as they marched back down to the harbour. Their retreat came as a bitter disappointment to him. He had only ended up in Boulogne in the first place because he was too honourable to flee to Dunkirk after the German advance blocked his advance towards the south. No one had ordered him to enter the town to take control of its defences. But once he had contacted Admiral Abrial, which he did shortly before midday on 23 May, he was trapped. Abrial ordered him to 'fight to the finish', adding that a 'powerful attack' would be made to relieve him and his garrison if they could only hold on for long enough.[43]

On hearing the British retreat, Lanquetot telephoned Abrial again and complained about the British desertion, and their failure to warn him they were about to go.[44] Abrial promised to take it up with the British high command, little realizing that Lanquetot's outburst was ill-informed and unfair. Protected as Lanquetot and his men were by the thick walls that encircled the Haute Ville, they were in no position to comprehend the hopeless position of the Welsh Guards. If Lanquetot had seen the horrific injuries suffered by some British soldiers, or how they had attempted to hold back the panzers lying in the open country, protected only by their trenches, without any adequate anti-tank barriers and with minimal artillery, his heart would surely have softened. As it was, his complaints further soured the Anglo-French relationship, and may have contributed to one of the great tragedies of the campaign: Churchill's decision to sacrifice the British garrison at Calais, which was made partly to demonstrate to the French that the British were not deserting their ally.

Lanquetot's anger might also have abated if he had seen the courageous efforts to hold back the panzers by British Pioneers (labourers in military uniform) on the left of the Welsh Guards' sector of the perimeter.[45] There were a number of undisciplined Pioneers in Boulogne: countless reports exist of how their officers and men were drunk and disorderly, and how they fired at their own troops when they were retreating.[46] But the Pioneers' 5 Group, who were filling a gap in the front line under the leadership of Lieutenant-Colonel Donald Dean VC, were very different. Because Dean and his Pioneers had no anti-tank guns, they had to improvise quickly when a tank finally lumbered up to the rudimentary 'barricade' they had erected, consisting of lorries and cars placed across the road, reinforced with furniture from bombed-out houses. The tank slowly pushed its way over the obstruction, but, as Dean wrote: 'We were prepared for this . . . I had some lorry petrol tanks punctured with a pick, the tank being unable to shell us during its crushing climb, and we set fire to the lot. A sheet of flame went up, and the tank backed hastily off . . . Our roadblock burned for quite a while, and allowed for a further block to be made under cover of smoke.'[47] This decisive action deterred the tank crews from attempting to breach 5 Group's barricades again, and thus, when the order came telling them to retreat, they were free to go back to join the Guards, who by this time were holding an inner perimeter around the harbour.

16: Evacuation of Boulogne

Boulogne, 23 May 1940
(See Map 11)

While the Guards and Lieutenant-Colonel Dean's Pioneers were still holding the outer perimeter around Boulogne, British ships had started to evacuate the 'useless mouths'. General Brownrigg was taken off with part of Rear GHQ shortly before dawn on 23 May, and the remainder boarded another destroyer at 12.20 p.m. on that same day.[1] At 3 p.m. a new phase in the evacuation commenced with the arrival of the destroyers HMS *Keith* and HMS *Whitshed* at Quai Chanzy, next to the Gare Maritime.[2] Lieutenant Graham Lumsden, navigator on *Keith*, has recorded what he witnessed: 'As we entered the harbour, we passed a number of British and French destroyers bombarding the aerodrome which was in German hands. Boulogne harbour is approached by a narrow channel between long stone piers with a kink to the right in the channel just before it enters the harbour proper . . . We secured at the railway quay.'[3]

The scenes on the quay were, if anything, even more frantic than those observed by the Irish Guards when they had arrived the previous morning. The civilians and Pioneers were described by more than one witness as 'a rabble'.[4] On the previous day, the refugees had made way for the Irish Guards when they saw them with bayonets at the ready. Now civilians and Pioneers alike surged forward, and rushed on to *Keith* as soon as they saw an opportunity. As the unwanted passengers were cleared from *Keith*'s deck, her crew were able to observe the antics of some of the wealthier refugees. They pushed their cars with mattresses on the roofs into the harbour, then approached the ships and begged the sailors to allow them on board. Most pleas fell on deaf ears. Captain David Simson, the forty-seven-year-old commander of *Keith*, was not allowing any French civilians on to his ship, but some British refugees were more than welcome: among the legitimate passengers were twelve pretty young women, described by gunner Iain Nethercott as 'Bluebell-style show girls'.[5] They came aboard with their suitcases as if departing on a pleasure cruise.[6]

The officer in charge on HMS *Whitshed*, the other destroyer at the quay, was the thirty-nine-year-old Commander Edward Conder. His name is unknown to most historians, but his coolness and bravery under fire was to be one of the most inspiring features of the evacuation. Fortunately, the part he played has been immortalized, thanks to a vivid account written by Sam Lombard-Hobson, *Whitshed*'s first lieutenant.[7] According to Lombard-Hobson, it was Conder who helped to prepare the Navy for the evacuation. When *Whitshed* had docked at the quay during the early hours of 22 May, his first act was to push through the crowd on the quay so that he could make contact with General Brownrigg at Wimereux. While Conder was in Brownrigg's office, he telephoned Vice-Admiral Bertram Ramsay at Dover, and told him it would take more than his ship to evacuate the 'useless mouths' still in the town.[8] Thanks to his swift intervention, an additional seven destroyers were made available over the next forty-eight hours to bring back British troops from Boulogne to Dover.

But his resolute action during the afternoon and evening of 23 May was even more remarkable. After rescuing seventy 'stretcher cases', and 150 'walking wounded', he decided to play an active role in the land battle that was raging by the time *Whitshed* steamed out of the harbour. The first target that tempted him was a machine-gun post in a warehouse, which was firing at some Irish Guards. Conder ordered that the warehouse should be demolished. The ship's 4.7-inch guns were immediately swung round, and two shells were fired at the target. Because it was only around a hundred yards away, which is point-blank range for such powerful guns, it was blown to pieces. On seeing the building collapse, 'a roar of cheering went up from the guardsmen', wrote Lombard-Hobson.[9] Next to catch Conder's eye was a series of flashes emanating from naval guns in Fort de la Crèche, to the north of Boulogne, which had been captured by the Germans earlier that day.[10] 'Open fire on that bloody fort,' roared Conder. The broadside must have hit a nearby ammunition dump because, as Lombard-Hobson noted, there followed 'a terrific explosion'. He also saw another shot being fired at a column of tanks moving down towards the quay. 'One huge tank disintegrated completely from a direct hit,' he recorded.[11]

Before *Whitshed* departed, Brigadier Fox-Pitt was told he had to hold Boulogne even if this meant that 20 Brigade fought to the last man.[12] On receiving this message, he talked to Conder and *Keith*'s commander,

Simson. They all agreed that while Boulogne might be held if artillery and aircraft cover were provided, it certainly could not be retained without such assistance. A reply to this effect was sent back to England.[13]

It has not been possible to find documents that explain why, during the afternoon of 23 May, the British Government decided that 20 Brigade should be evacuated. The most likely explanation is that Fox-Pitt's message woke the politicians in London to the risks they were running. Whatever the reason, at 5.49 p.m. a message was received on *Keith*, while she was still tied up at the quay, stating that Fox-Pitt was to evacuate Boulogne after all.[14]

To speed up the evacuation, HMS *Vimy*, another destroyer, was ordered to come into the port so that the two ships could be filled with troops simultaneously.[15] Don Harris, a rating on *Vimy*, has described what he saw as his ship was summoned:

On arrival [outside the harbour], we could clearly see large numbers of German Army advance units swarming down the high ground approaches leading to the city. They were being bombarded from offshore by four French destroyers. We signalled a request for one or two to accompany us into the port to evacuate as many troops [as possible] . . . [The] reply was . . .: 'No, it is suicidal to go in there. We will continue to bombard' . . . So we proceeded into the narrow harbour [alone].[16]

At this critical moment the Luftwaffe arrived, forcing Brigadier Fox-Pitt to scribble his evacuation order while taking cover under a train on the quay.[17] It contained the following words: 'Bde will evacuate Boulogne forthwith. All personnel of non-combatant units and other units now on quay will be evacuated first . . . All ranks will embark on any destroyer available on arrival at quay.'[18]

But before it could be distributed, the action in the port hotted up to such a degree that it began to look as if the evacuation would be terminated before it commenced. Lieutenant Lumsden's account demonstrates how the air raid affected those on *Keith*:

We had begun to embark the mass of people on the quay into the two ships so that they were blocking all the gangways and ladders down into the ships, when we heard and sighted a large force of enemy aircraft approaching from the north-east . . . As the attack began . . . the Captain . . . ordered bridge people below, because the bridge was just above quay-level, and therefore exposed to splinters from bombs bursting there. Finally he decided that, as we could do nothing useful, he and I would leave the bridge. I stood back to allow him down the bridge ladder to the wheelhouse, as courtesy and seniority demanded, but he signed me to precede him. No Captain likes to leave his bridge when under attack. I had taken one or two steps down when, alas, he fell down on top of me, shot in the chest by a German sniper's bullet . . . We laid [him] on the settee in the tiny charthouse . . . [Then] the Doctor arrived and pronounced him dead.[19]

On *Vimy*, which at the time of the air raid was tied up to *Keith*'s port side, Don Harris had to cope with a similar ordeal, as the following extract from his account reveals:

Automatic rifle fire . . . had been heard from the bridge before I noticed our Captain [Lieutenant-Commander Colin Donald] train his binoculars on a hotel diagonally opposite, but quite close to our ship. I heard another burst of firing from the snipers located in the hotel, and saw our Captain struck down. He fell on to his back, and as I leaped to his aid, I saw that a bullet had inflicted a frightful wound to his forehead, nose and eyes. He was choking in his own blood, so I moved him on to his side, and it was then that I received his final order. It was: 'Get the First Lieutenant on to the bridge urgently.' As I rose to my feet, more shots from the hotel swept the bridge, and the Sub-Lieutenant fell directly in front of me. I glanced down at him and saw four bullet holes in line across his chest. He must have been dead before he hit the deck.[20]

If twelve RAF planes had not arrived to head off at least some of the German planes, it is hard to imagine that the British destroyers, tied up as they were in the harbour, could have avoided being sunk. Even so, about thirty of the sixty German planes attacked the destroyers in the harbour with a similar number concentrating on the ships in the open sea. 'The only opposition to this formidable force was some scattered rifle and Lewis gun fire . . . and the single-barrelled two-pounder pom-poms in each destroyer when these could be brought to bear,' wrote *Keith*'s navigator. 'With what I had read of the capabilities of Stukas, I thought that both ships would be sunk as they lay.'[21]

Lombard-Hobson was equally impressed: 'The bombing . . . was vicious,' he wrote.

Every ship opened fire as the Stukas screamed down, with their angry hornet-like noise, to drop their bombs which sent up huge fountains of mud and water alongside the destroyers, drenching everyone on deck . . . To add to the bedlam, a splinter cut the wire to our fog siren, which wailed continuously, and must have sounded to others like the final death-throe . . . Miraculously *Whitshed* was not damaged.[22]

The skipper was not the only casualty on *Keith*. Iain Nethercott, whose action station was on the starboard side of the ship, near a pompom gun, saw one bomb drop on to the quay, just feet away from *Keith*, killing two sailors and sending lumps of concrete on to the deck.[23] A mortar shell that hit the deck gouged a deep hole, and covered the gunners, Nethercott included, with metal splinters. None of the stretcher cases lying on deck survived the German gunfire. But the most shocking injury of all occurred after Nethercott and his gun team began to fire at a warehouse on the northern side of the river. In the middle of this action, the gun swung off target, but when Nethercott turned to shout a warning to Dunbar, the gun-layer, he was confronted by a horrific sight. Dunbar had been decapitated by a shell, leaving his trunk, still spouting blood, sitting motionless in the seat, tied into position by the harness. Fortunately, perhaps, there was no time for the survivors to stand on ceremony. According to Nethercott: 'We dragged Dunbar off, and put him against the ready used lockers.'[24] Within minutes the gun was firing at the Germans again.

Don Harris has described how *Vimy* escaped from the harbour:

On the upper deck I located the First Lieutenant, and appraised him briefly of what had occurred. He immediately assumed command, and ordered all securing lines cast off, and full speed astern. He consulted me on the approximate location of the snipers in the nearby hotel, and after I had given my opinion, he ordered A gun's crew up forward to bear on the target, and fire a four inch shell at point blank range, [the target being] no more than one hundred yards [away]. The result was devastating indeed! Still at full speed astern, we reached the outer limits of the harbour, and then had to contend with German bombers . . . The planes broke away from us to attack the four French destroyers still at their task of bombarding the port. The first attack brought immediate results: the leading ship [the *Orage*] suffered a direct hit, and disappeared in a gigantic mushroom of flame and smoke.[25]

After Simson's death on *Keith*, her first lieutenant took charge, and insisted that everyone on the bridge should lie down flat. While they were taking cover in this way, Lumsden saw that *Vimy* was reversing out of the harbour. His account reveals how his ship followed *Vimy*'s lead:

The First Lieutenant, now our Captain, asked me if I could take the ship out . . . I found myself replying 'Of course I can Number One!' No communication was possible to men on the upper deck to slip the wires, so after ringing on main engines, I shouted engine orders . . . to make the ship surge ahead and astern, and so part the wires. When this was achieved, it was not too difficult to swing the stern off the quay and to start the ship moving astern. As we moved astern, I rushed up to the bridge more than once to improve my view astern at this critical stage, but very soon clattered down again when bullets whistled past me as soon as I showed my head. Keeping as close as I dared to the stone pier on the northern side of the channel, of which I could see something over our port quarter, I was mightily grateful to round the corner successfully . . . As we shot out of the harbour, we passed the destroyer *Whitshed*, normally our flotilla second in command . . . We shouted to him that Captain Simson had been killed, and warned him of the accurate enemy small arms fire from the northern side of the harbour.[26]

The surviving officers and ratings on *Keith* then steamed back to England, stopping only to bury her commander, and the other dead men on board, and leaving Conder in *Whitshed* to control the shipping off Boulogne.

Meanwhile there had been further manoeuvring inside the town itself. During the early afternoon, the Guards and Lieutenant-Colonel Dean's Pioneers had been ordered to retreat to the area around the quay but were ordered to advance again towards the Germans after Fox-Pitt received the message that they were to fight on.[27] When, following the air raid, a second order to retreat to the quay was given, an unfortunate mistake was made, which denied some soldiers their chance to escape. Lieutenant-Colonel Sir Alexander Stanier, the Welsh Guards' commander, was the only officer who knew where to find the headquarters of his 3 Company, and decided to visit it so that he could pass on the retreat order in person. He found the house where he had last seen the company's commander and, despite the bullets flying around outside, got out of his car to bang on the door. There was no answer. He waited outside the house for a while, but by the time a Welsh Guard inside had asked an officer if he might open up, Stanier, fearing that his men had moved on, had departed. Because of this, 3 Company never heard that the rest of the battalion was withdrawing. Stanier mentioned the missing men to Brigadier Fox-Pitt, who was standing on the bridge connecting north Boulogne with Quai Chanzy, but the brigadier told him it could not be helped, then gave the order for the bridge to be blown up.[28]

During the Guards' retreat to the quay, the Pioneers' indiscipline in the area around the harbour became a liability. According to 20 Brigade's war diary, they had been 'lined up as best as possible, and told to hold the barricades. They lined the windows of the quay sheds, and held the railway trucks on the quay.'[29] But as the war diary admitted, these men 'were for the most part drunk'. That was one reason why, when the Guards retreated, they were 'fired on by their own people in the backs'. It is likely, however, that the firing was not all the work of drunken Pioneers. At least two reports suggest that fifth-columnists were responsible too.[30] Historians who have claimed that fifth-columnists did not exist, and were merely the result of British soldiers' paranoia, would do well to read the following excerpt from 20 Brigade's war diary:

The snipers from the rooves, blocks of flats, churches, [and] office buildings, and men acting as observers for German artillery were innumerable – not counting the actual spies dressed as priests etc . . . One man was found with a collapsible machine gun . . . The gun was protruding from the man's coat, and he stood at an attic window. This man was pursued. He was captured, but tried to escape whilst being conducted back to Brigade Headquarters, and was bayoneted. Three men were discovered approaching [a] destroyer with time bombs. They were attacked . . . trussed up, and thrown overboard into the sea. There was even a man in the uniform of a Belgian colonel trying to get information for the German Force. He was granted a firing party of 5 men, which seemed a definite waste of ammunition. No-one could deny that some of these 5th columnists were brave. When one man saw that he was to be shot [at the brigade's HQ] – he had refused a bandage for his eyes – he said quite distinctly in English: 'I die once for myself and twice for my Führer.'[31]

Following the departure of the German and British planes, there was a temporary lull inside and outside the harbour. According to

Lombard-Hobson, 'All went quiet, except for occasional bursts of machine-gun fire.'[32] Nevertheless Conder sent an emergency signal to Admiral Ramsay at Dover, stating that he was not prepared to send another destroyer into Boulogne until he was given air support. It arrived shortly after 7.20 p.m.[33] Then, with a shout of 'In we go, boys,' Conder ordered his own ship, *Whitshed*, and the destroyer HMS *Vimiera* into the harbour.[34] 'The scene that greeted us on the quay was beyond description,' wrote Lombard-Hobson.

There was rubble and masonry along the quay, like the aftermath of an earthquake. Dead and dying were lying about everywhere, and being trampled on by the milling crowd of military and civilians, many of whom were either dazed or drunk. As sailors jumped ashore to secure our wires, the ship was again rushed by a mob of panic-stricken AMPC troops who had abandoned their weapons, and again we had to repel them at the point of the bayonet.[35]

Conder decided that the Welsh Guards, who were shooting at the Germans from a wood on the north side of the river, should be summoned on board first, and gave the order that they should move, shouting to them through a megaphone from the bridge. Some of the Irish Guards who had been defending the perimeter around the quay were ordered to board next. 'We were then to witness an incident which I . . . would not easily forget,' wrote Lombard-Hobson.

While a mixed party of men was forming up to embark, a single soldier, unable to take any more, broke ranks and made a dash for the gangway. Without a moment's hesitation, the subaltern in charge took out his revolver and shot the man through the heart, who lay motionless on the jetty. The young officer then turned to his section, and calmly told them that he only wanted fighting men with him. The effect was electric, and undoubtedly prevented a stampede by other troops awaiting evacuation.[36]

As the troops came aboard, Conder stood on the bridge fearlessly conducting operations in spite of the sporadic gunfire still being directed at the ship. 'I implored him to put on his steel helmet,' wrote Lombard-Hobson, 'reminding him that Captain D [Simson] had been killed that way; but all he said was that the damned thing did not fit, and gave him a headache.'[37] Conder only gave the order for *Whitshed* and *Vimiera* to leave the harbour after he had been informed that they could not safely take any more men on board. When they left, two tanks were engaged by *Whitshed*'s 4.7-inch guns. The tanks were obliterated and, according to Lombard-Hobson: 'The shout of triumph that went up from *Whitshed* was more suitable for the football ground than the field of battle; and order had to be restored by megaphone, also at point blank range!'[38]

Whitshed and *Vimiera* steamed out of the harbour at 8.25 p.m., each ship carrying more than five hundred and fifty men. Ten minutes later their places were taken by two more destroyers, HMS *Wild Swan* and *Venomous*.[39] It was while a third, HMS *Venetia*, was following the first two ships into the harbour five minutes later that the Germans made their most determined effort to nip the evacuation in the bud. The focus of the German efforts appears to have been *Venetia*, the idea being that if she could be sunk in the harbour mouth, the other destroyers would be unable to escape to the open sea, and the evacuation would have to be called off.

In the heat of the battle it was hard for the 2nd Panzer Division crews to be sure which destroyer they were targeting, but it seems likely that the following account by Franz Steinzer records the German reaction as *Venetia* steamed into the harbour:

Oberleutnant Jaworski [commander of 4 Company, the 3rd Panzer Regiment] spots a destroyer through his binoculars, and sees that it is heading for the harbour . . . 'Alarm! Get two heavy panzers ready to attack! Drivers start your motors,' he says . . . The company commander jumps on to the panzer, and takes cover behind the turret. I order my driver to go as fast as he can . . . and to knock down fences and trees, whatever it takes, to get to a point where we can see the port . . . We hear the commander's voice. It is almost jolly: 'Half right, distance 500 metres, destroyer!' Then the gunner says: 'Target is in my sights.' The first shell is fired. Fifty metres too far. I look through the binoculars, and see that the destroyer is ready to land. I can see troops clearly on deck. There is loads of activity. The gunner moves the gun, and the second shot hits the ship. Within seconds, a bright yellow flame shoots up five metres into the air, and bits of the ship are blown up. Because of the fire and dust, I can't see anything more . . . Additional shells are fired . . . The destroyer tries to escape from the shells . . . and at the same time it shoots back . . . The ground vibrates. Everything is shaking. [Then] there is a loud wailing sound, and our tank is hit . . . [But] no one panics inside the tank [although] . . . every time we look through the periscope we see a shell coming our way . . . [and] the air becomes unbreathable.[40]

Steinzer and his comrades believed they had sunk the British destroyer they were engaging, and after the battle even painted a picture of it on their tank's turret to celebrate the sinking. However, if *Venetia* was their target, their shelling was not as effective as they claimed. *Venetia*'s war diary confirms that she was hit aft by one shell, which set her on fire, but neither this shell nor the others that hit her during the battle succeeded in sinking her. Like the other destroyers that preceded her into the harbour, she made good her escape. (Details of *Venetia*'s escape, and the part played by HMS *Wild Swan* and *Venomous*, the next two destroyers to tie up alongside the Gare Maritime, are in note 41.)[41]

Unfortunately there was not enough room on the ships for everyone. The desperation felt by those left behind can be gauged from a note in 20 Brigade's war diary: it describes the departure of *Wild Swan* and *Venomous*, which had been tied up on the west and east sides of the Gare Maritime respectively:

The Irish Guards, after having got [their] wounded aboard, scrambled on to the deck of the Destroyer. The men dropped from the quay to the deck, but no-one [on] . . . the Irish Guards side actually dropped in the water. On the other side [of the Gare Maritime] however . . . as the Destroyer moved off, [some] men [who] jumped [did fall] into the water. They were rescued by rifle slings . . . tied together, and they were thus hauled aboard. One Welsh Guard who had found himself left behind . . . stripped . . . dived in and was hauled aboard the Destroyer as she was moving.[42]

Other Guardsmen left behind accepted their fate with a stiff upper lip. Charles Saunders has described how near he came to being rescued: 'To dodge the snipers, we'd break cover only two or three at a time and race across the dock to the boat. There were only four chaps in front of me and I thought I was home and dry. Then suddenly an incendiary bomb went off. The fire threatened to spread to the boat so the skipper cast off, leaving me and my mates stranded.'[43]

Sidney Pritchard was another Welsh Guard who literally missed the boat. He was about to step on to one of the ships with the stretcher he was carrying when he was tapped on the shoulder by a comrade, who said that he had a wife and child at home. 'I handed over the stretcher to him,' Pritchard remembered, 'so he got on board, and got away, [while] I went back to wait my turn in a black corrugated shed.'[44]

At 10.30 p.m. a message from Wild Swan revealed that her commander believed further evacuation to be 'impracticable'.[45] But two more destroyers were nevertheless sent into Boulogne during the night. The official report of the Boulogne evacuation records what was seen at 1.30 a.m. on 24 May by Lieutenant-Commander Roger Hicks, commander of HMS Vimiera, the last British destroyer to steam into the harbour: 'The silence was eerie. The only noise came from a burning lorry on the quay, the flames of which and a full moon gave plenty of light. Lieutenant Commander Hicks hailed the quay, but there was no sign of life. As he was preparing to back out, a voice answered. He found there were more than 1,000 soldiers waiting anxiously for a ship.'[46]

One of the soldiers was Lieutenant-Colonel Dean, who had been knocked unconscious by a near miss, but had recovered just in time. He was the most senior British officer remaining in Boulogne when Vimiera appeared for the second time that night. The brigadier had been evacuated on the destroyer HMS Windsor, which had left the harbour at 11.20 p.m.[47] Dean recorded the final stage of the evacuation in the following terms:

It was reported to me that a dark shadow was to be seen out at sea so I signalled S.O.S. with my torch in case it was a British ship . . . The Vimiera backed carefully in to the end of the mole, and we started embarking across planks, being much impeded by civilians trying to rush it . . . Some falling off the planks were swept away by the swift current. With my [Pioneer] Officers, we got a very orderly embarkation, and I then asked the Naval Officer to wait as I had more men to be brought up from the barricades. I ran off, and withdrew these as the Germans were not doing anything active there at the time, and I warned all others in sight to make for the end of the mole. I arrived back at the Vimiera breathless and sweating, and asked for [a] longer time, as there were still men thought to be under the trains [on the quay]. The Naval Officer said that he was already most dangerously overloaded and top heavy, that dawn would break shortly, that he would not wait a moment longer, and if I did not get on board he would leave without me . . . Not wishing to be taken prisoner, I walked aboard . . . I believe that I was the last to get away from Boulogne.[48]

The official war diary of the evacuation concluded: 'At 02.45/24 she [*Vimiera*] slipped regretfully leaving some 200 men on the jetty . . . [There were in fact many more left behind as specified in note 49.][49] [She] reached Dover at 0355/24 where she landed some 1,400 men.' As the report stated, this took the total number of men, women and children evacuated from Boulogne to 'roughly 4,368'.[50]

17: Calais and the French Complaint

Calais, 22–4 May 1940

(See Map 12. Also Map 1)

Three days prior to the last-minute evacuation of 20 Brigade from Boulogne, a much more ambitious exodus was already being planned. One of the first soldiers who observed what was being organized was Lieutenant Austin Evitts, a young signalman. On 20 May, he was summoned to the office of a Colonel Graveley in the War Office, where he was astonished to be told, 'Your mission is to do the wireless communications for the evacuation of the BEF.' When Evitts gasped, 'Evacuation of the BEF?' Graveley replied, 'Well, yes, if the worst comes to the worst,' adding that Evitts and his men were to go to France immediately, where they were to set up wireless stations at Dunkirk, Boulogne and Calais. Evitts and his No. 12 Wireless Section set out for Dover that same night, and by the evening of the next day he was in Calais.[1]

The clear, unguarded instructions given to Evitts were not matched by the rather mysterious orders that reached Lieutenant-Colonel John Ellison-Macartney, commanding officer of the 1st Battalion, Queen Victoria's Rifles (QVR), during the night of 21–2 May. The QVR were destined to be the first battalion sent to France to protect Calais. However, Ellison-Macartney was initially told only that his battalion was going 'overseas'.[2] Early next morning he and his men boarded the two trains laid on for them at Ashford, Kent, and were taken to Dover. There, he was handed instructions in a sealed envelope, which were only marginally more informative than those given to him the night before. His orders were to 'proceed to Calais and get in touch with the local commander, or if unable to do so, to take necessary steps to secure the town'.[3]

Lieutenant-Colonel Reggie Keller, commanding officer of the 3rd Battalion, the Royal Tank Regiment (3 RTR), was equally bemused by the instructions he received during the night of 21–2 May. He was ordered to take his battalion from Fordingbridge, Hampshire, to Southampton, but could only tell his men they were on their way to an 'unknown destination'.[4] His initial assumption was that they were going to Cherbourg to join the rest of the 1st Armoured Division, which was at that moment assembling south of the River Seine.[5] But such was the speed of the German advance that the original plan had to be changed during the night, and instructions were sent from the War Office to divert the personnel train. As a result, the battalion's tanks went to Southampton as originally planned, but the men ended up at Dover.

This unforeseen change upset Keller, as is evident from the report by Major Foote, from the Royal Armoured Corps Branch at the War Office, who drove down to Dover to brief 3 RTR's commanding officer: 'He was very angry,' Foote reported, 'and wanted to know what the hell was happening, and where his tanks were.'[6] Keller was told he and his men would be reunited with their tanks in Calais, where they were to back up British infantry in case the Germans attacked the town. Then he too was given a sealed envelope; it was addressed to the 'Senior Military Commander, Calais'.[7]

The ships taking the QVR and 3 RTR to Calais left Dover at 11 a.m. on 22 May, and arrived shortly after 1 p.m., that is, just a few hours after 20 Brigade disembarked at Boulogne.[8] They were greeted in Calais by a scene that these unblooded troops, who knew nothing of the events in France, could only describe as shocking. 'A dark pall of smoke sent up by the buildings on fire hung low over the town,' wrote RTR soldier Robert Watt. 'Ships lay dead in the water, and broken glass from a deserted hotel on the quayside covered the roadway. It crunched and cracked underfoot as a mixed group of dejected Allied soldiers, hoping to embark on our ship for the sanctuary of England, came towards us.'[9]

In an attempt to avoid being bombed in the harbour, the RTR's soldiers were instructed to vacate the ship, and were dispersed among the sand dunes where, it was thought, they would be safer. It was not long before this theory was put to the test. 'Suddenly,' wrote Watt, '[we heard] the drone of planes overhead [and] the scream of bombs, and the deafening crash of explosions left me clawing at the sand. This was for real. My first encounter with the reality of war. I was shaking with fear, and felt ashamed that others [might] see it on my face.'[10]

While his men were receiving their baptism of fire, Keller was reporting to Colonel Rupert Holland, Area Commandant of Calais, whose headquarters were in a medical centre in Boulevard Léon Gambetta.[11] Their discussion was inconclusive. After Holland had read the contents of Keller's sealed envelope, he could only give the RTR commander what amounted to another clue in this military version of a treasure hunt: Keller was to obtain his orders from 'GHQ'.[12]

The first GHQ officer Keller encountered was General Brownrigg, who had turned up in Calais in a destroyer.[13] Honouring his promise to Brigadier Fox-Pitt, Brownrigg instructed Keller to go quickly to Boulogne. If Keller had been ready to move, he and his tanks would have proceeded to Boulogne immediately, but that was impossible because the ship carrying the tanks did not arrive in Calais until around 4 p.m., and even then Keller had to wait while she was unloaded.[14] However, at 11 p.m. 3 RTR's orders were changed. A Major Ken Bailey had turned up with orders from GHQ, which were diametrically opposed to those Keller had been given by Brownrigg: 3 RTR's tanks were to go to St Omer, twenty-nine miles east of Boulogne.[15]

Unfortunately, by the time Bailey appeared, Brownrigg had departed, and therefore Keller could not ask him which orders he was supposed to obey. Sending the tanks to St Omer immediately in the hope that another GHQ officer could be contacted there would have been one way to resolve the conflict. However, that solution was also infeasible. Even if the unloading of the ship containing his tanks could have proceeded briskly, a long delay was built in because of the way the ship had been loaded: although it was obvious that Keller would need his heaviest tanks, the thirty cruisers, for any serious operation, the dockers at Southampton had placed them at the bottom of the vehicle ship.[16] That meant the upper levels had to be unloaded before the cruisers became accessible. The cutting off of the electricity supply and the downing of tools by the ship's staff for four and a half hours during the night of 22–3 May merely increased the delay.[17]

Keller's only consolation was that his predicament could have been worse: left to his own devices, the ship's commander would have steamed out of the harbour without unloading the tanks, so alarmed was he by the German bombing. He only changed his mind after a revolver, pointed at him by 3 RTR's second-in-command, persuaded him that leaving port with the tanks on board would be equally unwise.[18] There was another obstacle: once the tanks had been unloaded they could not go out on patrol immediately because their guns, which had been packed separately from the hulls, were coated with mineral jelly, and had to be cleaned before they could be mounted.[19]

While the ship was being unloaded an attempt was made to clarify the instructions. As soon as enough light tanks were on dry land, a small patrol was sent to search for GHQ. Unfortunately it returned having failed to find any GHQ staff officers at St Omer. This did not satisfy Major Bailey, who decided that he himself would accompany another patrol to St Omer during the morning of 23 May.

We know what happened to Bailey on this trip after he became separated from the escorting tanks thanks to a recently discovered account by Dick Page, another officer sent with instructions for Keller from Lord Gort's command post. Having delivered his message, Page agreed to act as Bailey's driver during the St Omer expedition. 'At a crossroad just outside Calais, we stopped to check our route on the map,' wrote Page.

Our belts and revolvers were on the back seat . . . Hardly had we done so, than a German soldier . . . sprang out of a deep ditch just by the car, fired a couple of shots into our bonnet from his sub-machine gun, and shouted 'Aus!' Bailey, being on the ditch side, tumbled out first, and was shot through the shoulder as he did so. I followed, but he [the German] did not fire again, and we got down into the bottom of the ditch. Our truck driver [who had been following in his truck] . . . seized his rifle and jumped down on to the road. The German pulled a stick grenade out of his belt, and threw it at him. It hit the road in front of him [the driver] and burst . . . He went down and did not move . . . He was dead.[20]

Page and Bailey had bumped into the advance guard of Guderian's 1st Panzer Division, which was supposed to be passing to the east of Calais on its way to Dunkirk.[21] The advance guard, including the German who had shot Bailey, withdrew after being attacked by men in a Royal Army Service Corps petrol-supply company which had fortuitously appeared on the scene in the nick of time. This permitted both Bailey and Page to escape back to Calais. Bailey, who reached Calais at around midday, was in time to tell Keller that although the Germans had reached the road to St Omer, 3 RTR should nevertheless still attempt to break through since the Germans had retreated after being stopped in their tracks.

Thus, twenty-four hours after his arrival in France Keller, who had been handed another message from Brownrigg confirming that the tanks should go to Boulogne, was still receiving conflicting orders from different officers.[22] His subsequent decision to comply with Bailey's command appears to have been influenced by the fact that officers in Calais assumed, incorrectly, that Boulogne had already fallen.[23] However, Keller, who, in addition to the information Bailey had given him about the Germans, had also been told by a French source that a column of German tanks had been spotted moving towards Calais from Marquise, was far from convinced that Bailey's command was still practicable.[24] As he wrote after the campaign, he eventually ordered his tanks to proceed at around 2.15 p.m. towards St Omer via Guînes 'against my better judgment'.[25]

It was a decision he was to regret. The British tanks were around one mile south-east of Hames-Boucres, when a German armoured column backed up with anti-tank guns and artillery was spotted on the road to the south running from Pihen-les-Guînes to Guînes. Battle was joined, and by the time Keller ordered his men to retreat at least seven of his tanks were out of action, and the battalion had suffered its first casualties.[26] This was brought home to the commander of one of the battalion's carriers as he was being driven back towards Calais when his driver 'nodded towards three bundles covered by groundsheets. Boots stuck out from under them.'[27]

During the fighting, Keller received a message stating that 'a Brigadier Nicholson' wished to talk to him.[28] An account attached to 3 RTR's war diary, when describing Keller's reaction to this message, states: 'Replied middle of battle. What does he want? Put on air.'[29] That was the polite version. 'Get off the air. I'm trying to fight a bloody battle!' was the version that circulated within the battalion.[30] Keller only discovered who Brigadier Nicholson was, and what he was doing in Calais, when the two men met during the early part of the evening. Brigadier Claude Nicholson was the new commander of all British troops in Calais, and he instructed Keller to take his remaining tanks back to the town centre.

Meanwhile the troops assembled to 'secure' Calais had been digging themselves in. When the QVR arrived on 22 May, they had gone beyond the town centre, and had placed roadblocks on most of the principal roads leading into Calais. The one exception was the road to Boulogne which was left to 3 RTR. However, one infantry battalion stretched over such a wide area could not be expected to hold off a determined attack for long, which was why the War Office arranged for two more battalions to arrive in Calais on the following day: the 1st Battalion, the Rifle Brigade and the 2nd Battalion, the King's Royal Rifle Corps (KRRC).[31] Once they had arrived, Nicholson was able to put in place a double-banked defence line. The Germans would have to pass through the QVR screen outside the town before reaching Calais's 'outer perimeter': a ring of nineteenth-century battlements punctuated by bastions, which, if covered by the Rifle Brigade and the KRRC, would, it was hoped, be more easily defended. The extra troops also provided Nicholson with an additional bonus: the men in these battalions were full-time regular soldiers, who might be expected to stiffen the resistance that might be supplied by the QVR's less experienced territorials.

That kind of logic did not impress everyone who saw off the troops at Southampton docks on 22 May. When KRRC officer Lieutenant Grismund Davies-Scourfield, while chatting at Southampton's docks to an embarkation sergeant-major, remarked, 'I suppose you're pretty busy just now, plenty of people sailing and all that,' the sergeant-major replied lugubriously, 'Not many sailing, but there'll be plenty coming home. The regiment's going the wrong way, if you ask me.'[32] It did not take Davies-Scourfield and his men long to discover what the sergeant-major meant. As they and their Rifle Brigade comrades walked off the ships at Calais during the early afternoon of 23 May, one of the first sights that caught their eyes was a long line of corpses laid out alongside an even longer line of wounded men on stretchers on a platform at the Gare Maritime.[33]

The it-will-never-happen-to-me feeling prevented any immediate panic, but later that afternoon, after ships carrying the battalions' vehicles and equipment had arrived, the KRRC's Private Eric Chambers witnessed a disturbing incident much closer to home.[34] On the way to Southampton from Fornham Park, west of Bury St Edmunds, where the KRRC had been based, the man sitting beside him had suddenly pointed to a woman in the distance who was paying a milkman, exclaiming, 'There's my wife!' The same man was shot in the forehead while seated beside Chambers in a KRRC truck in Calais's docks. He was the first KRRC casualty. The fifth-columnist who had killed him was quickly cornered in the house where he was lurking, and everyone in the area heard his terrified screams as he was bayoneted.[35] But long after the screams had died away, the idea that he and his comrades might not survive was the predominant thought in Chambers's mind as he wiped the man's blood off the seat, and drove from the docks to the town centre.

By 6.30 p.m., British soldiers were manning the battlements that constituted the outer perimeter.[36] They were only just in time. While German records show that the 1st Panzer Division had been ordered during the night of 22–3 May to head towards Dunkirk, which meant bypassing Calais, they might have been tempted to take the town, had it not been defended. (Details of actions fought by Searchlight Regiment troops which warned off the 1st Panzer Division are described in note 37).[37] On 23 May Guderian ordered the 10th Panzer Division to capture the town in the 1st Panzer Division's place.[38] General Ferdinand Schaal, the 10th Panzer Division's commander, then instructed his troops to try to take Calais that same night.[39] They backed off when met by gunfire that told them the town was strongly defended.

Although by this time Calais was protected by Nicholson's troops, he appears to have remained reluctant to fight it out in the town, which he felt would be 'difficult' to hold, even with reinforcements. (Additional difficulties experienced by Nicholson and his troops are mentioned in note 40.)[40] He was given an opportunity to find a way out during the afternoon of 23 May when the War Office instructed him to take 350,000 rations to Dunkirk. He was told that the task was to be given strict priority 'overriding all other considerations'.[41] With that in mind, he told Keller to send out another patrol to discover whether the road to Dunkirk via Gravelines was still passable.

Thirty-three-year-old Major Bill Reeves set off at 11 p.m. in his A13 cruiser tank escorted by three light tanks. He first realized it might be difficult to get through when he came across a series of barricades placed across the road. But when he drove past the first barricade without meeting any opposition, he appears to have dropped his guard. This might have had fatal consequences for, as he wrote in his report, after he had gone through a third roadblock, he discovered that 'the enemy were present in large numbers on either side of the road. [However] they did not seem in the least perturbed at seeing us, and I soon realized that they thought we were their own tanks. Some of the German troops waved to us as we passed, and we returned the compliment.'[42]

The mortal danger in which Reeves and his men found themselves was dramatically increased by the action of one of his tank commanders:

'Peter Williams stopped his tank on one occasion, thinking the soldiers were French, and said "Parlez-vous anglais?"' Disaster was only averted because the German soldier approached appeared to be as much in the dark as Williams. 'The German . . . merely shook his head and walked off,' wrote Reeves.[43]

Their journey through German lines continued for about two miles, after which, as Reeves recorded, 'they [the Germans] appeared to be getting suspicious, and one or two despatch riders came up and [pointed] torches at my tank, and moved off rapidly as if to report'. However, Reeves's group was forced to halt when they reached a hump-backed bridge spanning the canal at Marck, where a line of mines connected by a strip of metal had been placed across the road.[44] Reeves's account explains how even this obstacle was surmounted:

The only solution appeared to be to explode them by two pounder fire. I fired two rounds at them and exploded two, but the remaining six were intact. We decided that to go on firing would raise a hornets' nest, so Sergeant Cornwell volunteered to get out of his tank and remove the mines. This was an extremely nerve racking business, especially as we had seen two Germans on the other side of the bridge . . . There was dead silence as the Sergeant quietly crept from his tank, revolver in hand, and proceeded to attach the tow rope of his tank to the mines . . . The bright moonlight and the stillness seemed to accentuate the feeling of hidden danger . . .

Cornwell's own account describes what happened next: '[I] got back aboard and closed down, and we reversed away, and was able to pull them far enough to one side to make enough room to get past.'[45]

'Having crossed the bridge, our troubles were not over however,' wrote Reeves.

For we ran straight into coil after coil of anti-tank wire, which wound itself around our tanks and sprockets, and brought two tanks to a dead standstill. At that moment I thought our number was up . . . But . . . no Germans [were] yet in sight . . . The crews got out and proceeded to cut away the wire with wire cutters. This took about twenty minutes and we were once again on the move.

The tanks eventually reached Gravelines.

Unfortunately Reeves's good fortune did not help Keller and Nicholson, waiting anxiously for news in Calais. Reeves's radio did not work
properly, and all Keller heard from him was a couple of garbled snippets
which included, 'I've an important message for you,' and 'Canal bank
Gravelines'.[46] This initially led Keller to assume incorrectly that the way
was clear.[47] However, subsequent patrols sent out during the early hours
of 24 May were unable to force their way through the German anti-tank
guns, and the British patrols had to retreat back to Calais. It was only
then that Nicholson concluded Calais was indeed surrounded.[48]

But at 3 a.m. on 24 May, Nicholson received the following telegram
from Major-General Dewing at the War Office: 'Evacuation decided in
principle. When you have finished unloading your two MT [motor
transport] ships, commence embarkation of all personnel except fighting
personnel who will remain to cover final evacuation.'[49]

Three hours later Dewing warned Nicholson on the telephone that,
although Calais was to be abandoned, the evacuation would not take
place for at least twenty-four hours.[50] It was in the wake of this conversation that Nicholson, buoyed up by the knowledge that defiant resistance would probably lead to the successful rescue of his troops, prepared
to withstand the coming siege.

At this point the British and French paths in Calais started to diverge.
The French commander of land forces in Calais was Commandant
Raymond Le Tellier. He had set up his headquarters in the sixteenth-
century citadel situated on the western side of the Old Town where he
had the frustrating task of trying to cobble together a viable defence for
the areas of Calais he could control with the limited forces at his
disposal.[51] As if that was not difficult enough, his attempt to assert his
authority was undermined by his having to tiptoe round the wishes of
Commandant Carlos de Lambertye who, as Commandant du Front de
Mer, remained in command of the naval coastal batteries dotted in and
around Calais. Le Tellier also appears to have had mixed feelings about
Nicholson. The presence of the British commander with four battalions
at his disposal was welcome in that it meant the town could be defended.
However, it also underlined his own forces' weakness, and this may
have dented his pride.

Had the two men been acting together, they might have agreed to
tell their respective generals that Calais was impossible to defend against
a strong attack without substantial reinforcements. The Royal Navy

could then have been sent in to evacuate the troops, as had happened at Boulogne. However, instead of supporting Nicholson's wish to leave the town by giving his superiors a realistic appraisal of the town's inadequate defences, Le Tellier effectively stabbed his British counterpart in the back. During the early hours of 24 May, Le Tellier telephoned General Fagalde, who on 23 May had been placed in command of all land forces in the Channel ports, to complain that the British were about to evacuate Calais.[52] Fagalde, who appears not to have appreciated the weakness of the British defences, said that he would ask General Weygand to have the evacuation cancelled. As far as he was concerned, the British troops were to hold Calais whether they liked it or not.

If, in spite of this act of betrayal, the French were hoping to motivate the British troops, they could not have gone about achieving their aim in a more clumsy way. During the early hours of 24 May the French naval forces in Calais had given their British allies the impression that they intended to stand their ground. Coastal guns operated by French sailors had started firing at the Germans at 4.45 a.m., and had carried on even though they had become the prime target of the German artillery.[53] But then, in scenes reminiscent of what had happened at Boulogne, all but one of the French naval gun batteries were spiked between 10.30 and 11.30 a.m., and rather than being ordered to fight on as infantrymen, the gunners were told to go down to the harbour to catch French ships that were waiting for them. The last of this group of sailors, who had been occupying a gun battery in the docks, were told that if they were not down at the quay within five minutes, the ship would depart without them.[54] They smartly abandoned their position, and reached the ship shortly before she steamed out of the harbour.

It has not been possible to pinpoint with any certainty the order that permitted de Lambertye to authorize the French Navy's exodus. It is also unclear whether it was given with Le Tellier's consent. At least one witness has testified that the two men did not always see eye to eye.[55] It is just possible that de Lambertye was relying on an order given by Admiral Abrial on 20 May permitting the evacuation of naval personnel from the coastal batteries if they discovered they were no longer covered by Allied forces, which would have been the case if the British really had been withdrawn from the town.[56] Or perhaps de Lambertye had concluded that the gunners would only be in the way once their weapons had been spiked since they were not armed with rifles and machine-guns.

Whatever the reason, it was certainly not his own cowardice. Although de Lambertye was almost incapacitated by painful bouts of angina, he not only refused to depart but, shortly before the departure of the ships with around 1500 soldiers and sailors on board, made a passionate plea to those who were able and willing to listen to consider returning as volunteers to man some of the forts that had just been evacuated. Only one man from the ships volunteered, an artillery officer called Capitaine Michel Blanchardière, but he and de Lambertye managed to collect around fifty more Frenchmen who were willing to stay.[57] These volunteers can have been under no illusion about the danger of the mission they were being asked to fulfil. De Lambertye warned them that if they were not rescued, they must be prepared to die at their posts.[58] They did not let him down. After they had been placed in Bastion 11 on the western side of the outer perimeter, they held their section of the line around Calais until the end of the battle.

Notwithstanding this one notable exception, British soldiers were upset by the French forces' mass evacuation. But that did not justify the appalling treatment meted out to some troops who remained at their posts. The gunners who stayed were concentrated in Bastion 2 on the north-eastern side of the outer perimeter. Their commander, Lieutenant de Vaisseau Lavier, had prepared to depart as soon as he saw that the other bastions which had been occupied by the French were being abandoned. He even went so far as to cement up his guns. However, at midday on 24 May, when he was told to open fire, he dutifully had his men knock and rub off the cement, and instructed the gunners to aim at the targets given to him, beyond Coquelles, for about an hour.[59] And when he was told to shorten the range of his firing, he burst into tears of frustration at receiving an order he could not obey. As he remarked to his commander, if he went ahead and fired his guns as requested, they would probably kill more Allied troops and civilians than Germans. On hearing this, de Lambertye told Lavier to spike his guns, and retreat with his men to Dunkirk.[60]

Lavier's first attempt to escape failed. He and the five men who had remained with him after the departure of the others tried to board a British ship, tied up to the quay, only to be told that there was barely enough room for British evacuees and wounded, let alone Frenchmen. Lavier then drove with his men out of Calais into the countryside to the east of the outer perimeter, stopping on the way to pick up an

English map of Calais from a pile of British equipment. He and his party ended up driving into a farm, presumably hoping that they might be able to lie low there until the battle was over.[61]

The farm was held by a British officer and fifteen of his men. They were probably from or acting under the command of the Rifle Brigade, which was holding the eastern side of the perimeter. Even before Lavier and his group arrived there was enmity in the air between British and French soldiers on the farm. The British soldiers had already locked all of the French troops into a barn. This may have been prompted by an order from the Rifle Brigade's second-in-command, Major Alexander Allan, who had told his men that all Frenchmen without arms should be 'arrested' and guarded. He had added, 'No nonsense about safety catches; shoot them if they move.'[62]

Nevertheless, to begin with the British troops were nice to Lavier, inviting him and his right-hand man into the farm's kitchen to share their food. It only subsequently became clear to the Frenchmen that they were being subjected to a kind of interrogation. The atmosphere grew more oppressive when Lavier, who had not been based in Calais for long, was unable to answer questions about the town's civil administration. This made the British soldiers suspicious. Lavier's truck was searched. When the British map of Calais was discovered, the British officer decided that Lavier and his aide must be spies. Shortly afterwards the two Frenchmen were put up against a wall and shot. Lavier was killed, but his aide, who collapsed on to the floor as the shots were fired, crawled away in the dark despite his wounds and made good his escape.[63] The rest of Lavier's men, who had been locked up by the British, were captured by the Germans after the British retreated.

Although the Lavier incident remained a well-kept secret until after the battle, the fate of at least two QVR platoons was affected by the Anglo-French rift. On 23 May, Captain Tim Munby, the commander of a QVR scout-carrier platoon, was ordered to set up a roadblock on the road running from Calais to Boulogne. He placed it a little to the west of Fort Nieulay, the ruined eighteenth-century fortress, west of Calais, that dominates the main road.[64] During the afternoon of 23 May, his three carrier sections were reinforced by another QVR platoon. An hour later, prompted by an order from his colonel, he asked the French captain who was holding the fort with some forty soldiers whether the QVR troops could join the French inside the fort. After speaking to Le

Tellier on the telephone, the French Captain Herreman reluctantly agreed that Munby and his men could enter the fort provided that Munby promised not to retire later. This condition appears to have been a snide response to the British failure to fight to the finish at Boulogne.[65] Although the fort, which was perhaps better described as a five-acre field surrounded by thirty–forty-foot-high battlements, could not be expected to hold out against a determined siege, Munby agreed to comply with Herreman's request, a courageous gesture, given that he must have realized that if the Germans mounted a strong attack, everyone in his force would probably end up being taken prisoner if they survived at all.

But Captain Herreman and Le Tellier were not satisfied with this, and at 2.45 p.m. on 24 May, during the subsequent siege, Herreman complained to Le Tellier that the British were not allowing their tanks to be used to relieve the fort's garrison. The telephone line connecting them was cut in the middle of the discussion, but not before Herreman had indicated that he intended to fight to the finish, and that he would probably be overrun sooner or later. Rather than reflecting responsibly that it might not be fair to expect the British to sacrifice their tanks in a lost cause, Le Tellier, as he recorded in his diary, immediately decided 'to intervene in person with the English command, and to insist that they should order the officer in charge of their tanks . . . to go to the aid of their French comrades'.[66] Despite Le Tellier's request, the tanks were not sent to help Captain Herreman, and by 4.30 p.m. Herreman had surrendered, in the process condemning the British captain and his men, who had effectively been 'locked in' by the French demands, to five years as prisoners-of-war.[67]

18: Calais – Fight to the Finish

Calais, 24–7 May 1940
(See Map 12)

If Munby and his men had not linked up with the French, they might have been permitted to retreat during 24 May, along with other QVR platoons holding the roads into Calais, back to the outer perimeter of the town itself. (Details of the QVR's withdrawal are in note 1.)[1] That was where Lieutenant Davies-Scourfield and his comrades in KRRC's B Company were waiting during the early hours of 24 May. They were on the western side of the outer perimeter. Davies-Scourfield's own position was on and around Bastion 9. (The outer perimeter including Bastion 9, and the inner perimeter to which the KRRC subsequently retreated, are shown in Map 12 on pp. 526–7.)

Because he had been told that they were only expecting a 'weak column' of Germans, reinforced with 'a few guns . . . captured from the French', he was inclined to agree with his company commander's verdict that 'we jolly well ought to be able to stop them.'[2]

This attitude was encouraged by the weather: according to Davies-Scourfield, it 'promised to be a beautiful day . . . and as we set about improving our positions, my spirits rose'.[3] But his optimistic outlook was disturbed when he observed a solitary carrier coming down the road towards him rather than the three that had set out earlier that morning. 'Out of it jumped "old" Bateman [aged about thirty-five . . .] calling urgently for help,' wrote Davies-Scourfield.

In front of the carrier, slumped behind his Boys [anti-tank] rifle, sat Lance Corporal Smith, dead. Beside him, exhausted, and in pain, was the driver, Wilson, who had almost had his leg shot off. Blood was everywhere, and the armoured plating on the front of the vehicle was twisted and mangled . . . Bateman reported that . . . the two leading carriers . . . had been put out of action, and, he thought, their crews all killed.[4]

As Davies-Scourfield wrote in his memoirs: 'It no longer seemed such a lovely morning.'

That was just the beginning. Throughout the rest of the morning, the KRRC on the western ramparts had to endure shelling and machine-gun fire as the left wing of the German attack tried to soften up the defenders before advancing. At noon on 24 May, the British soldiers saw a long line of German tanks being deployed on the ridge overlooking their position. The KRRC had only three of the RTR's light tanks in support in case the Germans broke through but, as Davies-Scourfield later recalled, their presence at least gave him the opportunity to pose a question that he hoped might elicit a comforting response:

I asked [the RTR officer] whether the Redoubt would be of any use as an obstacle to the tanks, and whether our Boys rifles would be effective, at least at close range. I well remember his response. 'None whatsoever,' he said. 'They'll laugh at this bank, and your Boys rifles wouldn't blow a track off at point-blank range. Our only hope is to bluff them; [we have to] make them think we have a big force here.'[5]

Fortunately, the KRRC's bluff appeared to work. Although German tanks quickly targeted any British guns used in the front line, they never mounted a massed attack, which would almost certainly have succeeded. But even holding a position behind the KRRC's front line was an uncomfortable, life-threatening experience, according to the following extract from the account by 2nd Lieutenant Airey Neave, the Searchlight Regiment officer, and budding politician, who was hiding behind a wall in a side-street near the Pont Jourdan railway bridge (north-east of Bastion 9):

At . . . about 4 p.m. [24 May], a [British] cruiser tank moved forward . . . and an officer peered out of the turret. He fired two or three rounds, and then withdrew. The Germans replied with great violence. Tank shells and machine-gun bullets came thick and fast for twenty minutes. Ricochets off the walls and flying glass made my situation . . . rather exposed . . . The wall which sheltered me had ragged gaps where mortar bombs had flung bricks into the street . . . The enemy seemed dreadfully close, though I could see nothing but clouds of dust and smoke . . .

He went on to relate how, after putting up with the discomfort caused by the dust and heat for some time, he eventually moved across the street in a bid to reach a nearby café where he intended to quench his intolerable thirst: 'I waited for the fire to lift, and was about to cross, when I felt a sharp bruising pain in my left side. I collapsed to the pavement, my rifle clattering.' Fortunately he was able to get up, and stumbled across to the café. Inside, as he recalled, 'a medical orderly opened my battledress blouse . . . From far away, I heard him say: "You're a lucky one, sir. 'Arf an inch from the 'eart!" '⁶

As the fighting continued, it gradually became clear to Brigadier Nicholson that he could not hold the existing outer perimeter for another day. He would have to order his men to retreat to the inner perimeter he had selected. This still involved his forces retaining the northern ends of the lines of ramparts and bastions that ran from north to south on the west and east of the town. In other words the area of the outer perimeter near the sea was to be retained. But the depth of land held was to be drastically reduced, with Allied forces remaining in the Old Town to the north of Bassin de Batellerie, while allowing the Germans to take over the New Town.⁷ To fit in with his plan Davies-Scourfield and his men would have to abandon Bastion 9 without further fighting; they were then to move to their new position on the south side of the Old Town.

Not surprisingly, the British soldiers fighting in the front line knew nothing of the high-level discussions that were to decide their fate. During the morning of 24 May, the Anglo-French disagreement about whether Calais should be evacuated had become a talking-point in England. The following note, which records what Major-General Dewing told Vice-Admiral Ramsay in Dover at 10.40 a.m., shows how quickly Le Tellier's complaint about the planned evacuation was processed: 'Nick [Nicholson], the fellow over there, has got a perfectly clear order . . . That stands. But he and his fellows – the useful ones – are to go on doing their job for a minimum of twenty-four hours . . . But I must warn you that this business is now up on the very highest levels, and God knows what they will decide.'⁸

By the end of the afternoon, Nicholson was not alone in believing that the evacuation policy should be decided sooner rather than later. At 5.28 p.m., an hour after the destroyers patrolling outside the harbour had been attacked by German Junkers, resulting in one British destroyer sunk and two severely damaged, the commander of HMS *Wolfhound*, who, regardless of events in the harbour at Boulogne, had steamed into Calais's harbour, sent Dover the following warning from Calais's Principal Sea Transport Officer: 'Enemy now in southern portions of Calais. Brigadier is trying to organize a line in town. My private view is that situation is desperate unless reinforcements arrive forthwith.'[9] A further signal sent at 7.05 p.m. suggested that events were spinning out of Nicholson's control: 'Reinforcement urgent if whole garrison be not overwhelmed.'[10]

It is not clear when Nicholson first discovered that the evacuation was to be cancelled. At some point during the battle, 2nd Lieutenant Hugo Ironside, 3 RTR's intelligence officer, picked up a telephone that had been ringing in the citadel, and was surprised to find his distant cousin General Sir Edmund Ironside on the line. It must have been an embarrassing moment for the general, who had advised his young relation to go into the army rather than the air force for the sole purpose of avoiding death during the first six months of the war. Yet now he had to tell him that he must fight to the finish: there was to be no evacuation, and young Hugo was asked to pass on this unwelcome message to the brigadier.[11]

In case there was still any doubt in Nicholson's mind, the War Office sent him the following message via *Wolfhound* at 11.23 p.m.:

In spite of policy of evacuation given you this morning, fact that British forces in your area now under . . . [Fagalde], who has ordered no . . . evacuation, means that you must comply for sake of Allied solidarity. Your role is therefore to hold on, harbour being for present of no importance to BEF . . . No reinforcements . . . You will select best position and fight on.[12]

General Ironside also sent a message to Nicholson: 'General Fagalde appointed command [sic] all allied troops in North. Fagalde appoints you cammand [sic] allied troops in Calais and forbids evacuation. You will carry out the order . . . Yours are all regular troops, and I need not say more.'[13]

One can only speculate on what Nicholson must have felt when he received these callous signals. His torment must have been all the more acute because, having received the messages that morning telling him that the evacuation would take place, he had told Keller to burn his remaining tanks. This not only led to more complaints from the French but also seriously reduced his forces' firepower.[14] By the time this order was revoked, Keller had only four cruisers and ten light tanks left.[15]

Whatever his personal anguish, Nicholson duly gave the orders to what remained of his four battalions to retreat to the inner perimeter. His instructions were put into effect at 11.45 a.m. on 24 May in relation to the Rifle Brigade's section of the inner perimeter, and between 8.30 and 11.30 p.m. on 24 May in relation to the KRRC's section.[16] At least some of the men in the front line were then instructed that they must hold their new positions and fight to the last man and last round.[17]

Next morning the British defenders, cooped up inside Calais's Old Town, saw the ominous sight of the German flag, emblazoned with a swastika, fluttering over the Hôtel de Ville. It so excited Oberst Menny, the German commander leading the 10th Panzer Division's right-hand attacking group, that he jumped the gun, claiming Calais was already taken.[18] In some ways he was right, for with the Hôtel de Ville's bell-tower, Calais's equivalent of Big Ben, in German hands, German snipers were able to pick off anyone moving near the three main bridges spanning the canals and waterways that separated the German and British front lines. That made the defence of the Old Town very difficult, and it was almost inevitable that, sooner or later, once German tanks were deployed against the barricades by the bridges, even this new line would be breached.

However, it was not just the defenders who had problems. During the late afternoon of 24 May, Guderian warned General Schaal, the 10th Panzer Division's commander, that if Calais could not be taken without heavy German losses, his troops must be held back until Stuka attacks had softened up the British defences.[19] This explains why, at around 9 a.m. on 25 May, Schaal attempted to minimize casualties on both sides by sending André Gerschell, the Jewish mayor of Calais, who had bravely remained at his post until the Germans arrived, to ask Nicholson whether he would surrender. Nicholson's reaction to this was observed by Austin Evitts, who had been adopted as Nicholson's signalman within the citadel: ' "Surrender!" said the Brigadier in a decidedly brusque manner. "No, I shall not surrender. Tell the Germans that if they want Calais, they will have to fight for it." '[20]

The fighting recommenced. But at midday, Schaal decided to afford the British a further opportunity to give in before unleashing XIX Corps' heavy artillery, which had been brought up from Boulogne. The

deadline for Nicholson's reply to the new peace initiative was initially
1 p.m., but it was extended to 3.30 p.m. after Schaal discovered that the
German officer, who had orders to pass the peace overture to Nicholson,
had been detained by British soldiers at their front line, and had only
reached the citadel at around 2 p.m.[21] By then Nicholson's morale had
been buoyed up with the following stirring message from Anthony
Eden, Secretary of State for War:

To Brigadier Nicholson. Defence of Calais to the utmost is of vital importance
to our country as symbolising our continued co-operation with France. The
eyes of the Empire are upon the defence of Calais, and H.M. Government are
confident you and your gallant regiments will perform an exploit worthy of
the British name.[22]

Shortly afterwards, Nicholson's defiant reply to the German question,
asking whether he would surrender, was delivered to Schaal: 'The
answer is no, as it is the British Army's duty to fight as well as it is the
German's.'[23] The German response to this was a murderous artillery
barrage fired into the Old Town.[24]

Few accounts adequately record the suffering endured by British
soldiers in Calais during the fighting on 25 May. One that gives a better
taste than most was written by William Harding, the gunner whose
vivid description of his first visit to a French brothel is mentioned in
Chapter 2. After his guns were destroyed by German shelling in the
front line to the west of the outer perimeter, he was ordered to assist
the QVR and, acting as an infantryman, helped to hold the line in the
Old Town running from the lighthouse beside Place de Russie to the
sea.[25] The following extract from his account includes a description of
the kind of events and injuries that must have been commonplace
in the front line as British soldiers stood their ground on the inner
perimeter:

I heard a sobbing behind me, and on looking round I saw a soldier dragging
himself along by his elbows, leaving a trail of two red lines behind him. I saw
that both his feet were missing . . . At that moment, help arrived and he was
taken away.

The mortar fire became very heavy with bombs dropping all over the
place . . . I saw the Vickers pom-pom get a direct hit . . . I jumped up instinc-

tively, and ran over to the gun, but it was shattered, with its ammunition belts lying twisted over, its three gunners lying looking up out of dead eyes, with only their uniforms holding them together . . .

I returned to my position . . . I had just laid down in my spot . . . when some riflemen with bayonets fixed ran across our front. A tail end chap was hit by a mortar bomb, which resulted in a low wall looking as if buckets of red paint had been thrown over it. The man completely disintegrated, with his head resting on his neck, his arms and legs close by. His face had a slight smile on it. I ran over without thinking, and saw that his torso was stripped of clothing, [and] his abdomen [was also stripped of its flesh] revealing undisturbed intestines, such as is seen in a photograph in a medical book . . . It was a sickening sight.[26]

The reports by Major Alexander Allan, second-in-command of the Rifle Brigade, reveal what finally enabled the Germans to pierce the inner perimeter that afternoon. The French troops still in Calais had intercepted a German radio message that showed they were planning to launch a strong attack on the western sector of the perimeter, held by the KRRC. This prompted Nicholson to order the Rifle Brigade to launch a counter-attack of its own in an attempt to forestall the German offensive. The order that was delivered to the Rifle Brigade at 1 p.m. required them to release all of their carriers. Eleven carriers and two tanks were duly assembled for the counter-attack.[27] This British armour was to pass through the ramparts just to the north of the Bassin des Chasses de L'Est, and was then to speed round to the south in order to attack the German troops from the rear.[28] It must have appeared an attractive move to Nicholson, after all the defending his men had done.

Unfortunately, it was also ill-advised. The carriers and tanks were playing a vital role in shoring up the Rifle Brigade's line. But although the Rifle Brigade's commanding officer, Lieutenant-Colonel Chandos Hoskyns, protested that the manoeuvre would probably weaken the defences to such an extent that the Germans would break through, Colonel Holland, who had delivered Nicholson's command, insisted that the attack should nevertheless go ahead. Hoskyns was unable to appeal to Nicholson directly since the telephone line linking the Rifle Brigade with the brigadier was dead.

Radio contact with the brigadier was re-established before the attack could start, and Nicholson agreed that it should be cancelled as soon as he heard Hoskyns's objections. But it was too late. While the carriers had been away, the Germans made their first breakthrough. That did not mean the British defenders were defeated. The Rifle Brigade withdrew through the town to the north, fighting as they went. But while before they had been able to form up behind a single line of canals and ramparts, now each company was reduced to conducting its own guerrilla war, withdrawing from street to street, from building to building, as it retreated towards the harbour often without knowing where neighbouring units were holding.

Each time a section of the British front line was forced back, there was a risk that the rearguard holding up the Germans would be surrounded while the others retreated. This was what occurred at the south-eastern section of the inner perimeter when, as Hoskyns had predicted, the Rifle Brigade's front line was pushed back. Major Allan has described how, after a counter-attack aiming to rescue the rearguard was beaten back by machine-gun fire, those left behind on the front line made a courageous attempt to escape and join their comrades:

A French camion appeared full of wounded men belonging to [the] Company in charge of Corporal Lane, and driven by a fifth columnist at the point of a revolver. In spite of being waved on, the driver stopped under fire, and while the wounded who could, were getting out, to try to crawl across the road, [2nd Lieutenant] Edward Bird ran forward, climbed into the driver's seat, and endeavoured to start the lorry. In [the course of] this gallant effort, he was shot in the head, dying soon afterwards.

According to Allan, 'Few . . . were extricated from this imbroglio.'[29] Only some thirty of around 150 men in the sector were saved.[30] Lieutenant Bird was just one of four Rifle Brigade officers who received fatal wounds during the afternoon – another of whom was the battalion's commanding officer.

But of all the brave acts the Rifle Brigade soldiers performed that day, it is doubtful whether any were more heroic than that carried out by Platoon Sergeant-Major Richard 'Sybil' Johnston in front of the roadblock at rue Mollien as A Company withdrew from the inner perimeter.[31] It is mentioned in the following account by the Rifle Brigade's Doug Wheeler:

The block was made out of these big rolls of undersea cable . . . We got a visit from Major Brush. We used to call him 'Maggie' . . . he was wounded in the throat, and he had a first aid dressing round it, and two fingers missing from one hand. He told us: 'You will soon come under fire, and I want you to hold this position for as long as possible. It is imperative you hold it, even to the last man' . . .

Down the Rue Mollien, there were civilians and British soldiers crossing the road . . . towards the docks side, and there was a lot of firing going on . . . Sybil said we should fire . . . at the tops of the buildings to prevent the Germans from shooting the people crossing the road. [Then] Sybil . . . said that one of the soldiers trying to cross the road was wounded. He [the soldier] was crawling, because he couldn't stand up. He [Sybil] told us to charge down the road and bring him in, but the old soldiers were not stupid, and were not keen to go. Sybil was disgusted with this, and said: 'Cover me,' and he took a wheelbarrow we'd been using to make the roadblock, and ran . . . down the road.

One man watching through a chink in the barricade reported that he had seen Johnston stagger and fall over as he was hit by German gunfire. But his true fate was only discovered later, in testimony provided by a British prisoner-of-war who went out with the Germans after the battle to collect the dead. 'He said PSM Johnston was lying in the wheel-barrow, and it was almost full of blood. He must have been hit about a dozen times.'[32]

The fighting on 25 May reached its climax during the early evening. At 6 p.m. the artillery barrage, which had continued ever since the peace initiative during the afternoon, stopped abruptly, and German tanks moved forward in an attempt to storm the bridges leading from the New Town to the Old Town. According to the KRRC's regimental history:

At the left bridge [Pont Faidherbe], three tanks advanced, followed by a saloon car. One tank forced the block, but, with another, was put out of action. The third withdrew and the car was abandoned. Major Owen [KRRC's second-in-command] was killed at this point.

At the centre bridge [Pont Richelieu], the leading tank blew up on a mine and this attack also failed.

At the right bridge [Pont Freycinet] . . . enemy infantry and one tank, backed by heavy mortar fire . . . forced our posts nearer to the Citadel.[33]

The situation was only saved, as far as the KRRC were concerned, by a determined counter-attack, in the course of which yet another KRRC officer was fatally wounded.[34]

Meanwhile Major Allan, who had taken over as the commander of the Rifle Brigade, had become desperate. By early evening he had lost touch with Nicholson in the citadel, and at 7.55 p.m. he sent the following message to Dover: 'From Rifle Brigade Calais. Citadel a shambles. Brigadier's fate unknown. Casualties Rifle Brigade may be 60 per cent. Being heavily attacked and flanked, but attempting counter-attack. Am attempting contact with KRRCs fighting in the town. Are you sending ships? Quay intact in spite of very severe bombardment.'[35]

A similar signal was read out in London that night during a specially convened War Cabinet Defence Committee meeting, and was the starting point for a discussion on whether an attempt should be made after all to evacuate the troops from Calais. The Vice-Chief of the Naval Staff told the committee members that if the Army could hold the Germans, the Navy might still be able to evacuate the Calais garrison: although it might not be possible to get a destroyer into the harbour, smaller boats would have a better chance of going in and, once in, they might be able to ferry the soldiers out to destroyers, especially if they arrived at night.[36] The minutes of the meeting continued: 'The alternative was to tell our troops in Calais to hold on at all costs, although it must be realized that this would mean the loss of the garrison.'

Those who believed that it was permissible to sacrifice the soldiers for the greater good held sway. The minutes concluded: 'It was essential to hold on to Calais for as long as possible. If we attempted to withdraw our garrison from Calais, the German troops in Calais would immediately march on Dunkirk. A message should be sent to our troops in Calais telling them that every hour that they could hold out would be of immeasurable value to the British Army.'[37]

Back in Calais, the fierce fighting that had raged throughout the late afternoon and evening died down, prompting Austin Evitts in the citadel to note

how quiet it was, now that the shelling and bombing had stopped. There was a stillness in the air all around, and it was so peaceful we might have come into another world . . . Was it I wondered the peace before the storm? . . .
Then, sometime between 2100 and 2200 hours we looked up, and to our

great surprise, saw two or three ships lying just off shore and right opposite to our positions, and with their bows pointing a little to our left. They must have only just arrived, and we recognized them at once as British destroyers . . . A mighty cheer went up, as everyone went wild with delight. Soon lights were seen to come on here and there [on the ships], and it looked as if 'action stations' might have been called . . . As the seconds ticked away, we watched with excitement, anxious to see what was going to happen. Then, with a blinding flash, and a noise like the sharp crack of thunder, their guns suddenly opened fire. It was fairly obvious their target was the German gun positions at the rear of the town somewhere, and with all forward guns firing, they pounded them . . . How it gladdened our hearts. This was the naval support we had asked for. The bombardment continued for some time. The German guns made no reply, their gunners knowing only too well perhaps that they were no match for British destroyers. When it was all over, the lights gradually went out, and once more we were left in peace.[38]

The peace did not last long, according to Evitts. He recalled observing a series of incendiary bombs being dropped on the citadel:

Soon the [barrack] buildings were alight, throwing up enormous sheets of flame high into the sky [until] all around was like day . . . The buildings continued to blaze away well into the night, but they were not the only fires burning that night in Calais; over in the direction of the docks and harbour the sky . . . was ablaze with light, reflecting the flames of other buildings burning, and above it all hung a red glow in the sky. On the west side of the harbour too, I could see huge clouds of black smoke billowing higher and higher; it was from the large oil storage tanks on fire. They were being destroyed by the Royal Marines.[39]

Had it not been for Le Tellier's tampering, it is possible that the garrison might, even at this late stage, have been evacuated. In case the French commander had a change of heart, an armada of fifteen yachts and trawlers, with the boats they had towed over from England, assembled off the coast with enough room to take around 1800 men.[40] When the evacuation order never arrived, some nevertheless went into the harbour, to pick up French and British soldiers. One of the yachts was carrying yet another message for Nicholson: 'Hold out at all costs.'[41] It was duly delivered.

The strong British – and French – resistance led to a series of crisis meetings at the headquarters of the 10th Panzer Division. During a meeting held at 11 p.m. on 25 May, General Schaal was asked by Guderian's chief of staff whether it might not be wiser to delay the *coup de grâce* until 27 May, when extra Stukas could be made available. Schaal decided to continue with the attack on 26 May in case a delay enabled the British to bring in reinforcements.[42] An artillery barrage was laid on for between 8.30 and 9 a.m. on 26 May, and Schaal's infantry battalions were instructed to attack the Allied forces inside the inner perimeter only after the German gunners had stopped firing. Special provision was made for the citadel. German Stukas were to bomb it until 10 a.m., whereupon it was to be stormed.[43]

After the bombardment and bombing on the morning of 26 May when the British had still not given way, Guderian gave Schaal one final chance to break the deadlock. This time, Schaal had a deadline: if Calais's defences were not broken by 2 p.m. that afternoon, the 10th Panzer Division would be withdrawn, and the Luftwaffe would be instructed to destroy the town.[44] With the benefit of hindsight, it can be demonstrated that Guderian was being somewhat harsh, given how close the British were to surrendering. If he had heard the situation report sent out by the British defenders at 8 a.m. that morning, he might have been less worried about the final outcome, and might have given Schaal more time than he did. The British report included phrases such as 'Quay and harbour under MG fire . . . Troops dead beat, no tanks left . . . water essential . . . reinforcements would have to be on a considerable scale . . . [and] probably a forlorn hope.' The weakened British defences were contrasted with the growing strength of the Germans, who were said to 'hold greater part of Northern town' and to 'have plenty of ammo'.[45]

Nevertheless, Nicholson and his men came near to forcing Guderian to make good his threat. It was only at 1.30 p.m. that Schaal was able to tell Guderian that the attacks were finally making progress. He reported that Allied soldiers had been seen waving white handkerchiefs from the citadel, and he and his commanders stated that they would take Calais in a matter of hours.[46]

British and French accounts suggest that the crucial German breakthrough came somewhere between 1 and 1.30 p.m. During this period, the Germans overran Bastion 11, the stronghold held by the French volunteers, who only surrendered after they ran out of ammunition.[47]

The Germans also forced the KRRC to withdraw. At 1 p.m. the KRRC were ordered to retreat from the line of the three key bridges separating the Old Town from the New Town to a line further back, running from the harbour to the Old Town's cathedral.[48] However, there was a lot of fighting, and much blood was spilled, before that decision was taken. (Details of some of this fighting are in note 49.)[49]

At around 4 p.m., even the new line became untenable, and Lieutenant-Colonel Miller, the KRRC's commanding officer, told his troops that it was every man for himself. He advised the officers with whom he was still in contact to hide until dark, and then to try to escape. After that order, the only organized resistance among the rifle companies came from KRRC's B Company whose officers had not heard that they were to withdraw towards the harbour. Eventually even they were overrun and, in the process, most of their officers were either wounded or killed.[50] At the same time, the Rifle Brigade's and the QVR's positions on the east of the Old Town were also overrun.

Evitts, who by this time had taken refuge with most of the other officers in the citadel in a large dark chamber fifteen feet below ground, has described how during the afternoon of 26 May 'the shelling stopped, and [once again], it suddenly became very quiet'. The siege was coming to an end, and although it was only about 3 p.m., British officers in the citadel, realizing they were surrounded, began to talk about holding out until dark so that they might escape.[51] But as Evitts noted in his account, their hopes were to be quickly dashed: 'Not long afterwards the French naval liaison officer came hurrying into the fort, and in a very excited manner exclaimed so that everyone could hear: "Gentlemen, the French Commander has surrendered." Immediately a cheer rose from the small group of French soldiers at the back.'

Their defeatist attitude shocked the British soldiers, who could think of nothing worse than being forced to capitulate. The prospect of giving in horrified them. 'I looked across at the Brigadier,' Evitts reported.

The bitter agony of defeat lay unmistakably written on his face. Now he was about to suffer the humiliation of surrender . . . The French naval liaison officer again came into the fort. This time he went straight to the Brigadier and spoke quietly to him. Then Colonel Holland, after a few words with him, came over to me and said: 'The Germans have reached the Fort. I want you to go out and take the first ten men with you; there you will have to surrender.'

It was, as Evitts called it, 'the bitter end'. No one was in the citadel to hear the final message from Anthony Eden, which was intended to inspire the Calais defenders. It included the words: 'Am filled with admiration for your magnificent fight which is worthy of the highest tradition of the British Army.'[52]

Notwithstanding the surrender of the citadel, there was still time during the night of 26–7 May for one last gallant exploit by British forces in Calais. In spite of the order forbidding a general evacuation, a Lieutenant Brammall was ordered by Vice-Admiral Ramsay to transform his motor yacht *Gulzar* into a hospital ship by painting red crosses on her sides so that he could go over to Calais that night to pick up any wounded. It was to be a small-scale rescue operation: the medical team consisted of just one surgeon lieutenant and two sick-bay attendants, and sixty stretchers on the boat deck stood in for beds. Henry Granlund, a member of *Gulzar*'s crew, has described the scene he witnessed as the ship approached Calais's harbour at around 2 a.m. on 27 May:

The journey was uneventful as far as the Calais breakwaters. The town itself was in flames and could be seen as far away as Dover. Billowy black clouds of smoke reflected the red flames, and it was a straight course the whole way. The breakwater lighthouses at Calais are about a third of a mile from the port itself, and a narrow channel runs from the sea to the 'bassin avant'. Her diesel motors could not be heard at slow speeds and . . . the noise was drowned by the crackling of fires and the occasional rifle shot. The glare from the burning buildings and warehouses lit up the whole basin . . . and we were surprised that no notice was taken of us.[53]

In fact, *Gulzar* was being watched closely by some fifty British soldiers, who were still standing hopefully on the piles supporting the end of the eastern jetty. It had been separated from the landward section after the jetty was hit by a shell. Another soldier, the nineteen-year-old Leslie Wright, one of Evitts's signalmen, was also watching from the top of the isolated piece of jetty. He was so cold and exhausted that he had taken off his wet clothes, and climbed into the hut on the jetty to rest. When he heard the men outside shouting 'They're coming!', he had leaped up fearing that the Germans were attacking, and was astonished to see what he later referred to as a 'British launch' chugging into the harbour.

As Wright and his comrades watched, the 'launch' was tied up beside the Gare Maritime's deserted pier, and a group of men jumped off, disappearing into the station. They did not stay long. No sooner had they entered the station than they were challenged, and as they turned and fled, shots were fired at them. Fortunately it was half-tide, so the ship's deck was beneath the level of the Gare Maritime. Once the party was back on the boat, its members were no longer silhouetted against the glare given off by the fires. Nevertheless there was no time to untie the mooring ropes; they were cut with an axe, and the ship sped away, with guns firing at her from all sides, into the harbour's channel.[54]

On the eastern jetty the Royal Marine captain, whose rank had enabled him to take command, ordered every man to shout as loudly as he could and to flash torches as the 'launch' went past them towards the open sea. It is not certain whether it was the shouting or the torches that first attracted the attention of *Gulzar*'s crew, but the men on the jetty were overjoyed when they saw her turn round and edge back towards them. Only then did *Gulzar*'s crew see who had hailed her. According to Granlund, there were 'men hiding below the pier in amongst the piles and seaweed, and on the small platforms just above the water level. Some had no clothes or weapons, none had any ammunition, and many were in the last stages of exhaustion.'[55]

As *Gulzar* approached the pier, Lieutenant Brammall shouted that he could not tie up, and that the waiting soldiers would have to jump on board as he went past. Every man on the pier managed to leap on as *Gulzar* passed and, notwithstanding the guns being fired at them by the Germans, there were no casualties. Having completed the rescue – which took the total evacuated from Calais to around 440 – Brammall turned *Gulzar* once more so that she could motor out to sea and back to Dover.[56]

St Omer, La Bassée Canal, London, 22–6 May 1940
(See Maps 1, 10 and 13)

The first steps to form a line that would protect the BEF's rear, west of Arras and La Bassée, were only taken on 20 May, three days after GHQ's Lieutenant-Colonel Bridgeman had understood the extent of the French débâcle (see Chapter 11).[1] Even then Gort's initial measures were derisory. Major-General Harry Curtis was ordered to use all available forces to prevent the Germans crossing the line of canals running from Watten to St Omer, and from St Omer to La Bassée, some thirty-five miles as the crow flies.[2] On 23 May, Curtis's line was extended some fourteen miles further to the south-east so that he also ended up with responsibility for the canals connecting La Bassée with Raches, an area that had previously been the responsibility of another *ad hoc* force set up to protect the BEF's flank while it was engaged on the Escaut (see note 3).[3]

Gort's plan sounded fine in theory. But in practice it was less than satisfactory. The only full-strength infantry units made available to Curtis initially were a single battalion from his own 46 Division, plus a brigade from 50 Division.[4] Although Curtis was given to understand on 20 May that these forces were to be bulked up with men from the Royal Engineers and Royal Artillery, reinforcement troops and service personnel, he must have wondered how, with the units at his disposal, he could possibly be expected to hold forty-eight miles of canal line which in normal circumstances would have required at least nine divisions to make them secure.[5] This did not stop him trying to fulfil Gort's bidding. On 21 May he told Brigadier Gawthorpe, who was to assist him, that the canal line was to be held 'at all costs'.[6]

Curtis and Gawthorpe could not contemplate guarding the complete line with the troops at their disposal. The best they could do was to concentrate on the bridges. Even there, the firepower they could deploy was patchy. The minimal military presence placed at the bridges has been highlighted in a report by an unidentified officer from 2 Division's 'leave details', who at 11 a.m. on 22 May was ordered to guard the bridges at Arques and St Omer, and at St Momelin if he discovered it was not already guarded by French forces.[7] His company, consisting of a core of infantrymen from the Royal Berkshires and Royal Welch Fusiliers, was made up to strength with service personnel such as drivers from the Royal Army Service Corps (RASC) – that is, men who had not been trained to fight in the front line. Even had these men been of the right mettle, they would have found it difficult to repulse a German attack because of their equipment. 'We had no Bren guns or anti-tank rifles, [we had] 50 rounds per man only, [and] . . . no ammunition for officers' revolvers,' the officer reported. 'We [also] had no picks or shovels, grenades, mines, wire or medical appliances.'[8]

His report describes how he settled in one platoon by the Arques bridge during the afternoon of 22 May, and confirmed that the bridge at St Momelin was being held by another unit, before he drove back to St Omer where some of his men had taken over the bridge by the station: 'Having no tools for digging, we were unable to construct any defences [near the St Omer bridge], and the men were obliged to take up positions as darkness came on lying behind local obstacles, and in some cases in the open.'[9] There was no opportunity to complain about their situation to Brigadier Gawthorpe. Neither the officer nor anyone he contacted had any idea where the brigadier was located.

The only good news was provided by an officer from GHQ, who arrived at about 9.45 p.m., claiming he had come to meet 'an Armoured Division' that had landed at Calais the same day. However, the surge of optimism engendered by this news was misplaced. The tank 'division' to which he was referring was in reality the 3rd Battalion, the Royal Tank Regiment, and far from having already 'landed' at Calais, most of the tanks were still at the bottom of their transport ship in Calais harbour, waiting to be unloaded (see Chapter 17). Although the officer does not mention his disappointment in his report, disappointed he must have been, for when the Germans started shelling St Omer 'at about 2300 hours', no British tanks or any other reinforcements were to be seen.[10]

The officer hoped that he had fully complied with the orders given to him after his RASC personnel took over two of the other bridges in the St Omer area, the men reaching their positions after midnight on 22–3 May. But he then learned that the artillery unit that had been holding St Momelin had left. Consequently, at the very moment when he should have been concentrating on holding the bridges at St Omer, he was obliged to weaken those defences by sending his Royal Welch Fusiliers platoon to St Momelin. As if that was not bad enough, the Searchlight Regiment battery that had been holding the St Omer station bridge until his men relieved them insisted on taking away the three lorries that were being used as a barricade. 'I protested,' the officer reported, but the Searchlight battery major 'said they had valuable equipment inside, and insisted that his drivers drove them away forthwith'. Replacing them with other trucks was 'a difficult task', wrote the officer, because at first the drivers could not be found, and when they were 'they were very adverse to doing this job under shellfire . . . The Major took with him the two Bren guns and one anti-tank rifle which he had previously loaned us, but these he later returned to me just before dawn.'[11]

'When daylight came, I took immediate steps to reorganize my positions,' the officer continued.

First of all I took all personnel off the bridge, and arranged for it to be covered by the flank. I then ordered my one anti-tank rifle to occupy a shell hole position in the wall of a house on the other flank about 100 yards south of the bridge. As all had been quiet for about an hour or two, I ordered the men to stand down in small parties, and eat what breakfast they could.

At about 0630, a French colonel and staff officer arrived, and asked me to explain my dispositions. He stated that he would immediately arrange for two tanks and an anti-tank gun to be sent up to support me, and he would also send some mines for the bridge. At 0745, the French staff officer returned with news that the Germans were at the gates of the town . . . At about the same time a French horse-drawn anti-tank gun appeared, but while getting into action a burst of machine-gun fire broke out. The horse team bolted with the ammunition limber, thus rendering the anti-tank gun useless.

Simultaneously an enemy tank appeared round the corner of a house on the far side of the bridge, and then withdrew, returning almost immediately with three others, and from the far bank at a range of about 70 yards, they proceeded to plaster our position with gun and machine-gun fire. One of the first shells set our lorries [which were blocking the bridge] on fire, and a column of smoke went up. The firing was intense, and lasted until the lorries had almost burnt out, when the tanks proceeded to advance towards us across the bridge.[12]

At that point, the officer, deciding he had nothing with which to delay the tanks, abandoned his position with his remaining men. The canal line had been breached.

Thirty miles to the south-east, in the area around La Bassée, the canal banks were guarded by General Curtis's principal infantry unit: 25 Brigade. His best troops had been deployed in this sector since, with fighting raging around Arras, it was believed that this area would be attacked next. Their brief was to hold on until larger BEF units arrived, but that would only happen as units were freed up from the main body of British troops on their eastern front.

Gort had arranged this according to the following schedule. In the course of the night of 22–3 May, the main body of the BEF had been withdrawn from the Escaut to the so-called Gort Line on the Franco-Belgian border. (Details of the positions on the border on 24 May are shown in Map 10 on pp. 522–3 and explained in note 13.)[13] At the same time, Belgian troops were moving to their sector north of the Gort Line, which involved their digging in to the north, north-west and south-west of the River Lys and the Canal de dérivation de la Lys. During the afternoon of 23 May, and the night of 23–4 May, three British divisions, the 2nd, 44th and 48th, were to be relieved by French and Belgian forces from their positions on the new Allied line. (After 44 Division had been relieved, the southern part of the Belgian line ran from Menin [thirteen miles north-east of Lille] to Deinze [twenty-three miles north-east of Menin], and from Deinze to Maldegem [sixteen miles north-west of Deinze].)

The French and the Belgians had hoped that these British troops would be used in the counter-attack planned for 26 May. However, on 23 and 24 May, Gort issued orders that the relieved divisions should replace the patchwork of forces then holding the canal line, or where that had already been breached a line just behind it, to protect the remaining BEF divisions.[14]

The 2nd Battalion, the Royal Irish Fusiliers, was one of the units within 25 Brigade. Its troops had been holding their six-mile stretch of canal line – which ran from Avelette, near Hinges, to Cuinchy, near La Bassée – since 21 May.[15] This was a very long front for one battalion to hold, and Lieutenant-Colonel Guy Gough, the commanding officer, might well have wondered whether to regard it as a joke, or a compliment to him and his men. He appears to have taken it as a compliment, and he and the battalion spent the next two days preparing their positions and burning the many barges that might have served as stepping-stones for Germans anxious to cross the waterway without getting their feet wet.[16]

On 22 May a bridge spanning the canal in the Royal Irish Fusiliers' sector was blown up. This took place long before any Germans arrived at the canal line. The commander of the company holding the bridge, who authorized the demolition, believed he had heard panzers approaching, only discovering subsequently that the clanking had been made by French tanks.[17] The demolition of another bridge nearby was swiftly halted so that the French could cross there instead. But the premature explosion upset Gough, who had been ordered not to blow any bridges unless it was absolutely necessary. The holding of the canal line, with as many bridges as possible intact, was an essential requirement for the much talked-about counter-attack.[18]

Gough's order to leave the bridges intact until the last possible moment made life very difficult for those officers in the front line who had to decide when to blow them. The right to decide when to destroy the bridge leading to Essars was delegated to the Fusiliers' 2nd Lieutenant Mike Horsfall.[19] At 2 a.m. during the night of 23–4 May, Horsfall and his sergeant-major were on the southern, 'German', side of the canal near Essars when they heard a dog barking in the distance. Horsfall was immediately suspicious, but although he strained to listen, he could not at first hear anything untoward except that more dogs had begun to bark, and their barking was coming closer. Then it dawned on him that the usual background noises had changed. A new sound came and went, rising and fading, before growing louder and eventually becoming recognizable as the unmistakable sound of soldiers marching.

When Horsfall heard someone approaching the bridge, he fired his pistol, sending a white flare up into the air. The bright light revealed what he had feared: two lines of German soldiers marching up the ramp of the bridge towards him. Fortunately for Horsfall, rather than pursuing him, they dived off the ramp into the safety of the shadows as soon as the flare illuminated the area. Even as they were taking cover, Horsfall and his sergeant-major were sprinting back to the northern end of the bridge, screaming at the sappers that the Germans had arrived.

At this point the battalion's shortage of equipment was keenly felt. Given that the prearranged signal for the blowing up of the bridge was the firing of a white flare followed by a red flare, it would have been sensible to give Horsfall and his sergeant-major two pistols so that they merely had to press two triggers to raise the alarm. However, because they had only one pistol between them, Horsfall had to waste what might have been crucial seconds in ejecting the used cartridge after firing the white flare so that he could load his pistol with the second, the red one. His task would have been hard enough if everything had gone smoothly. But as he ran, he discovered that the first cartridge could not be ejected: it was stuck. There was nothing to be done other than to bang the gun against his leg in the hope that the impact would dislodge it. In the end, the banging worked, and Horsfall was finally able to reload the gun and shoot the red flare into the sky. Seconds later there was a huge explosion, and as Horsfall looked out from the area where he and the sergeant-major had in their turn taken cover, he saw huge concrete boulders bouncing on to the road in front of them. The engineers had blown the bridge in the nick of time.[20]

Thanks to Mike Horsfall and his comrades, who held the enemy at bay for some forty-eight hours, the Germans were unable to establish a strong bridgehead over the canal near their position.[21] Unfortunately, the British forces to their right were less successful: between 23 and 25 May, German infantry, in some cases backed by armoured vehicles, crossed the canal and established several bridgeheads on the north-eastern bank. (For details see note 22.)[22]

It was only then that the repercussions of the 21 May Arras counter-attack were realized, as German commanders, concerned about what the Allies might do next, reined in the panzer corps – for the second time in two days. The first reining in had occurred on 22 May when von Rundstedt, backed by Hitler, had demanded that Allied troops around Arras should be mastered before the advance continued.[23] Ironically this cautious attitude appears to have been unwittingly influenced by Rommel, the last man who would intentionally have asked for a halt. It seems that his exaggerated claim that his 7th Panzer Division had been attacked by 'hundreds of enemy tanks' around Arras may have been taken seriously by at least some of the German generals.[24] Although the attack on Boulogne began during the afternoon of 22 May (see Chapter 15), the 10th Panzer Division, which, after the Arras counter-attack, had been kept in reserve in case the Allies made further attacks, was only freed up to march on Calais some twenty-four hours later, leaving the 1st Panzer Division to concentrate on its advance towards Dunkirk, via Gravelines.[25]

   This delay turned out to be crucial. If the 10th Panzer Division had thrust through to Dunkirk on 22 May, which was what Guderian had originally intended, it is likely that the town would have been taken without much of a fight.[26] In that case the Germans would have been spared the second reining in, which took place on 23 May, after General Ewald von Kleist, commander of the Panzer Group Kleist that controlled the XIX and XLI Panzer Corps, complained that his panzer divisions would not be strong enough either to attack towards the east, or to ward off a strong Allied counter-attack unless Arras was dealt with first.[27] It seems that this persuaded the 4th Army's commander von Kluge to tell von Rundstedt during the afternoon of 23 May that the infantry should be allowed to catch up with the so-called 'fast troops'.[28] When von Rundstedt agreed, von Kluge issued the fateful order at 8 p.m. that night, which gave Gort the breathing space he needed: the Panzer Corps were to postpone their attack for around thirty-six hours in order to be ready to attack on 25 May.[29] So, although it is generally believed that it was Hitler who stopped the tanks with 'his' famous halt order, given shortly after 11.30 a.m. on 24 May, the tanks were by then already at a standstill and it was von Rundstedt, rather than Hitler, who proposed that the halting of the tanks should be extended. Hitler merely approved von Rundstedt's proposal. (An analysis of the halt order is in note 30.)[30]

   And it was von Rundstedt who, nominally at least, was given the final say on whether the halt order should remain in force after 24 May.[31] Therefore, it is not entirely correct to refer to 'Hitler's' halt order. This point was underlined by what happened after General Walther von Brauchitsch, Commander-in-Chief of the German Army, during the night of 24–5 May, gave permission for the troops under Army Group A to advance again, even though Hitler had not ruled that the halt order should be revoked. On 25 May von Rundstedt responded by stating that the postponement of the attack should nevertheless continue, not only to give the infantry more time to catch up, but also because he felt that insufficient notice would be given to the Luftwaffe if the attack were to proceed immediately. The fact that he stuck to this position emphasized the true situation: the control of the halt order had been delegated by Hitler to von Rundstedt, as expressly stated in Army Group A's war diary.[32] It was an extraordinary situation, which permitted the subordinate general to defy the Army's Commander-in-Chief with the blessing of the country's dictator.

This does not mean that von Rundstedt made his decision without being strongly influenced by Hitler. One can easily see how von Rundstedt, who knew that Hitler did not want the armour to cross the canal line until it was absolutely safe, might have been keen to ensure that his orders anticipated the Führer's wishes. His desire to ingratiate himself with Hitler is likely to have been all the stronger because, on 24 May, Hitler had cancelled the humiliating order issued by von Brauchitsch that von Rundstedt's Army Group A should surrender control of the armoured forces to General Fedor von Bock, Army Group B's commander, who, if von Brauchitsch had had his way, would have handled them with his infantry, which was advancing through Belgium.[33] Von Rundstedt's dependence on Hitler in relation to the resumption of the attack by the armour was clearly demonstrated on 26 May, when Hitler was consulted by von Rundstedt about his decision to cancel the halt order. Only after Hitler agreed with von Rundstedt's judgement was the order given, during the afternoon of 26 May, to resume the attack.[34]

By then, from the German viewpoint, everything had changed for the worse. The respite the BEF had enjoyed by the halting of the panzers had already enabled Gort to provide protection for his southern flank, using the divisions relieved by the French and Belgians. During the early evening of 25 May, Gort also took steps to protect his forces in the north, and decided that the reserve troops, which had been allocated to the Allies' counter-attack, would have to fill in.

Gort's decision, which was as significant to the outcome of the campaign as Hitler's and von Rundstedt's halt order, was influenced by many different factors. By 25 May it must have been clear to Gort that he could not count on being rescued by British troops advancing from the south. The BEF's 1st Armoured Division, whose first tanks had been landed at Cherbourg on 20 May, was unlikely to break through the German bridgehead holding the bridges over the Somme if its first attempt was anything to go by. Although on 23 May Gort had urged the War Office to order the Armoured Division to attack northwards from south of the Somme, no British tanks had crossed that river, notwithstanding a determined attempt on 24 May by an infantry battalion backed with British armour.[35] News pouring in from Belgium on

25 May was equally disheartening. The Germans had launched a savage attack on the Belgian Army stretched out along the River Lys and its Canal de dérivation to the north of the BEF's eastern front, and had penetrated the line.[36] However, evidence provided by at least one officer on Gort's staff suggests that while this worried the British Commander-in-Chief, he was only persuaded to act after another lucky break.[37]

On 25 May a British patrol, led by a Sergeant Burford of the 1st/7th Middlesex Regiment, had crossed the River Lys in a collapsible boat, and had come across Germans in a village between Comines and Menin.[38] One of Burford's men was killed, and a second man wounded during the ensuing firefight before the Germans withdrew. Then, to Burford's surprise, a blue German staff car came up the street towards the British soldiers. Burford, who was armed only with a pistol, emptied it into the car, killing the driver, and causing the car to crash. The passenger jumped out and escaped, leaving behind a briefcase full of documents, which Burford seized, before ordering the surviving members of his patrol to make their way back to British lines with their wounded comrade.[39]

The captured documents were passed to General Montgomery's 3 Division. It turned out that the escaped passenger was Lieutenant-Colonel Kinzel, the liaison officer between von Brauchitsch and the 6th Army's commander, General Walther von Reichenau, and the documents disclosed their next target.[40] The Germans intended to break through the Belgian line on the Lys, so that they could advance round the left flank of the main BEF formations, which were by this time dug in on the Franco-Belgian border. It was evident that, if successful, the Germans would be able to exploit a gap that had already appeared between the British left and the Belgian right. The principal thrust was to be made between the Belgian towns of Ypres and Comines.[41] By a happy coincidence, 3 Division's staff were crowding round these documents, laid out on a dining-room table, at the very moment when General Alan Brooke, 2 Corps' commander, visited Montgomery's headquarters. As soon as Brooke learned what they had captured, he made sure that the documents were passed immediately to Lord Gort.[42]

Whatever it was that finally convinced Gort that he had to shore up his northern flank, at around 6 p.m. on 25 May, he placed General Franklyn's 5 Division, one of two reserve divisions, under General Alan Brooke's command, and the troops therein were quickly sent up to the north to man the Ypres–Comines line, providing a new obstacle in the Germans' path behind the Belgians. This decision was not to be taken lightly: using 5 Division in this way effectively scuppered French hopes of making a strong Anglo-French counter-attack, spearheaded by 5 Division. It also laid Gort open to the charge that he had denied France the chance to snatch victory from defeat, at a time when he had only just persuaded the French politicians and generals, who had criticized him for having cut and run from Arras, that by withdrawing when he did, he had saved the troops who would otherwise not have been available for the counter-attack.[43] Gort also decided that the BEF's 50 Division, his second reserve unit, was to be used as well to block the Germans in the north.

Gort might have been less anguished about his 25 May decision if he had sat in on a meeting held at the Defence Ministry in Paris that day: Commandant Fauvelle, General Blanchard's aide, had told General Weygand and the Président du Conseil Reynaud that the French 1st Army was so weak it would be unwise to expect it ever to mount a counter-attack. When asked what the situation had been when he had left Blanchard, Fauvelle responded, 'I believe in a very early capitulation.'[44] This honest assessment, which appears to have been one of the first Weygand received, prompted the French Commander-in-Chief to send Blanchard a message giving him complete discretion concerning whether he should go ahead with the counter-attack.[45]

That evening, Gort was unable to speak to Blanchard, who was away from his headquarters. But Gort's message given to Blanchard's staff was passed on to Blanchard on the French general's return. It galvanized Blanchard, who had just been appointed commander of Army Group 1, to send the British Commander-in-Chief an order containing some of the same information that Gort wanted to tell him: the counter-attack was off, and the French and British Armies must retreat from the Franco-Belgian frontier to the River Lys. The message never reached Gort; the two men only came to an agreement about the retreat when they met at Attiches early the next day. (Details of the retreat are in note 46.)[46]

The news that Gort could not make the counter-attack, coupled with a devastating report on the dangers facing the BEF, made by General Dill, who had visited Gort on 25 May, finally concentrated the minds of the politicians in London on the true situation in France. After the

meeting with Blanchard, Gort received a message Anthony Eden had
sent during the night of 25–6 May, which included the following words:

Since Dill saw you today I have had information all of which goes to show
that French offensive from Somme cannot be made in sufficient strength to
hold any prospect of junction with your armies in the north. Should this prove
to be the case you will be faced with a situation in which safety of BEF will
be predominant consideration. In such conditions only course open to you
may be to fight your way back to west where all beaches and ports east of
Gravelines will be used for embarkation . . . Prime Minister is seeing M.
Reynaud tomorrow afternoon [in other words, during working hours on
26 May] . . . In meantime it is obvious that you should not discuss the possibility
of the move with French or Belgians.[47]

Gort replied: 'I must not conceal from you a great part of the BEF
and its equipment will inevitably be lost even in best of circumstances.'[48]

The fear that Britain without most of its army might soon have to
face the victorious Germans without any assistance from France was the
predominant subject at that day's War Cabinet meeting. The ministers
attending were concerned that Reynaud during his visit to London
might wish to inform Churchill that France was about to surrender.
They were right to be worried. Reynaud's Cabinet were expecting him
to ask Churchill whether Britain would permit the French to surrender
notwithstanding the treaty, which forbade such action without the
British Government's consent.[49]

The anxiety around the British War Cabinet table provoked a discussion that most people in Britain, still in the dark about the extreme
peril facing the BEF, would have found extraordinary. It revolved
around whether Britain, rather than fighting on, should attempt to reach
an accommodation with Hitler via Italy's Benito Mussolini.[50] The raising
of this sensitive topic by the Foreign Secretary Lord Halifax was recorded
in the meeting's minutes in the following terms:

Lord Halifax: said . . . we had to face the fact that it was not so much now a
question of imposing a complete defeat upon Germany, but of safeguarding
the independence of our own Empire . . . In this connection, he informed the
War Cabinet that he had had an interview with the Italian Ambassador the
previous evening, in which Signor [Giuseppe] Bastianini had clearly made

soundings as to the prospect of our agreeing to a conference. The Ambassador had said that Signor Mussolini's principal wish was to secure peace in Europe. The Foreign Secretary had replied that peace and security in Europe were equally our main object, and we should naturally be prepared to consider any proposals which might lead to this, provided our liberty and independence were assured.[51]

The War Cabinet's response to Edward Halifax's statement has also been preserved:

Churchill: said that peace and security might be achieved under a German domination of Europe. That we could never accept. We must ensure our complete liberty and independence. He was opposed to any negotiations which might lead to a derogation of our rights and power.

The meeting was adjourned to allow Churchill to meet Reynaud. After the two premiers had lunched together, the War Cabinet was convened again at 2 p.m. and Churchill passed on Reynaud's grim message: excluding troops in the Maginot Line, the French had only fifty divisions left, whereas the Germans could still field 150. Weygand had told Reynaud that if the Germans took Paris, the French Army would retire to the south-west. However, given their superiority in numbers and tanks, the Germans could pierce the French line and pass through it. Weygand 'did not think that France's resistance was likely to last very long against a determined German onslaught'. Reynaud had hinted that while he himself would not sign peace terms imposed on France, he might be forced to resign, leaving the way clear for someone who would.[52]

This pessimistic summary prompted Halifax to return to the question of whether an approach to Italy should be made, the minutes of the meeting once again recording the ensuing debate:

Churchill: doubted whether anything would come of an approach to Italy . . . If France could not defend herself, it was better that she should get out of the war, rather than that she should drag us into a settlement which involved intolerable terms . . .
Clement Attlee (Leader of the Labour Party): said that if France now went out of the war, Herr Hitler would be able to turn on us the sooner.

Churchill: said that he hoped that France would hang on. At the same time we must take care not to be forced into a weak position in which we went to Signor Mussolini, and invited him to go to Herr Hitler . . . [to] ask him to treat us nicely. We must not get entangled in a position of that kind before we had been involved in any serious fighting.[53]

Halifax: said that he did not disagree with this view, but . . . he was not quite convinced that the Prime Minister's diagnosis was correct, and that it was in Herr Hitler's interest to insist on outrageous terms. After all, he knew his own internal weaknesses. On this lay-out it might be possible to save France from the wreck. He [Halifax] would not like to see France subjected to the Gestapo.

Churchill: did not think that Germany was likely to attempt this in regard to France.

Halifax: said he was not so sure. Continuing, [he] thought that we might say to Signor Mussolini that if there was any suggestion of terms which affected our independence, we should not look at them for a moment. If however Signor Mussolini was as alarmed as we felt that he must be in regard to Herr Hitler's power, and was prepared to look at matters from the point of view of the balance of power, then we might consider Italian claims.

Arthur Greenwood (of the Labour Party): doubted . . . whether it was within Signor Mussolini's power to take a line independent of Herr Hitler.

Neville Chamberlain: M. Reynaud wanted us to say to Signor Mussolini that if he [Mussolini] did not come into the war against us, we were prepared to do a deal with him in regard to certain named places. We were not prepared to accept that proposition as it stood . . . The only advantage we should get was that France would be able to move away the ten divisions now on the Italian front. Signor Mussolini would get something for nothing, and what was offered would be only the starting point for new demands.

Churchill: thought that it was best to decide nothing until we saw how much of the Army we could re-embark from France. The operation might be a great failure. On the other hand, our troops might well fight magnificently, and we might save a considerable portion of the Force . . .

His general comment on the suggested approach to Signor Mussolini was that it implied that if we were prepared to give Germany back her colonies and to make certain concessions in the Mediterranean, it was possible for us to get out of our present difficulties. He thought that no such option was open to us. For example, the terms offered would certainly prevent us from completing our re-armament . . .

Halifax: said that, if so, the terms would be refused . . .

Churchill: said that Herr Hitler thought that he had the whip hand. The only thing to do was to show him that he could not conquer this country . . . At the same time, he [Churchill] did not raise objection to some approach being made to Signor Mussolini.

Greenwood: thought that Signor Mussolini would be out to get Malta, Gibraltar and Suez. He felt sure that negotiations would break down. But Herr Hitler would get to know of them, and it might have a bad effect on our prestige.

Chamberlain: thought that he [Mussolini] would make some extra demands on us . . . for example, Somaliland, Kenya or Uganda.

Halifax: thought that this was a good argument against mentioning particular matters in the approach . . . If we got to the point of discussing the terms of a general settlement, and found we could obtain terms which did not postulate the destruction of our independence, we should be foolish if we did not accept them.

Greenwood: said that the discussions contemplated would take some time. Meanwhile France would be getting into a worse position. If Paris was likely to be taken within a short time, was there really any chance that negotiations would serve any purpose?

The Cabinet eventually agreed that it would consider a draft communication to Italy, which would be prepared by Halifax for the next day, and the session was then terminated, the thoughts of those present switching, no doubt, to the subject on which everything else hinged: the evacuation of the BEF.

Later that day, Gort received another message from Anthony Eden, which stated:

Prime Minister has had conversation with Monsieur Reynaud this afternoon. Latter fully explained to him the situation and resources French Army. It is clear from this that it will not be possible for French to deliver attack on the south in sufficient strength to enable them to effect junction with the Northern Armies. In these circumstances no course open to you but to fall back upon the coast in accordance with terms my telegram . . . May 26. Monsieur Reynaud communicating General Weygand, and latter will no doubt issue orders in this sense forthwith. You are now authorised to operate towards coast forthwith in conjunction with French and Belgian armies.[54]

Shortly afterwards, in the words of Vice-Admiral Bertram Ramsay, who was to run the evacuation from Dover, 'The Vice-Admiral was informed by the Admiralty that it was imperative that "Dynamo" [the evacuation from Dunkirk] was to be implemented with the greatest vigour, with a view to lifting up to 45,000 of the BEF within two days, at the end of which it was probable that evacuation would be terminated by enemy action . . . Admiralty ordered Operation "Dynamo" to commence at 1857.'[55]

Unfortunately the message sent by Reynaud to Weygand earlier that afternoon did not include quite the same message as that given to Gort and Ramsay. Rather than mentioning the embarkation of troops, it said merely: 'I believe it will be desirable if you could tell General Blanchard immediately that you formally authorize him to retreat towards the ports.'[56] When it was drafted on Winston Churchill's 10 Downing Street notepaper to be read to General Weygand over the telephone at 4.05 p.m. on 26 May, the conflict between the orders sent to Gort and Weygand might have seemed insignificant.[57] But the conflict was to have the gravest of consequences, and was to contribute to one of the greatest turnabouts in history, which would see British and French men, who had started the war as allies, becoming sworn enemies.[58]

20: Siege at Cassel

Cassel and London, 27 May 1940
(See Maps 10, 14, 15, 16 and 20. Also Map 1)

The 26 May War Cabinet discussions about Britain giving up the fight commenced just as the BEF's generals were being cheered up with a glimmer of hope. The interception of the German signal two days earlier ordering what Pownall described as the discontinuation of 'the attack on the line Dunkirk–Hazebrouck–Merville' (mentioned in Chapter 19), and the Germans' subsequent failure to exploit the bridgeheads they had established over the Gravelines–La Bassée canal line, suggested that the BEF might be able to escape after all.[1] 'Can this be the turn of the tide?' Pownall wrote in his diary, after being shown the signal. 'It seems too much to hope for.'[2]

The halting of the tanks had been crucial: it had given Gort the chance at least to start the process of putting battalions from the three divisions relieved by the French and Belgians on 23 and 24 May into the new defence line running from Bergues, just outside Dunkirk, to Hazebrouck, and from Hazebrouck right down to the town of La Bassée in the south.[3] This British line was designed to prevent incursions from the south and south-west. German units approaching from the west were to be blocked by the French Army. On 23–4 May French units secured the eastern banks of the canal running from Watten to Gravelines before being forced back to the Mardyck Canal and Canal de la Haute Colme on the night of 27–8 May.[4] These new lines, taken in conjunction with the front that British troops were to hold in the north – between Ypres and Comines – created a kind of safety zone, or corridor, down which British and French troops, who had been fighting along the Franco-Belgian frontier and the French Escaut, could safely march on their way to Dunkirk. (The corridor is shown in Map 10 on pp. 522–3.)

But how strong was the new line in the south? There were clearly not enough men available to police every inch of land between Bergues and La Bassée. Gort therefore decided to do the next best thing, which was to man the main towns and villages in the line with a view to transforming them into 'stops' or strongpoints. The theory was that if they were defended staunchly, the German advance might just be delayed for long enough to permit the bulk of the BEF to reach Dunkirk.[5] The corridor would not have to be protected for long: from 26 May until the night of 29–30 May might be sufficient, if the retreat envisaged by Gort from the British sector of the Franco-Belgian frontier proceeded according to plan.[6] Assuming that a perimeter could also be formed and successfully defended around Dunkirk, Gort would have done everything in his power to ensure that the evacuation could take place. It would then be up to the RAF and the Navy.

A key figure in the setting-up of these strongpoints was Brigadier Nigel Somerset, the forty-six-year-old great-grandson of Lord Raglan, Commander-in-Chief of the British Army at the time of another desperate action: the Crimean War's charge of the Light Brigade.[7] Somerset had been a lieutenant-colonel – the commanding officer of the 2nd Battalion, the Gloucestershire Regiment – when the German offensive started. But like so many of the older officers his brigadier was not up to leading his men into battle and had been forced to return to England because he was ill. On 15 May Somerset became the acting brigadier. He and his 145 Brigade, part of 48 Division, left their positions on the Belgian Escaut on the night of 22–3 May and, after withdrawing to the sector of the Gort Line near Rumegies, on the frontier between France and Belgium, had been relieved by the French.[8] The French soldiers were a cavalier crew compared with 145 Brigade, as was observed by David Wild, the brigade's chaplain: 'Dressed in all kinds of uniform, they strolled along, rarely in any recognizable formation. Some were pushing perambulators loaded with their kit and hung round with fowls and other forms of loot. Twice I saw a man leave the ranks, enter a house and emerge with a bicycle, on which he cheerfully rode off ahead of his formation, waving farewell to his platoon commander.'[9]

The first French relief troops appeared during the afternoon of 23 May, and Wild's account describes their commander's arrival at Brigade Headquarters and his suggestion that Brigadier Somerset might care to inspect the French troops as they passed:

Knowing that the Brigadier by this time had some fairly lurid views on Frenchmen, we stood nearby to hear what he would say. He surveyed the motley rabble for a while, bicycles, chickens, perambulators and all, and then turning to the General said, 'Surely they are very big men for Frenchmen?'

In spite of the fact that they were mostly coloured colonial troops, the General seemed delighted with what he took for a compliment.[10]

Later that night the brigade retreated to Nomain, arriving at dawn, and the brigadier, the padre and the men were taken to their billets where they hoped to wash, shave and enjoy a well-earned rest.[11] However, at 7 a.m. on 24 May, they received new orders. Somerset was to command a group to be known as 'Somer Force', consisting of his brigade and some additional units, and was to be transported to Calais to relieve the siege there. 'So much for the first day in reserve and rest!' Somerset commented in his account.[12] Later that day Wild saw a 48 Division staff officer hand in another order at Brigade Headquarters. 'You are to proceed to Cassel,' the staff officer told the brigadier. 'We do not know where the enemy are, but we hope you will get there first . . . Troop transports will arrive this evening.'[13]

Wild's account continues:

During the evening, while I was hanging about . . . within reach of my car, I met the ever-cheerful [Major] Ronnie Cartland [the brother of author Barbara Cartland]. 'Come and have supper,' he said; 'Dick's [2nd Lieutenant Dick Troughton] coming too.' He led me into a small field on the other side of the road from HQ, and brought me to where his incomparable batman was setting out a marvellous picnic on a spotless tablecloth spread out on the grass. There, we sat down, Ronnie, his subaltern, Dick, and I. Except that there was no river, it might have been a river picnic by the Cherwell.[14] There were hedges around the field, and the long grass was full of kingcups. Overhead German planes were constantly passing to and fro, and [on] the other side of the hedge we heard a steady stream of DRs [dispatch riders] calling at HQ. Any one of them might be bringing the order for us to move. Four hundred yards away up the road, some of our troops had dragged a piano out of a farmhouse, and we could hear them singing all their most sentimental favourites. Our prospects that night were not exactly cheering, but others like ourselves seemed bent on enjoying that lovely summer evening, and a few hours' rest.

I could not forget that picnic. If it had not been impossible, I should have guessed that it came straight out of Fortnum and Mason. We had cold duck in aspic, followed by some specially good tinned fruit, and we washed it down with a wine that Ronnie said he could strongly recommend . . . At the end of supper he even produced a bottle of Cointreau, for my special benefit, he said.

At length there were signs of activity on the other side of the hedge, and we knew that it was time to go. As we walked to our cars, I said to Dick that if any of us failed to survive . . . I hope[d] that those [of us] who came through would tell those at home of that cheerful party and that unforgettable summer evening.

On the way to Cassel, a radio message instructed Somerset to send one of his three battalions to Hazebrouck, another of Gort's strongpoints. Somerset selected the 1st Bucks Battalion, the Oxfordshire and Buckinghamshire Light Infantry, for this task because they were at the back of the column.[15] That left just two infantry battalions – the 2nd Gloucestershire Regiment (2nd Glosters), and the 4th Oxfordshire and Buckinghamshire Light Infantry (4th Ox and Bucks) to defend Cassel – although they were to be supported by tanks and Bren-gun carriers from the 1st Light Armoured Reconnaissance Brigade, which included the 1st Fife and Forfar Yeomanry and the 1st East Riding Yeomanry.

As they approached the town on the morning of 25 May, Wild, who had gone ahead of the fighting troops, became more and more anxious about what he would find:

For all I knew, we were driving straight towards the enemy, supported by (just) two lorries of signal equipment and two trucks full of dry rations, cooks and typists. We were a little cheered however to see some of our artillery in position to the left of the road some two miles from Cassel. Evidently the Germans had not arrived.[16]

Wild's account goes on to describe what he saw as he drove into the town:

The road into Cassel is very picturesque; it rises out of the flat plain, through a series of well wooded foot hills, until suddenly the mass of the hill on which the town stands rises up ahead. The last long climb follows a series of zigzags up the steep face of the hill, until the road takes a sharp right angle bend straight into the narrow main street. The corner was not a cheering sight. Some . . . horse-drawn artillery had taken a direct hit at this point, and all over the road were scattered the remains of wagons, guns, horses and men. A hundred yards further up the street was a burned out six wheel lorry and several of the houses

. . . were just . . . empty shell[s]. After another right angle bend, we came out into the magnificent main square. Several of the largest buildings had cascaded their ruins into the street, but the desolation was relieved by the sight of a few British officers and men. Several of our Bren gun carriers, which had left Nomain some hours ahead of us, were in possession of the town.[17]

Private Melville Thomas, one of the Ox and Bucks soldiers, had even more vivid memories of what he saw as he marched into Cassel.

A whole column of French Army transports and supplies had been bombed and machine gunned from the air. I can still see a black pony in agony and terror with full shining teeth, and jaws apart. And a young French soldier who had fallen at his horse's head while [apparently] trying to calm the poor creature down, one hand on the animal's forehead, the other holding the reins. The catastrophe had been so rapid that it presented itself to our horrified gaze like a still photograph taken from a moving film. We soldiers stopped as often as we could to see if there was a human or animal alive, but there was none.[18]

From that moment on the spot where this carnage had taken place was invariably referred to by British soldiers as 'Dead Horse Corner'.

As soon as the brigadier arrived, the positions to be held by the two infantry battalions were allocated. The defence of the town was split into two halves with the Glosters holding the western portion, the Ox and Bucks the east. But a lot of work had to be done, much of it supervised by men from the Royal Engineers, to make Cassel defendable. Roadblocks were built on all the main roads leading into the town, and covered by the battery of guns allocated to Somer Force in addition to the brigade's nine anti-tank guns. The walls of buildings around the outer limits of the town were loopholed, and roofs and ceilings were shored up, until the whole town was converted into a kind of fortress, complete with outposts.

One such outpost was situated in a blockhouse to the north, and there were also outposts in Bavinchove and Zuytpeene, villages to the west of Cassel (see Map 14, p. 529).[19] These outposts were positioned so that they might warn the main force inside Cassel of the Germans' approach. Brigadier Somerset was also instructed to take command of the British forces at Hondeghem, a village some three miles to the south-east, and of those from his own brigade at Hazebrouck, which is around two miles south-east of Hondeghem. Thus 48 Division's Somer Force ended up holding a line of strongpoints facing south-west, which was tacked on to the line of strongpoints held by 48 Division's 144 Brigade to the north-west at Arneke, Ledringhem and Wormhout.[20]

Given the warlike preparations, and that Germans had already been seen to the west of Cassel – they had been fired on with an anti-tank gun on 26 May – it is perhaps surprising that Cassel should have been chosen as the venue for the meeting on 27 May of all the generals and the French admiral involved with the setting up of the perimeter defences around Dunkirk. At 7 a.m. on that day all of these senior officers drove into Cassel, little realizing that Hitler and von Rundstedt had at last ordered their Panzer Division commanders to advance, or that Cassel was one of their most cherished targets.[21]

The German keenness to capture Cassel had nothing to do with the town's natural beauty, which, prior to the German attack, was at its best in the cobbled streets leading up to the quaint main square enclosed by some of the finest buildings in Flanders. Nor was it just that the town could be turned into a fortress, thanks to the old gateways under arches that protected the town on both its northern and southern sides, and its narrow streets, which could be so easily barricaded. What made Cassel important from a soldier's point of view was its stunning views and dominating position relative to the five roads that passed close to the town. Apart from Mont des Recollets, a mile to the east, it is on the only hill in the area.

Those who enter the buildings on the south side of Cassel's main square, including the Hôtel du Sauvage where the meeting of Allied commanders took place, can look out across the plains, which stretch into the distance as far as the eyes can see. In 1940 an even better view to the north could be achieved from the back of the town's Gendarmerie, located on a street that branched off the smaller square further up the hill. And those who climbed even higher, to the summit of Mont Cassel, where two tall buildings originally designed as part of a leisure complex, including a casino, had been built, not only had the opportunity to admire the statue of the French General Foch, who used Cassel as his headquarters during the First World War, but they could see anything that moved for miles in any direction.

'It was a glorious morning,' wrote Colonel Robert Bridgeman in his account of the 27 May meeting.

I got safely to Cassel, parked the car in a side street and went to Hôtel du Sauvage in the square. It had been hit by a shell, and the staff had evidently bolted the day before, leaving the cloths on the tables in the dining room where the Conference was to be held, with its glorious [south-] westward view across the plain . . . On a table was a deserted bottle of Armagnac . . . which aroused my primeval looting instincts. But alas, I was no longer commanding 15 platoon 3 RB, nor had I Rifn George with the platoon pram. General Adam had arrived just before me. [On 26 May Lieutenant-General Sir Ronald Adam had been told by Gort to take charge of the setting up of the perimeter defences.][22] . . . Fortunately [General] Fagalde also came early, and armed with my precious map, I got them together on a side table, used by waiters in better times, and they had about ten minutes settling the occupation of the Dunkirk perimeter. It was done in a sensible and friendly way, and fortunately in English.[23]

Dunkirk's outer perimeter was to be established behind the line of the main canals that encircled both the town and the beaches on either side of it. (See Map 16 on pp. 532–3). It was agreed that it would run from the sea near Nieuport to Furnes in Belgium, and then on to the walled town of Bergues in France, before bending back north-westward towards the sea. Although Bridgeman, Adam and Fagalde intended Gravelines to be included when they met at Cassel, it eventually had to be excluded, and the western side of the perimeter was marked by the Mardyck Canal.[24] That made the perimeter some seven miles deep at its deepest point, between Dunkirk and Bergues, and twenty-three miles wide, between Mardyck and Nieuport. The British were to be responsible for the eastern sector, with the French taking command of the west. The canal between Dunkirk and Bergues was to be the dividing line between the French and British sectors.

In his report Bridgeman correctly confirms that there were no differences of opinion about the terrain to be held. But his analysis was less perspicacious when it came to dealing with Fagalde's feelings. Behind the smiles and handshakes, the French general was seething. What had upset him were the scenes, described in the following extract from his account, that he had witnessed on the way to the meeting:

The route nationale running from Dunkirk to Lille, which we took, was literally blocked from Dunkirk to Bergues by large English lorries abandoned by their drivers . . . I ended up by complaining about this to an English officer I came across. He told me shamefacedly that all the personnel were being told to leave their cars wherever they could, and to evacuate from Dunkirk![25]

The officer's statement had astonished Fagalde. Like Weygand, he had been given to understand that the French Army was to hold a perimeter around Dunkirk; neither man knew of Gort's instructions to evacuate. Consequently, he believed the British were behaving like rats deserting a sinking ship without having the decency to admit it.

Fagalde had another gripe: as Bridgeman had gathered, he had no problem with the allocation of the Dunkirk perimeter sections to be guarded by the French and British. But he was upset by Gort's decision to leave it to General Adam, 'a mere intermediary', to tell him and the other commanders what it was. Gort's instruction to Adam that he should say he would act in accordance with French orders not only failed to disarm Fagalde but had the opposite effect. Fagalde's suspicion that Adam's agreement to serve under French command was a piece of window-dressing was confirmed in his eyes after he had questioned Adam on how long the British intended to hold their perimeter sector. 'I only obtained vague replies, or no replies at all,' Fagalde reported. 'I then realized that it was all talk without substance, and I decided not to make any alteration to my plan to defend the entire perimeter with my troops.'

Fagalde was not the only person surprised by what was said. The British contingent, who believed that, like them, the French had been ordered to evacuate their troops, were appalled when General Louis Koeltz, General Weygand's representative at the meeting, stood up and started pontificating on the need to go on the offensive. Koeltz stated that the generals would not be doing their duty if they did not attack towards St Omer and Calais at the first opportunity, and preferably as soon as the retreat to the Lys had been completed. Koeltz was supported by Fagalde, who stated that it would be easy to seize Calais, if only he were given some tanks to support an attack.[26]

Had there been time for more leisurely discussion, such declarations might have led the BEF generals to suspect that the instructions given by the French Government to their generals did not correspond to those passed down to Gort by the British Government. Unfortunately, before inquiries could be made, German artillery started to shell Cassel, and the meeting was brought to a hasty conclusion, leaving the generals and Admiral Abrial to escape from the town as quickly as they could, and to speed off back to their respective headquarters.

They departed just in time. General Adam and his party were machine-gunned from the air as they left, and Major-General Pakenham-Walsh, the BEF's Engineer-in-Chief, who was supposed to be dealing with engineering tasks linked to the fortification of the Dunkirk perimeter, was hit in the arm. At 10.30 a.m. lookouts from the Glosters' A Company, which had a two-platoon garrison in the outpost at Zuytpeene, two and a half miles to the west of Cassel, saw their first Germans.[27] Fifteen minutes later they spotted some twenty tanks and a hundred German foot-soldiers approaching. Two runners were immediately sent back to warn the battalion's headquarters in the town, but forty-five minutes after the appearance of the first tanks, the runners arrived back to report that they could not get through to Cassel. The outpost was surrounded, and was duly overrun, but not before the Glosters had gallantly resisted all German attempts to overcome their defences for the best part of a day. The Germans also overran the position at Bavinchove after the Ox and Bucks garrison slipped away before they could be pinned down.

Cut off as he was from the outposts, Major Maurice Gilmore, the acting commanding officer of the Glosters after Somerset's promotion, was alarmed when A Company's commander, Major Bill Percy-Hardman, and his men failed to return from Zuytpeene. As Gilmore well knew, the outpost was not equipped to do more than break up the initial German attack. A series of dispatch riders were ordered to tell Percy-Hardman to withdraw, but they were no more successful at contacting A Company in Zuytpeene than the Zuytpeene runners had been in reaching Cassel. During the afternoon, two more men were sent in a carrier in a final attempt to break through the German cordon. They were never seen alive again by British eyes. A patrol subsequently sent out by Gilmore found their charred corpses sitting in their burned-out carrier.[28]

Percy-Hardman's action, which saw him and his thirty-one men holding out for an entire day against overwhelming odds, won him the Military Cross. But even this courageous performance was outshone by the third platoon in his company under the command of 2nd Lieutenant Roy Creswell, who somehow managed to hold out in the blockhouse, two miles north of Cassel, for more than two days.[29] Creswell and his thirteen men had first occupied the blockhouse during the evening of 26 May. Given that it was supposed to be turned into a mini-fortress, it did not at first sight look promising. It did not even have a front door. But following in the best tradition of British soldiers who have been called on to mount a spirited defence against overwhelming odds, Creswell and his men did their best to make good the defects.

They used sandbags to block the doorway, and to reduce the gun slits to manageable proportions, and they sawed through the poles supporting the wooden scaffolding that had not been taken down by the blockhouse builders. Once the scaffolding had been removed, they further improved the field of fire by carrying away the construction hut that had also been left behind by the builders, together with the sand, gravel and timber piled up beside it. Some of this material was used partially to block up the unfinished observation tower, which, in its uncompleted state, was basically a wide and tall chimney-like cylinder running from the floor at the back of the blockhouse to the roof above. Although this passage to the roof was obstructed, it was still a worry for the defenders, who feared that the Germans might use it as an entry point when attempting to storm the building: because the back of the blockhouse had no slits in it, it was obvious that once all the defenders were inside, determined attackers would be able to approach on its 'blind' side, climb on to the roof, and then either climb or drop smoke bombs down the tower. This would enable the Germans to smoke out the defenders, since there was no door that could be used to isolate the tower from the rest of the blockhouse interior.

It was 6 p.m. on 27 May when the first Germans were seen approaching the blockhouse. Its entrance was promptly sealed, after Creswell's men assembled inside. Between 7 and 8 p.m. the Germans launched what Creswell later described as a 'furious attack', which included firing anti-tank shells through the blockhouse gun slits. Splinters from one of these shells fatally wounded one member of the garrison, and the others must have wondered how long it would be before they joined him on the casualty list. However, their spirits were revived somewhat when one German who crept up and tried to break down the improvised 'front door' was killed by the blast from a grenade that one of Creswell's men dropped out of a gun slit. He was the first, and last, German to attempt to force an entry during the siege.

In spite of all the shooting, the blockhouse itself was not damaged during that first attack, and when the Germans eventually retired for the night, the only evidence of the battle visible from the interior was the flames from a nearby haystack, which burned all night. This helped the defenders: it enabled Creswell and his men to check that they were not being stalked.

During 28 May only one attack was made on the blockhouse, which was repulsed, like the assault the previous day. The main hardship the garrison endured resulted from the shortage of water. Much of what the fit men had in their waterbottles was given to their wounded comrade. The others had to supplement their ration with tots of rum.

Creswell started the 29 May entry in his account with the words: 'This was destined to be one of the worst days of our defence.' He then described what happened at 'about 0900 hours': 'A wounded British officer was seen to hobble round the west corner of the blockhouse shouting: "A wounded British officer here!"'

Unbeknown to Creswell, it was a Captain Lorraine, who had been pulled out of an ambulance and ordered at gunpoint to help the Germans capture the blockhouse. 'When I attempted to reply,' Creswell's account continues,

[the officer said] immediately: 'Don't answer back!' When he [Lorraine] reached the east end of the position, he looked down at a dead German, and said out loud: 'There are many English and German[s] like that round here.' At the same time, he looked up at the roof of the blockhouse very pointedly, an action which seemed to indicate the presence of someone on the roof. With that, he limped out of sight, leaving us all with the regret that we had been unable to help him, while at the same time, he obviously did not want us to open a door to let him in.

The German strategy was immediately obvious. Utilizing the distraction in front of us, the enemy had clambered up the blind side i.e. the rear . . . They then removed the cement from the top of the useless observation hole [in the blockhouse roof], poured a tin of petrol on the material serving as a block, and set it on fire with hand grenades . . . [The] explosions were the first indications of any real activity by the enemy.

Gas masks had to be worn until the fire, and clouds of smoke, could be got under control . . . A heavy quilt curtain brought from Cassel was place[d] across the entrance way leading to [the observation tower and] the fire, and [it] was kept damp, while water taken from a sump of dirty water was poured on the fire . . . The hole, when [the material blocking it had] burned away, was large enough to enable the enemy to lob grenades through it from the roof into the blockhouse itself.

Tortured by thirst, and fearing that the Germans might attack at any moment, the garrison continued to carry out the task they had been set, firing at a car moving down the Cassel–Dunkirk road, one hundred yards to the east, killing its occupants. Creswell finished his account for 29 May with the phlegmatic words: 'The remainder of the day passed without incident.' The blockhouse garrison only finally surrendered on 30 May, after the Germans fired through the slits again, this time using heavier weapons. The British soldiers' misery at having to give in might have been allayed somewhat had they known what the resistance at Cassel was helping to achieve. Unfortunately, they only heard the rationale for the defence of Cassel for the first time when, after their capture, a German officer nodded towards the smoke in the distance, and told Creswell, 'That's the English evacuating from Dunkirk.' At the time, Creswell thought the German was trying to trick him, and retorted, 'You're a bloody liar!' It was some time before the penny dropped.

While Creswell and his platoon were in the blockhouse, the gunners supporting the two infantry battalions in Cassel's town centre were fighting a deadly duel with tanks unleashed by the 6th Panzer Division. The riflemen and Bren gunners in the garrison had the capacity to stop German infantry. But tanks were another matter. Had it not been for the brigade's nine 25mm anti-tank guns, and the fifteen two-pounders deployed by the Worcestershire Yeomanry, it is doubtful that Cassel could have been held.[30] Men in the Worcestershire Yeomanry have claimed that as many as forty German tanks were dispatched by these guns alone in and around Cassel.[31]

Harry 'Wally' Munn, a gunner in the Worcestershire Yeomanry's 209 Battery, laid claim to three of these scalps. His two-pounder gun was sited in the west of the town, overlooking the road that led to Gravelines and Calais. When Major Cartland, the battery commander, called out, 'Tanks in your area, Bombardier,' Munn shouted back, 'I see them sir,' and from then on, he, as the number one in the three-man gun team, was left to deal with what might have been a life-threatening situation.

Munn has described seeing twenty-four tanks rumbling and clanking towards them:

As the tanks got nearer, we could clearly see the Swastika flags on the front . . . [They] reached a small wood at the base of the ridge, and halted there, out of sight of our position. Directly below us was a gap in the wood, where we expected the attack to come from, and sure enough, three tanks came through the gap about 600 yards from the gun site. One was a fairly large tank armed with a gun and twin machine guns, and two were smaller, armed with machine guns . . . I gave the order: 'Take post', and we manned the 2 pounder. As the Number 1, I gave the orders using the open sights on the gun which enabled the Number 3, layer Frank Barber, to pick up and follow the tank with his telescopic sight. The loader, Number 2, Bill Vaux, had loaded the gun, and the next order was 'Fire!' . . . The 2 pounder shell had a tracer base, and this enabled you to see where it went. Our first shot went straight and true for its target, but at almost the point of impact, the tank dipped into a small trough in the ground, and the shell passed in front of the turret.

From our point of view, this could not have been worse. The tracer base enabled the German tank commander to know he was under attack and from what direction. His gun turret turned in our direction, and he opened fire missing us by some fifty yards . . . Our next shot hit the tank just below the turret, and failed to penetrate the armour, but went up into the air like a rocket. We continued our duel with the tank. We fired, they moved, halted and fired back. After some 15 shells had been fired, Bill Vaux, the loader, who could not see what was going on, but knew from the lack of movement of the gun we were still engaging the original target, enquired: 'When are you going to hit the bloody thing?' By now the tank was less than 100 yards from our position, and we still could not penetrate its armour. The only thing I could think of was that the wheels that propelled the tank tracks were unprotected, and so I shouted to Frank: 'Hit [it] in the tracks, Frank!' The gun muzzle dipped slightly, and just as the tank moved, we fired, hitting the track propulsion wheels . . . The tank halted abruptly, swinging to one side. Still full of fight, they turned their gun in our direction, and fired again hitting the bank in front of the gun. Our next shell must have disabled the turret, as they opened the escape hatch and ran for their lives back towards their lines . . .

The other two tanks that came through with the one we had just stopped were on the right and left of our position. I decided to engage the one on the left as it was close to the outskirts of the town and firing . . . at a target in our

lines. It was a perfect target silhouetted against a small hillock. I gave the
necessary commands . . . Frank pressed the firing pedal, and this time the shell
penetrated the armour, exploded inside the tank and blew it into small pieces,
as its own ammunition went up. There were no survivors.

The third tank had not moved from the point where we had first sighted it,
and its turret moved slowly round searching for our gun . . . Frank [was]
following the tank, [which was] traversing left and right as it searched for our
position. Frank talked to himself as he followed the target. 'Keep still!' [he
said], and as the tank paused for a second he fired, completely destroying this
one, as we had the previous one.[32]

The gunners did not always come out on top, and the havoc caused
when German tanks were not dealt with promptly is illustrated by one
incident that occurred during the afternoon of 27 May. Things began
to get out of control when three tanks broke through the defence line
at the south-western side of the town's perimeter, overrunning the
Glosters' D Company's forward positions. The noise of the firing was
so loud that it disturbed Captain Bill Wilson, whose B Company was
holding the adjacent area. His account describes what he saw when he
went to investigate:

I found to my amazement about forty troops of D Company, and the Battalion
mortar platoon . . . standing like lost sheep in the lane opposite my HQ . . .
Thinking that something must have happened to [Captain] Cholmondeley, I
managed to get all D Coy back . . . into positions of some sort. I found
Cholmondeley in his HQ surrounded by wounded . . . Cholmondeley told
me that his anti-tank rifles were ineffectual against the tank in the grounds
[apparently the other two tanks had retreated], but I couldn't get clear information from him as to where exactly the tank was. He was very much upset.[33]

The best that Wilson could do was call on another officer in his own
company to come to the rescue. 2nd Lieutenant Julian Fane has described
what happened next:

The IO [Intelligence Officer] asked me to get an A/Tk rifle . . . [in order] to
engage the tank at close range. I called for a volunteer . . . Private Palmer
jumped at the job . . . We then crept up to within 50 yards of the tank's
position, and got ready to fire the rifle. We were lying in a hole in the ground,

and the tank was half hidden by some trees. Palmer fired the first shot, but it bounced off the tank. He was about to fire again when two mortar bombs, presumably from the [Glosters'] mortar platoon . . . burst in front of us. One of the bombs blew a hole in the back of Pte Palmer lying beside me, and twisted the anti-tank rifle into what looked like a piece of barbed wire. I got Palmer back into a trench, and after cutting away part of his tunic, placed a field dressing over his liver which had been exposed. There was complete chaos all round, and the wounded and dying were all calling out for water and groaning. I managed to grab hold of a distracted stretcher bearer, and left him with my wounded volunteer. I then hastened back to my own platoon, passing the remains of D Coy . . . There were very few of them.[34]

By this time Wilson had made it to the top of the château that was being used as D Company's headquarters to see how best to deal with the incursion. When he looked out of the window he was relieved: 'I saw the tank at the end of the grounds, conning tower open and smoke pouring out of it,' he wrote. 'Apparently in the meantime one of our anti-tank guns had been moved up into position, and dealt with it.'[35]

On the other side of town, some of the soldiers belonging to the Ox and Bucks had been softened up not by Germans but by the smartness of the houses they had to defend. Melville Thomas, who had been so affected by the carnage at Dead Horse Corner, has described how he and his comrades wilted after being positioned in a luxurious town house bedroom. 'We all gratefully inhaled a perfume that filled the room,' he wrote, before going on to mention 'the two sumptuous beds with gold silk covers. We sank on to them with all our gear on.'

During one of my rest periods I lay on the soft downy bed near the door, and I took out my wallet and reread letters from home, including one from a young lady with whom I had exchanged photographs. I had asked her to send me a photo of herself, which she did, and I received it while I was in France. As I gazed at Maria's pretty image, I very much regretted not having had enough time to visit her when I was in Oxford.[36]

Thomas and the other men in the bedroom were only brought to their senses by a sergeant from their company's headquarters, who marched in briskly and read out the following order, addressed to the battalion: 'You will fight to the last man, to the last round.'

Thomas's first testing assignment outside the bedroom required him to climb to the top of the building that served as his company's head-quarters to act as a lookout. He would have felt quite secure doing that had he not been told that the last lookout had been shot and killed. He nevertheless accepted the order with good grace and settled down in the room where he had been placed. 'From this elevated position, I had a wide panoramic view of the countryside around Cassel,' wrote Thomas.

I was amazed to see, only about a mile away, Jerry tanks, armoured vehicles and motor bikes with sidecars gathering at assembly points. I darted down the stairs to report what I had seen, but a group of . . . officers told me to get back to the observation post at once, and to only inform them of any significant developments . . . [Then] across the square came a cry from one of our lads. 'There's a tank down the street!' I could hear tremendous firing, and then an explosion.

The tank, like so many others, had been stopped in its tracks by an anti-tank gun.

The next day, the risks that came with being an anti-tank gunner in a fixed position were made clear to all. Captain Roger Dixie, the brigade's anti-tank gun commander, had rushed to supervise the firing of one of the 25mm guns at another group of tanks that had been approaching the Ox and Bucks' sector in the south-east corner of the town. Sergeant Jim Loftus was pleased to tell Dixie that his gun was winning the battle: two tanks were lying immobilized with their tracks shot off. Dixie appeared to find this exhilarating, and insisted that he should direct the gun crew. As he prepared to give the firing order, he shouted, 'Come on, you yellow bastard!' They were his last words. No sooner had he finished speaking than he was hit and killed by a German shell.

Loftus saw many dreadful sights while defending Cassel, but that was the one which affected him the most. He was in a daze as he stumbled back to Brigade HQ. The next thing he remembered was being asked by one of the brigadier's staff to hand over the grenade he must have picked up for protection while hurrying to report the terrible news.[37]

But it was the stretcher-bearers, medical orderlies and doctors who had to cope with more awful sights and injuries than anyone. Bill Small, a medical orderly who was working for the Ox and Bucks' medical officer, found one soldier with his lungs literally hanging out of his stomach after his chest had been split open by a shell.[38] 'Make sure everything's put back inside me,' the injured man bravely told him. Small decided to bandage up the wound with the lungs still outside the man's body before carrying him a hundred yards down the track leading to the town centre and safety. Fortunately Small had been a farmer before the war and was very strong.

Another job he never forgot was the collection of the corpses after the first day's fighting in Cassel. Dignity required that each one was wrapped in a blanket and the blanket secured with pins. The wrapped-up corpses were then placed on the back of Small's truck. It was an unpleasant task, but it became routine for Small, until a blanket fell open and a severed head rolled on to the ground. Even Small was shocked by this, but he took a deep breath, picked up the head, placed it back inside the blanket, before sealing it up more securely.

Eventually the Germans, who had been attacking throughout 27 May, withdrew, and Major Gilmore concluded his account for that day with the following commentary:

As the evening wore on, the attack and mortaring died down, and things became quiet. Brasso [Captain Brasington], the Quartermaster, came up for the last time with rations. He was fired at on the way at close quarters, and his vehicle drove into a shell hole in the square. After this, we had no rations, but had to depend on local resources. On the whole, we seemed to have successfully delayed the Germans at this particular point.[39]

★ ★ ★

The defence of Cassel was not the only rearguard action fought by troops acting under Brigadier Somerset's command that day. Three miles to the south-east, in the village of Hondeghem, an equally stalwart performance was delivered by K Battery, the 5th Regiment, Royal Horse Artillery. Armed with just four eighteen-pounder guns, plus some Bren guns and rifles, this small band of men held up the German panzers from 7.30 a.m. until 4 p.m. Then, after leaving the village to the Germans, they broke through German infantry who threatened to cut off their line of escape in the nearby village of St Sylvestre, by conducting two bayonet charges. These assaults, accompanied by blood-curdling shouts, stunned the enemy into temporary submission, giving the British soldiers the opportunity to escape. Most of those who survived the battle at Hondeghem managed to make it to the relative safety of Cassel.[40]

That is more than could be said for the Bucks Battalion, Oxfordshire and Buckinghamshire Light Infantry at Hazebrouck. This unit's resources had been stretched to their limit in attempting to provide equal firepower on all roads running into the town. Not surprisingly, the isolated thinly spread outposts were eventually overrun during 27 May, leaving just Battalion Headquarters in the town centre to carry on its hopeless resistance the next day. Nevertheless, this surrounded unit of around one hundred men refused to give in until, forced out of their headquarters by the smoke and flames ignited by the shelling, they were finally cornered in a garden, and surrendered during the early evening of 28 May.[41]

It would be wrong to say that BEF troops were only involved in tenacious rearguard actions during 27 May. At 5.30 a.m. on that day, another gallant but poorly prepared attempt was commenced by the BEF's 1st Armoured Division, acting under French orders, to break through the German bridgehead south of the Somme, aiming at the area between Pont-Remy, south-east of Abbeville, and St Valery-sur-Somme.[42] The Germans were particularly well established at Huppy (some six miles south-west of Abbeville).

The attack towards Huppy, which was to be carried out by the Armoured Division's 10th Royal Hussars, was only supposed to go ahead backed by French infantry after the Germans had been softened up with a barrage of shells fired by French artillery. But as happened so often during the campaign, French aid did not arrive on time, and the commander of the Armoured Division's 2nd Armoured Brigade tried to delay the attack. Unfortunately the messenger carrying this message was killed before he could reach the officer in charge of the 10th Royal Hussars. As a result, thirty relatively thin-skinned cruisers and light tanks rumbled in towards Huppy only to be ambushed by German anti-tank guns. The armour came off second best, and it was not long before the countryside around the village was littered with holed British tanks abandoned by those of their crews fortunate enough not to have been killed. Just ten tanks escaped from the battlefield.[43]

The Queen's Bays attacking on the right near Limeux fared little better, ending up losing twelve tanks, and by the time the 3rd Armoured Brigade, which had reached St Valery-sur-Somme, retreated, the

Armoured Division had lost sixty-five tanks in battle, while an additional fifty-five were out of action as a result of wear and tear without having fired a shot in anger.[44]

It was the last time the Armoured Division was used as an attacking strike force against well-entrenched positions, but only because its commander, General Roger Evans, eventually stood up to the French, refusing to allow any more of his tanks and their crews to be sacrificed in this way.[45] Subsequent equally fruitless attempts on 28–30 May to break through from the south to the Somme were spearheaded by de Gaulle's 4th Armoured Division.

Meanwhile at 4.30 p.m. on 27 May, when fighting in Cassel was at its fiercest, a different form of delaying action was being pursued in London, as opponents of the Mussolini peace initiative fought in the War Cabinet against those who wished to embrace it. The scale of the danger facing not only the BEF but also Britain itself undermined the case made by those who refused to countenance making peace with Hitler.

The extreme peril was emphasized by the War Cabinet's Chiefs of Staff Committee in their 25 May memorandum, whose contents were deemed so sensitive that even the title was encoded. It was headed: 'British Strategy In A Certain Eventuality'.[46] Its first words explained why it was so secret:

The object of this paper is to investigate the means whereby we could continue to fight single-handed if French resistance were to collapse completely, involving the loss of a substantial portion of the British Expeditionary Force, and the French Government were to make terms with Germany.

The note confirmed that Britain could carry on alone, but only for so long as she retained air superiority, which could not be guaranteed. It went on to visualize a nightmare scenario, which must have sent shivers up the spine of some, if not all, of those reading it: the Navy might not be able to head off invasion forces while under sustained attack from the air. Once an invasion force had landed, the Army would not be strong enough to repel it. A summary produced five days later spelt out the shortfall of men and equipment. Although fifteen divisions were available for the defence of the country, excluding those which had been or were still fighting in France and Norway, the soldiers in most of these units were untrained and did not even have sufficient hand-held weapons such as Bren guns and rifles let alone the artillery considered essential to block a German attack. Only two units had the seventy-two twenty-five-pounder guns that each division was supposed to possess. Another had two-thirds and another five had between ten and twenty-five per cent of this artillery establishment. But that was it. Anti-tank guns were also in short supply.[47] According to the 25 May note, the RAF's ability to maintain air superiority was equally vulnerable: it depended on the Germans not hitting two factories where all the engines for Britain's fighters were manufactured.

This troubling conclusion, which had underpinned Halifax's presentation at the War Cabinet on 26 May, was supported by the following chilling warnings in another document bearing the same title that was circulated after the 26 May War Cabinet meetings:

Supposing Germany gained complete air superiority, we consider that the Navy could hold up an invasion for a time, but not for an indefinite period.

If, with our Navy unable to prevent it, and our air force gone, Germany attempted an invasion, our coast and beach defences could not prevent German tanks and infantry getting a firm footing on our shores. In the circumstances envisaged . . . our land forces would be insufficient to deal with a serious invasion.

The crux of the matter is air superiority. Once Germany had attained this, she might attempt to subjugate this country by air attack alone . . . Germany could not gain complete air superiority unless she could knock out our air force, and the aircraft industries, some vital portions of which are concentrated at Coventry and Birmingham.

Air attacks on the aircraft factories would be made by day or by night. We consider that we should be able to inflict such casualties on the enemy by day as to prevent serious damage.

Whatever we do however by way of defensive measures . . . we cannot be sure of protecting the large industrial centres upon which our aircraft industries depend, from serious material damage by night attack. Whether the attacks succeed in eliminating the aircraft industry depends not only on the material damage by bombs, but on the moral effect on the work people, and their determination to carry on in the face of wholesale havoc and destruction . . .

If . . . the enemy presses home night attacks on our aircraft industry, he is likely to achieve such material and moral damage . . . as to bring all work to a standstill.[48]

Given this stark presentation of what lay ahead, the document's conclusion, which flew in the face of the statements the Chiefs of Staff Committee had made in the preceding analysis, was hardly reassuring:

To sum up, our conclusion is that . . . Germany has most of the cards. But the real test is whether the morale of our fighting personnel and civil population will counter balance the numerical and material advantages which Germany enjoys. We believe it will.

Having read the Chiefs of Staff Committee's verdict, members of the War Cabinet met again to reconsider the proposed Mussolini peace initiative. This time it was Neville Chamberlain, the Lord President of the Council, who put the case for the peace initiative:

Chamberlain: . . . thought that Signor Mussolini still had the idea that when the vital moment came, he could play an important part and get a share of the spoils. But he [Chamberlain] did not think he [Mussolini] would play any part in the game until Paris had been taken.

There remained, however, the attitude of the French . . . Was it that they intended to say that the French had had a magnificent [military] scheme, but that, owing to the withdrawal of the BEF, they had been unable to carry it out? . . . It would be unfortunate if they were to add to this that we had been unwilling even to allow them the chance of negotiations with Italy.

Churchill: said that the Lord President's argument amounted to this, that nothing would come of the approach, but that it was worth doing to sweeten relations with a failing ally.

Sir Archibald Sinclair (Secretary of State for Air and Leader of the Liberal Party): said . . . being in a tight corner, any weakness on our part would encourage the Germans and the Italians, and would tend to undermine morale both in this country and in the Dominions. The suggestion that we were prepared to barter away pieces of British territory would have a deplorable effect, and would make it difficult for us to continue the desperate struggle which faced us . . .

Halifax: referred to . . . the record of his discussion . . . with Signor Bastianini . . . in which he [Halifax] had said that we had always been willing to discuss the questions between our two countries, and to endeavour to find solutions satisfactory to both sides. The French were not really proposing to go much further than this, except in the direction of geographical precision, where he was not prepared to accept their views.

He doubted whether there was very much force in the argument that we must do nothing which gave an appearance of weakness, since Signor Mussolini would know that President Roosevelt's approach had been prompted by us. [On 26 May Roosevelt had written to Mussolini to ask whether he would like to mention Italy's grievances to Roosevelt so that the American President might pass them on to the Allies.][49]

Attlee: said the suggested approach would be of no practical effect, and would be very damaging to us. In effect the approach suggested would inevitably lead to our asking Signor Mussolini to intercede to obtain peace terms for us.

If we accepted the French idea of geographical precision, there was a danger that Signor Mussolini would at once ask for more, and we should still be in the same difficulty, that if we refused, we should be accused of letting the French down . . .

Greenwood: said that . . . if it got out that we sued for terms at the cost of ceding British territory, the consequences would be terrible . . . The Prime Minister and M. Reynaud had already made approaches to Italy which had not been well received. It would be heading for disaster to go any further with these approaches.

Churchill: said that he was increasingly oppressed with the futility of the suggested approach to Signor Mussolini, which the latter would certainly regard with contempt . . . The approach would ruin the integrity of our fighting position . . . Even if we did not include geographical precision . . . everybody would know what we had in mind . . .

At the moment our prestige in Europe was very low. The only way we could get it back was by showing the world that Germany had not beaten us. If, after two or three months, we could show that we were still unbeaten, our prestige would return. Even if we were beaten, we should be no worse off than we should be if we were now to abandon the struggle. Let us therefore avoid being dragged down the slippery slope with France. The whole of this manoeuvre was intended to get us so deeply involved in negotiations that we should be unable to turn back . . . The approach proposed was not only futile, but involved us in a deadly danger.

Chamberlain: said that while he agreed that the proposed approach would not serve any useful purpose, he thought we ought to go a little further with it, in order to keep the French in a good temper. He thought that our reply should not be a complete refusal. We had a good argument in that, since the previous day, we had heard that President Roosevelt had now made an approach . . . It . . . might jeopardise our chances of getting a favourable reply from President Roosevelt if we were now to barge in on our own . . .

Halifax: said that he saw no particular difficulty in taking the line suggested by the Lord President. Nevertheless, he was conscious of certain rather profound differences of points of view which he would like to make clear . . .

He could not recognise any resemblance between the actions which he proposed, and the suggestion that we were suing for terms and following a line which would lead us to disaster. In the discussion the previous day, he had asked the Prime Minister whether, if he was satisfied that matters vital to the independence of this country were unaffected, he would be prepared to discuss terms. The Prime Minister had said that he would be thankful to get out of our present difficulties on such terms, provided we retained the essentials and the elements of our vital strength, even at the cost of some cession of territory.

On the present occasion, however, the Prime Minister seemed to suggest that under no conditions would we contemplate any course except fighting to a finish . . . If . . . it was possible to obtain a settlement which did not impair those conditions, he, for his part, doubted if he would be able to accept the view now put forward by the Prime Minister.

The Prime Minister had said that two or three months would show whether we were able to stand up against the air risk. This meant that the future of this country turned on whether the enemy's bombs happened to hit our aircraft factories. He [Halifax] was prepared to take that risk if our independence was at stake. But if it was not . . . he would think it right to accept an offer which would save the country from avoidable disaster.

Churchill: said that he thought the issue which the War Cabinet was called upon to settle was difficult enough without getting involved in the discussion of an issue which was quite unreal and was most unlikely to arise. If Herr Hitler was prepared to make peace on the terms of the restoration of German colonies and the overlordship of Central Europe, that was one thing. But it was quite unlikely that he would make any such offer.

Halifax: said that he would like to put the following question. Suppose the French Army collapsed, and Herr Hitler made an offer of peace terms. Suppose the French Government said: 'We are unable to deal with an offer made to France alone, and you must deal with the Allies together.' Suppose Herr Hitler, being anxious to end the war through knowledge of his own internal weaknesses, offered terms to France and England, would the Prime Minister be prepared to discuss them?

Churchill: said he would not join France in asking for terms. But if he were told what the terms offered were, he would be prepared to consider them.

Greenwood: said that the immediate question was whether the French approach to Signor Mussolini would stave off French capitulation.

After Halifax had acknowledged that it would not have this effect, the Cabinet finally agreed that the compromise proposed by Chamberlain would be adopted: a letter would be sent to Reynaud telling him that they should wait to hear the Italian reaction to the American initiative before they approached Mussolini directly. It was an inconclusive end to the dispute, and Halifax's subsequent threat that he would resign if his views were not taken into account suggested that more stormy discussions lay ahead the next day when the issue was to be dealt with by the War Cabinet again.[50]

21: Surrounded at Le Paradis

Cornet Malo and Le Paradis, 24–7 May 1940
(See Map 13. Also Maps 1 and 10)

Delaying the German advance in a fortified town such as Cassel was hard enough, but attempting to do the same without such cover was somewhat more challenging. Nevertheless that was the task that had to be done on the canal line to the south-east of Cassel, and it was the three brigades in 2 Division that were ordered to do it. On 23 May, 2 Division's 4, 5 and 6 Brigades handed over their positions south of Bourghelles, on the Gort Line, to French troops. The next day they were ordered to man the twenty-one-mile stretch of the canal line running from the railway bridge south-east of Aire to La Bassée.[1]

As the troops moved, they little realized that they were being given the most difficult assignment handed to any unit in the BEF. The scale of the problems posed by what they were being asked to do can be gauged by the small number of soldiers who returned home. Figures are not available for all these units, but those given in 4 Brigade's war diary probably provide a conservative indication of the loss of life, health and liberty throughout the division. Of the 2500-odd men in 4 Brigade who started off the campaign, only around 650 made it back to England during the evacuation.[2] Equally gruesome figures have been recorded for some of the individual battalions within the other two brigades. (See note 3.)[3]

It is doubtful whether any battalion in these brigades suffered more torment on and around the canal line than the men in the 2nd Royal Norfolks, a 4 Brigade unit. The Royal Norfolks' Captain Hastings, the officer who found it so hard adapting to life in the front line on the River Dyle (see Chapter 6), has written an equally vivid and informative account describing difficulties encountered on and behind the canal line. To begin with, no one had anything like enough sleep. According to Hastings, this, combined with the need to be constantly alert, sometimes caused the most reasonable of officers to act out of character.

It certainly skewed his judgement. During the night of 23–4 May when a suspected fifth-columnist was handed over to him near Locon, at the battalion's first stopping-place on the way to the canal, Hastings seriously considered shooting the man even though there was little evidence to indicate that the 'fifth-columnist' intended to act against the Allies' interests.[4] The arrested man claimed he was Belgian, and wanted to visit his grandmother in Béthune, an area known to be held by the Germans. But that was all. Nevertheless Hastings threatened to shoot the prisoner if he carried on walking towards Béthune, and only released him after he agreed to go to La Bassée instead.[5] Later Hastings wrote of this episode: 'The peculiar atmosphere . . . must have had some effect on me. It seems shocking to me now that I should actually have thought of shooting this wretched man, against whom I was only half convinced that there was any case at all.'[6]

When the Royal Norfolks arrived at Locon, the officers believed that they were going to have a rest during what was expected to be a period in reserve. However, while Major Lisle Ryder, their thirty-seven-year-old acting commanding officer, was reconnoitring, his car and the following vehicle were fired at on both sides of the canal. It was clear some Germans at least had arrived before them. It was no surprise, therefore, when, in the course of the meeting convened at their temporary Locon headquarters during the night of 24–5 May, Ryder told the company commanders that they must abandon any thought of having a good sleep: instead they must prepare for action.

4 Brigade was to be the central unit within 2 Division's sector on the canal line, with 6 Brigade on its right, and 5 Brigade on its left. The Royal Norfolks ended up in the centre of 4 Brigade's position. (4, 5 and 6 Brigades' positions are shown in Map 13 on p. 528.) The battalion's companies were to move up to the canal line immediately, in the dark, flushing out any Germans they found in their path, and were to establish foxhole positions on the northern and eastern canal banks between Avelette and the Bois de Paqueaut.[7] It would have been a difficult assignment for a full-strength well-rested battalion, but it was immeasurably harder for an understrength unit whose men were suffering from varying degrees of sleep deprivation. At this point, the battalion consisted of just 450 officers and other ranks.[8]

The following extract from Hastings's account of the meeting chaired by Ryder highlights the way in which the acute shortage of sleep was almost bringing the battalion's headquarters to a standstill:

This is a scene I shall never forget. The room is lit by candles. The C.O. [commanding officer] is so tired that his head keeps nodding as he talks, and he falls asleep. [Captain] Charles Long [the adjutant] is standing by his shoulder. We let him sleep for a minute. Then Charles taps the bottom of the candle on the table – gently – louder – louder still. The C.O. wakes up, and gets out a few more sentences, and goes off again. The same process is gone through again. It is repeated several times until the orders are complete. There is only one map. The heads of all the company commanders are crowded round it. They are making what notes they can. Soon they leave.[9]

Ryder's original plan required the battalion's headquarters to be moved at the same time as the companies to a village enticingly named Le Paradis (Paradise).[10] However, while moving in the dark, without lights, signposts, or large-scale maps, Hastings, who had been given the task of selecting the site for the new HQ, lost his way, and ended up with the headquarters personnel near Le Cornet Malo.[11] It was only during the next night, 25–6 May, that the fateful decision was made to move the headquarters again to Le Paradis. Little did the officers who made the decision realize that life there was going to be anything but paradise.

Although several attacks were put in on the Royal Norfolks' section of the canal line on 25 May, and small bridgeheads were established on the north-east bank, officers at the battalion's headquarters believed that the companies, after suffering their first casualties, were still holding their own. That was thought to be the case notwithstanding the fact that during the previous night two of the front-line companies, which had also got lost in the dark, ending up mistakenly digging in alongside a tributary of the canal rather than on the canal line itself.[12] Like the battalion's headquarters personnel, the 'lost' companies reached their correct positions on the night of 25–6 May, and it was only the next morning that Ryder ordered that steps should be taken to form a true picture of his front line. One of these steps involved sending Hastings forward to the crossroads at Le Cornet Malo to find out what had happened to A Company, on the Royal Norfolks' right. 'At the cross roads I was surprised to see [2nd Lieutenant] Slater, who was now commanding A Company [after Captain Yallop's death on 25 May], and a group of six or seven men standing helplessly around him,' wrote Hastings.

Slater told me his position up by the canal had been overrun by tanks, and the company had been 'minced up'. All that remained, he said, were the few men standing about outside, and some others who were wounded, that he had got inside a building on the . . . corner of the cross roads. I went . . . and looked at the wounded. As I came out, another car was arriving, and Col. Money, commanding the Royal Scots, got out. He was anxious to hear Slater's story, which Slater retold, again using the expression 'minced up'.

'Minced up!' shouted Col. Money. 'How dare you say you have been minced up!' and he went on to describe the casualties his battalion had suffered, before concluding: 'Do I say I've been minced up? I'm far from being minced up' . . . Col. Money continued stormily in this strain for some time, and if anything could have stirred new life into these tired men, I think his 'conversation' might have done so. But at the end of it all, Slater and his men seemed more helpless than ever, and I formed the opinion that they couldn't make any further effort . . . Having formed this opinion . . . I acted on my own initiative, and told Slater to bring his seven men in to Battalion Headquarters.

Before I left, [Lieutenant] Edgeworth, commanding B Company [the company now holding the front on A Company's left], came running up . . . His Company too was much reduced in numbers . . . He had only 19 men. He had a position along the line of a hedge 200 or 300 yards in front of the cross roads. There were no tanks about at the moment, but he thought there were Germans in a village just beyond his position.

Hastings drove back to Le Paradis to tell Ryder what he had done, only to discover that

he did not agree to Slater's recall, and was angry that I had done it. 'Go back,' he said. 'Put the two companies together, and command them yourself.' The cross roads, he told me, were to be held at all costs – to the last man and the last round. He concluded his orders by saying: 'Keep them back with your own pistol if necessary.'

I saluted and left, feeling rather dispirited and incompetent . . . On the way I tried to form a plan, but I couldn't gather my thoughts, and realized with a shock that I wasn't going to be very much use.[13]

Hastings's account goes on to describe the state to which he, and no doubt some of the other officers, including Slater, had been driven thanks to their lack of sleep.

The symptoms are that you have got quite used to doing without sleep, and have ceased to desire it with any very intense feeling. Your mind is sluggish, and you don't like to trouble it to do more than you think is essential. You have no curiosity about anything, and with an effort you are able to do the job in hand which you are apt to think you are managing pretty well, whereas in reality you are not doing anything of the sort, for your vision has narrowed its limits to such an extent, that you take no account of things that should be very obvious.[14]

Nevertheless on returning to the crossroads, where Slater and his men were still lingering, Hastings was encouraged by the fortuitous arrival of what he called 'unexpected reinforcements'. As he arrived fifty to sixty Royal Scots came running out of the trees in front of him, the remnants of the company sent forward during the night of 25–6 May to hold up the German advance north of the canal.[15] 'I stood firmly in the middle of the road,' reported Hastings,

and grasped my revolver in my hand. When the leading men reached me, I shouted to them to stop, which they did. As the others caught up, I enquired who was in charge. A sergeant major [who, it was later discovered, was Sergeant-Major Johnstone] came forward, and I asked him what the devil he thought he was doing, and where he was going.

'Had orders to withdraw, Sir,' he said.

'Orders from whom?' I asked.

'Orders from Major Bucher, Sir.'[16]

'Where is Major Bucher?'

'Wounded Sir – in the wood. He told us to withdraw.'

'Where are you going now?'

'Back to Battalion Headquarters.'

Some of Colonel Money's remarks to Slater were still in my mind, and also . . . Ryder's remarks to me on the same matter, and yet here was the best part of a company of Colonel Money's own troops running out of their positions in no sort of order at all. I told the . . . Sergeant Major . . . that the cross roads had got to be held at all costs, and that there was to be no withdrawal of anybody beyond this point, and I should need his men to reinforce the position I was about to make. He made no demur. I think he was very pleased to have found an officer to tell him what to do.[17]

The fifty to sixty Royal Scots and the twenty-five odd men from the Royal Norfolks' A and B Companies mentioned earlier brought the total under Hastings's command to in excess of seventy-five. These men, plus some extra reinforcements subsequently brought up by Captain Long, were told to line up behind the hedge that had previously been held by Edgeworth. They were soon joined by Major Bucher, the commander of the Royal Scots company, who had hobbled back from where he had been wounded and insisted on remaining with his men. Later, when he had to give orders, he was carried round the position on Sergeant-Major Johnstone's broad back.[18] Having thus formed a new line, and handed over the control of it to Captain Hallett (the other Royal Norfolk officer quoted in Chapter 6), Hastings was instructed to return to the battalion's headquarters at Le Paradis.

There he was told to help transform the buildings they were occupying on the Duriez family's farm into a stronghold that could be defended from all four sides. Duriez Farm – whose position is indicated in Map 13, p. 528 – consisted of a central courtyard enclosed by the farmhouse to the south, stables and barns to the west and north, and a brick wall with a gate in it to the east. Under Hastings's supervision, loopholes were made in the walls of the brick buildings and in the wall that formed the outside of the perimeter, and when it came to dealing with the corrugated-iron barn on the north side of the courtyard, Hastings used a crow-bar, which he inserted between the corrugated-iron sheets to make a series of vertical slits. The corrugated-iron walls were then reinforced with bales of straw, which Hastings hoped would provide some protection against bullets.[19] It was no fortress, but it was the best that could be done with the material available.

Notwithstanding all these preparations, it was clear that the position could not withstand a long siege. However, both Hastings's and Ryder's spirits rose when a message arrived from 4 Brigade's Brigadier Warren stating that a counter-attack by the French was imminent, and a tank battalion was 'on its way'.[20] It was the first of several such messages that kept coming, even after the German attack commenced on the morning of 27 May. One message stated that French officers would arrive 'at any moment' to reconnoitre the Royal Norfolks' positions so that they could be relieved.[21]

Also inside what could now be loosely described as 'a stockade' was Captain Charles Long, the adjutant. His account of the 27 May events that were to constitute the Royal Norfolks' last stand began: 'The morning of the 27th was heralded by heavy enemy attacks by infantry and tanks, and was accompanied by intense artillery fire. All this noise woke me from one of the most refreshing sleeps I had ever known. It was 4.30 in the morning of the most desperate day of my life.'[22]

From that moment, the men in the farm were virtual prisoners. They were cut off from the outside world unless they went out in a carrier, which gave some protection against bullets. However, the battalion's signalmen and officers could speak on the radio to Brigade Headquarters, situated back from the fighting at L'Epinette, and, until they were disconnected, they could also converse with the remnants of the front-line companies using wires that had been laid for this purpose.[23] The news that came back down these wires was nothing if not grim, being full of reports about massing tanks. Apart from the morale-boosting promises that reinforcements would be forthcoming, there was to be little material help from Brigade during much of the ensuing battle. Appeals made to the brigadier to have the division's guns fired at the concentrations of German armour were answered almost invariably with the same discouraging response. There was 'no ammunition'.[24]

Because so few men from the front-line companies survived, it has been impossible to describe all the nail-biting incidents that doubtless took place as these men stood their ground against the much stronger enemy troops and armour. However, the account written by Captain Hallett, whom Hastings had left in charge of the men he had been directing, at least gives some idea of what they must all have had to endure.

Unlike Hastings, Hallett appears to have been relatively fresh, which enabled him to take a much more proactive approach to his command. Shortly after Hastings had departed during the morning of 26 May, Hallett led a patrol forward to the southern side of Le Cornet Malo and fired at Germans he saw approaching from the direction of the Canal. 'It was a pity we had no mortars, or we could have bombed them beautifully,' he reported enthusiastically.[25]

Nevertheless Hallett's group's rifle and Bren-gun fire must have stopped the Germans in their tracks. As his account records, when he ordered his men to advance again, they did so without opposition, and captured a wounded German soldier, who was in a ditch, plus some others who also surrendered without a fight. 'After all the frightful things the troops had threatened, it was amusing to see how well they treated the [wounded] prisoner,' Hallett noted. 'They gave him cigarettes and chocolate, and . . . [when] I started to question him . . . he was quite ready to talk. He said that there was about a division [facing] . . . us across the Canal, as I'd rather expected, instead of the odd hundred men . . . that I'd been told.'[26]

The Germans attacked again as it became dark, driving back Hallett's forward posts. Then, according to Hallett, 'they started digging hard just beyond the village where we could hear them all night, [and] just before midnight I heard unmistakable sounds of tanks'.[27] This prompted Hallett to take the initiative once again, and after sending out a small patrol, whose report enabled him to work out exactly where the Germans were digging, he gave orders for the mortars that had become available to be fired at them. 'From the shouts and shrieks, there must have been some direct hits,' Hallett observed.[28]

But, as Hallett's account confirms, that was the last time he was able to impose his will on the battle:

As it began to get light, [at] about 5 a.m. [on 27 May], the tanks arrived, huge fellows, and about a dozen. I phoned Battalion HQ . . . Then they cut the line. This was the last message I got to the Battalion. The forward sections came in, leaving their guns, and worse, the anti-tank rifles. And for a bit there was . . . chaos . . . Eventually we had a brainwave, and ran out below the tanks' angle of fire, and put Mills grenades in the tracks. It did not do the tanks much harm, but [it] frightened the drivers, and they ditched them. We got four that way . . . Then gradually some form of order was restored. We got the light machine-gun back in position, and the anti-tank rifles mounted.

Luckily the German infantry were a long way behind their tanks, so when they came, we were ready for them. And come they did, in masses. I never believed I'd see troops advancing shoulder to shoulder across the open, but these men did, and suffered accordingly. The Brens fired till they were red-hot, and also the riflemen. But we [also] suffered heavily, and in the end, I was left in a big farm [house in] . . . an attic, with an anti-tank rifle, and a rifle for myself, and one rifleman to help.[29]

After some further exchanges of fire, even Hallett's last remaining helper was killed, and he himself was captured while trying to escape. Back at Duriez Farm, the state of the front-line battalions was monitored from messages received in the 'signal office' in the cellar under the farmhouse kitchen. A similar pattern of signals emanated from each company. First, messages came through to say they were holding. Then a more desperate voice, which could barely be heard above the firing in the background, informed the commanding officer that they were involved in hand-to-hand fighting. Sometimes the signalman at the other end of the wire had a personal chat with his mate in the battalion signal office. When B Company was about to be overrun, their signalman Alf Blake confided to Bob Brown, the nineteen-year-old telegraphist: 'I'm afraid we're for it. Don't forget me. We've had some good times together. I don't know whether I'll ever be seeing you again.' It was the last message from B Company, and the last time Bob Brown ever heard Alf Blake speak. He must have been killed shortly afterwards, among the many who did not survive long enough to surrender.[30] There was no time for Brown to be sentimental: as soon as the line went dead, he shouted up the stairs to the officers in the kitchen, 'The line to B Company's been cut.'[31]

As the German attacks strengthened, everyone who could be spared was ordered to take their place around the farm's perimeter, and that included Bob Brown. Once all contact with the front-line companies had been lost, he could do no more as a signalman. He was glad to come out of the suffocatingly hot cellar. Apart from anything else, it gave him the chance to see for himself what he and his comrades were up against. He would never forget what he saw. The British soldier is often at his best when, against overwhelming odds, he has to go on fighting with his back against the wall, and that is what Brown witnessed when he joined his friends on the farm's perimeter. He could not but be impressed at the way Corporal Tom Warren, one of the men near him, carried on laughing and cracking jokes until the very end. Warren was mad keen on films about the Wild West, and rather than being terrified of the approaching Germans, like some of the others, he had decided to act as if this was his opportunity to play a starring role. Each time Warren thought he had brought down a German, he exclaimed, 'Another redskin bites the dust!' Then Brown would say, 'I hope you are still notching it up on your rifle,' to which Warren would respond, 'Yes, I am. There's not much of it left now.' And so he continued, inspiring all those around him to 'keep their peckers up' and carry on fighting.[32]

Before the lines to the companies were cut, it was discovered that the

Germans were attacking in two main lines: between the Royal Norfolks' left and 5 Brigade, and in the area held by Hallett and his men.[33] After overrunning the front-line companies, the German troops were free to concentrate on Battalion Headquarters, which they did with a vengeance, approaching Duriez Farm from the north, the east and the west in spite of the fire put down by the men in the courtyard. 'We engaged the enemy furiously,' Long reported.

[Then] suddenly the enemy on the right stopped advancing, and . . . ran back towards the wood. We had one moment of exultation. We felt the counter-attack had been successful somewhere, and the German line was falling back. But our exultation in one moment turned to consternation.

A sudden flurry of noise and rattle of shots was heard in front of the Battalion HQ [i.e. to the south]. A section of German motorcyclists had rushed up the road to Bn HQ. They were dealt with effectively, and fell back on the RAP [Regimental Aid Post] buildings [a short distance to the east, across the road from the farmhouse], leaving 2 dead in the road.[34] From the RAP they filled the air with shots, and it seemed impossible to get at them . . . It was a very awkward moment which was saved by RSM [Regimental Sergeant-Major] Cockaday. He seized a Bren, and rushed forward into the open. Taking up a position, he opened fire with the gun. In the course of this, he was wounded.[35]

Thanks to Cockaday, who was backed up by Ryder and Long, the Germans were eventually driven away from the south side of the farm, and an escape route, in theory at least, was kept open. Long attempted to secure it by ordering some of the men to hold a couple of neighbouring houses as outposts. However, the difficulties Long experienced in going to and from these houses must have convinced him that salvation might well be impossible. According to Long, the 'piece of open country [between the battalion and the houses] . . . was whipped with fire. The route [I took] was the only one possible, and I'm damned if I liked it. This was the only time I felt frightened. However we got there, and lost no men.'[36]

Holding these outposts became even more problematic when the brigade's artillery, probably reacting to a telephone call from Long telling the brigadier where the Germans were attacking, began to shell them. It was a frightening moment. After holding off the enemy so courageously, it seemed as if they were about to be annihilated by British guns. The barrage was only stopped when Long dashed back through another hail of bullets to telephone through an urgent request to the brigade to put an end to their unwelcome 'support'.

No sooner had the guns been silenced than another problem emerged. 'The men seemed to lose heart without anyone to command them,' Long wrote later. 'So once more, I dodged back again, and got the men in position and cheered up.' However, the situation in the outposts was only stabilized after he had placed an NCO in each of the two houses he had ordered his men to hold.[37] Long was then free to return to the farm.

Hastings has described what he witnessed there:

At one moment I am watching the movements of the enemy through glasses through a hole in the roof. Another moment I am firing a rifle. Now I am firing a Bren gun which stops . . . A party of Germans try to get past at short range. Everyone that can get a rifle gets some shooting. Richardson has a German Tommy gun taken from the dead motorcyclist in the road . . . Now the outlook is good. Now again it is bad . . . Now I am putting the Battalion papers and war diary in a sack and weighting it with stones, and tying it up ready to sink it in the farm pond. Now I am looking down from an upper window on the dead German motorcyclist who still lies in the road with his arm outstretched. A stream of blood has run from his head to the gutter. As I look, I see a soldier steal out at the peril of his life, and remove the wrist watch from the dead man's hand. He slips back as quickly and quietly as he slipped out . . .

Charles Long is a great success with the men. He is telling awful lies, but he talks as if he himself believes what he says . . . The men love him . . . He set a fine example by his disregard of personal danger, and certainly did more than any other officer to keep morale at a high level. He has a breezy manner, was always cheerful, and full of unbounded optimism . . . All this he managed to convey to the troops . . .

Something that looks like a tank approaches. Where is the anti-tank rifle? It is lying out in the road. I go to get it. A private soldier comes after me. 'Let me get it Sir,' he says. I don't let him, but I am touched at his offering. It has a hole in the side of the barrel, but it can still be fired. The tank stops behind a hillock. Its top can just be seen . . . It's an armoured troop carrier . . .

The CO is ringing up Brigade. He says: 'I shall not ring you up again. We are doing very well.'[38] . . . I think he [Ryder] is about to crack. He says to me:

'When I think of the magnificent battalion I took over only a few days ago . . .' He is unable to go on. I wonder why he does not abandon our position. I think we could still get some men away safely. We both know now there is no hope of holding on much longer. However, he says [that] others are depending on us. I think he knows more than I do. I glance at the Battalion papers in the sack. He nods his head, and I pitch the sack into the farm pond. It doesn't sink. I throw a bicycle on top of it. Now it sinks.

Now I am going round counting up rounds of ammunition. I see Richardson. He is quiet and very grim. He is watching the development of the enemy's attack from the side of the troop carrier. I am getting ammunition collected from the rifles and pouches of the wounded. Bren gun magazines must be broken up and the rounds distributed. We are very very short of ammunition, but everyone has a few rounds.[39]

Long was also finding the scenes at the farm increasingly hard to bear. The farmhouse cellar was full of wounded. Dead men were scattered around the courtyard. The farm was being shelled repeatedly. One shell went through the wall of the building where the battalion's petrol was stored. It was a miracle this did not cause a devastating explosion. Even the message received at 2.45 p.m. from the brigadier telling Ryder he was free to abandon the farm and escape with his men to the north-east brought no real comfort, since, as Long realized,

It was manifestly impossible that any could get away. The enemy were all round with tanks and guns . . . The CO called a conference of all available officers, and we discussed the matter. It was decided that should there be any left alive at dusk, they should attempt the escape. We had very little hope. I remember sitting on a chair for a minute or two thinking about my wife, and feeling very queer about it. She would be a widow, and we had only been married since September. Then I realized it wouldn't do. So I stood up.[40]

It seems likely that it was shortly after this conference that Ryder walked round the farm buildings to tell the men what the brigadier had said to him. They were told that they would not be disobeying orders if they broke away and escaped. However, he wanted to offer a choice to those who stayed: either they could all surrender or they could fight to the finish. Some men wanted to carry on fighting, but even they eventually agreed it was pointless to do so: the ammunition would probably only last another hour. In the end everyone agreed they must surrender.[41]

Hastings's and Long's accounts tell us what was going on in the farmhouse at this juncture. According to Hastings:

A shell detonates on the window sill of the room [inside the farmhouse]. Charles Long is knocked over. I see blood on the back of my hand, but I am not wounded. It is only some grit from the brickwork. [Lieutenant] Johnny Woodwark is standing next to me. He holds out a field dressing and is asking me to put it on his neck. We pass to the adjoining room. [Then] something happens in the room we have left.[42]

Long has described what that 'something' was: 'A soldier rushed into the room. "The whole roof is alight, Sir," he shouted. The CO then called for all men to come down, and he commenced to give the order to abandon the house and to fight it out outside. Then the house seemed to fall on me.'[43]

Somehow both Hastings and Long, together with some of the other officers and men, made it out of the burning, and partially ruined, farmhouse, ending up in the ditch running along the road on the farmhouse's south side. 'Then [Lieutenant] Draffin [the medical officer] appeared in the road,' wrote Hastings, 'shouting and holding up his Red X bag. Someone else produced a white towel . . . It was . . . unquestionably the right course, so I took the towel myself, and stood up in the road holding it above my head. The firing ceased.'[44]

Meanwhile Ryder had assembled in the barn on the west side of the courtyard all of the men who had been firing out of the slits around the farm's perimeter. There was not a moment to lose if they were to survive, since the Germans were still firing at the barn. When Private Bill O'Callaghan moved to pick up his backpack the man who took his place was killed by a shell that penetrated the brickwork.[45] A white towel was waved out of the door leading from the barn to the field on the west side of the farm. Then the first group of men walked out. But their attempt to surrender was greeted by a burst of machine-gun fire, which scythed them all down.

Inside the barn the remaining men began to panic, fearing that, in spite of all the talk, the Germans were not going to take any prisoners after all. But Ryder insisted they should try again and, five minutes later,

the towel was waved out of the door once more. This time there was
no firing. All that could be heard from the Germans gathered outside
was the sound of triumphant whooping, signifying to the men inside
the barn that it was all over at last.[46] Or was it?

Le Paradis, 27 May 1940
(See Map 13. Also Map 1)

While the Royal Norfolks were fighting to the last bullet, if not the last man, at Le Paradis, other units within 2 Division were doing their bit on or behind the canal line to either side of them. Unlike the Royal Norfolks, who were at least able to start out on the canal line, 6 Brigade's 1st Battalion, the Royal Welch Fusiliers (RWF), on their right, had to fight their way to their sector of the canal, since German troops serving under the 3rd Panzer Division arrived there first.[1] Troops from the SS Germania Regiment had already penetrated as far inland as St Floris by 24 May.[2] However, because of the 24 May halt order, there was little if any tank support for most of their troops north of the canal, and this enabled Lieutenant-Colonel 'Harry' Harrison and his Royal Welch Fusiliers to push the Germans back. An RWF base was established at St-Venant on 25 May, and on the same day the battalion's B Company moved into Robecq alongside the canal.[3]

Unfortunately for B Company, German troops had surrounded Robecq by the evening of 26 May. The acting commander, 2nd Lieutenant Michael Edwards, might nevertheless have extricated most of his men, had it not been for a series of unforeseen events. The first occurred shortly after Robecq was occupied by British troops. The company sergeant-major was relieved of his command on the ground that he was drunk, and was replaced by an NCO who unbeknown to Edwards had bad eyesight. Nevertheless the new acting sergeant-major was called upon to play a central role in the escape from Robecq. During the night of 26–7 May, Edwards ordered his men to creep in single file between two of the German posts to the north of the village. The first men had reached the line between the posts, which were around seventy-five yards apart, when the newly appointed sergeant-major, believing that they had already passed through the Germans, stood up suddenly and exclaimed: 'This is a bloody waste of time!' What one man described as a 'rabbit shoot' ensued. Most of the men were either killed or captured, including the sergeant-major and Lieutenant Edwards, and B Company effectively ceased to exist.[4]

The next morning another error led to further bloodshed. For a reason best known to 6 Brigade's brigadier, the remainder of the RWF and the 2nd Durham Light Infantry (2 DLI), its sister company in 6 Brigade, were sited on the south side of the Lys Canal, which runs to the north of St-Venant, rather than on its north side. As a result, they had no anti-tank barrier separating them from the Germans. Consequently, when tanks attacked between 7 and 8 a.m. on 27 May, at the same time as attacks were being put in all along the canal line, the front-line companies were swiftly overrun, and the bridge over the Lys Canal, representing the only exit from the town on its northern side, was raked by gunfire. (The location of the bridge is marked in Map 13 on p. 528.) Whether Brigadier Furlong of 6 Brigade was feeling guilty about this strategic error, or whether it was just that he was a very brave man who was trying to salvage as much of the brigade as possible after its safety had been jeopardized by orders coming from further up the hierarchy, he nevertheless crossed the bridge at around 11.45 a.m. to tell Harrison that both he and the DLI should retire.[5]

The RWF's Captain Walter Clough-Taylor has described how he first came to hear of the brigadier's decision after being ordered to report to his colonel near the bridge:

I found him in a ditch alongside our tumbledown hut which we had been using as a HQ. 'I want you,' he said, 'to form a defensive flank by the bridge. You had better start to thin them out now, Clough.' So accordingly, I stood like some grim P.T. instructor in the middle of the road launching each man on his perilous journey with a shout of 'Next, go!' They had to run the gauntlet over the bridge, which was now being literally plastered with fire from stationary tanks down the road. I saw many stagger and fall as they ran. Martin, my trusty servant, had his arm blown off.

At last it was my own turn. I summoned courage, waited for a burst of fire, and dashed forward. I was only a yard or so on to the bridge when I was hit in the leg . . . I recoiled, and staggered crazily back to the culvert. As I stood thinking wildly how I was to get across alive, I noticed there were girders, rising to about a foot in height in the centre, above the roadway. How I wished I had seen them before. I flung myself down, and caterpillaring madly along behind one of them arrived miraculously on the other side. I got up, and was at once hit again in the arm and hip. I staggered on to the shelter of some houses . . .

As I lay there, I heard Harry [Harrison] shouting: 'Why the hell don't they blow the bridge?' I thought vaguely that if they did, they would undoubtedly blow me [up] too, as I was only 20 yards away. But I was past caring . . . The next thing I heard was an unmistakable German voice. I was horrified. [Then] I saw . . . the first of about two dozen tanks, which, after hesitating at the bridge, rolled triumphantly past.[6]

Clough-Taylor was captured, and lived to tell his tale. Harrison was not so lucky: after crossing the bridge he was shot while trying to escape, making him one of the twenty-five officers and 490 other ranks from the battalion who were found either to have been killed or wounded or to be missing when the RWF formed up in England after the evacuation.[7]

Harrison and his Fusiliers were not the only soldiers to suffer because of British actions on 27 May. Even higher losses were endured by the men making up the 1st Battalion, the Queen's Own Cameron Highlanders, which was the left unit within 5 Brigade. Because 5 Brigade was 2 Division's left-hand unit it was also at the extreme left of the front held by the division. Those Germans who were not well up on Scottish regiments must have assumed that the Camerons were wearing skirts: they were the last battalion to wear kilts into battle. But there was no mistaking their toughness. At dawn on 27 May a half-company from the battalion of Camerons, backed by six French tanks, was ordered to counter-attack against a section of the 7th Panzer Division's Schützen-regiment 7, which had crossed the La Bassée Canal on the Camerons' right. The men in the Schützenregiment 7 came off worst, fleeing across the canal.[8]

It was this attack that upset Rommel as he was supervising the positioning of pontoons at Cuinchy, which were supposed to enable his panzers to cross the canal.[9] According to Rommel:

A report came in that a strong force of enemy tanks from La Bassée had attacked the 7th Rifle Regiment's eastern bridgehead and thrown Battalion Cramer back across the canal. The enemy tanks, which included several . . . heavies, were now standing on the northern bank, and spraying the southern bank with machine-gun and shell fire. We could hear the enemy fire a few hundred yards away to our right, and there was a grave danger that the enemy tanks would push on to the west along the canal bank, and attack the Battalion Bachmann, which still had no anti-tank weapons, apart from anti-tank rifles, on the northern bank, and also had no depth. If the enemy exploited his chance, he could be at the western crossing point in a few minutes.

The situation was extremely critical. I drove the sappers on to their utmost speed, and had the pontoons lashed roughly together in order to get at least a few guns and tanks across. With so many sunken barges and other obstacles jammed in the canal, it was impossible for the bridge to take a straight course, and its structure consequently had little strength. As the first Panzer III lumbered across, several pontoons gave noticeably, and it was touch and go whether or not the tank would slither bodily into the canal. While it was crossing, I sent off a Panzer IV 50 yards to the east along the high bank on our side of the canal with orders to open fire immediately on the enemy tanks attacking from La Bassée. The fire of this Panzer IV brought the leading enemy tank to a halt,

and the German defences were reinforced by a Panzer 3 that had made it to the north bank. Thus the French tanks' attack, backed up by the Camerons, was foiled.[10]

It is likely that it was panzers from this bridgehead that attacked the Camerons' positions around Violaines and La Bassée at about 2.30 p.m. on 27 May.[11] Wherever they came from, 5 Brigade's three-gun anti-tank platoon halted around twenty of the advancing panzers.[12] That might have stopped most tank commanders, but it was nothing compared with the number of tanks available to Rommel. At 3.15 p.m., 5 Brigade's Brigadier Gartlan ordered the Camerons' commanding officer, Lieutenant-Colonel Pat Rose-Miller, to withdraw.[13] In his hurry to get the companies out before they were surrounded, Rose-Miller sent a runner with a verbal instruction that they must retire immediately. However, when Major Maurice Wilson received the message, he sent the runner back to Rose-Miller with a request that the order should be confirmed in writing.[14] Although Wilson managed to obtain the confirmation he needed from a French unit he contacted before the runner returned, the withdrawal from the canal was delayed. Whether or not this made a difference, one fact was unfortunately certain: most of the men in the Camerons' front-line companies were either killed, wounded or captured, and the battalion only consisted of seventy-nine men when it was evacuated from Dunkirk, making it, if one excludes the 51st Highland Division battalions (whose exploits are dealt with in

Chapter 35), one of the hardest hit, if not the hardest hit, of all battalions in the BEF.[15]

However, even the heartbreaking losses incurred by the Camerons could not compete with the drawn-out torment that must have been suffered by one group of Royal Norfolk soldiers after they were captured at Le Paradis. According to a 1947 report compiled by the War Crimes Interrogation Unit entitled 'Le Paradis: The Murder Of Ninety Seven British Prisoners-of-war By Members Of The German Armed Forces At Le Paradis-Lestrem, Pas De Calais, France On 27th May, 1940', the captured soldiers were killed by members of the 1st Battalion, the SS Totenkopf Division's 2nd Infantry Regiment (1 Bn TIR 2).[16] Many of the victims had been with Major Ryder when they surrendered at Duriez Farm (see Chapter 21). The description of the massacre was so harrowing that it prompted Lieutenant-Colonel Alex Scotland, the writer of the report, to state at the beginning: 'The bringing to justice of those guilty of this brutal crime should become a crusade with every man serving in the Army today.'[17]

Nailing the criminals was particularly important because the murder of the Royal Norfolks was just one of a series of war crimes committed in the same area. According to the War Crimes report, French and German witnesses mentioned other massacres, which did not lead to prosecutions, presumably because none of the victims survived. British witnesses also mentioned two cases where massacres were only prevented thanks to the timely intervention of officers. (See note 18.)[18]

Evidence of a motive for the Le Paradis murders was provided by witnesses who described what happened during the morning of 27 May. The men in 3 Company, 1 Bn TIR 2, who had spearheaded the attack on Le Cornet Malo, were ordered to bury their dead in that village.[19] At least twelve German corpses were buried in a mass grave. Afterwards, SS-Hauptsturmführer Fritz Knöchlein, the company's commander, who was later to be tried by a war-crimes tribunal, gave a speech in the course of which he called for revenge.[20] His men represented a small proportion of the total casualties. On 29 May, a note sent to the German XVI Corps, under whose command the SS Totenkopf Division was operating, stated that no less than 710 SS soldiers had been killed, wounded or were missing after the battle.[21]

There were only two known survivors of the various massacres in this area: Royal Norfolk Privates Bert Pooley and Bill O'Callaghan.

However, their testimony has been sufficient to demonstrate how so many of these unfortunate men were dispatched. O'Callaghan received his first inkling that the prisoners were not going to be well treated shortly after he was captured at Duriez Farm. On being asked whether he was carrying a knife, he automatically replied in the negative. However, he had forgotten that he had one hanging from his belt, and he was punished for his forgetfulness with a heavy blow to his head, which almost knocked him over.[22]

This might have been put down to the legitimate jumpiness of a guard who feared his prisoner was trying to conceal a weapon. Not so easily excused was the treatment meted out to one of O'Callaghan's comrades. A guard asked him whether he would like one of the cigarettes that had been thrown on to the ground. However, when he stepped forward to pick one up, the German swung his rifle butt into the man's face, sending him staggering back with blood spurting out of his mouth and nose.[23] Pooley was also treated roughly. After taking up a guard's invitation to sit down as one of the wounded, he was brutally kicked in the ribs for his misdemeanour. Shortly afterwards, when he glanced at a guard who had liberated some cigarettes from his pockets, the guard, sensing no doubt that the look was disapproving, jabbed his rifle butt into Pooley's face, knocking out four teeth.[24]

The testimony collected by the War Crimes Interrogation Unit does not specify whether the rough handling of the prisoners occurred before or after their fate was determined. Although two of the interrogated German witnesses claimed they had been told what had been discussed by the 1 Bn TIR 2's company commanders – 1 Bn TIR 2's 1 Company's Hauptsturmführer Kaltofen and 3 Company's Hauptsturmführer Knöchlein – who wanted the prisoners to be shot, the witness statements do not mention when and where the discussion was supposed to have taken place. It probably happened while the captured British soldiers were being detained in a field some distance away from Duriez Farm, following the surrender. Pooley observed a group of SS officers having an animated discussion at this point.[25]

However, the interrogated Germans did reveal what the German officers had discussed. The officers alleged that the British soldiers had carried on shooting after misleadingly hoisting white flags and swastika banners, and had shot at German medical orderlies even though they could be recognized as such by their armbands. They also claimed that the British had used so-called dum–dum bullets (bullets with hollow points, which are designed to expand on impact and were prohibited under international law). All of this justified their killing the prisoners, according to the majority of those who took part in the conversation. The only officer who objected was 2 Company's acting commander, Obersturmführer Reinhold Loew, but he was branded a 'rabbit' and his opinion ignored.[26]

The British captives were subsequently marched to rue du Paradis, the road that runs past Duriez Farm, and ordered to enter another farm, further to the west, which was owned by a Monsieur Louis Creton.[27] (Creton's Farm is marked on Map 13 on p. 528.) There, they were taken to a meadow and lined up in front of a pit that ran along the front of a brick farm building. It was the presence of two machine-guns trained on them that first alerted Pooley to what might be in store for them.[28] He was not the only British soldier who guessed. O'Callaghan saw one man wheel round on entering the meadow as if intending to escape, and heard him exclaim, 'I'm not going to die like this.' Then the man changed his mind, and carried on walking in the column with the others.[29] The next event both O'Callaghan and Pooley remembered was the German order to the machine-gunners to open fire, whereupon both guns began to fire at them.[30]

O'Callaghan, who was shielded by the two soldiers beside him, dived to the ground as soon as he heard the machine-guns fire. Nevertheless, he felt a searing pain shoot up his left arm as he fell, which told him that he had been hit. He came to rest with his face in a patch of thistles, and he felt himself being pinned down by two comrades who had fallen on to his legs and right arm. As for Pooley, who had been in the middle of the column, he was initially only wounded superficially. He also fell to the ground, on top of another soldier.

Then the machine-gun stopped firing and, for a short period, all that could be heard were the cries and moans of the wounded and dying. This was quickly interrupted by a barked German command, followed by a metallic rattle, which told Pooley and O'Callaghan that bayonets were being fixed to rifles. Then there were more shots, accompanied by screams of terror and pain, as the German soldiers moved among the prisoners, shooting them with pistols and bayoneting them.[31]

A German witness, who gave evidence to the War Crimes Interrogation Unit, described a particularly poignant scene in the midst of the carnage. He recalled seeing an older man raise himself on one elbow and point with his other hand to his heart, as if asking to be finished off. If that was what he was asking, his wish was swiftly granted, and after being shot again, he collapsed in the pit along with the other British soldiers.[32] It is possible that this witness was describing the tragic death of Major Ryder who, at thirty-seven, was much older than most of the other soldiers. Ryder was certainly present. Pooley states that he saw his commanding officer, sitting with his back against the wall of the brick building, before the Germans moved in to deliver the *coups de grâce*.[33]

Both O'Callaghan and Pooley were lucky not to be bayoneted. Afterwards O'Callaghan described the moment when a German pulled away the corpse lying on top of him. Petrified, he waited for the bayonet thrust that he must have thought was inevitable. But the thrust never came. Perhaps O'Callaghan's own blood confused the German, or perhaps it was the blood that had leaked out of his comrade's corpse, but for whatever reason, the soldier passed over O'Callaghan, evidently believing he was already dead.

Pooley was not quite so fortunate. While the Germans were searching for any form of life, a man lying beneath him shuddered as he died. A German must have seen the movement, and fired at the pile of bodies. Both bullets hit Pooley in the leg. Then, to his horror, he saw a German stepping into the pit in front of the building where he and his British comrades were lying. But just as Pooley thought that his last moment had come, a whistle was blown, and the German climbed out, leaving Pooley shaking with fear, but very much alive.[34]

After the German voices had faded, both Pooley and O'Callaghan lost consciousness. Pooley only realized that someone else was alive when he heard O'Callaghan snoring in the darkness. O'Callaghan woke up when Pooley shook him, and after he had scrambled to his feet, he somehow managed to pull Pooley out of the pit. He then carried him away from the meadow on his back. He could not carry him far, and when Pooley, who was freezing cold, asked O'Callaghan to go back to fetch some blankets he had seen lying near the brick building where they had been shot, O'Callaghan reluctantly obliged. He had seen German soldiers sheltering from the rain in buildings near the corpses, and feared they might spot him.

It was while he was retrieving the blankets that O'Callaghan heard a sound that would haunt him for the rest of his life. Someone was moaning, 'Get me out of the rain.' On hearing this, O'Callaghan was tugged in two directions: he wanted to help his wounded comrade, but feared that if he stayed they would all be caught by the Germans in the nearby building. Repressing his humane thoughts, he tore himself away from the man's moans, and went back to Pooley. No sooner had he done so than both men heard a shot ring out, a shot that O'Callaghan must have half hoped and half feared had put an end to the moaning man's suffering. If, as O'Callaghan suspected, the shot really was fired at the wounded British soldier, it justified the decision he had made. It was obviously too risky to go back to check. Now Pooley's and O'Callaghan's only thought was how to save their own skins.[35]

★   ★   ★

It did not take long for the more law-abiding elements within the German Army to discover the evidence left behind by the SS at Le Paradis. On the day after the massacre, a German major wrote a report about it, which ended up on the desk of XVI Corps' General Hoepner. The major reported that he had seen eighty-nine dead English soldiers. 'It was apparently a case where the prisoners have been summarily executed by being shot in the head at very close range,' he wrote. 'In some cases, the whole skull has been smashed, a type of wound which could only have been inflicted by blows from rifle butts, or similar weapons.'[36]

At the same time a parallel investigation was being conducted by the Totenkopf Division. On 28 May, Gunter d'Alquen, a professional journalist who had been instructed to form a war-correspondents company in the Waffen-SS, was asked to escort Dr Thum, the Totenkopf Division's deputy legal adviser, to the meadow where the massacre had taken place. 'We came to a single small farm situated at right angles to a medium-sized country road,' d'Alquen wrote.

It was possible to look into the back yard from the road . . . [The corpses] in British uniform were lying in this yard near the buildings. They were lying in such a position that one can assume they were killed by machine-gun bursts. It struck me at once that the dead soldiers were not wearing helmets, nor did they have any equipment on them . . . I took pictures of the dead bodies and the whole farm. At Thum's request these were to be placed at the disposal of the Division . . . I believe I was already sitting in the vehicle when Thum . . . told me that in the field from which he had returned the equipment of the shot British soldiers was lying in a heap, from which he had come to the conclusion that a summary trial had taken place there.[37]

The two men then departed.

The next day General Eicke, the Totenkopf Division's commander, presumably reacting to a request for an explanation from his superior in XVI Corps, justified the execution with some of the same arguments as the company commanders had used to authorize it: the English had used dum-dum bullets, and 'a swastika flag was exhibited luring our soldiers from cover, whereupon they were ambushed and wiped out by machine-gun fire'. After specifying the total number of Totenkopf troops who had been killed or wounded, he stated that most of his troops were shot in the back, adding, 'It was in our interest to take our revenge for the treacherous and villainous fighting tactics adopted by the English by shooting the remainder of those who took part in the cowardly ambush following a court martial. Reports which give a different account of what happened are malicious and false.'

Evidently this report did not satisfy the officer dealing with the investigation at XVI Corps. He wrote back to ask a number of penetrating questions, which included: 'How many SS men were hit by dum-dum bullets, and how did you know that dum-dum bullets had been used?'; 'Where . . . was the swastika flag exhibited by the enemy? . . . Was it captured?'; 'Why was such an important fact, the use of dum-dum bullets by the enemy, not reported immediately?' and 'Why was the shooting of such a large number of prisoners not reported?' Fortunately for General Eicke, he was never forced to answer these questions, since before the matter could be pursued by XVI Corps, the SS Totenkopf Division was removed from its control, and it seems likely that after the file was passed up to the 6th Army, it was conveniently forgotten.[38]

23: Manhunt

Vinkt, Belgium, and London 25–8 May 1940
(See Map 17. Also Maps 1 and 10)

One of the great myths of the 1940 campaign is that the King of Belgium did not warn the BEF generals that he was about to surrender after the Germans broke through Belgian defences on the Lys. That does not mean that the King could not have done more to alert his British and French allies before capitulating. It is certainly the case that when the final decision to surrender was announced during the afternoon of 27 May it shocked British politicians and soldiers alike. It even surprised Lieutenant-Colonel George Davy, GHQ's liaison officer with the Belgian Army's headquarters, who had expected the Belgians to carry on fighting for another twenty-four hours at least.[1]

Surprising Davy took some doing, since, prompted by the Belgians, he, along with Lord Keyes, had throughout the previous day been desperately warning the War Office and staff at GHQ about the state of the Belgian front. The Germans had broken through the Belgian line on the River Lys and its main tributary, the Canal de dérivation de la Lys, in more than one place. Although a new line had been formed to the north-west of the original front line, doubts had arisen on 26 May as to how long it could hold.

It was these doubts that persuaded Keyes on 26 May to give Gort and Sir Archibald Sinclair, the Secretary of State for Air, what amounted to an ultimatum: only a British counter-attack against the Germans between the Lys and the Escaut, or fighter support provided by the RAF along the Belgian line, could save the Belgian Army from a 'disaster'. (See note 2 for details.)[2] On the same day, Gort was also told that if the Germans were not driven back from the Courtrai sector, the area where the most threatening breakthrough had taken place, 'the whole front might collapse'.[3] An equally alarming warning was handed to General Pierre Champon, the head of the French liaison mission at the Belgian King's headquarters, during the afternoon of 26 May. After summing up the positions of the Belgian Army, it concluded with the following words: 'The limit of the [Belgian Army's] resistance has nearly been reached.'[4]

These warnings precluded Gort from complaining that the Belgians had not kept him informed about developments on their front: as he admitted in his Despatches, he knew the Belgians were a spent force long before they surrendered.[5] That is not to say there were no other queries about the King's strategy. Had he been wrong at the 21 May Conference at Ypres to say he could relieve British forces even though this left him without sufficient reserves? Should he not have created reserves by retreating to the shorter line of the Yser Canal rather than making his final stand on the Lys? Although Van Overstraeten was concerned on 21 May that Belgian soldiers might not carry on fighting if ordered to retreat again, should the King not have attempted to put them to the test? Could he not have formed a new line to the south, thereby ensuring his troops stayed in touch with the British, after the Germans broke through on the Lys, rather than going north? And after he had told the British he was about to surrender could he not have continued the fight for an additional twenty-four hours by ordering his troops to steal away from the front line during the night of 27–8 May given that the Germans usually stopped fighting at night? This might have enabled the Belgian Army to hold out for a little longer further to the north and west.

We may never find complete answers to these questions. But one fact is certain. Although the Belgian King should have explicitly told his allies that if the Germans broke through his line again he might be forced to surrender immediately, it is quite wrong to say that Leopold surrendered without warning Gort of what was going to happen sooner or later. It was Keyes's message to Gort at 12.30 p.m. on 27 May that gave the British Commander-in-Chief the clearest indication. It included the words: 'He [King Leopold] fears a moment is rapidly approaching when he can no longer rely upon his troops to fight, or be of any further use to the BEF. He wishes you to realize that he will be obliged to surrender before a débâcle.'[6]

★　★　★

The Belgian fear that their army might not carry on fighting if another retreat was ordered is likely to have been influenced by one of the most shameful actions of the campaign, which had taken place two days before the surrender. On 25 May, sections of Belgium's 7th and 15th Regiments, which were holding the west bank of the Canal de dérivation de la Lys at Meigem, surrendered without firing a shot at the Germans.[7]

It seems that since the previous day the men had been demoralized, partly because they were exhausted and partly because they were disheartened at having had to yield so much Belgian soil to the invaders. In addition, they had been depressed by stories about their French allies, passed on to them by Belgian refugees. The French had apparently turned back Belgian refugees at the Franco-Belgian frontier after charging them exorbitant prices for basic items such as water and bread.[8] It seems that these complaints were the straw that broke the camel's back. What made the accounts of the regiments' surrender so alarming was that it was not just a case of men taking their lead from cowardly or defeatist officers, or of men giving up because they were not properly led. The men in the regiments in question had ignored their officers' orders to fight, and some had actually fired at officers or, in at least one case, shot them.[9]

The surrender by the 7th and 15th Regiments presented the Germans with another bridgehead on the Belgian side of the canal. It was the Belgian Army's courageous attempt to block the attempt to extend this bridgehead that infuriated German commanders, and led to the horror and terror that followed. The troops called in to block the German advance were from Belgium's élite Chasseurs Ardennais. They were ordered to defend a new line centred on Vinkt, a small Flemish village, some two and a half miles west of Meigem.[10] The wall of fire put down by the battalions within the 1st Chasseurs Ardennais Division enabled the Belgians to repulse attack after attack, launched initially by Germany's 56 Division on 25 and 26 May, and subsequently by 56 Division's replacement, 225 Division, on 26 and 27 May.

This committed defence of Vinkt dispelled another myth concerning the Belgians: that none of their soldiers had the will to stand and fight. But at 4 p.m. on 27 May, having made a stand as resolute as any by British forces on or to the north of the La Bassée Canal, the last Chasseurs Ardennais troops retreated from the village, leaving Vinkt's civilian population, who had been cowering in their cellars throughout the battle, to take the consequences.[11]

Those consequences were described by the prosecutor on the opening day of the 1948 war crimes trial of two officers from 225 Division who had played an active role in Vinkt on 27 May. According to the prosecutor, they were a series of 'atrocities carried out by a fierce and merciless battalion of soldiers on terrorized civilians', atrocities that he referred to as 'the Vinkt Massacres'.[12] The battalion to which he referred was the 1st Battalion of 225 Division's 377th Regiment, which had been involved in the fiercest fighting on the eastern side of the village during 26 and 27 May. After the battle ended, it was principally men from this battalion who were responsible for slaughtering seventy-eight civilians, including around forty in one short spell of frenzied killing in Vinkt's main street, a stone's throw from the village church. The remainder were murdered in the farms and cafés dotted around the surrounding countryside, with special attention being paid to men found inside buildings that had served as Belgian strongholds during the fighting.

As the Belgian War Crimes Commission, which carried out the investigation before the trial, pointed out, the atrocities did not appear to have been the acts of individual soldiers out of control, but were rather organized reprisals orchestrated by their commanding officers.[13] The fact that many killings took place in properties adjacent to the main road running from Meigem to Vinkt, along which the main thrust of the German attack had been made, is at least consistent with this theory.

Many more civilians would have been executed had it not been for the fact that by no means every German soldier agreed with the measures being taken. Time and again in the evidence prepared by the War Crimes Commission, there are records of civilians being saved from a German firing squad, thanks to the timely intervention of an officer who happened to be passing. This disapproval may explain why, after the war, some German soldiers were prepared to testify against their senior officers. However, since the soldiers giving evidence must in some cases have been worried that they themselves might be prosecuted and are likely to have tailored it to present themselves in a good light, their testimony has had to be treated with caution.

German soldiers' accounts reveal that, at some point during the late afternoon of 27 May, after Belgian battalions had left the area, Lieutenant-Colonel Hodissen, 377th Regiment's commanding officer, ordered that certain civilians were to be shot. Because Hodissen died in Russia before the investigation, he was never interviewed about what happened at Vinkt, and it is uncertain what his motives were for the killings. It is possible that he wanted revenge for the 184 Germans killed during the fighting, or perhaps he genuinely believed that Belgian civilians had shot at German soldiers during the battle.[14] In either case he was not entitled to sanction the indiscriminate killing of civilians without taking steps to find out what each man had done.

Oberleutnant Franz Lohmann, one of two men indicted at the 1948 War Crimes trial, stated that Hodissen initially talked about burning the whole village, presumably without evacuating it first, but had eventually decreed that the only civilians to be punished were those caught with or those seen using a firearm. They were to be shot.[15] Another witness claims that Hodissen had reined in Major Erwin Kühner, the second officer indicted, who had wanted to kill women as well as men. Hodissen apparently told Kühner that only the men should die.[16]

Evidence provided by Lieutenant Heinrich Klussmann, a member of Hodissen's staff, is particularly interesting, since it might include a description of the first instance when Hodissen passed the death sentence on a civilian. According to Klussmann, the battle was still being fought when Hodissen mentioned that one of his men had been shot at from a house and had consequently arrested the civilians he found inside. Hodissen said the civilians should be shot, whereupon Klussmann reminded him that there had to be a field tribunal hearing before such a sentence was carried out. This exasperated Hodissen, who retorted that when he had been fighting in Poland, they had never bothered with such niceties and, in any case, there was no time for a tribunal with the battle raging around them. As far as Hodissen was concerned, the report that the shooting had taken place sufficed.[17]

Klussmann's report does not specify exactly where the shooting by the civilians was said to have taken place. That makes it difficult to link it up with those identified in affidavits given to investigators acting for the War Crimes Commission. It is just possible, however, that he was referring to the one that took place at the Van Steenkiste family's farm, opposite Kühner's advanced headquarters, on the road leading from Meigem to Vinkt. (The location of this farm, and other Vinkt landmarks referred to in this chapter, are indicated in Map 17 on p. 534.) Two of the men who were to die there were arrested at the Vermeulen family's farm, further along the road towards Vinkt, where there had been bitter fighting before the Germans took control of it on 26 May.

Elza Vermeulen, the daughter of the farmer, was twenty-eight when the Vinkt massacre took place. In the statement she gave to the War Crimes Commission she described what happened at the Vermeulens' farm on 27 May when the battle to take control of it was over:

Our entire family of six [Elza, her parents, her brother and her two sisters] were taken outside the house by the Germans, and we were made to stand up against the stable wall after our hands had been tied up. The soldiers said to us: 'You've been shooting at us.' Then they lined up in front of us in order to kill us. But at that very moment, a superior arrived who said something to the soldiers.[18]

What was said appeared at first to amount to a reprieve, since the firing squad was stood down, but during the afternoon the Vermeulens were taken to a meadow attached to the Café den Haring, opposite the Van Steenkistes' farm, near to where the 377th Regiment's 1st Battalion's advanced headquarters were situated. There, they were detained along with other civilians from the area while their fate was decided. If the testimony given by the indicted Oberleutnant Lohmann is correct, the first he knew about what was in store for Elza Vermeulen's father and brother was when he received a note stating that Hodissen had ruled that they must be shot because they had been shooting at Germans.[19] Lohmann claimed he only then ordered one of his men to make the arrangements for the execution.

The first Elza Vermeulen knew of the sentence to be carried out was when

some Germans arrived, and after checking identity cards . . . one of them said: 'The women will live, but the men have been shooting, and they must die.' My father and brother were then taken away . . . Just before they left, my brother asked my mother for a little cross. One of the Germans, on seeing this, laughed and said: 'Give him the cross. It will be the last gift you will ever be able to give him on this earth. The next time you see him will be in the next world.'

After her father and brother's departure, Elza and the rest of the family lay on the ground in the meadow watched over by armed guards. But, according to Elza, the guards' behaviour failed to improve even after the men had left: 'When my fourteen-year-old sister asked for a drink, the Germans laughed, and shouted back: "You do not need to drink, dog's daughter, because you are going to die as well!" On hearing this, my sister burst into tears, which delighted the Germans.'

The next day when the Vermeulen women were finally allowed to go home, they found their farmhouse had been ransacked, and all their animals killed.

As for Elza's father and brother, they were taken across the road to the Van Steenkistes' farm where, without being given any chance to prove their innocence, they and three other civilians were shot. A Belgian prisoner-of-war, who was forced to bury them after watching them die, has described how the Germans made absolutely sure they were dead by bashing in their heads with their rifle butts.[20] At least this series of killings did not go unpunished. Lohmann's defence at the war crimes trial – that he had only arranged the execution because his superiors had ordered him to do so – failed to impress the court. It agreed with the prosecutor's argument, that Lohmann would have had to take active steps to check that a properly constituted tribunal had found the condemned men guilty of a war crime before such a defence could have succeeded.[21]

The killing at the Van Steenkiste's farm was just one of a series of crimes committed during the late afternoon and evening of 27 May as German troops went on the rampage. After the relatively orderly dispatch of the Vermeulens and their companions, the search for more victims developed into a kind of manhunt as German soldiers vied with each other to collect and kill the most prisoners. There was no standing on ceremony. They thought nothing of breaking into houses in Vinkt and dragging out any men, women and children they found. Similar searches were conducted at the farms in the surrounding area.

One can well imagine the terror experienced by those who were subject to the raids. Many witnesses stated that they were hauled out of their homes by German soldiers who were literally foaming at the mouth, and who invariably prefaced their brutal actions with the words 'Die Zivilisten haben geschossen [Civilians have been shooting]', as if this legitimized what they were doing.[22] Then the killing started. One crime that was committed as seven men and women and one fourteen-year-old child emerged from a cellar at De Spoele, another area on the Meigem to Vinkt road (east of Kruiswege), can only be described as horrific. As soon as they came out begging for mercy, German soldiers leaped on to the three men like freed caged lions, beating and kicking them until they fell to the ground. One of the surviving women stated that she saw one of the men hit with the soldiers' rifle butts; the hitting only stopped when he lay motionless, his head a bloody pulp.[23]

Meanwhile, the fourteen-year-old watched the dead man's brother, who had been wounded by a poorly aimed bullet, writhing on the ground in agony until he was put out of his misery with another shot fired at point-blank range.[24] The third man was also shot. Only the three women and the child survived.

The fate reserved for two members of the De Wulf family, who had also been picked up by one of the death squads, was, if anything, even more terrible. After he had seen his uncle gunned down in the fields beside the Meigem–Vinkt road, André De Wulf, aged twenty, was also shot as he tried to escape. However, a Belgian soldier, who was ordered to bury André, noticed that the young man was still blinking. This made no difference as far as the guard was concerned, who ordered the Belgian soldier to proceed with the burial regardless. It was only when André's body had already been covered with earth that the guard finally deigned to fire a bullet into the grave.[25]

Those who were arrested and accused of shooting at Germans were not necessarily killed immediately. Eleven men who were found hiding in and around Vinkt were initially taken to the headquarters of Lieutenant-Colonel Lorenz, commander of 225 Division's 376th Regiment, which had been operating to the north of Vinkt. This at first seemed a life-saver, since Lorenz did not believe that civilians were killing German soldiers. After the eleven men had been questioned, Lorenz ordered his interrogator to save the men's lives by sending them back to the rear so that they would be well clear of what might still be a combat zone. Unfortunately, the corporal escorting them was stopped by a battalion commander of the reserve regiment in the division who, notwithstanding the corporal's protests, insisted that all the men had to be killed. These innocent men were then taken into the garden of the Café Het Zwart Huizeke, another café alongside the Meigem–Vinkt road (near Meigem), where they were shot, and finished off with bayonets.[26]

Civilians who were discovered at around 6.30 p.m. on 27 May in the cellar of the Vinkt convent, which in peacetime served as a girls' school, an old people's home and a place of worship for nuns, received special attention.[27] During the fighting, the convent had been a prime site for the Belgian Chasseurs Ardennais, who had rained their fire down from the upper floors on any Germans attempting to approach Vinkt from the east. The Germans' perverted logic decreed that those who had benefited from cover provided by the Belgian gunners should be

29. *Above* British soldiers service their Matilda Mark 1 tanks in a farmyard near Arras before the 21 May counter-attack

30. *Middle* A German 88mm gun takes on two British tanks – believed to be those commanded by 7 RTR's Major John King and Sergeant Doyle

31. *Bottom left* Doyle's Matilda Mark 2 tank Good Luck after it was captured by the Germans

32. *Right* Lieutenant Dick Furness VC who died while heroically attacking a machine-gun post during the 23–4 May retreat from Arras

33. *Above* Just some of the soldiers who died when the 1st Panzer Division attacked and decimated the 7th Royal Sussex regiment near Amiens on 20 May

34. *Right* One of several British cruiser tanks ambushed and knocked out at Huppy during the abortive 27 May attempt by the BEF's 1st Armoured Division to reach the River Somme from the south

35. *Below* Boulogne's Hôtel Impérial, where Rear GHQ was based, after it was bombed during the night of 19–20 May

36. *Left* The Irish Guards unload their ship after arriving in Boulogne on 22 May

37. *Below* HMS *Venetia*, almost entirely hidden by the smoke emanating from a fire aft, backs out of Boulogne's harbour after being hit by German shells during the rescue of the Guards on 23 May

38. *Left* Germans from the 2nd Panzer Division pose to commemorate the 'sinking' of *Venetia*. In fact *Venetia* escaped back to England

39. *Above* The German staff car standing abandoned on the right side of Calais's Pont Faidherbe was left behind when the Germans tried and failed to break through the British roadblock at 6 p.m. on 25 May. This photograph was taken after the British garrison had capitulated

40. *Right* Brigadier Claude Nicholson, the commander at Calais, who refused to surrender on 25 May, saying, 'Tell the Germans if they want Calais they will have to fight for it'

41. *Bottom* A British corpse lying beside a truck that was part of a roadblock. There were many scenes like this around Calais on 27 May, the day after the British garrison finally surrendered

42. and 43. *Above* The blockhouse north of Cassel where
Lieutenant Roy Creswell (*below left*) and his platoon held out
for more than two days although they were surrounded

44. *Below middle* Brigadier Nigel Somerset, commander of the
Cassel garrison, who complained bitterly that he and his men
were being sacrificed while those evacuated were taking the
credit for the BEF's escape

45. *Below right* Lieutenant Julian Fane, one of the few
Glosters who made it back from Cassel, shortly after he
arrived in England.

MASSACRE AT LE PARADIS

46. *Right* A modern photograph showing Le Paradis, Duriez Farm where the Royal Norfolks made their last stand, and the barn in front of which some ninety-seven British prisoners were massacred on 27 May

Church

Approximate route taken by R. Norfolk PoWs

Duriez's farmhouse

Rue du Paradis

Louis Creton's barn

Massacre site

Approximate route taken by 2 survivors after massacre

47. *Left* The barn with the massacred soldiers in front of it

48. *Bottom left* Captain Nick Hallett, a Royal Norfolk, who was the last man left fighting in his sector near Le Cornet Malo before he too was captured

49. *Bottom middle* Major Lisle Ryder, the acting commanding officer of the Norfolks, who was executed along with many of his men

50 *Bottom right* Captain Fritz Knöchlein, seen here as a British prisoner, who was hanged after a court concluded he had ordered his men to carry out the massacre

51. and 52. *Left* Sepp Dietrich's shot-up Mercedes after it was ambushed by British gunners supporting the Royal Warwicks' B Company under Captain Edward Jerram (*below*)

53. *Middle left* Dead British soldiers believed to have been massacred after being captured near Wormhout

54. and 55. *Above* The barn where some 80–90 British prisoners were killed on 28 May, including Sergeant-Major Augustus Jennings (*above right*), who died after diving on to a grenade thrown by a German

56. *Bottom right* Captain James Lynn-Allen, who was shot after helping another British soldier escape from the barn where the massacre was taking place

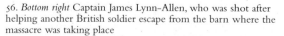

57. to 59. *Top left* Elza Vermeulen and her family lie in a field near Vinkt as they wait to hear their fate: the women were spared, but Elza's father and brother were taken to a nearby farm where they were shot along with other civilians. The execution was organized by Oberleutnant Franz Lohmann (*middle left*). After the executions, the dead men were buried by other prisoners urged on by their German captors (*middle right*)

60. Some of the massacred Belgian civilians lying beside the Vinkt presbytery wall after they were shot on 27 May

punished for the injuries the Belgian soldiers had inflicted. That appears to have been how they justified herding into the street all of the civilians who had been in the convent's cellar. They were not deterred by the fact that those they were assembling were a particularly harmless bunch, including some very elderly men and women, four monks and students, the Vicar of Vinkt's assistant, as well as the nuns. These prisoners were joined by the last of the civilians found hiding in Vinkt residences or the surrounding fields.

As they waited outside the convent, some heartbreaking scenes were played out, especially when recalled with the benefit of hindsight. The majority of those selected by the Germans were doomed, and were never to see their families again. That being the case, perhaps the most distressing parting involved a thirteen-year-old boy, Achiel Steyaert. When he was taken away from his mother, she protested vehemently, saying that he was her son, and had done nothing wrong. The German who had seized the boy retorted, 'That makes no difference. The pig!'[28]

Maurice Mertens, aged thirty-nine, and his family were also caught up in the unfolding tragedy. During the battle they had been sheltering in a Vinkt cellar, and had remained there until German soldiers entered the house and ordered everyone back to their own homes. If the Mertens family had hoped the coast was clear, however, they were to be quickly disillusioned. As they drove into Vinkt, they were flagged down and roughly forced out of their car. After their belongings had been thrown on to the ground, they were told to leave them and their car where they were, and to join the other men and women outside the convent.[29]

Only then was the crowd outside the convent ordered to start walking towards Meigem, the men and the thirteen-year-old boy leading the way, and the women following behind. A mile into their journey, the guard escorting them was approached by a man in a car, and he ordered the column to return immediately to Vinkt.[30] The women were instructed to peel off before entering the village, and were left in a meadow beside the road. For the men there was to be no such respite. They were marched on down Vinkt's main street. The older men were eventually halted outside the convent they had so recently vacated. A second group stopped on the south side of the road beside the vicarage garden wall, and a third, including Mertens, carried on towards the wall adjacent to the butcher's shop on the north side of the road. (See Map 17 on p. 534.) By this time, Mertens knew what was in store for them since, as they approached the village, he had overheard a terrifying conversation between their guard and a German officer. According to Mertens, 'Our guard approached him [the officer] . . . and asked: "What shall I do with these people?" He [the officer] replied, "They are all to be shot." '³¹

As Mertens approached the butcher's shop, he noticed they were being watched by some Germans armed with machine-guns. His statement records what happened next:

When I saw those soldiers, I said to my brother-in-law: 'They are going to shoot us.' He replied: 'No, they are only there to scare us.' [However] when we came up level with the Germans, we were ordered to stop [and] . . . they threatened us with [their] machine-guns, shouting: 'Everyone must stand against the wall' . . . We all obeyed, [although] I moved most reluctantly. I was watching the commander. The German escorting us approached him, and spoke to him. [Then] the commander raised one hand in the air, and shouted: 'Fire!' I immediately flung myself against the wall . . . The shooting lasted for one minute. Two bodies fell on to my back. They saved my life . . . After the firing stopped, a German in front of us fired another two bullets into the pile of bodies on top of me, thinking they were still alive.

But none of the bullets hit Mertens who, miraculously, had escaped without so much as a scratch. Although he lay spreadeagled on the ground, and must have appeared as dead as the others, he had in fact survived.

Mertens did not dare to move a muscle until all the Germans had left the centre of the village. Then he called out to see whether his brother-in-law and his friend were also alive. His brother-in-law did not answer, but his friend, who was pressed up against his leg, moved, showing that he was still in the land of the living. According to his statement, Mertens then said, 'Let's escape.'

He [Mertens' friend] replied: 'I can't. I've been shot in the leg and arms.'
    I said: 'I can carry you.'
    But he replied: 'No, they'll kill us.'
    I said: 'I'd rather be shot escaping than stay here.'

And after pulling himself out from under the bodies lying on top of him, Mertens rose like Lazarus from the dead, and crept away. He had barely gone two hundred yards, however, when he was spotted by a German soldier, who fired at him. He eventually made it into a house, only to be captured again the next day.

It was then that he had his second brush with death: he was taken to see the very officer who, the previous day, had pronounced his and the other civilians' death sentence. Apparently Mertens only avoided a similar fate by swearing that he came from Thielt, six miles west of Vinkt, and that the blood on his clothing was from wounded people whom he had cared for there. Because he was believed, his story had a happy ending, a rare commodity in Vinkt on 27–8 May 1940: he ended up being reunited with his wife, and they were both released during the afternoon of 28 May.[32]

In spite of the lengths to which the Germans had gone to kill all those assembled beside the butcher's wall, Mertens was not the only survivor. Two other men lived.[33] One was Hector Schollaert, a nineteen-year-old student refugee from the school run by Catholic brothers at Ostakker, near Ghent. He had not taken evasive action as quickly as Mertens, and had been hit by bullets in his back, hip and knee. He had then lost consciousness, and while alternating between complete oblivion and a feverish sleep, he had a heavenly dream. He dreamed he was walking under the pergola in his school's garden on a peaceful sunny day, and he was reading a book. Whether this symbolized his belief that he was about to die of his wounds and be judged at the entrance to Paradise, or whether it was just a piece of dreamed escapism, he had a terrible shock when he awoke to the harsh reality.

Like Mertens, Schollaert had been protected from some of the German bullets because he was lying under a pile of bodies. Two of his schoolfriends had been killed by the shooting. The only consolation was that Cyriel Gardinus Pieyns, another schoolfriend, had also survived. However, neither could think of escaping because their injuries were so severe, so both men carried on lying in the street, among the piled-up corpses, feigning death each time a German passed.

The Germans who did pass must have seen a hellish sight. Those walking from west to east would first have come across the group of nineteen bodies including Schollaert, Pieyns and, until he escaped, Mertens. A few yards further down the street, but on the other side of the street, near the vicarage wall, were the corpses of the fourteen civilians who appear to have been shot at about the same time as those by the butcher's shop.[34] Finally, outside the convent, at the eastern end of Vinkt's main street, lay the corpses of the seven elderly men – aged between sixty-one and eighty-nine – who had also been executed outside the building that had once been their refuge. None of the men from this group survived to describe their fate.[35]

The sight of what looked like forty massacred corpses clearly fascinated the German soldiers, and many stopped to take photographs that would later be passed around campaign veterans and treated as gruesome souvenirs. However, it was almost inevitable that, sooner or later, someone would notice that not all the bodies were dead. And that was what happened at 8 a.m. on 28 May. One German peered at the bodies by the butcher's wall for so long that Cyriel Pieyns, who had been holding his breath in an attempt to appear dead, breathed out. This was immediately seen by the German, who shouted to a comrade: 'This one's still alive!'

Pieyns quickly sat up, and began explaining that they had not done anything wrong, but had had the misfortune to be caught in cross-fire, only to be interrupted by the second German who stated that he was going to shoot him. Pieyns was only saved when the first man calmed down the would-be assassin and convinced him that he had done enough shooting. Seconds later, Schollaert scrambled to his feet, provoking a similar exchange. Eventually the two teenagers' lives were spared, taking the number of men who had survived the massacre at the centre of the village to four.[36]

One possible reason for the unexpectedly merciful treatment accorded to Pieyns and Schollaert was the fact that, unbeknown to them, the Belgian surrender had come into effect at 4 a.m. that morning.[37] That did not stop Major Kühner sanctioning another round of atrocities, which the prosecutor at the Vinkt war crimes trial characterized as 'sadism personified'.[38] By the morning of 28 May, all the surviving civilians still in Vinkt were gathered together in a field owned by a René D'Oosterlinck, and made to watch the atrocity unfold.

The spectacle was set up with chilling efficiency. First the women were separated from the men, and the inhabitants of Vinkt were separated from refugees. Then a table was set up, around which German officers were seated. Civilians brought before this panel were first taken to be photographed in a truck that had been converted into a photographic studio, with its own darkroom. This meant that when a civilian was brought before the tribunal at the table, the officers could be presented with a photograph of the accused, thereby giving a veneer of official formality to the proceedings.

The first man brought before this kangaroo court in the early morning of 28 May was Louis Van der Vennet, a wealthy bachelor in his mid forties who was a Vinkt councillor.[39] As an educated man he, unlike most of the Flemish inhabitants of Vinkt, read French newspapers and had French friends. This turned out to be his undoing, since when he was captured while trying to elude a German patrol, a letter in French was found in his pocket. The letter written in the language of France, Belgium's ally and Germany's enemy, gave the Germans the pretext to accuse him of espionage. To ensure that everyone knew his crime, the letter in question was stuffed under his collar. Then he was frogmarched through the crowd in the field to a property just across the road where he was ordered to dig his own grave.

As he passed through the crowd, he called out to his Vinkt friends, begging them to intercede on his behalf. One witness, who was a young girl at the time, remembers him shouting to her father, 'Please help me. Tell them I've done nothing wrong.'[40] But no one dared to speak up for him, for fear that they would be implicated in whatever he was said to have done. All they could do was watch, horrified, as he was shot down by a firing squad, and as he tumbled into the grave he had dug with his own hands. (The place where he was shot, and René D'Oosterlinck's field, are specified in Map 17 on p. 534.) Any hope that he might survive the shooting disappeared when a German stepped forward and fired a final shot into his body.

Five other civilians were dispatched in the same way that day. While this was going on, sadistic German guards patrolled among the crowd, forcing those at the front to kneel so that those at the back could see. In the course of these patrols, they warned that anyone seen averting their eyes would be executed as well. Similar threats were used to quieten those sections of the crowd who screamed and wailed at each shooting. After five such executions, which included the murder of a man who had done nothing more than confiscate from his child and put into his pocket a used cartridge, the 'entertainment' ended at around 2.30 p.m., and the survivors were finally allowed to go home.

★ ★ ★

Compared with the torment experienced at Vinkt, and the horrors and
hardships endured by many other Belgian soldiers and civilians in the
course of the 1940 campaign, King Leopold's suffering because of
his critics' verbal attacks was relatively minor. But by normal standards,
the psychological assaults he had to put up with were very fierce. On
28 May, when the Belgian surrender came into effect, the French Prime
Minister, Reynaud, accused the King of surrendering while the battle
was still raging, and claimed he had done so without warning his allies.
Churchill would have sanctioned an equally damning press release, had
it not been corrected at the last minute by the same Lieutenant-Colonel
Davy, who as head of the liaison mission at the King of Belgium's
headquarters, had been trying for at least twenty-four hours to warn
Gort that the Belgians were weakening. Fortunately Davy was back in
England by 28 May and attended that evening's Cabinet meeting where
the press release was discussed.[41]

As a result, the press release, and Churchill's first speech on the
subject in the House of Commons, reserved judgement on whether
King Leopold had done anything wrong. This reflected Churchill's
view, expressed in the course of the 27 May War Cabinet meeting, that
the King 'could not altogether be blamed now for the action he was
taking . . . Any grounds for recrimination lay rather in the Belgian action
on the outbreak of war . . . If Belgium had then invited us to enter
their country, we could have established ourselves in a strong defensive
position.'[42] And he might have added, with even more justification, the
French could as well. Perhaps he also had an eye on the political capital
he might reap from the surrender and exploit in his dealings with the
French over Reynaud's Mussolini peace initiative.

The War Cabinet met for a third time to discuss the peace initiative
at 4 p.m. on 28 May. Once again the minutes recorded the debate
between those in favour of and those against saving Britain by negotiating
with Hitler.

Churchill: said that it was clear that the French purpose was to see Signor
Mussolini acting as intermediary between ourselves and Herr Hitler. He was
determined not to get into this position.
Halifax: said that the proposal which had been discussed with M. Reynaud
on Sunday had been as follows: that we should say that we were prepared
to fight to the death for our independence, but that, provided this could be

secured, there were certain concessions that we were prepared to make to Italy.
Churchill: thought that the French were trying to get us on to the slippery slope . . .

Chamberlain: said that there could be no question of our making concessions to Italy while the war continued. The concessions which it was contemplated we might have to make, e.g. in regard to Malta and Gibraltar, would have to be part of a general settlement with Germany . . .

Sir Archibald Sinclair: said that on the previous day the War Cabinet had taken the line that nothing must be done to cut across President Roosevelt's approach. We had now learned that the President's approach had been ill-received.

Chamberlain: said that it did not necessarily follow that, because Signor Mussolini had not responded to President Roosevelt's approach, he would turn down an approach made by the French. It had been reported that Signor Mussolini had deeply resented President Roosevelt's interference.

He [Chamberlain] agreed with the Prime Minister's diagnosis that M. Reynaud wanted to get Signor Mussolini engaged in conversations. He would then try and turn these conversations into a conference. If we rejected the terms offered, he would abuse us as he had abused the Belgians that morning.

Halifax: agreed that there was little prospect that anything would result from an approach on the lines suggested by the French. At the same time, the larger issue was involved. Assuming that Signor Mussolini wished to play the part of mediator, and that he could produce terms which would not affect our independence, he thought that we ought to be prepared to consider such terms . . .

We must not ignore the fact that we might get better terms before France went out of the war and our aircraft factories were bombed, than we might get in three months' time.

Churchill: . . . The essential point was that M. Reynaud wanted to get us to the Conference table with Herr Hitler. If we once got to the table, we should then find that the terms offered us touched our independence and integrity. When, at this point, we got up to leave the Conference table, we should find that all the forces of resolution which were now at our disposal, would have vanished . . .

Chamberlain: said that, while he agreed with this general diagnosis, it was important to understand the French position . . . He thought that the essential elements in the reply to M. Reynaud should be on the following lines: that we regarded the suggested offer contained in his letter as a not very substantial one, which opened up no real prospect of influencing Signor Mussolini's attitude.

In our view, mediation at this stage, in the presence of a great disaster . . . could only have the most unfortunate results . . . We concluded, therefore, that, without prejudice to the future, the present was not the time at which advances should be made to Signor Mussolini . . .

Churchill: said that he came back to the point that the French wanted to get out of the war, but did not want to break their Treaty obligations to us . . . It was impossible to imagine that Herr Hitler would be so foolish as to let us continue our re-armament. In effect, his terms would put us completely at his mercy . . . A time might come when we felt that we had to put an end to the struggle, but the terms would not then be more mortal than those offered to us now.

Halifax: said that he still did not see what there was in the French suggestion of trying out the possibilities of mediation which the Prime Minister felt was so wrong.

Chamberlain: [said] . . . It was clear to the world that we were in a tight corner, and he did not see what we should lose if we said openly that, while we would fight to the end to preserve our independence, we were ready to consider decent terms if such were offered to us . . .[43] It was right to remember that the alternative to fighting on nevertheless involved a considerable gamble.

Greenwood: said that any course . . . was attended by great danger . . . But he did not feel that this was a time for ultimate capitulation.

Halifax: said that nothing in his suggestion could even remotely be described as ultimate capitulation.

Churchill: thought that the chances of decent terms being offered to us at the present time were a thousand to one against.

Chamberlain: said that . . . he felt bound to say that he was in agreement with the Foreign Secretary in taking the view that if we thought it was possible that we could now get terms which, although grievous, would not threaten our independence, we should be right to consider such terms.

. . . Looking at the matter realistically, he did not think it could be said that an approach to Signor Mussolini on the lines proposed by the French at the present time would be likely to produce an offer of decent terms, certainly not with Paris in Herr Hitler's grasp, but uncaptured. He therefore concluded that it was no good making an approach on the lines proposed by M. Reynaud at the present time. On the other hand, he thought that if we were not very careful as to the terms of our answer, France might give up the struggle at once. He did not want to give her any pretext for doing so.

[Chamberlain added that] while he thought that an approach to Italy was useless at the present time, it might be that we should take a different view in a short time, possibly even a week hence. The real question was, therefore, how to frame a reply to the French which, without rejecting their idea altogether, would persuade them that this was the wrong time to make it.

Attlee: said that it was necessary to pay regard to public opinion in this country. The War Cabinet, with full information, had watched the situation gradually unfold . . . But when the public realised the true position, they would sustain a severe shock. They would have to make a real effort to maintain their morale, and there was a grave danger that, if we did what France wanted, we should find it impossible to rally the morale of the people.[44]

At 6.15 p.m., the meeting was adjourned to allow Churchill to address his other ministers. What he said to them was recorded by Hugh Dalton, Minister of Economic Warfare, in the following terms:

[Churchill said] it was idle to think that, if we tried to make peace now, we should get better terms from Germany than if we went on and fought it out (and lost). The Germans would demand our fleet – that would be called 'disarmament' – our naval bases and much else. We should become a slave state, though a British Government which would be Hitler's puppet would be set up – 'under Mosley or some such person' . . . On the other side [that is if we fought on], we had immense reserves and advantages. Therefore . . . we shall go on and we shall fight it out, here or elsewhere, and if this long island story of ours is to end at last, let it end only when each one of us lies choking in his own blood upon the ground.[45]

The War Cabinet minutes describe the ministers' reaction to Churchill's address. After the Cabinet meeting was reconvened,

Churchill: said . . . they had not expressed alarm at the position in France, but had expressed the greatest satisfaction when he had told them there was no chance of our giving up the struggle. He did not remember having ever before heard a gathering of persons occupying high places in political life express themselves so emphatically.

The War Cabinet then approved the draft of the telegram that was to be sent that night to Reynaud, an extract from which is laid out below:

Since we last discussed this matter, the new fact which has occurred, namely the capitulation of the Belgian Army, has greatly changed our position for the worse, for it is evident that the chance of withdrawing the armies of Generals Blanchard and Gort from the Channel ports has become very problematical. The first effect of such a disaster must be to make it impossible at such a moment for Germany to put forward any terms likely to be acceptable . . .

We are convinced that at this moment, when Hitler is flushed with victory, and certainly counts on an early collapse of Allied resistance, it would be impossible for Signor Mussolini to put forward proposals for a conference with any success . . . Therefore, without excluding the possibility of an approach . . . at some time, we cannot feel that this would be the right moment.

You will ask, then, how is the situation to be improved. My reply is that by showing that after the loss of our two armies, and the support of our Belgian Ally, we still have stout hearts, and confidence in ourselves, we shall at once strengthen our hands in negotiations, and draw to ourselves the admiration, and perhaps the material help, of the USA . . .

We have reason to believe that the Germans too are working to a time-table, and that their losses and the hardships imposed on them, together with the fear of our air raids, is undermining their courage. It would indeed be a tragedy if by too hasty an acceptance of defeat, we throw away a chance that was almost within our grasp of securing an honourable issue from the struggle.[46]

Thus was Mussolini's peace initiative consigned to history, helped on its way by the Belgian capitulation, which provided the perfect excuse for the British Government to reject Reynaud's proposal. The peace initiative was never seriously contemplated again. But not all the consequences of the Belgian capitulation were to be so convenient for the British Government. Churchill's restraint concerning King Leopold upset Reynaud and, prompted by the French Prime Minister, General Edward Spears, Britain's liaison officer between Reynaud and Churchill, wrote on 29 May to complain:

The fact that a very mild attitude towards the King of the Belgians is being taken in London is causing considerable concern here [in France] . . . It is . . . said here . . . that Roger Keyes . . . has spoken to a great many people in London excusing the King. This is completely contrary to French policy, and a very great deal depends as far as morale here is concerned upon making him out to be the villain he certainly appears to be.[47]

The next day Spears developed the point in another letter:

Reynaud . . . really is very hurt and upset that a different line was taken by the Prime Minister to his own on the subject of the King of the Belgians. He says it might have been realized in London that there was good reason for the line he had taken. It is in fact such a heaven-sent excuse, and we ought not to commit the stupidity of not taking advantage of it.[48]

Reynaud's plea, which apparently suggested that King Leopold was to be made a scapegoat whether unfairly or not, did not fall on deaf ears. Churchill, like Reynaud, was prepared to do almost anything to keep the French fighting. On 4 June he stood up in the House of Commons and, putting to one side what he had been told by Lieutenant-Colonel Davy, issued the following rebuke: 'Suddenly, without prior consultation, with the least possible notice, without the advice of his Ministers, and upon his personal act, he [King Leopold] sent a plenipotentiary to the German Command, surrendered his army and exposed our whole flank and means of retreat.'[49]

24: Crisis in the North

Ypres–Comines line, 26–8 May 1940
(See Map 10 and 18. Also Map 1)

It is to Gort's and General Alan Brooke's credit that they managed to push British troops into position behind the crumbling Belgian Army before King Leopold surrendered. On 25 May, they had agreed that troops earmarked for the counter-attack should hold the so-called Ypres–Comines line, which was marked by the 'very nearly dry' canal running between the two towns (see Chapter 19).¹ Although this was an inadequate barrier, it was the best natural obstacle in the area. If British forces were able to secure the area west of the canal, it was clear that the line could be extended northwards along other canals to keep the Germans away from the all-important corridor to Dunkirk. (The way the troops on the Ypres–Comines line contributed to the securing of the corridor is shown in Map 10 on pp. 522–3.)

British forces under the command of 5 Division's General Franklyn started arriving at the canal line during the morning of 26 May.² They included 13 Brigade's 2nd Cameronians, a Scottish regiment commanded by the forty-five-year-old Lieutenant-Colonel George Gilmore, a larger-than-life gin-swilling Colonel Blimp character, full of the bluster that would not have looked out of place in a comic strip. If asked privately, at least some of his younger officers would have described him as a buffoon and would have expressed surprise that he had been decorated for bravery during the First World War. He certainly gave the impression that he was more interested in the culinary than the martial arts. It was presumably this that had given him the pot belly that led to his being nicknamed 'Pop'.³

But war has a habit of making heroes of the most unlikely types, and Gilmore, whose morale and commitment to making a success of the task in hand increased in direct proportion to the growth of obstacles placed in his path, was to be one of them. According to the following extract from his report, his ability to rise to the occasion first manifested itself during the morning of 26 May when his battalion's progress north of Warneton was blocked by a column of French ambulances:

I thought they had wounded in them, but when I looked, I found that if they were not empty, they had unwounded troops in them. As my task was operational and urgent – I had been ordered to be in position on the [Ypres-Comines] Canal by daylight, the sun was already up, and I was still a long way from the canal – I told them to stop. Not a bit of it. At last I deliberately stood in front of one ambulance with my back to it, and my orderly ready with his rifle to shoot the driver if he knocked me down. The driver came on as far as he dared, his vehicle actually touching my coat. But he came no further.[4]

Thanks to Gilmore, his battalion escaped from the traffic jam, and reached the canal line just in time.

Not being in the least perturbed by the warning from his brigadier that the Germans had broken through the Belgians to the east, and were likely to appear on the north-east banks of the canal at any minute, Gilmore proceeded to walk up the entire length of the line his battalion was to hold between Hollebeke and Houthem as soon as his troops arrived.[5]

When I reached the left of my position, the bridge there, over the canal, was being prepared by sappers for demolition. Nearby was a small prosperous farm, and an elderly couple . . . [came] to the gate of the garden to look at us. [As] they smiled and waved their hands . . . the bridge was blown, and simultaneously some German artillery opened fire.[6] That couple went straight away as they stood. They did not even turn back into the house. I went . . . [inside the house] later. There was a rocking chair by the kitchen fire, the mending on the table, and a half emptied bottle of red wine, some in a cup with a broken handle, and a slice of bread that had been put down in the act of eating, to see what was going on outside.[7]

It was not long before all the civilians in the area had cleared out, including the proprietors of the café where Gilmore and his men bought drinks to fortify themselves for the challenge ahead. Within hours, as Gilmore observed,

except for my troops, the countryside was deserted. The habitations were there, fires alight, as the smoke coming from the chimneys showed, but all human activity had ceased, like magic, during the actual performance of everyday tasks. It was as though all the inhabitants had been suddenly whisked off the earth. The sounds that will live long in my ears will be the lowing of unmilked cattle . . . and the barking of hungry tied up dogs. These people had lost everything that they held dear on this earth; the places where they had lived and brought up their families, and where they hoped to spend their last remaining days. The day before, this was so. Anything else was impossible, but the impossible had happened.[8]

There was some shooting on 26 May, but the main German attack, using troops from no less than three divisions, started, as was also the case on the south side of the corridor to Dunkirk, early the next morning. (Details of German units are in note 9.)[9] By then, the entire line between Ypres and Comines was guarded by soldiers from the three available British brigades; 5 Division's 13 Brigade, including the Cameronians, held the middle sector. (The troops' positions on the Ypres–Comines line are shown in Map 18 on p. 535.)[10]

'Just before dawn, there came a tremendous noise,' Gilmore reported. 'The Boche opened up with all . . . he had; this went on for about three hours.'[11] A series of fierce skirmishes ensued along the whole of the Ypres–Comines line, and many of the units holding the canal were pushed back to positions further west. After some of Gilmore's front-line sections were forced to retreat, his companies were instructed to form a new line on a ridge just over a mile back from the canal, which Gilmore was ordered to hold 'at all costs'.[12] Gilmore, who disappeared to talk to the commanding officer of the 2nd Wiltshires, another 13 Brigade battalion, shortly after he had issued the order to hold the ridge, was not in a position to check that his men complied with it. When he returned, he found to his dismay that around two hundred of them were congregated not on the ridge but on the Warneton–Ypres road, about half a mile to the west of it.[13]

His report describes how, at about 6.30 p.m., he marshalled his forces to correct the error:[14]

Standing in [a] carrier, I moved up and down the road, and got everyone into position . . . in a ditch. Then, dismounting, armed with a rifle and fixed sword [bayonet], I ordered [the men] to do the same. As far as I could gather, we mustered ten officers . . . about 180 men, and five carriers. Positioning the officers in front, with two carriers on either flank, and my own patrolling up and down in front of us as we advanced, I pointed to the high ground that we had left . . . and said: 'That is our objective. Advance!' And away we went: a line about 400 yards long, [with] no reserves . . . just a long line of determined men with rifles topped with steel.

Gilmore explained later why he had insisted his men should form up and advance in a long line:

This was done deliberately to give a show of strength . . . The strength of an attack on scattered forward troops . . . is often over estimated. By the time the reports reach senior command, the words 'large numbers of troops advancing' . . . can be given a meaning quite out of proportion to the number involved. This was the impression I meant to give, and I believe it succeeded in its object.[15]

But, as Gilmore conceded, infantry alone

would not have been enough . . . [They] all would have died in the attempt, had it not been for our carriers. They guarded our flanks, and when the enemy tried to get us with enfilade fire, they chased him away, or ran him down. My own carrier had no weapons, and the driver was cruising up and down in front of us, when presently two Boche light machine guns some distance in front opened fire, causing . . . a few casualties. When the Germans with one LMG [light machine gun] saw the carrier, they ran; there were only two of them. One went this way, and the other went that [way]. [Then] the carrier turned, and . . . a second machine gun team also went like the first. How we cheered and yelled!

One of the most courageous thrusts was made on the orders of 2nd Lieutenant Christopher Weir, who – spurred on, perhaps, because his driver was a pugnacious boxer, known in the regiment as 'Knocker' Knox – charged a machine-gun post even though its bullets had already destroyed their Bren gun. When the German gunners saw the carrier accelerating towards them, they abandoned their position and fled, only to be run over as the carrier chased after them and cut them down one by one. Weir won the Military Cross for this action, and Knox the Military Medal.[16]

German machine-gunners were not the only obstacle obstructing the advancing Cameronians. The artillery barrage laid on to assist the counter-attack failed to allow for the progress made by the British troops. 'When we reached the hill,' Gilmore complained, 'we found we could still advance, but the concentrations were still on . . . There was nothing for it, but to go through our own fire . . . It caused us casualties, but not as many [as there would have been] had we held back our advance.'

Notwithstanding the determined attempts by the carrier crews to snuff out the threats posed by the German machine-gunners before they could harm the advancing infantry, the Cameronians were eventually stopped in their tracks by cross-fire as soon as they reached the portion of the ridge nearest to the Warneton–Ypres road. This was sufficient to protect the road, but not quite far enough forward to achieve Gilmore's objective: to seize a position that would enable his men to dominate the land, including the canal, to the east. However, his plan to carry on had to be drastically revised after he discovered that seven of the ten officers who had started out with him had either been wounded, killed or gone missing.[17] That did not prevent Gilmore trying to press on with a small party of men after ordering Captain Pat Hendriks, the only officer still in contact with him, to hold the position they had reached.

It was a controversial decision. It was not long before all the men who accompanied him were either killed or wounded, or so pinned down by gunfire that they could not move. Even then Gilmore was not prepared to withdraw. His account describes how, after deciding initially to remain until dark in the position he now occupied with Rifleman Stephenson, his orderly, for company, he, as he put it, became 'restless' and began to fire at a German armed with an anti-tank rifle whom he had spotted around three hundred yards away. 'It was during this duel that I received my first wound,' wrote Gilmore.

I was kneeling . . . [and] firing when a shell burst practically on top of me . . . A large splinter entered the inside of my left thigh . . . I was a bit dazed. I knew I had been hit in the leg. There is no mistaking that numbing, burning feeling when you have been wounded before, and while I was trying to see the extent of the damage, I was hit again in the tummy . . . Down I went like a shot rabbit. I lay still for a moment, and then put my hand down, but . . . could not feel it touching my body. I pulled it up to look at it . . . It was covered with blood. I thought that the end had come at last, but strangely enough I did not worry overmuch. I felt detached and rather glad to think that all this worry and anxiety would trouble me no longer. It was only later, when I felt that I could get away, that I really became afraid and worried.

I remember Stephenson saying: 'Are you badly hit sir . . . ?' I told him not to worry, as I was finished. He fussed around with his field dressing . . . We could only dress one wound, and I decided that the leg was the more dangerous, because of the femoral artery . . . I think that soon after, I must have fainted . . . When I came to, I heard voices. But Stephenson was lying next to me with his finger on my lip. He shook a warning with his head, and I listened. They were Germans, in the same patch of crops on the edge of which we lay . . . Presently the talking ceased. I then tried to move, but I could only do so by lying on my side, the right side, and pushing myself along with my right leg, a matter of two or three inches at a time . . . The pain was intense. It was then that I really gave up hope . . . I was sad, and I thought of my wife and all that home meant.

However, as dusk fell Gilmore, encouraged and assisted by Stephenson, somehow summoned the strength to start staggering back to the ridge they had taken earlier. It was still held by 'Jemima [Puddle Duck]' Hendriks, whose ungainly gait had earned him his nickname. Whether or not this had irritated Gilmore on the parade ground, he must have been glad to see that Hendriks was still in command of the situation on the ridge, which was where, as Hendriks' own account of the episode reveals, the two men met up:

I had some 20 rifles and one Bren in a furrow on top of the hill. Jerry then opened up the very devil of an artillery and mortar concentration. When it had abated a bit, I was trying to discover if anyone was left on my left, when old Pop [Gilmore] appeared, supported by three chaps, and hit in a couple of places. He was very heroic, and said: 'Well, I leave you in sole charge. This position is vital to the BEF, and must be held at all costs.' I said I'd do my best – with 20 men![18]

Hendriks did as he promised, only to discover during the night that the Cameronians had been ordered to withdraw to the line near where the counter-attack had started. This must have prompted him and the soldiers accompanying him to wonder whether many of the 128 Cameronians who were put out of action had suffered needlessly.[19] The counter-attack had only secured the Warneton–Ypres road for a few hours, and no explicit reference to it in German records confirms that it led to more cautious advances the next day. However, combined with three other counter-attacks in the southern sector of the Ypres–Comines line, it is likely to have had that effect, and if it did, it resulted in an excellent dividend, since 13 Brigade was able to hold its front throughout the next day, and carried on dominating troops from the German 31 Division until it was ordered to withdraw at 10 p.m. during the night of 28–9 May.[20]

Gilmore's counter-attack had been mounted on the spur of the moment without recourse to higher authorities. The counter-attacks at the southern end of the Ypres–Comines line were much grander affairs. They were set up by General Franklyn after he had decided that the southern end of the line was more important than the north.[21] The best known attack was carried out shortly after Gilmore's, by the 3rd Battalion, the Grenadier Guards, which with two other battalions tried to recover the ground lost by 143 Brigade on 13 Brigade's right during the morning and early afternoon of 27 May.[22]

Unlike the soldiers in the 5 Division battalions, who, as reserves, could not have been surprised when asked to block a gap in the line of troops protecting the corridor leading to Dunkirk, 1 Division's troops, including the 3rd Grenadier Guards, were part of the main body of the BEF for which the corridor was being kept open. As such, they had been marched back from Roubaix on the Gort Line to Le Touquet (north of Armentières) on the Lys during the night of 26–7 May in accordance with the arrangements made between Gort and Blanchard. (See Chapter 19.)[23] During the middle of the afternoon of 27 May, the Grenadier Guards' commanding officer, Major Allan Adair, had just received the order to retreat to Dunkirk with a view to being evacuated when a counter-order, sending the battalion to assist 5 Division's General Franklyn, was presented to him by Major-General Harold Alexander's ADC. The order required Adair to move the battalion to Bois de Ploegsteert so that they would be well placed to do Franklyn's bidding.[24] The ADC has described how he received a mixed reception from the Grenadier Guards' two most senior officers:

Colonel Adair [in fact he was still a major] was his usual cheerful optimistic self, lying in a ditch with his feet up. He told me he was delighted to see the son of his 1917 Commanding Officer doing his bit, and of course the Battalion would set off at once to plug the gap [west of the Ypres–Comines line]. The Battalion Second in Command, Osbert Smith, took a different line, and said it was a pity I had not fallen off my bike miles away.[25]

Having had salvation dangled temptingly in front of their eyes before it was snatched away, the battalion proceeded to march to Ploegsteert Wood. Meanwhile Adair and the commanding officer of the 2nd Battalion, the North Staffordshire Regiment, another 1 Division unit that was to help in stopping up the gap, visited Franklyn at his headquarters, a villa in Ploegsteert. Afterwards Franklyn wrote:

I sat them down on each side of me on the steps of Ploegsteert Château and I remember feeling that I just had to impress these two with the importance and feasibility of the task which I was going to ask them to perform. The text books of the time laid it down that a counter-attack on a strength greater than one company must never be launched without most careful reconnaissance, yet I was proposing a counter-attack by two battalions over ground which they had never seen . . . I found [Lieutenant-Colonel] Butterworth [the North Staffordshire's commanding officer] somewhat dour, but I felt he was a determined person who could be relied upon. Adair was entirely different: [he was] gay and light-hearted. His laughter was akin to a giggle, and I wondered if he would succeed in tackling such a difficult problem.[26]

Adair, Butterworth and their men had not had an opportunity to sleep off the twenty-mile march they had made from the Gort Line to the Lys during the night of 26–7 May, but Franklyn believed he had no alternative but to send both of them back to their battalions with orders to move that evening. They were to counter-attack towards the east until they reached the Ypres–Comines Canal. The Grenadier Guards, with the 2nd North Staffordshires, who were to attack on their left, were to move forward at 8 p.m.

Describing all the manoeuvres and difficulties encountered by these two battalions during their night-time assault is impossible. However, an account left behind by Captain Roderick Brinckman, in command of the Grenadiers' right hand 2 Company during the counter-attack, does give some idea of the obstacles encountered and the resourcefulness needed to overcome them. The first words in Brinckman's account of the attack have an ominous, and familiar, ring about them: 'We were late getting to the starting line, and it was in fact getting dark when we did.'[27]

That did not appear to affect the morale of the troops, or the observers who watched them set out. One witness described their departure in the following terms: 'The whole battalion moved past my headquarters. The setting sun was shining on their bayonets. Their Bren-gun carriers were on either flank. In all my life I have never seen a finer and more awe-inspiring sight. They walked through the guns, and the men on them cheered . . . as they passed.'[28]

However, according to Brinckman, their advance

was considerably slowed down by innumerable fences which we had to climb over . . . added to which a fairly large copse and a stream about 5 ft. wide and 4 ft. deep, not marked on the map, were encountered . . . Having got through the wood, some stragglers of the Black Watch [who had just made their own counter-attack] came through our lines.[29] They appeared to be demoralized, and painted a depressing picture of conditions on their front . . . Shortly after we had crossed the stream, we advanced up a slope which led towards our objective: the canal. We were met with very heavy fire, and at this stage, I was hit by a piece of mortar bomb in my right eye. The men got down, but unfortunately . . . both my platoon commanders were killed, as indeed were . . . some of my section commanders. I went forward to the leading section of my right platoon . . . and in doing so, was hit in the right shoulder and left elbow by tommy gun fire . . . At that moment, to my right rear, I saw advancing more Grenadiers, and in the darkness I was able to see that it was Dick's [Lieutenant Dick Crompton-Roberts's 1] company [which, according to Brinckman, started out on his company's left, but had ended up on its right]. They were greeted with the same fire as we had been, and also got down . . . A great number of the men . . . in both Companies . . . [became] casualties immediately.

I ran across to Dick, and said: 'There is only one thing to do. We must charge these few Germans here at [the] point of [the] bayonet. When I get back to my company, I will blow a whistle, and we will get up and go for them.' This we did, and getting amongst the Germans, we disposed of them all on our side of the Canal. I received another wound in the left thigh . . . but nothing to count.

I seemed to have practically no men left now. In fact I had Sergeant Ryder ([who was] already wounded in the hip), and one guardsman. There was a cottage on the Canal which seemed to be a centre of activity . . . [for] some German soldiers. I had five hand grenades in my haversack, and four of these I threw into the windows of the cottage. Those Germans who were not killed or wounded fled back across a small bridge on to the other side of the Canal.

I said to Sergeant Ryder: 'We are on our objective, but we must get hold of some more men.' I sent the guardsman back to Major Adair along the railway line as I had previously arranged.[30] Sergeant Ryder and myself then proceeded to crawl back towards where I had left my reserve platoon. On the way back, I was hit again through the back of the right knee, and became unable to walk or crawl. I think Sergeant Ryder was also hit again . . . I lay there for some time, hoping that either my rear platoon commanders would come forward, or that if my runner succeeded in getting back to the battalion headquarters, we might perhaps receive more support. I found myself bleeding very heavily, and decided that my mortar wound was the worse. I put on my first field dressing, took off my tie and made a tourniquet above it. Probably due to fatigue and lack of sleep and also loss of blood, I think I must have fainted, because the next thing I remember was finding myself in daylight on a bed in the very cottage into which I had thrown the grenades the night before, with a German soldier, very much alive, standing over me, and two or three dead Germans lying on the floor around the bed. Through the door was another small bedroom, and on the bed there, I saw Sergeant Ryder . . . evidently in great pain.

Adair and the rest of the battalion had been following his front-line companies notwithstanding German gunfire directed over their heads. In his account, he has described what he saw as the leading companies reached the slope leading down to the canal.

We could see a farm blazing in front of Comines directly in 2 Company's line of advance, and shortly afterwards the leading sections . . . were silhouetted in the flames, as they went forward towards the canal bank. Meanwhile 1 Company pushed on down the hill, and as it advanced, came under terrific machine gun fire. The whole front was lit up by the enemy's tracer ammunition.[31]

After the initial thrust, the Grenadiers' 1 Company sent out a patrol to try to make contact with the remnants of Brinckman's 2 Company, in a courageous attempt to bring back the wounded. 'We never heard of any of this patrol again,' Adair wrote euphemistically.[32] In fact, the officer who was sent out had been severely wounded and captured.[33] Then, as members of the German 61 Division moved into the vacuum left behind the Grenadiers' vanguard, Adair gave orders that his men should form up about a quarter of a mile back from the canal in a field ditch that was deepened and transformed into a trench by the men digging with their bayonets.[34]

It was on this line that the remainder of the battalion stood its ground throughout 28 May with those of the North Staffordshires who had survived their own counter-attack on their left, and with the 1st/7th Battalion, the Royal Warwickshire Regiment, on the North Staffordshires' left. Like 13 Brigade, the Grenadier Guards were still in place at the end of the day and, also like 13 Brigade, were able to make an orderly withdrawal towards Dunkirk during the night of 28–9 May, albeit with far fewer men than had been in the battalion on their arrival. Just nine officers and 270 other ranks remained when the battalion left the battlefield. Other battalions who had stood their ground on the Ypres–Comines line were even worse off. For example, 143 Brigade's 8th Royal Warwicks could only count on eight officers and 134 other ranks by the time they made it to Dunkirk.[35]

In spite of the courageous counter-attacks, and the stoic defence of the Grenadier Guards' 13 and 143 Brigades, and the arrival just in time of the men in 4 Division, who had marched up to block an even more threatening German thrust against 17 Brigade's troops east of St Eloi at the north of the Ypres–Comines line, the Germans might still have broken through to the north-west of this line if they had moved more quickly.[36]

Some of the pressure to the north of Ypres was absorbed, thanks to General Montgomery, whose 3 Division made its celebrated drive from the Gort Line on the night of 27–8 May, passing under the arc of the German shells firing at British artillery on Mont Kemmel, and ending up at dawn on 28 May along the western banks of the Yser Canal, to the north of the 50 Division units, which had taken over Ypres, and the area just to its north and south.[37] But that still left a void to the north of Noordschote on the left of 3 Division's line.[38] Securing this sector could not be entrusted to infantry divisions or even battalions since none was available during the daylight hours of 28 May. The blocking was done by isolated groups from the 12th Royal Lancers in their armoured cars. They were assisted by David Smith, a twenty-six-year-old lieutenant in the 101st Royal Monmouthshire Field Company, a unit within the Royal Engineers. Of all the many men who played a role in protecting the corridor to Dunkirk, Smith's contribution is one of the least known. It was also somewhat different from most of the others in that rather than holding off the Germans with a gun or grenade he did so by blowing up bridges. His achievement was all the more remarkable because he accomplished it with just a lance-corporal and a driver as back-up.

The odyssey that was to take him north of the British line of infantry started at 4 p.m. on 27 May when he was ordered to blow up the main bridge near Ypres' Menin Gate.[39] This was complicated because there were British troops nearby. However, after ordering all the troops at the gate to put their fingers into their ears and open their mouths to prevent their hearing being damaged by the blast, he duly blew up the bridge without hurting anyone. The only casualty was the 4th East Yorkshire Regiment's commanding officer's carrier, which was crushed by capping stones thrown into the air by the explosion. Fearing a court-martial for that dereliction of duty, Smith made a quick exit and spent the rest of the day destroying barges on the Yser Canal.

But it was his work on 28 May that saved the BEF. Blowing up the bridges between Ypres and Noordschote was accomplished quickly because the explosives were already in place – all he had to do was press down the plungers to trigger the explosions. Dealing with the bridges to the north of Noordschote was more of a challenge, and after placing explosives at several crossing-points, and after blowing them up, Smith began to suffer from a splitting headache, caused by wiping sweat off his face using hands smeared with the weeping gelignite. There were moments of extreme peril. One wooden bridge to the south of Dixmude was still smouldering when he arrived, following a botched attempt to incinerate it.[40] This would not have mattered, had it not been that, as Smith pointed out, the bridge had already been prepared for demolition. Nevertheless, while his assistant shielded the explosives from the flames with a sandbag, Smith coolly walked across the bridge, fixed the detonating charge and, as he subsequently reported matter-of-factly: 'The bridge was destroyed without any more trouble.'

The events he witnessed that day at Dixmude were more dramatic.[41] He was chatting to Royal Lancer 2nd Lieutenant Ned Mann, who was guarding the Dixmude bridge with two armoured cars, when among the throng of refugees pouring across Smith caught sight of a black Mercedes car full of German officers. 'Look, Ned. They're German!' Smith exclaimed. Mann was not able to catch up with the car, as it sped away. But he sent out the following message, which has been recorded in the Royal Lancers' war diary: 'Calling all cars. Black car containing German staff officers last seen moving west from Dixmude. Expected to move North. Stop it, or shoot!'[42] The occupants of this car and of two similar vehicles were subsequently spotted by another Royal Lancer officer talking to Belgian soldiers at Nieuport.[43] However, because the British officer in question was only in an unarmed truck, he was unable to comply with Mann's urgent message. The cars were subsequently driven back over to the German side of the Yser, leaving Smith to blow up the Dixmude bridge before they returned with reinforcements.

Mann and Smith were diverted from their task after a man claiming to be a French major arrived, stating that he and his men had been ordered to take over the defence of the bridge. However, when Mann discovered that there were no French soldiers in the vicinity, he returned to the bridge convinced that he had been talking to a fifth-columnist. By this time the 'French major' had disappeared. Meanwhile Smith had found the leads laid by the Belgians when preparing the bridge for demolition, and after he had connected them to explosives, he finally triggered the blast. Any refugees unlucky enough to be on the bridge when it exploded went up with it.[44]

Minutes later, a column of German motorcyclists, followed by a long line of lorries, arrived at the eastern side of the Yser.[45] They were the first of around 250 German vehicles seen entering Dixmude that day and, thanks to Smith and Mann's four armoured cars (two more had arrived after the appearance of the first Germans), the west bank of the Yser at Dixmude remained a German-free zone.[46] Other troops of armoured cars also held the Germans at bay at crossing-points further to the north.[47]

Thus, linked by the thinnest of threads, the web of British soldiers reached all the way from Noordschote to the coast. During the night of 28–9 May, this line was extended to the south-west as 50 and 3 Divisions' troops fell back from the area around and to the north of Ypres to hold the line running from Poperinghe to Steenstraat via Woesten and Lizerne.[48] As a result, the escape route leading back to Dunkirk remained open.

25: Up the Glosters

Arneke and Ledringhem, 28 May 1940
(See Maps 10 and 14. Also Maps 1 and 18)

The fact that Weygand had not sanctioned an evacuation from Dunkirk had already led to growing tension between British and French generals at the 27 May conference at Cassel. That day, anticipating that similar difficulties might arise in the future, General Dill, the newly appointed Chief of the Imperial General Staff, sent the following note to Anthony Eden, the Secretary of State for War:

I think there may still be some doubt in Gort's mind as to how much liberty of action he has been given by His Majesty's Government in the matter of re-embarkment. From General Blanchard he has received orders to occupy a certain sector of the waterline covering Dunkerque 'from which there will then be no further retirement' . . . This appears to give him no freedom to embark any of his troops unless so ordered by Blanchard. On the other hand he has been told that no other course is open to him but to fall back on the coast in accordance with [the message dated 26 May]. These terms quite clearly indicated evacuation.

We have told him further that we expect that General Blanchard will issue orders in this sense after receipt of a message from Monsieur Reynaud. If Blanchard or Weygand orders evacuation, there will of course be no ambiguity. If on the other hand Gort receives no such orders from them, is he to be free to evacuate in order to ensure the security of as large a portion as possible of his command, or is he to be bound rigidly by his present orders from Blanchard?

I submit that this doubt about Lord Gort's freedom of action should be pointed out to the War Cabinet, and I suggest that a message should be sent to him making it quite clear that His Majesty's Government would expect him to appeal to them to liberate him from his obligation to continue to comply with orders issued by his French commander the moment that he judges that those orders entail unnecessarily increasing the risks to which his command is exposed.[1]

In case Gort really was still confused, Eden sent him a crystal-clear message that afternoon: 'Your sole task now is to evacuate to England maximum of your force possible.'[2]

Dill's concern for Gort's position did not stretch to the allocation of more troops to the BEF to facilitate the evacuation. In response to Gort's request that the Canadian Division should be sent to help out at Dunkirk, he wrote: 'My considered advice to H.M.G. is that . . . no Canadian Brigade should be sent,' adding: 'Militarily there is only a remote chance that any considerable formation of the BEF will be able to extricate themselves in the encircled position . . . The addition of 2 Brigade groups . . . or relief by the Canadians . . . cannot . . . make a difference between success and failure . . . No organized formation is likely to be extracted . . . This is not a case of throwing our last reserves into the battle; it is throwing them into a net.'[3]

But the British generals were not alone in having to muddle along without obtaining the support they required from their superiors. Incredible as it may seem today, at least some of the French generals, even after the Cassel conference, had still not been told that the BEF was to be evacuated. General Blanchard only found out the British Government's and Gort's true intentions thanks to a fortuitous break. On 27 May, a copy of a British 2 Corps order, instructing its divisions to retreat to the perimeter around Dunkirk, had been given to a French unit supporting the BEF, and the French unit had, in its turn, passed the 'incriminating' document to one of Blanchard's liaison officers.[4] When the order was received at Army Group 1's headquarters, a panic ensued because it conflicted with what Blanchard wanted. He had intended to stop both French and British troops at the River Lys.[5]

An attempt was made to contact Gort, but he could not at first be found.[6] Only later was it discovered that he had been looking for Blanchard at Admiral Abrial's command post in Dunkirk, and had then been delayed by traffic jams as he was driven back to his own head-quarters at Houtkerque.[7] The two generals finally met at Houtkerque shortly after 10 a.m. on 28 May, where they settled down with Pownall to discuss the ramifications of the British retreat.[8]

During the meeting, Gort explained that he had been instructed to do whatever was necessary to save as many BEF soldiers as he could, and after showing Blanchard Eden's 27 May telegram confirming that he must evacuate the BEF, he begged Blanchard to order the French

Army to retreat towards the Dunkirk perimeter during the coming night to conform with what the BEF would be doing.[9] According to Pownall's account of the meeting, Blanchard was 'horrified' when he saw the British Government's instructions to Gort, and was only 'pacified some-what' after being told that the order to evacuate had no doubt been mentioned to the French Government, which had not yet got round to passing on the evacuation order to him.[10] Gort's and Pownall's observa-tion that the main strongpoints on the south-western front at Cassel, Hazebrouck and Wormhout could not be relied on for another day appeared to strike a chord with Blanchard's two staff officers if not with Blanchard, especially when it was stressed that penetration through the strongpoints would enable the Germans to force themselves across Army Group 1's line of withdrawal. As Pownall drily put it, the two staff officers 'saw the not too obscure logic of the case', but 'Blanchard continued to make difficulties.'[11]

Blanchard said he could not agree to retreat in line with the BEF without contacting General Prioux, the commander of the French 1st Army since Blanchard's elevation to the top job in Army Group 1. Prioux would know whether the 1st Army troops were in a fit state to move. But Blanchard stated that the manoeuvre might be problematical, given that a large number of French soldiers had not yet reached the River Lys, and those who had were exhausted. While Gort and Pownall waited, a messenger was sent to Prioux's headquarters at Steenwerck, only to return stating that he had not been able to get through on the road via Watou.[12] Thereupon Blanchard said that he himself would go to see Prioux using another route. However, before terminating the meeting, he asked whether Gort was going to retreat even if the French troops could not leave the Lys that night, given that this would leave the French flanks completely unprotected, and the French 1st Army in a very difficult situation. Gort replied that the answer was yes; the BEF would abandon the Lys, whether or not the French complied.[13]

Had Blanchard known the difficulties that the French IV and V Corps troops had encountered during 27 and 28 May while fighting to make their way back to the Lys, his conversation with the British generals might have had a different outcome. The troops in these corps, which, as mentioned in Chapter 19 (see Chapter 19, note 13), had been holding the south-eastern end of the corridor, had been cut off because of the failure to man a second line of strongpoints to the north of Violaines and Givenchy. When, during the afternoon of 27 May, the Cameron Highlanders at Violaines were overrun, as described in Chapter 22, there was no serious obstacle to delay the German advance. Consequently, while panzers were free to speed up to Lomme in the north to cut off the escape route running from Lille to Armentières, German units also captured the bridges over the Deûle further to the south, thereby blocking the other roads that the French IV and V Corps troops had counted on for their salvation.

The French III Corps only escaped from the encirclement because the withdrawal routes allocated to their troops were to the north of those allocated to IV and V Corps, and this meant that even those III Corps troops who encountered German forces were able to sidestep to safety round the north of the German line. Many of III Corps' troops, after being blocked by German guns at Lomme, managed to escape on the Lambersart–Verlinghem–Frelinghien and Lambersart–Pérenchies–Houplines roads to the north of Lomme. Unfortunately, the troops in IV and V Corps had no such room for manoeuvre. As a result, the soldiers from these corps, whom Blanchard had been hoping would make it back to the Lys when he met up with Gort and Pownall during the morning of 28 May, found themselves bottled up in and around Lille at the end of that day with no way out unless they broke through the German cordon. (A description of IV and V Corps' thwarted 27–8 May attempt to escape to the Lys is in note 14.)[14]

The fate of these courageous French troops, condemned by their generals' errors to fight on at Lille until their ammunition ran out, illustrates only too well what would have been in store for British troops had it not been for the series of last-ditch stands made by BEF units to protect the corridor. During 27 May, those at Hazebrouck, Hondeghem and Cassel, as well as at various points along the La Bassée Canal, had delayed the Germans just long enough to allow the next layer of British forces to form up. But it was the tenacious action fought at Ledringhem on 28 May that included the most uplifting events on that critical day.[15]

Ledringhem was one of a pair of villages first occupied by the 5th Battalion, the Gloucestershire Regiment, on 26 May. The second was Arneke.[16] These villages had been garrisoned to provide a shield for Wormhout, another of the main strongpoints mentioned by Gort and Pownall during their 28 May meeting with Blanchard.[17] The 5th

Glosters, like the garrison at Cassel, were part of 48 Division, which was responsible for holding a line of strongpoints on the south-western front. The Ledringhem, Arneke and Wormhout strongpoints were all held by battalions in 48 Division's 144 Brigade. This permitted 144 Brigade's Brigadier 'Hammy' Hamilton to apply an overall strategy when it came to planning the defence of the three locations. Two Glosters' companies were positioned in and around Arneke. Another was placed in Ledringhem, and the fourth between the two villages.[18]

The companies were arranged in such a way that if, as expected, the Germans reached Arneke, the most westerly strongpoint, the BEF troops could retire to Ledringhem, the next in line. Ledringhem could then soak up some of what the German units might be planning to use against Wormhout. Of the three locations, Wormhout was furthest away from the Gravelines–La Bassée canal line where the Germans were assembling.

As expected, Arneke was attacked first, during the evening of 27 May. According to Captain Leslie Hauting, the Glosters' adjutant, the Germans were greeted with a hostile reception from the three 25mm guns, and the two-pounders that had been moved up to support the British garrison: 'Both enemy tanks and infantry suffered heavy losses as they approached the railway line [which runs from north to south through the village],' wrote Hauting, 'one 2 pounder alone accounting for five tanks and four armoured cars, and then directing its fire directly at the infantry as they swarmed over the railway.'[19]

Nevertheless, the German armour nearly overcame the Glosters in a matter of hours. At one point armoured fighting vehicles drove into the village, and fired from point-blank range into the *estaminet* (bar) being used as the garrison's headquarters.[20] The British response was furious: anti-tank rifles, Bren guns and rifles were fired out of the windows until all those vehicles which were not knocked out withdrew. This gave the Glosters an opportunity to withdraw from the village during the night. By the next afternoon the Arneke contingent, together with the rest of the 5th Glosters, were holding the perimeter around Ledringhem.

During the night of 27–8 May, word was received that Ledringhem should be held for a further twenty-four hours. Some of these hours elapsed before the village was attacked because the Germans set about surrounding the village before moving in to capture it. However, during the afternoon of 28 May, the soldiers within the garrison realized that their enemy must have achieved its preliminary objective after a German vehicle approached the village on the Wormhout–Ledringhem road, and crashed into the roadblock that had been built to cover the battalion's rear. Sergeant Ivor Organ, who, on hearing some loud explosions, ran out to investigate, has recorded what he saw:

The front of the enemy vehicle was embedded in a makeshift barricade, and a few yards further on, a pretty big German was lying on the ground. He had taken a bullet through the head and his brains were spilling out. We all felt sick. We searched the vehicle. Then one of us suggested we bury the dead man in the front garden of one of the houses. We dragged him by his feet . . . but just when we were about to bury him, [we found] the hole was too small. We had to dig some more at the foot end.

When we had finished the burial, we went back to the roadblock where some anti-tank gunners had arrived. They explained that they had lost some men not far away, and in spite of the danger, I went to see for myself. Some of our chaps were lying among farm equipment which had been piled together, but was now all over the place. I noticed a pair of boots and a human shape under a greatcoat. As I got nearer, I was horrified to see that it was another of my mates, with his head come away from his body.[21]

Only then was Ledringhem bombarded, part of the softening-up process that often preceded an attack. As the light faded, the Glosters' officers began to wonder whether they should be retreating, after a dispatch rider, who had been sent to seek instructions from Brigade Headquarters, located on the Wormhout–Wylder road, failed to re-appear.[22] But then, according to Hauting, 'as the enemy . . . commenced his attack, it was decided to give such an account of ourselves that the enemy would never forget'.

Before any such action could be taken, two runners arrived with instructions from Brigadier Hamilton, who urged the Glosters to make their way 'when you can' to Bambecque, part of the next line to be held by the BEF.[23] Unfortunately it was impossible to leave immediately as the Germans would have followed up too closely. There was nothing for it but to carry on fighting until there was a lull.

Sergeant Organ's account reveals his movements in Ledringhem when the German 20 Division advanced into the village:

Suddenly an officer burst into the room [of a house where some of the Glosters were resting] shouting that the enemy was attacking . . . He told us to go down the street as fast as possible to the school [which was also the mayor's office]. We got to the school, out of breath, and found the best part of the battalion there. There were machine-guns and rifles poking out of every window ready to fire. Apart from the glow of cigarette ends, the rooms were in total darkness, and we were squeezed in like sardines. We quickly realized that by setting the houses alight, the enemy were going to force us out into the open . . . We soon saw them running towards us. We opened fire. Each time I finished a round, the enemy retaliated blowing out doors and windows.[24]

According to Hauting, in spite of the German thrusts,

arrangements were made for withdrawal at 2215 hrs, but before this time arrived, the attack was so intense that an orderly withdrawal would have been impossible. The orders were consequently cancelled, and all our efforts concentrated on keeping the enemy out of the village. His method appeared to be a short and intense mortar bombardment, alternating with an infantry attack accompanied by as many noise-producing fireworks as possible.[25]

The climax of the battle came after the men holding one of the Glosters' positions at the southern end of the main street withdrew, enabling the Germans to establish a foothold. This created a problem for the Glosters since, with Germans able to watch their movements, they would have no opportunity to slip away unobserved. 2nd Lieutenant Michael Shephard, who until that point had been the officer in charge of the battalion's carriers, described the counter-measures called for by Lieutenant-Colonel Guy Buxton, the Glosters' commanding officer:

Seven officers and seven men with rifles and bayonets and a few hand grenades, and two men with Bren guns, prepared to attack the enemy 150 yards away. We waited against the wall of the HQ, and in the ditch on the other side of the road. Then we spread out, and began moving slowly down the street.

I expect every man there felt the same as I did. Not frightfully brave, doing it because it was absolutely essential . . . wondering whether it would hurt when it came, and taking courage and hope from the presence of others.

It was natural that we should take to some kind of war cry [which was]: 'Up

Gloucesters!', and shout encouraging words to each other, at the same time gaining confidence as we moved forward. Our pace increased, but we did not break into a run, for it was necessary to keep a look out for any enemy who might be lingering further up the street than we expected.

The burning houses cast an eerie glow against the church walls, and proved of assistance to us, for we were able to see the Germans cross the street ahead of us. They gave us a rather feeble volley, which was returned wholeheartedly by our rifles fired from the hip, and on we went. When we reached the bottom of the street, the Germans were quiet.[26]

However, no sooner had the British troops returned to their head-quarters than the Germans reappeared in force and established a machine-gun post at the southern end of the village, near Ledringhem's church. Then, according to Shephard, the whole process had to be repeated:

This time we had more men . . . Two more officers were with us, and most of the men were those who had been on fighting patrols in France [in the Saar region during the phoney war], the very medicine for the Boche. I think the German officer must have sensed that we meant business this time. We could hear him exhorting his men to meet our attack. The first sense of fear had left us, and it was almost thrilling moving down that street to get to grips with those grey clad infantrymen. So, cheering, thirty-odd men and officers moved steadily towards the corner by the church.

The blaze had grown greater, and we could see the figures of the enemy as they waited in the cover of walls and doorways. The light of his [own] making showed us the leader, who was shouting harshly to his men. I saw him at the same time that others did, and simultaneously our rifles cracked, and the German went down . . .

We lost men as we went forward . . . but that did not deter the others. Suddenly the road was illuminated by great explosions, as the enemy rolled and threw their stick bombs at us. Our own grenades replied, and one, neatly lobbed through a doorway, silenced the machine-gun for good. We fired another volley at the shadowy figures, and then . . . ran in.

On my right I saw a Tommy bayonet a man. I heard him shout triumphantly . . . Another Tommy ran past me and round the corner to bayonet a Boche, who crouched there with his bombs. Another German ran away . . . and fell at my feet before I realized that I had fired again from the hip. Everywhere

our men were doing the same thing, bayoneting, shooting and bombing. Everywhere we were pushing the enemy back from the village. It was
exhilarating!

Unfortunately Shephard had to retire from the fray, having been
temporarily blinded by a bloody flesh wound, before the last Germans
were pushed out of the street. But pushed out of the street they were,
and the Glosters were, in Shephard's words, 'more or less free to go'.
The three officers who had been severely wounded during the bayonet
'charge' were left in the school, but those still able to walk, and some
who were not, crept or were carried out of the village shortly after
midnight.[27] Lieutenant-Colonel Buxton, who had been wounded in the
leg, began the journey being pushed in a wheelbarrow before transferring
to a horse.[28] By some lucky chance, they managed to time their departure
so that they moved between German attacks, and therefore got away
without having to fight their way out.

Their move back to Bambecque was a story in itself. On the way
they came across a German battery and were forced to rush the sentries,
who would otherwise have alerted their comrades. They encountered
another obstacle as they crossed the Cassel–Wormhout road at Riet
Veld.[29] When they entered the village, a French woman saw them and
pointed out of her window at some German soldiers who were sleeping
beside the road. The Germans were allowed to sleep on undisturbed as,
like ghosts, the British troops moved silently through the village.[30]

Their arrival in Bambecque at dawn on 29 May was witnessed by an
astonished Captain Bill Haywood, adjutant of the 8th Worcestershire
Regiment, another 144 Brigade unit, who had only just been warned
by the brigadier that the Glosters were unlikely to make it back to
Bambecque since he had been unable to send any reinforcements.
'Suddenly we saw a strange and unforgettable sight,' wrote Haywood.

Round the corner, into the village street, came a slow, straggling column of
British troops, shuffling along in a state of almost complete exhaustion. For a
second I just stared. Then I recognized burly Colonel Buxton stumbling along
at the head of his men. Behind him was Hauting, the Adjutant, with two
prisoners. I spotted Major Mason and young Shephard with his head bandaged.
These were the survivors of the 5th Gloucesters. I ran forward, and Colonel
Buxton almost tottered into my arms. I said: 'You're hurt, sir.' He mumbled:

'I'm peppered all over, Bill. None of it serious' . . . I took Colonel Buxton indoors, and we spread a blanket on the floor for him. He said: 'Don't let me sit down, or I won't get up,' but I told him he had nothing to worry about, and eased him to the floor . . . I gave [him] a glass of red wine, but he had barely sipped it, before he fell fast asleep.[31]

26: Massacre at Wormhout

Wormhout, 26–8 May 1940
(See Map 14. Also Maps 1 and 10)

When Gort told Blanchard on 28 May that his front-line strongpoints would not hold out for another day, one of the towns he was thinking of was Wormhout (see Chapter 25). It was protected by two infantry battalions (the 8th Worcestershire Regiment and the 2nd Royal Warwickshire Regiment), some machine-gunners and a battery of anti-tank guns, a force that might have been expected to repulse an attack by German foot-soldiers but which could not be relied upon to hold out for long against tanks. The Worcesters had been ordered to hold the east of the town, and the 2nd Royal Warwicks had been instructed to shield Wormhout on its west and south-western sides, the area that the Germans were likely to attack first.

The Royal Warwicks had arrived in Wormhout at dawn on 26 May. In spite of the importance of their mission, and the fact that a German attack was imminent, its officers were not kept informed about either of these factors. The account by the Royal Warwicks' Captain Edward Jerram has shown just how long it took after the battalion's arrival in Wormhout for the British soldiers to appreciate the extreme peril that was facing them.[1] 'I don't think anybody visualized that there might be much activity here,' Jerram reported.

We had ostensibly been pulled out to rest, and [believed we] were in Corps reserve. [When we arrived on 26 May] I had my valise unrolled, and intended to sleep in it under a covering of truck hoods which I myself rigged up. [This took place near his B Company's 'HQ', a series of slit trenches at the western end of the château garden that also housed the battalion's headquarters. (The château's position is specified in Map 14 on p. 529.)] Just before lunch, or afterwards, I strolled into the town and had a look at the church, inside and out. From the outside, [I could see] it was a very pleasant Norman piece of work. It was raining, so I went back to Coy. HQ. I wrote a letter to Mother, and then found there was no post yet being collected.

Meanwhile the men in Jerram's B Company had dug themselves in so that they were facing north and north-west. They held the area between the roads leading to Dunkirk and Esquelbecq.[2] '11 Platoon were [on] the right,' Jerram recorded.

[Its headquarters were] based [in] a small cottage which appeared empty. [11 Platoon's Lieutenant] Dunwell made use of the bed [in the cottage] during this quiet period. The next day, the owner, a pretty lass, whose husband was at the front, returned and visited me with a policeman! Apparently a lot of her things had been purloined, and she had actually seen some of Dunwell's men wearing 'hubby's' belongings. However investigation didn't produce much, angry though I was.[3]

Dunwell's platoon might have been subjected to more intense scrutiny had it not been for some alarming news that had come in from the front on the twenty-sixth. Jerram's account describes how this put an end to the period of relaxation he had been enjoying since their arrival:

I was lazing over a book on a camp chair with the rain, now quite heavy, pattering on my 'roof'. To the west [I could hear] perpetual gun-fire – the French and Germans in combat. Behind me [I could hear] the Church bells ringing out. An orderly arrived with a message summoning me to a conference with the Colonel [Philip Hicks] . . .[4] The gist of [the] information [about the enemy] was there was an AFV [armoured fighting vehicle] column in Noordpeene . . . SW of Wormhout, and about ten miles off![5] It meant that they were behind or round the line the French were holding from St Omer to the sea coast.

This prompted a flurry of activity as the companies' positions were hastily rearranged. Jerram's B Company was moved to the south of the Wormhout–Esquelbecq road. A Company was placed on B Company's left, and D Company on A Company's left. C Company was in Esquelbecq. Those positions meant that, barring a sudden change of direction, the German armoured vehicles would have to overcome the men in the Royal Warwicks' newly sited trenches if they wanted to use the main road that runs from Cassel to Dunkirk via Wormhout.

However, as Jerram's account indicates, at dawn on 27 May there was no evidence of anything sinister coming their way, other than what was said to the company commanders at Major Hicks's early-morning conference: 'We received orders that we had to hold Wormhout at all costs in order that a big strategical operation could be successful. Personally I thought it might mean that the German mechanized column advancing towards us was going to be hit an almighty crack on its left flank. It was all very secret.' Captain Dick Tomes, the battalion's adjutant, recorded in his diary some of the actual words contained in the order: 'You will hold your present position at all costs to the last man and last round. This is essential in order that a vitally important operation may take place.'[6]

The first sign that Wormhout was about to be attacked came shortly after lunch on 27 May. While Jerram was inspecting some huts with a view to seeing whether he might sleep in one that night, some planes flew very low overhead. The next sounds he heard were a series of explosions.[7] 'I fell flat on my face on the floor,' wrote Jerram.

Then I got up. I discovered four enormous craters in a ploughed field, and at the side of the road . . . The other two fell in the square. They were obviously having a go at the transport there. One of these lifted our petrol lorry bodily, and planted it into the ditch. Luckily it never exploded . . . [But] a small child had its foot blown off. This . . . disgusted me . . .

The bombing put the battalion on red alert, and Jerram had to jettison the plans he had made to have a restful night with a roof over his head. 'Things looked like warming up, so that night I slept on the ground beside my trench,' he wrote. Next morning the men were woken up at 'about 3.15 a.m.', according to Jerram. Before doing anything else, he inspected his company's front-line positions, which looked even more inadequate than they had the day before. During the evening of 27 May, the battalion had been reduced from four to three companies. C Company, which had been in Esquelbecq, had been sent back to help guard the perimeter around Dunkirk, so the other companies had to hold wider fronts.[8]

Jerram's own company's positions had been further weakened by the order to place one of his platoons near the Wormhout–Dunkirk road to the north of the town. His one consolation was that B Company's positions had been reinforced by two platoons of Cheshire Regiment machine-gunners who had arrived at 7 p.m. on the twenty-seventh.

(The Warwicks' final positions, including Jerram's and the battalion's headquarters, are marked on Map 14 on p. 529.)⁹

'When I got back to my slit trench I found [10 Platoon's 2nd Lieutenant] "uncle" Gunnel having his breakfast,' wrote Jerram. 'My servant soon brought mine. It went down well. It was a lovely morning!' While they were eating, they heard the first shots. Gunnel was immediately ordered to go to the Wormhout–Esquelbecq road to investigate. Shortly afterwards, Jerram received his report. A German motorcycle patrol had appeared at the barricade blocking the road, along with crowds of refugees who were trying to pass through Wormhout. The motorcyclists had turned round and made off as soon as they saw the barricade. British machine-gunners had then opened up. 'The German attack proper started at 0940,' wrote Jerram.

A column of German lorries arrived. Their progress was prevented by . . . [the] roadblock of farm carts. The Bosch jumped out into the fields on either side, throwing something alight under the lorries, which, with our . . . shells, soon caused a terrific fire amongst them and the barricade . . . Bullets started zipping about all over the place. Shells began to fall around and amongst us. A battle had started in earnest.¹⁰

Because Jerram was behind his company's front-line positions, he was protected from the worst of the German firing and shelling. But bullets still whizzed over his head and thudded into the parapet shielding his trench. 'Shelling was [also] fairly intense and close,' he recorded. '[It was] close enough to duck down on several occasions. [Nevertheless] during these moments when one couldn't really do anything, I looked at a [Daily] Sketch [the newspaper]. I found it kept me calm, and it appeared to make the men close to me think light of the matter.'¹¹ However, Jerram's feigned nonchalance became increasingly difficult to sustain once the messages delivered by runners revealed the torments endured by those in the front line.

At first the messages were encouraging. The initial waves of the German attack were carried out by infantry alone, unsupported by tanks. But about an hour after the battle started, an incident took place that was dramatically to alter the balance of power. At 10.50 a.m., Obergruppenführer Josef 'Sepp' Dietrich, commander of the SS Leibstandarte Adolf Hitler Regiment, the infantry spearheading the attack, was being

driven eastward along the Esquelbecq–Wormhout road when his car
was halted by the roadblock covered by Jerram's B Company. At least
two of Dietrich's men got out of the car to remove the obstruction, but
before they could move on towards Wormhout the car was shot up by
gunners from the Worcestershire Yeomanry, who were concealed beside
the road some fifty yards to the east.[12] The shooting killed the driver,
but Dietrich and Hauptsturmführer Max Wünsche, the commander of
the Leibstandarte's 15 Company, who had accompanied Dietrich, dived
into the nearest ditch. Escaping from the ditch with their dignity intact
was quite another matter, however, and the unfortunate men were
pinned down for several hours by the British gunners who, although
unaware of their captives' identity, were determined to ensure that they
would play no further part in the battle.

It was a humiliating moment for Dietrich. Not only had his rash act
led to the death of at least one of his men, but it had also deprived his
regiment of its commander at the height of the battle. He and Wünsche
were trapped in the ditch for around four hours.[13] While there, he is
said to have caked himself with mud to avoid being burned by the
flaming oil and petrol from his car, which had been ignited by the
shooting. Wünsche fared even worse: he passed out after climbing into
a pipe, which he hoped would enable him to crawl away from the ditch
where they were effectively imprisoned.[14]

It was the SS troops' inability to free Dietrich that led to the tanks
being called in during the early afternoon to rescue him – a development
that was to have tragic repercussions for the British troops opposing
them.[15] Bill Cordrey, who was with one of the front-line platoons in
Jerram's B Company, has described the moment when he and his men
saw the German armour for the first time:

Suddenly Titch, who was on look out, shouted 'Quick Corporal, come and
have a look at this!' Even before I looked over the parapet, I knew what it
was. Subconsciously, I had been listening to a low hum, and the penny dropped.
Tanks! Sure enough, there they were, about 700 yards away, and making
towards us in an extended line. I made a dive for the Boys anti-tank rifle . . .

Everybody was opening up now, and the sections on my right were really
letting go . . . Sticking the Boys over the parapet, I picked out the most central
tank, and decided to let him have the full ten rounds . . . The previous year I
had been on an anti-tank rifle course, and our instructor had told us that these

.505 bullets would penetrate armour, spin around the inside of the tank, fragment, and kill all the occupants. What a joke! That bloody tank never faltered, and I knew I was hitting it . . .

The situation was getting really hot. We were being plastered with shells and automatic fire. What to do? . . . Every nerve in me was screaming 'Get out! Don't be a bloody fool, you've done your share.' But I was more scared of running than staying put . . . Suddenly Clancy said: 'Quick, Bill! Look! They're turning!' I took a quick look, and sure enough, the whole line had made a half-left incline, and the extreme right flank was going to miss us by at least a couple of hundred yards. I couldn't believe my eyes . . . As the tanks moved away, I expected to see the infantry following up behind them. But it was all clear.[16]

It was only later that Cordrey discovered that the section on his right had not been so lucky: 'Corporal Thomas . . . told me that a tank went right over his trench, and everyone was killed except himself . . . He lost both legs. He also said that the whole of the line to his right was wiped out.'[17]

Surviving German records do not specify which tank platoon within the 2nd Panzer Division's 3rd Panzer Regiment was seen by Cordrey. But testimony provided by an unnamed member of one panzer crew has highlighted the tough resistance his group encountered.[18] Even before his platoon was sent in to attack, another platoon from his company was all but annihilated by British anti-tank guns positioned on either side of the Esquelbecq–Wormhout road. Four tanks were put out of action, and seven men were either killed or severely wounded within five minutes.[19] After that calamitous start to the operation, it was decided to unleash the remainder of the 6th Panzer Company, backed up by tanks from two platoons of heavy and light tanks. The principal attack was to pass through B Company's positions on and around the Esquelbecq–Wormhout road, while a lighter attack was to be mounted simultaneously against positions held by the Royal Warwicks' A and D Companies to the south of the town.

The 6th Company's first task was to destroy the anti-tank guns beside the Esquelbecq–Wormhout road so that the tanks could drive with some degree of safety to Wormhout's centre. How this was accomplished is spelt out in the following extract from the report by its chronicler:

Nothing can be seen of the well-hidden anti-tank guns. Only after one of the guns fires at the commander's tank at a distance of around 300 metres is the gun spotted by the left tank's gunner, and it is put out of action with a well-aimed shot. Then we drive at top speed towards the hedge which has caused such problems for Lieutenant Cord's platoon.[20] Anyone who does not run away is just knocked down or driven over . . . The Tommies leave their positions, and run back towards the town centre . . .

We follow them at breakneck speed. The route we follow takes us into a large park . . . It is full of cars and lorries . . . and here and there we see huge stacks of English petrol containers and ammunition . . . The Commander sees an English command flag hanging out of the large house in the middle of the park . . . It is at the centre of lots of wires which all meet at the house. So this must be the Tommies' command post . . .

However, before we reach the house, thick smoke is smelt inside the tank . . . Is the tank burning? But when the Commander looks at the rear of the tank, he sees that it is not. The Tommies have opened some of the petrol canisters, and have poured petrol on to the tracks inside the park. They have then ignited the petrol . . . We beat a hasty retreat, passing the exploding ammunition dumps and the burning petrol cans, and knocking down any trees that get in our way. After several attempts, we knock down part of the park wall and escape to the open fields outside the park.

The British defenders had valiantly repulsed the first assaults. But they could not withstand stronger thrusts, and eventually the British front-line units were either overrun or pushed back, thereby permitting the tank crews to rescue Dietrich and Wünsche at around 3 p.m.[21]

Jerram had telephoned through his first situation report to Major Hicks at Battalion Headquarters while the tanks were still assembling in a wood about a thousand yards away from Jerram's ditch. The German armour was at that point just a distant threat. That was more than could be said for the German mortars. They terrorized Jerram's men, and in the end he was driven to ask Hicks if he had anything to help him neutralize them. All that Hicks could come up with was a solitary carrier, which was clearly insufficient.

This depressing news was matched by a message from one of the front-line platoons, which, Jerram says, 'shattered me'. The platoon had reported that it had run out of anti-tank .55 ammunition. 'If they had had their full complement at the beginning, this meant that they had fired 240 rounds!' Jerram remarked. He might have added that this suggested they were up against a large concentration of tanks. But there was nothing to be gained by fretting. All he could do was issue an order that more ammunition should be sent up to the platoon in a carrier.[22]

It was not long before the security of the men in his front line deteriorated sharply. A Lance-Corporal Handyside from 11 Platoon turned up with a bleeding forehead and a jammed Bren gun to tell Jerram that he was the only one left in his section, the rest having disappeared to the west. On his way to report to Jerram, he had seen two other lance-corporals, with some of their men, who had also abandoned their positions. Jerram's account explains that he was in two minds about how to react: 'I hoped for some runner to arrive with orders to withdraw . . . but until they came, I felt bound to hold my ground. All I knew was that an order of the day had been issued [along the following lines]: "Tell your men, with our backs to the wall, the Division stands and fights."' That order persuaded him that he could not release the lance-corporal just yet, so he instructed Handyside to collect all the men he could find close by and take them up to the front line once more. 'We got the Bren working again,' Jerram reported, 'and off he went. He was an exceedingly gallant and brave man.'

It was around this time that Jerram sent his last despairing message to Major Hicks, stating that his position was about to be pierced by tanks. 'Shortly afterwards I heard tanks rumbling down the road on my right,' Jerram concluded.

During most of the battle, the Royal Warwicks' headquarters had been situated not in the château spotted by the 3rd Panzer Regiment's tank crew, at the southern end of its park, but in a trench within the same park further to the north-west.[23] During the middle of the afternoon, when tanks were seen approaching again, Major Hicks turned to his intelligence officer, and said coolly: 'I think it's about time we got moving.'[24] Then, as if suddenly remembering that everyone was waiting for his lead, he shouted: 'It's *sauve qui peut!*' This command left at least one private in the dark: he turned to Captain Dick Tomes, the adjutant, and said, 'I don't know what he's talking about.' Tomes quickly provided a translation: 'It's every man for himself!' he shouted.[25] Major Hicks and his intelligence officer then left the park, somehow managing to avoid being captured, along with around eighty other men.[26]

Unfortunately Tomes was unable to take advantage of his own translation. As he attempted to escape, he was knocked unconscious by a bullet or splinter. When he came to, he found that he had been carried into the battalion's medical aid post along with the other wounded men. Feeling too faint to move, he remained where he was until he was eventually captured there with other men who were likewise too badly injured to make a run for it.

Jerram and what remained of his company's headquarters staff were luckier. They made it through the German lines to arrive at Rexpoede in time for breakfast on 29 May.[27] There, he was greeted by Major Hicks with the heartfelt words: 'Thank God you've arrived!' He and his men were revived with food and drink while sitting on the grass beside a track. However, as his account makes clear, he was not celebrating: 'I suppose [a sense of] anti-climax was getting a hold on me. Lumps kept on coming to my throat. There was next to nothing left of my company . . . It was depressing to see the remnants of the [rest of] the battalion . . . They didn't look more than a hundred . . . out of some 500 before the battle.'[28]

★   ★   ★

The men who fought at Wormhout deserve to be remembered, like those who did the same at other strongpoints, for standing their ground and thereby holding up the Germans for just long enough to allow the BEF to retreat up the secure corridor behind them to Dunkirk. But Wormhout veterans were to acquire a special notoriety, thanks to what happened there after the fighting ended. These post-battle events were the subject of a 1947 report written by the same War Crimes Interrogation Unit that had investigated the murder of the Royal Norfolk soldiers at Le Paradis (see Chapter 22).

The first paragraph of the Wormhout report's introduction says it all:

This report gives the known details of the wilful murder after capture by German soldiers of approximately 80 or 90 men of the 2nd Battalion, the Royal Warwickshire Regiment, the Cheshire Regiment and the Royal Artillery on the 28th of May 1940 near the village of Wormhout in northern France.[29]

According to the report, the killing was perpetrated by soldiers within the SS Leibstandarte Adolf Hitler Regiment, which the British defenders had resisted so fiercely. No judgement was made by the investigators on whether the murderers were influenced by Dietrich's incarceration. All that is certain is that after Dietrich had been confined to the ditch for some time, the order was given to at least some of the troops within the SS Leibstandarte Regiment that no prisoners were to be taken.[30] Some of the British prisoners-of-war were then shot.

The exact time of the shooting is hard to determine. But it is clear that when it took place, the 2nd Battalion of the SS Leibstandarte Regiment was commanded by Hauptsturmführer [Captain] Wilhelm Mohnke, who took over when his predecessor was wounded. This, and other evidence collected by the War Crimes Interrogation Unit, suggests that he might have been at least partially responsible for the brutal atrocity that is now generally referred to as 'the Wormhout Massacre'.[31]

The first crime perpetrated by SS Leibstandarte soldiers in breach of the Geneva Convention appears to have been committed in Wormhout's central square. Lance-Corporal Thomas Oxley of the 4th Cheshire Regiment has testified that he and other members of his battalion were guarding the Wormhout–Cassel road during the early afternoon of 28 May when all of a sudden they were instructed to board two trucks parked behind the village church. They were then driven to the main square. Oxley's report describes what he witnessed there:

We entered the square . . . and were surprised to see a large party of Germans at the other end . . . I observed the time on the church clock . . . It was 1.50 p.m. . . . [The Germans] appeared to be resting, but immediately they observed us, they opened fire. Most of the men on our two trucks were either killed or wounded. My truck gave a sudden turn, and I was thrown off . . . The truck went on.

I found that three other men had been thrown off our truck on the other side. I said to the other three that it looked as if there was nothing [for it] but to be taken prisoner. We therefore stood with our hands up. The Germans immediately crowded around us, shouting and storming, and pointing their weapons at us . . . They were fanatical, and some were dancing around us pointing their tommy guns at us . . .

After a matter of minutes, they fired on us. Whether they all fired, I cannot say, but definitely one of them, whom I had been watching, let go a burst on his tommy gun at the four of us. I was hit twice on the arm and leg, and was knocked out immediately.

After coming to, I saw some Germans sitting around the shop fronts. Others were eating and drinking, and others were going down the streets throwing grenades through bedroom windows. While all this was going on, I had the presence of mind to keep perfectly still, and watched them. Whilst doing so, three Germans brought an English sergeant, who was not known to me, out of a house. He appeared to be badly wounded, and a German officer immediately shot him down with a revolver. [Then] he emptied his revolver into the sergeant while he lay on the ground.

Oxley's account reveals that at about 4.50 p.m. the Germans left the square in a hurry, after bursts of gunfire were heard away from the town centre. This gave Oxley, and another wounded British soldier he encountered, the chance to escape.

I suggested to him that we should make for the British Dressing Station, a big red brick building . . . On arrival there we found the drive littered with corpses, some stripped naked, their bodies patterned with bullet holes, and others in uniform . . . There seemed [to be] no sign of any life. We therefore did not go further up the drive or into the house. I then suggested to this other soldier that we should make for the fields, which we did.[32]

Oxley and his new companion then made their way back to the new British front line, further to the north.

Their decision to get away spared them from witnessing the even worse scenes that occurred on the outskirts of the town that afternoon. The gratuitous violence meted out to British soldiers captured there was initially on a relatively small scale. In the case of at least one platoon of the Royal Warwicks' A Company, this was partly because few remained to be persecuted. A Cheshire Regiment man, Private F. Harbour, described in a brief letter he sent in 1944 to the War Office Casualty Branch the fate of some of the men who were taken prisoner with him on the Wormhout perimeter:

I was travelling in a 30 cwt truck which was driven by Sgt. Thompson with 19 other soldiers when we were ambushed. [Most of the soldiers were Royal Warwicks.] Tanks cut us off from both sides of the road. They set the truck on fire. Only two of us [and the driver who was badly wounded] survived intact. The others, including Ptes McKenzie and Williams, were burnt to death.[33]

According to Harbour, one of the survivors of this gruesome incident was Private Charles Daley, a Royal Warwick. It was Daley's experiences following the shooting up of the truck that suggested their German guards meant to treat them more harshly than captured British soldiers were entitled to expect. While Daley and Harbour were being hurried back to the SS Leibstandarte's 2nd Battalion's headquarters, near the Wormhout–Ledringhem road, a guard, without any justification, turned on Daley and, after accusing him of being an 'Engländer Schwein', shot him in his right shoulder.[34]

If that had been the only act of violence after the fighting ended that afternoon, the British soldiers involved might perhaps have put it down to a misunderstanding or mistake. But Alf Tombs, a Royal Warwick who had been at D Company's headquarters when captured, was to witness an incident about which there was no ambiguity. Before Tombs was taken prisoner, his company commander, Captain James Lynn-Allen, had sent him with a small party of men to pick up extra ammunition from the battalion's headquarters. On the way, one of his comrades caught the trigger of his gun on the branch of a tree they were passing. This resulted in his gun being discharged into the back of Private Gould, who was just in front of him. Gould slumped to the ground, unconscious, and when Tombs and the others all agreed that if they were to carry out their mission it would be impossible to take him along with them, Gould was propped up against a bank near a gate.

Unfortunately, gunfire coming from German lines prevented Tombs and his comrades reaching the château's park where the battalion's headquarters were located, and they retraced their steps so that they could tell Lynn-Allen. They had just reached his position when they were surrounded and forced to surrender. It was then that the shocking incident took place. As they and their guards marched towards Wormhout, they saw Private Gould who was lying motionless against the bank where they had left him. Rather than stopping to find out whether he could be helped, a guard marched over to where he lay, pointed his rifle at Gould's head and pulled the trigger, thereby putting an end to Gould's suffering, and his life.[35]

An even more horrific scene has been described by the Royal Warwicks' Private Bert Evans, who was captured with another group of D Company soldiers near the Wormhout–Cassel road: '[While being marched into Wormhout], I was looking to the left of the road at what looked like a factory. Fifteen to twenty men were lined up outside stripped to the waist, and opposite them were four machine-guns mounted on stands. Then the guns were fired and the men all fell down as if they were rag dolls. That is when I first began to think that we might be shot too.'[36]

Evans and the thirty or so men with him were joined on the Wormhout–Cassel road by Richard Parry, of the Royal Artillery, who had not been involved in the fighting at Wormhout but whose column had arrived after the battle was over and was then caught up in the bloody aftermath. After he joined the Royal Warwicks prisoners, they were all kept standing with their hands up outside an *estaminet* for about fifteen minutes until a German officer came out and told them they could put their hands down. They were then marched to the SS Leibstandarte's headquarters which was in a field on the western side of the Wormhout–Ledringhem road. There, they were put together with another group of about sixty men, including Charlie Daley, Private Harbour, and Thompson, their wounded lorry driver.[37]

It is interesting at this point to compare the statements of the British and German witnesses who observed the scene that followed from different viewpoints. When Richard Parry made his statement to the War Crimes Interrogation Unit he said: 'It was from this point [in the field] that I saw the German officer who looked like a Prussian. [In a previous statement Parry had described a German officer who looked like a Prussian and who wore a monocle.] He seemed a "big noise", wore a soft peaked cap (I think it was black) and was giving orders to his subordinates on the road, from his gestures, I should say about ourselves. He was raving blue murder!'[38]

The German who described this scene was Oskar Senf, a corporal in the Leibstandarte Regiment's 2nd Battalion's 7th Company. He was the only German who has claimed he saw one of his officers ordering that no prisoners should be taken. From his testimony, it can be deduced that Senf was probably one of the Germans who escorted Evans, Parry and the other thirty men in a northerly direction up the Cassel–Wormhout road, and then in a south-westerly direction down the Wormhout–Ledringhem road until they reached his battalion's headquarters. In his statement he recalled how

Just a little way in front of the Battalion Battle HQ Hauptsturmführer Mohnke, Company commander of 5 Company who had just taken over the command of the battalion, came up to us and reprimanded SS-Untersturmführer [2nd Lieutenant] Heinrichs in our presence, because he had, contrary to orders, brought in prisoners. His words were: 'What do you mean by bringing in prisoners contrary to orders?' I do not know what Heinrichs replied to that . . .

We arrived at the Battalion Battle headquarters [where] we waited with the prisoners. Heinrichs went to the Battalion Battle HQ, which was at the time in the open, and wanted to hand the prisoners over there. Meanwhile the prisoners were standing in loose formation, along the edge of the road. Several were smoking . . .

After . . . about half an hour, Heinrichs came back to us, and brought some ten men of the battalion . . . from another company. That was late in the afternoon, around six o'clock. It was raining and misty. Heinrichs ordered us to bring back the prisoners with the other men. When I asked: 'Where?', he said that the men, that is the other ten men . . . 'knew what to do'. I then asked the men where we were going, and was told that they had orders from Mohnke to shoot the prisoners . . . I felt . . . incensed, and stated that we were not in agreement. The men who had joined us told us that they would do it alright. I told Heinrichs again before he left us that this was not in my line . . . Heinrichs replied that we had just heard ourselves how Mohnke had shouted at him.[39]

One of the prisoners, who spoke German, understood what was being said and blurted out, 'My God! They're taking no prisoners!'[40] However, before he was able to impart this information to everyone else, the British soldiers found themselves being escorted across the fields away from Wormhout. On the way more rough treatment was meted out, one man being clubbed with a rifle butt when he could not keep up, and another being stabbed in the chest with a bayonet.[41] None of the prisoners dared to stop for long enough to see whether these assaults were fatal, and they ran on until shepherded into a barn in another field. (Its location is marked on Map 14 on p. 529.) Daley, who in spite of his painful shoulder managed to make it to the barn without being attacked again, has described what happened next:

Captain Lynn-Allen, who was commanding D Company, and who was the only officer amongst the prisoners, protested against what appeared to be the intention, namely to massacre the prisoners. He also protested that there were a number of wounded, and that the accommodation was insufficient to give them room to lie down. The German soldier shouted back: 'Yellow Englishman, there will be plenty of room where you're all going to.' This man spoke fluent English with a strong American accent. He and others then threw bombs into the barn.[42]

The precise chronology of the events that followed is hard to reconstruct from the conflicting testimonies of the shocked men inside the barn, but Bert Evans remembered clearly what happened to him:

I was standing next to Captain Lynn-Allen, just inside the door of the barn, when the Germans began throwing grenades in. I had my right arm shattered by one of the first explosions. Then, while I was still feeling dazed, and as another grenade come in through the door, Captain Lynn-Allen, who was at this time unwounded, seized me, and dragged me out through the door, and round the corner, while the Germans who had thrown the grenades were taking cover against the explosions. Captain Lynn-Allen practically dragged, or supported me the whole way to a clump of trees which was about 200 yards away. When we got inside the trees, we found there was a small stagnant and deep pond in the centre. We got down into the pond with the water up to our chests. Captain Lynn-Allen was standing some little distance from the edge. I, because of my condition, stood closer to the bank, and presumably lower in the water.

It was then that Lynn-Allen said to Evans: 'I wonder whether we've escaped.'

According to Evans, his rhetorical question was answered seconds later: 'Suddenly, without warning, a German appeared on the bank of the pond just above us, showing that we must have been spotted before we gained the cover of the trees.' As he approached them, Lynn-Allen shouted out: 'Oh my God!' as he saw the German raising his pistol to fire, and Evans just had time to see Lynn-Allen's head split open by the first bullet, before he himself was hit in the neck. He immediately collapsed into the water. The fact that Evans lost consciousness might have caused him to drown. Instead, as it turned out, it saved his life. While he was lying motionless in the water, the German must have returned to the barn, satisfied that Evans, as well as Lynn-Allen, had been safely dispatched. That is why when Evans, after a brief spell under water, came to his senses and stood up again, the German soldier had vanished.

Although Evans suspected that Lynn-Allen must have been killed by the shot to his head, he nevertheless waded around in the pond trying to find his body. However, his search was fruitless, and it suddenly dawned on him that he was in mortal peril and must get away before he was seen again. Regardless of the terrible injuries to his arm and his wounded neck, he crawled into a ditch, encouraged no doubt by the gunfire that he could still hear crackling beside the barn. Although he was hit in the shoulder by a stray bullet, he finally reached a nearby farmhouse, which was occupied by a German ambulance unit. He was a prisoner-of-war once again, but this time captivity meant security.[43]

After Evans's flight from the barn, the ordeal continued for those inside it. Brian Fahey, another Royal Artillery man who had been captured, then brought to the barn with the others, has described what he witnessed:

The German officer in charge said, 'Raus! five men' . . . [Five men] were taken out and stood there . . . There were five Germans with rifles, and . . . [the German officer] counted 'Eins, zwei, drei, vier, fünf', and as he said each number, another man was shot by the firing squad. I then made up my mind that, wounded as I was, I would be in the next five . . . He said: 'Another five men!' and I got up and . . . because I couldn't walk properly, a boy helped me; I put my arm round his shoulder, and we took our positions. I was number five in the second five, and they made us turn round so we were actually shot in the back . . . The shot went right through my body. I thought I was dead, and I suppose I passed out.[44]

Nobody volunteered to go outside when the next five were summoned, and so it was that the climax of the massacre was reached. After ordering those nearest the entrance, including Charles Daley, to turn round, the Germans shot them in the back.[45] The Germans then rushed into the barn firing machine-guns and throwing grenades. It was this final burst of frenzied killing that accounted for most of those who remained in the barn, and left most of the survivors with terrible injuries. One has described how he felt physically sick when he saw how another man's leg, almost severed at the thigh, had twisted round inside his trousers. Almost as bad was the noise that emanated from his mouth. He was screaming, and thumping the ground, as if he could not bear the agony he was suffering.[46] Daley, who had survived being shot in the back, was left with a shattered right leg, and a bullet in his left leg.[47] Incredibly, Parry lived although a bullet had been fired into his mouth at point-blank range.[48]

In the midst of all this carnage, the courage exhibited by two Royal Warwicks' soldiers stood out. On seeing the first grenades thrown into the barn, Sergeant Moore and Sergeant-Major Augustus Jennings had pounced on them, either hoping to pick them up and throw them back at their captors or perhaps intending to sacrifice their own lives to shield their men from the blast. Whatever their intentions, their bravery went so far beyond the call of duty that no one who witnessed it could have denied that their valour matched that of those BEF soldiers who won the Victoria Cross. Unfortunately, even if they had been rewarded with the highest accolade for valour, the explosion, which killed both of them instantly, would have made both VCs posthumous.

When the first bout of firing and shooting had died down, one young lad cried out at the back of the barn: 'Shoot me! Shoot me!' until eventually a German walked over to him and shot him between the eyes.[49] The Germans then left the barn, and the din that had been made by the firing and explosions was replaced by absolute silence. It was broken when another lad was heard reciting the Lord's Prayer, the recital only stopping as he expired.

Given what had happened inside the barn, it is perhaps surprising that any of the British soldiers survived. However, nine men, including Evans and Tombs, escaped under their own steam, and at least eight other men were still alive when troops from a regular German Army unit entered the barn two days later. Of these eight, one died shortly afterwards.[50]

The horror of the massacre overshadowed the other injuries and killings that had occurred during the Wormhout battle, but it is no exaggeration to say that the 2nd Battalion, the Royal Warwicks were sacrificed so that the road to Dunkirk could be protected. According to the regimental history, of the three companies who stood their ground and fought at Wormhout, only seven officers and 130 men were counted when the remnants of the battalion made it back to Dunkirk.[51]

27: Escape to Dunkirk

West Cappel and Cassel, 28–9 May 1940
(See Maps 10, 14 and 15. Also Map 1)

If the defences protecting the south-western side of the corridor to
Dunkirk had been breached when Wormhout, Hazebrouck and
Ledringhem were overrun on 28 May, the German Army might yet
have cut off Allied troops on their way to the sea. But Gort, and his
subordinate commanders, had given the line more than one layer.[1] So
when the front line of strongpoints fell under German control, others
were being occupied, albeit with fewer troops and guns, further back.
Thus, rather than finding the road to Dunkirk open after passing through
the outer crust of the British positions, German troops during the late
afternoon of 28 May and on 29 May had another line to contend with,
running from Vyfweg to Bambecque via West Cappel in the north and
from Caestre to Vieux Berquin via Strazeele in the south.[2] The two
sectors of the new line were like a bird's wings on either side of Cassel,
which jutted forward in a salient towards the south-west.

The knowledge that this weaker back-up line could not be expected
to hold up the Germans for long must have been another worry for
Gort at his 28 May meeting with Blanchard. At that meeting (described
in Chapter 25), Blanchard had stated that he must see General Prioux
before deciding whether the French soldiers within the 1st Army could
withdraw to the Dunkirk perimeter during the coming night. The two
French generals finally met that afternoon, and Blanchard gave Prioux
and his three Army corps (III, IV and V Corps) permission to retreat to
the coast if they could.[3] This was duly passed on to General de La
Laurencie, commander of the French III Corps, the only French corps
to have made it back to the Lys. (Details of the failed attempt by the
French IV and V Corps to escape from Lille are in note 4.)[4] De La
Laurencie told Prioux that he would retreat that very night if it was
feasible. Prioux on the other hand decided that, with two of his corps
still attempting to break through the German cordon placed around
Lille, it would be dishonourable to withdraw. He elected to remain at
his Steenwerck headquarters in case he could help them.[5]

De La Laurencie's plan to retreat to Dunkirk could not be put into effect without his generals' consent, and at first that was not forthcoming. When he mentioned the withdrawal to them at 6 p.m. that night, two of them objected that their troops were too tired to move. De La Laurencie coolly listened to what they had to say. Then he famously came up with the strategy that was to overcome their objections. He told them that if, after checking with their commanders, they still felt the same, he would go along with their decision, provided that they signed a document stating that they took full responsibility for their divisions' surrender, which would then be inevitable. That persuaded them at least to try to escape up the corridor to Dunkirk, and it was eventually agreed that de La Laurencie's three divisions – General Paul de Camas' 1st Motorized Division, General Louis Janssen's 12 Division, and General Maurice Lucas' 32 Division – should commence their retreat at 11 p.m.[6]

General Prioux should have told the British Major-General Edmund Osborne, whose 44 Division was still covering the southern end of the corridor from Caestre to Vieux Berquin, what had been decided. Osborne might then have had time to organize his own troops' retreat to Dunkirk that night. But Prioux failed to let Osborne know.

The omission was made even more indefensible because of what Osborne had said to Prioux earlier that afternoon, before Blanchard's meeting with Prioux. Osborne had begged Prioux to withdraw his troops while there was still time, only for Prioux to retort that there was no point in doing so since, if there was to be an evacuation, the British would leave the French behind.[7] He would rather they remained where they were even if that meant they would have to surrender than subject them to an arduous forced march and the risk that they would be abandoned at Dunkirk. However, before Osborne left the 1st Army's headquarters, Prioux had reluctantly agreed at least to send a message to his superiors, asking whether his men might be allowed to withdraw up the corridor, and Osborne had specifically requested that Prioux should let him know as soon as he received the answer. Prioux, while agreeing to comply with Osborne's request, had commented, '*C'est inutile* [It's pointless],' thereby expressing his defeatist frame of mind.

In view of Prioux's undertaking, Osborne was upset when, during his 8.30 p.m. meeting with IV Corps' General Aymes, the French general mentioned that some of Prioux's troops were to retreat after all.[8] Osborne was advised to confront Prioux immediately.

'I found him in a room with two candles and a couple of staff officers,' Osborne reported. After recording Prioux's confirmation that his troops were going to move up the corridor, Osborne added, 'As far as I could make out, he had made no attempt to acquaint me with his decision . . . The whole essence of his conversation was that he had left me in ignorance of his decision, as I afforded extra protection to his left. In spite of all the demands . . . that I should hold firm the western flank, [and] should come under their orders . . . we were to be jettisoned as soon as it suited them.'

Osborne's report recalls some of the indignant questions he put to Prioux in response. These included: 'Why had I not been warned?' and 'By what right was I being treated like this?' Eventually, however, Osborne, evidently realizing that his protests were not achieving anything other than the relief of his own exasperation, took Prioux's advice, which was to decide on his division's next movement after talking to de La Laurencie.[9]

The interview with de La Laurencie was to be even more uncomfortable: 'This officer received us with informal rudeness,' wrote Osborne.

He admitted that he was commanding the 2 columns, but [stated] that he was leaving at 2300 hrs. that night, and not [at] mid-day [on the] next day as Prioux had ordered.[10] I pointed out that [it] was now nearly 2130 hrs, and that I was in contact along the whole line . . . to protect their left flank. His manner was practically insulting. He merely said . . . that he was going at 2300 hrs. To any statement of mine, he merely answered 'onze heures'.

At this point, an infuriated Osborne accused de La Laurencie of having committed the 'grossest treachery', then stalked out of the room.[11] Osborne concluded his note of their meeting: 'This officer was intolerable.' Eventually, he decided his troops would retreat just six miles that night to a tankproof locality on Mont des Cats, and would only complete their journey to Dunkirk the following night.[12]

★ ★ ★

Even as 44 Division started out on the first leg of its journey towards the sea, thereby removing the shield that had been protecting the southern end of the corridor, another group of BEF troops and armour were on their way to guard a northern section of the road to Dunkirk down which 44 Division would be marching on the twenty-ninth. Brigadier Charles Norman's force, consisting of the 1st Fife and Forfar Yeomanry's tanks and carriers, and the 1st Welsh Guards' foot-soldiers, had been ordered to hold a line that ran from Bergues to West Cappel.[13] It was clear that these two units, backed by the 6th Green Howards, did not have enough men to hold this four-mile line securely, but Brigadier Norman was determined that they would at least delay any Germans who tried to reach the Poperinghe–Bergues road, using the roads that passed through Vyfweg and West Cappel.[14]

His confidence took a knock at dawn on 29 May, however, when Lieutenant-Colonel Steel, commanding officer of the 6th Green Howards, came to see him with the following disheartening message:

My battalion is a labour battalion of 20-year-old boys. They were sent out to dig trenches, and are armed only with rifles. They have been put into an unsuccessful counter-attack near Gravelines in which they lost heavily. They have been down to the beaches, and told they were going home. They were then brought back, and put on the ground where they are now. They will stay just as long as they do not see a German. At the first sight of the enemy, they will bolt to a man.[15]

In fact, the Green Howards only fled later that afternoon after they had been overrun by tanks, and Brigadier Norman, who had taken refuge at the bottom of a ditch near the crossroads at Rattekot, had to be rescued by a section of the artillery which he had wisely placed nearby.[16] Their guns, firing over open sights, persuaded the tank crews to withdraw.

Fortunately for the BEF, the part of the line that passed through West Cappel, where one of the strongest German thrusts was to be made that day, was held by 2 Company of the Welsh Guards, regular soldiers who were unlikely to bolt. Although their three platoons were spread out thinly around the village, they nevertheless held their ground when attacked at 3 p.m., and defied the Germans until it was too late for them to exploit their breakthrough that night.[17] The order to retreat to a château in the village was only given after the Guards' front-line positions were pierced.[18]

The order came too late for two platoons holding 2 Company's two flanks. They were overrun. But parts of 5 Platoon in the centre, which had been facing the Germans advancing from the south, made a relatively orderly withdrawal, thanks to the gallantry of one of its youngest officers. Nineteen-year-old 2nd Lieutenant Rhidian Llewellyn ordered his surviving men to double back to the château in the village behind them, while he remained behind with Guardsman Warwick as the rearguard.

The hard tactics adopted and the torments endured by soldiers who carried out what could almost be described as suicide missions in order to keep the corridor to Dunkirk open have rarely been described in history books; that is what makes Rhidian Llewellyn's frank account so noteworthy. His first quandary concerned a Guardsman Fizackerley, who had been wounded on the way to the château. The wounded man was lying about a hundred yards behind the trench that Llewellyn and Guardsman Warwick were holding. Before giving the order to withdraw Llewellyn ran back to see what could be done for Fizackerley while Warwick fired at the Germans with a Bren gun. One look at Fizackerley's wounds told Llewellyn that the guardsman was too severely injured to be moved in the middle of a running battle. But he could not bring himself to spell this out. So instead he told a white lie: he and Warwick were going to withdraw, and Fizackerley would have to stay where he was for now, but they would be back just as soon as they could with reinforcements. Wondering no doubt whether Fizackerley believed him, he ran back to Warwick in the front-line trench.

Llewellyn's second moral difficulty occurred as he and Warwick made their dash for freedom. They did not follow the direct route to the château, which was covered by German guns. Instead, they looped round to the east, a route that, Llewellyn hoped, would take them to the rear of the château after passing around its eastern side. Llewellyn realized that he had miscalculated, when he found their path obstructed by hundreds of Germans. However, rather than calling on the two Welsh Guardsmen to throw down their weapons – including the Bren gun that Llewellyn was holding – the Germans put up their hands to surrender. For a fraction of a second Llewellyn hesitated, wondering what he should do: if he stopped to take prisoners, he might himself be shot or overpowered by the Germans pursuing him. If he tried to walk through the Germans in his path, they might overpower him and Warwick. Deciding that he valued his and Warwick's life and liberty more than any moral scruples, he opened fire with the Bren gun, killing and wounding as many Germans as was necessary to persuade the others to leave their way clear. He and Warwick then fled to the château.

But Llewellyn's troubles were only just beginning. He was put in charge of another group of guardsmen, and ordered to hold the main entrance on the northern perimeter of the château's parkland. They stayed there until they were attacked by tanks, whereupon Llewellyn instructed those who could to take refuge inside the château. Most of the men who were not injured or killed ran into the château across the bridge spanning the moat. But Llewellyn, who had waited for the last man to cross, was forced to dive with a Guardsman Andrews into the moat in order to escape an approaching tank.

The next two hours were the most uncomfortable of Llewellyn's life. He and Andrews stood in the moat under the bridge with cold water up to their necks while the battle between the Germans and the Welsh Guards inside the château raged over their heads. Their discomfort was exacerbated by their fear that the Germans inside the tank that had come to a grinding halt on the bridge would spot them if they so much as moved. Their ordeal was only terminated when, during a lull in the fighting, an officer slipped out of one of the château's side doors, and whispered to Llewellyn and Andrews that it was safe to come inside.

It was not long before Llewellyn and Andrews took the next step in their bid to escape from the Germans. As it grew dark, they and the other men in the château crept outside, and after dodging the bullets fired by the watching Germans, most of the survivors made for Dunkirk. The last line of 2 Company's war diary, written by its commanding officer, Captain Jocelyn Gurney, revealed the toll taken by the fighting. Of 139 men in the company at 3 p.m. on 29 May, 'Coy had 3 officers (2 wounded), 21 Ors [other ranks] left.'[19] The majority of these men who arrived in Dunkirk belonged to Llewellyn's platoon, and notwithstanding, or perhaps because of, the ruthless tactics he had adopted, he was subsequently awarded the Military Cross.[20]

Due to an oversight, an even smaller percentage of the garrison holding Cassel reached Dunkirk. By the evening of 28 May, the garrison had fulfilled its mission, but because no message arrived ordering Brigadier Somerset to retreat, he and his men were forced to hold on. In fact, a message ordering the retreat had been sent by dispatch rider during the evening of 28 May. But the motorcyclist lost his way, and only reached Cassel on the twenty-ninth after spending most of the night in a ditch.[21]

In the short term, the principal problem the Cassel garrison faced was not the danger posed by the Germans, who gave the town a wide berth on 28 May, but their own morale. Looking out from their vantage-points in the town, they could see that the Germans were moving across their line of retreat to the north, as well as appearing in the south. As if that was not demoralizing enough, their deteriorating living conditions made life in Cassel unpleasant to say the least. The entries in a diary written up by Lieutenant Tom Carmichael, an officer in the East Riding Yeomanry whose tanks and carriers had been ordered to hold the road winding up to the eastern side of the town, gives a vivid snapshot of what it was like to enter Cassel on 28 May:

The ascent into Cassel was the last place I should have cared to take up a position. There was . . . evidence that the enemy guns were ranged accurately on the road. The trees were shattered, two 2 pounders showed signs of direct hits, and a little heap huddled under a groundsheet marked the remains of one of the crew. But this was not the worst [sight]. On turning into the town, a 3 tonner . . . carrying personnel had suffered a direct hit . . . The mangled remains [were] ghastly. The tortuous [position] of the dead was eloquent [to the fact] that very few had escaped. And there they lay, exactly as death had overtaken them, [the sight] made more terrible by the cold and the rain.

Cassel [itself] was mainly in ruins from air bombing. Lorries destroyed by fire, together with the debris from the houses, and telephone wires blocked the streets. Smoke here and there marked the dying embers of burnt buildings.[22]

Even 145 Brigade's commander was somewhat disenchanted. When Brigadier Somerset heard from the Ox and Bucks' quartermaster, who had somehow made it past the Germans with rations for his battalion, that the bulk of the BEF was being evacuated from Dunkirk, he was more than a little upset. He later wrote in his account of the campaign: 'I now fully realized that we were "the Joe Soaps" of Dunkirk. That we were being sacrificed so that as many British and French [as possible] could get away from Dunkirk, and get all the kudos for that. I felt very bitter.'[23] However, he quickly pulled himself together, adding: 'I had this kept secret, making him [the quartermaster] swear he'd tell no-one.'

The dispatch rider bearing the order to withdraw turned up in Cassel on the morning of 29 May. By then it was daylight, which made it impossible to vacate the town without being spotted. Therefore Somerset decided that there was nothing for it but to wait until nightfall, and in the short term at least no one within the garrison, apart from the commanding officers, was to be told what was coming.[24]

On 29 May, the Germans attacked the town again, making several attempts to break through the defences around the perimeter. At one stage they nearly succeeded, getting to within thirty yards of an outpost in a farm on the north-west side of the town, before being driven off by men from the Glosters' B Company.[25] The perimeter line might have been pierced if the Germans had followed up their shelling of this outpost with a strong thrust. After a shell killed the commander of the battalion's 10 Platoon which had been guarding it, most of his men retreated to B Company's headquarters. (The farm and B Company's headquarters are marked in Map 15 on p. 531.) Fortunately Captain Bill Wilson, B Company's commander, was able to stop up the breach, as is revealed by the following extract from his account:

Pulling the rather shaken 10 Pl[atoon] together, I started to lead them back to their position. [But] we had just got into the tiny yard at the back of HQ, when a shell landed in the kitchen doorway. L/Cpl Badnell, one of my signallers, was killed outright. [He was] dreadfully mutilated. About ten others were badly injured. Pte Phelps next to me had both [his] legs blown off, save for tiny threads of muscle. I was for the third time amazingly lucky, receiving only a small piece of shrapnel in the thigh. With the SBs [stretcher-bearers] down at [the] 10 Pl position, we did what we could, but that was little enough, and the wounded . . . suffered greatly.[26]

The position was only finally shored up after Wilson placed the 10 Platoon survivors in trenches that had been dug by some Cheshire Regiment gunners who had also withdrawn, and armed them with the Cheshires' machine-guns.

Equally shocking was the damage caused by shells fired into the centre of the town. The placing of a gun next to the town's Gendarmerie, whose cellar, lit by two flickering candles, served as the headquarters for both the Ox and Bucks and the East Riding Yeomanry, was, according to Lieutenant Tom Carmichael, 'asking for trouble'. As he stated tersely

in his account: 'Trouble came.' His account vividly describes the ensuing
bombardment:

I was lying full length on the floor . . . As the fire became more intense, I
pulled my helmet over the side of my face . . . A major . . . came into the cellar
for shelter, and was standing at my feet. In spite of the racket and the banging,
I was almost asleep, when we were electrified by a terrific explosion. [There
was] an acrid smell, and a shower of masonry [fell] on my head. I had almost
freed myself, when another great weight from above pinned me down again
. . . I . . . scrambled free, [and] . . . began looking round.

The floor above my head had been blown away completely, and the chest
of drawers which had contained last night's dinner service, [which had been
in] the room above, was the second weight that descended upon me. As the
dust cleared, I found the remains of another less fortunate than us. It was the
Major who had taken shelter in our cellar. He was in two halves.

Carmichael was so shaken by what he had seen that he nevertheless
asked the medical officer whether he could do anything for the dead
man. The doctor looked at the decapitated body, which had ended up
on a shelf running along one of the cellar walls, and raised his hands in
a gesture of complete impotence. The officer, who seconds earlier had
been Major Joe Thorne, the Ox and Bucks' second-in-command, was
now a lifeless shell.[27]

Brigadier Somerset's first inkling that the shelling had led to casualties
was when an Ox and Bucks officer stumbled into his headquarters,
which had been moved to Place du Château at the summit of Mont
Cassel, announcing that everyone else in the cellar had been wiped
out.[28] (Somerset's 29 May headquarters and the Gendarmerie are both
marked on Map 15 on p. 531.) '[He] collapsed on reaching me. He was
covered in the remains of some of his comrades,' Somerset noted.[29] In
fact, Major Thorne was the only man in the cellar who died, though
many more were injured. But there was little that Somerset, sitting in
the brigade's headquarters in Cassel's keep, could do other than to
breathe a sigh of relief that he himself was still in one piece. Until the
previous night, his headquarters had also been in the Gendarmerie.

This horrific incident made Somerset even keener to abandon Cassel.
But during the afternoon of 29 May there was a setback. The East
Riding Yeomanry tank troop, which he had sent to Winnezeele, a

village some four miles to the north-east of Cassel, to check whether the escape route out of the town was still open, failed to report back. This led Somerset to conclude that 'they must have met the enemy in force, and had been unable to send back anyone with information . . . I . . . began to realize that unless our own troops from Dunkirk or the north put in a counter-attack, our chances of getting out of Cassel were remote – let alone [our chances of] reaching the Dunkirk perimeter.'[30]

Nevertheless, Somerset was determined to try their luck, and at 9.30 p.m. the first of his troops marched silently out of the town. It was not long before the silence was broken. While the troops that had been withdrawn from the perimeter were being assembled on the road to the east of the town, a man near Somerset fired his anti-tank rifle by mistake. This terrified many of those who could not see what had happened; they assumed Somer Force was under attack. However, order was soon restored, and the long column finally snaked away from the town towards the north-east.

Unfortunately, as Somerset had feared, the Germans were waiting for them. The first of the garrison's troops had not passed Winnezeele before they were fired on by German guns. This represented the end of the orderly phase of the retreat, as units which had started off intending to march in a line, split into many separate groups and attempted to make good their escape. From this point on it is impossible to track the progress of all the men coherently. The soldiers in each group had their own story to tell. Suffice it to say that after a series of firefights, most of those who had been in the column were either killed, wounded or, like Somerset, captured.[31] It was a sorry end to what had been a brave, and successful, rearguard action.

However, there were exceptions to the rule. Three Glosters' officers and the men under their command reached Dunkirk.[32] The officers included Julian Fane, the nineteen-year-old 2nd lieutenant who had tried to disable the tank that broke through the Glosters' defences at Cassel (see Chapter 20). His description of his journey to Dunkirk with nine Glosters' other ranks shows what many British soldiers must have endured as they marched up the disintegrating corridor. When the Germans ambushed the column, Fane's B Company was one of three Glosters companies that took refuge in the Bois St Acaire, a large wood to the north of Winnezeele.[33] 'We tried to get there without being seen by the enemy,' Fane reported.

But we must have been spotted by the Hun, for we had not been there long, before the whole area around the wood resounded with the cries of 'Kamerad! Kamerad!' There were quite a lot of troops shouting this treacherous word at the top of their voices. Then they all stopped, and a voice started speaking in clear tones in very good English. The words the man spoke were 'Come out! Come out! Hitler is winning the war. You are beaten. Come out, or we will shell you out. Lay down your arms and come out running.' It was a nasty moment . . . for we all realized the hopeless position we were in. One false move and we would all be shelled to hell.[34]

Some of the British men in the wood were shot, and many captured.[35] However, by keeping quiet and frequently shifting their position, the soldiers with Fane somehow avoided the shells that rained down through the trees. At nightfall when they finally emerged from the wood, they were surprised to find that there were no Germans to be seen. If that did not make them suspicious, any thoughts that they were metaphorically as well as physically out of the woods were soon swept away when, about an hour after they started moving, they were ambushed again, this time while they were crossing an open field. 'Everyone threw themselves to the ground,' wrote Fane. 'Lieutenant Dick Olive, who was in front of me, caught a blast of machine gun fire in the chest. His lungs began to fill, and I shall never forget the rasping noise of his breathing. It took about two minutes before he drowned in his own blood.'

Company quartermaster Sergeant Farmer's death was even more spectacular, according to Fane. Tracer bullets that hit him in the back ignited the rounds in the rifle bullet bandoleer slung over his shoulder, which went on exploding long after he had fallen. Fane was also wounded in his right arm. However, after they had scrambled down the ditch beside an adjacent road, Fane and some eleven men shook off their ambushers. It was a small number compared with around 450 officers and men from the battalion who appear to have accompanied Fane when the Glosters left Cassel.[36]

Fane quickly decided that it was not safe to move by day. He told his men that if they were to avoid the Germans they would have to walk all night, and rest during daylight hours. This certainly ensured that their marches were relatively secure. But their night-time manoeuvres were like a recurring nightmare: there were hours of endless plodding, punctuated with frustrating halts, as they worked out the best way to cross the many barbed-wire fences and streams in their path. If anything, the days were even worse: they had to lie up more or less immobile in ditches or farm buildings, ever fearful they might be discovered.

They also had to cope with great physical discomfort. Given that their uniforms were frequently soaking wet after wading through streams, they were lucky not to be struck down with pneumonia. They all suffered from a mild form of trench foot, caused by their feet being constantly damp. Those who tried to counter this by taking off their boots during rest periods found that it was impossible to put them on again because their feet were so swollen. The only remedy to counter this was to slit the leather with a knife, but this led to further difficulties. The loosened boots rubbed against the wearer's skin, causing agonizing blisters.

As if that was not enough, Fane also had his wounded arm to worry about. It was throbbing and very swollen. They were also hungry: when they had set out they only possessed a packet of biscuits and three tins of processed food plus some extra rations that two men produced out of their backpacks. Fortunately, they were not short of cigarettes, and discovered that smoking took the edge off their hunger. But they only finally put an end to the weakness they experienced due to lack of food when, during their third night since leaving Cassel, they broke into a house and feasted on the food, wine and beer they found there.

But what bothered them most during their four-night journey were their many close encounters with Germans. They were able to gauge where some of the enemy were from the flares that frequently shot up into the sky. However, when they came across soldiers in the dark it was difficult if not impossible to differentiate the Germans from Allied troops without speaking to them. One mistake made by Fane nearly ended with the whole party being put in the bag. This occurred near Oost Cappel during their third night on the move, on 31 May–1 June, when they came across a column of horse-drawn artillery.[37] Believing it to be French, Fane walked up to a man near the front of the column and spoke to him in French. The man replied in German but, luckily, was too tired to check why Fane was walking around in the dark. Before the penny could drop, Fane beat a hasty retreat.

The following day they had an equally fortunate escape. While they were resting in a barn some Germans came in, and Fane and his men only avoided capture because they were hidden behind some piled-up bales of hay. Nevertheless Fane almost had a heart-attack when, before the Germans departed, a man climbed the ladder that had been left in front of the bales and looked over the top of their 'barricade'. Fane and his men could not have been more relieved when they saw that the face looking at them over the top of the hay belonged to a French civilian rather than a German stormtrooper. The Frenchman, who was probably the farmer, climbed down the ladder and walked away discreetly after Fane's Corporal Eldridge signalled to him that he should not say a word. The men were so shaken by this incident that Fane permitted them to smoke a cigarette, regardless of the risk, after the last German and the civilian had left the barn. They were all glad when night fell again, and they were able to leave.

However, the next night there were more shocks in store for them. At one stage, Fane was pulled up short by the group's scout, who pointed to a large dark shape above their heads. It was a gun barrel, which might have been German. Without waiting to find out, they scurried away. Later that night, Corporal Eldridge saved the day again when he suddenly gripped Fane's shoulder, and whispered, 'My God, Sir. Look out!' Fane looked down, and saw a German sleeping on the ground at their feet. They quietly stepped around him, and left him to his slumber.

It was only at dawn on 2 June, after four nights on the run, that they finally reached the first of the canals running round the Dunkirk perimeter. On the far side, there was a scuttled boat that had not quite sunk. After Corporal Eldridge had swum across and brought it back to their side of the canal, they set up a kind of ferry service, with men clinging to the half-submerged boat, while it was pulled back and forth across the canal with string. During this manoeuvre, a French farmer emerged from one of the houses on the Dunkirk side of the canal and confirmed that the Germans had not yet crossed that waterway. It was Fane's and his group's first indication that they had reached their goal. But they were only just in time.

28: The Dunkirk Armada

Sheerness, Ramsgate and Dunkirk 19–29 May 1940
(See Maps 16 and 19. Also Maps 1 and 10)

The first step taken in France that was to pave the way for the BEF's evacuation from Dunkirk was taken on 19 May. That was when General Brownrigg told Colonel Whitfield, whom he had just appointed as Dunkirk's commandant, to evacuate all 'useless mouths', mirroring similar operations in Boulogne and Calais.[1] The initial stages of the Dunkirk evacuation then proceeded calmly, with Whitfield at first appearing to have no difficulty dovetailing in with arrangements organized by Admiral Abrial, the overall Allied commander in the town.

However, harmonious Anglo-French relations in Dunkirk were shattered when Whitfield began to ask awkward questions about how the French proposed to deal with a German attack. He wanted to know, for example, whether explosives were to be placed on the bridges spanning the canals around the town so that they could be quickly demolished if the Germans arrived.[2] Whitfield's sensible inquiry was rebuffed by a French general who was supposed to be dealing with the town's defence.[3] According to Whitfield's account:

His attitude to me was not even bordering on one of cordiality, and the atmosphere throughout the interview was far from pleasant. The General evidently resented such inquiries being made, and I was obliged to remind him that the Admiral himself had asked for the information. The General finally informed me that none of the bridges were ready for destruction, and that no recce had been made.

Whitfield's subsequent attempt to appeal over the general's head to Admiral Abrial met with a similarly unsympathetic response. Abrial was unavailable to see him so he had to make do with Admiral Leclerc, Abrial's chief of staff, whom he described as 'a very difficult man to deal with'. According to Whitfield, 'he [Leclerc] treated all motives with suspicion, and was unable to see the British point of view. When on this occasion I asked for the necessary permission to prepare the bridges for demolition, his only comment was: "So you wish to blow up the town, do you?"' He only agreed to Whitfield's suggestion after 'considerable argument'.

Whitfield's precautionary move was justified: even the French generals and admirals became jumpy when they were shown an order, retrieved during the night of 25–6 May from a shot-up German car on the west side of the canal near the destroyed bridge at Watten, revealing that Dunkirk was to be attacked sooner rather than later.[4] The fact that an attack was imminent became clearer still when the Luftwaffe stepped up the frequency of its bombing raids 'culminating', as Whitfield put it, 'with the almost complete destruction of town and docks on Monday 27th May . . . By nightfall, the main oil tanks and most of the city were on fire.'[5]

Anglo-French relations deteriorated still further after the French complained that British soldiers entering the town were misbehaving. 'These complaints were made with some venom,' wrote Whitfield, adding:

Misbehaviour is, I think, the wrong term to use. By far the majority of complaints were made against men who were wandering about trying to find their way to the docks or boats, and were often in the last stages of exhaustion, and sought cover in the Bastion. [He was referring to Bastion 32, the French Headquarters at Dunkirk]. I was finally obliged to point out with some asperity that . . . French soldiers were looting British lorries, stealing without question any car or motorbike they happened to see, and in fact taking away from the dumps intended for the British troops all food supplies.[6]

The arguing allies would have been better advised to concentrate on resolving a more intractable problem: how to set up adequate defences around Dunkirk's outer perimeter until enough organized British and French units arrived to defend it. (Dunkirk's outer perimeter is shown in Map 16 on pp. 532–3.)

By 28 May, the western side of the perimeter was guarded by the French 68 Division.[7] But the rest of the perimeter, though defended, was hardly equipped to withstand a determined German assault. This was particularly worrying in relation to the eastern sector, since this was where troops in Germany's Army Group B, freed up by the Belgian capitulation, were likely to approach first.

The defence of this critical eastern sector was initially entrusted to the

British Brigadier Clifton who had started the campaign as the commander of the light tanks and carriers in the 2nd Light Armoured Reconnaissance Brigade (it contained 15th/19th The King's Royal Hussars and the 5th Royal Inniskilling Dragoon Guards). He was instructed to defend the line of canals running round the edge of the Dunkirk perimeter from Wulpen via Nieuport to the sea.[8] But, as is mentioned in Clifton's report, it was the area surrounding Nieuport itself that represented his biggest headache. One of the principal problems was the failure to blow up all the bridges over the canals running from Nieuport to the sea. Although Clifton had four eighteen-pounder guns covering the main canal crossing-points leading from Nieuport into the perimeter, his artillery commander admitted he was worried about German tanks 'to stop which he had no weapons immediately available'. During 28 May the German tanks that did appear were only held up by a squadron of the 12th Lancers within the perimeter 'making ugly faces'.[9]

British infantry was also in short supply. When Clifton arrived inside the perimeter at 1 p.m. on 28 May, he only had 270 men at his disposal, most of them armed with mere rifles. It was 5 p.m. before the first reinforcements arrived in six lorries. But they could not by any stretch of the imagination be equated with the organized battalions that were needed. They included soldiers from all sorts of different units, and only two-thirds had rifles. Nevertheless, in the best tradition of British Army officers faced with superior opposition, Clifton resolved to make the most of his meagre resources and he explained to his new recruits that they had to hold the line for twenty-four hours until the organized brigades turned up. Although this pep talk appeared to put fire into the bellies of men who had arrived looking tired, hungry and bewildered, even Clifton had misgivings as the following extract from his report reveals:

About 0200 hrs [during the night 28–9 May] I was somewhat perturbed by a visit from a R.E. Officer . . . He stated that he was holding a portion of the Nieuport sector, that most of his men were old, specially trained pioneers and could hardly use a rifle . . . He was certain they would give way if they came under heavy fire. Could I relieve him? I told him that I had no troops with which to relieve him, and that it was imperative he should maintain his position.[10]

Clifton's cobbled-together defences could not keep the Germans out of Nieuport.[11] But all German attempts to form a bridgehead inside the perimeter to the west of Nieuport and in the area around Wulpen failed. They were also denied an opening on the land between these two centres, thanks to frequent patrols by Clifton's light tanks. They cannot be said to have failed for want of trying. Some Germans attempted to walk over the bridge at Wulpen dressed as nuns. Others concealed themselves between horses and cattle.[12] They also tried to cross the canals separating them from the perimeter in rubber boats. However, all of these relatively small-scale incursions were driven off, so that in spite of some difficult moments, the perimeter line in Clifton's sector was intact when it was handed over to the BEF's 4 Division during the night of 29–30 May. Over the next twenty-four hours, the rest of the perimeter line was taken over by French and British front-line troops, including many who, thanks to Lord Gort's insistence, had abandoned their positions on and around the River Lys during the night of 28–9 May. (See Chapter 25.)

The British admirals in London did not wait for the perimeter defences to be established before setting in motion their part of the evacuation plan. On 27 May the Admiralty contacted those men whose names had been placed on the small-vessels register to commandeer their boats.[13] Although cross-Channel ferries and armed boarding vessels had begun to collect soldiers from Dunkirk's quays during the night of 26–7 May, it had quickly become evident that they alone would not be able to rescue all the BEF troops; smaller boats were needed if men were also to be collected from the beaches.[14] One of the first small-boat owners contacted was Basil Smith, a London doctor, who had registered his motor yacht *Constant Nymph* with the Admiralty following an appeal broadcast by the BBC on 14 May.[15] His account describes how he first heard that his assistance was required:

00.10 27th May 1940. Admiralty rang up to confirm that my boat was ready for sea, and arranged for four hours' notice. Not being a subject of good habits, I did not have to get up to answer this call!

08.45. Admiralty rang again and asked me to go to the boat. Having already put a few things in a bag, I went to Isleworth [near Twickenham in West London] as soon as possible, and arrived there between 10.00 and 11.00.[16]

Smith, like many of the owners contacted, was instructed to take his boat to Sheerness, one of the principal assembly points for the small boats commandeered.[17] However, he was not allowed to motor up the Thames without a permit so he was forced to wait at the boatyard until the naval officer commandeering other boats appeared. 'When the officer arrived,' wrote Smith, 'he did not seem to think there was any tremendous hurry.' Consequently, even though the boats were desperately needed off Dunkirk, there was a delay in Isleworth until the permits were issued later that afternoon. Smith and his mate, who had in the meantime joined him on *Constant Nymph*, were unable to reach Sheerness that night, and it was breakfast time on 28 May before they arrived there. 'We were informed that we could sign on for one month,' wrote Smith, 'but [we] did not then know for what purpose we were required, although I [had] been told by the pleasant-voiced man who spoke to me from the Admiralty that it was dangerous.'

There were further delays at Sheerness while Smith tried to find someone who would permit him to sign on. Eventually he approached the dockyard commodore, who was supervising the provision of fuel and food for the small-boat crews. This had the desired effect, and within an hour, as Smith later reported: 'I was signed on, and . . . was making my way out of the basin with a crew of two young ratings, a full tank and [a] deck cargo of petrol . . . and enough provisions to last my little gang for about a week, including a large lump of raw beef and two small sacks of potatoes.'

Unfortunately, the delays he had encountered had wasted valuable time. It was now almost two days since he had first been contacted. This had a knock-on effect, since, leaving Sheerness as he did at 6 p.m. on 28 May, he was not able to reach Ramsgate, the next staging-post in the journey, before dark, and he decided to stop for the night on the way.[18] It was a decision he must have regretted. Sleeping on a twenty-four-foot boat at sea can be uncomfortable at the best of times, and Smith has described how his and his crew's sleep was frequently interrupted by their need to pop up to the deck to be sick.

It was lunchtime on 29 May – the third day since he had been contacted – when they arrived at Ramsgate. There, Smith calculated it would take some twenty-four hours for him to complete the round trip to Dunkirk following the so-called 'Route Y', indicated on Map 19 on p. 536, which amounted to approximately 175 sea miles. Route Y had to be taken at this time because German guns at Calais and Gravelines could fire at boats using the more direct 'Route Z', which constituted an eighty-mile round trip. On hearing Smith's travel-time estimate, the naval commander liaising with the small boats at Ramsgate advised him to get a good night's sleep that night. But he was to get up at the crack of dawn the next day to meet up with a cargo boat outside Ramsgate harbour: he would then be towed to Dunkirk. Smith made the rendez-vous, but more delays occurred before they set off. Thus it was only at 3.30 p.m. on 30 May – the fourth day since he was contacted – that Smith and his crew finally began their journey to France, arriving at Dunkirk at dusk.

Meanwhile, back at the Admiralty in London, on 27 May an emer-gency meeting had been convened to work out how more small boats could be made available, and how this could be achieved quickly. The additional boats were required because many of the craft offered after the BBC appeal had been unsuitable.[19] It was during this meeting that Vice-Admiral Sir Lionel Preston, director of the Small Vessels Pool, decided that naval officers should be sent that day to boatyards between Teddington (near Kingston-upon-Thames), Brightlingsea (near Col-chester, Essex), and Burham (near Maidstone, Kent) with authority to commandeer small boats on the spot. They were to look for 'small handy motor cruisers, fast if possible . . . with not more than 3 foot 6 inches draught for beaching purposes'. Crews prepared to take their vessels to Sheerness could be paid 'reasonable expenses' and would then be offered the opportunity to serve with them.

By the end of the day, forty-three small boats had been commandeered using this new fast-track procedure. They were just some of the 588 small vessels that were eventually selected by the Admiralty during the evacuation.[20] Lieutenant Dann, a naval officer who went with the first convoy of small boats to Dunkirk, has described what he witnessed when they were first assembled at Sheerness:

The first assembly was typical of the whole of this miniature armada. A dozen or so motor yachts from 20 to 50 feet in length, nicely equipped and smartly maintained by proud individual owners, a cluster of cheap 'conversion' jobs' mainly the work of amateur craftsmen, who had set to work in their spare time to convert a ship's lifeboat or any old half discarded hull into a cabin cruiser of sorts . . . [and] half a dozen Thames river launches resembling nothing so much as the upper decks of elongated motor buses with their rows of slatted seats, but given a tang of the waterside by rows of painted lifebuoys slung around the upper sails. The very names of these latter craft are redolent of the quiet of Richmond, Teddington and Hampton Court: *Skylark*, *Elizabeth* and *Queen Boadicea*. A strange flotilla indeed to be taking an active part in what has been described as the greatest naval epic in history.[21]

One of the boats involved in that first assembly was the motor launch *Advance*, owned by a Colin Dick, a man whose political leanings might have disqualified him for the task of rescuing British soldiers from Hitler's army: unbeknown to those summoning him, both he and at least one of his companions on *Advance* were, or had been, members of Oswald Mosley's Blackshirts, and the British Union of Fascists and National Socialists had owned the launch before selling it on to Dick.[22]

But Dick's support for Fascism did not prevent him fighting for Britain against Germany, and his report describes what he did when, during the afternoon of 27 May, he was telephoned by the Admiralty and given to understand that his launch might be needed: 'We [that is Dick and two boating friends, one of whom was Eric Hamilton-Piercy, a prominent Blackshirt] were to go at once to Teddington to remove any private gear remaining on board.'[23] There, they volunteered to take the boat to Sheerness. They were told to depart the next morning, which they did, arriving in Sheerness at lunchtime on 28 May. 'At the time, we had no idea what the boats were wanted for,' wrote Dick. But after making inquiries, they were referred to HMS *Wildfire* in Sheerness where they signed on.

Dick's report does not disclose whether he told the naval officers on HMS *Wildfire* that he had only just left a nursing-home where he had been confined with 'internal trouble'. Nor does it mention whether the Navy were ever informed that one of his companions had been examined recently by a medical board and declared unfit for any kind of national service. It does reveal, however, that Hamilton-Piercy, his second companion, a married man with four children, had no chance to tell his family where he was going before he set off. It was lucky Hamilton-Piercy did not drop out because, as Dick admitted, 'Piercy . . . the only physically fit member of the party, managed to relieve his rather invalid shipmates of a great deal of exertion.'

That night Dick and his crew chugged from Sheerness to Dover.

Dick's account describes how after arriving there during the early hours of 29 May, 'an officer came down the jetty, and at last told us what we were wanted to do, that it would be dangerous, but was very important, and that we should have ample support from the RAF.' Then, after turning down their last opportunity to go ashore, they set out for Dunkirk that same morning 'in company with other boats'.

Dick and his companions were not required to do anything especially dramatic at Dunkirk. But the mere fact that these civilians, like the other civilian small-boat owners, stuck to their task so persistently and phlegmatically in the face of considerable discomfort and danger deserves the highest commendation. *Advance* and the other small boats accompanying Dick and his crew reached the area off Dunkirk at around midday on 29 May. Theirs was the first convoy of small boats to arrive. It was not long before they saw what they were up against. As they approached Dunkirk, they realized that what they had taken for a cloud bank was in fact the smoke given off by the burning town.

No sooner had they arrived off the beaches than they were machine-gunned by two German planes, which flew so low overhead that one is believed to have torn away *Advance*'s signal mast. Dick and his companions, who had never before been exposed to gunfire, could have been forgiven if they had been overwhelmed by what they must have regarded at the time as a very lucky escape. But it merely strengthened their resolve. Lieutenant Dann, who was leading the convoy, has described how, after this first murderous machine-gun attack from the air, 'three cheerful bearded grinning faces appeared above the [*Advance*'s] fore cabin roof, and three pairs of hands were clasped and shaken overhead as a signal that all was well. Only the Jolly Roger was lacking to complete the picture.'[24]

Once off the beaches, they were instructed to operate a kind of relay service. *Advance* was to pull a whaler as near to the beach as Dick dared, and then he was to stay put while the others rowed the whaler closer to the beach. The plan was that the whaler would be filled with soldiers and rowed back to *Advance*, which would then tow it out to a destroyer waiting further out to sea. But this procedure, which sounded so simple in theory, was not easy to apply in practice. On the first trip, the whaler capsized near the beach, and the two oarsmen had to be helped to bale out the water before the rescuing of soldiers could commence. During the third trip, the whaler, which was full of soldiers, hit an underwater obstacle, and sank beneath them. Fortunately Dick in *Advance* and another vessel were able to rescue all of the soldiers as well as Dick's companions. The rescue operation was able to continue using the same procedure as before because on their way back to this beach Dick and his crew came across an abandoned whaler and seized it.

During the next trip, however, disaster struck while *Advance* was alongside a destroyer. German aircraft appeared in the skies above them while soldiers were clambering up the nets lowered over the destroyer's side. On seeing the planes, the destroyer lurched forward without warning the *Advance* crew to take evasive action and, as Dick reported, 'Three or four men were seen to fall overboard, some being crushed between the destroyer's side and *Advance*'s port quarter.' Dick and his companions only managed to rescue one of these men, who was lucky to escape with his life and what appeared to be a broken thigh. The others must have died either before or after they sank beneath the waves.

Undaunted, Dick and his companions just carried on, turning the tiller and going in to the beaches yet again. As they towed the next whalerful of soldiers out to the destroyer, a bomb was dropped near *Advance* throwing Dick off his feet, and sinking the whaler. This time all of the men were rescued, and were duly placed on larger ships. But *Advance*'s hull was left leaking, and a large hole was visible above the water line.

Dick and his crew nevertheless continued with their fetching and carrying duties but, from that moment on, stopped operating their own whaler, preferring to pick up men from any vessel they found floating near the beach, which included other ships' whalers, pontoons and even canoes. It was only later that evening, when they realized their petrol supply was running low, that they finally decided they could do no more and returned to Ramsgate, pleased no doubt to have done their bit, and grateful to have lived to tell their tale.

29: Beached

There are many soldiers who have described what they witnessed as they entered the Dunkirk perimeter. An account by Gunner Lieutenant Elliman is as good as any to set the scene for 29 May, the day when the Germans made their first major attempt to disrupt the evacuation. On 28 May he thought he had struck lucky when, while inland at Poperinghe, he had tossed a coin with a brother officer for the privilege of taking an advance party to the coast and won.[1] Only later did he discover that spending extra time on the Dunkirk beaches could hardly be considered a prize.

In his account, he has described his feelings as he prepared to make a swift getaway from Poperinghe: 'I collected about 40 men . . . and squeezed them into a couple of 3 tonners, then bade farewell to Dick Strahan and the TSM [Troop Sergeant-Major], wondering if I should ever see them again. The chances of their being captured seemed fairly large, as we realized by then that the BEF was surrounded.'

Elliman was driven away in a Humber Snipe eight-hundredweight truck, but at times, as the truck and lorries proceeded along the road towards Dunkirk, there were so many troops in their way, and their progress was so slow, that they would have travelled just as quickly if they had walked. They could, however, be grateful for one aspect of their journey. During at least part of the day they crawled along in what Elliman described as driving rain and a thunderstorm: 'I repeatedly thanked God for the bad weather,' he wrote. If the weather had been good, they would have made easy targets for the Luftwaffe.

The extent of Elliman's and his comrades' good fortune only became clear later. A note in the German 6th Army's war diary records that at 3.40 p.m. (French time) the next day, German troops approaching Poperinghe from two directions, the south-east and south-west, finally made contact, encircling all Allied soldiers who were not already west of the meeting point. Most of those encircled were captured, including General Prioux and many of his men in IV and V Corps who had not been able to escape from Lille.[2] But as the war diary confirmed, the encircling movement had been completed too late as far as the majority of the British Army was concerned. Most British soldiers, and certain French units that had made it back to the Lys and were consequently free to move westwards, had, like Elliman and his men, already moved out of the Germans' reach, after passing through Poperinghe.[3]

There was another reason why the British and French soldiers had an easier time withdrawing to the coast than might have been the case had the full might of the German Army been unleashed against them. On 28–9 May Guderian, von Kleist and von Kluge decided that it would be wrong to use their panzers against the fleeing Allies, given the extra losses this would entail. The Army Group B infantry was much better suited to fighting in the marshy ground between Poperinghe and Dunkirk, and saving the tanks would enable the panzer divisions to be strengthened before the next phase of the campaign, which was to be against the French south of the Somme.[4] This decision, which appears to have been taken by the generals without any prompting from Hitler, has been overshadowed by the more famous halt order issued on 24 May. But it appears to have played an equally important part in enabling the evacuation to go ahead.

Shortly before Elliman's group reached the village of Warhem, three-quarters of a mile south of the Canal de la Basse Colme, which ringed the southern boundary of the Dunkirk perimeter, they were stopped by military police. They were then directed to abandon their transport in a field that was already full of abandoned vehicles. Some of the cars and lorries were on fire or had already been burned out, but others had simply been left in perfect working order with all their supplies and guns inside. This enabled Elliman and his men to equip themselves with rifles and food. After the other ranks had fallen in, Elliman observed that 'away from their guns they looked lost and dismayed'. He was also upset at the prospect of leaving his equipment behind, and when he looked one last time at what he referred to as 'my beautiful Humber', with all his possessions in the back, he could not bear to set it alight in case he might get the chance to come back for it. It was, as he wrote in his report, 'a sad parting'.

He and his men spent the night near Warhem, and at about 10 a.m. on 29 May, spurred on by a French officer's report that Germans were already approaching Bergues, just over two miles to the east, they began their final march towards the Dunkirk beaches. The fact that the path they took was the only feature in the vicinity above the flooded countryside, and that it was being used by a long column of BEF soldiers in addition to his own, heightened his sense that they were dangerously unprotected and liable to be scythed down if the Luftwaffe made an appearance. However, after crossing a bridge that led into the outer perimeter, they eventually came to a bridge spanning yet another canal, possibly the Canal des Chats, which, later on, would mark the line of the inner perimeter. (The two perimeters are marked in Map 16, on pp. 532–3.) There, as Elliman recorded, he was faced with the first of many dilemmas:

Suddenly I heard a swish! and an explosion. A cloud of smoke and earth was pitched into the air just to the left of the bridge . . . Crum[b]s! I thought, they can't be very far behind . . . A couple of officers climbed down, and swam across the canal. But . . . I decided to go on to within 50 yards of the bridge, and then sprint across to the other side . . . So I dumped my haversack and . . . we made our dash, and got well into the fields beyond the canal before pausing for breath. Whoof! We'd made it. As I learned later, the enemy scored a direct hit on the bridge five minutes after we crossed it, and just after my last gunner had got across.

But if Elliman and his men thought they were home and dry, they were mistaken. Their ordeal, shared by many British soldiers, was only just beginning. Elliman's account describes the scene on the beach between Dunkirk's eastern jetty, generally referred to as 'the mole', and Malo-les-Bains, when they arrived there during the early afternoon.[5]

The tide was fairly low. A steamer lay on her side at the water's edge. The sandy beach was about 100 yards wide. Down the centre stood the line of men, three abreast. The smoke . . . from the burning oil tanks drifted eastwards over the town. A few officers walked up and down. All was quiet.

And then it started! A formation of high fliers came up from the west, and dropped stick after stick of bombs . . . This first attack . . . was most unnerving. You felt so completely exposed on the beach . . . For a time some of us huddled under the hull of the wrecked steamer, but as nothing happened for some time, I called in all my men, and formed them up in the queue again for fear we should lose our place.

As Elliman's account bears witness, this scene was repeated again and again, with the men scattering each time planes passed overhead, then rushing back to form up at the end of each attack. Given that Elliman and his men planned to end up on one of the destroyers they could see some distance from the coast, it was perhaps not surprising that they should find the attacks on these warships more disturbing than anything. 'The destroyers pumped shells into the air,' he wrote, 'and . . . disappeared behind 80 foot high walls of spray thrown up . . . [by] near misses . . . While these attacks were in progress, the Stukas were diving, zooming, screeching and wheeling over our heads like a flock of huge infernal seagulls.'

During most of the afternoon, the planes failed to hit any of the men on the beach: they were concentrating on the ships. But during the early evening a bomber dropped its load on to the beach where Elliman and his men were lying: 'I heard the Stuka coming down in a vertical dive right on top of me,' Elliman reported.

I was by now dulled by hours . . . of explosions . . . so that the imminence of death aroused no great feeling of fear . . . Either the bomb would land on me, or it wouldn't . . . I thought . . . of Margaret in those few seconds of suspense, and she brought me a sort of peace of the spirit. The next moment: Crash! Darkness! And then a vision of falling sand in front of me . . . I realized I had been missed, and . . . I could hear the plane climbing away over Dunkirk. The attack was over.

Elliman had been spared, but some of his men were less fortunate: his medical orderly's right cheek had been blown away. Two other men had been killed. The telephonist was so shocked by the injuries he saw that, as Elliman put it, he went 'wackers' and was carried away laughing uncontrollably.

After the bombing ended, a different kind of torture ensued. By this time Elliman and his men had abandoned their original plan to get on to a boat off the beach at Malo-les-Bains, and had joined another queue, which led up to the mole. 'Thousands of men stretched away behind us,' wrote Elliman. 'But we failed to move forward . . . Only the wounded were got away that night . . . As the hours went by, the spirits of all must have been sinking . . . Mine certainly were. Sleep was impossible. It was just waiting, waiting, waiting.'

The shortage of destroyers at the mole during the night of 29–30 May was down to a mistake.[6] That afternoon German bombs had hit many of the ships beside the mole, and a junior naval officer was so shaken by what he had seen that he panicked and drove to La Panne to telephone Vice-Admiral Ramsay's staff in Dover. The warning he gave was unambiguous: the mole was unusable. It was this that prompted Ramsay to order that no ship should dock at the mole that night.[7] The true situation was only discovered the following morning.

The ferocity of the attacks on the ships off Dunkirk explains why some naval officers' nerves were at breaking point: 29 May was a nightmare for the Royal and Merchant Navies, as ship after ship was sunk or put out of action. The first of the many sinkings that day took place in the early hours of the morning near Kwinte Whistle Buoy, which marked the easternmost point on Route Y. (The buoy is marked in Map 19 on p. 536, as are Route Y and the other routes to Dunkirk.) Lieutenant-Commander Rodolph Haig, in charge of the minesweeper HMS *Lydd*, one of four ships most involved in the tragic events near the buoy, reported how he first became aware that something was amiss in the following terms:

When passing the Kwinte Buoy, flares were sighted, and shouting heard close at hand. The light from an Aldis lamp revealed the bow and stern portions of [the destroyer] HMS *Wakeful* appearing above water with men clinging to them.[8] I immediately lowered a whaler, and two carley floats. Shortly after this, HMS *Gossamer*, which was close by, ordered us to put my light out and drop a depth charge. I could not at once comply with the latter order as I was too close to the wreck, and would have killed the men in the water . . . I kept the ship moving while the whaler and carley floats were picking up survivors, and had just got 20 alongside when HMS *Grafton* appeared.[9] I asked her if she would pick up the rest, and she asked us to circle round her in case of enemy submarines. It was then discovered from one of the survivors that *Wakeful* had been torpedoed by an MTB [motor torpedo boat].[10]

Grafton's Commander Cecil Robinson had been right to be concerned about U-boats since, unbeknown to him, one was stalking his ship from just over a mile away at that very moment. It was *U-62*.[11] No testimony has been found that describes the manoeuvring that was being plotted inside the German vessels in the area, as *Lydd*'s and *Grafton*'s commanders signalled to each other. All that is known is what is in *U-62*'s and the British ships' war diaries. *Grafton*'s Lieutenant Hugh McRea, writing his ship's report in place of Commander Robinson who was killed during the action, mentioned that after *Grafton*'s boats had been in the water for about ten minutes, Robinson saw a 'small darkened vessel on the port quarter at about three cables [600 yards]', which *Grafton*'s commander took to be a British drifter. Robinson even had a signal sent to her asking her commander to pick up survivors. The identity and nationality of this ship have never been established. It is possible that it was *U-62*. If so, and if her commander, Oberleutnant Hans-Bernhard Michalowski, had read Robinson's message, he might have had qualms about shooting at a warship engaged in a rescue operation. However, there is evidence that it was another German ship: Michalowski's war diary suggests that the U-boat was further away than the ship that had been spotted and the war diaries of the British ships in the area state they were on *Grafton*'s starboard side. It was probably a German motor torpedo boat. Whether or not Michalowski did read Robinson's signal, he nevertheless gave the order for two torpedoes to be fired, one of which hit *Grafton* two minutes ten seconds later, according to the U-boat's war diary. After the torpedo had hit its target, the watching submariners noted with satisfaction that there was an explosion at the stern of the British warship. But they did not hang around to shoot up the second ship they had seen. Fearing that another British vessel proceeding towards *U-62* might be a destroyer preparing to attack, Michalowski gave the order to dive and, in the words he jotted down in his war diary, the U-boat 'disappeared'.[12]

Unbeknown to Michalowski, his U-boat's torpedo was not the only missile that had struck *Grafton*. Seconds afterwards, *Grafton*'s Lieutenant McRea heard another explosion. A shell or grenade fired by another ship, possibly the 'darkened' vessel' seen by Robinson, had hit *Grafton*'s bridge, killing Robinson, another officer and two other seamen. McRea's report also describes the damage caused by *U-62*'s torpedo. *Grafton*'s stern aft of the after-magazine bulkhead had been blown off.

Lydd's Commander Haig first realized that *Grafton* was in trouble when he heard an explosion at her stern: 'I continued my circle to port,' he reported, and sighting [what looked like] an MTB about 50 yards away on the starboard beam, Sub-Lieutenant . . . Britton, who was on the bridge, opened fire with the starboard pair of Lewis guns, and raked her up the stern, bullets being seen to hit her wheelhouse and superstructure in a cloud of sparks. It was thought she was disabled. I then closed *Grafton* with the idea of taking off survivors . . . but as she appeared to be all right, I circled round to starboard to finish off the 'MTB'. A dark object was sighted ahead in the direction in which the 'MTB' was last seen, and fire was opened with Lewis guns and 4 inch. *Grafton* also opened fire . . . The supposed MTB was then rammed, and split in half. As she was hit, figures sprang at the ship, and it was thought that an attempt was being made to board . . . Fire was therefore opened with rifles.[13]

But as *Lydd*'s commander later discovered, the dark object he had taken for an MTB was in fact *Comfort*, a British drifter, and the boarders, far from being Germans trying to kill his crew, were British sailors trying to save their own lives. Few succeeded. One of the survivors was *Wakeful*'s Lieutenant-Commander Ralph Fisher, who had been rescued by *Comfort* shortly before the ramming, and it is thanks to his testimony that it is possible to piece together the evidence explaining how *Comfort*'s tragic loss occurred.

From what should have been the relative security of *Comfort*'s bridge, Fisher had spotted some of his men still clinging to *Wakeful*'s stern, which, like the bow, was poking out from under the water. Courageously, but as it turned out ill-advisedly, he directed *Comfort*'s commander to go alongside to take them off. Their rescue mission was only abandoned when, on approaching the wreck, they saw that the stern had moved and all the survivors were in the sea. Arguably, *Comfort* at that point should have made way immediately to get out of the danger zone. Instead, Fisher found time to warn *Grafton*'s commander that she might find herself on the receiving end of a torpedo, if she hung around much longer. They were the last words he spoke as a passenger on *Comfort*. No sooner had he finished speaking than *Grafton* was hit by one of the two torpedoes fired by *U-62*. The resulting explosion blasted *Comfort* out of the water, and as she was dumped back into the sea, her deck was swamped, and Fisher was swept overboard once again.

There, he watched the next episode in the drama unfold: the two British ships fired at *Comfort*, and she was rammed. Fisher remembered shouting, in a desperate attempt to limit the bloodshed, 'For God's sake, stop! We're all English!' but his protests were drowned by the noise of the guns. According to Fisher, all of *Comfort*'s crew and all of the survivors she had rescued from *Wakeful* were killed during the mêlée apart from himself, two men who jumped aboard *Lydd*, and two other crew members, later discovered in the sea in *Comfort*'s skiff.[14] Fortunately most of *Grafton*'s crew and the troops on board were saved: they were transferred on to another ship.[15] But that did not alter the fact that a terrible disaster had occurred.

The prospect that Operation Dynamo might be brought to a premature halt by German submarines and motor torpedo boats was, however, averted during the afternoon of 29 May by a simple remedy: the opening up of the new Route X (see Map 19 on p. 536), which passed to the south-west of where *U-62* and the German vessels had been patrolling.[16] But just as one obstacle was overcome, another reared its head: the Luftwaffe. Hitler had told the Luftwaffe's Commander-in-Chief Hermann Göring to finish off the BEF and, during 29 May, the Luftwaffe went a long way towards achieving that objective: in the course of that day no less than ten destroyers and eight personnel ships and paddle-steamers were either sunk or put out of action in addition to an assortment of smaller craft, many of them thanks to the Luftwaffe's efforts.[17] Small wonder, then, that the admirals in London and Dover, upset by the losses, swiftly withdrew the seven remaining fleet destroyers, which were larger and more modern than the fifteen allowed to carry on.[18] Vice-Admiral Ramsay was only permitted to deploy them again during the following afternoon when it became clear that without them the evacuation could not be completed quickly enough.[19]

The Luftwaffe's most impressive series of attacks targeted ten British ships, which, during the afternoon of 29 May, were tied up alongside Dunkirk's mole. Between 3.30 p.m. and 6 p.m., three air raids put seven of these ships out of action. The German scalps included the destroyer HMS *Grenade*, whose wreck might have blocked the harbour entrance had the ship not been towed clear shortly before she was sunk by an explosion. The consequences of some of these attacks were not as spectacular as that on HMS *Wakeful*, since many of the ships, although disabled, did not sink. But the scene conjured up by the words 'put out of action', which appears in so many of the ships' reports, does not begin to describe the damage and carnage that was caused.

One of the ships tied up around the mole that afternoon was the destroyer HMS *Jaguar*.[20] It was her second trip to Dunkirk during Operation Dynamo. The previous day, her commander, Lieutenant-Commander John Hine, had attempted to collect soldiers from beaches to the east of Dunkirk using whalers and skiffs to do the ferrying between the shallows and his destroyer.[21] *Jaguar*'s Stoker Arnold Saunders never forgot what he saw as the ship approached Bray-Dunes beach on 28 May: 'My first impression of the coast was [that I was looking at] a beautiful stretch of sand, with what looked like shrubs on the beach, until they all started moving into lines. It was [only] then that we realized what our job was to be. Up until then we were not told anything.'[22]

It was a scene observed by countless sailors as they approached the beaches for the first time. But on 29 May, partly because the rough sea made it difficult to use the beaches, *Jaguar* and other large ships were ordered to congregate at the mole in the hope that frequent RAF patrols would head off any strong attacks.[23] Unfortunately for the Royal Navy, large formations of German planes arrived over Dunkirk on three occasions during the afternoon when there were no Hurricanes or Spitfires patrolling, with disastrous results for the British.

Jaguar had taken on board around a thousand soldiers at the mole, and was steaming away from the harbour when she was bombed at around 4 p.m. during the second of the three successful Luftwaffe attacks.[24] No bomb actually hit the ship, but one of her officers reported seeing one land in the sea just a couple of yards away. It then exploded, following which there was a terrifying roar, as steam was let off from the ship's fractured steampipes. Then the ship's engines stopped and there was what the officer described as 'a deathly hush'.[25] Another destroyer was on hand to take off her troops and tow *Jaguar* away, but not before those on board had seen the terrible injuries inflicted. While searching for a line near the ship's bow, Stoker Saunders saw one soldier whose leg had been blown off, his only hope of survival being the assistance provided by his comrade, who was attempting to stem the bleeding with a tourniquet. Another image remembered by many survivors was a man who had had half of his head blown off. 'His brains were literally hanging out,' Saunders remembered.

But it was the burned men on some of the other bombed ships who appear to have suffered most. One of the worst cases was Bob Bloom, a nineteen-year-old sickbay attendant on HMS *Grenade*, which had been tied up to the mole alongside *Jaguar* while the latter was taking soldiers on board. At around 6 p.m., *Grenade* was hit by a bomb dropped by a plane flying with the third wave of bombers, and Bloom has described how that affected him:[26]

I was coming down a ladder leading from the sickbay to the mess deck when a bomb went down the ship's forward funnel and exploded. I was thrown up in the air and hit the deckhead. Then I fell back into the blast given off by the bomb. As it hit me, I put my hands up to my face to protect it. It felt as if I had been hit six times on the face with a whip. I was in such pain that I prayed to God to take me. But someone picked me up, and pushed me outside, and I ended up on the upper deck.

There I saw one of the stokers I knew who was just sitting there with his seaman's cap on and everything. I said something to him, but then I noticed his ribs were sticking out through his chest. He was dead. I looked at my hands. The skin was hanging off both of them as if I was trying to pull gloves off. My face was stinging like mad. My lips were swelling up all the time. I did not realize this at the time, but my nose had all but disappeared. Only the septum was left. Then I heard someone shout 'Abandon ship!'

Bloom somehow jumped over the side into the water, and climbed on to the mole. From there he staggered on to *Crested Eagle*, a paddle-steamer moored to the other side of the mole. Shortly afterwards, having also taken on board wounded men from *Fenella*, another personnel vessel beside the mole that had been bombed, *Crested Eagle* got under way, only to be hit by four bombs dropped during yet another air raid.[27] Bloom, who had been lying prostrate on a bunk in the ship's restaurant, which had been transformed into a sickbay, knew he was in trouble again when the lights went out. Before he could be burned again, by the fires the bombing had ignited, he jumped into the sea for the second time that day. *Crested Eagle* was eventually beached near Bray-Dunes where she became a landmark for small ships striving to find the beach. In the meantime those in the water swam for their lives.[28]

'By this time, my face was so swollen that I could hardly see,' Bloom remembered. 'But my life was saved by two soldiers who were hanging on to what looked like a barn door with a ring fixed to it. They hung on to it and kicked with their legs, while I sat on it holding the ring.' Hours later they were rescued by another ship which took him to Ramsgate. Not that he knew much about the journey. Mercifully, while he was lying in the wardroom, somebody slipped a morphine capsule under his tongue whereupon he lost consciousness.

He was already in England when he woke up. He had been laid out with other wounded men in a marquee. There he was reassured by a nurse who had him lifted on to a stretcher so that he could be taken to hospital. 'You'll be safe soon,' she told him, as he was moved. Bloom's last words to her before he lost consciousness again were 'Will you please tell my parents I'm OK.'[29]

A completely different atmosphere prevailed among the crew from the U-boat *U-62* when their submarine subsequently docked at Helgoland on the way back to Wilhelmshaven. According to crew member Kurt Wendler, the men attended a wild celebration at a restaurant called Aunt Anna. Even the commander, Michalowski, who normally did not socialize with his men, was so pleased at having sunk an Allied warship that he joined in the party. He bet one of the under-officers that he could do a moving handstand down the eight-metre table at which they were eating, and won.

Their boisterous behaviour continued after dinner. On the way back to their billets, Michalowski had to rescue his paralytically drunk engineer who had broken into a bakery and covered himself with flour. However, before they left the restaurant, the proprietress had reminded them that they would not win the war by sinking just one ship. 'If you sink any more, come back,' she told them, 'and then everything's on the house.'[30]

30: Entente Cordiale

Dunkirk perimeter and bastion, 29–31 May 1940
(See Map 16. Also Maps 1 and 10)

May 29 was not only a testing time for the Navy. It was also to be a critical day for the BEF soldiers holding the Dunkirk perimeter. If the Germans had broken through the British defences that day, and had gone on to capture the town, the number of troops evacuated would barely have exceeded the pessimistic forecast that the Admiralty mentioned to Vice-Admiral Ramsay at the beginning of Operation Dynamo (see Chapter 19). Approximately 58,000 men were evacuated prior to dawn on 29 May. (Evacuation figures are explained in this chapter's note 1 and Appendix B on pp. 540–41.)[1]

The security of the perimeter depended on whether the BEF could prepare its defences before the Germans arrived in force. On 29 May, this looked particularly doubtful around the market town of Furnes, one of the linchpins of the British sector. A report by one Grenadier Guardsman, whose battalion was to form part of the Furnes garrison, describes the ominous sight he saw that day as he and his unit approached the town: 'About a mile away and out of range as far as we were concerned, a party of Germans could be seen marching and wheeling bicycles at about the same speed as our own column. Friend and foe arrived in Furnes at about the same time. We took up positions on one side of the canal, and most of the Germans [on] the other.'[2]

The dangers awaiting the Guards at Furnes as they moved into the town became all too apparent during the late afternoon.[3] As Lieutenant-Colonel Jack Lloyd, the 2nd Grenadier Guards' commanding officer, prepared to pace out the battalion's positions along the canal bank accompanied by two of his officers, they were warned by a passing sapper: 'Don't go any further. There are snipers.'[4] But they carried on regardless. All of a sudden, three shots rang out, and all three officers fell. The Grenadier Guards' war diary records what happened next:

Captain Harrison reported back to Major Rupert Colvin that the enemy had broken through, and [had] already reached the line of the canal. Also that the recce party under the Comdg. Offr. [had] . . . been surprised, and it was feared that the Comdg Offr., Major Pakenham and Captain Jeffreys had been killed. Major Colvin immediately proceeded forward in a carrier, and found that these three officers had been pulled into the cover of a house by 2/Lt [Jack] Jones. Mr Jones had displayed great gallantry and complete disregard to personal risk, standing [his ground] under heavy rifle and MG fire while he carried the Comdg. Offr. who was dead, and Major Pakenham and Captain Jeffreys into the house. The front of the house was under such heavy fire that it was quite impossible for stretcher bearers to approach it. 2/Lt Hennessy arranged with the French tanks who were then present in the town to go up to the front of the building and endeavour to extract the wounded. Even this was impossible as A/Tk weapons were immediately brought to bear. Meanwhile 2/Lt Jones assisted by [two other officers] . . . made an entrance through the back of the house and extricated them.[5]

The war diary goes on to disclose the opposition encountered as the front-line companies moved into position on the east side of the town:

The centre and left Coys. had considerable difficulty in occupying their pos-itions being under fire from both 5th column on the near bank of the canal and German snipers and LMG on the far bank. The position was finally occupied by about 2130. [Prior to that,] Bn. HQ had been established in a cellar in the centre of the town. The cellar had been occupied by a 5th columnist who was discovered, and executed.[6]

As at Nieuport, the Germans had missed a golden opportunity to break through and finish off the BEF before the perimeter was properly defended, but as the Grenadier Guards' war diarist observed:

The . . . loss of life . . . might have been avoided if the British troops holding the town on the previous day had not been drunk when the Bn. entered it, as were a great proportion of the French soldiers.

[During] the evening . . . Lt-Col. Lloyd and Capt. Jeffreys were buried in the Close of Furnes Cathedral.[7]

But sad as the losses suffered by 3 Division's Grenadier Guards were, they were nothing compared with the casualties inflicted on the 4th Royal Berkshire Regiment, another 3 Division unit, even before they arrived in Furnes. According to an account by the Berkshires' Captain Francis Waldron, by the time he made it back to Furnes during the early hours of 30 May, the battalion was in what he calls a 'truly parlous state'.[8] The Berkshires had been all but decimated in their last rearguard action at Elverdinghe to the west of the Ypres Canal.[9] Over four hundred men had been killed, wounded or were missing after that battle and they had also lost their fearsome commanding officer, Lieutenant-Colonel Geoffrey Bull, a stiff archetypical Grenadier Guardsman referred to as 'the Bull' by everyone who had been licked into shape by him. He had been mortally wounded during the retreat to Furnes. Only ten of the thirty officers who had started the campaign were still with the battalion on 30 May. The casualties might have included Douglas Jardine, England's former cricket captain, had he not returned to England shortly before the fighting started.[10]

The surviving officers had only eighty other ranks to command when they first arrived at Furnes, thirty of whom were wounded. Nevertheless, depleted as they were, fifty men were still able to fire their rifles, and that same night they were ordered to man the section of canal running from Furnes to Nieuport just to the north-east of the 2nd Grenadiers. (The positions held by BEF units in the Furnes to Nieuport sector are shown in Map 16 on pp. 532–3.)[11]

Initially, Waldron, the twenty-seven-year-old adjutant, remained at the battalion's headquarters, in a cottage about a quarter of a mile north of the canal line, to carry out his organizational duties. But in his account he has described how, by the end of the day, even he had to help out at the front:

As evening drew in, [Major] Roper [the acting commanding officer] came back and said that things were really serious in the front line. [2nd Lieutenant] Partridge and Captain Ryland were the only two officers up there. They were both almost falling asleep on their feet. The sappers to our left had broken back, and our own men, after the heavy enemy mortar fire, had also broken back. This meant that we had nobody on the canal bank. If the enemy should choose to attack, there was nothing to stop him.[12]

Waldron's account goes on to explain what steps he took after being sent forward, his garrison eventually being reinforced with thirty to forty extra men who turned up at his headquarters:

When we got to the edge of the canal, we crawled on all fours to look over. Partridge, always a bloodthirsty fellow, as indicated by his flaming red hair, suggested it would be a good idea to throw a few hand grenades over to the other side, as there was no doubt the enemy was there. This, in my view, was a quite absurd suggestion, for we still had to get our men into position, and to draw their fire on us was asking for trouble.[13]

As the men were coaxed into their foxholes behind the canal bank, Waldron heard firing to their right. He found out later that the Germans had crossed the canal in front of their right-hand neighbours, the 1st Coldstream Guards, another 3 Division unit that had taken over part of the Berkshires' area. During the ensuing firefight the Germans shot two of the Guards' officers. It was to be the first of a series of battles fought by the Coldstream Guards that night, in the course of which they lost five officers and around forty men.[14] 'I was thankful that it was dark,' Waldron explained, 'for if the Hun had seen the precarious situation we were in for the next few hours, nothing would have stopped him getting more men across.'

At this juncture, Waldron's judgement, like Partridge's, appears to have been impaired by exhaustion, and his account reveals the suicidal action he now proposed. 'I still remember the message I sent to my commanding officer: "Suggest immediate counter-attack with our men across Coldstream front. The Germans have two machine-guns already over the canal."' Fortunately the new acting commanding officer was more cautious: the order came back that he was 'on no account' to stage an attack in the Coldstream Guards' area.

Waldron's account mentions the steps he took to ensure that at least the Berkshires' sector of the canal was held more or less securely. He placed most of the men in their dugouts behind the canal bank. However, he insisted that at least two from each dugout should climb to the top of the canal bank, a difficult order to enforce, given that, as Waldron noted, 'many dead bodies of their own comrades were lying stiff on the edge of the bank, killed doing the work which they were now detailed to do'.

Then they waited expectantly. At dawn on 31 May, the two barges floating in the canal to the left of their position suddenly burst into flames. Fearing that the Germans were about to attack, Waldron summoned all his men on to the canal bank, ready to repulse whatever might be thrown at them. But it was a false alarm, and later that morning Waldron decided to go back to his battalion's headquarters to request that a fresh officer be sent up to replace him. He thought about taking Captain Ryland with him, but reluctantly decided against it. As he recorded in his account, 'Captain Ryland was . . . suffering severely from shock, and [was] sitting in the corner of his dugout. It was necessary, however, for the morale of the men that I should leave an officer there, whatever state his mind might be in.'[15]

By the time Waldron returned with rations for the men Ryland's shell-shock had taken a turn for the worse. It had been exacerbated by the fact that the Germans were now firing at the position, and shelling them with mortars. 'All he could ask me was: would it be possible for him to go back and change into warmer clothes, as he was terribly cold,' Waldron recorded. 'I . . . told him that I would see what I could manage. In the meantime he was to do his best to encourage the men.'[16]

But Waldron's own state of mind deteriorated sharply before he could relieve Ryland. His account describes how, after returning to the battalion's headquarters, he was given some unpalatable tidings from which he never recovered. They were delivered by 8 Brigade's Brigadier Woolner, who had come to check that all was well.

He was evidently very overwrought. I asked him how long we should have to hold out, being careful to mention the battalion's dire state. He said that as far as he knew it would be another five or six days!

He then informed me that he had never seen an officer in such a dirty condition, and I was to go and wash immediately. It probably had not dawned on him that I had not had any sleep that night, or for that matter the night before.[17]

After the brigadier had departed, Waldron received a report that told him it would be impossible to get rations to the front because of heavy German cross-fire. That did not preclude the officers from sitting down to eat their own lunch – which consisted of bully-beef, 'the food so . . . [criticized] by our troops', commented Waldron, washed down with Perrier Jouet '28, 'the most expensive [champagne] we could have at any luxury residence in London'. However, while they were eating, there was a sudden deafening crash. The next thing Waldron remembered was picking himself up from the floor, having registered that their house had been hit by a shell.

As the dust cleared, he found himself in the midst of a scene of complete devastation. Where, seconds before, there had been a civilized room with china on the mantelpiece, antimacassars on the chairs and family pictures around the walls, now it looked more like a building site. The outside wall of the house had been knocked down, and the room was covered with bits of broken plaster. Waldron staggered over to help up another officer, who was sitting dazed on the floor. He spoke to him, but the reply he received made no sense: the officer was another victim of shell-shock and, for the moment at least, he was blind. 'Across the room, the battalion's doctor lay quietly with his head resting on the table,' Waldron remembered. 'I went over to him, and was able to lift his small body in my arms, and with the assistance of one of the men, we carried him quickly down the street to his own first-aid post.' It was to no avail, for as Waldron soon discovered, he had been killed by the explosion.

Some men in Waldron's position might have celebrated their survival. But he found that his morale, which was already low, was further depressed by the Germans' continued attempts to shell them out of their position. 'My own reaction was that I must do something. If I had not had anything to do, I should have screamed,' Waldron wrote, 'for I was getting very near breaking point.' He was cheered up by his batman Josey, who produced a flask of brandy. 'This helped to pull me round,' Waldron recalled, which must have relieved the batman for Waldron's appearance really was shocking now: his face was bleeding, and his trousers were soaked with the doctor's blood.

The desperate situation at the battalion's headquarters was echoed by news that came in from the front. Apparently the Germans had broken through on the Berkshires' left, which, if true, made it difficult if not impossible to go up to the canal line without being shot at. However, as Waldron stated: 'I felt that I must continue to do things, or my brain would snap. I asked [Roper] . . . if it would be all right if I went forward to make a reconnaissance, to find out exactly where the Germans were. Anything . . . to get out of headquarters, which was constantly being bombed and shelled. Roper said it was a good idea.'[18]

Roper could not have been more wrong. As Waldron and Josey scurried forward across fields and through ditches towards the left side of the front line, shells landed within a few yards of them, both to their left and right. If this had happened a few days earlier, Waldron would have been frightened out of his wits, but as his account demonstrates, he was now living in a dream world. 'The thought of danger, the fear of being hurt, had entirely left [me] ... Everything seemed remote, as though I ... was watching an exceedingly dramatic film in the cinema,' Waldron noted.[19]

On their way to the canal, Waldron and Josey came across an officer commanding a section of Coldstream Guards who had come to help the Berkshires. The officer in charge swore that the reports of Germans across the waterway were just rumours. Hardly had he said it than, as Waldron recalled, 'Josey let out a yell, and fell backwards.' He had been hit in the shoulder. 'I leant over [Josey] ... and [then] I felt a blow ... as if I had been hit by a sledge hammer in my back.' It was from a German bullet, which pierced the top of his lung and left him lying on the ground gasping for breath. He was not the only one to be shocked: 'I shall never forget the face of the Coldstream officer sitting opposite me on the other side of the ditch when it slowly dawned on him that we had been hit,' wrote Waldron. ' "By God," he exclaimed, "they must be there after all!" ' Then, after promising to send someone to fetch Waldron and Josey – if anyone could be spared, given the counter-attack that had to be made – the officer departed, and Waldron and Josey were left lying on the ground, alone.

It is interesting to hear what they thought about as they lay talking to each other. One moment nothing mattered any more. The next they were terrified by the prospect that they would be bayoneted when the Germans found them. They thought of their families and promised each other that, if only one of them survived, he would be sure to tell the other's family what had happened. Their semi-delirious ramblings were interrupted by the arrival of some more Coldstream Guards. The officer had been as good as his word, and both Waldron and Josey were manhandled back down yet another ditch, and sent by truck to La Panne.[20]

Meanwhile those left behind to the north of the Furnes–Nieuport Canal were supposed to carry on resisting. Some were unable, or unwilling, to comply with this instruction. According to the 2nd Grenadier Guards' war diary, the line was only patched up, thanks to the Grenadiers' 2nd Lieutenant Jack Jones, and the battalion's carriers. Jones and two carrier sections had been sent to investigate what assistance might be required shortly after noon on 31 May after it became clear that the front-line troops in the Berkshires and the 1st Suffolk Regiment on their left had been cut off from their headquarters. The war diarist reported:

When he arrived, he had found that the Royal Berkshires and Royal Suffolk Regiments, accompanied by men of the 246 Field Company R.E. [Royal Engineers], who had been put in the line, were about to withdraw without orders. An effort was made by one of their officers to rally them, but they broke under heavy enemy shell fire before they could be reorganized. Mr Jones found it necessary to shoot some of the men, and his NCOs turned others around at the point of the bayonet. However he succeeded in restoring order, and himself led the remains of both Bns. and the R.E.s back to the line of the canal.[21]

At 2 p.m. Jones returned to his battalion's headquarters 'and reported that the position had now been stabilized'.[22] By then the 2nd Grenadier Guards had already been told that they, along with the rest of 2 Corps, which was holding the eastern section of the outer Dunkirk perimeter, were to be evacuated that night.[23] However, the fate of the battalions acting under the command of 1 Corps, whose job it was to carry on holding the perimeter to the west of 2 Corps, was still hanging in the balance. It seems incredible to us now, given what we know of the evacuation, that there was ever any real doubt that everyone would get away. But witnesses who visited Gort's headquarters at La Panne during the evening of 30 May have described seeing small groups of staff officers huddled around guttering candles earnestly discussing the best way to surrender.[24]

Contingency plans had already been put in place to ensure that the Germans would not capture Gort. That evening, at a meeting of corps and divisional commanders, Gort announced that he was going back to England, albeit reluctantly, to deprive the Germans of any chance of staging a propaganda coup by capturing the BEF's Commander-in-Chief.[25] General Alan Brooke also said his farewells at the same meeting, leaving a day before the evacuation of his 2 Corps commenced.

Before he went, he told Major-General Martel of 50 Division, who had fought under his command, that he and his men were to form part of the Dunkirk perimeter rearguard.[26] 50 Division, with the rest of 1 Corps, under whose command Martel was to be placed, were to carry on fighting until their ammunition ran out to allow the maximum number of troops to get away. However, Brooke said he did not know what Martel should say to his division's brigadiers, given that there was only a small chance that they and their men would be extricated. As Gort had confirmed, it was unlikely that the rearguard would get away, since the French evacuation arrangements were bad, and the French would not want to leave while there was still the possibility that French 1st Army units were struggling back to the perimeter.[27] After Brooke had departed, Martel took advice from a staff officer on what he should say to his brigadiers. They eventually decided to keep mum about their chances of escape.

In the middle of the meeting chaired by Gort, 1 Corps' commander, General Michael Barker, walked into the room, whereupon he was told that he must stay behind with his men. If and when the time came for the capitulation, he was to contact Admiral Abrial so that they could reach an agreement on how to surrender. At that point, he was to send his staff home, but he was to remain with his troops.

According to General Montgomery, Barker began talking incoherently after being told he had drawn the short straw.[28] Whether or not he started off behaving in a confused manner, he ended up putting a brave face on it, and said brightly, 'Right. Now I know where I am.' In fact, he perked up enough to encourage the more fortunate generals who knew they were going home to joke about his being 'entertained in a château on the Rhine'.[29] However, after the meeting was concluded, he went for a stroll with a member of his staff, in the course of which he indicated that the idea of surrender was repugnant to him, adding: 'I damned well won't surrender. That is a contingency they don't seem to have allowed for.'[30]

While Barker was coming to terms with his bleak future, Montgomery gave Gort a piece of his mind about 1 Corps' commander: no one could say whether 1 Corps would have an opportunity to slip away, but it would never do so under Barker, who almost had a nervous breakdown whenever anything went wrong. General Harold Alexander was likely to be a much better bet, Montgomery stated.[31] Prompted by this intervention, Gort subsequently relieved Barker of his command, and at 12.30 p.m. on 31 May, Alexander was told he should immediately take charge of all BEF troops remaining at Dunkirk.[32]

In spite of all the talk of surrender, Gort failed initially to inform Alexander that he had been sent a telegram that gave him permission to surrender if he was no longer in contact with the politicians in London, and if he was no longer in a position to inflict further damage on the enemy.[33] Gort's aide, Colonel Bridgeman, on noticing the omission, was so nervous about uttering the word 'surrender' in his Commander-in-Chief's presence that, instead of asking Gort a straight question, he showed Gort the telegram in question, and asked if the instructions should be passed on to Alexander. Gort said they should.[34]

Alexander took over the command at a time when contradictory signals were being given by the generals and politicians in London about the risks to be taken to accommodate the French. At 11 a.m. on 31 May Gort had telephoned Anthony Eden to ask whether he was expected to hold the perimeter for as long as possible so that the maximum number of Frenchmen were evacuated or whether he was supposed to withdraw when it became unsafe. Eden told him to withdraw when it became unsafe.[35] Alexander received similar instructions from Major-General Percival, the Assistant Chief of the Imperial General Staff.[36] Yet on 30 May, Dill had told Gort that he must give the French a 'fair' number of places on British ships even if that resulted in fewer British soldiers getting out.[37] Given the inconsistency of his orders, it is not surprising that Alexander plumped for the safety-first option. However, it was a decision that was to lead to bitter in-fighting between British and French commanders.

The flames of the conflict were fanned by the physical 'battles' between French and British troops on the beaches. Some of the earliest scuffles were provoked by confusion as to where the French troops were supposed to congregate. The initial agreement was that the British would go to La Panne and Malo-les-Bains, leaving Bray-Dunes to the French.[38] Unfortunately no one in authority had informed the French rank and file of this as they passed through the perimeter. As a result, there were what Capitaine Georges Meric, liaison officer to 2 Corps, referred to as 'angry scenes' as French soldiers found themselves being turned away at barriers erected by their allies to safeguard the British beaches, and forced to make their way along to the French beach through crowds of soldiers and vehicles attempting to move in the opposite direction.

The angry scenes reached crisis point on 29 May near the British GHQ at La Panne: Meric watched nervously as a group of French soldiers threatened to use their guns to break through the British barriers. The unedifying spectacle of ally shooting it out with ally was only avoided thanks to a German bombardment of the town, which at the last minute scattered the rebels. This prevented what Meric euphemistically referred to as 'any regrettable acts'.

It was not only the French troops who were at fault. General Voruz, head of the French liaison section, described how, while he was waiting on the Quai Félix-Faure in the Dunkirk harbour area, a panic-stricken British captain rushed up and seized his car.[39] The British officer would not leave the car until forced to do so. Even more alarming were the hundreds of British troops who stormed a ship set aside for French soldiers including Voruz and his men. According to Voruz, there was trouble even after the ship set sail. Her commander was reduced to brandishing his revolver in an attempt to restore order. But this did not work for long since the British troops continued to insult the French. Worse still, when the British soldiers heard that the ship was to dock at Cherbourg before she went on to Dover, they were so upset that they went on the rampage, throwing any guns they could find into the sea, presumably hoping that if they arrived back in France unarmed, they would not be asked to carry on fighting.

One of the principal British gripes was that the French soldiers were ignoring orders to abandon their haversacks and equipment when they queued up to embark. There was nothing more infuriating for an exhausted British soldier who had reluctantly left behind his belongings than to be barged in the back by French soldiers who insisted on carrying theirs. One Sherwood Forester later confessed that he and his mates were so incensed by two French soldiers who had jostled them that they told them, 'It's your country; you defend it!' and pushed them off the mole into the harbour.[40] These soldiers were not alone; there are many similar tales of French troops trying to board boats, only to be thrown back into the sea.

The treatment meted out to General Champon, head of the French Mission to Belgium, and his staff must have been particularly upsetting for the French. Champon had been told that the British Admiralty would evacuate his ninety-man mission on a British ship, but during the morning of 28 May, the GHQ officer dealing with his case only offered him berths for ten men.[41] Although Champon immediately telephoned the naval attaché in London to complain, there was no immediate solution to the problem. At 5 p.m. on 28 May his hopes were raised when he was told that he and his men could be taken on a

British destroyer that afternoon. But when they presented themselves at the barriers cordoning off the beach at La Panne, they were at first not permitted to pass, and after they were finally allowed on to the sand, the destroyer never appeared.

On 29 May, two of Champon's officers were given permission to embark on a boat, but after they had waded out to board it, the naval officer in charge swore at them and said he was only taking British soldiers. By this stage Champon appears to have abandoned all hope of a dignified departure: he told his men to walk up and down the beach so that they could interrogate the sailors in each boat as it arrived to find out whether it had been sent for his Mission. Fortunately for Champon, and Anglo-French relations, he and his men had not been completely forgotten and, in the end, they did manage to embark on two ships, but it is likely that the indignities they had suffered at the hands of the British soldiers prior to their departure added to the ill-feeling that was already growing in the minds of the French commanders.

The Champon story was just one of many complaints that reached Admiral Abrial and General Fagalde in Bastion 32, their command post at Dunkirk. (Its location is shown in Map 16 on pp. 532–3.) Fagalde was incensed, and warned General Adam in writing that if it continued he would be forced to order his troops to defend themselves with their guns. Fagalde was mollified somewhat when Adam immediately visited the bastion, and promised to issue an order that the anti-French behaviour was to stop. But Fagalde was hopping mad again when he learned that, far from remaining *in situ* to ensure that his order was complied with, Adam had shortly afterwards boarded a ship bound for England.[42]

From all of this it can be seen that Admiral Abrial and General Fagalde had grounds for feeling aggrieved by British soldiers' behaviour even before difficulties arose with the BEF's top generals. The first of these problems came to light while Gort was still in France: Abrial and Fagalde could not at first persuade him to commit BEF troops for Dunkirk's ongoing defence. During the morning of 31 May, however, Gort sent a letter to Abrial stating that 1 Corps under General Barker, 'a fighter *magnifique*', was to be put under French command.[43]

Abrial would have been perfectly happy with this, had the British troops been made available unconditionally. But at around 3.30 p.m., he and Fagalde were visited by General Alexander, his staff officer

Brigadier William Morgan, and Captain Bill Tennant, Senior British Naval Officer in Dunkirk, and told that Alexander, rather than Barker, was to be the new British commander, and that important conditions were attached to the provision of British troops. There is no British report that includes a verbatim account of this tense meeting. But the following minutes, compiled it seems by a French Anglophobe, at least give the French gloss on what was said, if not the whole story:

Admiral Abrial: 'Lord Gort has just given me a letter in which he has told me that he is leaving three British divisions in France to defend the Dunkirk bridgehead along with French forces in order to permit French and English soldiers to embark. He is putting these three divisions under the command of General Alexander, who in his turn is to serve under the General commanding the [French] 16 Corps [General Fagalde].'

General Alexander: 'Yes,' spoken without conviction.

General Fagalde: 'I am asking General Alexander to place these divisions after their retreat in the following positions: one division in the region of Bray Dunes to support the French 12 Division, one division in the Uxem region, and one division to the east of Bergues on the Canal de la Basse Colme.'[44]

Alexander: 'My divisions are so tired that they cannot hold the front you have specified. They are lacking in guns thanks to the battles they have fought. Also Lord Gort has not told me to hold a sector of the Dunkirk bridgehead with French troops; he has told me that all the English troops are to be evacuated.'

Abrial: 'I do not know what Lord Gort has told you. I only know that I have this letter which we can read together to see if we are in agreement.'

Fagalde: Reads the Lord Gort letter in English, and translates different passages as he reads them.

Alexander: seeking support from his chief of staff [Brigadier William Morgan]. 'Lord Gort's never told me to co-operate with French troops to hold Dunkirk; he told me to save as many English troops as I can, and then to evacuate them on the boats.'

Alexander's chief of staff [Morgan]: agrees with what Alexander said.

Fagalde: 'So you are saying that the French Army should cover the evacuation of the British Army while the British Army gives no assistance to the French Army for its retreat.'

Alexander: 'I want nothing more than to co-operate with you. I am just telling you that my troops will abandon their positions . . . in accordance with orders I have received from Lord Gort.'

Abrial: 'If you do this, the French soldiers will not have even started to evacuate, because there have not been enough boats. The 5000 places which the English Navy has put at our disposal for the last two nights are insufficient to evacuate the 100,000 Frenchmen who are defending Dunkirk.'

Alexander: 'I am sorry about this . . . However, the Germans are at the gates of Dunkirk, and those who do not leave . . . will be captured. Everything that can be saved will be saved.'

Capitaine de Frégate de Laperouse: 'No, General, it is still possible to save honour.'

(Long silence. General Alexander stares at the table in front of him. He wipes his forehead and pretends he does not understand.)

General Altmayer: 'I must insist we should act honourably. We have been fighting to save everything that can be saved, English and French, but we should not leave this place without making sure we have done our duty. We have not yet fulfilled our commitments. We can do more if the British agree to help us.'

Alexander: 'I have received the order to evacuate . . .'

Altmayer: 'But, General, we have a mission which has been given to us by Admiral Abrial and by General Fagalde, and it has been explicitly confirmed by Lord Gort. It is to defend Dunkirk with all the French forces available, and with three British divisions. We must accomplish this mission.'

Alexander: 'I have not been told to do this by Lord Gort.'

Abrial: 'To sum up, the letter that Lord Gort has written, the only one that in my eyes is important, has been contradicted by the verbal orders he has given to you, General. I propose that we go to see Lord Gort so that we can all act in agreement. It is 4.30 p.m., and he told me he will not embark until 7 p.m.'

Laperouse: 'Can you warn Lord Gort we are coming?'

Alexander: 'There is no point going to see Lord Gort. He left at 4 p.m.'

(Long silence – disappointment.)

Abrial: 'Since we cannot count on English co-operation, General, I will fulfil my mission using French troops. We French have a mission which is to fight to the last man to save as many soldiers as possible from Dunkirk. Until we have achieved this goal, we will remain at our posts.'

Doubtless, there is some truth in the French account of the meeting. Other witnesses, however, suggest that the minutes do not cover everything that was said. For example, General Fagalde remembered that when he first mentioned the inner perimeter he intended to hold,

Alexander replied, 'You must be joking!'[45] Alexander's own account explains why he particularly disapproved of the eastern sector of the French general's proposed inner perimeter, which was to run from Bergues through Uxem, Ghyvelde and Basse Plaine to the sea: 'The line which they proposed to hold south-east and east of Dunkirk was so close to the harbour and beaches that the enemy would speedily render further evacuation impossible with artillery fire at short range.'[46]

Alexander's General Staff Brigadier, William Morgan, recalled that, whatever is claimed to have been said in the above minutes, the essential difference between the two sides was that Abrial refused to accept that the French should evacuate the bridgehead in the short term. His idea was that only non-combatant troops would be evacuated, leaving the fighting troops to carry on holding the perimeter.[47]

Whatever was said at the meeting, no one disputes what happened next. Alexander stated that he would ring up Anthony Eden to ask for his instructions, which he did at around 7.15 p.m. that evening.[48] Half an hour later, Alexander's recommendations were discussed in an emergency sitting of the War Cabinet's Defence Committee. The minutes of that discussion reveal how a decision was reached on the thorny issue of when the evacuation should terminate, before it was telephoned through to Alexander.[49] The discussion was given an extra urgent twist after Eden told the Committee's members that General Alexander had telephoned his report through from La Panne, and that he might not be able to be reached on the telephone after another hour or so. 'An immediate decision was therefore called for,' the meeting's minutes state.

During the meeting, it was pointed out that the French intended to hold out more or less indefinitely, even though, according to the minutes, 'it was fairly clear that any French troops left to garrison Dunkirk – after the BEF departed – would be rapidly captured'. But it was Alexander's view on the evacuation that swayed the seven Defence Committee members. They accepted his advice that fewer, not more, troops would be extricated if the BEF had to hold on after the night of 1–2 June, and ruled that the evacuation should end then. Even though Eden had said that a serious disagreement with the French might lead Abrial to deny the BEF access to the mole – at the meeting in France Abrial had threatened to close the port if the British did not co-operate with the French – the last words of the minutes stated: 'It would be entirely wrong to sacrifice our men by attempting to hold out longer in order to please the French.'[50]

Eden must have moved very quickly after the Defence Committee meeting. At 8.15 p.m., just an hour after Alexander had telephoned him, he rang Alexander to confirm what had been agreed.[51] The written instructions that followed almost three hours later stated: 'You should withdraw your force as rapidly as possible on a fifty–fifty basis with the French . . . aiming at completion by the night of the 1st/2nd June.'[52] Later that night Alexander showed these new instructions to Abrial and Fagalde. They provoked another protest from Fagalde, who in the meantime had seen the telegram sent to Abrial summarizing what had been agreed in Paris that afternoon at the Supreme War Council attended by Churchill, Reynaud and Weygand.

The meeting in Paris represented an important landmark for those who wanted to see as many British troops as possible back in Britain ready to repulse a German invasion: before Dunkirk was discussed, Reynaud and Churchill agreed that the evacuation of all Allied troops from Norway should commence on 2 June. Reaching an agreement about what to do at Dunkirk was more complicated since Weygand believed that there were still many French soldiers marching back to the coast. In fact, most of the troops who had escaped the encirclement, including those in the French III Corps, had arrived at Dunkirk two days earlier.[53] However, Weygand acknowledged that there was probably no hope for the French troops surrounded at Lille. They duly surrendered that night, enabling the Germans to round up some 35,000 prisoners.[54]

Weygand's coming to terms with what was happening at Lille, and his admission that the troops there would be unlikely to make it back to the perimeter, helped Churchill convince Weygand that there was no need to hold on at Dunkirk indefinitely. Nevertheless, as was mentioned by General Sir Edward Spears in his vivid account of the War Council, Churchill had to make concessions in order to bring the French into line after Reynaud complained that only 15,000 French soldiers had been evacuated compared with 150,000 British troops. As well as agreeing that a higher proportion of those evacuated while the perimeter was being held should be French, Churchill famously interrupted when Admiral François Darlan, the head of the French Navy, stated that the BEF rearguard would be evacuated before the French:

'Certainly not,' he boomed.

'Monsieur Churchill refuse d'accepter que les troupes anglaises soient les premières embarquées,' translated Roland de Margerie in clipped, precise, literary French.

But now the Prime Minister was doing his own translating. 'Nong,' he roared. 'Partage – bras dessus, bras dessous.' The gesture he made, effectively camouflaging his accent, conveyed better than the words that he wished the French and British soldiers to leave Dunkirk arm in arm.[55]

Fortunately for Alexander and the troops in Dunkirk, Churchill's generous gesture, which, if accepted by him and his team, would have been at the BEF soldiers' expense, was not fully reflected in the telegram the War Council members sent to Abrial. It stated that the Dunkirk bridgehead was to be held until Abrial reached the conclusion that no more troops were capable of reaching the perimeter, whereupon the town was to be evacuated. The War Council's instructions concerning the British troops' participation was less clearly defined: they were to fight as part of the rearguard for 'as long as possible'.[56]

Nevertheless, this still appeared to be inconsistent with Eden's telephoned instructions to Alexander, and Fagalde demanded that Alexander should obey his prime minister, who, after all, was Eden's boss: 'As at the first meeting, this caused Alexander to roar with laughter,' Fagalde later recalled.[57] 'The idea that the British Army should be called on to provide the final rearguard and to sacrifice itself appeared to be an enormous joke to him.'

Alexander replied that he did not answer to the Prime Minister, but only to the Secretary of State for War. 'I told him that his attitude was not that of a real soldier,' Fagalde remembered, 'that he was flagrantly disobeying his Commander-in-Chief's orders, that he was abandoning his comrades at a critical moment, that he could go ahead and embark with his troops, that we would protect the evacuation . . . and that we would show him that whatever he said, we could remain for several extra days at Dunkirk without being captured. I then finished by saying: "Your decision to evacuate with your three divisions represents a disgrace for England."' Fagalde's note terminated dramatically: 'General Alexander, looking very embarrassed, and not daring to look at me, took his leave and disappeared. We were now on our own!'[58]

31: Evacuation

Dunkirk, Lancashire and London, 31 May–1 June 1940
(See Map 16. Also Map 1)

During the early evening of 31 May, Rear-Admiral William Wake-Walker, who was in charge of shipping off Dunkirk, saw a sight that gladdened his heart: 'I saw for the first time that strange procession of craft of all kinds that has become famous. Tugs towing dinghies, lifeboats and all manner of pulling boats, small motor yachts, motor launches, drifters, Dutch schoots, Thames barges, fishing boats [and] pleasure steamers,' arriving in the nick of time to rescue Britain's surrounded Army.[1]

The boats were all the more welcome after the day's difficulties. That morning it had been difficult, if not impossible, to use small boats off the beaches on account of the swell caused by the wind. Many of those that had attempted to pick up soldiers had been swamped. Wake-Walker had only been able to announce that conditions had improved at 5 p.m.[2] Then the armada had arrived, appearing as if conjured up thanks to a miracle, just when Wake-Walker needed them most. A special effort was made to have these small boats in place ready to pick up 2 Corps' battalions, which were to retreat to the beaches that night.

Given the large number, it is not surprising that some never made it home. One of the most celebrated disasters involved a fleet of six cockle-fishing boats from Leigh-on-Sea, Essex, which arrived off the Dunkirk beaches at dusk on 31 May. Jimmy Dench, skipper of the cockle-boat *Letitia*, which was towed over from England by one of the faster boats in the fleet, has described how, after seeing that the swell was not conducive to picking up soldiers from the seashore, the cockle-boats moved on to the north-eastern side of the mole. From there, they operated the same kind of shuttle service as that mentioned in Chapter 28: they collected men from the jetty and ferried them to larger ships further out at sea.[3]

Dench's description of an incident that occurred during the penultimate ferrying trip from the mole provides an example of the perils facing the small ships' crews, and the phlegmatic steadfastness that enabled them to carry on regardless: 'On going in for a third time, a shell burst in between the last boat . . . and us. We turned back to go out, but the signaller that we had on board, and had only been "out" for about six weeks, and never been under fire, said: "We've got to go in again." So we went in.'

Dench's account goes on to record how they loaded up with soldiers one last time, and delivered them to the trawler that was to tow *Letitia* home:

Soon we saw another boat coming up behind us. It was the *Renown*, and, yelling that they had engine trouble, they made fast to our stern . . . We towed them [the trawler towing *Letitia*, which in her turn towed *Renown*], 3.5 fathoms of rope being the distance between us. That was at 1.15 a.m. [1 June] . . . Tired out, the engineer, seaman and signaller went to turn in, as our work seemed nearly done. We were congratulating ourselves, when, at about 1.50 a.m., a terrible explosion took place, and a hail of wood splinters came down on our deck. In the pitch dark, you could see nothing, and we could do nothing . . . except pull in the tow rope which was just as we passed it to the *Renown* about three-quarters of an hour before.

It was clear to everyone on *Letitia* that *Renown* had been blown to smithereens by a mine.

Three fishermen from Leigh-on-Sea died in the *Renown* disaster, along with one young seaman from the Merchant Navy who had also volunteered. Each fisherman lost represented a tragedy for his family: they were all in their twenties. But the death of the eighteen-year-old sailor, Harold Porter, was particularly poignant.[4] He had only just left school when he went to Dunkirk. At school, he believed that he had been a failure, although his chances of success there had been lessened by recurrent ill-health. Nevertheless he had hoped to redeem himself, and had told his father at the end of one of his last terms that one day he would do something to make the school proud of him. When his parents received the letter telling them that their son had 'done well', and had 'died doing his duty . . . helping to evacuate troops from the coast of Belgium', they were comforted by the knowledge that not only had he made them proud of him, but he had also done something that, had he lived, would have made him proud of himself.

Among the soldiers who were to make use of the lines of small boats towed to the beaches were the 2nd Grenadier Guards. Although acting commanding officer Major Colvin knew by 6 a.m. on 31 May that the battalion was likely to be evacuated that night, the good news did not filter down to some of the other ranks until much later in the day. An account by the signalman George Jones, who because of the shelling was cooped up in a cellar on the Grande Place in Furnes, reveals the feeling of hopelessness that he and his comrades experienced as they waited to learn their fate:

Pinned down, movement outside became impossible, but at least the same could be said for the enemy, and since our . . . cellar remained impervious to shot and shell, we . . . [sat] back to rest, wait, and hope for the best.

Someone scrounging around found a portable wireless, and at around 2 p.m., we heard the news that 'Over two-thirds of the forces encircled in the area of Dunkirk have now been evacuated and are safely in England.' [The number of troops landed in England was in excess of 160,000 by the end of 30–31 May. See note 5.][5] In the gloom . . . [and] dark corners of the cellar, looks and silence betrayed the thoughts of every one of us. Here we were miles inland, and virtually trapped in a town collapsing from bombardments from both sides. Meanwhile the best part of the Army was safely back in England. It felt very lonely.[6]

This despondency can be contrasted with the elation that greeted the order that they were to escape to the coast after all. Jones's spirits rose higher still when, just before he and his comrades were scheduled to leave their cellar, the bombardment that had kept them prisoner for much of the day suddenly ceased:

For us, our first miracle of Dunkirk . . . began [then]. This curtain of ragged steel began to lift just before 10 p.m., and in the bright glow of a hundred fires, we walked from Furnes without a bomb, shell or bullet arriving within half a mile of our scrambling single files. Twice we took wrong turnings, almost walking down the throat of the enemy, but stumbling over piles of rubble, bricks, broken glass and tangled telephone wires, at last we were clear.[7]

One of the guardsmen making up the rearguard at a junction on the way to the beaches wrote of his fear that the Germans would get to them before they could escape:

When we arrived at the junction, all was quiet, and we set up positions covering the roads from Furnes and Nieuport. Our own Battalion started coming through at about 2 a.m. . . . Then, as if the Germans had woken up to the fact that Furnes was quiet, we were treated to shelling which was very accurate on [our] . . . area . . . [Some of our men] were wounded . . . and we could hear the wounded crying out . . .

Then we heard the noise of horses galloping towards us from Furnes . . . We quickly got behind the hedge, and at least 40 horses . . . raced past. But no Germans followed.[8]

They eventually joined the other 2 Corps men on the beaches.

Most of the surviving Grenadier Guards abandoned their positions between 11.30 p.m. on 31 May and 2.30 a.m. on 1 June.[9] No German resistance obstructed their withdrawal to the sea. But any hopes they might have had that they would be compensated for their trials on the perimeter front line with an uncomplicated passage home were to be quickly dispelled. 'Of ships there were plenty,' wrote Colvin, 'but they were a long way off-shore, and the tide was only just starting to flow. Of staff officers . . . there was no sign, and consequently nobody knew what was expected of them.'[10] Guided by signals from the destroyers, thousands of men, described by Colvin as 'a solid mass five miles in length and about one hundred yards broad', began to walk along the beach towards Dunkirk.

If Colvin and his men had made it to the beach at Bray-Dunes, they would have discovered that steps had been taken to facilitate their evacuation.[11] On 30 May Royal Engineers had devised a way of setting up makeshift jetties. Around fifteen three-ton lorries had been placed side by side on Bray-Dunes' hard sand during low tide. Bullets fired at their tyres punctured them, and this together with the sand thrown into the backs of the lorries, and the fact that the lorries were lashed together after the covers were stripped off their superstructure ensured that they did not move when the tide came in. Decking panels from a bridging truck laid across the backs of the lorries, along with planks liberated from a local timber yard, served as the walkway along which soldiers could go out to the launches and boats that came in to collect them.[12]

But the aids awaiting them at Bray-Dunes did not make it any easier getting there. Attempting to march along the beach turned out to be a dangerous strategy. 'Squadrons of Messerschmitts periodically attacked,' wrote Colvin, 'and there were many unpleasant sights of wounded men left on the sands to die, or be drowned by the flood tide.'

Fearing that they might be hit by bombs, Colvin and some of his men stopped before reaching Bray-Dunes. They then waded out to a grounded steamer in the hope that they would be picked up from there, and ferried out to a destroyer. 'After some time, a motor boat towing a chain of empty ships' boats came out to us,' wrote Colvin. But the relief he and his men must have felt as they were taken off the steamer was to be short-lived. 'As we neared the destroyer, it was attacked by ... dive-bombers and hit in the engines,' Colvin remembered. 'She put to sea as quickly as possible with clouds of smoke pouring from her, and was subsequently abandoned.'[13]

Colvin appears to have been watching the first stage of the demise of the destroyer HMS *Keith*, which was finally sunk after being bombed again later that morning.[14] She was the first of many ships sunk that day, making 1 June the second worst day of the evacuation for the Royal and Merchant Navies in terms of large ships disabled: nine destroyers and personnel ships were sunk, or put out of action, plus numerous smaller vessels.[15] This was one of the principal reasons why the evacuation figures were sharply reduced: the number of soldiers evacuated plunged from over 60,000 the day before to some 31,000 during 1–2 June.[16]

The losses reflected the RAF's inability to fly fighters continuously over the perimeter. Although it was obvious that a back-to-back air umbrella would have reduced the losses at sea, there were not enough planes available for the three- to four-squadron patrols to be airborne all of the time. It was while no British fighters were overhead that large Luftwaffe formations struck, making 1 June a repeat performance of 29 May, only this time the sinking and killing occurred away from the mole.

Colvin's account confirms that he and his men were caught in the middle of the most effective series of air raids, which took place between 7.30 and 10 a.m. During the raids, he and his men were taken on board the tug *St Abbs*, which was rescuing *Keith*'s survivors from the water, along with others from the minesweeper *Skipjack*, another ship sunk by the bombers. 'Most of them were practically dead with cold,' wrote Colvin, 'being coated in thick oil, and some were terribly injured.' One of the most horrific cases was a man who had survived thanks to his lifejacket, but whose arms had both been blown off at the elbow.[17]

These were all injuries caused by one wave of bombing. Further raids put the destroyer *Basilisk* out of action – she had been picking up soldiers from a beach further to the east. The Luftwaffe also targeted *St Abbs*, splitting her in half with four delayed-action bombs dropped into the water ahead of her.[18] The ship sank in just forty-five seconds, the men trapped below deck going down with her. They included Lieutenant Turner, *Keith*'s surgeon, who, after surviving the bombing of that destroyer, had carried on caring for the survivors on *St Abbs* when she was attacked. It seems that the man from *Skipjack*, who had lost both forearms during the sinking of his ship, was less 'fortunate' on this occasion; he was not mentioned again in surviving witnesses' accounts, and probably went down with the ship.

His fate can be contrasted with that of Lieutenant Graham Lumsden, *Keith*'s navigator. Lumsden had already seen men dying; his commander had been killed beside him at Boulogne (see Chapter 16). Lumsden was lucky for a second time when rescued by *St Abbs* from the bombed *Keith* minutes before she was sunk by another bomb, and he was lucky for a third time during the bombing of *St Abbs*. Being on the bridge when *St Abbs* was bombed, he was able to scramble over the guardrail into the sea as the bow of the ship reared into the air, then sank backwards under the waves, following the stern. He had no opportunity to take off his uniform before he went into the water. Nevertheless, supported as he was by his lifejacket, he was able to swim slowly but surely towards the beach, thereby cheating death once again. It was a long haul, and Lumsden's account describes how he psyched himself into the right frame of mind to encourage himself to keep swimming: 'Thinking of something that would powerfully reinforce my will to swim on, I found myself picturing my wife's small but beautiful back-side. This provided a good fillip, and I was able to laugh at myself for the thought.'[19] He eventually landed near the squat red-brick fort at Bray-Dunes, and was evacuated later from the mole.

Colvin was equally fortunate as the following extracts from his account demonstrate. There were not enough lifebelts on *St Abbs* for everyone. But he had grabbed one from a soldier who died beside him on the ship's deck, and had only just put it on before she was hit: 'I remember being knocked down, and trying to get up again, only to find I had one leg out of action,' he reported.

The ship then heeled right over, and everything came crashing down. Everyone made a rush for the side, and I remember a horrid feeling of going down . . . into a bottomless pit. I took a deep breath, said a short prayer, and thought this was the one end I least desired. I had the sensation of being pushed through the water at great speed . . . The next thing I realized was that my head was above water, and that I was some fifty yards away from a lot of wreckage and struggling people. This probably saved my life, as most of the soldiers drowned each other through panic.

Men were now dying every moment from cramp, and their cries for help were pathetic. It was the second time that day that many of these sailors had faced death by drowning. We were all very near the end of our tether, when we realized that the tide was carrying us towards a wrecked steamer which was lying with her stern nearly under water. I remember discarding my Sam Browne belt, and wishing I could do the same with my boots, and then striking out as best I could towards the ship. As good fortune would have it, the tide took us right under the hull of the ship . . . I grabbed a rope ladder hanging from the fo'c's'le, but owing to my damaged leg, the tide . . . carried my legs away, and I couldn't get a footing on the bottom rung, so I had to give up my last hope, and cast away. The tide washed along the side of the ship very fast, and as I passed under her stern, I saw an old gangway hanging in the water. This I got hold of, and was able to drag myself up on to the bottom rung. It was so smashed about that I doubted it would bear my weight, and great was the relief when I pitched over on to the deck. Cramp in both legs made it impossible to move, and the cold was so intense that I couldn't even speak . . .[20]

But Colvin's ordeal was not over yet: 'Presumably the Germans could see us moving on the decks, and they came and bombed us again, but failed to score a direct hit. One simply prayed for a quick end, or anything rather than be cast into that cold water again.'[21]

Aboard SS *Clan Macalister*, the ship on which Colvin had ended up, was John Beeley, *Keith*'s telegraphist. His account describes how he half recognized another man dressed in white shirt and trousers who was near what he took to be the galley: 'Just for something to say, I said to him: "It's a f— good job we've got a cook with us", but this only produced a scowl . . . so I just thought "Miserable so and so," and went on my way.' It was only when Beeley heard other survivors on the ship addressing 'the cook' as 'Sir' that he realized the man with a vaguely familiar face was none other than *Keith*'s commander, Captain Edward Berthon.[22]

Berthon had been shocked by the terrible injuries he had seen inflicted when German planes had bombed his men who were swimming for their lives in the sea. After he, along with the other survivors on *Clan Macalister*, was picked up by a barge-like vessel that in peacetime was a yard craft in Sheerness dockyard, and taken to Dover harbour, he had a nervous breakdown triggered, apparently, by other men on board insisting that they must report to the harbour's examination vessel. When he heard this, Berthon became abusive, shouting that he was Captain D (the officer in charge of his flotilla), and as such did not have to report to any 'bloody' examination vessel, especially after what he had been through. He was only pacified when told that the guns on the breakwater were training round on to their boat, whereupon Beeley used his torch to signal that their boat was carrying Captain D of the 19th Destroyer Flotilla, together with survivors from *Keith* and some fifty military followed by 'Request permission to enter.' Shortly afterwards, the signal station flashed back, allowing them to proceed into the harbour. When they landed, Berthon was taken to hospital with Colvin and the other wounded men.

Little has been written about the doctors and nurses who dealt with wounded men rescued from Dunkirk. There were not enough beds for all of them in hospitals near the main ports in Kent used in the course of Operation Dynamo, so many casualties were transported to other locations around the country. Nancy Harker, then a twenty-nine-year-old nurse, never forgot the day she met the first Dunkirk hospital train that reached Whalley in Lancashire.[23] As the train, covered with red crosses, steamed into the station, she asked a colleague, 'Why ever have these poor things had to come all the way to the north of England after all they've been through?' The answer stunned her. 'Because hospitals in the south are being emptied for the invasion.'

The first injured soldiers off the train were carried into Calderstone's, a psychiatric institution that had been converted into a hospital, where Nurse Harker worked, at the beginning of the afternoon. It was the beginning of a long-drawn-out nightmare. 'The stench of gangrene still comes back to me,' she wrote in her account of that first day. She also mentions 'the wounds that cried out for immediate treatment [which] had had to wait for days to be treated'.

The delay in providing treatment also explained why maggots were found all too often under the soldiers' plasters. Nurse Harker has described how she came across this phenomenon for the first time on a patient whom she knew as Coveney: 'I remember holding his leg up, whilst a doctor removed his plaster, and how the maggots escaped and crawled up my arm. The look the doctor gave me was meant to freeze me into silence. He need not have worried. What harm could maggots do to me surrounded as I was with all this suffering?' Coveney refused to have his leg amputated, and died as a result.

Nurse Harker's favourite Dunkirk survivor was a young man called Bert Heath, one of the many 'GSWs' (gunshot wound cases). His right leg had been amputated in France, and his right arm had to go too as soon as he arrived at Calderstone's. He quickly won over Nurse Harker by nicknaming the leg's stump 'Baby', and by promising her that as soon as he was given a 'peg leg', he would race her up and down the ward. His bravery inspired the man in the next bed, a multiple GSW, who insisted that Nurse Harker should give him 'the needle' to stop him groaning in case he disturbed his neighbour.

During the first night after the sixty-four Dunkirk survivors were brought into the hospital, Harker and the other nurses were rushed off their feet trying to deal with their patients' physical needs. However, even then she forced herself to make time to accommodate the pastoral side of her job, which for some of the men was just as important as any medical treatment. One forty-seven-year-old man, who had 'gone over' as a baker, was so traumatized by the atrocities he had seen he could not sleep. There was not much Nurse Harker could do in such cases. But she laid a soothing hand on his forehead, then held his hand and said a silent prayer. To her surprise, such human contact appeared to make a difference. After a while, the baker finally let himself go, and drifted off to sleep.

Nurse Harker, along with the other Calderstone's nurses, was less sympathetic to three Frenchmen who arrived on stretchers only to leap up as soon as they were inside the hospital to declare that they had been shamming to get away. Although they may well have lived through traumas every bit as dreadful as those haunting the British wounded, they were sent to Coventry by the nurses, and abandoned in the laundry cupboard during that first night, where they sat listening to the news about what was happening in France. 'No time for them,' wrote Nurse

Harker, in her account. 'Only saw them when I went to get linen.'

Meanwhile, in London, the War Cabinet met at 11.30 a.m. on 1 June to discuss the decision to complete the evacuation that night.[24] It was acknowledged that the French were more than a little 'disturbed' by what Eden had told Alexander on 31 May, but Churchill initially fell into line, telling Eden that, whatever had been said at the 31 May Supreme War Council in Paris (see Chapter 30), Gort's opinion that holding out was impossible changed everything. Those attending also believed that British troops should not be penalized by being forced to carry on holding the line merely because the French were not evacuating their troops efficiently. For example, rather than using French ships to take their soldiers on the relatively short journey to Dover, some of the French ships were transporting the evacuated troops to ports as far away as Le Havre, thereby reducing the number of trips they could make to Dunkirk and the number of soldiers they could evacuate.

However, as the hours passed, the hard line advocated by Alexander and Eden appeared to be wavering. After the French Military Attaché, General Albert Lelong, had spoken to General Percival, General Dill's number two, he telegraphed back to his masters in France at around 3 p.m. that Eden's instruction to Alexander 'only indicated completion tonight as an objective, and not as a firm order'.[25] An hour later, Lelong sent a much more pessimistic message to Weygand:

The Chief of the Imperial General Staff, whom I saw at 3.20 p.m., is much more pessimistic than his deputy . . . The British Navy lost six ships this morning . . . In view of this, it is thought that they will not be able to hold on till tomorrow night. I have insisted that the question should be discussed by the Chiefs of Staff and the War Cabinet . . . [But] I fear this will not change what I'm telling you now.[26]

The Chiefs of Staff met later that day. Dill explained that when he had met Lelong, the French Military Attaché was 'in a great state of excitement'. According to Lelong:

it was one thing to be driven out and forced to evacuate, but it was quite different if an order from London were issued that the evacuation should . . . be completed that night. Such an order might have a disastrous effect on the Alliance in view of the conclusions reached at the Supreme War Council the day before to the effect that the evacuation should be continued until completed under the directions of Admiral Abrial.[27]

His point could not have been phrased more persuasively, since Churchill would do almost anything to encourage the French to carry on fighting, and the minutes of the discussion include Churchill's ruling:

The Germans might not break through, and it might be possible to continue for another night. The success or failure of our efforts to rescue the remnants of the French Army might have great results on the Alliance. As long as the front held, the evacuation should be continued – even at the cost of naval losses.

Later that evening, Alexander was told:

We do not order any fixed moment for evacuation. You are to hold on as long as possible in order that the maximum number of French and British may be evacuated. Impossible from here to judge local situation. In close co-operation with Admiral Abrial, you must act in this matter on your own judgment.[28]

The following telegram was then sent by Churchill to Weygand:

Crisis in evacuation now reached. Five fighter squadrons acting almost continuously is most we can do, but six ships, several filled with troops, sunk by bombing this morning. Artillery fire menacing only practical channel. Enemy closing in on reduced bridgehead. By trying to hold tomorrow, we may lose all. By going tonight, much may certainly be saved, though much will be lost. Situation cannot be fully judged only by Admiral Abrial in the fortress, nor by you, nor by us here. We have therefore ordered General Alexander, commanding British sector of bridgehead, to judge, in consultation with Admiral Abrial, whether to try to stay over tomorrow or not. Trust you will agree.[29]

32: Rearguard

The soldiers with 1 Corps, whom Churchill was prepared to sacrifice in order to keep the French fighting, included the men in the 1st Guards Brigade. Until 31 May their commander had been Brigadier Beckwith-Smith, known to everyone as 'Becky', a jolly character with a partiality for shooting pheasants. Both characteristics were in evidence when he attempted to cheer up 2nd Lieutenant Jimmy Langley of the 2nd Coldstream Guards, one of the brigade's battalions, after learning that they were to form part of the rearguard around the Dunkirk perimeter.[1]

Langley's account includes a description of the moment during 28 May when Becky tipped him off about the coming ordeal during a rest break on the sixty-mile march from the Franco-Belgian frontier to Hondschoote:

Suddenly Brigadier Beckwith-Smith . . . drove up in his car. 'Marvellous news, Jimmy,' he shouted. 'The best ever! . . . It is splendid . . . We have been given the supreme honour of being the rearguard at Dunkirk. Tell your platoon, Jimmy. Come on, tell them the good news.' After all the months together, I knew 15 Platoon very well, and had not the slightest doubt that they would accept this information with the usual tolerance and good humour . . . However I did not think they would class it as 'marvellous' and 'the best ever'.

'I think it had better come from you sir.'

'Right . . .' he replied . . . and after telling them to remain seated, made known to them the change of plan. [They had previously been told they were to be evacuated.] Then to my delight . . . he recalled his . . . instruction . . . as to how to deal with Stuka dive-bombers. 'Stand up to them. Shoot at them with a Bren gun from the shoulder. Take them like a high pheasant. Give them plenty of lead. Remember, five pounds to any man who brings one down. I have already paid out ten pounds.'[2]

The next day, having reached the perimeter, the 2nd Coldstream Guards occupied their designated 2200-yard sector of the Bergues–

Furnes Canal to the south of Uxem. (It is shown in Map 16 on pp. 532–3.) 3 Company, which included Langley's platoon, was sand-wiched between two other companies, 1 Company being on Langley's right, and 2 Company on his left. Langley's headquarters were in a small cottage a little way back from the canal, which gave him and his men a good view to the south, especially when they looked out of a hole they had made in the roof by removing a few tiles.

Fortunately Langley and his men saw no Germans during their first three days on the canal, which gave them time to prepare for the coming action. After increasing the company's firepower, by collecting Bren guns and anti-tank rifles plus 30,000 rounds of ammunition from BEF vehicles abandoned on the south side of the canal, and after having his men dig themselves in, the first Germans Langley saw at dawn on 1 June represented something of an anti-climax. Rather than charging towards the canal in the tanks that Langley and his men had heard so much about, the Germans who appeared around six hundred yards away out of the morning mist were not even armed with rifles. They just stood around holding spades, presumably given to them so that they could dig their own trenches. That did not stop Langley's men ambushing them, the resulting massacre enabling his platoon to get their eyes in, but leaving their commander feeling 'slightly sick'.[3]

Firing at the diggers, and the subsequent shooting to repulse German attempts to advance, inevitably betrayed their position, and at about midday, after Langley had observed the Germans manoeuvring what looked like an anti-tank gun on wheels, the cottage roof was hit by five shells. Fortunately this first attempt to knock out their stronghold was less successful than the 'friendly' fire from their rear, which had disturbed them during the previous night: a stray shell from a British gun had hit a small barn where some of Langley's troops were sleeping, killing two of his men.[4] When the first German shell hit the cottage, the men inside ran for their lives, and took cover in the trenches they had dug outside. However, as soon as the shelling ceased, they returned to the cottage – probably justifying the order to do so with the saying that over the years has comforted so many soldiers: shells never fall twice in the same place.

Shortly afterwards, Langley returned to the ditch, fifty yards back from the cottage, where the main company headquarters was located. There he was able to talk to 3 Company's commander, Major Angus McCorquodale, another larger-than-life character who liked to wear a papier-mâché mock-up of a helmet rather than the real thing, adopting the principle that if a shell was directed at his head, it would kill him whatever he was wearing so he might as well be comfortable. McCorquodale also adapted the conventional BEF uniform, making a feature of his trademark green socks and brown shoes, which he wore even during pitched battles. While they were chatting, Langley mentioned an interview with a BEF soldier he had heard broadcast on a portable radio in which the interviewee claimed he was 'the last man out of Dunkirk'. The two officers had a good laugh together about that.[5]

But the next crisis that came their way was no laughing matter. Langley's account has described how their conversation was interrupted by an officer commanding the unit to the right of the battalion, who claimed he had been sent over to talk to them by Lieutenant Evan Gibbs of the Coldstream Guards' 1 Company:

He [the officer from the other unit] informed us that the Germans were massing for an attack on the bridgehead, that his men were exhausted, and that he proposed to withdraw while the going was good. Angus merely said: 'I order you to stay put, and fight it out.'

'You cannot do that. I have over-riding orders from my colonel to withdraw when I think fit,' came the reply.

Angus did not beat about the bush: 'You see that big poplar tree on the road with the white milestone beside it? The moment you or any of your men go back beyond that tree, we will shoot you.' The captain started to expostulate, but Angus cut him short. 'Get back, or I will shoot you now, and send one of my officers to take command,' and his hand moved towards his revolver. The captain departed without further words. 'Get a rifle,' Angus ordered me, picking up one that was lying nearby. When I returned with mine, he said: 'Sights at 250. You will shoot to kill the moment he passes that tree. Are you clear?'

'Yes.'

We had not long to wait before the captain appeared, followed by two men. They stood for a time by the tree, and then the captain walked on. Both our rifles went off simultaneously: he dropped out of sight, and the two men ran back.[6]

Langley's account does not say whether their shots hit the officer. But McCorquodale's radical solution to the problem at least meant that the soldiers within the unit to their right remained at their posts, and the line along the canal was retained for a while longer.[7]

Unfortunately for 3 Company, the men on the battalion's right did not hold out for long. Whether this was because of the strength of the German thrust, or because the unit on the right withdrew as soon as McCorquodale's back was turned, may never be discovered. No war diary or testimony has been found that throws light on the issue. Whatever the reason, the Germans were able to cross the canal and apply such strong pressure on 1 Company, the Coldstream Guards' unit on 3 Company's right, that the soldiers in 1 Company were in the end obliged to retreat eastwards to join up with McCorquodale's men.[8]

Before the retreat, Langley was sent to see how 1 Company was faring. The report he brought back to McCorquodale was grim. While he had been with 1 Company, Lieutenant Gibbs had rushed forward to where a Bren gun had been abandoned, after the gunner had been shot, only to be wounded himself. Although a guardsman ran out to carry him back, Gibbs died soon afterwards. This was very bad news, but what bothered McCorquodale as much was Langley telling him that 2nd Lieutenant Ronnie Speed, an inexperienced officer who had only just joined the battalion in France, was intending to retire with 1 Company on to 3 Company. Langley's account describes McCorquodale's reaction:

Angus replied quietly: 'Is your flask full?'

I told him it was nearly empty.

'Take mine, and make Ronnie drink all of it,' [Angus said]. 'If he won't, or still talks of retiring . . . take command of the company. They are not to retire.'[9]

Ronnie was looking miserable, standing in a ditch up to his waist in water, and shivering. I offered Angus' flask and advised him to drink it, which he did. 'You are not to retire. Do you understand?' [I told him.]

Speed nodded, and 1 Company carried on where they were.[10] But again McCorquodale's solution only won a temporary respite. Half an hour later, the Germans attacked, and drove the remains of 1 Company on to 3 Company, thereby raising the possibility that McCorquodale and his men might be surrounded and attacked simultaneously from the front, side and rear.

There is nothing in the battalion war diary, or in any known account, which states that McCorquodale sent a runner back to his colonel to ask whether his men might be permitted to withdraw now that the Germans had established a bridgehead over the canal. If a runner was sent, it is unlikely that McCorquodale received a reply before Langley, having placed some of his men with Bren guns in the cottage attic, went back to him again to ask for orders. This time, as the following extract from Langley's account makes clear, it was McCorquodale who was weakening:

He was lying on top of the trench [Langley reported], half curled up, still in 'service dress': Sam Browne breeches, green stockings and brown shoes . . . He no longer wore his famous papier-mâché helmet. A dead guardsman was lying beside him. I told him I thought we could hold the enemy from the cottage, but I am not sure he understood. 'I am . . . so very tired,' he said, and then with a half smile, he rallied, and gave me his last order. 'Get back to the cottage Jimmy, and carry on.'[11]

Obeying McCorquodale's command, Langley returned to the cottage attic, and after watching his Bren gunners neutralize a German position established in a building across the canal, he was forced to reorganize his defences because one of the Bren guns was no longer working; according to Langley, the firing pin had melted, putting it out of action. Langley ordered the man with the remaining Bren gun to take up a position downstairs while he remained in the attic with his rifle. He intended to fire at anything that moved on the other side of the canal, a strategy that he hoped would keep the Germans' heads down, and convince them that the position was still strongly defended.

'I had just fired five most satisfactory shots,' wrote Langley,

and, convinced I had chalked up another 'kill', was kneeling, pushing another clip into the rifle, when there was a most frightful crash, and a great wave of heat, dust and debris knocked me over. A shell had burst on the roof. There was a long silence, and I heard a small voice saying, 'I've been hit,' which I suddenly realized was mine. That couldn't be right; so I called out, 'Anybody been hit?' A reply from behind –

'No, sir, we are all right.'

'Well,' I replied more firmly, 'I have.'[12]

Langley had been wounded in his left arm and head; whatever the Germans threw at them now, it was the end of the battle as far as he was concerned. With blood from his arm splattered all over his battle dress, he was helped down from the attic, taken to the rear in a wheel-barrow and transported in an ambulance to the hospital at Rosendaël, just to the south of Malo-les-Bains.[13]

Various accounts by soldiers in the 2nd Coldstream Guards have made what might be interpreted as critical remarks about the unit that had been on the 1st Guards Brigade's right on the Bergues–Furnes Canal.[14] In case these comments are taken to cast aspersions on the fighting performance of the 1st East Lancashire Regiment (the 'East Lancs', part of 42 Division's 126 Brigade), whose soldiers were at one stage on the Coldstream Guards' right, it is only fair to mention the evidence that vindicates their reputation. It is certainly true that the East Lancs were ordered at first to hold the canal line to the right of 1st Guards Brigade. However, before the Germans attacked on 1 June, men from another unit were placed between the Guards and the East Lancs, leaving the latter with a reduced front.[15] It appears to have been this other unit, the 5th Borders, that gave way on 1 June when the Germans attacked.

Given the large sector of the canal line allocated to the East Lancs on 30 May, no one could have complained if they had followed suit. Even before the last-ditch stand, which was to win them great distinction, and a Victoria Cross for one of their officers, it was realized that they had been given a most difficult assignment. With two companies up near the canal, and two in reserve, they were asked in the first place to hold a 3000-yard front that would have been difficult for three battalions to secure, let alone one.[16] Their task was made much more difficult because the southern bank, on the German side of the canal, was considerably higher in some areas than the northern, British, side. This was particularly the case near the destroyed bridge at Bentie-Meulen, which in peacetime had been the direct route from outside the perimeter to the village of Galghoeck. (The Bentie-Meulen bridge which is between Pont de Syckine and Pont à Moutons is shown in Map 16 on pp. 532–3.)[17]

The danger this posed was understood only too well by East Lancs officer 2nd Lieutenant John Arrigo whose D Company sections had been ordered to hold the canal line facing the spot where the bridge had stood. During the morning of 31 May, two of his soldiers near the bridge site were shot and killed in their foxholes. Their bodies could not be recovered until the German firing died down that night, and by the time Arrigo lifted one man out of his hole, the corpse was stiff from rigor mortis.[18] The dead man was still wearing his helmet, but there was a bullet hole in it and a corresponding one in his head, and another bullet had punched a neat hole in his forehead. Arrigo did not know whether the dead man had been imprudently standing up when shot, or whether he had been hit while crouching in the foxhole. Whatever had happened, it was a sad sight for the twenty-one-year-old officer to behold, and Arrigo was grateful for the failing light because it meant that none of his men could see him sobbing silently in the dark. It was the first time he had touched a dead man.

This is not to say that Arrigo had never before seen blood spilled. That same morning, he had seen what had happened to an unfortunate French dispatch rider who had driven up to the destroyed bridge, apparently unaware that it was the front line, before the British soldiers could stop him. He was shot, possibly by the same sniper who subsequently killed Arrigo's soldiers. Then, on discovering that no one could reach him, he wrote his last words in a notebook, before shooting himself in the head with his pistol, thereby ending his own life. Later that night, Arrigo was told that his platoon should retire with the rest of D Company to the stop line in Uxem, after being relieved by the battalion's B Company, commanded by Captain Marcus Ervine-Andrews.

Charles Best, who was transferred from another company to act as one of B Company's stretcher-bearers, has described the scene he witnessed in the field to the rear where Ervine-Andrews gave last-minute briefings to his NCOs before they moved into the front line: 'It was a beautiful evening. Colonel Pendlebury [the East Lancs' commanding officer] walked around shaking hands with everybody, telling them: "I know you can do it. I'll see you back in England." When I heard him say that, I realized we were in serious trouble.'

Best's sense of foreboding was heightened when Ervine-Andrews turned to him and said, 'It looks like we're going to need you.' After he had marched up a track in the dark to the farm just behind the front line where the relieving was to take place, Best asked some of D Company's men how things were up at the canal. The answer could not have been more discouraging: 'It's hell up there,' one of them said.[19]

The insertion of the 5th Borders into the front line on the East Lancs' left during the night of 31 May–1 June gave Ervine-Andrews and his men a more manageable one thousand yards to hold, but they had little time to settle in. At dawn on 1 June, the Germans attacked. It is impossible to describe in detail the actions fought by each section within the company as they stood their ground to the north of the canal. The fact that the actions witnessed by one section can be described is thanks to an account by Private Frank Curry, who was just eighteen years old at the time, one of the youngest members of the battalion. Curry watched the repeated attempts by Germans to rush up to the canal regardless of B Company's gunfire. They suffered heavy casualties, but kept coming back for more. Curry's description of one such attack reveals how Ervine-Andrews was able to marshal his defences from a barn a short distance behind Curry's position:

Suddenly Captain Andrews yelled: 'They are advancing!' . . . Minutes passed by. Then opposite, we saw the enemy creeping up amongst the long grass opposite. [They were] about a hundred strong, and [to] their rear we noticed several [of them] carrying rubber dinghies. 'Wait for it!' yelled Captain Andrews. 'Hold your fire until I blow my whistle!' . . . Then the whistle blew, and several shots [fired by] Captain Andrews with his revolver from . . . the barn was a signal for us to blast away into the enemy.

The East Lancs' gunfire stopped the men opposite Curry's section, but to his right some six Germans crossed the canal. Four were shot down, but two appeared to be struggling to their feet. 'We should have allowed them to live,' wrote Curry, 'for they were not in a position to put up any fight.' But maddened by the noise of the shooting and the bloodthirsty cries of Paddy Kavanagh, an East Lancs veteran in his forties who had taken Curry under his wing, Curry leaped forward and bayoneted one of the two Germans in the groin while Kavanagh dispatched the other. 'I felt sick,' wrote Curry, 'but in the heat of the moment, I was not sane.'[20]

At about 10 a.m., the East Lancs' hopes of holding out were undermined by news that Germans had got over the canal on both flanks. It was only because of covering fire from the battalion's carriers, and the flooded land to their left, that the enemy was pinned down, and prevented from surrounding Ervine-Andrews's men. Around two hours later, an even more threatening attack was made on the East Lancs' own front, and was only beaten off thanks to the personal intervention of Ervine-Andrews. No witness alive today observed at first hand what occurred when he went into action. But the following extract from the 30 July 1940 citation, announcing the award to Ervine-Andrews of the Victoria Cross for his 'most conspicuous gallantry', at least gives an idea as to how he took the steam out of the German attack:

There being danger of one of his platoons being driven in, he [Ervine-Andrews] called for volunteers to fill the gap, and then, going forward, climbed on to the top of a straw-roofed barn, from which he engaged the enemy with rifle and light automatic fire, though at the time, the enemy were sending mortar bombs and armour-piercing bullets through the roof. Captain Ervine-Andrews personally accounted for seventeen of the enemy with his rifle, and for many more with a Bren gun. Later, when the house which he held had been shattered by enemy fire and set alight, and all his ammunition had been expended, he sent back his wounded in the remaining carrier. Captain Ervine-Andrews then collected the remaining eight men of his company from this forward position, and, when almost completely surrounded, led them back to the cover afforded by the company in the rear, swimming or wading up to the chin in water for over a mile.[21]

As so often, the summary of the action in the citation does not include the full story. While it is correct that Ervine-Andrews did most of the shooting from the barn during the crucial stage of the battle, when the Bren gun had become jammed, he and his volunteers could not have held on to their position had it not been for an equally valiant act by another East Lancs officer. B Company's 2nd Lieutenant Cêtre, known to everyone as 'Joe' because of his bushy Joe-Stalinesque moustache, was as brave as his facial hair was long.[22] Although by 2 p.m. the area around the farm that served as the company headquarters was being shelled, and the position was being raked by gunfire from the flanks, Cêtre nevertheless raced back to the battalion's headquarters at Uxem to report that their ammunition was running out, and it would be impossible to hold out much longer. Before he returned to B Company, he collected the last available ammunition, and personally carried it back to Ervine-Andrews, along with instructions that they must fight on to the last round. Only then were they to withdraw through the battalion's A and D Companies, which were keeping open the line of retreat to the rear. Cêtre later received the Military Cross for his act of valour, which ensured that the position was held for an extra two hours.

Their ammunition finally ran out at 4.30 p.m., whereupon Ervine-Andrews gave the order to retire. By that stage only a handful of men were in a fit state to take advantage of it, and only those who moved quickly escaped. As Curry's account makes clear, Ervine-Andrews did not lead all of the men in the front line to safety: for at least some it was every man for himself.

'We started to run,' Curry reported.

I looked back. German soldiers [were] crossing the canal . . . in . . . small boats. As they climbed up the bank, they commenced firing at us. Suddenly I heard a cry from old Paddy. He had been hit in his back and [had fallen] to the ground. Corporal Johnson knelt beside . . . [him], and cradled him in his arms as blood began oozing from his mouth. Then Johnson yelled out 'Get going!' To my dying day I shall never [forget] that moment of terror. I threw my rifle on the ground, and turning, I dashed away, running towards the thick hedge in front of me.[23]

Back at Uxem, Arrigo's platoon and the rest of D Company were still holding the back-up line when the first men from B Company arrived. Their sergeant-major told Arrigo that he would not be seeing Ervine-Andrews again, unless it was after the war, because he had been captured. So everyone was astonished when Ervine-Andrews showed up, soaking wet, having waded through flooded fields and ditches on his way back.[24] Both Ervine-Andrews and the men with whom he was reunited at Uxem, and Curry, eventually made their way back to Dunkirk.

The 3 Brigade war diary, which describes conditions on the Bergues–Furnes Canal to the east of those areas held by the East Lancs and the Coldstream Guards, highlights difficulties experienced by many soldiers entering the perimeter in this sector, and explains how the Germans were nevertheless held at bay. Like many troops who poured into the perimeter on 28 May after passing through Hondschoote, 3 Brigade's crossed the canal into the perimeter at the bridge known as Pont-aux-Cerfs, some seven miles south of the beach at Bray-Dunes.[25] At the bridge they were greeted by what the war diarist refers to as 'a completely over-wrought staff officer who was brandishing a revolver and ordering all vehicles . . . off the road into the fields to be burnt. The site he chose for his task, and the comprehensiveness with which he tried to carry it out had considerable effects on subsequent operations.'[26]

While the staff officer's orders might have been justified for troops who were merely entering the perimeter to be evacuated, they were hardly appropriate for units that, like 3 Brigade, had to fight on. The staff within 1 Division's headquarters, which was in charge of 3 Brigade as well as of the 1st Guards Brigade including the Coldstream Guards, were left with neither a wireless nor the cables required for the division to be able to communicate with troops under its command. 'The . . . staff officer on . . . Pont-aux-Cerfs had ordered it all to be burnt,' wrote 3 Brigade's war diarist.

Next morning, the positioning of the front-line troops along the north side of the canal was aided by the flooding. It was obvious that the Germans would only be able to advance along the roads since the fields in between were under water. Consequently there was no need to guard the entire length of the brigade's front. Instead it sufficed to place a group of soldiers every 150–200 yards, thereby covering all roads and paths leading into the perimeter. Thus the brigade's strongest battalion, the 1st Duke of Wellington's Regiment, which was to hold the Pont-aux-Cerfs bridge, and subsequently its ruins after it was blown up the next day, and the adjacent canal, was able just about to cover some 5000 yards of the canal line with support from a company of Sherwood Foresters.[27]

On the other hand the Dukes quickly discovered that their line of fire was obstructed by the burned vehicles ordered off the road on the south side of the canal by the over-zealous staff officer. This may have bothered the men, but the officers appear to have been, initially at least, more upset by what had happened to their 'cellar' which had been in the commanding officer's car when it had been abandoned.[28] Their spirits were only revived after two slaughtermen were found who killed some pigs and cows thereby ensuring that the whole battalion could have a good meal.

Meanwhile the staff officers in 1 Division moved to Bray–Dunes. 'The road Les Moeres–Bray-Dunes was [also] lined with ditched vehicles and guns of every description and calibre,' 3 Brigade's war diarist continued. 'The only way to get back from Div HQ in many places was to go over the tops of abandoned vehicles.' The road was only cleared thanks to strenuous efforts made by a Royal Artillery unit whose guns had not yet been called upon to fire at the Germans.

The diarist also recorded what happened at 10 a.m. on 30 May when the Duke of Wellington's troops saw the enemy for the first time. The Germans had marched up to the canal without bothering to conceal themselves and had called on the British troops to surrender: 'Having held their fire till all [Germans] were collected in a bunch, the DWR post suddenly opened fire at point-blank range killing eleven and wounding one . . . whom they . . . captured. He [the captured German] said that they had been told that we were only awaiting their arrival to surrender, [and] that the war was virtually won.'

The Germans who followed this vanguard were much less accommo-dating, and soon British soldiers were cursing the staff officer by the bridge once again after seeing their comrades being hit by bullets fired by snipers who had taken cover behind the abandoned vehicles on the other side of the canal.

Additional British casualties might have been suffered after a Lysander, a British plane, swooped down over the perimeter at 4.30 p.m. 'We had had similar experiences before with Lysanders and [had] always been bombed or shelled immediately after,' wrote the diarist. 'Accordingly Division were at once asked if we might open fire on it.' The answer that reached the Duke of Wellingtons' commanding officer was 'For . . . sake don't fire at it. The Commander-in-Chief is in it!'

On the morning of 31 May, 3 Brigade's Brigadier Wilson heard that his men would not be evacuated for one or even two days, this being the decision reached at La Panne the day before (see Chapter 30). 1 Division was to remain in position as the rearguard. Nevertheless it was decided that 3 Brigade's headquarters should go to the beach at Bray-Dunes that night so as to be ready when the evacuation order was given. The war diarist has described what he witnessed during the move:

The scenery provided a . . . picture of the abomination of desolation. Ruined and burnt out houses . . . salt water spreading everywhere, vehicles abandoned, many of them charred relics of twisted metal on the roadside and overturned in the ditches. Light tanks and guns poking up out of the [floods]. Horses dead or dying from want of water. Here and there civilian or French Army corpses lying in the open. An unforgettable spectacle.

Only then did the Germans attack, crossing the canal on the brigade's right during the morning of 1 June and penetrating between the Duke of Wellingtons' front-line posts. Although the battalion was hastily ordered back behind the Digue des Glaises, a waterway north of the canal, the command came too late for those men in the battalion's right-hand company, which had heavy casualties. 'Few of them were left,' the war diarist concluded. Also shells hit both the Dukes' regimental aid post and the farmhouse serving as the battalion's headquarters, and it was sheer good fortune that there were not more dead British soldiers in this sector than there were. In the former case the medical officer was out searching for supplies, and in the latter, the commanding officer survived in spite of the roof caving in around him. The position was only saved thanks to the arrival of a squadron of carriers operated by the 5th Royal Inniskilling Dragoon Guards, whose presence, according to the war diarist, had 'a most calming influence on the enemy's enthusiasm'.

Fortunately for the front-line soldiers who retired from the Bergues–Furnes Canal, the Germans who had crossed the waterway did not immediately seek to expand the bridgeheads. As a result, British troops held a line of sorts, partly on the canal and partly further back, until that night, when the order issued that morning obliging all 1 Corps units to retire was put into effect.[29] Churchill's 1 June instruction to Alexander (quoted in Chapter 31) arrived too late to persuade him to alter the plans made that morning.[30] At 8 a.m. on 1 June, Alexander had told Abrial and Fagalde that while he still intended to abandon the canal line around the perimeter during the coming night, he would hold an inner perimeter line around part of Dunkirk during 2 June if any troops could not get away. Then he would evacuate the last BEF troops during the night of 2–3 June.[31]

This willingness to remain in Dunkirk for an extra day was not governed by any desire to fit in with the French. Although there was a contingency plan in case some troops failed to board ships during the night of 1–2 June, Alexander had hoped that all the remaining British troops would be evacuated that night. It was only during the late afternoon on 1 June when, following shipping losses at the hands of the

Luftwaffe, an order was given that there would be no further evacuation during daylight hours, that it was realized it might be impossible to take off some of the remaining BEF troops until the next night. (Other reasons for the delayed evacuation are in note 32.)[32]

Alexander cannot have been particularly happy about the extra twenty-four hours in Dunkirk. In spite of his intention to cover the harbour with a small number of British troops, it was clear that, from the moment 1 Corps moved back during the night of 1–2 June, the security of the 3000-odd soldiers who constituted the British rearguard, and any other 2 Corps troops not already evacuated, could only be safeguarded if French troops successfully held the new inner perimeter to the east of Dunkirk, and some kind of line to the west of Dunkirk, where they were already having difficulty holding the Germans south-west of Spycker. (The inner perimeter east of Dunkirk is shown in Map 16 on pp. 532–3.)[33] By the morning of 2 June some 261,000 Allied troops had been evacuated, including around 179,000 BEF soldiers.[34] But given the French Army's performance on the Meuse, Alexander would not have been human if he did not question whether his ally's soldiers were up to the task of holding on until the remainder were picked up.

The decision to hold on meant prolonged torment for wounded soldiers inside the perimeter before they could be properly treated by German doctors. Medical aid in the BEF's overcrowded casualty clearing stations within the perimeter was basic to say the least. Perhaps because so many of those 'cared for' died, accounts describing the prevailing conditions are few and far between. However, there is one account by a Corporal Adams, a nursing orderly who served in the La Panne casualty clearing station, which contains an authentic description of what these mobile hospitals were like.[35]

Adams's first posting in France had been with the 11th Casualty Clearing Station (11th CCS). As it had moved around France during the fighting, he had become accustomed to coping with horrific injuries. But it had taken some time before that stage was reached. When the fighting started, he and his fellow orderlies were far from ready for the awful sights they were to encounter. Early on one of his colleagues was traumatized when an amputated leg was carried out of the operating theatre and handed to him. Adams was equally shockable. His most traumatic experience occurred when he took a dressing off a patient's face only to find himself gazing into a crimson hole: the eyeball was stuck to the dressing. Even such terrible wounds failed to move him by the end of May 1940. When the 11th CCS was set up in the cinema and casino at La Panne, he was ready for anything. There were no beds and no sheets at the casualty clearing station. Wounded patients were brought in by the field-ambulance units, and had their operations on their stretchers. Those same stretchers were then laid on the floor, and covered with blankets that, according to Adams, were often 'blood-soaked and reeking'. No medical officers were available to deal with patients after the surgeons had operated. Nursing orderlies were expected to deal with post-operative pain by administering shots of morphine. They were also supposed to keep everything running smoothly.

That was more easily said than done, given the facilities at La Panne. The water supply gave out while the La Panne CCS was still operating. Peace and quiet was non-existent, which must have doubled the work for the staff, since alert patients are much more trouble than those who can forget their discomfort by sleeping. Heaven help patients who were shell-shocked. The sands and promenade at La Panne were bristling with machine-guns and artillery, and Adams has recalled how when planes attacked and the gunners went into action 'some patients nearly went mad' with terror. Given the limited resources at his disposal, one can hardly blame Adams for relying on a cocktail of trickery and bluffing in order to keep his patients quiet. Time and again he had to act the part of a delirious soldier's sweetheart or wife to soothe his patient's feverish rambling.

One man, whose legs were paralysed after he had been wounded in the bladder, kept asking when he would be treated by the surgeon. To calm him down, Adams arranged for the bandages to be removed and a new Elastoplast placed over the wound next time the man was given morphine, so that when the man woke up, he could tell him he had had his operation while he was asleep. On being told this, the man felt the plaster, smiled peacefully, and went back to sleep. He was still alive when he was sent off to be evacuated from Dunkirk. Another strategy Adams used to reduce his workload involved making himself scarce, except when patients called out for him. Even then, he had to creep around the ward, especially when he was carrying the urine bottle: if he was seen with it, the patients started clamouring, competing with each other to use it first.

Notwithstanding these difficult conditions, Adams was ashamed at how callous he became. At times he could not stop himself hoping that wounded men would hurry up and die so that he would have room to take in new cases who were queuing up for a place inside the CCS. On the other hand, his account reveals that even after all the terrible injuries he witnessed he still retained a modicum of compassion: 'I was surprised at the peaceful way death came,' Adams reported. 'I never saw any man who showed signs of fright, or who struggled to live. They just slipped away, as if they were relieved and happy to go . . . One moment they were [lying] silent with grey tortured faces. The next they looked placidly up, and the pain vanished from their eyes.'

Ironically, some of the men received their best treatment after they had died. All dead men were washed, their wounds were dressed, and they were then clothed in clean pyjamas. Finally they were sewn into a blanket before being buried. Every dead man was given a proper burial service.

By the time 2nd Lieutenant Langley was wounded on 1 June, the La Panne casualty clearing station had been evacuated. That explains how he came to be lying in an ambulance in the driveway leading up to Château Coquelle in Rosendaël, a large house that BEF soldiers knew as 'Chapeau Rouge' (Red Hat). It was a nickname inspired as much by the series of hat-like shapes covered with red tiles that stuck up from its roof as by the fact that it was adjacent to an area called Chapeau Rouge. (See Map 16 on pp. 532–3.)[36] This was the temporary base for the 12th Casualty Clearing Station, which doubled as a clearing house for wounded soldiers about to be evacuated to England. Langley could not have arrived at a worse time: the 12th CCS was overflowing. The time was long past when all wounded patients could be accommodated inside the house: newcomers were either left in tents in the grounds or, like Langley, lay abandoned and forgotten in the ambulances in which they had arrived.

There was another reason why Langley had to wait a long time for treatment. Philip Newman, a twenty-eight-year-old surgeon working at the CCS, had become demoralized by his inability to keep up with the number of essential operations as well as by the conditions. When the first shells landed near the house, he had thought it prudent to move down to the cellar where the 'operating theatre' was lit by one electric light. Then the electricity failed, and from that moment on, he had to make do with candles. It was in these circumstances that he decided he would do more good by going to the mole to help evacuate the many wounded there. It 'seemed to put saving the odd life by operation very much in the shade', he reported.[37]

On 1 June, Newman returned to the Chapeau Rouge château to find:

Something new was in the air. New orders had arrived. We were to pull out, but one medical officer and ten men were to stay behind for every 100 wounded ... At 2.30 [p.m.] we gathered in the mess for the ballot. Of the 17 officers, three only were to stay, so my chances seemed quite rosy. As the CO [commanding officer] shuffled the papers, my heart was pounding. Cocky O'Shea, the RC [Roman Catholic] padre, drew the papers. The last 4 were Herbert, Hewer, Williamson ... and [me] Newman. I was 17th, and down the drain anyhow. At least I knew the worst ... The rest were leaving at 8 p.m. for the boat.

I shall never forget those 5 hours before they went: trying to look efficient and 'don't carish', and everyone dreading to speak to me ... The CO called us all together and spoke. I gave 3 cheers for him. He did not seem anxious to catch my eye. I hope it was because he felt a great deal ... Eventually they went, and I was very glad to see them go.[38]

33: Mission Accomplished

Dunkirk's mole, and Rosendaël, 2–3 June 1940
(See Map 16. Also Maps 1 and 10)

Churchill's War Cabinet had many unpleasant shocks during the battles in France. But one of the most upsetting must have been Air Chief Marshal Dowding's 3 June assessment of Britain's strength in the air, taking into account the 250 fighters already lost during the campaign. According to Dowding, although there were 524 operational fighters in Britain (280 Spitfires and 244 Hurricanes) in addition to the three fighter squadrons still in France, if the Luftwaffe attacked Britain 'heavily', he could not guarantee air superiority for more than forty-eight hours.[1]

Dowding's downbeat analysis made it easy for the War Cabinet to deal with France's call for extra planes. None would be sent apart from those that were necessary to bring up to strength the squadrons already there. Had Dowding's assessment been made public, it would also have answered those critics serving in the BEF who, with good reason, asked why they had been bombed by so many German planes over Dunkirk. With the resources at Dowding's disposal, it was impossible both to retain enough planes to protect Britain, and to shield the evacuation with a continuous air umbrella.

Dowding mentioned another difficulty to the War Cabinet. He was convinced that his pilots' morale would suffer if he was forced to send out inadequately trained crews or weak patrols in order to comply with the Cabinet's demands. His concern was not just a device to save his planes for the defence of Britain. An account by Spitfire pilot Allan Wright, then a twenty-year-old officer in 92 Squadron, has highlighted the danger and psychological trauma endured by those who attempted to keep the Germans at bay in the air.[2] His first patrol over France was on 23 May. British soldiers and sailors in Boulogne on that day might say that the support from the RAF was woefully inadequate, but 92 Squadron's pilots in general, and Allan Wright in particular, did everything that could have been expected of them. Wright's account records that they were outnumbered by the large number of Messerschmitt (Me.) 109s (single-seater fighters like the Spitfires) and Me. 110s (manned by a pilot and rear gunner) that they encountered over Boulogne during their afternoon patrol, the second that day. But he and his chums did not hesitate to take on this formidable German force that was protecting the bombers flying below them.

Wright not only survived that action, but also shot down one Me. 110. Any triumphant feelings concerning his own performance were, however, tempered by the knowledge that four planes in 92 Squadron had been shot down, including the Spitfire flown by his best friend Pat Learmond, who had been unable to bale out before his plane hit the ground. The news that Learmond had been killed did not sink in immediately, but it did later that night, as Wright's account reveals:

[During the evening] I lay soaking in my bath. How lucky we were as fliers to be able to enjoy the luxuries of mess life when not required for duty. Pat's loss that morning now came home to me. I was overcome, and wept for him. I wasn't used to sudden death. How could it be possible that he was gone, not ever to come back? He so clearly had the potential for a brilliant career. Now gone.

I was aware that this hopeless and helpless feeling of loss was in itself a stranger to me. I had not cried since I was a child. Yet there was little personal fear for tomorrow. That came later.[3]

After surviving several subsequent patrols over Dunkirk, Wright and 92 Squadron patrolled over Dunkirk again on 2 June. By this time the RAF commanders had decided that it was better to fly less frequent multi-squadron patrols rather than extra single-squadron patrols. On this occasion, 92 Squadron was with three other squadrons. Nevertheless, Wright and his comrades were once again outnumbered by Me. 109s. That did not hold back 92 Squadron: they scattered the German formation they encountered. But even chasing away one German plane was extremely dangerous, as the following extract from Wright's account of a dogfight demonstrates:

Down we both went, each coaxing as much speed as we could out of our aircraft . . . The controls stiffened. Elevators were trimmed. It became almost impossible to get the sight steady on the target again. All my strength and concentration was needed. As the range closed, I fired several times. I got the sight on again once more, and with the last of my ammunition, his engine caught fire, and his dive steepened. He was about to hit the ground when there was an almighty bang in my cockpit. My first thought was that the speed had been too much, and my aircraft was breaking up. Smoke and an unfamiliar smell filled the cockpit.

Wright's plane had been hit by explosive shells fired by another Me. 109 on his tail. The shells penetrated the outer skin of his plane, causing the smoke and whiff of cordite inside the cockpit. But, as Wright's account reveals, he could not immediately investigate what had occurred:

I was still in a deep dive, and going much too fast to be able to manoeuvre. Streets, gardens and houses were expanding before my eyes . . . I closed the throttle, and was now heaving back on the stick with all my strength to drag the aircraft up and around.

Fortunately for Wright he succeeded, and although he had no more ammunition, he frightened off his pursuer by turning sharply, exploiting the Spitfire's ability to do so faster than its German rival, until he was on the Me. 109's tail. He then made for home. Only after he had landed at Duxford, near Royston, did he realize how lucky he had been: no less than sixteen bullet holes were found in his plane. However, there was no time to dwell on what might have happened. That evening he flew back to Martlesham Heath, the base in East Anglia whence he had taken off, to be ready for the next patrol.

That same day there was a less happy outcome to an incident at sea, which has become part of the Dunkirk legend. It was witnessed by Sub-Lieutenant Martin Solomon, who two days earlier had led the convoy of cockle-fishing boats to Dunkirk (see Chapter 31).[4] In the course of a subsequent trip to the mole, during the night of 1–2 June, he overheard a naval officer ask if anyone could help him deal with the French. Because Solomon spoke the language, he volunteered, and set about sorting out the log-jam blocking the mole.

He soon discovered what was behind the problem. The French soldiers were not being uncooperative: they thought that certain ships had been set aside for them, and believed they were to remain with their own units when boarding. As a result, one area on the mole became clogged up with troops, while no one was using the ships further along.

British officers had tried to resolve the situation by shouting, *'Allez!'* combined with gesticulations intended to indicate where the French soldiers were to go. But this merely aggravated the problem, since the French, believing they were being insulted, became stubborn, and refused to comply. Working alongside Commander Campbell Clouston, the thirty-nine-year-old naval officer in charge of embarkation on the mole, Solomon was able to sort out the problem, as he put it, 'to a certain extent', telling the officers in command of the French regiments what to do.[5] When he had done all he could, he took that night's last destroyer back to Dover, arriving on 2 June.

There, he was given permission to return to Dunkirk with Clouston. They set out that afternoon in one of two RAF motor boats full of naval officers and men who were being sent over to supervise that night's evacuation of the remainder of the BEF.[6] On the way, they were attacked by German aircraft, and their boat sank. After the sinking, their boat's bow was still visible above the waves, but it was clear that the men in the water could not bring her to the surface. The commander of the other boat offered to take Clouston on board but Clouston refused to desert his men and ordered the other boat to leave them, and press on to Dunkirk. It was probably the correct decision. Soon afterwards, this second motor boat was attacked, and hit by incendiary bullets, putting the starboard engine out of action. The commander subsequently reported that if survivors from Clouston's boat had been on board, their arrival at Dunkirk would have been 'most unlikely'.[7] As it was, they reached the harbour at around 9 p.m., later than expected, but in time to do the job for which they had been sent.

Solomon has described the fate of the men left in the water with him.

[The] French officer clinging to [the] bows of [the] wreck informed us that he saw an empty boat about 6 miles off in the direction of Gravelines. [I] asked permission of Commander Clouston to try to reach [it], and he and I decided to go off together. Commander Clouston however shortly abandoned the swim, and returned to cling to the remains of the wreck. As the water was slightly rough, it was impossible to see the open boat, and [it was] only [possible to see] the shore occasionally, but at 2230, I sighted a large empty destroyer cutter . . . which may, or may not, have been the original I set out for. [I] reached [the] same, but [I] was unable to climb aboard, as [the] sides were too high, and [I] was suffering slightly from exhaustion.

[At] 2300 [I] decided to swim for [the] 'German' shore, but fortunately, before abandoning [the] boat, [I] swam to [the] other side, where I found a fender hanging down. With the aid of the fender, and the remains of my kit used as a ladder, I was able to get aboard. [I] lashed [the] helm hard over, and attempted to row [the] cutter with one oar in [the] direction I imagined survivors might be. After approximately one hour, I abandoned the attempt, as [the] cutter was too large, [the] distance too far, and it was already getting dark.[8]

He was eventually picked up by a French fishing-boat.

Commander Clouston and all but one of the men in the water with him were less fortunate. Only one man was still clinging to the remains of the motor boat when a passing destroyer picked him up. The other men were said to have either died of exposure or drowned. The survivor stated that he had seen Clouston's corpse floating in the water some time before he was rescued. But Solomon's report includes a glowing tribute to what he referred to as 'the extraordinary courage of all the poor fellows in the water', which must have been based in part on what the other survivor reported:

Even though they must have known that the end was near, they never grumbled, nor were they afraid; they even went so far as to ask permission of Commander Clouston before removing their tin hats. When I left them clinging around the wreck, although already suffering from exposure, they were singing and discussing old times together. Commander Clouston's example must have helped them all, as it helped me. Although exhausted himself, he continued to chat, encourage and white lie to the end.[9]

One of the soldiers who might have been helped by Clouston that night, had the naval commander made it to the mole, was 2nd Lieutenant Julian Warde-Aldam of the 2nd Coldstream Guards. His battalion – minus Langley and McCorquodale and several other wounded, killed or missing officers and men – had reached the mole the night before, only to be ordered to return to the shore after waiting many hours in vain for a ship. That left the Coldstream Guardsmen with the prospect of waiting for an additional twenty-four hours on or near the beaches. An announcement was made confirming that there would be no more ships until the next night.

The announcement seemed all the more alarming, because while Warde-Aldam had been queuing up on the mole, he had seen one of many German shells fired into the area around the harbour land a hundred yards away, in the middle of a company of Frenchmen. The result was horrible to behold. This shelling initially persuaded the guardsmen that they would be much safer if they waited on the sand beside the mole where shells buried themselves before exploding, thereby smothering part of the blast. But Warde-Aldam's account describes how, after being summoned to take refuge in a casemate within the town, he and his comrades walked past the Frenchmen's remains: 'The ground was flowing (literally) in blood, and the cries of the wounded, as they clutched at our ankles as we went past, were heartrending. [Unfortunately] there was nothing we could do for them.'[10]

Warde-Aldam's account mentions another horrific scene he witnessed when he and his men returned to the mole at 9 p.m. on 2–3 June: 'As we went along the mole, I saw 4 horses in the water. They had obviously no hope of getting ashore, as their way was blocked by enormous boulders. Suddenly a Bren gun spat. The sea was red with blood, and 3 of the horses reared up and died. But one was left swimming about, snorting bloody spray at intervals, with its eyes just out of the water. I felt physically sick.'[11] Warde-Aldam's fear that he might vomit if he did any violent exercise appears to explain why he refused to jump down ten feet on to the boat he was to board along with the other guardsmen. Instead he boarded more sedately, after finding a ladder further along the mole.

The Frenchmen seen by Warde-Aldam were not the only victims of German artillery on 2 June. Earlier that morning, hospital staff at the 12th Casualty Clearing Station in Rosendaël were woken by what Major Philip Newman described as 'a terrific crash'. A shell had hit the front room of the château, the former operating theatre, injuring about a dozen of 'the poor chaps' whom Newman found there. 'One lad had a slab of concrete on his face,' wrote Newman. 'Everywhere patients were yelling.' For a time, the area around the house was full of naked men, some wounded and some burned, who were crawling about on the grass with bombs exploding around them.[12]

It appears to have been this shelling, combined with the deteriorating conditions at the CCS, which finally persuaded Newman that he should go down to the bastion at the harbour once again to see whether there was anything he could do to help. While there, he was ushered in to see General Alexander. Newman was surprised to find anyone as important as Alexander still in Dunkirk, but took the chance to tell the general about the 'hopeless' situation at the 'Château'.[13] Alexander immediately had a message sent to Ramsay in Dover asking for hospital ships. Unfortunately, although Alexander's message was sent *en clair* in the hope that the Germans would intercept it, and not bomb ships on a mercy mission, the two hospital ships which attempted to reach Dunkirk later that day were both attacked. One sank, and the other returned, damaged, to England.[14]

Meanwhile Newman returned to the château to await developments. The first was an invitation that evening to send all of the walking wounded to the mole. Newman and his staff quickly went round the house and grounds, and collected a hundred men who were willing, and just about able, to shuffle along. They were packed into four lorries. 'It was amazing who could walk,' Newman wrote in his account.[15] Captain Francis Waldron, who had suffered so much on the perimeter canal line near Furnes, was among them (see Chapter 30). His account reveals that the men transported were not really 'walking wounded' at all: 'Two men I vividly remember . . . Both their faces and parts of their bodies had been terrifyingly burnt, and they must have been in acute pain, and were quite unrecognisable.'[16]

On the way to the harbour it looked as if Waldron, along with everyone on his lorry, might also end up being burned. By the time they made it to the only road leading to the harbour, a burning oil tank beside the road made the driver question whether it was safe to pass. 'Do you or don't you get away?' the driver asked rhetorically, before accelerating past the danger spot at fifty miles per hour, ignoring the great heat that made them fear that at any minute they would be burned to a frazzle. In spite of this obstacle, the lorries arrived safely at the base of the mole, where their fragile human cargo, including Waldron, was unloaded. The men then limped down the mole, and were helped on to a waiting destroyer.[17]

'About 9.45 [p.m.],' wrote Newman, 'just as the light was failing, we got a message [in the Château] to say a hospital ship was coming in. I called all the men together, and told them there was [a] slight chance, and that if we worked really hard all night, [and] got rid of all the wounded, we could get on the boat.'[18] This galvanized everyone at the

CCS into action, and five ambulances full of wounded men were driven through the night, which Newman describes as being 'red with burning buildings', to the mole.

'We waited for an hour,' Newman noted:

[but] no [hospital] boat came. At [about] 11 p.m. I saw the last of the BEF file past. We, with some marines, rushed a few of the stretchers half a mile up the jetty, and put them on a boat. At about 11.30 p.m., the 4 commanders and brigadiers, and anybody else who was English, left in a pinnace, and there we were, left standing alone. Forsaken by England, and only the Germans to look forward to. I can never forget that moment as long as I live. It gave me the greatest feeling of desolation I have ever had.

The rest of the stretchers we begged the French soldiers to take with them on to the boats, which they did with an ill grace. So we did at least do our duty, and [helped] 25 more men to safety. One man on a stretcher, we actually chucked over, as the ship . . . left the quay. He landed safely.

We arrived back at the Château. The boys had worked very hard to get the convoy ready, and then, exhausted, had given up hope, and simply gone to sleep on the ground in utter despair.

The last ships carrying BEF soldiers left Dunkirk shortly before 11 p.m. That, together with French soldiers rescued during the night, and around 6900 wounded men not mentioned in the extract from the Dover Report in Appendix B (see pp. 540–41), took the total number of soldiers evacuated to 288,000 (including some 193,000 BEF troops), a miraculous figure compared with the 45,000 the Admiralty had originally mentioned to Ramsay.[19] Alexander and Tennant then toured the beaches and the harbour in a motor boat, calling for any British soldiers to show themselves. None did, and at 11.30 p.m. Tennant sent the following signal to Dover, which at the beginning of Operation Dynamo he had never imagined would be appropriate: 'BEF evacuated . . .'[20]

34: Payback

Dunkirk perimeter, and mole, 3–4 June 1940
(See Map 16. Also Maps 1 and 10)

Even before the ships had arrived at the mole during the night of 2–3 June to pick up the last British soldiers, the French were asking their British allies to return the next night for their troops. A message from General Koeltz included the following plea:

In addition to the 25,000 French troops who are defending the Dunkirk bridgehead, there are still around 22,000 Frenchmen. All the British soldiers are going tonight. As we are hoping to evacuate these 22,000 men during the coming night, there will still be 25,000 defenders here tomorrow. Admiral North [Abrial] is asking that all ships and aircraft are made available tomorrow night in order to evacuate the 25,000 fighters who have stayed behind in order to allow the last British troops to be evacuated . . . We are asking you in the name of the Commander-in-Chief to comply with Admiral North's request, and we should say that the alliance demands that the rearguard should not be sacrificed.[1]

The French request on this occasion could not have been more reasonable and, at around 10 a.m. on 3 June, Vice-Admiral Ramsay issued the following directions to all those who would have to pull together if the evacuation of the French was to be completed during the night of 3–4 June:

I hoped and believed that last night would see us through, but the French, who were covering the retirement of the British rearguard, had to repel a strong German attack, and so were unable to send their troops to the pier in time to be embarked. We cannot leave our allies in the lurch, and I must call on all officers and men detailed for further evacuation tonight, and let the world see that we never let down an ally.[2]

However, an acerbic message from Churchill reminded the French commanders that an opportunity to evacuate many more Frenchmen the previous night had been missed: 'We are coming back for your men tonight. Pray make sure that all facilities are used promptly. Last night for three hours many ships waited idly at much cost and danger.'[3] Although some French soldiers had been taken off the western jetty at Dunkirk during the night of 2–3 June, at least five large ships that went to Dunkirk during the night were forced to return with no troops, or hardly any troops, on board. It is estimated that around ten thousand more men could have been evacuated had the French been able to fill these ships.[4] That would have taken the total number of Frenchmen evacuated to 105,000 instead of the 95,000 who appear to have left before dawn on 3 June.[5] No one spared a thought for Major Newman and the wounded British soldiers at the 12th Casualty Clearing Station, who could all have been rescued had Newman only been kept informed.

It is no wonder that Churchill and the naval staff in London were upset. They would have had further grounds for complaint had they known that General Fagalde had decided as early as 8.30 a.m. on 2 June that most of his troops would not be evacuated that night. He had even sent a note to his generals to that effect.[6] Unfortunately General Alexander and Captain Bill Tennant do not appear to have been on the circulation list for this very important instruction, highlighting the difficulty of working with an ally where relations have all but broken down.

It was not just the British who were upset during the night of 2–3 June. French troops who were initially directed to the beaches only learned at 10.30 p.m. that the ships coming for them were berthing at the mole. After discovering that a mistake had been made, they had walked miles to the harbour, by which time the British ships had been and gone. They complained bitterly to General Fagalde's aide, Commandant René Lehr, not forgetting to describe the obstacles they had overcome to reach the mole while running the gauntlet of the German shelling.

Their complaints might have been less strident had they realized that Lehr had spent the night desperately attempting to shore up the front line with a patchwork of French units. In his account, he wrote: 'I admit that I was disgusted by such base sentiments.' As he pointed out to the complainers, they 'were not stopping to think about those in the front line who were still fighting even though they would also like to be evacuated'.[7] The French soldiers' morale was not helped by the terrible conditions at Dunkirk, hinted at in the following extract from Lehr's report: 'Entire columns of soldiers had been annihilated by the bombardment. Not far from Bastion 32 lay a line of corpses who had fallen on top of each other; it was as if a gust of wind had blown over a row of wooden soldiers. The dark road was so full of obstructions that it was impossible to avoid some of the corpses, which were run over by my car.'[8]

No soldiers were more demoralized than those in the French 32nd Division. During the night of 1–2 June, they had been ordered to go to the beaches to the west of Dunkirk.[9] Although they were officially Fagalde's reserves, they had naturally concluded they were to be evacuated that night. They could hardly have been more disappointed when, in the course of the following day, they were told that, far from being permitted to go home, they would be needed for a dangerous counter-attack. General Lucas, commander of 32 Division, felt that putting them into the front line was a bad idea, and in the following terms warned Fagalde what might happen if they were recalled:

It is impossible to produce an effective fighting force from the Division. The fact that they were allowed to go to the coast . . . has led them all to assume . . . that they were about to be evacuated . . . Asking these troops to go to the front again, in spite of the fact they have not been given fresh supplies during the 300 kilometre retreat, has so weakened their morale that the smallest incident would transform them into a disorganized rabble, and would lead to more of the depressing scenes which we have already seen at Camp des Dunes.[10]

The counter-attack being discussed was a legacy of the British retreat on 1 June from the canal line marking the southern extremity of the original outer perimeter. After the British withdrawal, the Germans had crossed the canal at Pont à Moutons and Pont de Syckine, as well as at the bridge at Bentie-Meulen, which had been held by Captain Ervine-Andrews and his men (see Chapter 32). The French had established a new line along the Canal des Moëres (south of Téteghem) under General Robert Barthélemy, commander of the Secteur Fortifié des Flandres (SFF). But French chances of mounting a winning counter-attack, which could have pushed back the enemy to the line of the outer perimeter, were undermined by Barthélemy's tactics. Rather than complying with Fagalde's command to use extra troops made available in the counter-attack, Barthélemy used them up bolstering the defences in his front line, insisting that if he did not do so it would be breached.[11] This infuriated Lehr, who had himself written the original 1 June order requiring Barthélemy to counter-attack. It contained the following words: 'The SFF has only one objective. It must do whatever is necessary to recover the lost terrain, failing which the evacuation will be impossible.'[12]

The counter-attack spearheaded by two of 32 Division's infantry battalions eventually commenced at 4 a.m. on 3 June, but its chances of succeeding were further reduced by poor planning.[13] Although tanks supported the advance of the left-hand battalion (111/122nd Regiment), they did not materialize on the right (to support the 111/143rd Regiment) until two hours after the counter-attack had started. By the time they arrived, the German anti-tank gunners were waiting for them, and they were quickly hit, and put out of action.[14] Because of the late arrival of the tanks which were supposed to support the right-hand wing of the attack, the infantry battalions did not advance simultaneously and the battalion on the left, which had advanced, was fired on unexpectedly from its unprotected right flank.[15] There were many casualties which might have been avoided had the build-up been co-ordinated.

But the officers leading their men could not say they had not been warned that progress would be hard. The 111/143rd's Sous-Lieutenant Joseph Andrieu has recalled that General Lucas described the counter-attack as a 'suicide mission'.[16] At the time Andrieu did not take this assessment seriously. He, like most soldiers, believed that he would survive somehow whatever the odds. However, he never forgot the reaction of his brother officer, Sous-Lieutenant Arnaud de la Portalière, a monk who had nevertheless agreed to serve in the French Army. Ten minutes before the counter-attack started, he told Andrieu that, if he was killed, Andrieu should take his wallet and give a hundred francs to each man in their section. He also mentioned a letter he had written to his mother, and asked Andrieu to try to make sure it was sent to her.

Andrieu never found out whether de la Portalière really believed he was going to die. All he knew was that, from the outset, his friend showed immense courage: he was one of the first to make it into the nearest ditch that had been held by the Germans. It was only then that de la Portalière began to behave strangely, refusing to follow Andrieu's suggestion that they should continue their advance. 'I don't want to dirty my boots,' he joked, referring to a pair he had recently acquired

Dunkirk

in Dunkirk. As he spoke Andrieu observed a puff of white smoke around his friend's head, and de la Portalière fell to the ground. A religious man might have wondered whether the smoke was a product of heat given off as de la Portalière conversed with God. There was, unfortunately, a more mundane explanation. It was smoke from a German grenade that had exploded nearby.

Andrieu had ducked down as the Germans attacked. In the course of the ensuing firefight, he was wounded, and his orderly was killed trying to protect him. They were just three of the many victims of the badly thought-out counter-attack, which saw his battalion reduced to around a hundred men.[17] By 12.30 p.m. it was clear that the counter-attack had failed, and those survivors who had not been captured, and who could still walk, returned to the northern banks of the Canal des Moëres where they had started.

It was only then that Andrieu, who had been captured, learned his friend's fate. De la Portalière lay where he had fallen, his skull split open by the grenade's blast. His wallet was still in his pocket and, inside it, Andrieu found the letter, which de la Portalière must have written to his mother during the battalion's first contact with the Germans in Belgium. It did not include anything that could not be found in thousands of similar letters written by young men on the eve of dangerous actions. However, it touched Andrieu's heart, and before forwarding it to his friend's mother, he jotted down what it said. It reads as follows:

My dear Mother,
Tomorrow is the big day. We must receive the 'Fritz'. I am with my section in a dangerous place that I have demanded. Everything is going well. I am currently in a Belgian farm not far from the Germans. It is 10 p.m. It is not very nice. If tomorrow I manage to survive, and I doubt I will, I will write to you. If not, I would like to tell you that I am happy to die for France, and I willingly give my life for you all. I will not send this letter, but I will keep it in my wallet. The ideals I have always espoused are sustaining me, and I hope that the little I have sacrificed in this life will not be forgotten in the other.
I am sending you 100,000 kisses.
Arnaud[18]

The counter-attack had failed to reach the objective specified by Fagalde. But it, combined with other courageous stands south of Téteghem, held up the Germans for just long enough to delay the attack on the north bank of the Canal de Dunkerque à Furnes where the French had intended to make their last stand. This line was probed, but never troubled by a serious German attack, and since the other parts of the inner perimeter were also not breached, even the troops left behind in the front line until the early hours of 4 June could have been rescued if enough ships had been provided.

General Fagalde gave the French troops holding the final inner perimeter specific times at which they were allowed to leave their posts to make for the harbour and the beaches where they were to be evacuated. The thinning-out process could begin at 8.30 p.m., 3 June, but the French soldiers were not permitted to present themselves for embarkation before 10 p.m.[19] Thin 'crusts' of troops were to remain on the inner perimeter line just in case the Germans did show up. They were to hold their positions until the early hours of 4 June when they, too, would be released if there had been no German attack by then.

Admiral Abrial, General Fagalde and his staff left Bastion 32 shortly before 9 p.m., to catch the motor boat laid on for them on the hour.[20] Captain Partiot, who left with Fagalde's staff, described the funereal scene he saw on the way to the mole:

We walk along the beach which is obstructed by isolated soldiers, cars, English cannons, dead men and dead horses . . . all the time expecting to see shells exploding around us as they have been doing on the beach, especially at Malo-les-Bains, all afternoon. This suburb is sinister. It is completely ruined, and burned, with more dead horses and unimaginable disorder. None of the cars have tyres any more; they have been taken and used as life belts.

Surprisingly there are no shells. We arrive at the mole which seems to be about two kilometres long . . . We step over three or four English corpses, and three or four holes caused by bombs. Then we queue up at the end . . . The fishing boats arrive at around 10.30 p.m. . . . . Then larger ships arrive.[21]

The final night's evacuation had begun.

Partiot and Lehr boarded one of the first ships to tie up at the mole. But by the time General Barthélemy and his troops left their positions, Dunkirk and the adjoining suburbs and beaches had been transformed by the crowds of soldiers queuing up to be evacuated. What shocked Barthélemy most when he reached the ruined Malo-les-Bains was not so much the lines of fighting troops, but what he called 'the military population' who had been living in the cellars. 'How long had they been there? Who was in charge of them?' he wondered, before deciding: 'They must be the queue jumpers, wanderers, and fugitives, come to look for shelter near the embarkation quays. Now that we are going, they are coming out all over the place . . . Men are bunched up together so as not to get lost, and they shout if anyone gets in their way. It is a human tide which is following its nose to safety, towards the beach.'[22]

The situation near the base of the mole was even more worrying, given that Barthélemy was hoping to lead his fighters through the mêlée. 'Troops keep on appearing out of the darkness,' he noted. 'Streams of men emerge from all sides and converge on the jetty, where they take on the appearance of an immense river, an impressive structure, which appears to be almost fixed to the ground.'[23]

His account reveals how he and his staff attempted to establish a system to prevent jams near the mole:

I form the men into groups. I do not allow any group to proceed until the last is out of the way. I try to stop the smart alecs who run to join the columns of men that have already been formed. For three hours, I do not stop. Some men I have to revive; others I have to calm down. At first I have some success, and there is some kind of order. But in the dark, as men push in from all sides, impatient to embark, the formed up units disintegrate, and the pushing and shoving begins all over again.[24]

One can well imagine the sense of panic and hopelessness that Barthélemy must have experienced as the hands on his watch reached 2 a.m. on 4 June, leaving just half an hour before the evacuation was supposed to end.[25] He was still seeing what he referred to as 'service troops' crowding around the mole, and this prompted him to observe ruefully: 'I had been looking for men all day to help me fill the gaps in our defences, and to bolster up the counter-attack.' Yet only now that there was a chance of escaping did these men appear, arriving just when they were not wanted, to steal the rightful places of those who had stood their ground and fought so bravely.

By 2.30 a.m. it was clear that most of the front-line troops would not escape. That being the case, it is sad to reveal there was no contingency plan for such an eventuality. Rather than turning the front-line troops around, and returning them to their positions, the last stages of the withdrawal were continued, as if nothing had gone wrong. In spite of the crowds at the mole, the final rearguard 'crust', who had dutifully maintained their watch on the northern bank of the Dunkerque–Furnes Canal, were called in, as were those holding the final positions on the flanks of the inner perimeter, their arrival at the mole and Dunkirk's other jetties only adding to the crush and confusion.[26] (Dunkirk's three main jetties are shown on Map 16 on pp. 532–3.)

Barthélemy's account records what he witnessed near the mole as the deadline for terminating the evacuation approached: 'The stars are growing paler. The sky is becoming lighter. The new day is dawning. The crowd on the jetty moves forward very slowly. I cannot see any boats at the end of the jetty . . . I realize that only those in the queue will be able to get on a boat. Our men will have no chance if they wait to be called up as a unit.'[27] Consequently, he allowed the men he had been holding back to join the other units in the queue. Then, apparently pulling rank to enable him to pass through the soldiers on the mole, he arrived at the far end just in time to board the destroyer *Shikari*, which cast off at 3.40 a.m., making her the last large British ship to leave. Meanwhile, ships that were to be used to block the entrance to Dunkirk were sunk in the harbour mouth.[28]

Much has been written in this and other books about the lack of character demonstrated by French troops during the battle for France and Belgium. It is good, therefore, to note that they ended the first part of the campaign with a courageous and dignified performance. The French war diaries bear witness to the resolute way their troops had held the lines of the inner perimeter after the British units departed. But it is thanks to a British account that we know how the French soldiers on at least one of Dunkirk's jetties coped with their unenviable predicament: Commander Troup, a British piermaster who had been supervising the exodus during that final night, has written of the 'wonderful discipline of the French troops' as the last British motor boat was about to leave what he refers to as 'the centre pier', the guiding jetty between the western jetty and the mole, with the French 32 Division's General Lucas on board:

About 1000 men stood to attention four deep about halfway along the pier, the General and his staff [being] about fifty feet away . . . After having faced the troops, whose faces were indiscernible in the dawn light, the flames behind them showing up their steel helmets, the officers clicked their heels, saluted, and then turned about, and came down to the boat with me. We left at 0305.[29]

The 1000 men who had saluted so smartly on the guiding jetty were just some of the French troops captured when, between 7 and 8 a.m. on 4 June, the Germans entered Dunkirk and Bray-Dunes. At least 40,000 were taken prisoner.[30] However, more than 120,000 Frenchmen were evacuated to England during Operation Dynamo, including some 27,000 during the night of 3–4 June, taking the total number of evacuees to in excess of 300,000. (More detailed evacuation statistics and analysis are to be found in Appendix B, below, and Chapter 30, note 1.)

Notwithstanding all the disagreements with the British, and the fact that so many French soldiers were left behind, Admiral Abrial was in the end grateful for what the Royal Navy had achieved. At 8.30 a.m. on 4 June the following telegram was sent from London to the French High Command:

Number of men evacuated last night were probably as many as 25,000. The evacuation started with the Germans in Rosendael, and finished under the fire of German machine guns. Nothing more could have been done. Admirals Abrial, Platon, and Leclerc are at Dover, as is General Fagalde. Admiral Abrial thinks the work of the English last night was magnificent.[31]

French soldiers abandoned in Dunkirk might have offered a less rosy view of the evacuation. Not only were they prisoners-of-war, but everywhere they looked they saw the utter devastation that symbolized the depths to which their beloved country had sunk. It has been hard to find reports by Frenchmen describing what they witnessed on the day they were captured, but a German staff officer who entered Dunkirk on 4 June wrote up what he saw in the following terms:

It's a complete mess. There are guns everywhere, as well as countless vehicles, corpses, wounded men, and dead horses. The heat makes the whole place stink. Dunkirk itself has been completely destroyed. There are lots of fires burning. Amongst the prisoners are Frenchmen, and blacks . . . some of them not wearing uniforms, real villains, scum of the earth.

We move to Coxyde Bains by the beach. But we cannot swim since the water is full of oil from the sunk ships, and is also full of corpses . . . Horses roam around. They have no food, or water. They cannot drink out of the canals since the water is polluted by dead horses' bodies . . . There are tens of thousands of cars, tanks, ammunition cases, guns and items of clothing . . . At midnight, there is a thanksgiving ceremony on the . . . beach, which we watch, while looking at the waves in the sea, and the flames in the distance, which show that Dunkirk is still burning.[32]

PART 3: AFTER DUNKIRK

35: Sacrifice of the 51st Highland Division

Incheville and St Valery, 5–13 June 1940
(See Maps 20 and 21. Also Map 1)

The signal 'Operation Dynamo now completed' circulated by the Admiralty at 2.23 p.m. on 4 June by no means implied that all BEF troops had been evacuated from France.[1] There were still more than 100,000 British soldiers south of the River Somme, a figure which rose to around 160,000 within days as new units were sent to France in an effort to persuade the French that they should carry on fighting.[2]

It is hardly surprising that General Weygand needed convincing. The battle for France, which had commenced with approximately the same number of soldiers on both sides, was now stacked heavily in favour of the Germans. Of around 140 divisions available, the Germans had mustered 104 for their 'Fall Rot' (Plan/Operation Red), the code name for the attack towards the south with a view to breaking through the Allied line along the Somme and Aisne.[3] To combat this, Weygand only had forty-five infantry divisions, including two BEF units, to hold the 225-mile front line running from Longuyon on the River Chiers to the mouth of the Somme. Even when the depleted French cavalry divisions and her fortress troops were added in, the total units available to Weygand still barely added up to sixty-five divisions.[4]

The German strength was buttressed by growing air superiority. Although Churchill was prepared to bring up to strength the nine RAF squadrons (three of fighters and six of bombers) in France, and to make available a further six squadrons (two of fighters and four of bombers), he informed Reynaud on 5 June that he could not provide the twenty fighter squadrons requested by the French. The remaining British planes had to be retained for the coming Battle of Britain.[5]

The wide fronts allocated to the British 51st Highland Division units on the left of the Allied line illustrate only too clearly the weakness of the Allied armies. When on 5 June Germany commenced her Fall Rot attack, the Highland Division, with the French 31st Division under command, had to secure nineteen miles of the front line. This meant that 154 Brigade, on the 51st Division's extreme left, was responsible for an eight-mile front, an impossible task against such a well-equipped professional army. Only strongpoints could be held, leaving gaps through which the Germans were able to penetrate with disastrous results, in particular for the battalions on the left. The war diary for one of them, the 7th Argyll and Sutherland Highlanders, ends its description of the fighting on 5 June with the words: 'On this day alone 23 officers and over 500 other ranks were missing, wounded or killed . . . June 5th must have been the blackest day in the history of the battalion.'[6]

Much has been said about the way the Highlander warriors stood their ground, thereby ensuring that the 51st Division's front was never completely pierced.[7] But hardly anything has been written about the battalions brought up to support them, and in particular about the epic contribution of the 4th Battalion, the Border Regiment, which was part of another BEF unit known as Beauman Division's A Brigade.[8] The Borders' D Company, numbering around a hundred men, was first placed in the front line on the River Bresle, to which the 51st Division retreated from the Somme during the night of 6–7 June. By 7 June this company was holding the village of Incheville, just to the south of an important bridge over the river, in the middle of the 51st Division's line.[9] At that time the 51st Division was holding the portion of the river running from Gamaches to Le Tréport.[10] The Borders were ordered to hold the village and the bridge 'at all costs'.[11] This, D Company proceeded to do. After being cut off from the rest of the battalion, and from other troops commanded by the 51st Division's Major-General Victor Fortune, it doggedly held on, and in the words of one writer: 'It went on fighting, and five days later, there was still a nest of wrathful indomitable Englishmen maintaining their cause in the Incheville wood.'[12]

When the 4th Borders' commanding officer Lieutenant-Colonel Tomlinson visited Incheville during 7 June, it took him just ten words to tell D Company's commander Major John Hopkinson what was expected of him: ' "For God's sake see that no one comes over that bridge!" he said indicating the bridge to the north of the village.'[13] After inspecting D Company's positions, Tomlinson departed, so that he could mastermind the battalion's movements from the south. Shortly afterwards the first Germans appeared, and although no immediate attempt was made by the enemy to enter the village, bullets zipped in and shells rained down on the Borders from all sides leaving the British garrison in no doubt that their enemy had crossed the Bresle at another crossing-point and they were surrounded.

The first crisis in Incheville occurred on 8 June after a company of Sherwood Foresters was sent up from the south to reinforce the Borders. This company from the Sherwood Foresters' 1st/5th Battalion had been ordered to attack Germans who had crossed the Bresle to the west of Incheville.[14] Unfortunately the artillery barrage from the south, laid on to assist their attack, all but neutralized it after shells landed near where the Foresters were lining up. Several men were killed but, just as importantly, the friendly fire combined with the German ambush, which eventually repulsed the raid, destroyed the Foresters' morale.

The consequences had to be dealt with by the Borders' Lieutenant Williamson who had taken over as garrison commander after Major Hopkinson was wounded. At 4 p.m. on 8 June, Williamson was warned by a look-out that a column of German transport was approaching the Incheville bridge from the north. They were following a similar route to that taken by hundreds of German troops whose progress towards the river had already been abruptly checked by the Borders' guns. 'I saw through my binoculars that they were lorries full of infantry,' Williamson wrote in his Incheville report:

. . . I . . . rushed back to my HQ where . . . to my astonishment I saw [Captain Bernard] Butler and his Foresters, who should have been making ready to stand fast, rushing about in all directions, and starting up the engines of their transports . . . I was staggered . . . [but 2nd Lieutenant] Crossley who was with me said that as . . . [Butler] was so yellow-bellied, and his men so unreliable . . . it would be better if he went. I was now [very] angry, and [told Butler] what I really thought of him . . . I [took] . . . my revolver out, and nearly shot him.[15]

. . . Then I thought of the wounded. I went up to a large three ton lorry, and saw that one of my [men] . . . was sitting along[side] the driver in the cab. I pointed my revolver at him, and told him if he did not get back to his post he was a dead man. I then made the driver stop his engine and get out together with all the men, and [ordered them to] carry all the wounded from the 'hospital' . . . [to] the lorry. When they had done this, I let the rotten crowd go.

The 'amusing' sequel is that the Boche was not coming for us, but . . .

crossed the river by the bridge [to the west, which] Butler had originally been sent to take. The roads from this bridge and Incheville converged some way [to the south] outside Incheville, and Butler and his Foresters ran into this convoy and were . . . captured.

Williamson's sentiments are uncharitable. But they appear less churlish when put in context. He had done as much as if not more than any other man in the garrison to ensure it survived: after the barrage had hit the Foresters during the morning of 8 June, Major Hopkinson had entrusted the fortification of the village to him, and as the following extract from his report makes clear, he had taken his orders very seriously:

I spent the rest of the morning . . . having holes knocked in walls and [roofs] . . . in order that a clear field of vision was obtained on all sides. I then had staggered barricades erected on all roads leading into Incheville. The idea of these . . . barricades was that they would not stop vehicles or tanks trying to enter Incheville, but would cause them to slow [down], and go diagonally across the road, so making an easy target for the anti-tank gun and Bren gun that I had trained on each barricade.

An account by Lieutenant John Watton, another 4th Borders officer, describes the additional measures taken: 'We fortified five houses in the village, using empty ammunition boxes filled with stones to block the windows . . . We gathered all bedding . . . we could find to lie on. [Then] we waited to ambush any Germans who came in range.'[16]

They did not have long to wait. A series of German staff cars and motorcycles were shot up and their occupants and riders either killed or put to flight as they attempted to pass through the village. After Williamson's men had killed the soldiers in the first car, they burned it with its driver and passenger still inside. If it was hoped that this would dissuade other Germans from attempting to enter the village, the men manning the barricades must have been disappointed. Watton has described how, shortly afterwards, a second car was halted in the same way. This time the Germans ran for their lives, and escaped, whereupon, as Watton wrote:

[the] heavily bearded . . . Williamson got into the car, smashed the opaque windscreen, and drove the vehicle into the back of the smouldering remains

of the first car with its by now skeletal occupants. Williamson [then] shouted: 'Loot it you fools, loot it!' I was hiding in a cellar at the time, but the thought of loot drove me to run to the car, open the boot, [and] tumble out suitcases full of German uniforms, great coats, chocolates and cigars. I only wanted the chocolates . . .

The cigars he distributed as prizes of war to his men.[17]

It was not long before a third car appeared at the barricade watched by Watton. His account describes how there were 'four Germans [inside. It] drove in fast, [and] overturned at our roadblock, [skidding] on its roof. I [will always] remember the terrible sound of screams and screaming metal. Three of the [four] Germans were killed.'

The gruesome dispatch of yet another German soldier, mown down by a Bren gun after riding his motorcycle up to one of the barriers, is described in Williamson's account: 'Crossley and I went up to investigate, and found the Boche lying on the road alongside his machine, terribly wounded in the small of the back and buttocks. He was still alive however, and [he was] moaning, and occasionally shouting "Achtung!" . . . As he was so badly hurt, I told Crossley to shoot him through the head with his revolver, which he did.' Luckily for Williamson and Crossley, there were no other Germans around who might have accused them of carrying out a war crime rather than a mercy killing.

By this time Williamson was in his element, and his account reveals the pleasure he took in destroying another car that his men shot up, with its contents. He also revelled in the number of Germans he had killed the previous day. 'I sent a fellow up to inspect the bodies,' he wrote. 'He returned with a German machine-gun and . . . reported that there were many corpses lying about. We returned to my HQ where we had roast goose, new potatoes and some good Burgundy. I was pleased to see that everybody was much more cheerful.'

Unfortunately not all those caught by the roadblocks were German. 'Just as I was finishing breakfast [on the third day of the siege], I heard the booming explosion of an anti-tank rifle from 2nd Lieutenant Crossley's HQ across the road,' wrote Williamson.

Upon investigation I saw an old French car stopped at the road barrier with two men in it. One appeared to be wounded, as the bullet from the anti-tank rifle had gone through the bonnet and body of the car, and out the back, striking the passenger in the arm . . . splintering and ripping it open. He got out with it hanging [down] limply, and moaning terribly all the time. It [turned out] that they lived in the village, and were an old man and his son who had fled before the German advance. [They had been] returning to their home . . . I ordered my medical orderly to amputate the old man's arm with his jack knife after filling him with brandy. [But] in the evening he died, and his son buried him in the hotel garden . . . Lt Watton read an RC service for him. Before Incheville fell, the son's house was smashed by shells and . . . burned to the ground. Such is the fortune of war.

By the beginning of their third day in Incheville Williamson and his officers were beginning to get itchy feet. However, because Germans held the terrain on all sides of the village they were effectively cut off from the battalion's headquarters to the south. They had no radios. Two messengers sent out failed to return. 'I concluded that [they] must have been captured or shot,' Williamson wrote. '. . . My next idea was to send a [messenger] with a pigeon with orders to release [it] before capture or death. The pigeon, which had easily distinguished markings, returned that night . . . After some discussion it was decided that we should carry on [defending] Incheville until relieved, or until we received orders to withdraw.'

As the days passed, the discomfort endured by the besieged British soldiers increased. Watton's account discloses that they had no running water. Because of this, 'there was no sewage disposal', although any inconvenience was minimized by 'one volunteer [who] worked full time clearing out the overflowing lavatory "basins"'. Drink was another problem, but as Watton admitted, 'We looted wine and cider from the cellars . . . No-one washed or shaved. Our sweat washed white lines down our filthy bearded faces. [After our] food had all gone . . . one of us, a butcher, shot a cow for us to eat.'

Williamson's Borders were still holding out in Incheville during the evening of 13 June. According to Watton, they shared their dinner that night with a German naval officer, one of the few enemy servicemen who had entered the village and survived the Borders' bloodthirsty reprisals: 'We lent him a tin hat to protect him from bits of ceiling . . . We dined on liver from the cow we had shot, and new potatoes dug from a garden. Houses across the street were on fire. Our faces were half red from the light of the flames, and half green from the green evening light from the woods behind the house. The meal ended with the ceiling falling [down].'

It was to be their last supper in Incheville. The next morning most of the garrison surrendered, having learned from a captured British officer sent into the village by the Germans that their Highlander comrades, for whom they had fought so long and hard, had either escaped back to England, or had themselves capitulated.[18]

If only the French had been as solicitous about the 51st Division's welfare, the entire division might have escaped. But as General Spears could have told Major-General Victor Fortune, the division's commander, as early as 6 June, having on that day attended a French War Committee meeting, there was little chance of that, if Weygand's hostile behaviour was anything to go by. 'I . . . was surprised by . . . [Weygand's] new line of approach,' Spears wrote later. 'This time General Fortune . . . was . . . [Weygand's] target . . . [Fortune] had, it seemed, fallen back without orders. It was quite intolerable. How could he, Weygand, conduct operations when such elements were included in his own "reliable and disciplined forces"?' He concluded: 'Your General should be called "Misfortune".'[19]

In fact Fortune, like Gort before him, was being unfairly criticized by Weygand. Fortune had admittedly complained on 6 June that the width of his front was 'ridiculous', and that it was 'sheer murder' to ask him to hold a nineteen-mile front for another day, but he only withdrew to the Bresle after the staff of General Robert Altmayer, commander of the French 10th Army, under whose command he fell, had given him permission to do so.[20] Although Fortune's front on the Bresle was reduced to a more manageable ten miles, Lieutenant-General James Marshall-Cornwall, liaison officer between the 10th Army and the War Office, that night nevertheless sent the War Office the following warning, the first of many, in the hope that the 51st Division could be extricated before it was too late: '51 Division is hardly fit for more fighting, and may crack if seriously attacked even on the Bresle position. If politically undesirable to withdraw all British troops from front line, I would urge that two more British divisions . . . be sent urgently to France.'[21]

Intelligence contained in a document snatched from an abandoned German car was even more worrying than what Marshall-Cornwall had learned from General Fortune. The document was shown to Marshall-

Cornwall at the 10th Army's Lyons-la-Forêt headquarters on 7 June.[22] It revealed that the 5th and 7th Panzer Divisions, which had broken through the Somme–Aisne line further to the east, were aiming to thrust through to Rouen, passing through the Conteville–Formerie and the Forges-les-Eaux–Doudeauville lines.[23] This intelligence should have set the alarm bells ringing at the French headquarters, and persuaded the French generals to order the 51st Division to retreat. The units standing in the path of the 5th and 7th Panzer Divisions were very weak. For example, the fourteen-mile Aumale–Forges-les-Eaux line, which ran at right angles to the 51st Division's front, was guarded by one isolated British battalion: the unblooded 2nd/6th East Surreys.[24] Once this flank was pierced, any troops that remained at the western end of the Bresle would be as good as surrounded.

Admittedly there were some fifty tanks from the BEF's 1st Armoured Division, which could make a stand on the Andelle behind the Aumale–Forge-les-Eaux line. But, as was revealed at the 7 June meeting attended by General Roger Evans, commander of the 1st Armoured Division, and Weygand at the 10th Army's HQ, he only had light tanks and cruisers at his disposal, none of which possessed armour thick enough to withstand shells fired by German guns. Also, the British tanks were not backed up by the artillery or infantry that would normally have been part and parcel of an armoured division. The infantry from Beauman's Division, a cobbled-together unit consisting of Pioneers and reinforcement troops, which Weygand said would back up Evans on the Andelle, was hardly a satisfactory substitute.

But Weygand, rather than calmly analysing what was feasible, and issuing the command that might well have saved the 51st Division, instead attempted to rouse Evans to do the impossible with rhetoric that might have been effective had it only been backed up with the provision of the reinforcements necessary to achieve what was being commanded. Marshall-Cornwall, who had accompanied Evans to the meeting, has described his impression of what was said:

As we entered the room, [Weygand] . . . shouted hysterically to Altmayer: 'If the Germans cross the Seine, I shall advise the Government to seek an armistice.' Then turning to us he screamed: 'It's the decisive battle of the war. Every man must stand and fight. Each tank must become a fortress! Every man must attack! He must bite the enemy like a dog – seize him with his teeth!' . . . He then stormed out of the room. Altmayer looked at me ruefully with a shrug of his shoulders, as if to say, 'The man's mad.'[25]

After attending a long conference with Altmayer's staff, who, according to Marshall-Cornwall, tried to reconcile Weygand's incoherent directive with the fluid situation on their rapidly crumbling front, the British liaison officer sent the following damning message to General Dill in London at 1 a.m. on 8 June:

Regret I have lost confidence in ability of French . . . to stop German drive to the Seine . . . Have requested 10th Army Commander to order 51st Division . . . to withdraw quietly to River Béthune, [around eighteen miles south-west of the Bresle]. Otherwise they will be trapped. Army Commander refuses to do so without orders from higher authority. I suggest you come over and see Weygand immediately. Otherwise we shall have to evacuate 51st from Dieppe beach.[26]

At 10.30 a.m. that same morning, Marshall-Cornwall once again tried to convince Altmayer that time was running out for the 51st Division, following which he sent another desperate plea to Dill: 'General Altmayer is broken down and incapable of commanding,' he wrote. 'I consider 51st Division is in imminent danger of having its communications cut, and may have to be . . . partially evacuated from the coast.'[27] Thus by midday on 8 June, all concerned, including Dill in London, had been warned of the mortal danger facing the 51st Division.

Notwithstanding all these efforts, it was only during the evening of 8 June, twenty-three hours after the need for it became apparent, that Marshall-Cornwall, having finally persuaded Altmayer to sanction the 51st Division's retreat to Rouen, had a message written out advising General Fortune that the French had given him permission to withdraw.[28] But by then all means of communicating between the 10th Army and the division had been cut, and Marshall-Cornwall, whose messenger was captured by the Germans before he could reach General Fortune, had no alternative but to notify the War Office at 2 a.m. on 9 June as to what had been agreed. In his telegram, he recommended that a man should be sent in an aeroplane or a destroyer to deliver the message to the 51st Division.[29]

Fortunately, although no message authorizing the withdrawal reached

Fortune directly, General Marcel Ihler, commander of the French IX Corps, under whose command Fortune had been placed the night before, was informed during 8 June.[30] And so it was only during the night 8–9 June, just as German tanks, unbeknown to Ihler and Fortune, were cutting off their Rouen escape route, that IX Corps along with the 51st Highland Division carried out the first stage of their retreat, leaving behind Lieutenant Williamson and his men at Incheville, who could not be contacted.[31]

Much of what followed at the 51st Division's various headquarters as it withdrew to the south is known thanks to a report written by Lieutenant-Colonel Henry Swinburn, General Fortune's senior staff officer.[32] According to Swinburn, a very dejected Ihler turned up at Fortune's headquarters at La Chaussée, some seven miles south-east of Dieppe, at about midday on 9 June to confirm that his entire corps, including the 51st Division, was as good as lost. Ihler had learned that the Germans had reached Rouen; this meant that he and his troops had been cut off from the town to which he had been ordered to retreat. Ihler only perked up after Fortune came up with a plan that at least gave them a chance of making it back to Le Havre whence they could hopefully be evacuated.[33] The plan involved Fortune sending a force, including the remnants of the 51st Division's 154 Brigade, ahead of the main body of the men, so that these British troops could hold the line running from Fécamp to Lillebonne.[34] If this line could be held by Fortune's force and some French troops already there, the roads down which the main force needed to retreat during the last part of their journey to Le Havre would be shielded. In other words, the final section of the 51st Division's and IX Corps' escape route would be secured.

It was a big 'if'. When Fortune gave his instructions to Brigadier Arthur Stanley-Clarke, commander of the force that was to do the shielding, the 51st Division's commander insisted that Stanley-Clarke should go ahead and evacuate his troops from Le Havre if the German panzers cut him off from the rest of the division. At 11.37 p.m. on 9 June Fortune, who had already informed the War Office that he was intending to retreat to Le Havre, also warned London: 'If enemy cut me off from Le Havre, will attempt pivot on one of Northern ports . . . in hope of evacuating a few men behind bridgehead.'[35]

It was a message that, for all the brave talk in front of General Ihler, demonstrated that Fortune believed the odds against his whole force

making it safely to Le Havre were very long. Nevertheless, notwithstanding Fortune's fears, the force, which was to be known as 'Ark Force',
taking its name from Arques-la-Bataille, where Fortune's instructions
were passed to Stanley-Clarke, set out that night hoping to do for the
planned exit from Le Havre what the 2nd and 48th Divisions had done
for the earlier evacuation from Dunkirk.

The first report that told Fortune his plan to reach Le Havre was
foiled appears to have come from a mobile wireless truck sent out during
the morning on 10 June to maintain contact with Ark Force. It ran into
German armour near Cany-Barville, on the road leading to Fécamp,
but its occupants managed to notify Fortune before being captured.[36]
This was followed by a series of similar reports from a variety of sources,
and at 10.45 p.m. on 10 June Fortune warned Admiral Sir William
James, Commander-in-Chief Portsmouth, that he might be forced to
evacuate his division between the mouth of the River Durdent and
St Valery-en-Caux.[37]

As if Fortune's task was not being made hard enough by the Germans,
the French high command also appears to have been doing everything
it could to obstruct the evacuation. At 7.30 p.m. that same evening
Colonel Butler, commander of the garrison at Le Havre, telephoned
the War Office with a disturbing message emanating from Weygand.
Although the Germans had already cut off Ihler and Fortune from the
Seine, the French generalissimo was still asking IX Corps, with the 51st
Division attached, to retreat to the area around 'Caudebec', which
presumably was a reference to Caudebec-en-Caux, just north of the
Seine some nine miles east of Lillebonne, and was insisting that under
no circumstances should the troops be evacuated from Le Havre. If
General Percival, Assistant Chief of the Imperial General Staff, who
took the call, had felt himself at liberty to save the 51st Division,
whatever the consequences as far as the French were concerned, he
might have instructed Butler to ignore Weygand's order, which was
clearly absurd given that the Germans were already holding the roads
leading to Caudebec. Instead the notes of the conversation record him
telling Butler that in view of Weygand's order 'he must not now allow
the evacuation of any fighting troops from the Le Havre area'.[38]

However, the Le Havre war diary relating to the evacuation of the
51st Division includes the following entry for 12.30 a.m. on 11 June:
'Telegram to 51 Div from War Office reference General Weygand's

orders to move south to bridge the Seine. War Office explained importance of acting strictly in conformity with any orders issued by 9th
Corps Commander.'[39] Although appearing at first sight to reinforce the
principle that French commands must be obeyed, this telegram in fact
represented a softening of the hard line that had originally been taken. No
longer was there insistence that Fortune must comply with Weygand's
demands, however unreasonable, as long as it was the French commander on the spot who ordered the transgression. This gave Fortune
an out, which he accepted with alacrity, replying brusquely at 10.10 a.m.
on 11 June: 'Physical impossibility [IX] Corps Cdr. approach Seine. In
same boat as me.'[40]

Fortune's response to War Office concerns suggests that he was understandably vexed at the way the lives of his men were being traded for
political gain. He can have had no such grievance in relation to the
Navy. Far from obstructing the evacuation, Admiral James was clearly
doing his best to anticipate Fortune's needs. As well as presiding over
the collection of sixty-seven merchant ships and 140 smaller vessels to
pick up British soldiers from the Le Havre area, as part of Operation
Cycle, he also took a proactive role by working out where else they
might be needed.[41]

Rather than waiting for Fortune's demands to arrive in Portsmouth,
James had sped over to Le Havre in a motor boat on 10 June where he
picked up intelligence he would never have received had he remained
behind his desk. While in France, he learned that the German advance
made it highly likely that St Valery-en-Caux would be where General
Fortune would end up. With that in mind, at 3 p.m. he ordered that all
available ships should be assembled off the coast at St Valery.[42] Then,
having returned to Portsmouth during the late afternoon, he refused to
be put off by the 8.15 p.m. notification from the War Office that
Fortune's troops would be withdrawing to the Seine, and that there was
to be no evacuation after all.[43] His visit to Le Havre had convinced him
that not only would there be an evacuation, but it would have to be
carried out sooner rather than later.

He was only to discover how soon after a British naval officer visited
St Valery's harbour during the early hours of 11 June in order to collect
the wounded. The officer in question could not have had a better
pedigree when it came to daring acts. It was Sub-Lieutenant Peter Scott,
the son of the legendary Scott of the Antarctic. He certainly needed a

cool head. As he and a small party of sailors from the destroyer HMS *Broke* chugged into the harbour in a motor boat at 2.30 a.m. on 11 June, he was struck by the silence, which was only broken by a solitary whistle. Scott whistled back, without eliciting any reply. Although two green Very flares had been fired from the pier, the prearranged signal that the coast was clear, he wondered whether they were sailing into a trap. 'Telling the coxswain . . . that I would be back in five minutes, I climbed ashore, drew my revolver and ran to some houses,' Scott reported. 'I saw the legs of a sitting sentry showing round a corner. Brandishing my pistol without much conviction, I popped around the corner and said: "Hands up." He jumped up and said: "Yes sir, certainly sir."'

Scott eventually discovered that there were around a hundred wounded soldiers to evacuate. As they were being carried on to other boats, which were then summoned, Scott told Fortune's chief of staff it was probably too dangerous to attempt to evacuate the rest of the division during daylight hours, especially as three British destroyers had already been damaged by German gunfire and bombs the day before. But he was prepared to signal to *Broke* to request that the evacuation should start immediately if the following night would be too late. 'No, I think we can hold on till tonight,' the chief of staff replied. 'But no longer.' Scott then signalled to *Broke* that the ships gathered around the destroyer outside the harbour should disperse for the moment and, before finally departing, assured the chief of staff they would be back that night.[44]

But even as ships were being assembled off the coast, a train of events was unfolding on land that was to ambush Scott's and Admiral James's well-laid plans. According to a diary completed by Major Murray Grant, second-in-command of the 2nd Seaforth Highlanders, it was neither the action carried out by the Germans nor the French high command that can alone be held responsible for what happened next.[45] The failure by Fortune and Ihler to ensure that the retreat was carried out in an orderly manner also played its part in jeopardizing the evacuation.

Grant has described how Fortune ordered the 2nd Seaforths to set off from the area near Ouville-la-Rivière before the other troops in order to act as the corps' advanced guard.[46] The battalion's initial task was to secure the ground south-west of St Valery up to the River Durdent.[47] Grant and his men moved off in trucks at 8.30 p.m. on 10 June: 'We had [a] . . . nightmare drive to St Valery,' wrote Grant.

All drove full out. It was still broad daylight, and we expected to be bombed out of existence at any moment. By pure luck we got through just before the roads became completely jammed with French military and civilian vehicles 'flying' to St Valery. At 22.15, the Bn column . . . arrived in the square at St Valery, which . . . was fairly clear of troops and vehicles. An hour later it was a seething mass [of soldiers and their transport].[48]

However, before deploying to the west, he and his men discovered that the Germans were already in control of the position on the Durdent they had been ordered to secure. It was therefore agreed that Grant should drive back to ask Fortune whether the battalion should instead place itself on a perimeter line nearer to St Valery. The line he proposed to hold started on the cliffs overlooking St Valery near Le Tot, and then ran more or less at right angles to the seashore, passing through the villages of Le Tot, St Sylvain and Néville.[49] Grant's diary refers to 'the extraordinary congestion on the road' that he encountered to the north of St Valery, and although he left at 10.30 p.m., it was past midnight before he had driven the fourteen miles separating St Valery from the divisional headquarters at Ouville-la-Rivière. Having persuaded Fortune's staff to rubber-stamp his recommendation, Grant attempted to return to St Valery, only to find he was delayed once again by traffic jams. 'French columns of MT had cut in on the main road allotted to 51 Div,' he recorded, 'and in trying to pass our columns, had created solid blocks of vehicles 3 abreast for stretches up to a mile long.'[50] It was 4.30 a.m. before he made it back to St Valery.

Grant's recollection of the growing chaos is corroborated by the testimony of Sergeant John Mackenzie, the 2nd Seaforth Highlander who, two months earlier, had been so shocked by French behaviour near the Maginot Line (see Chapter 2):

We . . . drove down a long slope into the little seaside resort of St Valery-en-Caux, passing cavalry, guns and infantry of the French Army, all in the last stages of demoralisation. We reached the square just as night was drawing in. A scene of indescribable confusion met us as our truck came to a halt. The town had been badly smashed by an air raid, and many houses were alight. Thousands of drunken French soldiers were looting cafés, shops and houses, blazing away at anything with their rifles. Someone took a couple of pot shots at me as I was talking to the driver of a light tank which was guarding the road into St Valery, sending me back to my truck in a hurry.[51]

In spite of the crowds, the troops in Grant's battalion were in place on the western portion of the perimeter that was to be held around St Valery in the early morning on 11 June. They held the section nearest to the sea, the line being extended by three other battalions on their left, two of them being Highlander units, as shown in Map 21, p. 538. There was an equivalent perimeter line to the east of St Valery running from Veules-les-Roses on the coast to Houdetot via St Pierre-le-Viger.[52] The approaches to the southern side of the town were blocked by French troops when they finally arrived and relieved the three squadrons of British tanks and carriers that had been filling in.

However, it was the western section of the perimeter that was to be attacked first, and at this juncture the delay caused by traffic jams was critical. First, the French unit that was supposed to take over the line from the edge of the cliffs overlooking St Valery to Le Tot had not arrived. Second, the 2nd Seaforths were not backed up by any anti-tank guns or artillery. According to Grant's war diary: 'The position was obviously untenable against AFV [armoured fighting vehicle] attack without artillery and A/Tk [anti-tank] support, and Major Grant was sent again to HQ Division, now at Cailleville, to . . . ask for this support as a matter of urgency.'[53]

Fortune agreed to send the guns as soon as possible but, presumably because of the traffic jams, and the failure to ensure that the necessary artillery and anti-tank guns were moved before they could be obstructed by the rest of the corps, neither the required units nor the guns had materialized by the time the first German panzers from Rommel's 7th Panzer Division appeared at around 2.30 p.m. By all accounts some ninety tanks attacked the thin line of Highlanders and Royal Norfolks holding the western side of the perimeter, and although once again they stood their ground, the German panzers brushed aside any resistance offered and pierced their front line. 'The fire [from the tanks] was severe,' wrote Grant, 'and we suffered between 30 and 40 killed and wounded . . . within a few minutes. Three enemy tanks were knocked out by [anti-tank] rifle fire . . . It is thought that . . . the knocking out of these tanks saved us from being completely overrun, because after a few minutes, which seemed like hours, the main part of the attack swept on to St Valery.'[54] Shortly afterwards German guns were spotted on the cliffs near Le Tot which dominated St Valery's harbour.

The sector held by the 2nd Seaforths was not the only one pierced. The panzer crews showed no mercy when they came across the 7th Royal Norfolks filling in between the 2nd Seaforths at St Sylvain and the 1st Gordon Highlanders holding St Riquier, some one and a half miles to the south.[55] 2nd Lieutenant Ran Ogilvie, an officer from the Gordons who went to inspect the Norfolks' weapon pits after the panzers had disappeared to their rear, reported: 'The carnage was terrible. Heavy calibre machine-guns had torn bodies terribly. Tank tracks had caught any[one] . . . in the open.' Ogilvie only had one field dressing, and he used it on a man whose head had been split open by shrapnel. Part of the man's skull was missing. 'He was screaming, though not fully conscious,' Ogilvie remembered.[56]

Equally hard hit was the 2nd Seaforths' regimental aid post situated in a barn at St Sylvain. According to 2nd Lieutenant Philip Mitford, he had just walked out of the barn leaving the doctor Murdoch McKillop to deal with the more seriously wounded men, when it was hit by a mortar shell. 'Quite a few were killed inside, and McKillop was severely wounded,' Mitford wrote later. 'One [of McKillop's] leg[s] was blown off and the other broken in three places. In spite of this, he tried to direct operations, and refused to be moved until the last man still alive had been rescued.'[57]

Because the barn was on fire, the wounded had to be hauled out without any ceremony. 'It was a ghastly task,' wrote Grant. 'We had no stretchers and only a few gates and doors on which to move the worst cases. The others had to be pulled out anyhow if we were to save them from being burned.' It was too dangerous to bring out the dead as well. After checking that no one else inside the barn was alive, Grant ordered that those remaining should be left to be incinerated because, as he noted in his diary: 'Owing to the flames and the enemy fire which was causing more casualties, it was impossible to get them out without further loss of life.'[58] Unfortunately Dr McKillop also died later that evening.

The 2nd Seaforths' survival in their position was no thanks to some French cavalrymen who were present when the Germans attacked. According to Grant, as soon as the first rounds were fired, 'They cut loose their horses, and instead of assisting us in defending the position, the majority rushed about trying to find cover. Eventually their commander was found, and told that he and his men would either fight under our orders or be cleared out of the position. They chose the former, but as the fire slackened, about half his men crept away into the village.'[59]

That does not mean that all the French holding the perimeter around St Valery behaved as spinelessly. The following account by a Black Watch officer, whose men were holding the section of the eastern side of the perimeter around St Pierre-le-Viger, includes a description of one of the most courageous acts of the campaign carried out by a French officer who rode up with his men to offer their support:

The horses were the first to suffer [when mortar fire was directed at the position]. Their screams of pain and fright were unnerving. A . . . French officer detailed some of his men to shoot the wounded animals, and let the others go free. [Then] . . . a burst of mortar fire landed about six feet from me. I was lying flat [and was unharmed], but the French officer was standing up . . . directing his men. It took me by surprise to see his arm leave his body, and drop at his [feet] . . . He still [carried on and] gave out his orders to his men . . . [while they] attended to him, applying dressing[s] and [a] tourniquet. They fixed up a makeshift stretcher, and wanted to take him to our . . . first aid post, but he refused to go, and insisted they carry him around the position.[60]

Such devotion to duty had a stiffening effect on all who saw him, and contributed to the fact that, notwithstanding the strength of the attack, the eastern perimeter line was held.[61]

Despite the German breakthrough on the western side of the perimeter, and the German guns on the cliffs, Fortune still believed that the evacuation from St Valery could go ahead as long as it was carried out in the dark. At 8.30 p.m. on 11 June, he sent Admiral James a signal containing the following words: 'Consider to-night last possible chance of evacuation of 51 Division. French authority given. Strength: British, 12,000. Equal numbers French. Total 24,000.'[62] The French authority Fortune referred to had not come from Weygand, but from the French admiral at Le Havre, whose permission to evacuate, finally given in writing at 6.45 p.m., was deemed adequate by the War Office.[63]

The position viewed through the eyes of those at sea who would have to run the gauntlet of the German battery on the cliffs to the west of the harbour was considerably less sanguine. One such sailor was Lieutenant-Commander House, whose tug *Fairplay* had towed nine drifters to the area off St Valery in spite of the fog, which at times was thick. At 8.55 p.m. an officer on the destroyer HMS *Saladin* hailed him, and shouted his orders through a megaphone. House was to take control of two nearby schuyts and, with their assistance, he was to pick up soldiers from the shore on the western side of St Valery. A series of white Very flares would tell him when the troops were being sent down to the beaches.

At 12.35 a.m. on 12 June he approached the harbour. After seeing white Very flares fired from the shore, he decided to send his boats in to the section of the western side where they would be away from the glare given off by burning buildings. However, no sooner had he clambered into one of the first boats to be taken into the harbour than the Germans on the cliff began to fire at them. Within minutes two of the boats were sunk. As House mentioned in his report, the situation was 'quite untenable': two more boats were 'riddled with shot' and sunk as they tried to escape. Realizing that if they carried on there would be a bloodbath, House, in the absence of any other orders, decided to call it a day, and he and his charges beat a hasty retreat before returning to Newhaven, the nearest British port.[64]

By 2 a.m. on 12 June Captain Armstrong in HMS *Saladin* had reached a similar conclusion, and sent the following signal to Captain Warren, his superior officer in the destroyer HMS *Codrington*: 'Have investigated St Valery which appears full of enemy, and beach is under heavy fire. Am now moving to Veules[-les-Roses].'[65] It was this signal, combined with Captain Warren's own experiences off St Valery, that led him to conclude it was 'quite impracticable as a place for evacuation'. As he wrote in his report: 'I could see the place was burning fiercely, and a lot of machine-gun and artillery fire was being directed on the beach. Also enemy star shell.'[66] On seeing this, he smartly called off the evacuation from St Valery itself, and joined *Saladin* off Veules-les-Roses.

The fog off St Valery had already proved to be an obstacle during the initial marshalling of boats for the evacuation. It was now to come into the reckoning again, making it much harder to locate those ships whose commanders needed to know about the change of plan if they were to play a role in the rescue. Many of those skippers who had not already been put off by the German guns seen firing at St Valery's harbour returned to England for want of clear instructions.[67] Nevertheless by the time *Codrington*'s beach parties were landed at Veules at around 4 a.m. on 12 June, several boats were to be seen ferrying soldiers, who had been queuing up at the water's edge, out to the three personnel ships and six coasters off shore. There were also ten French ships, mostly trawlers and drifters.[68]

Many of the British soldiers rescued were from the 2nd/7th Battalion, the Duke of Wellington's Regiment, whose station on the eastern perimeter was next to Veules. However, as the following account by Company Quartermaster Sergeant Jim Smith demonstrates, their position, which required them to drop down from high cliffs if they wanted to make it on to the beach, was in some ways disadvantageous compared with that of soldiers at St Valery, who could just walk to Veules along the seashore:

We took out hundreds of blankets from my truck [situated at the top of the cliffs], and knotted them all together, interspersed with rifle slings, and tied the end with a double knot onto the front of a[nother] three-ton truck . . . We had no idea if the first rope had hit the bottom, and the first few who volunteered to go down didn't know where they were in the dark. Of the first twelve, I think about seven were killed. One shouted up: 'We need more length at the bottom.' So we passed more rifle slings to the boys who were going down, and they tied them until eventually they made the ground. Quite a number got down that way along with me.[69]

Meanwhile, blissfully ignorant about the Navy's inability to get boats into St Valery's harbour, the men who had been holding the perimeter until shortly after midnight abandoned their positions so that they could be evacuated. Theirs was an alarming march, as the following report by 4th Queen's Own Cameron Highlander Major Bertie MacLeay, whose men had been holding part of the western perimeter, bears witness:

The run to St Valery is one which will never be forgotten by anyone who took part in it. It was macabre in the extreme, and reminded one of Dante and his Inferno. We passed blazing cottages, chateaux [and] trucks . . . all of the way . . . Normally people would be rushing away from a doomed and blazing town, [yet] . . . here were we bringing another 500 men into it. As we reached the town, the glare became brighter and brighter, and [although it was still night-time] it was like daylight as we went down the steep street into the upper square.[70]

It was only then that MacLeay was told that no boats had come in, and no one seemed to know whether any were expected.

British soldiers are taught to bear hardship with a stiff upper lip. It is not surprising, therefore, to find a dearth of accounts describing the Highlanders' feelings when no ships steamed into St Valery's harbour. They must have been bitterly disappointed and dispirited as they stood on the esplanade in the pouring rain, peering out to sea, waiting fruitlessly for the Navy. It was a replay of what French soldiers, left behind at Dunkirk, must have experienced. A hint of the growing desperation is to be found in the following message sent by the 51st Division's naval liaison officer to the Commander-in-Chief Portsmouth at 1.15 a.m. on 12 June: 'When may ships be expected? Situation most critical at Veules St Valery.'[71] Admiral James replied reassuringly, 'At any moment I hope,' little realizing that on this occasion the Navy was powerless to help.[72]

No explicit message ever reached the men in St Valery to tell them the evacuation there was off for that night, but they eventually reached that conclusion on their own. This prompted Captain Derek Lang, adjutant of the 4th Camerons, who had spotted ships off Veules-les-Roses, to attempt to walk there during the early hours of 12 June in order to ask the Navy whether something might still be arranged for the next night.[73] 'We had to keep close in to the rocks to avoid attracting machine-gun fire from the cliff tops,' Lang recalled.

As it was, there were places where we could only advance by diving from cover to cover. As we progressed, we came across the bodies of many of our soldiers and Frenchmen who been caught in the cross-fire of the guns. Some lay at the water's edge, washed by the tide. Others were poised in standing or crouching positions against the rocks where they had been shot. They looked so lifelike that we approached several of them to talk to them only to find their eyes sightless and their bodies rigid in death. These dreadful corpses reminded me vividly of P.C. Wren's book *Beau Geste*, in which the dead bodies were propped up on the battlement of the Fort . . .

Evidently some of the troops had tried to descend the three-hundred-foot high cliffs on ropes. Few could have succeeded judging by the smashed bodies lying on the beach, while a hundred and fifty feet above we could see the frayed ends of their broken ropes. Most appalling of all were the wounded. They were everywhere, and on our approach called out to us for water, or to help bind up their wounds. There was nothing we could do for them as any delay endangered the success of our mission . . .'[74]

Unfortunately, by the time Lang arrived at Veules, most of the ships had departed with the last of the 1350 British and 930 French troops rescued in this sector during Operation Cycle.[75] The ships had been scared off at around 9.30 a.m. on 12 June by German gunfire from both east and west.[76] His account refers to just two ships, one of which was flying the British white ensign. The other boat was French. German artillery on the cliffs near St Valery initially concentrated on sinking the French ship, first straddling it, and then hitting its deck, which was packed with rescued soldiers. 'A few minutes later the . . . hulk slid over on its side,' Lang recorded.

The guns were then directed at the other ship, *Hebe 2*, a Dutch coaster with a British crew, one of several to have sailed to France from Poole on 9 June. She had been grounded while attempting to pick up the last soldiers at Veules. Realizing it was now or never if he was to find a wireless set on board that might enable him to contact the Navy, Lang raced towards the ship. But he need not have bothered: like so many of the vessels involved in Operation Cycle, *Hebe 2* had no wireless, or any other means of conversing with His Majesty's destroyers off France.

He nevertheless hoped that the ship might be refloated, and having returned to the shore to collect volunteers who might help to ward off the Germans, he climbed back on to *Hebe 2*. His hopes were swiftly dashed. Shortly after he made it back to the ship, she was hit by a shell. The explosion knocked out Lang, wounded his brigadier, who had followed him on to the ship, and made a bloody hole in one of skipper Lieutenant Dennis Bennett-Jones's legs. Even that did not depress everyone's spirits. The junior officer on board, a sub-Lieutenant John Pryor, was still planning to sail the ship out to sea once the tide came in, and he was shocked when one of the army officers on board lowered the white ensign without reference to him to signify that they were surrendering. The Germans arrived soon afterwards to take them all prisoner.[77]

Back at St Valery, Fortune had ordered the troops to form an inner perimeter around the town in case they could hold off the Germans for another day. However, as is described in Colonel Swinburn's war diary, Fortune's hopes plummeted when he visited General Ihler's headquarters in the town centre, and was told that the French general intended to surrender. Ihler then asked Fortune to send a signal to Weygand confirming this. Fortune responded by stating that he could not give in until he was certain he could not evacuate his men; he was of the opinion that the evacuation might still go ahead if they could only recapture the heights near Le Tot. Although Ihler felt this was impossible, he gave Fortune to understand that he would not take any action until he heard back from Fortune after the British commander had spoken to his superiors. Believing that this assurance had bought him some time, Fortune ordered the 4th Seaforths to attack the Le Tot heights, while the 5th Gordons were given the task of holding the cliffs to the east of the town.

According to Colonel Swinburn, the execution of Fortune's plan was interrupted when at 8.15 a.m. he noticed a white flag fluttering from a nearby church steeple. After demanding that it be taken down, he was upset to discover from the Frenchman responsible for putting it there that General Ihler had surrendered. This was confirmed by a note handed to him by another Frenchman, which stated: '9 Corps will cease fire at 8 a.m.'[78] On seeing this, Fortune asked his staff to send the following message to the War Office:

I have been ordered to cease fire as from 0800 hrs by Comdt Ninth Corps. I am in the process of trying to clear enemy machine guns from cliffs overlooking harbour. A difficult situation exists in St Valery as all French elements have ceased fire and . . . [are] hanging out white flags. I have informed Corps Comdt that my policy is that I cannot, repeat not, comply with his orders until I am satisfied that there is no possibility of evacuating by boat any of my division later.[79]

Fortune's spirit is to be commended, but it was not long before he concluded that Ihler's defeatist stance was not so unreasonable after all. The moment when Fortune changed his mind was witnessed by 2nd Lieutenant Andrew Biggar, a signalman, who visited the 51st Division's headquarters at about 10.30 a.m., shortly after Fortune's last message was written: 'The General was gamely hesitating to obey the order and was considering the . . . position,' Biggar recalled.

Just then enemy shells started whizzing over the roof top of the small house we were in. They seemed to come nearer and nearer until it sounded as if they were just missing the chimney pots. With an anguish which I will never forget, the General reluctantly decided that he had little option but to obey the orders, and he said: 'Tell somebody to hoist that bloody flag on the church tower.' . . . The General [then] instructed me to take the news to Colonel Hunter . . . and to tell him to march all fit men up to Divisional Headquarters in a smarter manner than they had ever marched before.[80]

On hearing Fortune's order, efforts were quickly made to stop the assault on the heights near Le Tot. At the same time the 5th Gordons, who were just moving into position on the east of the town, found their line of fire blocked by a column of Frenchmen with white bandages tied to their rifles. This shielded the German troops who were arriving behind the Frenchmen. By the time the French soldiers had passed, the German tanks had approached, leaving the Gordons with no alternative but to surrender as well.[81]

Back at Fortune's headquarters inside the town, another signalman, who had just completed the transmission of Fortune's last message, had the presence of mind to tack on the following words at the end: 'I have now ordered cease fire.'[82] This last sentence, contradicting as it did what Fortune had been saying in the earlier part of the message, confused Admiral James. The Commander-in-Chief Portsmouth at first thought that there might have been a transcription error in London, and that Fortune had intended to say, 'I have *not* ordered cease fire.' That explains why, an hour and a half after the message was sent, James was still attempting to contact Fortune to assure him that they would come back for his men that night.[83] It was only after the Admiralty assured James that the message passed to him had been correctly transcribed that he came to terms with the awful reality.[84] Some eight thousand British soldiers had been captured and, as Colonel Swinburn wrote in his war diary, 'The activities of the 51st Highland Division [had] ceased.'[85]

36: The Sinking of the *Lancastria*

St Nazaire, 17 June 1940
(See Map 1)

Churchill might have been unable, or unwilling, to save the 51st Highland Division, but there were limits to what he was prepared to do to keep the French fighting. Minutes of the War Cabinet meeting held during the afternoon of 12 June report Churchill as saying 'that the British commanders in the Havre peninsula must not accept any further orders from the French who had let us down badly. They had not allowed the 51st Division to retire on Rouen, and had then kept it waiting until it was no longer possible for it to reach Havre. Finally they had compelled it to capitulate with their own troops. Any remaining troops must be evacuated that night without fail.'[1]

As it turned out, no French opposition to the evacuation was raised, and by midday on 13 June some 11,200 men, including the 51st Division's Ark Force, had been evacuated from areas in and around Le Havre, the last ship sailing as the first Germans approached the town, according to the British Commander Le Havre's war diary.[2]

So was the sacrifice of the 51st Division worthwhile? It is easy to say now that it did not encourage the French to hold out for much longer than they would have done even had the Highlanders been permitted to cut and run without reference to Weygand. But that is speaking with the benefit of hindsight. At the time when the 51st Division's retreat should have commenced, British ministers were still hoping that Reynaud would hold off the defeatist elements in his cabinet, whose influence had been growing ever since the appointment of Marshal Philippe Pétain as Deputy Premier on 18 May. It was only on 13 June, the day after the 51st Division's capitulation, that Reynaud finally asked Churchill to let France negotiate a peace settlement with Germany. This was a crucial stage on the road to France's surrender, given the March 1940 pledge that no such action would be taken by either party to the Anglo-French alliance without the other's permission. Churchill refused to give his consent, and at the end of his 13 June meeting with Reynaud at Tours, the French Government having left Paris three days earlier, there was still a faint hope, notwithstanding Reynaud's question, that France might carry on fighting.[3] Reynaud agreed that Roosevelt should be asked once and for all whether he would come into the war on the Allies' side before any irrevocable decision was taken.[4]

It was against this unpromising backdrop that the recently knighted General Sir Alan Brooke set foot on French soil again, as the Commander-in-Chief of the 2nd BEF.[5] His mission was nominally to help the French resist the Germans. But as Brooke told Anthony Eden when discussing his appointment, there was little chance of the British troops being able to turn the tide. According to Brooke, Britain had only just escaped a major disaster at Dunkirk, yet here they were risking another catastrophe. He realized there was a political rationale for returning to France, but he wanted Eden to know that there was no chance of it being a military success.[6]

This gloomy forecast was naturally kept secret from the men under Brooke's command. They included the 52nd Lowland Division, sent to France between 7 and 12 June, and some of the 1st Canadian Division, which commenced its flow of troops to France during the night 12–13 June, as well as the remnants of the 1st Armoured Division and Beauman's Division, which had never left France.[7]

Captain Jack Lambert, of 52 Division's 4th/5th Royal Scots Fusiliers, has described the sense of unreality that was predominant when he was shipped off to war on a luxury liner:

I carried a ridiculous amount of personal luggage, including of all things my walking out dress. Some officers even took their blue patrols in case there might be dancing . . . [On the liner] I . . . remember being asked to take luncheon with the Captain. We were served cocktails first, and then followed a wonderful lunch with the appropriate wine for each course. Naturally each place was set with a beautiful white starched napkin.[8]

The only indication that he might not be able to travel in such style on the way back was the lecture he was given before setting out on how to escape if captured. He was presented with two silk maps of Germany, which he sewed into his battledress trousers, and a miniature compass, which he concealed under a pip on his shoulder.[9]

Lambert's idyllic journey to France could not have been more different from that endured by General Alan Brooke on 12 June. The British

Commander-in-Chief had to make do with the facilities, or lack of them, on a dirty little Dutch steamer: they were a far cry from what might have been expected for such a senior soldier. There was not so much as a canteen on board to fortify Brooke and his staff for the ordeal ahead. He was forced to fall back on sandwiches given to him by his wife as they parted. Brooke's ship arrived off Cherbourg at 9.30 p.m. on 12 June, but he was then told he must wait until the next morning before landing. 'When the pilot boat came alongside, I said I would go ashore in it,' Brooke wrote. '[But] I was informed by the French officials that this was quite impossible; that passengers were strictly forbidden from travelling on the pilot's boat. It was evident that the war had not yet reached Cherbourg.'[10]

It was midnight before he was rescued by the British commander in Cherbourg. 'Apparently he had never been even warned by the War Office of my arrival,' Brooke commented. His treatment after landing was scarcely better. 'After being first of all rushed to a dugout in spite of my remonstrating that I did not believe there was a single German plane about, I was finally taken to the [British commander's] château . . . at 2 a.m. [on 13 June].'[11] It was an inauspicious start to the new campaign.

At 8 p.m. on 13 June Brooke finally reached Weygand's headquarters at Briare, south-east of Orléans, but it was 14 June before the French Commander-in-Chief, who had been travelling the night before, was able to see him. Brooke also visited General Georges' headquarters. Only then was he able to see for himself the extent to which the French Army had disintegrated. It was plain from the map shown to him by Weygand that large inroads had been made into the French line by the German panzers. Paris was not being defended and was duly taken by the Germans that day. And that was not the only bad news. Brooke was given to understand that the French did not have sufficient reserves to launch a viable counter-attack.[12]

Brooke was so shocked by Weygand's, and subsequently General Georges', report, and the French generals' main remedy – which was to place the 2nd BEF's divisions, backed by some French units, in front of Rennes to cover a security zone in Brittany – that when at 4 p.m. he arrived back at the Lines of Communication Headquarters at Le Mans, he immediately rang Dill to complain about the manoeuvres Weygand had requested.[13] During their conversations, Dill confirmed that he would halt the movement of British troops to France, and that, with one exception, all BEF troops already there should retire to the coast immediately. They were to be evacuated from ports such as Cherbourg, St Malo, Brest, St Nazaire and La Rochelle. The one exception was 52 Division's 157 Brigade, which, since 12–13 June, had been holding the line of the River Risle west of Conches-en-Ouche under the command of the French 10th Army.[14] Dill also agreed that Brooke was no longer to be under Weygand's command, and therefore had no obligation to comply with the French plan to hold Brittany.[15]

At about 8 p.m., however, Dill rang Brooke back, and asked what he was currently doing with 52 Division. When Brooke replied that he was complying with what they had arranged during their previous conversations, Dill responded, as Brooke reported in his notes:

'The Prime Minister does not want you to do that,' and I think I answered: 'What the hell does he want?' At any rate, Dill's next reply was: 'He wants to speak to you,' and he handed the receiver over to him . . . [Churchill] told me . . . I had been sent to France to make the French feel that we were supporting them. I replied that it was impossible to make a corpse feel, and that the French Army was, to all intents and purposes, dead . . . He insisted that we should make them feel we were supporting them, and I insisted that this . . . would only result in throwing away good troops to no avail.

Our talk lasted for close on half an hour, and on many occasions his arguments were so formed as to give me the impression that he considered that I was suffering from 'cold feet' because I did not wish to comply with his wishes. This was so infuriating that I was repeatedly on the verge of losing my temper. Fortunately while I was talking to him I was looking through the window at [Major-General James] Drew [52 Division's commander] and [Brigadier John] Kennedy [his artillery commander] sitting on a garden seat under a tree. Their presence there acted as a continual reminder of the human element of the 52nd Division and of the unwarranted decision to sacrifice them with no attainable object in view.

At last, when I was in an exhausted condition, he said: 'All right, I agree with you.'[16]

Unlike the situation prior to Dunkirk, when Gort had failed to make a stand against the politicians and War Office until it was almost too late, Brooke had stood up to Churchill sooner rather than later, and appeared

to win. At least, that was how the conversation must have been interpreted by Brooke as he wearily put down the phone. General Drew was
ordered to transport all his troops, excluding 157 Brigade, to Cherbourg
as soon as possible.

But that was far from the end of the vacillations concerning the 2nd
BEF. The next day Brooke was told that the 52nd Division's brigades
at Cherbourg were not to be evacuated after all 'for political reasons'.
He was only finally given the go-ahead to send them back to England
on 16 June.[17]

That still left the 52nd Division's 157 Brigade backed by the remnants of the 1st Armoured Division, both of which had been placed
under the command of General Marshall-Cornwall, plus the RAF
ground crews and line-of-communications troops for many of whom
St Nazaire was the nearest port. On 16 June Brooke, speaking on the
telephone from Redon, twenty-five miles north-east of St Nazaire,
warned Dill: 'At St Nazaire the Boche have become troublesome with
bombing and machine-gunning, and soon we shall be in the same
position as the 51st. I am afraid Marshall-Cornwall's force may suffer
the same fate.'

'I know,' Dill replied. 'But they must share the same fate as the 10th
Army.'[18]

But Brooke had already proved himself to be more than a match for
the politicians and their mouthpiece at the War Office, and the following
notes of his conversation with Dill at 10.30 a.m. on 17 June show what
could be achieved by standing up to them:

Brooke: 'Had a message last night from Marshall-Cornwall saying that if the
10th Army were pushed back from their present position they would disintegrate, and he would withdraw on Cherbourg.'
Dill: 'It is against all his orders to break away from the 10th Army so long as
he can co-operate with them.'
Brooke: 'Do you want him to disintegrate also?'
Dill: 'No, but there is a very delicate political game on now which is of vital
importance.'
Brooke: 'I dare say, but Marshall-Cornwall's lines of communications are based
in Cherbourg, and if he is to extricate himself, it is his only way.'
Dill: 'Can't you get the 10th Army to come with him?'
Brooke: 'That is what he is trying to do, but some of them are still bent on that

ridiculous operation down south [i.e. the plan to hold the Brittany peninsula]
. . . I am no longer in touch with him, and I gather the French are really in
the same state as they were when we were with them before.'
Dill: 'You can't control anything any longer?'[19]

Brooke gave Dill to understand that he could not, and if he was
being economical with the truth, Dill was in no position to intervene.
Therefore Marshall-Cornwall was permitted to continue his retreat from
the Verneuil–Mortagne-au-Perche road, where 157 Brigade had been
holding the line on 16 June, to Cherbourg, where the last of his troops
were eventually evacuated on 17–18 June with the advanced guard
belonging to Rommel's 7th Panzer Division just three miles away.[20]
Together Marshall-Cornwall and Brooke had engineered that these
troops at least should escape, notwithstanding the best efforts of the
politicians and War Office to obstruct their evacuation.

Nevertheless Dill, prompted by Churchill, initially ordered Brooke
to remain in France, notwithstanding the fact that there was no army
for Brooke to command any more. Dill admitted that it was for political
reasons. Brooke was only released from this obligation after Dill rang
him at 1.15 p.m. on 17 June to tell him that Marshal Pétain, the
eighty-four-year-old soldier-cum-politician who had replaced Reynaud
as the Président du Conseil the previous night, had just made a broadcast
stating that the French should stop fighting while he negotiated an
armistice.[21] The failure to forewarn Brooke was just another symptom
of the disintegration of the Anglo-French relationship. However, from
Brooke's point of view, the news of the broadcast had one happy
consequence: it freed him up to move to St Nazaire with a view to
being evacuated along with the remaining British troops and servicemen
in the area.

★ ★ ★

By 17 June, 57,000 of the 124,000 British servicemen from the Army
and RAF, who were eventually evacuated between 14 June and the
22 June Armistice, had left France.[22] But there were still 67,000 who
needed to get away, and many were relying on ships assembled off
St Nazaire to rescue them. The first boats carrying these desperate men
out to the larger ships off the coast commenced their ferrying early that
morning, and soon they were joined by a larger group of lighters, tenders
and British destroyers. Throughout the morning the boats moved to

and fro between the larger ships and the shore. The men they were carrying were for the most part a motley collection of reinforcement soldiers and line-of-communication troops. Many of the latter were tradesmen and labourers dressed as soldiers, including mechanics, engineers from the Royal Army Service Corps (RASC), and Pioneers. There were also men from the RAF maintenance units, which, until two days earlier, had been based in the huts beside the aerodrome at Nantes.[23]

Among the vessels gathered off St Nazaire was a group of merchant ships. There were also railway ferries that before the war had carried passengers from Dover to Calais. But of all the ships that had come to take the British forces home, one of the largest was the 16,243-ton Cunard ocean-going liner SS *Lancastria*, which had dropped her anchor some eleven miles south-west of the port.[24] During peacetime this ship was permitted to carry 1700 passengers, which, with her 375-man crew, took the total to just over 2100.[25] However, 17 June 1940 was no ordinary day, and the number boarding the liner crept up from 5000 to in excess of 6000, if the statements of the crew, overheard by those who boarded her, are to be believed.[26] Her skipper, Captain Rudolf Sharp, was certainly put under pressure to crowd in many more passengers than he would have deemed safe for a normal excursion.

Harry Grattidge, the ship's chief officer under Sharp, recorded in his memoirs how his captain first learned what was expected:

A naval transport officer came aboard, and told Captain Sharp that we must prepare to take as many troops as could be loaded, without regard to the limits laid down by international law. 'Is this,' I asked, with bitter memories of [the evacuation from] Norway [a few days earlier], 'another capitulation?'

The NTO looked shocked. 'Don't even mention the word,' he said. 'It's merely a temporary movement of troops.'[27]

The passengers did not just consist of men from the armed forces. There were also around forty civilians, including some embassy staff and some men from the Fairey Aviation company in Belgium, who with their families had to escape along with the troops. There were also a few dogs, notwithstanding Grattidge's initial determination to allow no pets on board for fear of contravening quarantine regulations. When it came to it, he did not have the heart to enforce his own order after seeing tears welling in the eyes of one little boy whose mother had just been told that their dog had to be shipped back to St Nazaire.[28]

As the troops and civilians boarded, *Lancastria*'s crew could not help being touched by the relief expressed by their new passengers. The first words uttered by one lady in her late twenties who came on board with two young children were 'Thank God we are on an English ship.'[29] Some of the soldiers were even more demonstrably appreciative: they fell on their knees and literally kissed the deck. As far as they were concerned they were as good as home.[30]

The first passengers were impressed by the crew's efficiency. It could have been the beginning of a regular cruise. As the men, women and children boarded, they were handed tickets telling them where on the ship they should sit, and the time when they could go to one of the dining areas for a meal.[31] Those who then ventured into the *Lancastria*'s plush dining room were reassured by the sight of waiters dressed in white jackets and bow-ties hurrying between tables covered with white tablecloths and silver cutlery. For many of the soldiers it was a welcome return to the life they had known before they had gone off to war.[32]

As the ship filled up, however, the crew's discipline lapsed somewhat. Men were seen boarding without being counted, and as a result no one has ever been sure exactly how many were taken. The testimony of Private Jess Fenton, a Sherwood Forester, gives some indication. When at around midday yet another lighter approached, he heard Chief Officer Grattidge shout to Sharp, 'We can't take any more! We've already got 6,700 on board.' To which Sharp replied, 'We'll just take this lot, but no more!'[33]

Grattidge has described how he and Sharp stood on *Lancastria*'s bridge nervously keeping an eye on what was going on overhead:

We . . . watched the planes quivering above us in the blue sky. Sometimes the afternoon sun caught their wings in a fine flash of scintillating light, like dragonflies cast in silver. Every so often came the sharp-edged snarl of a bomb, the rocking explosion, the fountains of spray that spattered our decks like spring rain. The Nazi planes were trying, [initially] without success, to hit the *Oronsay* [a 20,000-ton liner owned by the Orient Steam Navigation Company which was anchored about half a mile away].[34]

The air raid that should have acted as a warning to Captain Sharp took place at 1.50 p.m. when the *Oronsay* was finally hit by a bomb. Although it did not sink the ship, it destroyed part of her bridge, and might have alerted Sharp and Grattidge as to what could come their way unless they took evasive action.[35] Sharp was certainly given the option to depart. Captain Barry Stevens on the destroyer HMS *Havelock* advised him to leave immediately. Sharp would have gone if he could have persuaded a destroyer to escort him. But his signal asking for protection on the way home went unanswered, and after thinking for some time about which was the better of two evils, he turned to Grattidge and said: 'I think that we'll do better to wait for the *Oronsay* and go together.' Grattidge agreed, thinking, 'What chance would we stand on our own against a submarine attack?'[36] Unfortunately neither man had the presence of mind to suggest that they should at least pull up their anchor, and steam around rather than remaining stationary, a sitting duck for any German pilot who cared to attack.[37]

At 3.45 p.m. yet another air raid started, and minutes later Captain Field, an officer in the Medical Corps who was lying on one of the *Lancastria*'s aft decks, caught sight of a single German plane diving towards him. 'I heard men shout "Here he comes,"' he recalled. 'I heard the troops trying to tell a gunner where to shoot, but he kept saying "Where? Where?" . . . The scream of the bomb replaced the noise of the diving plane . . . Then . . . [came] the sound of [the] impact. [It was] like someone bursting a child's tin kettle drum with a hammer. [This was followed by] clouds of steam, smoke and fragments raining down.'[38]

The bomb was one of three or possibly four that hit the ship. RASC soldier Private Mansfield remembers what happened after he flung himself down on to the deck as the bomb nearest to him exploded:

A fiery cloud of red-hot flame engulfed us, [and] the deck below us shuddered and bumped as if in an earthquake. [It was as if] red-hot ashes were being scattered across us . . . This, [along] with the thunder of the explosion, seemed to go on for some . . . [time. When] finally I opened my eyes, [all I could see was] . . . blackness. I thought I had been buried under something . . . But when I took another look, [the] blackness was going grey . . . and I realized it was black fumes from the explosion that [had] enveloped us.[39]

While the men on the top decks were peering through the smoke, trying to find their bearings, some of those in the corridors and companionways inside the ship were picking themselves up after being knocked off their feet by the blast. Sergeant Tom Payne, one of the RAF ground crew on board, has described how he was thrown the entire length of the passage where he had been standing: 'I struggled up in a daze. My head felt numb . . . I stumbled forward to find myself gazing into the dining room. Everything was strangely quiet. A couple of chaps were standing beside me staring at what appeared to be a large gaping hole in the centre of the dining room floor . . . Clouds of smoke began to fill the room . . . Only then did I realize the stark reality: that we were hit.'[40]

Gallantly rushing down to one of the holds where he hoped to find his friend 'Pikey', he came across what he referred to as 'a terrible sight': 'The only way out from the hold, a temporary wooden staircase, had collapsed in the first rush of the men to get out, and now there was no exit. Ropes were being thrown down to [the men trapped inside] . . . but the struggling mass of men trying [unsuccessfully] to reach [these lifelines] was sickening to watch. [Then] the ship lurched to one side, and . . . [in a] panic, I rushed upstairs to the top deck.'

Oblivious to the horrific scenes down below, at least some of those inside the ship did not even realize they had been hit. The thud that had shaken her could just as easily have been a heavy weight dropping on deck. Or so they thought. However, as Gunner Garretts recalled: 'We looked at one another not knowing what to do,' only to be reassured by a group of sailors who announced authoritatively: 'It's all right. That one went over the side.'

'We all breathed a sigh of relief,' Garretts reported, 'and tried to make conversation . . . [But then] suddenly we [felt] . . . ourselves going over at an angle. Chairs started sliding across the floor, cups and saucers began crashing [off] . . . the tables, and that started a mad rush to get up on deck.'[41]

What had scared Garretts and his companions was the sensation of the *Lancastria* keeling over on to her starboard side. Orders were quickly shouted out from the bridge that all men should go to the port side in the hope that this would restore the ship's balance. The ship did indeed right itself for a while only to end up keeling over irrevocably to port, unbalanced, it seems, by the large hole that one of the bombs had blown out of the hull on her port side.[42]

Grattidge was lying on a bunk in his cabin when he heard the air-raid warning blow out over St Nazaire's harbour. He leaped up, but could only stand frozen to the spot as he listened to what he described as 'the chilling banshee scream' of bombs falling. 'Four times the *Lancastria* bucked and shuddered like an animal in pain,' he wrote later, before recalling how he raced up to the bridge.

'How many down number-two hold?' Sharp shouted to him as he arrived.

'About eight hundred RAF, sir. Why?'

'I think that first one struck there and blew away their exit.'

Another bomb had gone into number-three hold releasing tons of fuel oil. '. . . Over and again I could hear the signalmen repeating: "Hello . . . hello . . . engine room," ' Grattidge recorded. 'But there was no reply . . . All contact with the engine room had been cut off.

'For a moment it was impossible to see anything,' Grattidge recalled. '. . . Vast clouds of inky smoke came pumping over us.' Then it drifted away and, as Grattidge reported: 'We saw the most terrible sight the *Lancastria* could offer: the mess of blood . . . oil and splintered woodwork that littered the deck, and the furious white core of water that came roaring from the bottom of the ship in No. 4 hold.'

One look at Sharp was enough to tell Grattidge that his captain had also lost all hope of saving the ship. On seeing this, Grattidge seized the bridge megaphone and, in the polite and restrained language that only a British cruise-liner officer could adopt at such a moment of crisis, calmly announced: 'Your attention please. Clear away the [life]boats!'[43]

After the sinking of the *Titanic* twenty-eight years earlier, a lot had been said about never allowing a ship to go to sea again without sufficient lifeboats. But this had understandably been forgotten in the state of emergency that existed off the coast of France in June 1940. There were clearly not enough lifeboats for all the passengers on the *Lancastria*. There were barely enough for the women and children on board, many boats having been damaged by the bombs and lost when the ship keeled over. That explains why there was a panic-stricken rush towards the few lifeboats remaining.

'The first boat [to be lowered] was heavily loaded with women and children, and a few men to do the rowing,' wrote RASC Sergeant-Major Picken, who was stationed nearby. 'One woman didn't want to get in . . . and tearfully watched as her husband searched around the deck for their . . . daughter. [Eventually] the woman was forced into the boat . . . [but] as it touched the water . . . [it] capsized, spilling its passengers overboard.' They were only saved because a second boat, which was empty, was swiftly lowered; those who climbed into it owed their lives to a naval officer who stood beside it before it descended brandishing his pistol to make sure that no one on the ship climbed into it. The soldiers and RAF personnel in a third boat were less lucky. The davits did not support the lifeboat and its human cargo, and when it crashed into the water, its bottom stove in, the boat was swamped, and all those inside had to swim for their lives.[44]

Another report, which demonstrates that being allocated a seat in a lifeboat was a mixed blessing, was made by the woman who in 1940 was thirteen-year-old Emilie Legroux. She and Roger, her eleven-year-old brother, were placed in a lifeboat along with their parents. But before it could be lowered, some soldiers jumped into the boat on top of them. In the course of the mêlée that followed, the boat tipped up, dropping men, women and children into the sea. Roger Legroux came to the surface beside his mother, but neither his father nor his sister was anywhere to be seen.[45] Emilie's account reveals that her life was saved after a man she initially mistook for her father allowed her to hold on to his back. Ironically her father, the only one in the family who could swim properly, did not survive. He probably drowned.[46]

After the lifeboats were 'launched', another order was shouted from the bridge that would have had a familiar ring about it for anyone who had come up against the German panzers. It was: 'Every man for himself!'[47] The panic that this order caused had to be seen to be believed. All of a sudden, men began to hurl themselves over the starboard side of the ship. Their progress was watched by a phlegmatic forty-four-year-old Pioneer named Clement Stott, who noted that the ship had keeled over to port to such an extent by this time that 'most of those that jumped, instead of reaching the water, were crashing . . . head first on to the steel plates of the hull, or the edges of the port holes, and amid terrible screams, were killing themselves.'[48]

Sergeant Tom Payne, the RAF man who, as mentioned earlier, had raced up to the deck after searching in vain for his friend Pikey in one of the ship's holds, recorded how some of the first men to make it into the sea died: 'By my side [on the deck] some men picked up a latticed wooden raft and heaved it overboard. It landed on top of a number of men, and I saw a few still bodies float away . . . their necks [apparently] broken.'[49]

Some of the men who jumped from the deck while wearing their lifejackets died just as quickly. The starboard side of the top deck was at this stage so high relative to the sea that the wearers' heads were jerked upwards by the movement of the lifejackets as they hit the water. This resulted in a broken neck and instantaneous death for anyone who had not been taught how to lessen the impact by bending their legs and tugging the lifejacket down sharply as they fell. It was some time before it became clear that another way had to be found to disembark. By then the sea was full of what looked like floating coconuts bobbing around in the oily water. Only on closer inspection could it be seen that the 'coconuts' were in fact the heads of those killed in this way.[50]

Those who waited until the *Lancastria* had sunk further into the water found leaving the ship much easier. They were able to walk down the starboard side of the hull and plopped gently into the sea. Their relief at being able to avoid a long drop was only marred by what they saw through the portholes as they stepped over them: their doomed comrades trapped inside the ship.[51]

The account by Harry Pettit, an RASC sergeant, suggests that he was too frightened to wait until the last moment. He has described what happened to him as he slid down the ship's hull plates into the sea:

I sank below the water, and . . . kept going down . . . until my lungs seemed on the point of bursting. I was quite convinced at that moment that I was dying, and, with a clear calm picture in my mind of home and . . . [my] widowed mother, I wished that death by drowning did not take so long . . . Almost unconscious, I must have shot up to the surface quickly, because the next thing I knew was that I was choking and gasping amidst the dreadful scene[s] on the surface.[52]

One such scene involved Pettit himself. Because he and some of his comrades did not have lifejackets, they had linked up with some men who did, clinging to each other so that they were all buoyant. This co-operative effort was interrupted by a screaming man who tried to seize one of their lifejackets. Fortunately they were strong enough to throw him off, but he then attacked another man who was floating by himself nearby. What Pettit described as 'an awful struggle' ensued, which only ended when the lone swimmer eventually came out on top, and the assailant disappeared once and for all beneath the waves.[53]

There were countless other dramas. An officer on a lifeboat was forced to push another man who had gone berserk into the sea in order to save the other passengers.[54] Two men famously shot each other in a maritime version of a suicide pact. As if the swimmers did not have enough to contend with, German planes swooped down, machine-guns firing. Some also dropped flares in a bid to ignite the oil on the water. Fortunately this attempt to kill off the shipwrecked men failed for the most part, but those unlucky enough to be caught by patches of burning oil were, as one survivor put it, 'fried like sausages in a frying pan'.[55]

These events represented the horrific side of the disaster. But it seems that far and away the biggest killer was the sheer exhaustion and failing morale that overwhelmed so many of those in the water. At first most of the men and women who had managed to swim away from the *Lancastria*, and had found means of staying afloat using floating debris such as wooden oars and crates, deckchairs and tables, seemed to have a good chance of surviving. But gradually the effort of keeping their heads out of the oily water took its toll, and demoralization set in. There are countless tales of men just giving up, and slipping silently under the waves, never to appear again. Many of those who survived only did so because they cheered themselves up with thoughts of home and their family.[56]

It is very difficult to imagine the thoughts that must have been churning through the minds of the men, presumably non-swimmers, who had remained on the ship's hull. When Gunner Garretts looked back after swimming away from the *Lancastria*, he saw the scene that must have stirred the hearts of so many of those lucky enough to have swum away from the wreck: 'By this time . . . [the *Lancastria*] was right over on . . . [her] side,' he remembered, 'and one could not see much of the plates for all the troops that were sitting along the side. [There was] one chap standing up in front beating out the time while they all sang "Roll out the barrel" at the top of their voices. The next time I turned round she was gone.'[57] And so had most of those whom he had seen singing that jaunty song.

Nevertheless their spirit lived on. One survivor has described how, long after the ship had disappeared, he heard an echo of their courageous singing: 'As I floated . . . I heard something,' he wrote, 'or was it my imagination? Over the sea came a whisper, wafted it seemed from a thousand miles away. It was another song, a hymn. Very faintly, I followed the tune, but clearly . . . heard the last line [which ended with the words] ". . . to our eternal home".'[58] Far from being an aural 'mirage', it was probably yet another example of a group of men keeping their spirits up in the water with a rousing chorus. There are many reports of survivors being buoyed up by such singing.

It may have helped Gunner Garretts, but he was only just picked up in time: he was losing consciousness by the time a trawler's crew fished him out of the water.[59] That made him one of the lucky ones. Less than fifty per cent of those on the *Lancastria* appear to have survived. Figures released in the British press over a month after the tragedy suggested that only 2477 out of all the men, women and children on board had been saved.[60] If this figure is more or less correct, and if there really were over six thousand passengers on board, it means that more than 3500 had been killed, making it the worst maritime disaster in British history.

General Alan Brooke was fortunate enough to miss the sinking. But because of it his transport back to England was no more fitting for Britain's Commander-in-Chief than it had been on the way out to France five days earlier. When he boarded the trawler *Cambridgeshire*, after she had rescued nine hundred men who had been swimming in fuel oil, she was, as Brooke later wrote, 'covered in that foul-smelling black treacly substance. Heaps of clothes on the decks oozed out oil, whilst in the tiny cabin below, the carpet was soaked with it.'[61] However, as they steamed with the convoy away from France on 18 June, Brooke recalled himself 'thanking God that we were safely out of France for the second time. Luckily it was a lovely calm day, and, in spite of the stink of fuel oil, conditions were quite pleasant.'[62] His restful journey home was only disturbed by one of the ship's stokers, who was so disturbed by what he had seen off St Nazaire on the previous day that he had a mental breakdown, and had to be held down by Brooke and his staff on two occasions until he finally quietened down.[63]

One of the ships that, like *Cambridgeshire*, was steaming away from the mouth of the River Loire towards England during the night of

17–18 June was the merchant ship *Floristan* with around two thousand men on board. They were just some of the 27,000 servicemen and civilians evacuated from St Nazaire that night.[64] Some 144,000 British servicemen were eventually evacuated from France south of the Somme, if one includes those picked up after the 25 June Franco-German Armistice. A further 47,000 Allied soldiers were also evacuated from south of the Somme (most were French and Polish), taking the total number evacuated post-Operation Dynamo to more than 191,000.[65]

The number that reached England might have been considerably lower if the crew in a German bomber, which spotted the convoy at about midnight on 17–18 June, had had their way. The crew inside the bomber, a Junker 88, focused their attention on *Floristan*. However, because, unlike *Lancastria*, the ship was not at anchor, her skipper was able to turn her away from the plane's line of attack, and at the same time soldiers on board shot at the plane with their Bren guns. 'The Army gunners knew their job,' observed Colin Dee, an RAF maintenance unit sergeant on *Floristan*, who witnessed the attack. 'We saw the [plane's windscreen] ... disintegrate and fly away in the moonlight ... The German crew must have been cut to pieces. The aircraft was now so low, it seemed to be about to crash into us, but just cleared our funnel, removing the tops of the masts and our aerial. We saw it stagger on and finally dive into the sea missing all the other ships [as well].'[66]

During the moments following the crash, there was an eerie hush, but the silence was broken by clapping, cheering and shouting, which emanated from the other ships in the convoy.[67] It was a welcome sound for those on *Floristan* who, only seconds before, had believed they would end up in the sea like *Lancastria*'s passengers. It also came as a relief for those who had watched *Floristan* repulse the attack. It told them that even after the many grim events that had taken place since the BEF first arrived in France with such high expectations nine months earlier, culminating in the worst disaster of all earlier that afternoon, the British bulldog spirit was unbroken: it had survived to help its army, navy and air force fight another day.

Epilogue
Where did they go?

See Map 1

Significant events in the lives of some of the principal characters after they appeared for the last time in this book.

The Belgian

The King

King Leopold refused to flee to Britain, the solution proposed by Churchill. He was initially put under house arrest inside Belgium after he had surrendered, but was later deported to Germany where he remained until the end of the war. His subsequent attempt to carry on as the King of Belgium was met by bitter opposition, much of it prompted by the feeling that he had acted incorrectly in May 1940. In 1951 he abdicated, allowing his eldest son to become the new king.

The Dutch

The Whistleblower

Major Gijsbertus Sas' 'tomorrow at dawn' message sent from Berlin to Holland on 9 May 1940 was intercepted by a telephone tap placed on the Dutch Legation line by Hermann Göring's Forschungsamt. He was nevertheless permitted to leave Germany along with the other Dutch diplomats during the night 20–21 May, ending up in neutral Switzerland where he was reunited with his wife and son. From there he travelled to London, and then on to Canada where he was part of the Dutch military mission. He survived the war, and in 1946 became Holland's Military Attaché in Washington. In 1948 he described the role he had played at an inquest into what had gone wrong when Holland was invaded. By then he had become a major-general. But fate decreed that he was not to enjoy his new-found status for long: his bitterness at the way he had been treated contributed to the disintegration of his marriage. In 1948 he decided to divorce his wife, but tragically, before he could remarry, he was killed shortly afterwards in a plane crash.[1]

The Germans

The Spy

Colonel Hans Oster's involvement in the tip-offs given to the Allies about the German invasion plans was never discovered by the German authorities. But as a leading member of the resistance movement in Germany, it was almost inevitable that he would eventually fall foul of the Nazi regime. That moment came in April 1943: he was dismissed from the Abwehr after attempting to obstruct a surprise raid on their offices, and was arrested the day after the 20 July 1944 attempt to assassinate Hitler. On 9 April 1945 he was hanged at Flossenbürg concentration camp. According to his daughter Barbara, some people in Germany still regard him as a traitor.[2]

The Aviators

Majors Erich Hoenmanns and **Helmuth Reinberger** were both sent as prisoners-of-war to England and then to Canada when the Germans invaded Belgium. Hoenmanns was never able to make it up to his wife for his infidelity; she died prior to the invasion after suffering from a liver infection. Both Hoenmanns and Reinberger also became ill while in Canada, their complaints being exacerbated no doubt by their anxiety about how their reputations had suffered in Germany. In 1943 and 1944 respectively they were repatriated to Germany where they were interrogated so that their evidence could be presented to the Reichs War Tribunal. They were accused of 'negligently endangering' the Fatherland. Reinberger's final interrogation, according to the documents in Prague, was in March 1945. It is possible that the war ended before his case was heard. As for Hoenmanns, his story had a happy ending: after his return to Germany, he had a friendly meeting with Göring and was then formally exonerated in January 1944. He married a medical technician who had looked after him in the German hospital where he was treated following his repatriation, and had two more children having lost the two sons by his first marriage who were both killed during the war.[3]

War Criminals

Oberleutnant Franz Lohmann, who had organized the execution of at least two of the civilians massacred at Vinkt, was wounded while fighting in Russia, but survived the war. In 1946 he was arrested and charged with war crimes, and was sentenced to life imprisonment during his 1948 trial. However, he did not serve his full sentence, and died a free man. **Major Erwin Kühner**, who was also convicted, escaped with a twenty-year sentence.

Captain Fritz Knöchlein, one of the company commanders in the SS Totenkopf battalion implicated in the massacre at Le Paradis, was put on trial for murder in 1948, and found guilty. He was sentenced to death and was hanged on 28 January 1949.[4]

The Suspect

Captain Wilhelm Mohnke, commander of the SS Leibstandarte's 2nd Battalion, who was said by at least two witnesses to have been implicated in the Wormhout massacre, was captured by the Russians when Berlin was taken, and only returned to Germany in 1955. Once freed, he became a successful businessman. Post-war attempts to indict him for the killing at Wormhout failed after a key witness died. The only other evidence against him was based on hearsay. A suspicion that he was implicated in two other massacres in France in 1944 could also not be backed up with hard facts. He always denied having committed war crimes.

The Generals

General Heinz Guderian's attempt during Operation Barbarossa, the June 1941 invasion of Russia, to use similar tactics to those he had used in France – i.e. pressing ahead with his panzers without waiting for the infantry to catch up, and not being diverted by subsidiary targets on his flanks – led to conflict with his superiors. Although he had been promoted to the rank of colonel-general and put in charge of a panzer group, he still had to obey orders. Ironically, when he was eventually relieved of his command in December 1941, it was not because he had advanced too enthusiastically, but rather because he had allowed his troops to retreat. Since this contravened Hitler's express orders, Guderian's dismissal was almost inevitable. It turned out to be a blessing in disguise, however: when Guderian returned to Germany, he was found to be suffering from a heart condition that might have killed him had he carried on. It was fourteen months before his next big job: he was made the Inspector-General of Armoured Troops, and after the abortive July 1944 plot to assassinate Hitler, he was appointed Chief of the Army's General Staff, a position he held until March 1945 when he was sacked again: he had asked Himmler to persuade Hitler to surrender.[5]

General Erwin Rommel was for a time the scourge of British troops in North Africa. Shortly after arriving there in February 1941, he and his Afrika Korps advanced from Tripolitania through Libya to the Egyptian border, an advance that led to his being given his field-marshal's baton in June 1942 at the age of fifty. After a subsequent retreat and renewed offensive in 1942, he was eventually defeated by General Montgomery (see below) at the battle of El Alamein. Monty's victory ended the Afrika Korps' winning streak, and Rommel was recalled to Germany in March 1943. In November that year he was appointed the commander of Army Group B under von Rundstedt (see below) with responsibility for the coast from Holland to Bordeaux. However, his preparations were not enough to prevent the Allied landings in Normandy, masterminded by his old foe Montgomery. This persuaded him that Germany was all but defeated and it appears to have turned him against his Führer. He was not directly involved in the July 1944 plan to assassinate Hitler, but he might just as well have been. On 14 October 1944 Hitler sent generals to offer Rommel the chance to commit suicide before he could be tried for treason. Rommel accepted the offer, and after being driven away from his home, he took the poison that the generals had brought with them. Minutes later he was dead.

General Gerd von Rundstedt, like Guderian (see above), was also relieved of his command during Operation Barbarossa, the invasion of Russia. At the end of November 1941 Field Marshal von Rundstedt's Army Group South had retreated from Rostov at a time when Hitler was insisting that withdrawal was not an option. Rundstedt was subsequently sent to build up the defences along the Atlantic Coast, only to be dismissed again after the June 1944 Normandy invasion by the Allies.

The British

The Massacre Survivors

Bert Evans, the Royal Warwick who had been shot while in the pond near Wormhout, was taken to a hospital in Boulogne where his injured arm was amputated. After three years as a prisoner-of-war, he was repatriated to England, and discharged from the Army. The loss of his arm meant he could not go back to work in the factory where he had earned his living before the war, and he was reduced to scrubbing steps and floors. He only escaped this drudgery when a passing man took pity on him, and gave him an office job as a clerk.[6]

Private Bert Pooley, the Royal Norfolk soldier who survived the massacre at Le Paradis, escaped from the SS troops who had murdered his comrades, thanks to assistance from **Bill O'Callaghan**, the only other survivor. They hid in a farm near the massacre site, assisted by the farmer's wife, for several days, eventually surrendering to regular German troops. Pooley, who had been badly wounded in the leg, was repatriated to England in October 1943. After the war both men gave evidence at the murder trial of Fritz Knöchlein, one of the SS officers who had sanctioned the massacre (see above).[7]

The Prisoner

Brigadier Claude Nicholson, the commander at Calais, was taken prisoner, and incarcerated at Rotenberg am Fulda, a castle south of Frankfurt. Tragically he died there on 26 June 1943. He was just forty-four years old.[8]

The Wounded

2nd Lieutenant Jimmy Langley, the 2nd Coldstream Guards officer wounded on the Bergues–Furnes section of the Dunkirk perimeter, survived to become a PoW. However, his arm was amputated by surgeon Philip Newman (see below), and in February 1941 he was repatriated to England. The Germans might have thought twice about freeing him, however, if they had known what he would do next: he became one of the leading lights at MI9, the organization that, in partnership with MI6, helped prisoners-of-war to escape and travel back to England.[9]

The Surgeon

Philip Newman was captured by the Germans along with the wounded at the 'Chapeau Rouge' château near Dunkirk, but in January 1942 he escaped for the second time (he was recaptured after his first escape) and made it back to England. After the war he became one of Britain's leading orthopaedic surgeons working at the Middlesex Hospital, London. In 1962 he operated on Churchill, who had broken his hip, and in 1976 he was appointed CBE.[10]

The Generals and the Admiral

General Harold Alexander's star was riding high after his success at Dunkirk. In August 1942 he was given the crucial post of Commander-in-Chief, Middle East, so that he was in overall command when the Allies' first victories were won in that theatre: at El Alamein (October 1942) and in Tunisia (May 1943). He later commanded the 15th Army Group, which, after much hard fighting, overran Italy in May 1945 shortly before Germany surrendered. By then he was a field-marshal. After the war, he was knighted, made a viscount (of Tunis and Errigal), and after serving as Governor-General in Canada, and as Minister of Defence in Churchill's government, an earl.

General Alan Brooke was rightly praised for what he and 2 Corps had achieved on the Ypres–Comines line. Within two years he was promoted to the leading position in the Army: he was the Chief of the Imperial General Staff (CIGS) from December 1941 until the end of

DUNKIRK'S PERIMETER: FURNES

61. *Top left* Lieutenant David Smith, the Royal Engineer who on 28 May blew up the bridges between Ypres and Dixmude

62. *Top right* Captain Francis Waldron, who has described the Berkshires' torment on the Furnes to Nieuport section of the Dunkirk perimeter

63. *Right* Captain Marcus Ervine-Andrews (*left*) on the day King George VI (*second from right*) presented him with the VC for his 'most conspicuous gallantry' on the Bergues to Furnes section of the Dunkirk perimeter on 1 June

64. *Below* Soldiers from Montgomery's 3 Division take cover in their slit trenches in the flat countryside within the Dunkirk perimeter near Furnes on 30 or 31 May

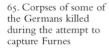

65. Corpses of some of the Germans killed during the attempt to capture Furnes

66. *Above* Troops queuing opposite Zuydcoote's sanatorium, between Bray-Dunes and Malo-les-Bains

67. *Left* A 3 Division unit (Royal Ulster Rifles) on the beach, probably taken after their withdrawal from the Dunkirk perimeter on the night of 31 May–1 June

68. *Right* Some of the little boats used to ferry rescued soldiers out to the larger ships waiting off shore

69. *Bottom left* Men in the shallows waiting to be picked up

70. *Bottom right* Commander Campbell Clouston, seen here at his wedding, who was in charge on the mole until he was tragically drowned

71. *Left* Vice-Admiral Bertram Ramsay who master-minded the naval side of the evacuation

72. *Below* The destroyer HMS *Grenade* after she was hit by German bombs on 29 May 1940, the day when the Luftwaffe nearly halted the evacuation

73. and 74. *Left* Soldiers had to negotiate planks and ladders when boarding the waiting destroyers HMS *Wolsey* (*left*) and *Vanquisher* (*far left*) which were tied up beside the mole

75. *Top left* Admiral Jean Abrial (*right*) with General Corap in front of Bastion 32, Abrial's Dunkirk headquarters

76. and 77. *Right* General Robert Fagalde and *far right* the BEF's General Harold Alexander (*right*), who rowed about the British refusal to carry on fighting in Dunkirk

78. to 80. *Left* The 'Chapeau Rouge' château in Rosendaël where surgeon Philip Newman (*bottom left*) treated Lieutenant Jimmy Langley (*below right*) seated on the left of his company commander Major Angus McCorquodale. Newman was left behind to look after the wounded after he and his medical team drew lots

81. to 83. *Top* One of the soldiers who did not make it home, unlike those (*left*) seen going back to England on the destroyer HMS *Wolsey*. Notwithstanding the criticism of the RAF, the position would have been worse still had the evacuation not been covered for a substantial period by pilots such as Allan Wright, who is seen (*bottom*) in his shot-up Spitfire after a patrol over Dunkirk. He wept after a friend was shot down during his first patrol over France

84. *Above* Germans inspect a line of lorries that had been used as a jetty during the evacuation

85. *Right* After capturing Dunkirk on 4 May, the Germans gathered on the beaches

86. *Bottom* The funnels of the sunk ships beside the mole after the evacuation bear witness to what might have happened if the Luftwaffe had been given a free rein over Dunkirk

87. *Above* Some of the 'little ships' commandeered during Operation Dynamo are towed past the Houses of Parliament after the end of the evacuation

88. *Left* Germans guarding French prisoners taken at Dunkirk and the surrounding beaches. Some reports state that over 80,000 Frenchmen were captured at Dunkirk

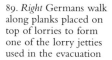
89. *Right* Germans walk along planks placed on top of lorries to form one of the lorry jetties used in the evacuation

90. *Left* General Marcel Ihler (*foreground facing left*) talks to one of his captors at St Valery after surrendering on 12 June. Rommel (with Knight's Cross) and General Victor Fortune (*far right*) look on

91. *Below* Survivors from the 51st Highland Division march into captivity at St Valery

92. *Below* General Sir Alan Brooke poses on the trawler *Cambridgeshire* on the way back to England after ordering the last of the 2nd BEF to leave France on 17 June

93. *Right* HMT *Lancastria* sinks after being bombed on 17 June. Some 3500 passengers are believed to have perished

the war. Once in position, he was all the more effective because, unlike his predecessors, he was quite prepared to stand up to Churchill just as he had done while Commander-in-Chief of the 2nd BEF in France. He was made a field-marshal before Germany surrendered, and afterwards a viscount. He was known thereafter as Lord Alanbrooke.

General Sir John Dill's star as a military commander waned after Dunkirk although he was made a field-marshal. Churchill felt that he was a negative Chief of Imperial General Staff and nicknamed him 'Dilly-Dally'. He was retired from his position in December 1941. However, while he did not get on with Churchill, he was highly thought of by the Americans. He could not have been more successful as the leader of Britain's staff mission in Washington. Sadly, in spite of this posting, he did not live to see the end of the war. He died in November 1944.

Lord Gort never commanded a field force again after Dunkirk. Although Churchill flirted with the idea of making him Commander-in-Chief, Middle East, in August 1942, General Brooke, who had criticized him so harshly for the way he had commanded the 1939–40 BEF, vetoed the idea. Gort was not entirely unappreciated, however: he was given the governorship of Malta, and won much praise for preparing and helping the island to withstand the siege. Subsequently he was the High Commissioner in Palestine. In spite of the stalling of his military career after Dunkirk, he became a field-marshal, and an English viscount (his inherited title was Irish). He did not survive for long after the war. He was diagnosed with cancer and died in March 1946.

General Edmond Ironside was encouraged to resign from his job as Commander-in-Chief, Home Forces, in July 1940 after General Brooke (see above) questioned the number of mobile reserves he provided for the defence of Britain. He was nevertheless made a field-marshal and a peer.

General Bernard Montgomery's advancement within the Army is believed to have been slower than it might otherwise have been because of his eccentric style of management and his insistence he should speak his mind. He could be tactless. He was only made commander of the 8th Army in North Africa in August 1942 after the first choice for the post died in a plane crash. He never looked back, winning famous victories at Alam Halfa, El Alamein, Medenine and Mareth before going on to command the 21st Army Group, under the overall leadership of General Eisenhower, which successfully invaded France during Operation Overlord on 6 June 1944. He also helped the Americans to halt the German advance through the Ardennes in December 1944. After the war he became the Chief of the Imperial General Staff, and ended his life as a peer and field-marshal.

General Henry Pownall was promoted to be the Vice-CIGS in 1941, and was given various commands in the East, as well as being Mountbatten's chief of staff in South East Asia. But his career never reached the heights of some of his peers. He was knighted but retired because of ill health in early 1945.

Vice-Admiral Bertram Ramsay was so highly thought of after Operation Dynamo that he was appointed as the Allied Naval Commander, Expeditionary Forces, in October 1943: as such he was given the task of transporting Allied troops to the Normandy beaches for the June 1944 invasion of France. Ramsay's execution of this task was one of the great achievements of the war, and Eisenhower paid him the ultimate tribute stating that only Ramsay could have organized such a large-scale landing. By then he was a full admiral and had been knighted. Unfortunately he did not live to see the fruits of what he had achieved: he was killed in a plane crash in January 1945.

The French

Admiral Jean Abrial was rewarded for what he had achieved at Dunkirk by being made Governor-General of Algeria (July 1940–July 1941), and subsequently Secretary of State for the French Navy (18 November 1942–26 March 1943). Although the French Fleet at Toulon was scuttled during his time in office in order to keep it out of German hands, thereby complying with a pledge given by Darlan to the British, Abrial was arrested after the war and in 1946 he was sentenced to ten years' forced labour because of his membership of the Vichy government. He was eventually released in 1947, however, and was granted an amnesty in 1953. When he died in 1962, he was given all military honours appropriate to his rank.

Marshal Philippe Pétain became the head of the unoccupied – southern – portion of France known as 'Vichy', a 'state' that came into existence after the armistice. It took its name from the town Vichy, north-east of Clermont-Ferrand, where his government was based.

After the war, he was tried and imprisoned for his collaboration with the Germans, and remained a prisoner until his death at the age of ninety-five.

Paul Reynaud had his first reverse following the armistice on 28 June 1940 when he crashed his car in the South of France and his mistress, the Comtesse de Portes, was killed. He spent the remainder of the war in various prisons, but he survived, and afterwards became a minister again. His story has a happy ending: after divorcing his first wife, he remarried in 1949, aged seventy-one, and had three children. He was almost eighty when his last child was born.

General Maxime Weygand had been one of the first French leaders to call for an armistice, and after it was signed he was the Vichy government's Defence Minister. However, even he had his green line which he would not cross: he refused to allow the Germans to overstep the limits set in the armistice agreement. That disqualified him from continuing in Pétain's government, and in October 1940 he was sent to Algeria where he was the French Delegate General, and Commander-in-Chief of forces in French Africa. As such he opposed German attempts to establish supply routes through his territory to Rommel (see above) and his Afrika Korps – a clear breach of the armistice terms. The Germans had their revenge when they insisted he be brought back to France in November 1941, and when they arrested him a year later following their move into what had previously been Unoccupied France. He was to remain in German custody for the rest of the war. Afterwards he was arrested and imprisoned by the French after being accused of collaboration with the Germans. But the charges did not stick: he was freed and exonerated in 1948.[11]

Fall of France

France finally 'surrendered' on 22 June 1940 when General Huntziger signed the armistice agreement at Rethondes (five miles north-east of Compiègne). By then the Germans had reached a line running from Royan (north of Bordeaux) in the west to Clermont-Ferrand and St Étienne in the east. In the process they encircled the French troops in the area south and west of the Maginot Line. The troops in the Maginot Line itself carried on fighting and defending their forts until the end. (The line reached by 22 June 1940 is shown on the inset on Map 1 on pp. 508–9). The armistice terms formally became operative three days later, after Italy, which had declared war on France on 10 June, also agreed to the ending of hostilities.

The Missing

Exact figures for Frenchmen killed, wounded and missing during the 1940 campaign in France, Belgium and Holland are unavailable. The statistics given below for the other countries involved may also be approximations, and should perhaps be regarded as best estimates:

British[12]
Killed and died of wounds: 11,014
Wounded: 14,074
Missing/PoWs: 41,338
Total: 66,426

Guns destroyed/damaged/left behind in France: 2472 out of 2794 shipped to France. Vehicles destroyed/damaged/left behind in France: 63,879 out of 68,618 shipped to France.[13] The RAF lost 931 planes including 477 fighters during the 1940 battles in France and Belgium.[14] Twenty-five of the Royal Navy's destroyers were lost or damaged at Dunkirk. They were just some of at least 170 ships and boats which were lost and damaged during the evacuation.[15]

French[16]
Killed: around 90,000
Wounded: around 200,000

Belgian
Casualties: 23,350

Dutch
Casualties: 9779

German
Killed: 27,074
Wounded: 111,034
Missing: 18,384
Planes lost: 1284

Maps

The maps on the following pages have been produced using Second World War maps, most of which have the scale 1:50,000 and 1:250,000, and are to be found in the British Library and the National Archives/Public Record Office. Readers should note, however, that the positions of towns, villages and other features on the maps, and the distances between them are only approximately correct. Details about the units' positions have been taken wherever possible from the original war diaries for these units, which are to be found in the NA/PRO in London, SHAT in Vincennes, near Paris, and BA-MA in Freiburg, Germany. I have also been assisted, particularly in relation to those units whose actions are not the main focus of this book, by maps in the following books: Horne, *To Lose a Battle,* Frieser, *Guerre-éclair,* Ellis, *War In France,* and Blaxland, *Destination Dunkirk.* In relation to some of the maps I have obtained expert assistance from those who have specialist knowledge of the battles that took place in the sectors in question either on account of books they have written or because they participated in the battles. The full details of what they have written or witnessed appear in the end notes of the chapters to which their works or memories have contributed, but I have mentioned their names in the Maps' section of the notes.

The chapter numbers specified on the maps indicate the principal chapters to which the maps relate. However, the maps should also be used to help readers follow the action in other chapters (see the map numbers specified under the title for each chapter).

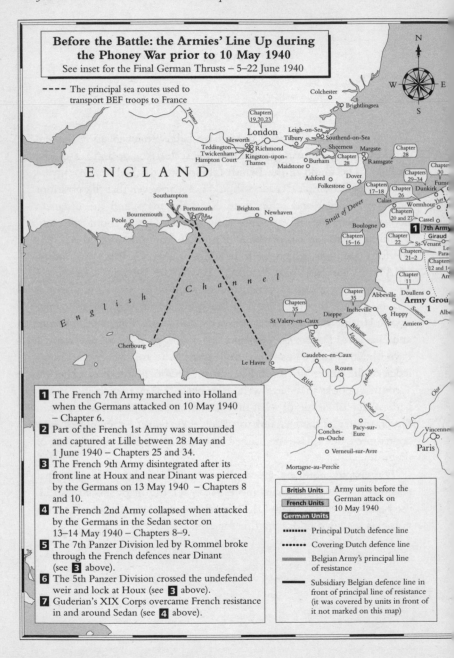

Before the Battle: the Armies' Line Up during the Phoney War prior to 10 May 1940

See inset for the Final German Thrusts – 5–22 June 1940

- - - - The principal sea routes used to transport BEF troops to France

1 The French 7th Army marched into Holland when the Germans attacked on 10 May 1940 – Chapter 6.

2 Part of the French 1st Army was surrounded and captured at Lille between 28 May and 1 June 1940 – Chapters 25 and 34.

3 The French 9th Army disintegrated after its front line at Houx and near Dinant was pierced by the Germans on 13 May 1940 – Chapters 8 and 10.

4 The French 2nd Army collapsed when attacked by the Germans in the Sedan sector on 13–14 May 1940 – Chapters 8–9.

5 The 7th Panzer Division led by Rommel broke through the French defences near Dinant (see 3 above).

6 The 5th Panzer Division crossed the undefended weir and lock at Houx (see 3 above).

7 Guderian's XIX Corps overcame French resistance in and around Sedan (see 4 above).

British Units	Army units before the
French Units	German attack on
German Units	10 May 1940

········· Principal Dutch defence line

······· Covering Dutch defence line

━━━━━ Belgian Army's principal line of resistance

━━━━━ Subsidiary Belgian defence line in front of principal line of resistance (it was covered by units in front of it not marked on this map)

Amsterdam

Baarn
Hilversum
Amersfoort

Haag

Rotterdam
Ochten

Ijsselmeer

Ijsel

Münster

| 0 | 20 | 40 | 60 | 80 miles |

National borders

Hellevoetsluis

Moerdijk

HOLLAND

Breda
Tilburg

Megen

Maas

Waal

Gennep

18th Army
von Küchler

A [Chapter] pointing at a town or village
shows the chapter in this book where the
place indicated is featured.

*Canal de dérivation
de la Lys*

Bruges

Ostende
Chapter
24
Vinkt

St-Lenaarts

Terneuzen
Antwerp

Maldegem
Ghent

Chapter
23

Escaut

Turnhout

Albert Canal

Venlo

Chapter
3

Roermond

Mechelen

6th Army
von Reichenau

Maastricht

Köln

Army Group B
von Bock

GERMANY

Ypres

Courtrai
Halluin

Lys

Oudenarde
Renaix

Brussels

Louvain

Wavre

Dijle

Hannut

Gembloux

Liège

Huy

Meuse

Rhine

Koblenz

Lille

Tournai

Chapter
6

Namur

Charleroi

BELGIUM

Houx

4th Army
von Kluge (including Hoth's
XV Corps' 7th Pz Div **5**
and 5th Pz Div **6**)

Bourghelles

Maulde
Douai

Valenciennes

Dinant

Chapter
8

Beaumont

Cambrai

BEF
Lord Gort

British
GHQ

2 1st Army
Blanchard until 25 May/
Prioux after 25 May

12th Army
List backing up Kleist's Panzer Group
(including Guderian's XIX Corps **7**)

Army Group A
von Rundstedt

Péronne

St Quentin

3 9th Army
Corap

Hirson

Chapter
8

LUXEMBOURG

16th Army
Busch

Chauny

Laon
Folembray

Amifontaine

Montcornet

4 2nd Army
Huntziger

Sedan

Chiers

Junglinster

Luxembourg

Dippach

Longwy

Army Group C
von Leeb

Compiègne

Rethondes

Aisne

Rethel

Guignicourt

FRANCE

Longuyon

Meuse

3rd Army
Condé

1st Army

Chapter
1

Rheims

La Ferté-sous-Jouarre

Metz

Army Group
2

4th Army
Requin

5th Army
Bourret

7th Army

M
A
G
I
N
O
T

L
I
N
E

Inset map — Principal German thrusts 5–22 June 1940

Principal German thrusts
5–22 June 1940

| 0 | 50 | 100 miles |

Calais

Boulogne

Lille

Arras

GERMANY

Dieppe

Somme

Cherbourg

Le Havre

Rouen

Longwy

Army
Group
3

MAGINOT LINE

8th Army
Garchery

Freiburg

St Malo

Brest

BRITTANY
Rennes

Paris

Alençon
Le Mans

Troyes

Chapter
36

Vannes

Redon

Loire

Nantes

Orléans

Briare

Dijon

SWITZ.

St Nazaire

Tours

Basel

Briare

La Rochelle

FRANCE

Vichy

Clermont-Ferrand

St Étienne

Lyons

Geneva

SWITZERLAND

Royan

Bordeaux

Principal thrust by
German units

Map 2   511

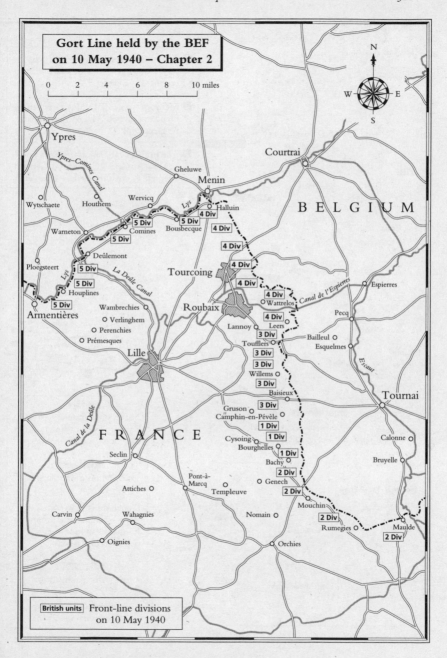

**Gort Line held by the BEF
on 10 May 1940 – Chapter 2**

0   2   4   6   8   10 miles

N
W — E
S

Ypres

Ypres–Comines Canal

Courtrai

Gheluwe

Menin

BELGIUM

Wytschaete   Houthem   Wervicq   *Lys*

Warneton   **5 Div**   Comines   Halluin   **4 Div**
     5 Div   Bousbecque   **5 Div**
     5 Div   **4 Div**

Ploegsteert   Deûlemont   **4 Div**
     5 Div   *La Deûle Canal*   **4 Div**
     5 Div   Houplines   **4 Div**   Espierres
     5 Div   Tourcoing   **4 Div**   *Canal de l'Espierres*
Armentières   Wambrechies   Roubaix   **4 Div**   Pecq
          Verlinghem   Wattrelos
          Perenchies   Lannoy   Leers   Bailleul   Esquelmes
          Prémesques   Toufflers   **3 Div**
                    Lille   **3 Div**
                         3 Div   Willems
                         3 Div
                              Baisieux   Tournai
FRANCE   Gruson   **3 Div**
     Canal de la Deûle   Camphin-en-Pévèle   **1 Div**   Calonne
          Cysoing   **1 Div**   Bruyelle
Seclin   Bourghelles
                    1 Div   Bachy
          Pont-à-   Genech
          Marcq   **2 Div**
Attiches   Templeuve
                    Nomain   Mouchin
Carvin   Wahagnies   **2 Div**   Maulde
                    Orchies   Rumegies   **2 Div**
Oignies

Escaut

British units Front-line divisions
on 10 May 1940

Map 3²

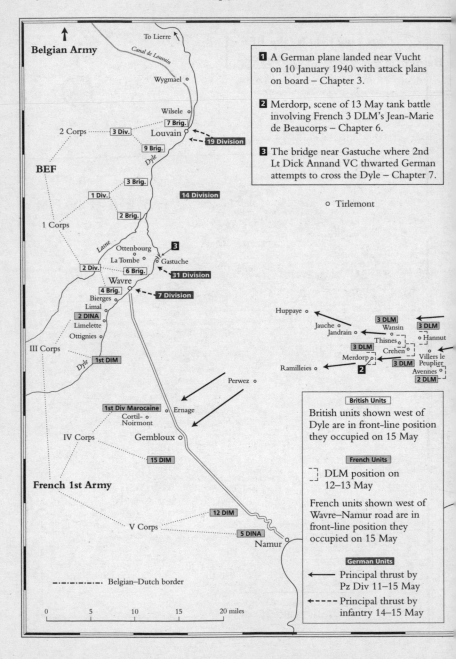

Belgian Army

To Lierre

Canal de Louvain

Wygmael

Wilsele

2 Corps — 3 Div. ····· Louvain

BEF

9 Brig.

19 Division

Dyle

3 Brig.

1 Div.

14 Division

2 Brig.

1 Corps

Lasne

Ottenbourg

La Tombe

3

Gastuche

2 Div.

6 Brig.

31 Division

Wavre

4 Brig.

7 Division

Bierges

Limal

2 DINA

Limelette

Ottignies

III Corps

Dyle

1st DIM

Perwez

1st Div Marocaine

Ernage

Cortil-
Noirmont

IV Corps

Gembloux

15 DIM

French 1st Army

12 DIM

V Corps

5 DINA

Namur

o Tirlemont

Huppaye

Jauche   3 DLM   3 DLM

Jandrain   Wansin

Thisnes   Hannut

3 DLM   Crehen

Merdorp   Villers le
Peuplier

Ramillies   3 DLM   Avennes

2   2 DLM

---

1 A German plane landed near Vucht
on 10 January 1940 with attack plans
on board – Chapter 3.

2 Merdorp, scene of 13 May tank battle
involving French 3 DLM's Jean-Marie
de Beaucorps – Chapter 6.

3 The bridge near Gastuche where 2nd
Lt Dick Annand VC thwarted German
attempts to cross the Dyle – Chapter 7.

British Units

British units shown west of
Dyle are in front-line position
they occupied on 15 May

French Units

DLM position on
12–13 May

French units shown west of
Wavre–Namur road are in
front-line position they
occupied on 15 May

German Units

⟵ Principal thrust by
Pz Div 11–15 May

◀╌╌ Principal thrust by
infantry 14–15 May

·—·—· Belgian–Dutch border

0   5   10   15   20 miles

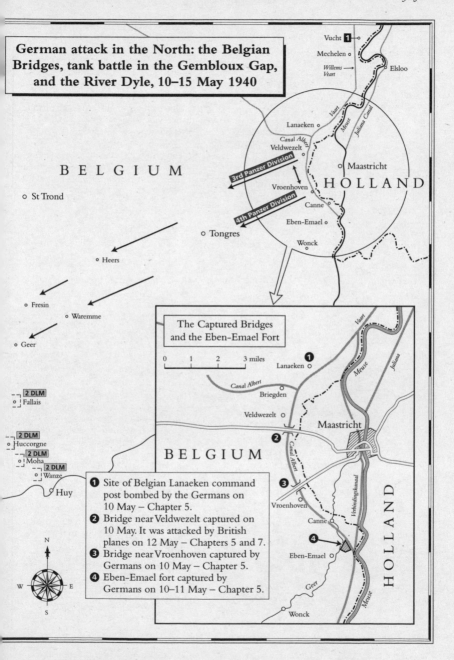

German attack in the North: the Belgian Bridges, tank battle in the Gembloux Gap, and the River Dyle, 10–15 May 1940

BELGIUM

HOLLAND

Vucht **1**
Mechelen
Willems → Veart
Elsloo

Lanaeken
Canal Albert
Veldwezelt
3rd Panzer Division
Maastricht
Vroenhoven
4th Panzer Division
Canne
Eben-Emael
Wonck

St Trond

Tongres

Heers

Fresin
Waremme

Geer

The Captured Bridges and the Eben-Emael Fort

0   1   2   3 miles

Lanaeken **1**

Canal Albert
Briegden

Veldwezelt

Maastricht

BELGIUM

2 *Canal Albert*

3

Vroenhoven

Canne

4

Eben-Emael

HOLLAND

Geer

Wonck

2 DLM
Fallais

2 DLM
Huccorgne
2 DLM
Moha
2 DLM
Wanze

Huy

1 Site of Belgian Lanaeken command post bombed by the Germans on 10 May – Chapter 5.
2 Bridge near Veldwezelt captured on 10 May. It was attacked by British planes on 12 May – Chapters 5 and 7.
3 Bridge near Vroenhoven captured by Germans on 10 May – Chapter 5.
4 Eben-Emael fort captured by Germans on 10–11 May – Chapter 5.

N
W   E
S

Map 4

515

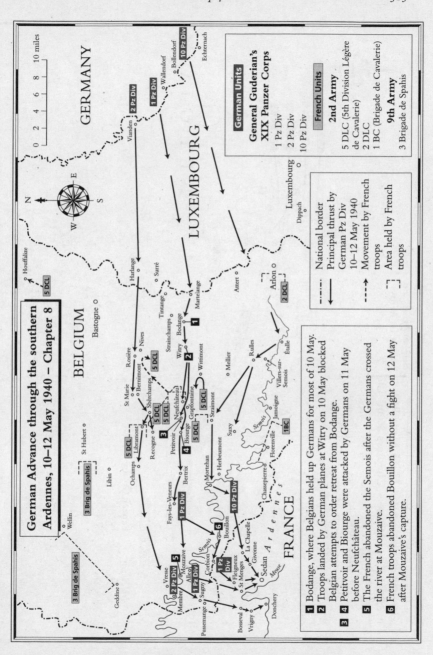

German Advance through the southern Ardennes, 10–12 May 1940 – Chapter 8

GERMANY

BELGIUM

LUXEMBOURG

FRANCE

Ardennes

German Units

General Guderian's XIX Panzer Corps

1 Pz Div
2 Pz Div
10 Pz Div

French Units

2nd Army

5 DLC (5th Division Légère de Cavalerie)
2 DLC
1 BC (Brigade de Cavalerie)

9th Army

3 Brigade de Spahis

.... National border
⬇ Principal thrust by German Pz Div 10–12 May 1940
- - -▶ Movement by French troops
⌐ ¬ Area held by French
∟ ┘ troops

1 Bodange, where Belgians held up Germans for most of 10 May.

2 Troops landed by German planes at Witry on 10 May blocked Belgian attempts to order retreat from Bodange.

3 Petitvoir and Biourge were attacked by Germans on 11 May before Neufchâteau.

4

5 The French abandoned the Semois after the Germans crossed the river at Mouzaive.

6 French troops abandoned Bouillon without a fight on 12 May after Mouzaive's capture.

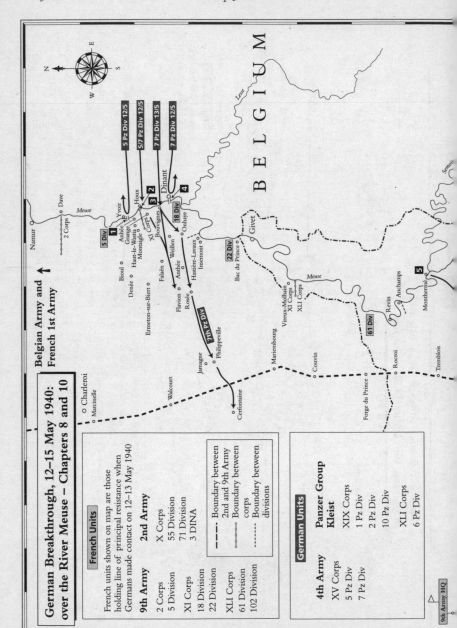

German Breakthrough, 12–15 May 1940: over the River Meuse – Chapters 8 and 10

Belgian Army and French 1st Army

French Units

French units shown on map are those holding line of principal resistance when Germans made contact on 12–13 May 1940

2nd Army

X Corps
55 Division
71 Division
3 DINA

9th Army

2 Corps
5 Division
XI Corps
18 Division
22 Division
XLI Corps
61 Division
102 Division

— · — · — Boundary between 2nd and 9th Army
— o — o — Boundary between corps
— — — — — Boundary between divisions

German Units

4th Army
XV Corps
5 Pz Div
7 Pz Div

Panzer Group Kleist
XIX Corps
1 Pz Div
2 Pz Div
10 Pz Div
XLI Corps
6 Pz Div

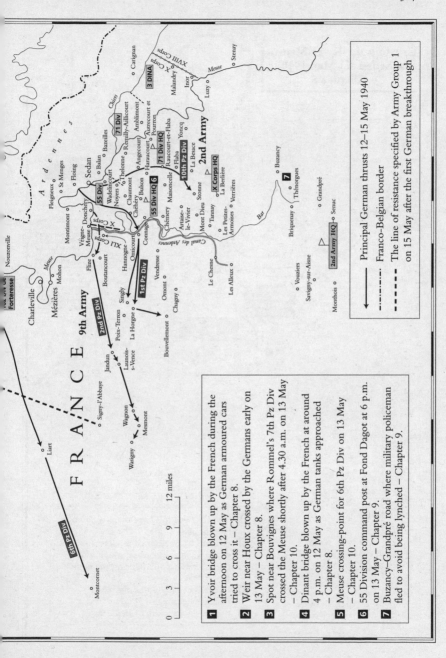

FRANCE

9th Army

2nd Army

Ardennes

Principal German thrusts 12–15 May 1940

Franco-Belgian border

The line of resistance specified by Army Group 1 on 15 May after the first German breakthrough

1 Yvoir bridge blown up by the French during the afternoon on 12 May as German armoured cars tried to cross it – Chapter 8.

2 Weir near Houx crossed by the Germans early on 13 May – Chapter 8.

3 Spot near Bouvignes where Rommel's 7th Pz Div crossed the Meuse shortly after 4.30 a.m. on 13 May – Chapter 10.

4 Dinant bridge blown up by the French as German tanks approached 4 p.m. on 12 May – Chapter 8.

5 Meuse crossing-point for 6th Pz Div on 13 May – Chapter 10.

6 55 Division command post at Fond Dagot at 6 p.m. on 13 May – Chapter 9.

7 Buzancy–Grandpré road where military policeman fled to avoid being lynched – Chapter 9.

0   3   6   9   12 miles

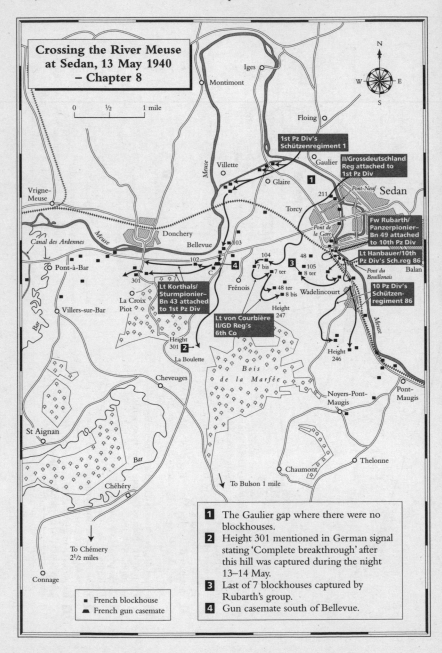

Crossing the River Meuse at Sedan, 13 May 1940 – Chapter 8

0   ½   1 mile

N
W   E
S

Iges
Montimont
Floing

1st Pz Div's Schützenregiment 1

II/Grossdeutschland Reg attached to 1st Pz Div

Villette
Gaulier
1
211
Pont-Neuf
Sedan

Glaire
Torcy

Vrigne-Meuse
Meuse
Donchery
Bellevue
Pont de la Gare

Fw Rubarth/Panzerpionier-Bn 49 attached to 10th Pz Div

Canal des Ardennes
102   103
4
104   48
7 bis   **3**   105
7 ter   8 ter

Lt Hanbauer/10th Pz Div's Sch.reg 86
Pont du Bouillonais
Balan

Pont-à-Bar
301
C
Frénois
48 ter
8 bis
Wadelincourt

10 Pz Div's Schützen-regiment 86

Lt Korthals/Sturmpionier-Bn 43 attached to 1st Pz Div

La Croix Piot

Villers-sur-Bar

Bar

Height 301
2
La Boulette

Lt von Courbière II/GD Reg's 6th Co

Height 247

Height 246

Cheveuges

Bois de la Marfée

Noyers-Pont-Maugis
Pont-Maugis

Meuse

St Aignan

Bar

Chéhéry

Chaumont
Thelonne

To Chémery 2½ miles

To Bulson 1 mile

Connage

■ French blockhouse
▲ French gun casemate

1 The Gaulier gap where there were no blockhouses.
2 Height 301 mentioned in German signal stating 'Complete breakthrough' after this hill was captured during the night 13–14 May.
3 Last of 7 blockhouses captured by Rubarth's group.
4 Gun casemate south of Bellevue.

Map 7

519

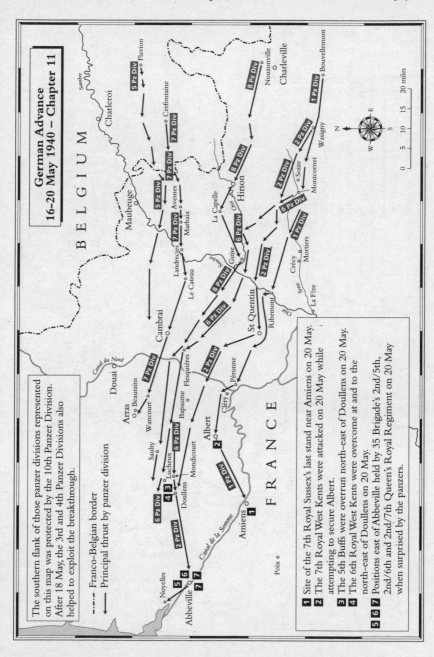

**German Advance
16-20 May 1940 – Chapter 11**

The southern flank of those panzer divisions represented on this map was protected by the 10th Panzer Division. After 18 May, the 3rd and 4th Panzer Divisions also helped to exploit the breakthrough.

-·-·-·- Franco-Belgian border
⟶ Principal thrust by panzer division

1 Site of the 7th Royal Sussex's last stand near Amiens on 20 May.

2 The 7th Royal West Kents were attacked on 20 May while attempting to secure Albert.

3 The 5th Buffs were overrun north-east of Doullens on 20 May.

4 The 6th Royal West Kents were overcome at and to the north-east of Doullens on 20 May.

5 **6** **7** Positions east of Abbeville held by 35 Brigade's 2nd/5th, 2nd/6th and 2nd/7th Queen's Royal Regiment on 20 May when surprised by the panzers.

BELGIUM

FRANCE

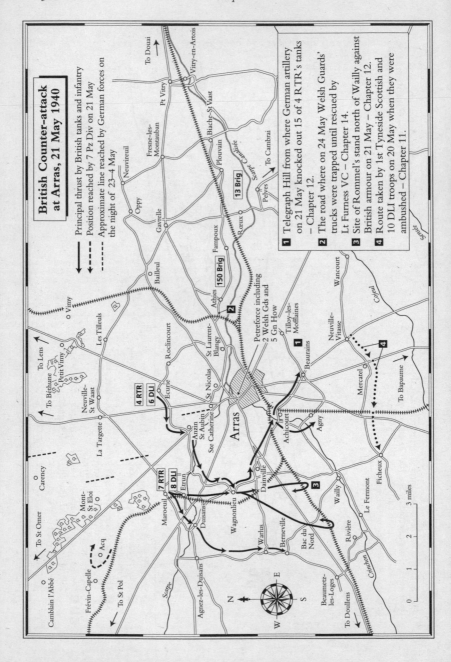

Map 8⁴

**British Counter-attack
at Arras, 21 May 1940**

— Principal thrust by British tanks and infantry

--- Position reached by 7 Pz Div on 21 May

···· Approximate line reached by German forces on
the night of 23–4 May

1 Telegraph Hill from where German artillery
on 21 May knocked out 15 of 4 RTR's tanks
– Chapter 12.

2 The road where on 24 May Welsh Guards'
trucks were trapped until rescued by
Lt Furness VC – Chapter 14.

3 Site of Rommel's stand north of Wailly against
British armour on 21 May – Chapter 12.

4 Route taken by 1st Tyneside Scottish and
10 DLI troops on 20 May when they were
ambushed – Chapter 11.

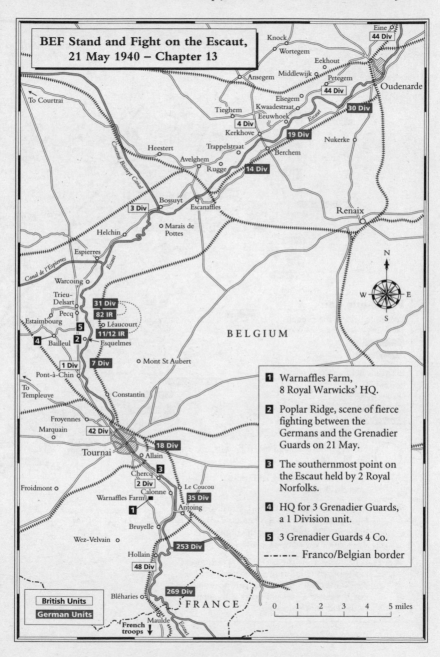

**BEF Stand and Fight on the Escaut,
21 May 1940 – Chapter 13**

To Courtrai

Knock

Eine
44 Div

Wortegem

Eekhout

Middlewijk

Ansegem

Petegem

44 Div

Oudenarde

Elsegem

Tieghem

Kwaadestraat

Eeuwhoek

30 Div

4 Div

Kerkhove

19 Div

Nukerke

Heestert

Trappelstraat

Berchem

Avelghem

Rugge

14 Div

Bossuyt

Escanaffles

Renaix

3 Div

Marais de Pottes

Helchin

Espierres

Canal de l'Espierres

Warcoing

Trieu-Delsart

Pecq

31 Div

82 IR

Estaimbourg

5

Léaucourt

11/12 IR

Bailleul

4

2

Esquelmes

1 Div

7 Div

Pont-à-Chin

Mont St Aubert

To Templeuve

Constantin

BELGIUM

Froyennes

Marquain

42 Div

Tournai

18 Div

Allain

Chercq

3

2 Div

Froidmont

Calonne

Le Coucou

Warnaffles Farm

1

Antoing

35 Div

Bruyelle

Wez-Velvain

253 Div

Hollain

48 Div

Bléharies

269 Div

FRANCE

Maulde

French troops ↓

N W E S

1 Warnaffles Farm,
8 Royal Warwicks' HQ.

2 Poplar Ridge, scene of fierce
fighting between the
Germans and the Grenadier
Guards on 21 May.

3 The southernmost point on
the Escaut held by 2 Royal
Norfolks.

4 HQ for 3 Grenadier Guards,
a 1 Division unit.

5 3 Grenadier Guards 4 Co.

–·–·– Franco/Belgian border

British Units
German Units

0 1 2 3 4 5 miles

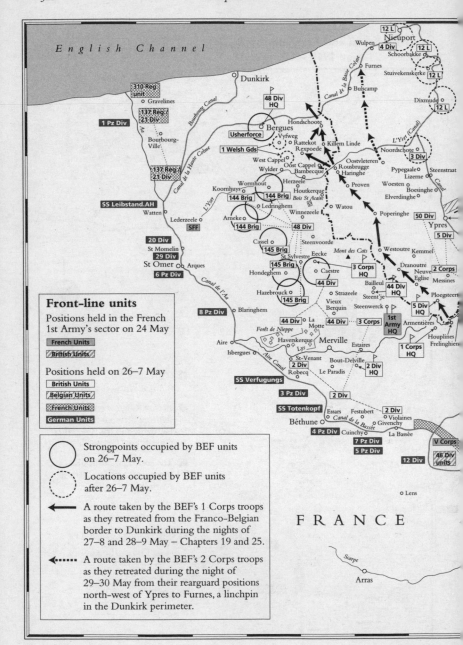

Front-line units

Positions held in the French
1st Army's sector on 24 May

French Units
British Units
Positions held on 26–7 May

British Units
Belgian Units
French Units
German Units

◯ Strongpoints occupied by BEF units
on 26–7 May.

◌ Locations occupied by BEF units
after 26–7 May.

← A route taken by the BEF's 1 Corps troops
as they retreated from the Franco-Belgian
border to Dunkirk during the nights of
27–8 and 28–9 May – Chapters 19 and 25.

◂···· A route taken by the BEF's 2 Corps troops
as they retreated during the night of
29–30 May from their rearguard positions
north-west of Ypres to Furnes, a linchpin
in the Dunkirk perimeter.

The Corridor to Dunkirk,
26–7 May 1940
– Chapters 20–27

Map 11 [6]

525

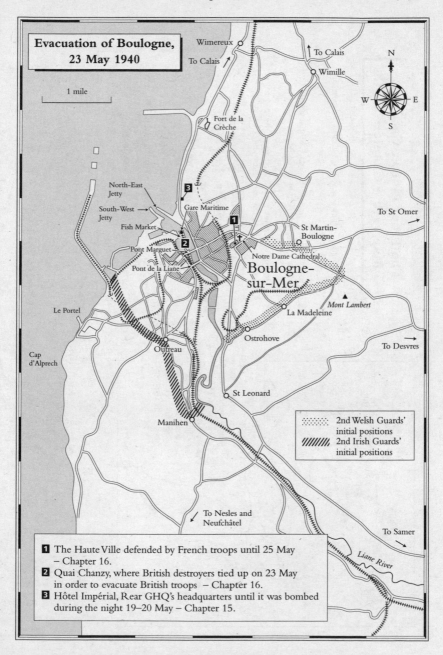

**Evacuation of Boulogne,
23 May 1940**

1 mile

Wimereux

To Calais

To Calais

Wimille

N

W   E

S

Fort de la
Crèche

To St Omer

North-East
Jetty

3

South-West
Jetty

Gare Maritime

1

St Martin-
Boulogne

Fish Market

Notre Dame Cathedral

2

Pont Marguet

Pont de la Liane

**Boulogne-
sur-Mer**

Mont Lambert

Le Portel

La Madeleine

Cap
d'Alprech

Ostrohove

To Desvres

Outreau

St Leonard

Manihen

2nd Welsh Guards'
initial positions
2nd Irish Guards'
initial positions

To Nesles and
Neufchâtel

To Samer

Liane River

1 The Haute Ville defended by French troops until 25 May
  – Chapter 16.
2 Quai Chanzy, where British destroyers tied up on 23 May
  in order to evacuate British troops – Chapter 16.
3 Hôtel Impérial, Rear GHQ's headquarters until it was bombed
  during the night 19–20 May – Chapter 15.

The Front Line at Calais,
23–5 May 1940 – Chapters 17–18

1 Calais's citadel, which was surrendered by its garrison on 26 May.

2 Bastion 9, held by the KRRC's B Company until they withdrew to the Old Town on 24 May.

3 Around fifty men were picked up from the end of the Eastern Jetty during the early hours of 27 May.

Outer perimeter 23–4 May

– – – KRRC supported by QVR.

······· Rifle Brig supported by QVR.

Inner perimeter 23–5 May

▬▬▬ KRRC, except that the French and KRRC troops held Bastion 11 and the battlements just to the left, and French troops held the Citadel.

○—○—○ Rifle Brig.

QVR patrol till 24 May evening

1 Fort Nieulay.

2 The spot where a German column was attacked by British tanks during the afternoon of 23 May 1940.

3 Les Attaques crossroads held by Searchlight Regiment troops during the afternoon of 23 May 1940 when attacked by German tanks.

To Gravelines

QVR roadblock till 24 May evening

To Marck

QVR roadblock till 24 May evening

To Dunkirk

QVR roadblock till 24 May evening

QVR roadblock till 23 May p.m.

To St Omer via Ardres

Bastion 3

Bastion 4

Bastion 5

Bastion 6

Porte de Gravelines

Canal de Marck

Porte de Dunkerque

Bd de l'Égalité

Bd Victor Hugo

Rue Mollien

Pont St Pierre

Quai de la Loire

Bassin Carnot

Rue Mollien

Pont Mollien

Canal de Calais

Bd Lafayette

Place de Russie

Place de Suède

Place de l'Angleterre

Place de Norvège

Avant Port de l'Est

Ponts Henri Hénon

Lighthouse

Bd des Alliés

Notre Dame

Place de Norvège

Pont Notre Dame

Rue Notre Dame

Pont de Richelieu

Place Faidherbe

Parc de Richelieu

Hôtel de Ville

Bd Jacquard

Place Albert

Fort Risban

Bassin des Chasses de l'Ouest

Place d'Armes

Place de Richelieu

Parc de Batellerie

Pont Freycinet

Pont Richelieu

Parc St Pierre

Railway Station

Bd Léon Gambetta

Citadel

Esplanade de la Citadel

To Les Fontinettes and QVR roadblocks 22–4 May a.m.

Cemetery

Bastion 10

Pont Jourdan

Bastion 9

To Boulogne

Bastion 11

QVR roadblock 22–4 May p.m.

To Oyez Farm

Les Baraques

To Sangatte

QVR roadblock till 9 p.m. 23 May; Fort Nieulay 200 yards: held by QVR/French garrison from 9 p.m. 23 May till 4.30 p.m. 24 May

1500 yards

1000

500

0

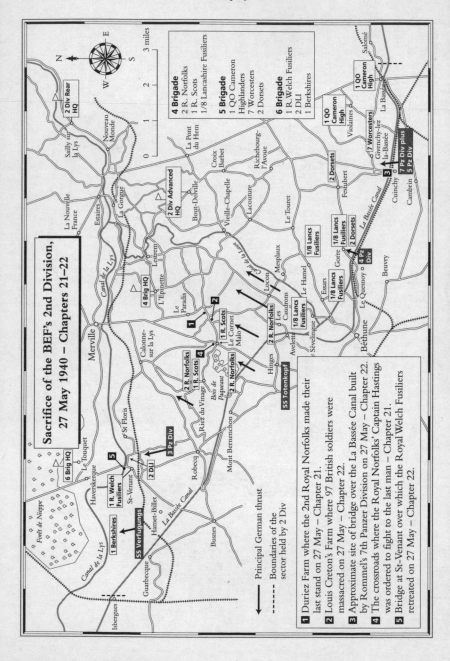

Sacrifice of the BEF's 2nd Division, 27 May 1940 – Chapters 21–22

4 Brigade
2 R. Norfolks
1 R. Scots
1/8 Lancashire Fusiliers

5 Brigade
1 QO Cameron Highlanders
7 Worcesters
2 Dorsets

6 Brigade
1 R. Welch Fusiliers
1 DLI
1 Berkshires

→ Principal German thrust

┄┄ Boundaries of the sector held by 2 Div

1 Duriez Farm where the 2nd Royal Norfolks made their last stand on 27 May – Chapter 21.

2 Louis Creton's Farm where 97 British soldiers were massacred on 27 May – Chapter 22.

3 Approximate site of bridge over the La Bassée Canal built by Rommel's 7th Panzer Division on 27 May – Chapter 22.

4 The crossroads where the Royal Norfolks' Captain Hastings was ordered to fight to the last man – Chapter 21.

5 Bridge at St-Venant over which the Royal Welch Fusiliers retreated on 27 May – Chapter 22.

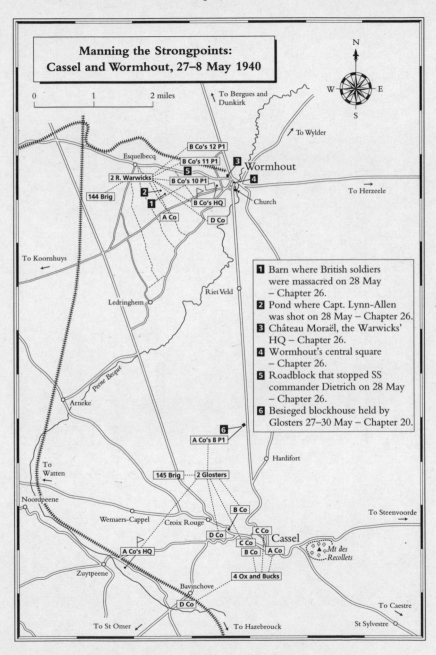

Manning the Strongpoints: Cassel and Wormhout, 27–8 May 1940

N
W · E
S

0   1   2 miles

To Bergues and Dunkirk

To Wylder

B Co's 12 P1

Esquelbecq

B Co's 11 P1

3 Wormhout

5

2 R. Warwicks

B Co's 10 P1

4

144 Brig

2

To Herzeele

1

B Co's HQ

Church

A Co

D Co

To Koornhuys

Riet Veld

Ledringhem

Peene Becque

Arneke

6

A Co's 8 P1

To Watten

Hardifort

145 Brig ···· 2 Glosters

Noordpeene

B Co

To Steenvoorde

Wemaers-Cappel   Croix Rouge

D Co   C Co   **Cassel**

A Co's HQ   C Co   A Co   ▲ *Mt des Recollets*

B Co

Zuytpeene

4 Ox and Bucks

Bavinchove

D Co

To St Omer   To Hazebrouck   St Sylvestre

To Caestre

1 Barn where British soldiers were massacred on 28 May – Chapter 26.

2 Pond where Capt. Lynn-Allen was shot on 28 May – Chapter 26.

3 Château Moraël, the Warwicks' HQ – Chapter 26.

4 Wormhout's central square – Chapter 26.

5 Roadblock that stopped SS commander Dietrich on 28 May – Chapter 26.

6 Besieged blockhouse held by Glosters 27–30 May – Chapter 20.

Map 15 531

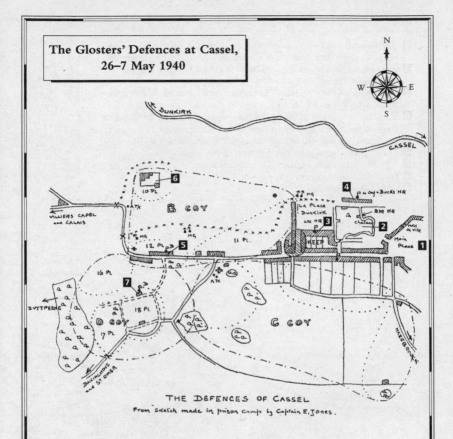

THE DEFENCES OF CASSEL

From sketch made in prison camp by Captain E. Jones.

1 La Grande Place, the lowest of the three main squares in Cassel.

2 Place du Château, the highest of the three main squares in Cassel, where 145 Brigade's HQ was situated.

3 The bank used as an HQ by the 2nd Glosters. It was situated in La Place du Général Plumer, which is higher than La Grande Place but lower than Place du Château.

4 Cassel's Gendarmerie, used as an HQ by 4 Ox and Bucks and E. Riding Yeomanry.

5 Glosters' B Company HQ. It was on the same level as the 2nd Glosters' HQ (see **3** above).

6 Farmhouse occupied by Glosters' B Company's 10 Platoon.

7 Château used by Glosters' D Company's HQ.

1. Approximate site of barn where Captain Marcus Ervine-Andrews VC of the E. Lancashire Regt made a stand on 1 June 1940 – Chapter 32.
2. Approximate site of cottage held by 2/Lt Jimmy Langley and his Coldstream Guards on 1 June 1940 – Chapter 32.
3. Canal line held by 4th Berkshires under Captain Francis Waldron on 30–31 May – Chapter 30.
4. Canal sector taken over by the 2nd Grenadier Guards on 29 May after three of the battalion's officers were killed – Chapter 30.
5. Château Coquelle, site of 12th Casualty Clearing Station – Chapter 32.
6. Guiding jetty, sometimes referred to as 'centre pier'.
7. The Mole, Dunkirk's principal evacuation point.
8. Bastion 32, headquarters occupied by Admiral Abrial.
9. Quai Félix-Faure.

Dunkirk: the Outer and Inner Perimeters, 30 May–2 June 1940

Front-line Units

British Units
French Units
German Units

A div, brig or bn linked on this map by a ········ or a ———— to a corps, div or brig respectively was under the command of that corps, div or brig either on or after 31 May 1940.

6 BW
Nieuport Bains
12 Brig   1 So. Lancs
Nieuport
4 Div   2 R Fusils
10 Brig   1/6 E.Surr
2 DCLI   256 Div
Coxyde Bains   2 Beds and H
2 Corps   XXVI Corps
8 Brig   2 E. Yorks   Canal de Furnes à Nieuport
La Panne Bains   Coxyde   1 Suff   Wulpen
La Panne   4 Berks   3
3 Div
7 Brig
Bray-Dunes Plage   1 Cold Gds
1/8 Zouaves   2 Gren Gds   4
Bray-Dunes   1 Gren Gds
2/8 Zouaves   Adinkerque   Furnes
12 Div   2/150 RI   Basse Plaine   2 RUR
Ghyvelde   9 Brig
1/150 RI
GRDI 92   1 KOSB
Moëres   9 DLI   Bulscamp
50 Div   56 Div
1 Corps   151 Brig
150 Brig   BELGIUM
Les Moëres   6 DLI
5 Gn How
4 E. Yorks   IX Corps
1 Div   Houthem
1 Brig   3 Brig   4 Gn How   216 Div
Digue des Glaises
2 Cold Gds   1 D of Welling
2   Pont Pauwhens Werve   Pont-aux-Cerfs
Hondschoote
14 Div
X Corps
18 Div
Rexpoede

············· Outer perimeter on 30–31 May
– – – – – Inner perimeter (east of Canal de Bergues) in place by 2 June early p.m.
···▬···▬··· Franco-Belgian border
++++++++++ Railways
———— Roads
———— Canal/rivers
– – – – Flooded area
M Forts

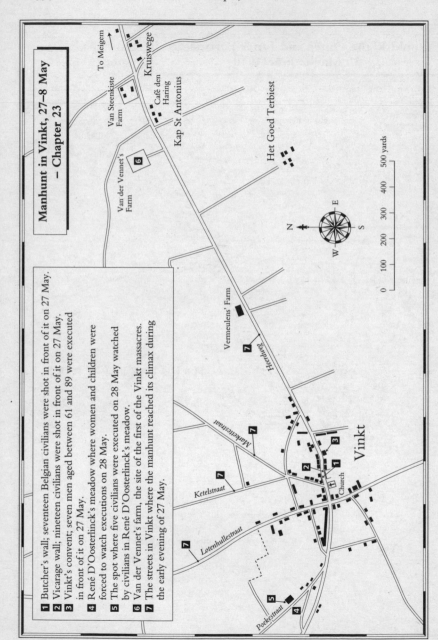

Manhunt in Vinkt, 27–8 May – Chapter 23

1. Butcher's wall; seventeen Belgian civilians were shot in front of it on 27 May.
2. Vicarage wall; nineteen civilians were shot in front of it on 27 May.
3. Vinkt's convent; seven men aged between 61 and 89 were executed in front of it on 27 May.
4. René D'Oosterlinck's meadow where women and children were forced to watch executions on 28 May.
5. The spot where five civilians were executed on 28 May watched by civilians in René D'Oosterlinck's meadow.
6. Van der Vennet's farm, the site of the first of the Vinkt massacres.
7. The streets in Vinkt where the manhunt reached its climax during the early evening of 27 May.

Map 18 535

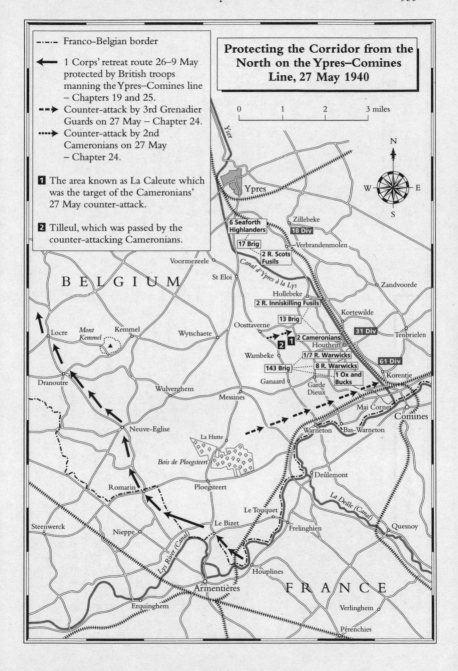

Protecting the Corridor from the
North on the Ypres–Comines
Line, 27 May 1940

Legend:

- -··-··- Franco-Belgian border

- ⟵ 1 Corps' retreat route 26–9 May
  protected by British troops
  manning the Ypres–Comines line
  – Chapters 19 and 25.

- --⟶ Counter-attack by 3rd Grenadier
  Guards on 27 May – Chapter 24.

- ····⟶ Counter-attack by 2nd
  Cameronians on 27 May
  – Chapter 24.

- **1** The area known as La Caleute which
  was the target of the Cameronians'
  27 May counter-attack.

- **2** Tilleul, which was passed by the
  counter-attacking Cameronians.

0   1   2   3 miles

N
W — E
S

BELGIUM

FRANCE

Ypres
Zillebeke
6 Seaforth Highlanders
18 Div
17 Brig
Verbrandenmolen
2 R. Scots Fusils
Voormezeele
Canal d'Ypres à la Lys
St Eloi
Zandvoorde
Hollebeke
2 R. Inniskilling Fusils
Kortewilde
13 Brig
Oosttaverne
31 Div
Tenbrielen
2 Cameronians
Houthem
Locre
Mont Kemmel
Kemmel
Wytschaete
Wambeke
1/7 R. Warwicks
61 Div
Dranoutre
143 Brig
8 R. Warwicks
Ganaard
1 Ox and Bucks
Korentje
Garde Dieux
Wulverghem
Mai Cornet
Comines
Messines
Neuve-Eglise
La Hutte
Warneton
Bas-Warneton
Bois de Ploegsteert
Deûlemont
Romarin
Ploegsteert
La Deûle (Canal)
Steenwerck
Le Touquet
Frelinghien
Quesnoy
Nieppe
Le Bizet
Lys River Canal
Houplines
Armentières
Erquinghem
Verlinghem
Pérenchies
Yser

Map 19

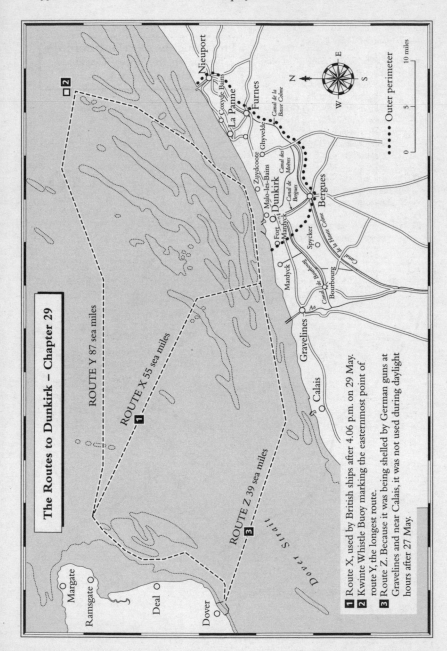

The Routes to Dunkirk – Chapter 29

1 Route X, used by British ships after 4.06 p.m. on 29 May.
2 Kwinte Whistle Buoy marking the easternmost point of route Y, the longest route.
3 Route Z. Because it was being shelled by German guns at Gravelines and near Calais, it was not used during daylight hours after 27 May.

Map 20 537

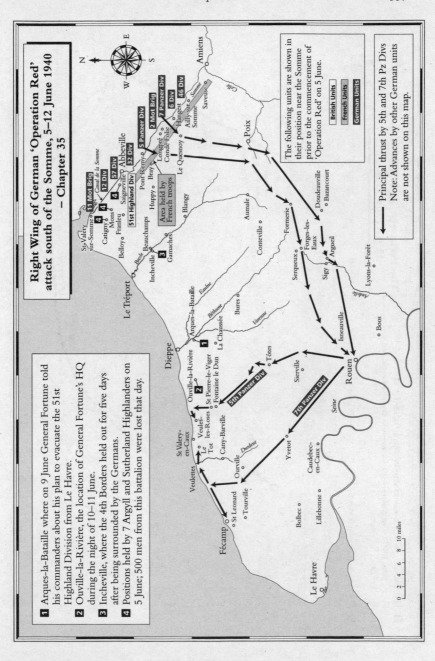

Right Wing of German 'Operation Red' attack south of the Somme, 5–12 June 1940 – Chapter 35

The following units are shown in their position prior to the commencement of 'Operation Red' on 5 June.

British Units
French Units
German Units

→ Principal thrust by 5th and 7th Pz Divs
Note: Advances by other German units are not shown on this map.

1. Arques-la-Bataille where on 9 June General Fortune told his commanders about his plan to evacuate the 51st Highland Division from Le Havre.
2. Ouville-la-Rivière, the location of General Fortune's HQ during the night of 10–11 June.
3. Incheville, where the 4th Borders held out for five days after being surrounded by the Germans.
4. Positions held by 7 Argyll and Sutherland Highlanders on 5 June; 500 men from this battalion were lost that day.

0 2 4 6 8 10 miles

Map 21[12]

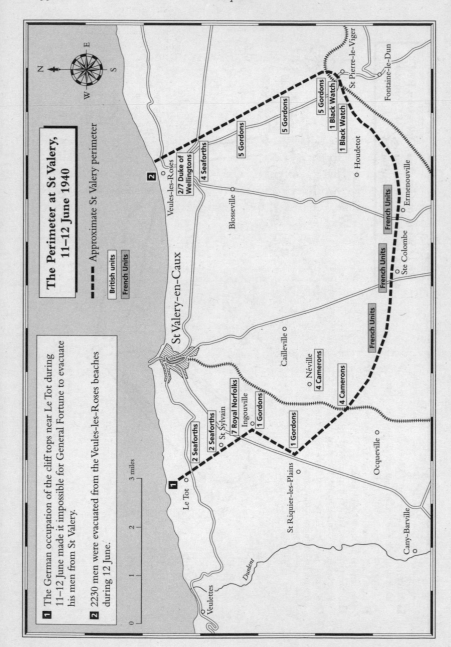

The Perimeter at St Valery, 11–12 June 1940

-------- Approximate St Valery perimeter

[ ] British units

[ ] French units

1 The German occupation of the cliff tops near Le Tot during 11–12 June made it impossible for General Fortune to evacuate his men from St Valery.

2 2230 men were evacuated from the Veules-les-Roses beaches during 12 June.

0 1 2 3 miles

St Valery-en-Caux

Le Tot

2 Seaforths

2 Seaforths

St Sylvain

7 Royal Norfolks

Ingouville

1 Gordons

1 Gordons

Veulettes

Durdent

St Riquier-les-Plains

Ocqueville

Cany-Barville

Cailleville

Néville

4 Camerons

4 Camerons

French Units

French Units

French Units

French Units

Ste Colombe

Ermenouville

Houdetot

Blosseville

Veules-les-Roses

2/7 Duke of Wellingtons

4 Seaforths

5 Gordons

5 Gordons

5 Gordons

5 Gordons

1 Black Watch

1 Black Watch

St Pierre-le-Viger

Fontaine-le-Dun

Readers' Reminder

Readers wanting to consult the Appendices, Dramatis Personae, Abbreviations and chapter Notes, which were on pp. 539–644 in the first edition of this book, can either purchase a copy of the original edition while stocks last, or they can borrow it from a library. Alternatively they will be included on Hugh Sebag-Montefiore's website: http://www. hughsebagmontefiore.com. The pages on the Internet will have the same page numbers on them as they had in the first edition of this book.

Personal Account 1

Sacrifice of the Royal Norfolk Regiment
(See Map 13)

The front line at Le Cornet Malo

On 26 May 1940, just hours before the German tanks were unleashed following the famous halt order (see Postscript p. 681), Captain Nick Hallett of the 2nd Battalion the Royal Norfolk Regiment was having his first decent sleep for four days near the Battalion Transport Section's headquarters at Lestrem. This was three miles north-east of Le Cornet Malo, where the Royal Norfolk's front-line companies were, even as he slept, bracing themselves for the onslaught which was to engulf them. In the extract from his memoirs laid out below, he describes how what started as a peaceful beginning of the day was quickly transformed into a nightmare from which there was to be no escape.[1]

26 May

I woke up late and in great comfort. There was real hot water for washing and shaving, and an excellent prospect of breakfast . . . Then came the bombshell: a dispatch rider arrived from Battalion HQ saying that I was wanted down there at once. As I was only just dressed, I went straight away with no equipment, shoes instead of boots and a pistol in my pocket. Daffin drove me . . . and we reached Le Paradis about ten minutes later. There the Colonel produced the big surprise. He said they were very short of officers and I'd got to hand over the Motor Transport section . . . and take command of two companies in the line right away . . .

Daffin drove me down to Le Cornet Malo [about three miles from Lestrem, and a mile and a quarter north of the La Bassée Canal] . . . Here I found A and B Companies' HQ's in a café on the crossroads . . . I sneaked up the road which was under long range machine gun fire and found the remains of the two companies plus A Company [1st Battalion the] Royal Scots all lying in one ditch.

More details about this ditch appear in the account written by Hallett's brother officer, Captain Hastings. He reported that the 'line [occupied by these companies] extended along the foot of a long hedge and ditch which ran parallel to the road, about 200–300 yards in front of the cross-roads. The hedge was high and thick and had the advantage that it afforded an approach that was completely screened from view, though not from bullets. Where the hedge was thinned out at the base it was possible to get a fair field of fire to the front, [although] not by any means as good as one would have liked . . . [It was also possible] to cover the road to the right . . . It was an unsatisfactory position: the ditch was not really deep enough to give much protection as a trench, and although the little mound of earth round the roots of the hedge offered meagre cover from the front, there was no protection from the rear, which is almost as important in the case of mortar fire, as these shells have a very high trajectory, fall to the ground practically vertically, and . . . their shrapnel [spray] pretty evenly in all directions . . . If one falls behind you, it is likely you will get it in your back if you have no protection. But it was the best there was in an emergency. [And even before Hallett turned up], the men set to work to improve [the position] . . . [They] scratched at the earth with their bayonets and scooped it out with their hands.' Hallett's account reveals what happened next:

[Captain] Hastings and [2nd Lieutenant Willeson,] our Intelligence Officer, . . . showed me round. The place was considerably battered by mortar bombs and everyone seemed a bit shaken. After a bit we . . . sorted . . . them into companies and [Hastings and Willeson] went back [to Battalion HQ]. That left me with [2nd Lieutenant] Slater in A Company and Lieutenant [Edgeworth] in B Company.

As things seemed very quiet, I took out a patrol . . . We went to the forward edge of the village unchecked, and there we saw about 50 or 60 enemy leaving a farm about half a mile down the canal road. [They were] . . . advancing towards the village. When they got a bit closer, we started to pick them off with rifle fire. But they still came on . . . We withdrew . . .

After a short while in the company line, . . . we went forward again . . . We found a wounded German corporal in a ditch and took four or five unwounded prisoners. We sent the unwounded ones straight back to Battalion HQ and on to Brigade. After all the frightful things the troops had threatened, it was amusing to see how well they treated the [wounded] prisoner. They gave him cigarettes and chocolate ... Then I started to question him . . . He was quite ready to talk. He said that there was about a division [facing] . . . us across the Canal, as I'd rather expected, instead of the odd hundred (men) . . . that I'd been told . . .

That evening the mortar platoon arrived under Platoon Sergeant Major Ireland . . . [It] got into action straight away . . . At dusk I sent A Company over to a farm about 200 yards to our left . . . There was a big gap between us and D Company . . .

Then, as it got dark, the enemy attacked again and drove in our forward posts. They started digging hard just beyond the village where we could hear them all night. Just before midnight, I heard unmistakeable sounds of tanks . . . I phoned through [to Battalion HQ] and asked for anti-tank mines, which were not available, and hand grenades, which were. Soon after dark Company Quartermaster Sergeant Milne arrived with hot stew which was . . . badly needed. Troops came back in relays to collect the food and take it forward.

27 May

Soon after midnight I ordered out a small recce patrol . . . They found the enemy digging and measured the distance to the mortar position. Then Ireland did some . . . shooting in the pitch dark using sound to direct [his guns]. From the shouts and shrieks, there must have been some direct hits. I sent up white Very lights occasionally but never saw any . . . [of the enemy].

Before first light the tanks started to move . . . We got the dannert wire off the mortar trucks and made a small road block. As it began to get light, [at] about 5 a.m., the tanks arrived, huge fellows and about a dozen. I phoned Battalion HQ and then they cut the line. This was the last message I got to the Battalion. The forward sections came in leaving their guns and worse the anti-tank rifles. And for a bit there was . . . chaos. Some of the mortar platoon [were] . . . captured, but Ireland got away with the guns in [a] . . . truck.

Eventually we had a brainwave, and ran out below the tanks' angle of fire, and put Mills grenades in the tracks. It did not do the tanks much harm but [it] frightened the drivers and they ditched them. We got four that way . . . Then gradually some form of order was restored. We got the light machine gun back in position and the anti-tank rifles mounted.

Luckily the German infantry were a long way behind their tanks, so when they came, we were ready for them. And come they did, in masses. I never believed I'd see troops advancing shoulder to shoulder across the open, but these men did, and suffered accordingly. The Brens fired till they were red-hot, and also the riflemen. But we also suffered heavily, and in the end, [almost everyone was either killed or wounded, and] I was left in a big farm[house in] . . . an attic with an anti-tank rifle and a rifle for myself, and one rifleman to help. We dodged around, firing at the tanks and sniping, until a chance shot killed the other man, and left me alone.

For a long time our position had been surrounded . . . I went across the road to join A Company, Royal Scots, . . . [who] were all in a big farm and had hardly suffered at all . . . I stayed there a bit, and had a much needed cigarette. [I] also helped pat out a fire in their ammunition store which the tanks had set alight. While I was in the house, one of the tanks shelled it, [which was] very unpleasant, since the small armour-piercing shells came straight through the wall. Eventually . . . I decided to try and contact C Company . . . Royal Scots on the right [and attempt to] get help and information.

Directly I got outside . . . I was hit in the side. It burned a bit, but was not serious . . . I ran along a ditch under cover into the wood . . . Then . . . I left the wood and started to slink back along a hedge between two fields towards the road. [Unfortunately] . . . an enemy machine-gun post saw me and opened fire . . . I was hit in the arm and . . . lay down . . . I lay still shamming [death] . . . My arm was obviously broken . . . I decided to stay there till dusk. As it was now about midday, it was a longish wait [given that] . . . I was bleeding pretty badly.

At dusk I got up, rather painfully, and leaving my rifle, I crept along the fence to a farm by the road. It was deserted . . . I went in and rested a while on a bed. Soon however, I heard a car stop outside, and some Germans came in. At first they did not discover me . . . I tried to creep out of the window. Unfortunately I was so weak that I slipped [and broke] . . . the glass. And there they found me, sitting in the courtyard.

Interrogation in a barn at Locon

Shortly before Hallett was captured, resistance at Duriez Farm in Le Paradis had likewise come to an end, and Captain Hastings and those who had taken refuge alongside him in the ditch outside the burning farmhouse had also become prisoners of war (see p. 291). They were swiftly marched away to the German rear, but although they could consider themselves fortunate in that they avoided the fate of the ninety-seven British prisoners massacred at Le Paradis, some of their lives were still in jeopardy, as Hastings's memoirs bear witness:[2]

[On the way to Locon, around 3 and a half miles south-east of Le Paradis,] we . . . saw a number of dead British soldiers. One party I noticed especially, looked as if they had been caught by machine gun fire as they emerged from a wood, the edge of which was about ten yards behind them. The feet of some of them were bare . . . It looked as if their boots had been stolen . . . It began to rain again and [it] continued to rain until we got to Locon.

At Locon, we were put into a barn, the floor of which was covered with straw . . . There were many other British troops in the barn. Amongst them [were] members of our own C Company, whose fate up till then we had not known about. They had been mopped up that morning and the Company Commander, Major J. H. Elwes, had been killed in circumstances of great gallantry. He had, I was told, heroically led a bayonet attack against Tommy guns . . . and had been shot dead . . . About 50 men of his Company were prisoners.[3]

I . . . [was] called over to the centre of the barn to be interrogated by a German officer who spoke fluent English in a very loud truculent . . . way . . . He had before him PSM Barrett and PSM Howlett of the 2nd Norfolks and CSM Kelly of the 2nd Manchesters. I did not hear the beginning of the story, but he was saying that certain articles of German equipment, including respirators belonging to German soldiers, had been found in some buildings which he was alleging had been used by C Company as a headquarters two days ago. The accusation was that the equipment belonged to the

German soldiers who, it was alleged, we had had as prisoners and had murdered before we ourselves had been captured.

The whole case appeared to turn on identifying the building in which the articles were found as being the same building that C Company had occupied. If the case was proved, said the German officer, the three sergeant majors were to be shot. Each sergeant major . . . had told the German what buildings had been used by our formations, but the German did not believe them. He now asked me if I would like to tell him where the HQ of the Company to which these warrant officers belonged, had been two nights ago.

I was inclined to demur at first, not being sure yet whether such information might still be of military value. He cut me short, [saying]: 'Do you think I should come to you if I wanted military information? I should not waste my time questioning an officer. I should question your men.' This very wordy German officer bragged a good deal more in this strain, but it was evident, with C Company mopped up and the whole area now in German hands, that there was no military value in giving corroboration to the sergeant majors' story. I asked if he would accept my corroboration as evidence to acquit the sergeant majors, and he agreed that he would, as I had not been present when they made their statement and could not have known what they had said. I then drew a sketch map showing where C Company had been the night before last, and hoped for the best. It turned out not to be the place where the equipment had been found and the sergeant majors were acquitted . . . They were much relieved. They had looked pretty glum throughout the argument . . . It was rough justice and a pretty queer sort of trial . . . One didn't feel sure until it was over that the verdict would . . . go the right way.

Personal Account 2

Defence of the Blockhouse outside Cassel
(See Map 14)

When Cassel was nominated as one of the strongpoints which was to delay the German advance, Brigadier Somerset was ordered to garrison an isolated blockhouse, two miles to the north, that overlooked the road leading to Dunkirk. It was one of the outposts that was expected to ensure that the main force in the fortified town was not taken by surprise. At the same time it was well placed to enable its occupants to fire at German vehicles and troops moving up the road. On 26 May 1940, the first day of the Dunkirk evacuation, Roy Creswell, a twenty-two-year-old 2nd Lieutenant in the 2nd Battalion, the Gloucestershire Regiment, was told to investigate what steps had to be taken to make the blockhouse defendable (see page 263). What followed was one of the backs to the wall rearguard actions which typified the tenacious spirit of the British soldiers who were ordered to hold up the Germans so that as many of their brother soldiers as possible could be evacuated. After the war, Creswell described the action at the blockhouse in the following words.[4]

26 May

At 1430 I was ordered to take two pioneers and three men [from Cassel], armed as for a patrol, to carry out a . . . recce of a blockhouse on . . . the Dunkirk road . . .

Information required was as follows:
(1) Was entry by force necessary? If so what tools and help was needed?
(2) What was the state of its defence and what improvements were necessary?
(3) What was the extent of the field of fire?
(4) Would Engineer help be needed?

The patrol returned [to Cassel] at 1700 hrs and reported that no force was necessary to effect an entry into the blockhouse whose construction was incomplete. It lacked doors, the observation tower was not in place . . . [and] the gun slits were [unfinished]. The wooden scaffolding was still in position around the building [and] . . . a builder's hut totally blocked its field of fire to the west. On the south side, piles of building materials, shingle and sand reduced the field of fire to a maximum of 100 yards. The eastern side possessed a fair field of fire [although it would be] . . . hampered by piles of earth from an unfinished tank trap. The north was totally blind, there being no gun slits in the northern wall, and because the observation tower was useless in its present condition. [The blockhouse] was occupied by a number of refugees.

This report, was made to the Commanding Officer, [Major Maurice Gilmore], who consulted Brigade HQ, but the order stood . . . The position had to be held at all costs as part of the defensive plan. The task was given to 8 Platoon which began to pack immediately. Its departure from Cassel was delayed as the platoon truck did not arrive until 2000 hours. They left eventually at 2045, reaching the blockhouse at 2145.

The truck was unloaded in the dark, while the refugees were persuaded to leave. Little could be done to improve the defences until dawn. Alarm posts were arranged, sentries posted, and the rest of the platoon rested.

27 May

Early in the morning a start was made to improve the fortifications and state of defence. Before this was properly underway, the only meal which we were destined to receive, arrived, consisting of tea, a nearly full tin of ration biscuits, and 56 small tins of meat paste. To this could be added a few tins of provisions and eggs brought down by the platoon itself.

To block up the two entrances, lengths of concrete, reinforced with iron bars, and sandbags, were utilized, the blocking of the side door being just completed as the Germans were sighted in the evening. With sandbags, the gun slits were reduced to a reasonable size in which the Bren gun and one anti-tank rifle was mounted, parts of the scaffolding being sawn away to enlarge the field of fire.

Another major task was the removal of the builder's hut to the west, [which was] piled high with stores of all kinds. A little after midday this was completed, a part of the contents being utilized to block up the observation tower entrance, on the top of which was poured some cement, found lying around in sacks. An attempt was also made to level off the piles of gravel and sand to the south and to cut down or at least cut gaps in the hedges, but the time at our disposal was insufficient to allow for the completion of this task.

At 1800 hours the Germans were seen advancing in open order across the western skyline. The side entrance was immediately blocked up and a heavy fire was brought to bear on the advancing enemy, upon whom several casualties must have been inflicted at a range of 600 yards.

Between 1900 and 2000 hrs. a furious attack was launched against us, which was eventually beaten off, the only lasting effect being that one nearby haystack was fired by tracer. This proved to be advantageous, since it burnt all night, and the light thus caused made the work of the lookouts slightly easier. In this attack the enemy used a type of shell which was about two inches long and which burst inside the blockhouse. Part of one of these hit Lance Corporal Ruddy who was severely wounded in the head and throat. The rest of the evening and night was spent in comparative quietness.

28 May

The night was passed without any marked action by the enemy. During the morning a second attack was made, which was eventually beaten off without any loss or injury to the garrison.

Today a rigid rationing of the remaining food and water had to be introduced owing to the failure of the cooks' truck to reach us the previous evening, as had been promised. The suffering of Lance Corporal Ruddy resulted in most of the water being sacrificed to his needs, the rest of the platoon existing on very little water and rum, which had been found in Cassel.

Around midday and in the early afternoon, spasmodic firing, as if from heavy guns, could be heard in the vicinity. We could never find out for sure the direction or point of origin of this, although the flight of the projectile seemed to indicate that the firing was not directed against Cassel or ourselves. During the evening we watched enemy mechanized columns moving round to the east of

Cassel. Unfortunately they were not within the range of our weapons. This development led to much speculation as to what was happening to the Battalion in Cassel.

29 May

This was destined to be one of the worst days we had experienced in the blockhouse. Dawn broke without any activity by the enemy, but about 0900 hours a wounded British artillery captain was seen hobbling on a crutch round the west corner of the blockhouse, shouting: 'A wounded British officer here!' When I attempted to reply, he answered immediately: 'Don't answer back'. When he reached the east end of the position he looked down at a dead German and said out loud 'There are many English and German(s) like that round here.' At the same time he looked up at the roof of the blockhouse very pointedly, an action which seemed to indicate the presence of someone on the roof. With that, he limped out of sight, leaving us all with the regret that we had been unable to help him, while at the same time, he obviously did not want us to open a door to let him in.

The German strategy was immediately obvious. Utilizing the distraction in front of us, the enemy had clambered up the blind side i.e. the rear . . . They then removed the cement from the top of the useless observation hole [in the blockhouse roof], poured a tin of petrol on the material serving as a block, and set it on fire with hand grenades . . . [The] explosions were the first indications of any real activity of the enemy. Gas masks had to be worn until the fire, and clouds of smoke could be got under control . . . A heavy quilt curtain brought from Cassel was place[d] across the entrance way leading to [the observation tower hole and] the fire, and [it] was kept damp, while water taken from a sump of dirty water was poured on the fire . . . The hole, when [the material blocking it had] burned away, was large enough to enable the enemy to lob grenades through it from the roof into the blockhouse itself. [But] . . . their strategy failed, for they failed to smoke us out into the open.

Later efforts to boil water on this fire failed to render it drinkable, although several eggs were successfully boiled on it. [They] had [also] improved the warmth inside [the blockhouse], which was particularly appreciated for it had been very cold inside.

During the afternoon an open car was put out of action by Bren and anti-tank rifle fire, its occupants being killed or wounded. The rest of the day passed off without incident.

30 May

The fire was kept under control all night and nothing interesting took place until midday when our Bren gun fire again forced the Germans to abandon a large car on the Dunkirk road.

At about 1400 hours a party of four Germans approached us from the road. They were fired upon at once and disappeared from view. After our capture we learnt that it was a recce party. A period of inactivity on the part of the Germans followed, which was broken by the firing of a haystack to the West and an attack from the East. This was beaten off, but they returned to the attack, bringing heavy automatic fire to bear on every gun slit and against the entrances. Any attempt on our part to fire through the slits was suicidal, for the enemy shots sprayed through the slits with amazing accuracy.

When even heavier weapons were brought to bear on us, further resistance became impossible. It was therefore decided to surrender, our hopes of making a break out that night being dashed to the ground. An attempt [to break out] had been decided upon, since the silence in Cassel had made it obvious that resistance had ceased there [too], while even the distant rumbling of gunfire had completely faded away.

No account of this episode can be [complete] ... without a tribute to the men of my platoon. Throughout the whole of our sojourn in the blockhouse, their morale, grit, fortitude and perseverance was excellent. Despite the order of 'One hour on, one hour off' resulting in very little rest, despite the lack of food and drink, they remained cheerful throughout and fought well until the very end.

Personal Account 3

Holding the Front Line in the Dunkirk Perimeter
(See Map 16)

If there is one account which highlights the narrow margin separating British success at holding back the German vanguard on the fringes of the Dunkirk perimeter from failure, it is to be found in the memoirs of Captain Francis Waldron of the 4th Battalion, the Royal Berkshire Regiment (see p. 397). He has described the torment suffered by officers and men alike as, exhausted, and in some cases shell-shocked by what they had seen and done, they somehow managed to summon up just enough energy and courage to keep the enemy at bay whatever was thrown at them. In the following extract, he describes the tense situation, northeast of Furnes, behind the canal running round the edge of the Dunkirk perimeter, during the night of 30–31 May 1940, as he struggled to work out how, with the limited resources at his disposal, he could best organize the troops so that they could hold his battalion's section of the front line.[5]

As evening drew in, [Major] Roper, [the acting Commanding Officer] came back [to Battalion Headquarters, about a quarter of a mile behind the canal which our men were defending], and said that things were really serious in the front line. [2nd Lieutenant] Partridge and Captain Ryland were the only two officers up there. They were both almost falling asleep on their feet. The sappers to our left had broken back, and our own men, after heavy enemy mortar fire, had also broken back. This meant we had nobody on the canal bank. If the enemy should choose to attack, there was nothing to stop him. [Although] I myself was feeling the strain, . . . [having been] sitting all day under shellfire, . . . Roper said he would like me to take over for a time. Partridge would show me the line we were supposed to be holding.

It was now . . . nearly dark, but the Very lights, gun fire and fires made the country quite visible . . . We got all [the] men [who had fled] lined up at Company Headquarters, [which was between

Battalion HQ and the canal], and then proceeded to take them up a long winding ditch . . . When we got to the edge of the canal, we crawled on all fours to look over. Partridge, always a blood thirsty fellow, as indicated by his flaming red hair, suggested it would be a good idea to throw a few hand grenades over to the other side, as there was no doubt the enemy was there. This, in my view, was a quite absurd suggestion, for we still had to get our men into position . . . to draw their fire on us was asking for trouble . . .

It was at this time that heavy machine-gun fire broke out to our right. It was evident the enemy had got over the canal there . . . Going back to the right of our line, I was met by two Coldstream Guardsmen. They told me the enemy had got two machine guns across the canal, (and) had shot their Platoon Sergeant Major and also two of their officers . . . I was thankful that it was dark, for if the Hun had seen the precarious situation we were in for the next few hours, nothing would have stopped him getting more men across.

I still remember the message I sent to my Commanding Officer: 'Suggest immediate counter-attack with our men across Coldstream front. The Germans have two machine-guns over the canal.' A quarter of an hour later, the answer came back that on no account was I to do anything on the Coldstream front. They had said they would be fully responsible for their own line.

My object now was to get [the recently arrived group of] thirty men forward to bolster . . . our meagre front line. There was a heavy cross-fire from these two machine gun posts, and [that made] it necessary to crawl up the ditch, showing [ourselves] as little as possible. The swish of bullets [passing] overhead left us in no doubt as to what would happen [to us if we got in their way.]

Having led the last thirty men up to the canal, Waldron, who appears to have made several trips back to the headquarters, eventually rejoined the troops in the front line and set about reorganizing the position.

In the front line . . . only one officer, Captain Ryland, was with the men, and he was suffering from shock to the extent that he was useless. My only NCOs were Sergeant Jenkins and Lance Corporal Branch.

I [should] describe the [situation at the] canal in more detail. The canal . . . water was four or five feet below the bank. The towpath was raised above the landscape on our side. Behind the towpath was a ditch, in some places ten feet deep. Into this [ditch], every twenty or thirty yards, sappers had built dug-outs. In these dug-outs, [I concluded], it would be possible to leave four or five men who could rest. [While they rested], . . . men . . . [could] be on guard on the canal bank a few yards above their heads.

There was still a sapper company to our left. These men, if we had had a full battalion, we could have relieved a long time before. I crawled along and, after making enquiries, discovered the officer in charge . . . I told him the situation, and explained the impossibility of being able to relieve him whilst we had so few men. He said that if that was the case, his men would hold on.

Crawling back to the beginning of our line, I got hold of Lance Corporal Branch and put him in charge of the northern end. The men we had placed in [the] dug-outs were already asleep. I decided to put one on the bank as [a] guard, and then realized it would be necessary to have two. It was [an eerie] . . . process [which involved] waking up a couple of fellows [in each dug-out] and telling them to get out on to the edge of the bank. Flares and Very lights were continually going up, and each time this happened, it was necessary to keep absolutely [still] . . .

The first two men to be put on the edge were [from] . . . my own . . . (A) Company. The implicit trust they were prepared to place in [me as their] . . . officer was amazing. If we only had [had more of our] officers, the men would [have been] . . . in much better fettle. Two more men were put on the edge from the next dug out. As we scrambled onto the edge of the canal, I kept up a constant stream of conversation to encourage them on their way. Many dead bodies of their own comrades were lying stiff on the edge of the bank, killed doing the work which they were now detailed to do.

I placed Sergeant [Jenkins] in charge of the right sector. [My] instructions were to keep up a spasmodic fire unless the enemy showed any signs of attacking in force, [in which case] . . . every man would immediately be called to the edge of the canal bank. This [was designed to] . . . keep the enemy guessing as to the strength of our forces . . . and at the same time, there would not be enough fire to cause him to retaliate to any great extent. Our Vickers gun had temporarily silenced the [enemy] . . . But as the night advanced, the shouting of the Germans, and an occasional splash in the canal, [told us] . . . they were still trying to get men across.

Directly on our left front, between ourselves and the sappers, were two barges. These, half filling the canal, were an excellent crossing stage for anybody wishing to attack. On the far bank, beyond the barges, was a farmhouse. From time to time, flashes would appear from the windows, and our men would return the fire . . . Dawn would be the time to fear an attack . . . I had two Bren guns trained directly upon the canal which, from time to time, we let off.

It was beginning to get light, and I was lying on the edge of the bank with Branch, when the two barges suddenly went up in flames. They were soaked in oil, and the heat was terrific. Who had set them on fire? We called all our men onto the edge of the bank. It was obvious, we thought, the enemy were now going [to] attack. As luck would have it, [however], the wind had veered, and the smoke in great billows drifted towards the enemy lines. It became lighter and lighter, and no attack occurred, and at last [we believed] it . . . unlikely that anything would happen for the next few hours. I told Branch and Sergeant Jenkins I was returning to [Battalion] Headquarters, and that . . . Partridge would come back and take over from me. Captain Ryland was still suffering severely from shock, and sitting in the corner of his dug-out. It was necessary however for the morale of the men that I should leave an officer there, whatever state his mind might be in.

At Battalion Headquarters . . . I found one of our men who had come forward with a certain amount of rations . . . and together we crept up the hedgerow to where Branch was holding the sector I had left to him. The bully-beef was a welcome sight to the men, for they had only eaten what they could carry with them since the morning before. I went down the whole line running between the different dug-outs and jumping into them. The enemy fire was on the increase once more. Apart from enemy rifle and machine-gun fire, they were now dropping mortar bombs [over the canal] with great accuracy. We should have had most of our men wiped out . . . if they had not had their dug-outs to sleep in.

At the far end of the line, Captain Ryland had somewhat regained his senses, but [he] was [still] suffering . . . All he could ask me was: would it be possible for him to go back and change into warmer clothes, as he was terribly cold. I thought . . . that, with Partridge coming up in the near future, it would be possible to get him back that morning, and told him that I would see what I could manage; in the meantime he was to do his best to encourage the men.

Back along the line to the left, I picked up three men who had been wounded by mortar fire . . . [They] would have to be evacuated. With difficulty, for one of them was seriously hit in the leg, we were able to get them back . . .

And so to our headquarters [once again] . . . It must have been late in the morning when the question of food arose [for us. We needed to] . . . have something to eat. In the little salon of our headquarters, a meal was laid: bully-beef and Perrier Jouet '28 – the food so . . . [criticized] by our troops, the wine, the most expensive [champagne] we could have had at any luxury residence in London. We sat down in the small room to eat, myself against the wall, the gunner officer on my left, the doctor opposite me and Derek Russell on my right. The room had all the appearance of a suburban villa: china pieces on the mantelpiece, anti-macassars on the chairs, pictures of the [house owner's] family round the walls, and all the ornaments one would expect to find in the best parlour in the suburbs.

We were getting well used to shell fire by now, and were prepared to enjoy this short respite. But the Hun gunners decided otherwise. One has always been told that as long as one hears the whistle of a shell, one is safe. On this occasion we heard no whistle. All I can remember to this day was a terrific crash. That is the only way I can describe it. And then I was picking myself up from the corner of the room, a champagne glass still held firmly in my hand. The enemy had scored a direct hit on the building; the whole of the side wall had come down. Derek, on my right, was white from head to foot from showers of plaster from the wall. He was sitting down dazed. Opposite, across the room, the [courageous little Scottish] doctor lay quietly, with his head resting on the table. I got Derek up and looked for a chair to put him on. No chairs were left with the exception of the one the doctor was still sitting on] . . . I . . . staggered across to him.

By this time Josey, [my batman], and a couple of the other batmen, had come in. [A] fire had started in the outside room, and this they quickly [extinguished] . . . The Doctor was evidently badly hit. I went over to him. [I] . . . was able to lift his small body in my arms and, with the assistance of one of the men, we carried him quickly down the street to his own first-aid post, and there handed him over to [the] Sergeant . . . [But there was nothing he could do]. The Doctor was dead. His death must have been almost instantaneous.

I somehow got back to Headquarters again. Derek, still white from head to foot, [and] suffering severely from shock, had temporarily lost his eyesight. My trousers were one mass of blood, not from myself, but from the Doctor, whom I had carried down the road. My face was bleeding, and to this day, I carry a scar on my lower jaw [where it was cut] by a chunk of that champagne glass I was grasping when the shell fell. However, things might have been worse. Headquarters was still there, and I still had my one Lance Corporal in the Orderly Room. We were still operating.

Sometime in the evening, a message came in. [It stated] that the Germans had . . . broken through to our left. Things, evidently, were becoming desperate . . . I . . . felt that I must continue to do things, or my brain would snap. I asked [Roper] . . . if it would be all right if I went forward to make a reconnaissance, to find out exactly where the Germans were. Roper said it was a good idea.

I knew of the heavy cross-fire . . . which had stopped our rations coming forward. But this was some hours previously, and if the Hun had got over, it was obvious that his cross-fire would now have stopped, for fear of hitting his own men. So I borrowed a rifle and, with a pair of field glasses, which had been given me by my father, round my neck, [and with] Josey [holding] . . . another rifle . . . we started, going forward [on] . . . the left flank.

The sharp crack of . . . mortars going off as [they] . . . landed within a few yards of us, first on our right, and then on our left, and then seemingly all around us, left me, where a few days before

I should have been frightened out of my [wits] . . . in a state of complete inertia. The thought of danger, the fear of being hurt, had entirely left [me] . . . Everything seemed remote, as though [I] . . . was watching a . . . dramatic film in the cinema.

I met an officer from the Coldstream [Guards]. The Coldstream [Guards] had heard of the break-through to the left, and this officer, with a party of men, had been sent to give us . . . assistance. I walked back with him to the ditch where the section of Guards had taken up their position. He insisted that no Germans had got through at all and [that] it was all rumour. I, for my part, was not [so] certain.

Josey [sat down] . . . next to me on the edge of the ditch, the Coldstream officer opposite [us]. The Coldstream officer and I were chatting . . . Suddenly [something which felt] . . . like a red hot [piece of] iron hit my left arm. It did not worry me particularly; nothing could worry me a great deal at that moment . . . I thought it was probably a fragment of something that had burst somewhere close [by]. The next second, however, Josey let out a yell and fell backwards. [I] did not [register] exactly what had happened [even] when he asked me to loosen his equipment. He was evidently in great pain. I leant over to get his respirator undone. It was tied in the approved army style, tightly across his chest . . . [Then] I felt a blow . . . [as if I had been hit by] a sledge hammer [on] . . . my back. This knocked me [down] . . . I shall never forget the face of the Coldstream officer sitting opposite me on the other side of the ditch, when it slowly dawned on him that we had been hit. 'By God,' he exclaimed, 'they must be there after all.'

As luck would have it, a message reached him at that time, telling him to take all his men out of the ditch back to Headquarters . . . It could not have been long [however] before another Coldstream officer came strolling across from where our headquarters was. He evidently did not know what had just happened, and was astonished to find us both lying incapable of moving. [With difficulty] I told him . . . what had transpired . . . My breath[ing] was very bad, for they had got me through the top of the lung . . . He [also] had no idea the enemy were over. He told us he would do his best to send some of his men to us if they were not needed for counter-attacking, and so Josey and I were left together again. We must have got very near delirium: all kinds of thoughts went through [my] . . . mind. Nothing mattered, and then [I thought about] the Germans and their bayonets. This meant the finish, and [I thought about my] home. We made promises to each other that if either of us got back, we would tell our families what had happened to the other . . .

Later . . . a sergeant of the Coldstream appeared on the scene. He and five or six other men had crawled along the ditch under heavy fire, under orders from their officer, to try to come and get us out . . . [Thanks to them], we got back at last to the Coldstream headquarters.

Evacuation from the 12th Casualty Clearing Station at Dunkirk

Waldron eventually ended up in the 12th Casualty Clearing Station at Château Coquelle in Rosendaël, a district of Dunkirk (see pp. 438 and 446, and see also Personal Account 5, by surgeon Philip Newman). As he takes up the story, he is lying in a tent in the Château's grounds on 2 June 1940 along with around twenty other wounded men.

It was dark when the doctor came in that evening and asked everybody to listen to him. He said that he had bad news for us. The Germans were not more than two miles away; they were expected [at] any minute. They had broadcast the hospital and the wounded would be looked after. We were on no account to be rude to them. There was not a chance of getting any of us away . . .

[Later, however, the Welsh ambulance driver, who had been handing out food and drinks of water,] told us there was still hope: all those who could call themselves 'walking wounded' might be able to get to the hospital ship [after all]. Lorries would [soon] be getting away. The next hour was agony: we were all trying to get onto our feet. I found myself walking with the help of [another] . . . man and a broomstick which the Welsh driver had brought over from the hospital.

My little Welsh friend helped me along to the lorry and, not without difficulty, hoisted me into the front seat. I was to act as his spare driver, though God knows I could never have coped, even for an instant, with the steering wheel. Our lorry was packed up with wounded, of whom perhaps five per cent could have been called 'walking wounded'. Two men I vividly remember. One of them said he could remember me at Division, but both their faces and parts of their bodies had been terrifyingly burnt, and they must have been in acute pain ... [They] were quite unrecognizable.

[We had been told] there were only two ways open to the docks. All the other roads were wrecked. [However] the first road we took turned out to be hopeless. The whole side of a building had fallen down, and rubble rose to about ten feet high across the highway. It was quite impossible to get round or across it. Back again to where we had started from and, as the little Welsh driver cheerfully remarked: 'Do you, or don't you get away?' The second road was apparently clear, but an oil tank was blazing on one side of it. He must have got the lorry up to a speed of about fifty miles [per hour], but even then, as we passed, the heat was terrific.

The streets were deserted. As we neared the docks, we saw [a few] French soldier[s. Apart from them], ... there were no signs of humanity. We reached the gates [leading] to the Mole. [It was here] ... the difficulty started. How were we going to get 'walking wounded' half a mile down the Mole? Three of us linked arms. I had to be on the outside, for the whole of my left arm and side was numbed. Half way down the quay, we were overtaken by a battalion of fighting men. I think they were the Hampshires, marching in threes, perfectly equipped. They looked as though they had walked straight out of barracks and not as though they were returning from the fighting line. Two destroyers lay alongside ... the Mole. They both seemed to be overladen with men, but with difficulty, we got onto the first one, and then our legs just collapsed. There was nothing more for us to do. If we got to the other side, we should be lucky.

Slowly, the destroyer pulled away from the side of the quay and headed into deeper water. A warship had been sunk just ahead of us, and numerous other craft could be seen, some nearly submerged, others with part of their structures standing out of the water. We . . . slowed down, a tempting target for German aircraft, and they were not long in spotting us. The decks of the destroyer were equipped with [guns] . . . and the gunners [fired] . . . at the . . . planes. The reason for our stop was that we could not go forward until the other destroyer was ready . . . Our ship had been shelled and the steering compass had been wrecked. The other destroyer at length pulled out and started ahead of us, and for the next twenty minutes, we knew something of the speed of destroyers. We tore through the water at what [felt like] . . . 40 miles per hour.

Dover was reached at last [and there followed] a very different landing from the many . . . [I had had when arriving] in Dover Harbour [as a civilian] . . . from the Continent. A hospital train, and then a clean white bed in hospital saw the end of that hectic, tragic time of fighting and retreating in France and Belgium.

Personal Account 4

Escape to Dunkirk
(See Map 10)

Following the evacuation of Cassel during the night of 29–30 May 1940, the British garrison found their route to the coast blocked by German tanks and troops north of Winnezeele (see p. 371). Most of the British soldiers were either killed or captured, but there were exceptions: one of the men who made it back to Dunkirk was Julian Fane, a nineteen-year-old 2nd Lieutenant in the 2nd Battalion, the Gloucestershire Regiment. In the following extract from his memoirs, he describes his eventful journey to the coast along with a small group of other ranks. The action starts shortly after the Gloucestershire Regiment's commanding officer had summoned his company commanders to discuss how they might evade the Germans who had barred their line of escape to the north.[6]

B and D Company's commanders returned and told us we were to return to the Bois St Acaire . . . just to the rear of our present position. We tried to get there without being seen by the enemy by crawling along . . . ditches and behind hedges. But we must have been spotted by the Hun, for we had not been there long before the whole area around the wood resounded with the cries of 'Kamerad! Kamerad!' There were quite a lot of troops shouting this treacherous word at the top of their voices. Then they all stopped, and a voice started speaking in clear tones in very good English. The words the man spoke were: 'Come out! Come out! Hitler is winning the war. You are beaten. Come out, or we will shell you out. Lay down your arms and come out running.' It was a nasty moment for us, for we all realized the hopeless position we were in; one false move and we would all be shelled to hell.

[Nevertheless] we decided to stay where we were and fight till the last. As the Germans knew our position, the first thing we had to do was to choose another. There was . . . [another] wood about 100 yards away . . . and we decided to make for that. So, bunching on the edge of the wood we were in, the men waited for the signal to run forward across the open ground. When it came, we all ran like hares. Hardly had we left the wood [than] machine gun bullets started whistling all around us. Never before have I run so hard. [Men] were dropping all around me, but I managed to get across the area and plunge into a thick bush intact. Luckily the casualties were not too severe, [although] one of my corporals was hit in the arm and lost a lot of blood before we managed to bind it up. [However] . . . we were no better off, for the Germans had spotted us again.

There was no shelter [from their guns when] . . . they started shelling, which they did before very long. [But] we stayed there all day . . . [While this was going on], we discussed our chances of survival. Things looked absolutely hopeless, for what chance had two companies against a superior force of Germans backed by tanks . . . [and] mortars as well as machine guns?

Darkness fell at last, and we prepared to leave the wood. The plan was to slip through the German lines under cover of [the night] . . . We started out in single file, [trying to be] . . . as silent as possible and keeping to all available cover. We had been marching about an hour . . . when . . . a red Very light [went] . . . up. We had walked . . . into a trap and [had been] . . . ambushed . . . Lieutenant Dick Olive, who was in front of me, caught a blast of machine-gun fire in the chest. His lungs began to fill and I shall never forget the rasping noise of his breathing; it took about two minutes before he drowned in his own blood. Company Quarter Master Sergeant Farmer, also next to me . . . was killed [when he] received a burst of tracer bullets in [his] back which set off the rounds he was carrying in a bandolier over his shoulder.

We [thought] we had absolutely no hope, for right behind us was a haystack which the enemy had set alight with incendiary bullets. We were silhouetted against this burning glow . . . [Then] a piece of shrapnel . . . glanced off my helmet. Temporarily numbed, I soon realized that I had been [wounded] . . . when I felt a warm trickle of blood running down my right arm. My first thought was [that I should] get up and charge the enemy. However, reasoning that there were few who could or would rally to the call, I . . . decided to worm [my] way [forward] until I fell into the ditch running along the road [towards] which we had been heading . . . [There], I . . . collected as many men as possible . . . and crawled . . . about 100 yards . . . then called a halt.

The group he had collected consisted of fifteen soldiers including Fane, although before long, that was reduced to twelve, after one man who had been sent to retrieve the maps Fane had left behind never reappeared, and two, who could not keep up, dropped out. Fane's account goes on to describe their adventures on the way to the coast.

We set out in the darkness with the object of getting to Dunkirk . . . Luckily . . . red flares that [the Germans] . . . kept sending up told us where they were. All night we kept on [walking], across barbed wire and through . . . streams. When dawn began to break, we had to look for some cover [where we could] . . . lie up during the day . . . I found a very deep ditch which was fairly large and covered with brambles and nettles. We [did not dare] to go on, so we spent the day in it. We watched where the sun rose so that we could judge [where] . . . North [was] . . . We were not far from a village . . . It was occupied by Germans . . . We saw their vehicles going in and out at odd intervals.

Things were very unpleasant until the sun came out. Our boots were full of water, and we all had a mild form of trench [foot] . . . Our battledress was soaking . . . [But the sun] helped [to] cheer us [up]. I took my boots off to dry my feet, [although I] only just got them on again . . . For food, we still had my loaf of bread, one tin of crab, two iron rations and a packet of biscuits . . . We . . . spent the . . . day sleeping and smoking, [although] I did not get much sleep, as my hand and arm began to swell up and started throbbing . . . It did not get dark until 10.30 that night, but as soon as it did, we left our shelter and made for the village in front of us . . .

As I approached the road running past the outskirts of the village, I heard the sound of a convoy approaching . . . We . . . decided . . . it must . . . [be] French. I told the men to take cover and I walked . . . across the field . . . and saw . . . it was an artillery group with field guns [drawn by horses] . . . I walked up . . . [to] a man on a bicycle in front of the lead vehicle and asked him in French if he was returning from Dunkirk. He answered in

German that he did not understand and moved forward. Realizing my . . . mistake, I waved, turned around and walked . . . back across the field towards where I had left the others, . . . (expecting at any moment to) get a bullet in [my] . . . back.

After the column had passed, . . . we broke into a house in the main street [of the village which turned out to be Oost Cappel (around 8 miles south-east of Bergues, the most southerly point on the Dunkirk perimeter). There] . . . we found some food, wine and beer. It was with great difficulty that I got the men out of the house in order to resume our trek . . . The only way to keep [going in the right] direction was to march by the flash of the guns on the coast and by the burning farmhouses which the Hun set alight to show their progress to the flanking troops. We had been going for a short time down a track through a small copse when I saw some black objects looming ahead . . . We all dropped to the ground by the side of the track. They were German tanks, that rolled by, just missing my legs [which were] hidden by the bracken . . . [Then] . . . we came to a road, but whenever we tried to cross it, a German car or dispatch rider drove by. There was one man who seemed to make regular trips up and down on a little two stroke. How we cursed him! Eventually we got over . . .

When [it was] 3 a.m., I had [once again] to find somewhere to hide . . . before dawn broke . . . We decided to put up in a barn . . . We climbed up onto the straw bales on one side and formed a barrier with the bales behind which we could hide . . . [However] I soon . . . had reason to regret the selection of our hiding place . . . I heard German voices in the yard outside. [During] the afternoon some of the Germans entered the barn and started sorting through the items in the wagons below . . . Suddenly I heard footsteps on a ladder laid against the hay bales, and a face appeared over the barricade of bales behind which we lay. [Luckily] it was a civilian. He said one word: 'Schlafen', and Corporal Eldridge beckoned to him to keep quiet and [to] go away, which he did . . . So unnerved were we, that when all the Germans had left the barn, I told the men they could smoke . . .

At 10.30 p.m., we climbed down [and] left the barn. We had not gone far before [our] scouts stopped us and told me that we were passing . . . underneath a large gun barrel. I looked up, and there it was . . . I decided to go on quietly [rather than going] around the gun position. Suddenly I felt Eldridge's hand on my shoulder, and a hoarse voice whispered in my ear: 'My God, Sir. Look out!' I looked down and saw a Hun sleeping . . . We all stepped quietly over him and continued on our way.

As dawn was breaking, we reached a large canal which was about three miles outside Dunkirk . . . On the far side was a boat which had previously been scuttled . . . Corporal Eldridge . . . offered to swim across in the bitterly cold water [to] . . . bring the boat [to where we were standing] . . . We then tied a string to the bow and one to the stern and so arranged a sort of ferry . . . A French peasant came out of one of the houses [nearby] and told me that so far the Germans had not arrived [on] this side of the canal. [However] they were not far behind us . . . A few bullets whistled past us as we [moved on].

After further misadventures, Fane eventually made it to the mole at Dunkirk, from where he was taken by ship back to England. His account's concluding paragraph describes his impressions as his long journey finally came to an end.

The sound of the ship's sirens, the clatter of the dock as we came alongside and the noises of the crowds must have woken me, as I was still dead to the world. I walked down the gangplank and was led to a waiting hospital train on a nearby siding. I had not washed for weeks. I had lived in ditches and slept in hay barns. I had had no proper food or clean drinking water for ages and felt desperately weary . . . I found myself lying on a top bunk and looking out of the window as the train moved off through the Kent countryside on a lovely summer's day. People were playing cricket in their whites on carefully tended grass, girls were playing tennis on hard courts in shorts and blouses and life was going on all around, as if there was no war. I ended up in Queen Mary's Hospital, Roehampton.

Personal Account 5
Inside Dunkirk's Casualty Clearing Station
(See Map 16)

No one showed more devotion to duty inside the Dunkirk perimeter than the medics who agreed to stay behind to care for the wounded and dying rather than joining the rest of the British Army on the boats going back home. Major Philip Newman, a twenty-eight-year-old surgeon, was one of the staff at the 12th Casualty Clearing Station, which operated during most of the Operation Dynamo period from Château Coquelle in the Rosendaël district of Dunkirk (see p. 438). As the following extract from Newman's memoirs reveals, he arrived at the Château on 28 May 1940, that is during the third day of the evacuation, and he was still there when the Germans finally took over the town on 4 June. He takes up the story after reaching Dunkirk at 1 a.m. on 27 May with a party of forty men in three lorries.[7]

28 May
In the morning there was a hectic drive to Chapeau Rouge (a district adjacent to Rosendaël, mentioned below) just after another air raid. Picked up two soldiers burnt to a cinder and arrived at the chateau in Rosendaël on the outskirts of Dunkirk. We now knew that we were left holding the baby, and that the BEF were pouring as hard as they could out of Dunkirk. Straightaway I organized a theatre in the drawing room of the Château, and within two hours had two operating teams going.

There was an awful languid feeling about this starting to get down to hard work again when everyone else was going home. Cowell arrived and told us to expect 700 wounded.

Bombing around us was frequent. This first day, we plodded on steadily with the operating, with the promise of relief in the evening by some field ambulance people. They never turned up; they had bunked off home. Slept that night on some luggage in the officers' mess.

29–31 May

[Our days] . . . started at about 5 a.m. Casualties were fast pouring in . . . They were hectic days in the extreme. Food was all tinned and only dished up in a very jumbly and small room, [where we had] to feed twenty officers. Almost every meal consisted of bully-beef and biscuits . . . One ate it standing up.

Shelling and bombing became worse; a 500 pound bomb fell within 50 yards of the house and a smaller one within twenty yards. Wounded increased until the house was packed full and the driveway was full of ambulances loaded up. I shifted my operating theatre to the cellar with one electric lamp.

The Commanding Officer (CO), Munro and Longridge got very busy with [the] evacuation and did many perilous journeys to the Mole at Dunkirk Harbour. The CO was marvellous, but I think pretty well exhausted. Munro was very brave and dashing; Longridge was very persistent and also exhausted. Gordi and Wills were grand with the patients. Others on the Unit showed considerable wear and tear . . . I myself was close to exhaustion. Some of the men were very good; others spent most of the time in the cellar.

The state of the wounded piling up in our grounds and the hopeless state of evacuation seemed to put saving the odd life by operation very much in the shade. I decided to take my share in the evacuation . . . instead of operating. I drove the CO down to the Mole and saw Dunkirk for the first time in three days. It was a sight of great devastation, and one drove very fast to lessen the risk of getting hit by shells. I spent from 10 [a.m.]–1.30 [p.m.] and 2.30–5.00 p.m. on the Mole and on that day, we got rid of some 700 wounded. I was very impressed by the four naval commanders and listened as they directed the evacuation ships with great authority. There was such an air of confidence after the awful army dithering.

It was a weary day with shells zipping over regularly in batches of about ten every fifteen minutes. Bombers dive-bombed the fleet. The jetty itself was a sight: . . . dead horses, overturned ambulances, columns of German prisoners, sunken boats and God knows what else. An ammunition dump went up just close by to add to the variety. The troops filed past ... The 'Retreat from Moscow' was never in it ...

These three days ... at the Chapeau Rouge (a nickname for the chateau, as well as the adjacent district) were tiring in the extreme, but at least the whole unit was there and at least there was somebody [other than] ... myself to take the responsibilities. At the time I thought those days were just hell. But I didn't know (what was coming)!

On the night of 30 May we had all been told that we were going home at 11 p.m. With everybody packed and ready in ... the ambulances, a message came through to wait until 4 a.m. At 4 a.m. another message [arrived]: '12th CCS to remain open; only patients to go.' This was just one of the many disappointments ... One of the [demoralizing] ... aspects of those days was the way anyone in authority seemed to forsake his post and jump on a boat for home. Col R, who promised to stay to see us home, hopped onto a boat the next day. Various 'big wigs' came out for a trip to organize, failed, and then caught the next boat home, leaving a few juniors behind to stand the racket.

1 June

Things were in an awful mess. Shells were bursting very close to the house and the wounded were in a terrible state. The Germans were reported near and might be in tomorrow. Munro and I decided that something must be done ... The CO was open to any suggestions. We set off in a state of desolation and went to two hospitals and a nunnery in Dunkirk [to see whether they could take our patients. They] all refused us and in sheer despair Munro and I decided to sit in a dug out and smoke a cigarette 'in peace'. Almost immediately another air raid started. But we had our first 15 minutes of quiet thought in days.

Returning to the Chapeau Rouge, something new was in the air. New orders had arrived. We were to pull out, but one medical officer and ten men were to stay behind for every 100 wounded. I decided to operate again. We only had candlelight in the cellar by this time and I had to do two leg amputations. One was a little French boy; I had to interview his weeping mother. I dropped into bed about 3.00 a.m. that night.

At 2.30 [p.m.] we gathered in the mess for the ballot. Of the 17 officers, three only were to stay, so my chances seemed quite rosy. As the CO shuffled the papers, my heart was pounding. Cocky O'Shea, the RC padre, drew the papers. The last 4 were Herbert, Hewer, Williamson and, [last but not least, me,] Newman; I was 17th and down the drain anyhow. At least I knew the worst. Hewer might get away if we could get sixty patients away, but we didn't.

The rest were leaving at 8 p.m. for the boat. I shall never forget those 5 hours before they went. Trying to look efficient and 'don't carish', and everyone dreading to speak to me. Cocky and I had a talk and a weep, and he gave me his cross, which I value more than anything in my possession. Lissy and I had a talk and a weep, and he gave me his copy of the New Testament. Munro bravely offered to stay instead, but retracted when put to the test.

We got more patients away, and it soon became obvious that Hewer, Williamson and I were to stay. The CO called us all together and spoke. I gave 3 cheers for him. He did not seem anxious to catch my eye. I hope it was because he felt a great deal. I'm sure it was. But everyone was so glad to leave. They associated us three with something that was a nightmare. Eventually they went and I was very glad to see them go. A few minutes before going, Lissy had a little service at the top of the house. It was very short and very worthy of the occasion. Away they went and there we were, left with over 300 wounded and the Germans to come.

Hewer, Williamson and I gathered in what was the Mess and decided to try and get a little order out of the chaos. The mess was to be in the cellar. Whitehall, the mess orderly, got this organized and proved to be the one shining light in [the] many dark days to come. We drank a few drinks and tried to take count of what we had. There were ambulances strewn all over the place, patients in tents, corpses and the house stinking like a cesspool. This evening we had hopes of a boat, but none came. Realizing the hopelessness of the situation, we decided to get a night's rest. Whitehall was great. He had actually prepared a meal on a table and had got the beds ready.

2 June

We slept for a few hours and then were awakened by a terrific crash. A shell had come into the front room, the operating theatre that was. In the very dim early morning light, we sorted out patients and masonry, and carried the patients outside. There were about a dozen of the poor chaps. One lad had a slab of concrete on his face. We soon realized what we were up against. Everywhere patients were yelling . . . 'Water!' and 'Orderly!' Naked men, wounded and burnt, were crawling about on the grass with shells bursting nearby.

During the morning, the French field ambulance was bombed . . . Six men were killed and the major wounded. Commander St Pol was my great mainstay. Whatever happened, I felt: at least he is there and is an old soldier and he will know what to do. But now he was wounded. There was nobody else I could appeal to for help.

I was now the owner of three cars: a Humber Super Snipe, a Lincoln Zephyr, and an Austin Seven. I chose the Zephyr and beetled down to the Bastion in Dunkirk Harbour (the Allied HQ). I eventually got into a meeting and found Major General Alexander. It was grand to find that there was anyone so big as this still in France! I told him that conditions were hopeless and that unless we had help, all we could do was to prevent [the]. . . wounded from dying from thirst. He immediately wirelessed for two hospital ships. Here at last was a straw to cling to.

Returning to the Château, I drove the old Zephyr like mad through hanging electric cables, [avoiding] shell holes [in my path] . . . I told the lads, and a little hope came into their eyes. Forsyth had now joined us from some field ambulance unit, and also a chap called Gaze, a building contractor from Diss, . . . a really good egg.

This evening, I think, was . . . the most dramatic yet. A message came through for all walking wounded to go. I had four lorries driven up and even had one of the wounded soldiers driving one of them . . . It was amazing who could walk. Chaps [were] going to England in a shirt, a blanket and bare feet, some with large running wounds in their backs and legs; [they were] hobbling along, [leaning] on the shoulders of others. I packed about 100 into the lorries and they really were a grand sight as we wished them good luck [and] as they drew away. As far as I know, they got safely on board a boat for England. Good luck to them.

About 9.45 [p.m.], just as the light was failing, we [received] . . . a message . . . [telling us] a hospital ship was coming in. I called all the men together and told them there was [a] slight chance, and that if we worked really hard all night [so that we] got rid of all the wounded, we could get on the boat. It was amazing what this ray of hope did. Five ambulances set off immediately . . . [driven by] . . . Gaze, Me, Hewer, Williamson and Evans. Gaze and I got separated from the rest. It was a most hair raising drive, with the streets almost impassable, many houses in flames, . . . the whole night red with burning buildings. Eventually we arrived at the Mole, and [then we] waited. The Navy had seen nothing of the ship.

Hewer arrived by another route and ended up with two wheels of his ambulance on a huge balk of timber and damned nearly overturned it. How he managed to unload the thing by himself, I have never found out. We waited for an hour. No boat came.

At about 11 p.m. I saw the last of the BEF file past. We, with some marines, rushed a few of the stretchers half a mile up the jetty, and put them on a boat. At about 11.30 [p.m.] the four commanders and brigadiers, and anybody else who was English, left in a pinnace, and there we were, left standing alone. Forsaken by England, and only the Germans to look forward to. I can never forget that moment as long as I live. It gave me the greatest feeling of desolation I have ever had.

The rest of the stretchers we begged the French soldiers to take with them onto the boats, which they did with an ill grace. So we did at least do our duty and [helped] . . . twenty-five more men to safety. One man on a stretcher, we actually chucked over, as the ship . . . left the quay. He landed safely. Now we were left on the quay, with just the last of the French troops filing past, and all hope for a hospital ship gone. Evans had bunked off on a ship with the tall lance corporal. The other four of us wearily found our way back to the ambulances.

I drove back [although I] could hardly see where we were going, and we became separated again. We arrived back at the Château. The boys had worked very hard to get the convoy ready and then, [exhausted], had given up hope and simply gone to sleep on the ground in utter despair . . . It was now about 1 a.m. On the way back, we had seen two white Very lights in the sky close by, indicating the German front line. As they looked objectionably near, we decided to take precautions. [The] four doctors and four NCOs took the watches in shifts, one of each to stay up for two hours. We quickly made a red illuminated cross and put it outside the front door. [But] the Germans did not come. The night was complete pandemonium, with the heavy French battery either side of us, [ships] . . . behind us off the coast, and shells bursting all around.

I remember I dropped onto the stone floor of the kitchen, absolutely dog-tired, and [was soon] . . . sound asleep. That night was hell, although no shell actually hit the house. The night before we had slept in the cellar, and although it did not strike me at the time, I remember now that we left three dying men in there, as it served as an operating theatre also. Captain Bartlett was one [of the men] who was dead in the morning. He was a really grand chap and now rests in what will be the Rosendaël cemetery.

June 3

. . . All day we were under shellfire, and there was dive-bombing all around. The French battery had now shifted back a bit. The pump was dry and there had been no water supply for two days. Patients everywhere were yelling for water. The situation was acute, until Gaze came up with gold and found another well. It was almost impossible to do any theatre work. All we could do was to carry patients to places of comparative safety, stop them from dying of thirst, and bury our dead. I had four men continually burying the [corpses] . . .; we had about 150 in our cemetery [by this time].

There was a first class air fight and we saw two (of our planes) . . . bring down three enemy planes. It was great to see some of our own planes for a change. I don't wish to describe the state of the ambulances. They were sheer death traps and hygienically appalling.

During the middle of the day three shells hit the house. The first hit the front steps, collapsing the cellar underneath with ten men in it. We pulled them all out and it was amazing how little they were hurt. Another hit the top [of the house. That shell] . . .

wounded a few men and almost got Williamson. The third hit the old mess room. A few men were killed in the ambulances and others wounded. The casualties were not as high as they might have been, but were quite considerable.

A very real danger was fast approaching. The Germans were coming, and the French were taking up their position on the canal not 200 yards away from the house. Forsyth and I went to see a French captain, and begged him to keep his troops out of the park. But he could offer us little hope. Later in the day the French began to dig in on the canal side of the park and we felt that we were now bound to be for it. We thought it was obvious that the French would retreat through the park where all the wounded lay on stretchers and perhaps hide in our cellars. This could result in nothing short of hand-to-hand fighting inside the house.

Just before dark, we contacted a French commandant and he promised us that he would see that they would not retreat through the park. This gave us some hope. As night drew on, the air became still. We posted our German pilot officer prisoner, Helmut, near the front door, together with our illuminated red cross. Rapidly we learnt the German for such things as 'Red Cross' and Don't Shoot' . . . I organized the senior NCOs and officers in a watch routine through the night. We all took our hour at the front door, and at the back of our minds we were all hoping that a Mills bomb wouldn't arrive [before the Germans] . . .

During my hour, nothing happened at all. But just afterwards, there was masses of rifle fire, and we thought that at last the French and the Germans were fighting on either side of the canal. Then we suddenly realized that there were no bullets coming past the house, and that they were all going off in the same place. Somebody had set fire to an ammunition dump. We did not know then, but it must have been the French retreating.

4 June
My duty over, and with a little extra excitement, I went to bed at 4 a.m. I knew nothing more, until I was hurriedly woken by a voice saying, 'The Germans are here.' I quickly put on my tunic, belt and cap and went to the front steps. The Germans were sitting all over the place talking to the patients, showing them photos and

fetching them water. It was a lovely morning and the Golden Ori-
ole was singing in the big oak tree in the park. There was peace at
last. What a relief! I felt very enamoured [with] the Germans that
day. Apparently Forsyth had been up near the front gate and seen
them walking aimlessly in with their rifles slung. Helmut was a
great help in the first ten minutes and did a lot to help us I think.
It was a great relief to feel at last one could get down to work
without running for shelter, . . . that the patients need not be
moved every hour to try to get them out of the shellfire, and that
the German aeroplanes were now 'friendly'.

   That day we were left almost entirely alone. They seemed to
take an interest in our food [however], so we quickly got some of
it stowed away in the cellars. They had a great liking for our tinned
fruit and milk, and demanded most of it. Gaze went down [to the
well] with a German guard and drew water, and tried his German
to great advantage. The patients were in an appalling state, especially in the ambulances. So we got everyone out of the ambulances
and put them all on the grass where they could at least [breathe] . . .
some fresh air. The house itself was very, very smelly, overcrowded
and in a shocking state. The burnt cases all seemed to be going off
their heads and were really in a deplorable state. I think some of
the Germans felt that war was an awful thing when they saw
them.

   That day we had regular meals for a change . . . It was a great
treat. The German field battery came and shared the park with us,
and showed us some really fine horses. I showed the German officer round the park, while he strutted round on a horse, of which
he was very proud. The Germans brought round some soup to the
men in the evening, which was greatly appreciated. Soon the
patients began to appeal to the Germans rather than our own
orderlies. We had a good night's sleep that night and life seemed
almost worth living.

Postscript

Stopping the German Tanks

Some people still believe that Hitler stopped his all-conquering tanks on 24 May 1940 (the famous halt order, see p. 246), because he wanted the British Army to escape from Dunkirk. According to this theory, Hitler preferred to enter into peace negotiations with the British Government on more or less equal terms rather than to force his terms down the throat of a vanquished country. The following extracts from the German Army Group A war diary however suggest that the tanks were halted on military grounds rather than because of Hitler's secret unvoiced desire to reach an agreement with Britain.[8] The same applies to the less well-known halt two days earlier. Arguably, the common reason behind both halts was the success of the British tanks' counter-attack near Arras on 21 May 1940; it had shown the German high command what could happen if they attacked recklessly without first consolidating their victorious advance. It seems there was a realization by at least some of the German military commanders that they might throw everything away if they did not ensure the tanks only advanced after the infantry had caught up with them. Little did they know that the British armour had shot its bolt, and that if they had carried on with their tanks immediately, total victory would almost certainly have been theirs for the taking.

Halting the tanks after the British counter-attack near Arras

After the British 21 May 1940 tank attack near Arras threatened to break through the German lines, Army Group A's war diary reported:

22 May 1940
0130 Telephone call from Colonel Schmundt, on General Staff, the Führer's adjutant for the Armed Forces: The Führer wants to

know about the situation at Arras. The enemy had attacked in strength and attempted to break through to the south of Arras. They had succeeded in pushing back the 7th Panzer Division at a limited number of points. Eventually the thrust was stopped . . .

The Commander-in-Chief of 4 Army [Colonel-General von Kluge] asks for a decision as to whether Group von Kleist (the tanks in XIX and XLI Panzer Corps) is to be launched against Boulogne and Calais as ordered by the Supreme Commander of the Land Forces on 21 May, or whether they should await clarification of the situation at Arras.

The Commander-in-Chief of Army Group (A, Colonel-General Gerd von Rundstedt) decides that the situation at Arras must be cleared up, and only then should the Group von Kleist push on to Calais and Boulogne.

At 0900 Colonel-General Keitel (from the Supreme Command of the Armed Forces HQ) arrives. He brings with him the directions of the Führer which had been transmitted by telephone during the night, and finds out what measures have been taken by the Army Group Command. After his return to the Supreme Command of the Armed Forces HQ, . . . Keitel . . . telephoned to say that the Führer was in full agreement with the measures [already] taken by . . . von Rundstedt. He added that the Führer had special confidence in . . . von Rundstedt and that he had again and again expressed his satisfaction concerning the leadership of Army Group A.

Hitler's famous halt order

The following extract from the 24 May 1940 entry in the Army Group A war diary appears to suggest that von Rundstedt had already decided that the tanks should not attack towards the North on that day before Hitler confirmed he agreed. However, it would be misleading not to mention that what is written in the war diary is ambiguous. Was Hitler just rubber-stamping von Rundstedt's decision, or was von Rundstedt persuaded by Hitler? Even if Hitler did not explicitly specify what he wanted to happen prior to von Rundstedt making up his mind, it is possible that von Rundstedt was ingratiating himself with his leader whose risk averse views concerning the tanks' advances he already appreciated.

Hitler had already made these views known in the course of approving the earlier 16 May halt order (see p. 125).

The same cannot be said of the Army Group A war diary entries for 25 and 26 May which are also laid out below. They clearly give the impression that the decision to continue the halt order until 26 May was for military reasons alone. However, even that does not settle the controversy once and for all. The written documents do not disclose whether von Rundstedt only decided what should be done after Hitler persuaded him in the course of conversations not recorded in the war diary.

The fact that General Franz Halder, the German Army's Chief of Staff, clearly believed that there was no valid military reason for not permitting the tanks to advance immediately certainly makes one wonder how von Rundstedt could have come to such a different conclusion about what was feasible. Halder's diary entry for 24 May contained the sceptical words: 'So the left wing consisting of tanks and motorized forces, which has no enemy in front of it, is being stopped in its tracks upon direct orders of the Führer!' His diary entry for 25 May is even more explicit: 'Political command has formed the fixed idea that the crucial battle should not be fought on Flemish soil, but should rather take place in Northern France. To camouflage this political move, the assertion is made that Flanders, criss-crossed by lots of waterways, is not suitable for tank warfare.' Such comments will encourage conspiracy theorists to carry on arguing, rightly or wrongly, that von Rundstedt would have reached another decision if purely military considerations had been taken into account.

24 May 1940

. . . At 11.30 the Führer arrives and has . . . [von Rundstedt] fill him in on the situation. He fully agrees with the opinion that . . . the quick troops (tanks) can be halted on the line which has been reached, i.e. Lens-Béthune-Aire-St Omer-Gravelines, in order to hold up the enemy who are being hard pressed by Army Group B [which is attacking from the North and East]. He emphasizes that there is a need to preserve the armoured forces for the coming operations and that a further tightening of the encircled space would merely result in a most unwelcome curtailment of the German air force.

At 12.45 orders based on the above are issued to 4 Army . . .

25 May 1940

At 00.45 new orders are received by telephone from the Supreme
Command of the Land Forces . . . permitting Group von Kleist
(tanks) to cross the canal line in connection with the continuation
of the offensive on 25 May. [However] this order is not passed on
to 4 Army. [Von Rundstedt] . . . having been particularly asked by
the Führer to determine the line of action for 4 Army, considers
that as a matter of urgency the motorized groups should be
allowed to close up within their own units . . . Also there is not
enough time to reach an agreement with the German air force,
which would have to be arranged if the canal line were crossed . . .

At 12.35 the Führer's command, which has been transmitted once
more by telephone, states that the canal is not to be crossed, that the
tanks must be preserved, and that Boulogne and Calais should be
attacked only if it seems that there will not be large tank losses . . .

26 May

It appears quite possible that the enemy group south of the
Somme is to push forward to the North-East or North, and that
it is to co-operate with the enemy's northern groups. Whilst there
is no serious danger, the grouping of our forces being as it is, there
nevertheless arises the need to bring the fighting in Northern
France to a conclusion as quickly as possible, thereby gaining freedom of action in the South.

In connection with the above, we should work out whether it
is still necessary to restrain the quick troops (tanks) . . . The Army
Group command believes that an advance beyond the line Bét-
hune-St Omer-Gravelines would be sensible.

These deliberations finally persuade the Führer to allow Group
von Kleist to advance.

1. Hastings's Report (see end notes for Chapter 21).
2. Hallett's Report (see end notes for Chapter 21).
3. *Report on Battle of La Bassee Canal – 24th–28th May 1940,* based on reports by officers
   in *Oflag* V1/B, a German camp for prisoners of war, describes this action.
4. Based on accounts supplied by Major Claud Rebbeck of the Gloucestershire
   Regiment, Roy Creswell and his daughter Sheila.

5. This extract which was given to me by Francis Waldron is printed here following his death thanks to permission from his children Alexandra, Brind and Rosemary, and technical assistance from his son-in-law John.

6. Based on memoirs supplied by the Gloucestershire Regiment's Major Claud Rebbeck and Julian Fane. The extracts are printed here following Julian Fane's death with the agreement of Diana, his widow, and his children Diney, Alexandra, Andrew and Anthony.

7. This extract is published with the agreement of Philip Newman's children Tony and Penny. This 75th Anniversary edition was conceived after the death of his other son Richard who brought the account to my attention before the publication of this book's 1st edition.

8. Based on translation of Army Group A War Diary, IWM Foreign Documents, AL1428.

Bibliography and Sources

Where there is no declared author of a particular document or book, the following procedure is adhered to in this section: if the document or book has been referred to in the Notes using an abbreviated definition, this definition has been placed in inverted commas in front of the full title in the following lists; if no abbreviated definition has been used, the document's or book's full title has been printed without any other details. Documents or books whose titles begin with a number are listed before those whose titles begin with a letter of the alphabet, and when determining where a document or book is placed, the word 'The' has been ignored.

Select List of Published Books

If in the Notes I have specified page numbers from an edition of a book with different pagination from that in the book's original hardback edition, I have in this list of books mentioned the details applicable to the original hardback edition followed by square brackets containing the details of the edition I have used in the Notes.

The 10th Royal Hussars In The Second World War, compiled under the direction of a regimental committee, Aldershot, 1948

Adair, Major-General Sir Allan: see Lindsay, Oliver

Aitken, Leslie, *Massacre On The Road To Dunkirk: Wormhout 1940*, London, 1977

Amersfoort, H., and Kamphuis, P. H. (eds), *Je Maintiendrai: A Concise History of the Dutch Army*, The Hague, 1985

Astier de la Vigerie, Général François d', *Le Ciel N'Était Pas Vide: 1940*, Paris, 1952

Barclay, Brigadier C. N., *The History of the Cameronians (Scottish Rifles), Volume 3, 1933–1946*, London, 1947

The History of the Royal Northumberland Fusiliers In The Second World War, Britain, 1952

(ed.), *The History Of The Duke Of Wellington's Regiment 1919–1952*, Britain, 1953

Barker, A. J., *Dunkirk: The Great Escape*, London, 1977

Baudouin, Paul, *Neuf Mois au Gouvernement (Avril–Décembre 1940)*, Paris, 1948 [*The Private Diaries (March 1940 to January 1941) of Paul Baudouin*, London, 1948]

Beaucorps, Jean-Marie de, *Soldat De Plomb*, Paris, 1997

Beaufre, Général André, *Le Drame de 1940*, Paris, 1965

Beddington, Major-General W. R., *A History Of The Queen's Bays (The 2nd Dragoon Guards) 1929–45*, England, 1954

Berben, Paul, and Iselin, Bernard, *Les Panzers Passent la Meuse (13 May 1940)*, France, 1967 [J'ai Lu, paperback edition, undated]

Blacow, Norman W. (ed.), *Martindale: The Extra Pharmacopoeia*, 32nd edition, London, 2005

Blaxland, Gregory, *Destination Dunkirk: The story of Gort's army*, London, 1973

Bollmann, Albert, and Flörke, Hermann, *Das Infanterie-Regiment 12 (3. Folge von 1933–1945): Sein Kriegsschicksal im Verbande der 31. (Löwen-) Division*, Göttingen, 1975

Bond, Brian, *British Military Policy Between the Two World Wars*, Oxford, 1980

⸻ (ed.), *Chief of Staff: The Diaries of Lieutenant-General Sir Henry Pownall, Volume 1, 1933–1940*, London, 1972

Bond, Brian, and Taylor, Michael (eds), *The Battle for France and Flanders 1940 Sixty Years On*, Britain, 2001

Bouver, Roman de, *2000 Duitse Soldaten Op Het Ehrenfriedhof Van Deinze En Vinkt*, Deinze, 2000

Brereton, J. M., and Savory, A. C. S., *The History of the Duke of Wellington's Regiment (West Riding) 1702–1992*, Huddersfield, 1993

Bullitt, Orville H. (ed.), *For The President: Personal and Secret: Correspondence Between Franklin D. Roosevelt and William C. Bullitt*, London, 1973

'Cameron Highlanders' Historical Records': *Historical Records of the Queen's Own Cameron Highlanders 1932–1948: Second World War: Volume 1*, no named author, Britain, 1952

Chaplin, Colonel H. D., *The Queen's Own Royal West Kent Regiment 1920–1950*, London, 1954

Churchill, Winston, *The Second World War, Volume 2*, London, 1949

Close, Major Bill, *View From The Turret: A History Of The 3rd Royal Tank Regiment In The Second World War*, Tewkesbury, Gloucestershire, 1998

Colville, J. R., *Man of Valour: The Life of Field-Marshal The Viscount Gort V.C.*, London, 1972

Cooksey, Jon, *Calais: A Fight To The Finish – May 1940*, Britain, 2000

⸻ *Boulogne: 20 Guards Brigade's Fighting Defence – May 1940*, Britain, 2002

Courage, Major G., *The History Of 15/19 The King's Royal Hussars 1939–1945*, Aldershot, 1949

Crabb, Brian James, *The Forgotten Tragedy: The Story of The Sinking Of HMT Lancastria*, Donnington, Lincolnshire, 2002

Cras, Hervé, *Jaguar Chacal Léopard: La Deuxième Division de Contre-Torpilleurs A Dunkerque*, Paris, 1942

Cunliffe, Marcus, *History of the Royal Warwickshire Regiment 1919–1955*, London, 1956

David, Saul, *Churchill's Sacrifice of the Highland Division: France 1940*, London, 1994

Davies-Scourfield, Grismund, *In The Presence of My Foes*, Britain, 1991

Davignon, Vicomte Jacques, *Berlin 1936–1940: Souvenirs d'une Mission*, Paris and Brussels, 1951

Doughty, Robert Allan, *The Breaking Point: Sedan and the Fall of France, 1940*, Connecticut, USA, 1990

Ellis, Major L. F., *Welsh Guards At War*, Aldershot, 1946

⸻ *The War In France and Flanders 1939–1940*, London, 1953

Enquêtecommissie Regeringsbeleid 1940–1945, *Enquêtecommissie Regeringsbeleid 1940–1945, Verslag houdende de uitkomsten van het onderzoek, Deel 1c, Algemene Inleiding/Militair Beleid 1939–1940, Verhoren* (Investigating Committee 1940–1945: *Report on the outcome of the enquiry, Volume 1c: General Introduction/Military Policy 1939–40: Interrogations*), The Hague, Holland, 1949

Fenby, Jonathan, *The Sinking of the Lancastria: Britain's Greatest Maritime Disaster and Churchill's Cover-Up*, London, 2005

Fire and Movement, a Royal Armoured Corps Tank Museum publication, Bovington Camp, Dorset, 1975

Fitzgerald, Major D. J. L., *History of the Irish Guards In The Second World War*, Britain, 1949

Forbes, Patrick, *The Grenadier Guards In The War Of 1939–1945, Volume 1: The Campaigns in North-West Europe*, Aldershot, 1949

Foster, Major R. C. G., *History of The Queen's Royal Regiment, Volume VIII: 1924–1948*, Aldershot, 1953

Franklyn, Sir Harold E., *The Story Of One Green Howard In The Dunkirk Campaign*, Richmond, Yorkshire, 1966

Franks, Norman, *Valiant Wings: The Battle and Blenheim Squadrons over France 1940*, Britain, 1988

Frieser, Karl-Heinz, *Blitzkrieg-Legende: Der Westfeldzug 1940*, Munich, 1995 [*Le Mythe de la guerre-éclair: La campagne de l'Ouest de 1940*, Paris, 2003]

Gamelin, Général Maurice, *Servir: La Guerre (Septembre 1939–19 Mai 1940), Volume 3*, Paris, 1947

Gardner, W. J. R. (ed.), *The Evacuation From Dunkirk: Operation Dynamo 26 May–4 June 1940*, London, 2000

Gates, Major L. C., *The History of The Tenth Foot 1919–1950*, Aldershot, 1953

Gough, Brigadier Guy, *Thirty Days To Dunkirk*, Wrexham, Clywd, 1990

Grandsard, Général Charles, *Le 10e Corps D'Armée Dans La Bataille: 1939–1940*, Paris, 1949

Grattidge, Harry, *Captain Of The Queens*, London, 1956

Graves, Charles, *The Royal Ulster Rifles, Volume III*, England, 1950

Guderian, Heinz, *Panzer Leader*, USA, 1952 [London, 2000]

Guttery, D. R., *The Queen's Own Worcestershire Hussars 1922–1956*, Stourbridge, Worcestershire, 1958

Halder, Diaries: see Lissance, Arnold

Harding, William, *A Cockney Soldier: Duty Before Pleasure: an autobiography 1918–46*, Britain, 1989

Hart, Peter, *At The Sharp End: From Le Paradis to Kohima: 2nd Battalion The Royal Norfolk Regiment*, Britain, 1998

Harvey, Richard, *Yeoman Soldier Prussian Farmer: an autobiography of the war years*, Yorkshire, 1981

Horne, Alistair, *To Lose a Battle: France 1940*, London, 1969 [paperback, London, 1990]

Horsfall, John, *Say Not the Struggle*, Kineton, Warwickshire, 1977

Howard, Michael, and Sparrow, John, *The Coldstream Guards 1920–1946*, London, 1951

Ironside, Diaries: see Macleod and Kelly

Ismay, Lord, *The Memoirs of General The Lord Ismay*, London, 1960

Jacobsen, Hans-Adolf, *Dünkirchen*, Germany, 1958

Jervois, Brigadier W. J., *The History of the Northamptonshire Regiment 1934–1948*, Britain, 1953

Jolly, Cyril, *The Vengeance of Private Pooley*, London, 1956

Jong, Dr L. de, *Het Koninkrijk der Nederlanden in de Tweede Wereldoorlog 1939–1945, Deel 2, Neutraal*, The Hague, 1969

Keyes, Roger, *Outrageous Fortune: The Tragedy of Leopold III of the Belgians 1901–1941*, London, 1984 [*Outrageous Fortune: King Leopold III Of The Belgians: Volume I 1901–1940: The Scapegoat Who Saved The British From Defeat In 1940*, London, 1990]

Knight, Colonel C. R. B., *Historical Record of the Buffs (Royal East Kent Regiment) 3rd Foot 1919–1948*, London, 1951

Ladd, James, *The Royal Marines 1919–1980*, London, 1980

Lang, General Sir Derek, *Return To St Valery: The story of an escape through wartime France and Syria*, London, 1989

Langley, Lieutenant-Colonel Jimmy, *Fight Another Day*, London, 1974

La Laurencie, Général Benoit de Fornel de, *Les Opérations Du IIIe Corps D'Armée En 1939–1940*, Paris, 1948

Lewis, Major P. J., and English, Major I. R., *The 8th Battalion: The Durham Light Infantry 1939–1945*, Newcastle, 1949

Lhoest, Jean-Louis, *Les Paras Allemands Au Canal Albert: Mai 1940*, Paris, 1964

Liddell Hart, B. H., *The Other Side Of The Hill: Germany's Generals, their rise and fall, with their own account of military events, 1939–1945*, London, 1948 [paperback, London, 1999]

    The Tanks: The History of the Royal Tank Regiment and its predecessors Heavy Branch Machine-gun corps Tank Corps and Royal Tank Corps 1914–1945, Volume 2, 1939–1945, London, 1969

    (ed.), *The Rommel Papers*, London, 1953

Lindsay, Oliver (ed.), *A Guards' General: The Memoirs of Major General Sir Allan Adair*, London, 1986

Linklater, Eric, *The Highland Division*, London, 1942

Lissance, Arnold (ed.), *The Halder Diaries: The Private War Journals of Colonel General Franz Halder*, USA, 1976

Lombard-Hobson, Sam, *A Sailor's War*, London, 1983

Lyet, Pierre, *La Bataille De France: Mai-Juin 1940*, Paris, 1947

MacDonald, Gregor, *A Cameron Never Can Yield: A Prisoner of War's Escape from Germany to Gibraltar*, Inverness, 1999

Macleod, Colonel Roderick, and Kelly, Denis (eds.), *The Ironside Diaries: 1937–1940*, London, 1962

Manstein, Field-Marshal Erich von, *Verloren Siege*, Bonn, 1955 [*Lost Victories*, USA, 1994]

Marshall-Cornwall, Lieutenant-General James, *Wars And Rumours Of Wars: A Memoir*, London, 1984

Martineau, G. D., *A History Of The Royal Sussex Regiment: A History Of The Old Belfast Regiment And The Regiment Of Sussex 1701–1953*, Chichester, 1953

Michem, Frans, *Vinkt in mei 1940*, Vinkt, Belgium 1968 [*Vinkt 1940*, Belgium, 1977]

Miller, Major-General Charles H., *History of the 13th/18th Royal Hussars (Queen Mary's Own) 1922–1947*, London, 1949

Mills, Brigadier Giles, and Nixon, Lieutenant-Colonel Roger, *The Annals of the King's Royal Rifle Corps, Volume VI, 1921–1941*, London, 1971

Minart, Jacques, *P. C. Vincennes: Secteur 4 Volume 2*, Paris, 1945

Mit Den Panzern In Ost Und West, Berlin, 1942

Montgomery, Brian, *A Field-Marshal in the Family*, London, 1973

Moore, Lieutenant-Commander Robert J., *A Hard Fought Ship: The Story of HMS Venomous*, Loughborough, Leicestershire, 1990

Morgan, Thelma, and Vanderbilt, Gloria, *Double Exposure*, London, 1959

Moses, Harry, *The Faithful Sixth: A History of the Sixth Battalion, the Durham Light Infantry*, Durham, 1995

Mrazek, Colonel James E., *The Fall Of Eben Emael: Prelude To Dunkerque*, USA, 1970

Muir, Augustus, *The First of Foot*, Britain, 1961

Neave, Airey, *The Flames of Calais: A Soldiers' Battle 1940*, London, 1972

Neville, Lieutenant-Colonel J. E. H. (ed.), *The Oxfordshire and Buckinghamshire Light Infantry Chronicle: Volume 1: September 1939–June 1940: The Record of the 43rd, 52nd, 4th, 5th and 1st Buckinghamshire Battalions in the Second German War*, Britain, 1949

Nicolson, Nigel, *Alex: The Life of Field Marshal Earl Alexander of Tunis*, London, 1973

Overstraeten, Général Raoul Van, *Albert I–Leopold III: Vingt Ans De Politique Militaire Belge 1920–1940*, Bruges, n.d.

Paillat, Claude, *Dossiers secrets de la France contemporaine: Tome V: Le Désastre de 1940: La Guerre éclair: 10 mai–24 juin 1940*, Paris, 1985

Parkyn, Major H. G. (ed.), *The Rifle Brigade Chronicle 1945*, Britain, 1946

Perrett, Bryan, *Armour In Action: The Matilda*, London, 1973

Pimlott, Ben (ed.), *The Second World War Diary of Hugh Dalton 1940–5*, London, 1986

Plato, Anton von, *Die Geschichte Der 5. Panzerdivision 1938 bis 1945*, Germany, 1978

Pownall, Diaries: see Bond, Brian

Prioux, Général René, *Souvenirs De Guerre, 1939–1943*, France, 1947

Quilter, D. C. (ed.), *No Dishonourable Name*, London, 1947

Reynaud, Paul, *Au Coeur de la Mêlée 1930–1945*, Paris, 1951 [*In The Thick Of The Fight, 1930–1945*, London, 1955]

Richards, Denis, *Royal Air Force 1939–45: Volume 1: The Fight At Odds*, London, 1974

Rissik, David, *The DLI At War: The History of the Durham Light Infantry 1939–1945*, Britain, 1952

Roberts, Andrew, *'The Holy Fox': The Life of Lord Halifax*, London, 1991 [paperback, London, 1997]

Rommel Papers: see Liddell Hart, B. H.

Rommelaere, Guy, *Le massacre oublié*, France, 2000 [*May 1940 In Flanders: Esquelbecq, Wormhout, Ledringhem: The forgotten massacre*, Britain, 2001]

Roton, Général G., *Années Cruciales: La Course Aux Armements (1933–1939), La Campagne (1939–1940)*, Paris, 1947

Ruby, Général Edmond, *Sedan: Terre D'Épreuve: Avec La IIe Armée Mai–Juin 1940*, Paris, 1948

Saint-Martin, Gérard, *L'Arme Blindée Française: Tome 1: Mai-juin 1940! Les blindés français dans la tourmente*, Paris, 1998

Sarkar, Dilip, *Guards VC: Blitzkrieg 1940*, Worcester, 1999

Schick, Albert, *Die Zehnte P.D.: Die Geschichte der 10. Panzer-Division 1939–1943*, Germany, 1943

Scott, Anthony, Packer, Cole, and Groves, J., *Record of a Reconnaissance Regiment: A History of the 43rd Reconnaissance Regiment (the Gloucestershire Regiment) 1939–1945*, Bristol, 1949

Scott, Peter, *The Eye Of The Wind*, London, 1961 [revised hardback, London, 1977]

Simpson, Bill, *One of Our Pilots Is Safe*, London, 1942

Spears, Major-General Sir Edward, *Prelude to Dunkirk and The Fall of France*, London, 1954 [*Assignment To Catastrophe*, London, 1956]

Stewart, Captain P. F., *The History of the XII Royal Lancers (Prince of Wales's)*, London, 1950

Taghon, Peter, *Mai 40*, Belgium, 1989 [Belgium, 2000]

Touzin, Pierre, *Les Véhicules Blindés Français 1920–1944*, France, 1979

Vanwelkenhuyzen, Jean, *Les avertissements qui venaient de Berlin: 9 octobre 1939–10 mai 1940*, Paris and Brussels, 1982

    1940: Pleins feux sur un désastre, Brussels, 1995

('Vinkt War Crimes Commission Report'): *Les Crimes De Guerre: commis lors de l'invasion du territoire national Mai 1940: Les Massacres De Vinkt*, compiled by Royaume de Belgique Ministère de la Justice, Commission des Crimes de Guerre, Liège, 1948

West, John L. (ed.), *The Loss Of 'Lancastria'*, Rossendale, Lancashire, 1988

Weygand, Général Maxime, *Mémoires: Rappelé Au Service*, Paris, 1952 [*Recalled To Service: The Memoirs of General Maxime Weygand Of The Académie Française*, London, 1952]

White B. T., *British Tanks and Fighting Vehicles 1914–1945*, Shepperton, 1970

Wilson, Patrick, *Dunkirk: From Disaster To Deliverance*, Britain, 1999

Select List of Other Sources: Documents, Reports, Accounts, Articles and Interviews

The following list does not include those documents, reports, accounts and interviews specified in the Notes that have not been given an abbreviated title.

The abbreviated title used in the Notes for each item in the following list has been placed in square brackets beside the full title of the item in question.

British, French and German war diaries whose titles have been abbreviated, as mentioned above, have been placed in separate sections.

Books mentioned in Published Books above are marked★.

['1940 Campaign History'], a history of the 1940 campaign, in NA/PRO CAB 106/222

Abrial, Admiral Jean, account in SHM 1BB2 207 ['Abrial's Report']

Alexander, Major-General Hon. H. R. L. G., 'Report by Major-General Hon.

H. R. L. G. Alexander on the operations of 1st Corps BEF from 1200 31st May till midnight 2/3 June 1940', in NA/PRO WO 167/124 ['Alexander's Report']

Allan, Major Alexander, report in NA/PRO WO 217/3, and another report in Major H. G. Parkyn (ed.), *The Rifle Brigade Chronicle 1945*,★ pp. 50–71 [together referred to as 'Allan's Reports']

Allen, Lieutenant-Colonel E. H., report in NA/PRO WO 217/28 ['Allen's Report']

Ambrosius, Hauptmann Lothar, 'Der Schelde-Übergang des II./I.R. 12 am 21. Mai 1940', in Bollmann, Albert, and Flörke, Hermann, *Das Infanterie-Regiment 12 (3. Folge von 1933–1945): Sein Kriegsschicksar im Verbande der 31. (Lowen-Division)*★ ['Ambrosius' Report']

Andrieu, Lieutenant-Colonel Joseph, my 2003 interview with him '[Andrieu Interview']

Archdale, O. A., account in IWM Documents 78/52/1 ['Archdale's Report']

Arnoul, Chef de Bataillon, in SHAT 34N174 ['Arnoul's Report']

Arrigo, John, my 2003 interview with him ['Arrigo Interview']

Baggs, C. H., report in IWM Documents 94/49/1 ['Baggs's Report']

Barclay, Brigadier C. N., 'The Action of the 2nd Cameronians (Scottish Rifles) on the 27th May', *Covenanter*, July 1957, pp. 27–8 ['Barclay's Report']

Barthélemy, Général Robert, report in SHAT 33N4 ['Barthélemy's Report']

Beeley, John, report, held by him ['Beeley's Report']

Behr, Rudolf, account 'Dann Ist Uns Der Panzer Ein Eisernes Grab' ['Behr's Report'], in *Mit Den Panzern In Ost Und West*★

Bergen, Édouard Van den, note to the Minister of Defence, dated 21 January 1940, in Carton A Farde 2 CIV, in CDH ['Van den Bergen's Report']

Blanchard's Report: see French War Diaries, Army Group section below

Bougrain, Général Gabriel, '2e Division Légère Mécanique: Relation par le Général Bougrain, Commandant De Cette Grande Unité Au Cours De La Campagne 1939–1940' ['Bougrain's Report'], in SHAT 32N494 Dossier 4

Bourgeois, Henri, 'The Battle Of The Ypres–Comines Canal 1940', held by his family [the 'Bourgeois Report']

Bridgeman, Lord, account held by his family ['Bridgeman's Report']

Brooke, General Alan, 'Notes On My Life Volume 3', in LHC, Alanbrooke 5/2/15 ['Alan Brooke, Notes']

Brownrigg, General Sir Douglas, report, in NA/PRO CAB 106/243 ['Brownrigg's Report']

Buisseret, Major Léon, account, dated 15 March 1946, in A Farde 2 CV, in CDH ['Buisseret's Report']

Callander, Lieutenant Donald, taped interview in IWM Sound Archive 7166 ['Callander's Tape']

Cardes, Colonel de, report, in SHAT 27N188 ['Cardes' Report']

Carmichael, Tom, 'Active Service Diary 1940', held by him ['Carmichael's Diary']

Claeys, Marcel, his 20 June 1945 statement ['Claeys' Statement'] to the Vinkt War Crimes Commission

Clarke, Len, my interview with him ['Len Clarke Interview']

['Clay's Obituary']: The Queen's Own Royal West Kent's Lieutenant-Colonel B. L. Clay's obituary in the December 1981 regimental newsletter

Clifton, Brigadier A. J., 'Report On Operation In Vicinity of Nieuport 28–30 May 1940', in NA/PRO WO 197/119 ['Clifton's Report']

Cole, Eric, 'The Hell Where Youth and Laughter Go', held by the Welsh Guards ['Cole's Report']

Colvin, Major Rupert, account ['Colvin's Report'], appears in Forbes, *Grenadier Guards In The War Of 1939–1945, Volume 1: The Campaigns in North-West Europe*, Aldershot, 1949★

Craemer, Léonard, report dated 19 April 1945 ['Craemer's Report'], Albert Canal Bridges file, in CDH

Crousse, Commandant, report, in SHAT 34N145 ['Crousse's Report']

Curry, Frank, his unpublished account 'Escape From Dunkirk' ['Curry's Reports'], as told to Raymond Walsh, held by Curry, and my 2001 interviews with him

Daley, Charlie, statement ['Daley's Report'], in Appendix C of the Wormhout Massacre Report (mentioned below)

Dann, Lieutenant A., report ['Dann's Report'], in NA/PRO ADM 199/788

Daumont, Capitaine, 'Replis Successifs de l'Artillerie Durant Les Journées des 13 et 14 Mai 1940' ['Daumont's Report'], in SHAT 32N295

Dean, Lieutenant-Colonel Donald, 'Notes On Lt Colonel D. J. Dean's Experiences in Late 1939 and Early 1940 with the Auxiliary Military Pioneer Corps' ['Dean's Report'], held in Lieutenant Colonel John Starling's private archive, which he maintains on behalf of the Royal Pioneer Corps Association

Delilis, Marcel, report ['Delilis' Report'], in SHM TTE10

Drescher, Hauptmann, account ['Drescher's Report'], in BA-MA RH20–18/37

Drinkwater, Les, article, 'Reminiscences' ['Drinkwater's Report'], in *Grenadier Gazette*, issue 5, 1982, pp. 32–4

Duffet, Général Camille, '18 D.I.: Campagne de 1939–40' ['Duffet's Report'], in SHAT 32N99

Duhautois, L., report ['Duhautois' Report'], in SHAT 30N82

Dunoyer, Général, report ['Dunoyer's Report'], in SHAT 32N15

['Dutfoy's Appeal'], the 5 September 1947 report, in SHM TTE6, given on behalf of the Ministre de la Marine to Monsieur le Garde des Sceaux, Ministre de la Justice Maritime (Direction des Affaires Criminelles) in connection with the judicial procedure at the Service Central de la Justice Maritime

['Eben-Emael Report']: 'Rapport sur la défense du fort d'Eben-Emael en mai 1940', written by the Commission Militaire Centrale Commission des Forts, in CDH, Eben-Emael file

Edwards, Mr, report, dated 27 May 1940 ['Edwards's Report'], in NA/PRO MT40/36

Evans, Major-General Roger, report ['Evans's Report'], held by his son

Evitts, Austin, 'Calais 1940 Remembered', *Journal of the Royal Signals Institution*, Winter 1971, Volume X, No. 3 ['Evitts, Calais 1940']. A copy can be found in LHC, Wright LW1/2

Fagalde, Général Robert, 'Notes du Général Fagalde: Commandant le XVIème C.A. sur les agissements anglais à Dunkerque, en mai et juin 1940' ['Fagalde's Report'], in SHAT T604 and ANP 3W 289

Faivre, Dominique, 'Robecq-Saint-Venant et la région: De la drôle de guerre aux combats de mai 1940', a copy of which is held by Sinnett/RWF

Fane, Julian, my interviews with him and two reports. One is held by the Soldiers of Gloucestershire Museum, Gloucester, and the other by him ['Fane's Reports']

Fenton, Jess, my 2004 interview with him ['Fenton Interview']

Flavigny, Général Robert, 'Journal de Marche de la 21ième Corps' ['Flavigny's Report']

Foque, Capitaine, report ['Foque's Report'], in SHAT 34N130

Foucault, Captain, report ['Foucault's Report'], in SHAT 34N178

Fox-Pitt, Brigadier Billy, transcript of interview in IWM Sound Archive 7038 ['Fox-Pitt's Transcript']

Franklyn, General, account ['Franklyn's Report'], held by the Green Howards

Gamber, Claude ['Gamber's Report'], in SHAT 34N130

Garretts, A., account ['Garretts's Statement'], held by Lancastria Association

Gartlan, Brigadier G. I. report ['Gartlan's Report'], in NA/PRO WO 167/354

Gawthorpe, Brigadier J. B., '137 Infantry Brigade: A Formation of the TA in the First Year of the War, 1939/40' ['Gawthorpe's Report']

Georges, General Alphonse, 'Journal du Cabinet' ['Georges' Journal'], in SHAT27N148

Gilmore, Lieutenant-Colonel George, 'The Story of an Eventful Month, May 1940' [Cameronians/Gilmore Report], *Covenanter*, November 1957, pp. 78–9, and January 1958, pp. 104–6

Gilmore, Lieutenant-Colonel Maurice, account ['Glosters/Gilmore Report'], held by his son

Gort, Lord, Despatches in Supplement To *The London Gazette* Of Friday, the 10th of October, 1941, published on 17 October 1941 ['Gort, Despatches']

Gouvello, Commandant, report ['Gouvello's Report'], in SHAT 32N99

Grandsard, Général Charles, account ['Grandsard's Report'], in SHAT 30N82

Granlund, Henry, report ['Granlund's Report'], in IWM Documents 84/45/1

Grant, Major Murray, Personal Diary, ['Grant's Diary']

Griffin, George, '1st Battalion Welsh Guards At Arras – May 1940' ['Griffin's Report']

Hallett, Captain Nick, 'A Diary of the Blitzkrieg and After: May 1940' ['Hallett's Report'], made available by his daughter

Hanbury, Peter, 'A Not Very Military Experience' ['Hanbury's Report'], held by him

Harding, William, taped interview ['Harding's Tape'], in IWM Sound Archive 6323

Harris, Don, account ['Harris's Report'], in IWM Documents under 87/15/1

Hastings, Captain R. J., 'Recollections of the Blitz' ['Hastings's Report']

Hautecler, Capitaine-Commandant Georges, 'Défense et sautage du pont d'Yvoir', *L'Armée et La Nation*, May 1959 ['Hautecler's Yvoir Article']

Hauting, Captain L. C., 'Diary of Captain L. C. Hauting Adjt. 5 Glosters: 13–30 May 1940' ['Hauting's Report'], held by his daughter

Hoenmanns, Erich, his 29 October 1943 statement, in the Reichskriegsgericht files held by the Historicky Ustav Armady Ceske Republiky in Prague, Czech Republic, and the account held by his wife and son ['Hoenmanns' Statements']

Hopkinson, Major John, 'D Company, 4th Battalion: In France, May and June 1940' ['Hopkinson's Report'], held by his son

Humbert, Colonel, note describing events on 28 May in Annex 11 to Blanchard's Report (see French War Diaries below) ['Humbert's Report'], in SHAT 1K130

Jerram, Edward, account, 'Diary of Edward J. Jerram, Captain, The Royal Warwickshire Regiment: Commanding B Coy' ['Jerram's Report'], held by his son

Jodl, General Alfred, diary [Jodl's Diary], translation, in IWM Foreign Documents, AL 977/2/2 and AL 977/3/1

Jones, Captain E., report [the 'Glosters/Jones Report'], in NA/PRO CAB 106/292

Jottrand, Major Jean, 'Souvenirs Personnels' ['Jottrand Souvenirs'], in CDH

Keller, Lieutenant-Colonel Reginald: three of his four reports ['Keller's Reports'] are to be found in the Tank Museum, Bovington, and the fourth is in NA/PRO CAB 106/233

Keyes, Admiral of the Fleet Sir Roger, 'Diary of Belgian Campaign', made available by the second Lord Keyes ['Keyes, Diary']

King, John, 25 November 1943 account ['King's Report'], in the Tank Museum, Bovington

Kissack, Major Harry, report, 'D Company: Report of Action in Belgium: May 1940' ['Kissack's Report'], held by his grandson

['Koch Report']: Storm Group Koch war diary, in BA-MA RL33/97

La Barbarie, Chef d'Escadron, 'Historique' ['La Barbarie's Report'], in SHAT 32N251

Labarthe, Lieutenant-Colonel Pierre, 'Déroulement des Événements' ['Labarthe's Report'], in SHAT 34N165

Lanquetot, Général Pierre, documents ['Lanquetot Documents'], in SHAT 1K678

Lehr, Commandant René, 'Historique Du 16ème Corps d'Armée Rédigé En Décembre 1940' ['Lehr's Report'], in SHAT 30N179

Libaud, Général Emmanuel, 'Extrait du Rapport' ['Libaud's Report'], in SHAT 30N247

Long, Captain Charles, 'Battle of La Bassée Canal, 24–25–26–27 May 1940' ['Long's Report'], held by Norfolk Museums and Archaeology Service, Norwich

Lumsden, Lieutenant Graham, report ['Lumsden's Report'], in IWM Documents, 66/24/1, p. 6

MacGrath, Capitaine de Vaisseau, 25 May 1940 report ['MacGrath's Report'], in SHM TTE6

MacKenzie, John A., 'Forty Years Ago with the 78th To St Valery: Contact with the enemy', *The Queen's Own Highlander*, vol. 20, no. 58, 1980 ['Mackenzie's Report']

Mansfield, J., account ['Mansfield's Account'], held by the Lancastria Association

Martin, Général Julien, 'Notes Sur Les Engagements Du 11 Corps Du 10 Au–23 Mai 1940' ['Martin's Report'], in SHAT 30N123

Mertens, Maurice, statement to the Vinkt War Crimes Commission ['Mertens' Statement']

Miller, Lieutenant-Colonel, report ['Miller's Report'], in NA/PRO WO 217/5

Montgomery, General Bernard, report ['Montgomery's Report'], in IWM Documents BLM 19 and 22

Monjoie, Colonel R., report ['Monjoie's Report'], Carton A Farde 2 CIII, in CDH

Munn, Wally, report ['Munn's Report'], held by Sam Hardy, President of the Worcestershire Yeomanry's Old Comrades Association

Nash, Lieutenant-Colonel W., report ['Nash's Report'], in NA/PRO WO 217/20

Nethercott, Iain, taped interview in IWM Sound Archive 7186, and my interviews with him ['Nethercott's Reports']

Newman, Major Philip, report ['Newman's Report'], held by his son

Nicholson, Brigadier Claude, report ['Nicholson's Report'], in NA/PRO WO 217/1

Osborne, Major-General E. A., 'Extract From Diary of Maj-Gen E.A. Osborne, DSO' ['Osborne's Diary'], in NA/PRO WO167/275

Oster, Barbara, my interview with her ['Barbara Oster Interview']

O'Sullivan, Captain Hugh, account ['O'Sullivan's Report'], in NA/PRO WO 167/458

['Paradis XVI Corps Investigation'] included in the Appendix to the German XVI Corps war diary, in BA-MA RH21–4/527

['Paradis War Crimes Report'], dated 24 January 1947, report held by Norfolk Museums and Archaeology Service, Norwich

Parry, Richard, reports to the War Crimes Interrogation Unit in the Wormhout Massacre Report ['Parry's Reports'], pp. 62–3 and 68

Patterson, Gordon, 'The Personal Autobiography of Gordon Nelson Patterson' ['Patterson, Personal Autobiography']

Payne, Tom, account ['Payne's Statement'], held by Lancastria Association

Penneman, Corporal, 6 April 1945 report ['Penneman's Report'], in Albert Canal Bridges file, in CDH

Petit de La Villeon, Capitaine de Frégate Loic, report dated 5 September 1940 ['Petit's Report'], in SHM TTE6

Picken, Sergeant-Major A., account ['Picken's Statement'], in West, *The Loss Of 'Lancastria'*,*

Pieyns' statement to the Vinkt War Crimes Commission ['Pieyns' Statement']

Pinaud, Lieutenant-Colonel, report ['Pinaud's Report'], in SHAT 34N174

Quenard, Capitaine, 28 August 1940 note ['Quenard's Report'], in Weygand's files, in SHAT 1K130 Carton 3 Dossier 13

Ramsay, Vice-Admiral Bertram, 18 June 1940 dispatch ['Ramsay's Report'], in Supplement to *London Gazette*, 17 July 1947

Reeves, Bill, report, 'Tanks In Calais', and my 2002 interviews with him ['Reeves's Reports']

Reid, Miles, account ['Reid's Report'], in IWM Documents 83/37/1

Reinberger, Helmuth, 13 September 1944 statement ['Reinberger's Statement'], in Reichskriegsgericht documents at the Historicky Ustav Armady Ceske Republiky in Prague, Czech Republic

Rigby, Brigadier Bernard, history of the Cheshire Regiment ['Rigby, Cheshires' Regimental History'], held by the Cheshire Regiment

['RO1']: 'Activités de RO1 au début des Hostilités', March 1956, in the 3rd Chasseurs Ardennais Regiment's file, in CDH

['RO2']: 'Des Reconnaissances Frontières du Groupement des Ardennes', in the 3rd Chasseurs Ardennais Regiment's file, in CDH

['RO4']: 'Rapport sur la Reconnaissance d'Officier no.4 1939–1940', dated 17 July 1956, in the 3rd Chasseurs Ardennais Regiment's file, in CDH

Rose-Miller, Lieutenant-Colonel Patrick, account and tape of reminiscences held by his daughter ['Rose-Miller Reports']

Sas, Gijsbertus (junior), 'Het begon in mei 1940', in *De Spiegel*, 17 October 1953 ['De Spiegel']

Schollaert, Hector, statement to the Vinkt War Crimes Commission and Sofie De Smet's 2004 interview with him ['Schollaert's Statement']

Senf, Oskar, statement ['Senf's Report'], in the Wormhout Massacre Report, pp. 46–8

Smith, Charlie, my interview with him ['Charlie Smith Interview']

Smith, David, account ['Smith's Report'], held by him

Solomon, Martin, report ['Solomon's Report'], in NA/PRO ADM 199/788A

Somerset, Brigadier Nigel, two reports held by his son ['Somerset's Reports']

Spiegel, De: see Sas

Stott, Captain Clement, 'I Led Fifty Men To The Lancastria' ['Stott's Story'], held by Lancastria Association

Sweeney, Joe, account ['Sweeney's Report'], in IWM Documents 85/18/1

Swinburn, Lieutenant-Colonel Henry, 'History of the 51st Highland Division – 26 May to 12 June 1940' ['Swinburn's History'], held by his son

Swinburne, Hugh, report ['Swinburne's Report'], held by his daughter

Tallec, Paul Le, report dated 8 October 1949 ['Le Tallec's Report'], in Weygand's file, in SHAT 1K130 Carton 3 Dossier 11

Taylor, Toby, account ['Taylor's Report'], held by him

Tellier, Chef de Bataillon Raymond Le, report dated 25 August 1940 ['Le Tellier's Report'], in SHM TTE6

Tennant, Captain William, report ['Tennant's Report'], in NA/PRO ADM 199/788A.

Thomas, Melville, 'Don't You Know There's A War On' ['Thomas's Report']

Timpson, Major Theodore, 'The 1st Bn. Queen Victoria's Rifles, at Calais, May 1940', in NA/PRO WO 217/4, and another report 'Calais, May 1940' held by his grandson Rupert Fordham ['Timpson's Reports']

Tombs, Alf, my 2000 interview with him ['Tombs Interview']

Tomes, Captain Dick, 'Personal Diary' ['Tomes's Diary'], held by his family, and my 2001 interviews with him ['Tomes's Interviews']

Véron, Colonel, 'Notes Sur La 9eme Armée, Les Opérations Auxquelles Elle A Participé' ['Véron's Report'], in SHAT 29N441

['Vinkt Prosecution's Introduction']: In Zake Vinkt – Not. Nr. 104-V/48 in Archief van het Auditoraat General: Krijgsauditoraat in Brussels

Voguë, Capitaine de, 'Notes prises par le Capitaine de Voguë Officier de liaison entre le GA1 et le BEF sur la période du 10 au 29 mai', dated 14 July 1940 ['De Voguë's Report']

['Vroenhoven Report']: the October 1940 report on Operation Beton in the Koch Report (see above)

Waldron, Francis, account ['Waldron's Report'], held by him

Weller, Hauptmann, 'Calonne 1940' ['Weller, Calonne'], an article unearthed by Henri Bourgeois. The journal where the article appeared is unknown

Whitehead, Major Denis, 'From The Desert – May 1942: 5th Green Howards, BEF' ['Whitehead's Report']

Whitfield, Colonel G. H. P., account ['Whitfield's Report'], in NA/PRO WO 197/ 119

Wild, David, 'With the 145th Infantry Brigade: May 1940' ['Wild's Report']

Wilson, Captain Bill, account ['Wilson's Report'], held by his son

['Wormhout Massacre Report']: the report WCIU/IDC/1650 on the Wormhout Massacre by the War Crimes Interrogation Unit, in NA/PRO WO 309/1814

Wright, Leslie, 'Personal Experiences In The Defence Of Calais' ['Wright's Report'], in LHC, Wright, LW 1/3/2

Yardin, Dr, 'La Tragique Évacuation Du Bastion 2', in *La Voix Du Nord*, 25 May 1956 ['Yardin's Bastion 2 Article']. A copy is to be found in SHM TTE6

British War Diaries

Army

GHQ

['GHQ's War Diary']: GHQ's war diary, in NA/PRO WO 167/28

BRIGADES

['4 Brigade's War Diary']: 4 Brigade's war diary, in NA/PRO WO 167/352

['5 Brigade's War Diary']: 5 Brigade's war diary, in NA/PRO WO 167/354

['6 Brigade's War Diary']: 6 Brigade's war diary in NA/PRO WO 167/357

['20 Brigade's Boulogne War Diary'], held by Bill Heber Percy

BATTALIONS

['Cameronians' War Diary']: 2nd Cameronians' war diary, in NA/PRO WO 167/ 721

['2nd Coldstream Guards' War Diary']: 2nd Coldstream Guards' war diary, held by Coldstream Guards

['2 DLI's War Diary']: 2nd Durham Light Infantry's war diary, in NA/PRO WO 167/728

['Irish Guards' Boulogne War Diary']: 'Report On The Operations Of The 2nd Battalion Irish Guards In The Boulogne Area From Tuesday 21st May 1940 To Thursday 23rd May 1940', held by the Irish Guards

['RWF War Diary']: The 1st Royal Welch Fusiliers war diary, in NA/PRO WO 167/843

['Welsh Guards 1st Company War Diary']: 1st Welsh Guards' Prince of Wales 1st Company's war diary, held by the Welsh Guards

['Welsh Guards' Carrier Platoon War Diary']: Welsh Guards' carrier platoon's war diary completed on 28 October 1940, held by Welsh Guards

AD HOC FORCES AND PORT WAR DIARIES

['Le Havre War Diary']: 'War Diary Relating to the Evacuation of the 51st Division from Havre and St Valery: 9th to 13th June 1940', in NA/PRO WO 167/314

['Macforce Report']: 'Summary of Composition, Moves and Dispositions of Macforce 17–25 May', in NA/PRO WO 197/118

['Polforce Report']: 'Report on the operations of Polforce 20–25 May', in NA/PRO WO 197/118

['St Omer Report']: 'St Omer – Activities of No. 3 Company 2 Div leave details, May 1940', in NA/PRO CAB 106/221

MEETING MINUTES/REPORTS

[The '30 May La Panne Minutes']: 'Note On Conference At GHQ (La Panne) On Evening 30th May 1940', in NA/PRO WO 167/124

Navy

OPERATIONS

['Boulogne War Diary']: 'Operations Vice Admiral Dover, May 18th–24th 1940: Evacuation At Boulogne', in NA/PRO ADM 199/795

['Calais War Diary']: 'Narrative of operations conducted from Dover, May 21–26, 1940: Calais', in NA/PRO ADM 199/795

['Cycle Report']: Operation Cycle report, in NA/PRO ADM 199/2206

['Warren's Narrative']: Captain Warren's 'Narrative Of Operation Cycle', sent to Admiral James on 15 June 1940, in NA/PRO ADM 179/158

LOGS

['12 Wireless Section Log Book']: 'Extract of messages between Dover and Calais according to Log kept by Control Wireless Station of No.12 Wireless Section at Vice-Admiralty Dover', in LHC, Wright, LW 1/16

SHIPS

['*Crested Eagle*'s Report']: Lieutenant-Commander Bernard Booth, 31 May 1940 report, in NA/PRO ADM 199/787

['*Grafton*'s Report']: Lieutenant Hugh McRea, 3 June 1940 report, in NA/PRO ADM 199/786

['*Jaguar*'s Report']: Lieutenant-Commander John Hine, 1 June 1940, in NA/PRO ADM 199/786

['Lydd/Haig Report']: Lieutenant-Commander Rodolph Haig, 7 June 1940 report, in NA/PRO ADM 199/786

['*Venetia*'s War Diary']: dated 30 May 1940, in NA/PRO ADM 199/795

['*Venomous*'s War Diary']: dated 26 May 1940, supplied by Lieutenant-Commander Robert Moore

['*Wakeful*'s Report']: Commander Ralph Fisher, 30 May 1940 report, in NA/PRO ADM 199/789

French War Diaries

Army Group

['Blanchard's Report']: 'Compte Rendu du Général Blanchard sur les rapports entre les forces Britanniques et le G.A. No. 1 pendant la période du 10 mai au 1er juin' in Weygand's files, in SHAT 1K130

Army

['1st Army War Diary']: 'La 1ière Armée du 26 Mai au 4 Juin', in 1st Army file, in SHAT 29N1

Divisions

['1 DCR JDM']: definition used to refer to both of the following documents: 'Journal des Marches et Opérations de la 1 Division Cuirassée' and 'Journal des Opérations', in SHAT 32N447

['3ième Division Cuirassée History']: 'La 3ième Division Cuirassée Dans La Bataille Des Ardennes', in SHAT 32N470

['French 21 Division War Diary']: 'Journal de Marche de la 21ième Division' dated 14 February 1942, p. 11, in Lanquetot Documents (see above)

['Récit des Événements ID 55']: 'Récit des Événements vécus par l'I.D. 55 du 10 au 15 mai 1940', in SHAT 32N254

Battalions

['111/122nd Regiment's Counter-Attack Report']: 'Rôle du 3ième Bataillon du 122ième constitué en Bataillon de marche sous les ordres du Capitaine Arbola, les 2 et 3 Juin', in SHAT 32N202 Dossier 3

['111/143rd Regiment's Counter-Attack Report']: 'Le 3ième Bataillon du 143ième à la Contre-Attaque de Téteghem le 3 Juin 1940', written by Chef de Bataillon Carbonnel, in SHAT 34N141

German War Diaries

Army Group

['Army Group A War Diary']: Army Group A war diary, English translation, in IWM Foreign Documents, AL 1428

['Army Group B War Diary']: Army Group B war diary, English translation, in IWM Foreign Documents, AL 1433

Panzer Divisions' Units

['2/Schützenregiment 7 War Diary']: the battalion war diary, supplied by 7th Panzer Division's Helmut Gutzschhahn

['6th Panzer Company Report']: report by unnamed German from the 6th Company of the 3rd Panzer Regiment of the 2nd Panzer Division, pp. 16–17 using the numbers at the top right of the page, in BA-MA RH27-2/93

['10 Panzer Division War Diary']: 10th Panzer Division's war diary, in BA-MA RH21-10/9

['Rommelalbum']: 'Rommelalbum: Geschichte der 7 Panzer Division: Kurzer Abriss über den Einsatz im Westen vom 9 Mai–19 Juni 1940', in BA-MA RH27-7/44

Regiment

['Leibstandarte War Diary']: SS Leibstandarte Adolf Hitler war diary, in BA-MA RS4/1211

Acknowledgements

The romance of Paul Gallico's heartbreaking novel *The Snow Goose* sparked off my life-long interest in Dunkirk. I read it when I was a child. Since then I have read most of what has been written about the evacuation. But I was only inspired to write my own version of what happened after reading two books that showed me there was a gap in the market.

The first was Sir Alistair Horne's masterly *To Lose a Battle: France 1940*, which is to history what Tolstoy's *War and Peace* is to novels: unlike most military history books, it begins with a lengthy account of what happened before war was declared, explaining how the political and military situation in France between the two world wars weakened the morale and strength of the French armed forces, before going on to explain how the Germans defeated the supposedly great French Army in a matter of days. Here at last I had found a fascinating description of the events that made Dunkirk necessary, something that had been missing from the books I had read on the subject. But it was Patrick Wilson's relatively unknown book *Dunkirk: From Disaster To Deliverance* that showed me there was another aspect of the famous evacuation story, which had not been fully explored: the British last-ditch stands outside the town that made the evacuation possible. They had been mentioned in the classic works on the retreat to Dunkirk, L. F. Ellis's official history *The War In France and Flanders: 1939–1940* and Gregory Blaxland's *Destination Dunkirk: The story of Gort's army*, but the details ferreted out by Patrick Wilson showed that the stark facts contained in these admirable books could be brought to life.

Once I had started my research I was helped particularly by four other historians: Jean Vanwelkenhuyzen's *Les avertissements qui venaient de Berlin: 9 octobre 1939–10 mai 1940* showed me that some of the most interesting material relating to the 1940 campaign occurred before the fighting commenced. This book about the twilight world of spies and military attachés in Berlin during 1939 to 1940 contains material that would not be out of place in a spy novel, only it was all true and meticulously researched and sourced by Vanwelkenhuyzen. He has also written two books on the 1940 campaign itself, as well as a seminal work on the so-called Mechelen incident (described in this book's Chapter 3), and when I contacted him to see whether I could consult some of the sources to which he had referred, he immediately came to my aid and pointed me in the right direction.[1] Secondly, I am indebted to Oberstleutnant Dr Karl-Heinz Frieser of the Militärgeschichtliches Forschungsamt, author of *Blitzkrieg-Legende: Der Westfeldzug 1940*, not only because his book with its mass of new material about the German attack on France and Belgium makes his work as important as Alistair Horne's for anyone researching the 1940 campaign, but also because he gave me any assistance he could whenever I put questions to him on his subject, and sent me a bundle of panzer division war diaries he had found to help me on my way. He also showed me how to contact German veterans. Thirdly, I would not have been able to find the best sources for my chapters on the battles in Boulogne and Calais had it not been for the assistance provided by Jon Cooksey, author of *Boulogne: 20 Guards Brigade's Fighting Defence – May 1940* and *Calais: A Fight To The Finish*. He advised me on how best to deal with these battles, and he also lent me all his source material so that I did not have to spend time digging for what he had already found. Saul David, author of *Churchill's Sacrifice of the Highland Division: France 1940*, was just as generous concerning the material he had accumulated when writing his book, lending me all of his source material, and telling me how to contact the veterans and their families who had helped him describe what happened to the 51st Highland Division at St Valery after the evacuation from Dunkirk. The fruits of his aid are in the penultimate chapter of this book.

I should also mention Jeroen Huygelier, an archivist at the Centre de Documentation Historique in Brussels, who, in addition to bringing to my attention all relevant files and books relating to the May 1940 battles in Belgium, allowed me to read and refer to the unpublished documents on the Mechelen incident, which he unearthed in the Czech Republic, and Peter Taghon, author of *Mai 40*, who gave me copies of all the documents about the massacres at Vinkt (described in Chapter 23), which he found in a Belgian archive, as well as the chilling photographs showing the corpses of those who were shot. He also brought to my attention various accounts, war diaries and photographs he had collected from German veterans and archives.

The second Lord Keyes, author of *Outrageous Fortune: The Tragedy of Leopold III of the Belgians 1901–1941*, made available all documents passed down to him by his father, the first Lord Keyes, along with books and documents collected while writing his own book, and introduced me to Lode Willems and Baron Thierry de Gruben who have been the Belgian ambassadors in London while I was researching this book. Thanks to Lord Keyes's introduction, they both offered me all the support they could, and allowed me to study books sent from the Centre de Documentation Historique, Brussels, in their London embassy where I was also assisted by the defence attachés Captain Albert Kockx and Colonel Daniel de Cock, and their secretary Claudine Stroobants.

The author Ian McEwan, whose novel *Atonement* includes memorable scenes about the retreat to Dunkirk and about the nurses who treated the wounded returning from Dunkirk, convinced me that I should include in my book the scenes describing the march to Dunkirk, which I have placed in my Chapter 27, and also told me how to find material about 1940 nurses.

I cannot begin to mention and thank in this short section all the people who have kindly given me accounts about the 1940 campaign, or advice on how to find soldiers, and the families of those soldiers who might have written such accounts. There were literally hundreds of them. Those whose documents or testimony I have used are specified in the chapter end notes. But the following documents are particularly important: Captain R. J. Hastings's and Captain Nick Hallett's accounts shine a ray of light into what happened in and around Le Paradis before the captured Royal Norfolks were massacred there; Captain Edward Jerram's account provides similar details of the fighting before the Wormhout massacre. 2nd Lieutenant Roy Creswell's describes one of the most stirring actions of the campaign: his platoon held out in a blockhouse outside Cassel for more than two days even though Germans climbed on to the roof and dropped grenades down the hole left for the observation tower, and even though the barricade keeping the Germans out was on fire. Captain Francis Waldron's account represents one of the few detailed descriptions of the torments suffered by British soldiers in the front line inside Dunkirk's perimeter. The surgeon Philip Newman's record of events during the final hours at Dunkirk's casualty clearing station provides an unexpected gloss on the evacuation: he was one of those left behind to care for the wounded when the last British ships sailed back to England. The accounts by Major John Hopkinson, Lieutenant Williamson and John Watton should also be highlighted: they chronicle the highs and lows experienced by an isolated company from the Border Regiment during the battles that took place south of the River Somme after Dunkirk. Although this small group of men, which was holding the village of Incheville near the River Bresle, was surrounded, they held out for more than five days and only surrendered after learning that their comrades in the 51st Highland Division, whom they had been supporting, had capitulated.

The following association personnel, historians, librarians, editors, liaison officers and archivists assisted and advised me, or permitted me to use their collections, address lists and databases:

In Britain

Association of Dunkirk Little Ships: John Slater and Rob Stokes.
British Library: *Maps*: Jeff Armitage, map collections reading room manager, and Nicola Beech, Jo Dansie, Debbie Hall, Steve Martin and Debbie Rughooputh. *Newspapers*: Brian Huff, book delivery manager.
Camden, London Borough of, Library Service: Sonia Winifred, deputy head, Tony Adams, Denis Chase, Roberto Cioccari, Yasmin Hounsell, Louise Shapiro; *Inter Library Loans*: June Gronland and Richard Wheatley.
Churchill College, Cambridge: *Churchill Archives Centre*: Allen Packwood. *Library*: Mary Kendall, the librarian.
Dunkirk Veterans Association: Jim Horton, general secretary, and secretaries of all branches around Britain.
House of Lords Record Office: Jennie Lynch.
Imperial War Museum: *Documents*: Roderick Suddaby, head of department, Anthony Richards, Simon Robbins; *Foreign Documents*: Stephen Walton; *Photograph Archive*: Roger Smither, keeper, Hilary Roberts, head of department, David Bell, Sarah Martin, Yvonne Oliver, Elizabeth Selby; *Printed Books*: Jane Rosen; *Sound Archive*: Margaret Brooks, head of department, Peter Hart, Jo Lancaster, John Stopford-Pickering.
Kensington and Chelsea Library: John McEachen, head of Libraries and Arts.
Liddell Hart Centre for Military Archives, King's College, London: Alan Lucie, Kate O'Brien.
Maritime Museum, Ramsgate: Michael Hunt.

Ministry of Defence: *Admiralty Library*: Jenny Rate; *Air Historical Branch*: Flight Lieutenant Mary Hudson, Clive Richards; *Naval Historical Branch*: Jock Gardner, historian, Kate Tildesley, foreign documents curator; *Naval Manning Agency*: Graham Smith; *Naval Career Management Reserves*: Stuart Harley.

The National Archives (formerly the Public Record Office): Geoff Baxter, François Belhomme, and Hazel Pocock.

Navy News: Michael Gray, an editor.

Royal Chelsea Hospital, London: Brigadier Kim Ross.

The Second World War Experience Centre, Leeds: Dr Peter Liddle, director, Robert Carrington, and John Larder.

The Tank Museum, Bovington: David Fletcher.

In France

Archives d'Histoire Contemporaine: Dominique Parcollet.

Association Mémoriale du Souvenir: Lucien Dayan, president.

Archives Nationales: Françoise Adnès, Jean Pouessel.

Boulogne Archives Municipales: Cécile Noël.

Comité de Coordination des Sociétés Patriotiques de Dunkerque: Jean Becaert, president.

Dunkerque Archives Municipales: Nicolas Fournier, Christine Harbion, Catherine Lesage, Olivier Ryckebusch.

École de St Cyr Coëtquidan: Lieutenant-Colonel Tim Carmichael, British Liaison Officer, and Andy Ribbans.

Établissement De Communication Et De Production Audiovisuelle De La Défense (ecpad): Olivier Simoncelli, Sébastien Isern, Nathalie Riou and Élisabeth Szlezys.

Institut Géographique National, France: Jean-Claude Dupuis.

Service Historique de la Défense: *Service Historique de l'Armée de Terre*, Vincennes: Generals Michel Berlaud and Jean Jacques Senant, the consecutive heads of the service, Michelle Decuber, reading room, Sandrine Einhorne-Heiser, communication, Colonel Frédéric Guelton, directeur du département recherches, Hervé Lemoine, head conservator, Lieutenant-Colonel Paul Malmassari, head of division des traditions et de la symbolique militaires, and adjutant-chef Philippe Lafargue, Raphael Masson, former head of the library, Marie-Martine Renard, private documents, Henri Vaudable, head of documentation, Marie Anne de Villèle, head of the library. *Service Historique de la Marine*, Vincennes: Contre Amiral Alain Bellot, head of the service, Karine Leboucq, head of archives, Annie Molton and Monique Frêlon, reading room, Alain Morgat, head of library.

In Germany

Bundesarchiv-Bildarchiv, Koblenz: Martina Caspers.
Bundesarchiv-Militärarchiv, Freiberg: Jana Brabant, Helmut Doringhoff, Renate Jansen.
Institut Für Zeitgeschichte, Munich: Karin Popp.
U-Boot Archiv, Altenbruch: Horst Bredow and Horst Schwenk.

In Belgium

Centrum Voor Historische Documentatie (Centre de Documentation Historique), Brussels: Jeroen Huygelier and Eva Muys.
Historian: Dirk Decuypere, author of *Dorp Zonder Grenzen: 1940–1945 Epicentrum Geluwe*.

In Holland

Centraal bureau voor genealogie, The Hague: Sytske Visscher.
Instituut voor Militaire Geschiednis, The Hague: Peet Kamphuis and Herman Amersfoort.
Nederlands Instituut voor Oorlogsdocumentatie, Amsterdam: René Kruis.

In the USA

The National Archives, Washington, Edward Maccarter, Photographic Section.

Children of Politicians, Soldiers and Admirals

Evelyne Demey, Paul Reynaud's daughter, and Jean Daladier, Édouard Daladier's son, gave me permission to use documents in their fathers' files in the Centre Historique des Archives Nationales, Paris. Guy de Chassey, Admiral Jean Abrial's grandson, helped me describe his grandfather's treatment after the war. William Neave gave me permission to use his father's documents in the House of Lords Record Office, London.

I have been helped by the following advisers, researchers, journalists and photographers: Alexander Bainbridge, Henri Becquart, an expert on events at Cassel, and his son David, Jacob Van der Beugel, Gilbert Bloch, Daniel Brewing, Professor Geoffrey and Nomi Burnstock, Maud Capelle, André Coilliot, expert on events at Arras, Eloïse Comert, Agnès Delahaye, Dominique Faivre, expert on events at St-Venant, Dalila de Freitas, Sara Gertjegerdes, Clemence Graffin, Sarah Harrison, James Holland, Dr Gabriel

Jaffé, Isabelle Kernot, Annika Klein, Knut Klemme, Mirja Kraemer, Andrea Lehmann, Eve Leroux, Jan Linke, Juliana Lopoukhine, Gorette Martins, Fiona Morell, Mara-Luisa Muller, Hedda Plecher, Dr Rudiger Overmanns, Anna Plodeck, Alanus Radecki, Niesje Burggraaff and Frits Sas, Kathrin Schiff, Anna Schultz, the following members of the Sebag-Montefiore family: David, Harold, Bishop Hugh, Ruth, Saul and Simon, Karen Serres, Peter Sheridan, Sofie De Smet, Charlotte Soehngen, Will Stewart, Graf Romedio von Thun-Hohenstein, and Sam Warshaw.

I must mention my former agent Mike Shaw from Curtis Brown, who retired after advising me to write this book and selling the idea to Penguin, but not before he had given me sound advice about how to research it and what to include in it, my new agent Jonathan Lloyd also of Curtis Brown, who ensured that I was given the time I needed to complete it notwithstanding the many years it took to do so, and Eleo Gordon, the editorial director at Penguin, who commissioned it in spite of the fact that there are already lots of books about Dunkirk, who stuck with it when there were delays in completing it, and who advised me wisely on what to leave out from my first draft and what to insert into the final manuscript. John Gilkes has designed the very user-friendly maps. Hazel Orme was the copy-editor. She has expertly tidied up text and chapter end notes alike and has gently coaxed me into smoothing off the book's roughest edges.

Her complicated job was made much easier than it would otherwise have been thanks to the editing of the first draft by Aviva Burnstock my wife, and my parents Stephen and April Sebag-Montefiore, who have not only helped me make the text more readable but who, after correcting the first draft, have given me many useful historical tips, as well as invaluable suggestions which along with those made by Eleo Gordon helped me to restructure the manuscript.

Index

on Gort Line 6, 7, *511*; its
strength 59; its commander-in-
chief 3, 24, 175, 402, 503; its
adjutant-general 188, its engineer-in-
chief 263; its staff 544; Rear
GHQ 188; GHQ *509*; overall French
commander in control of 20, 23,
550n; its armour 8–9, 247, 272; its
light cavalry 142; support from and
action by RAF 64, 130, 440, 560;
deficiencies 9, 17; some of its troops
to go to Scandinavia 20; and the
pillbox affair 21–2; saw French
deficiencies 17, 19; and sex 10–16;
march into Belgium 7, 22, 25, 59, 62,
68, 76, 80; positions on Dyle 75–6,
156, 512m; Germans approach for first
time 75–6; retreat from Dyle 79,
581n; positions and actions on
Escaut 156, *521*, 587n; action on
Escaut 156–172; danger to caused by
impenetrable Ardennes theory 80;
danger caused by German
breakthrough 129–30, 141, 144, 156,
175–6, 249–50, 273, 384; Germans
encircle from north 248; danger to
BEF increased by Ironside 24, 176; its
digging divisions 130; retreat to
Somme considered 144–5; counter-
attack considered 144; its generals'
animosity to French generals 144–5;
suspected by troops of being in
trouble 156; retreat from Escaut 164,
176; guarding its flank and use of
strongpoints 177, 240–41, 243, 256,
279, *522*, *528*; protecting north of
corridor 327, 333, 338–40, 353,
364–5, 368, *522*; retreat to Dunkirk
considered/planned/executed 143,
176, 212, *522*; retreat to Lys 605n,
607n; retreat from Lys 337, 619n;
escaping up corridor 328; safety of
predominant 250, 336, 630n;
evacuation of by Operation
Dynamo 253–4, 275, 375, 443, 447,
629n; generals hope can be saved 255;
its hard-hit battalions 297; Belgian
request for counter-attack 614n;
warned Belgians would

surrender 303–4; no extra troops to
help 336; French learn BEF to be
evacuated 336–7; small boats needed
to evacuate 378; troops in
perimeter 386; Luftwaffe to finish
off 391; guarding Dunkirk
perimeter 403, 435–6; conflict with
French 406, 409; evacuation of
rearguard 410–11, 633n; abandoned
vehicles 424; number of evacuees and
left behind 436, 458; medical aid
for 436, 438
British Expeditionary Force (BEF), 2nd xxiii;
commander-in-chief 176, 482, 503;
armour 465; plan to protect
Brittany 483; order to retreat to
coast 484; delayed evacuation 485
British-French disintegrating relations:
British rudeness/offhand
behaviour 188–9, 406; British
attempt to be conciliatory 406 ;
French threats 406; fear French
would stop evacuation/be upset 409,
421; generals quarrel 406–9, 411;
physical conflict 404, 405;
consequences/symptoms of broken
down relations 449, 486; French
gratitude in spite of
disagreements 456
British Government xxii, 6, 8, 19, 34, 37,
202, 250, 262, 319–20, 336–7
British Navy
FLOTILLA
19th Destroyer Flotilla 419
DESTROYERS
Basilisk 417, 631n
Broke 470
Codrington 475–6
Gossamer 388
Grafton 388–91, 627n, 699
Grenade xi, 391–3, 628n
Havelock 489, 641n
Jaguar 392, 628n, 699
Keith 200–5, 416–19, 631n
Saladin 475
Shikari 455, 635n
Vanquisher xi
Venetia x, 208–9, 593–4n, 699
Venomous 208–9, 594n, 690, 699